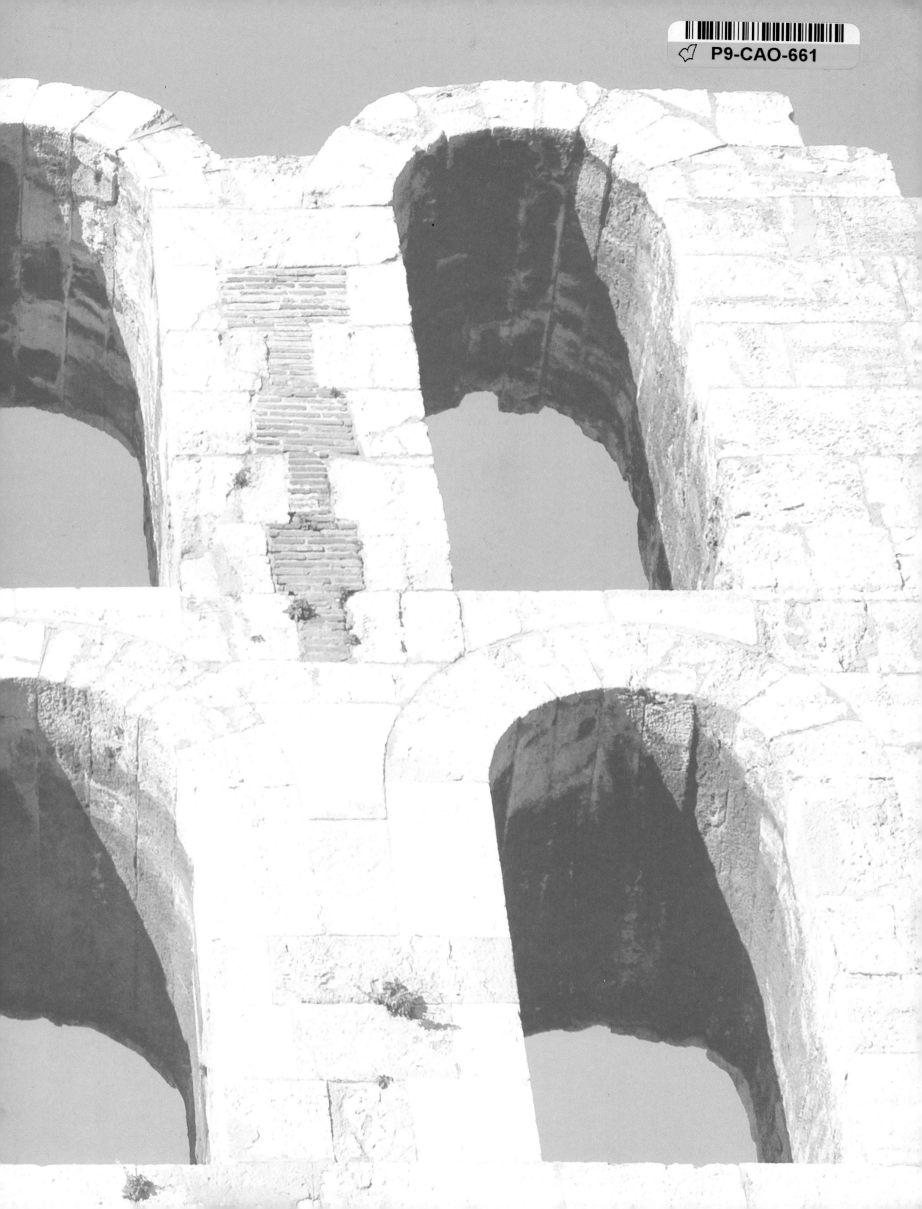

Architectura

ELEMENTS OF ARCHITECTURAL STYLE

Architectura

ELEMENTS OF ARCHITECTURAL STYLE

GENERAL EDITOR
Professor Miles Lewis

BARRON'S

First edition for the United States, its territories, and Canada published in 2008 by Barron's Educational Series, Inc.

All inquiries should be addressed to:
Barron's Educational Series, Inc.
250 Wireless Boulevard
Hauppauge, New York 11788
www.barronseduc.com

ISBN-13: 978-0-7641-6170-4
ISBN-10: 0-7641-6170-9

Library of Congress Control No.: 2008929852

The moral rights of all contributors have been asserted.

Printed in China by 1010 Printing International
Film separation by Pica Digital Pte Ltd, Singapore

Conceived and produced by
Global Book Publishing
Level 8, 15 Orion Road
Lane Cove, NSW 2066
Australia
Ph: (612) 9425 5800
Fax: (612) 9425 5804
Email: rightsmanager@globalpub.com.au

FRONT COVER

Interior of the Reichstag, Berlin, Germany

MANAGING DIRECTOR
Chryl Campbell

PUBLISHING DIRECTOR
Sarah Anderson

ART DIRECTOR
Kylie Mulquin

PROJECT MANAGERS
Dannielle Doggett
Catherine du Peloux Menagé

GENERAL EDITOR
Professor Miles Lewis

CONTRIBUTORS
Dr. Oya Demirbilek, Associate Professor Nur
Demirbilek, Adjunct Assistant Professor Lisa
Richardson Elkins, Assistant Professor J. Philip
Gruen, Associate Professor Rumiko Handa,
Professor Robert Harbison, Sue Harris, Chris How,
Douglas Lloyd Jenkins, Associate Professor June
Komisar, Professor Miles Lewis, Bill Millard, Ron
Powell, Craig Reynolds, Professor Elizabeth H.
Riorden, Roger Sandall, Dr. Jeffrey John Turnbull

COMMISSIONING EDITOR
Dannielle Doggett

EDITORS
Scott Forbes, John Mapps, Bronwyn Sweeney,
Mary Trewby

COVER DESIGN
Kylie Mulquin

DESIGNERS
Cathy Campbell, Lena Lowe, Kylie Mulquin,
Mark Thacker

JUNIOR DESIGNER
Althea Aseoche

DESIGN CONCEPT
Kylie Mulquin, John Witzig

PICTURE RESEARCH
Linda Braidwood, Shirley Cachia-Baldwin,
Jude Fowler-Smith

ILLUSTRATION EDITOR
Selena Quintrell

ILLUSTRATOR
Irene Still

INDEX
Jon Jermey

PROOFREADER
Kevin Diletti

PRODUCTION
Ian Coles

CONTRACTS
Alan Edwards

FOREIGN RIGHTS
Kate Hill

PUBLISHING ASSISTANT
Christine Leonards

Contributors

General Editor and Contributor

Professor Miles Lewis is an architectural historian with a special interest in the cultural history of building technology, prefabrication, and vernacular architecture. He is an Honorary Life Member of the Comité International d'Architecture Vernaculaire, a Fellow of the International Advisory Council of the Royal Institute of Architects, a Fellow of the Australian Academy of Humanities, a Member of the Order of Australia, and Professor of Architecture in the Faculty of Architecture, Building and Planning, University of Melbourne, Australia.

His publications include *Victorian Primitive*, *Don John of Balaclava*, *The Essential Maldon*, *Two Hundred Years of Concrete in Australia*, *Victorian Churches*, *Melbourne: The City's History*, *Suburban Backlash*, and numerous articles and papers on architectural and building history, urban conservation, urban renewal, and housing policy, as well as numerous addresses at international conferences on various aspects of architecture.

Dr. Oya Demirbilek is Head of the Industrial Design Program at the Faculty of the Built Environment, University of New South Wales (UNSW), Australia. Dr Demirbilek's professional experience includes appointments as instructor in product design, Art Center College of Design (Europe); freelance designer for ceramic products, Hardegger Handels, Bern, Switzerland; Research Assistant, Lecturer, and Assistant Professor in Industrial Design, Middle East Technical University, Ankara, Turkey; Lecturer and Senior Lecturer in Industrial Design, Faculty of the Built Environment, UNSW.

Dr. Demirbilek's current research interests include universal design, participatory design, design for aging populations, and emotional responses to products.

Associate Professor Nur Demirbilek teaches architecture in the Faculty of Built Environment and Engineering, Queensland University of Technology (QUT), Australia. Associate Professor Demirbilek's experience includes appointments as researcher at the Environmental Systems Unit of the Building Research Institute, Scientific and Technical Research Council of Turkey; Instructor, Assistant Professor, and Associate Professor at the Middle East Technical University, Ankara, Turkey; Visiting Lecturer at the Faculty of the Built Environment, UNSW, University of Sydney, and UTS for one year; and Senior Lecturer and Associate Professor at QUT.

Her research areas includes climate responsive building design, and thermal performance analysis of buildings, lighting, and color.

Adjunct Assistant Professor Lisa Richardson Elkins teaches undergraduate architecture at the University of Illinois at Chicago, United States.

She has experience in Chicago, San Francisco, and London, and she has been designing architecture and furniture professionally for more than ten years.

In 2006 she founded *2 point perspective, inc.*, a design firm specializing in environmentally responsible architecture, interiors, and furniture design. She is accredited by the Leadership in Energy and Environmental Design program (LEED) of the US Green Building Council.

Assistant Professor J. Philip Gruen teaches architectural history and theory in the School of Architecture and Construction Management at Washington State University, United States. He received his PhD in Architecture from the University of California at Berkeley, and has also taught classes at the California College of the Arts and the University of Oregon. His general research interests concern the architecture and urbanism of the United States. More specifically, they regard the interaction between tourists and the built environment, both past and present.

Assistant Professor Gruen is currently working on a book about late-nineteenth-century tourism in the urban American West.

Associate Professor Rumiko Handa teaches in the Department of Architecture at the University of Nebraska-Lincoln, United States where she is Graduate Committee chair. She taught at the University of Michigan and Texas Tech University, United States, and was a guest lecturer and critic at several institutions in Japan and the United States. She is the recipient of the 2002 National Educator Honor Award from the American Institute of Architecture Students.

Associate Professor Handa has written for the *Journals of the Bibliographical Society of America*, the *Encyclopedia of Twentieth-Century Architecture*, *Design Research Society*, N*exus:Architecture and Mathematics*, as well as other journals. She is currently co-editing a book on the role of architecture in eighteenth- and nineteenth-century historical fiction.

Professor Robert Harbison teaches at London Metropolitan University, England where he heads the MA in Architectural History, Theory and Interpretation.

He is the author of many books on architecture and wider cultural themes, including *Eccentric Spaces, The Built, the Unbuilt and the Unbuildable, Reflections on Baroque*, as well as a forthcoming History of Western Architecture.

Sue Harris was educated in architecture, welfare work, and language in Sydney, Australia and in Canada where she lived and worked for many years. Sue has spent much of her career working with architects, specializing in managing and administering the process. She also has extensive experience in stonework conservation for the Department of Public Works in New South Wales, Australia.

Chris How has a variety of experience in investigation and design, including bridges, below ground, and large span structures in steel, timber, and reinforced concrete. He was in private practice from 1976 until 2004 in western Victoria, Australia and is the author of a number of unpublished reports on heritage buildings.

His publications are 'Translated Tradition in the Portland Bay Settlement,' in Malcolm Duncan et al. [eds.], *Proceedings of the Second International Congress on Construction History Volume 2* (Cambridge 2006); 'Stability and Survival,' in John Ashurst [ed.], *Conservation of Ruins* (Oxford, 2006); 'Medieval Traces in a Modern Garner', in Miles Lewis [ed.], *The Victorian Barn*, Conference: Melbourne University. (Melbourne, 2007); 'The Balanced Ledger; the Steam Packet Inn,' *Building Connections*, Spring 2005 (Melbourne, 2005).

Douglas Lloyd Jenkins is a writer, historian, and academic. He is one of New Zealand's best known and most highly respected design, art, and architecture writers. He was awarded the Montana Medal for Non Fiction for his book *At Home: A Century of New Zealand Design*. Described by Wallpaper magazine as "one of the most influential design writers in the Southern Hemisphere," he is currently the director of Hawke's Bay Museum and Art Gallery, Napier, New Zealand.

Associate Professor June Komisar is an architect, and teaches in the Department of Architectural Science at Ryerson University, Toronto, Canada. She holds an MA in Architecture from Yale University and a PhD in Architecture from the University of Michigan. She is an associate of the Centre for Studies in Food Security, and the principal investigator of a multidisciplinary research facility—the "REAL Lab" at Ryerson.

Her research includes Brazilian architecture, the design process, and the connections between urban agriculture and sustainable architecture.

Bill Millard has a PhD from Rutgers University, United States and works as a writer, editor, and consultant. His work appears in *icon*; *Oculus* and *e-Oculus,* the American Institute of Architects' journal and e-journal; *The Architect's Newspaper*; *BD*; the *RIBA Journal*; *Architect*; the *LEAF Review*; *Sites*; *OMA's Content* (Köln:Taschen, 2004); and in Bechir Kenzari [ed.], *Architecture and Violence* (Barcelona, 2008). He is currently working on a book about the American built environment, with support from the Graham Foundation for Advanced Studies in the Fine Arts.

Ron Powell holds a Bachelor in Architecture, a Graduate Diploma in Landscape Design from the University of New South Wales, Australia as well as a Graduate Diploma in Environmental Studies from Macquarie University, Australia. As an architecture student, he worked on the Sydney Opera House.

Ron has worked on major public open spaces including Sydney's Darling Harbour and Bicentennial Park. At the present time, he is overseeing the conservation of Sydney's nineteenth-century sandstone buildings.

Craig Reynolds holds an MA in Architectural History from Virginia Commonwealth University, United States. In 2006, he was awarded the Frederic Lindley Morgan Architecture Research Award from the University of Louisville, where he is currently pursuing a PhD. He was previously awarded a research internship at the Thomas Jefferson Library, Monticello, and a grant from the Virginia Department of Historic Resources for the study of Jeffersonian architecture. He has also worked in the publications office of the Virginia Historical Society and as a preservation advocate for both government and not-for-profit historic preservation organizations.

Professor Elizabeth H. Riorden has taught architecture at the University of Cincinnati, United States since 2002. She practiced architecture for ten years, and became a Registered Architect in the State of New York in 1988. In 1992, she moved to Tübingen, Germany, to work on the documentation and conservation of the archaeological site of Troy, located in northwestern Turkey, on a full-time basis. She is a member of the American Institute of Architects and is a Fellow of the American Academy in Rome.

Roger Sandall holds a degree in archaeology and anthropology from the University of Auckland, New Zealand. He did postgraduate work in fine arts and theater at Columbia University in New York. He has worked in an architectural studio specializing in town planning and urban design. He has also written on literature, philosophy, and the arts in *Art International*, *Commentary*, *The New Criterion*, the German cultural journal *Merkur*, and the former UK publication *Encounter*. In the past year, he has participated in radio broadcasts on the Australian programs *The Philosopher's Zone* and *Counterpoint*.

Dr. Jeffrey John Turnbull is Senior Fellow in the Faculty of Architecture, Building and Planning, University of Melbourne, Australia. He teaches architectural design and architectural history.

His PhD thesis, "The Architecture of Newman College," is a new interpretation of the work of the Chicago architect Walter Burley Griffin. Dr. Turnbull was a Visiting Professorial Fellow for the Griffin Exchange Program at the University of Illinois at Urbana-Champaign during 1988. An outcome of this exchange was the 450-page volume: Jeff Turnbull and Peter Navaretti [eds.], *The Griffins in Australia and India: the complete works of Walter Burley Griffin and Marion Mahony Griffin* (Melbourne: Miegunyah Press, 1998).

Contents

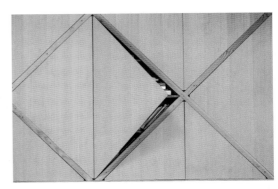

Foreword

Architecture is a universal art and a universal science, because it affects everyone. It is more than just the creation of buildings that work effectively: and it is more than just the development of design style or fashion. It creates the icons that define our culture—the temple, the house, the monument, the skyscraper, and so on.

Buildings (including engineering works amongst them), are also our greatest permanent investment, and for most families in the world the construction, purchase, or rental of a dwelling is their greatest material commitment.

But the creation of architecture can be looked at it in another way as well. Building processes themselves—not just the results of them—are part of our culture. How you thatch a roof depends upon what you learnt from your ancestors and from your neighbors, and how you then accommodate those lessons to the materials and conditions before you. How you form an opera house or an art gallery is the result of the interaction between design ideas, civic aspirations, material constraints, and much more.

Frank Gehry's designs are specific to our age, because they depend upon computer software which has existed for only two or three decades. But Glen Murcutt's designs are also of our age because they reconfigure, in terms of contemporary sensibilities, ideas about shade and ventilation which are timeless, and a material, corrugated iron, which is almost two centuries old.

When you look at the elements of architecture, as we do in this book, you find so much in common between the past and the present, and between one nation and another. And the differences are as instructive as the similarities. An approach that looks at the roof as a universal phenomenon across cultures, and at the window or door as forms that evolved over thousands of years, takes us to the essence of how built forms are created and where they come from.

We do not know the inventor of the hipped roof, any more than we know the inventor of the wheel, but both are enormously important developments. The first person to tip a stone upright and fix it in place fulfilled a universal desire for monumentality, and his stone, no doubt, immediately acquired symbolic and sacred associations. How can one evaluate the significance of this?

Historically the great task of the builder has been to enclose space, and the first person to create a space in which hundreds of people could meet—perhaps a Hittite architect—created the conditions that would allow complex social developments up to and including democracy.

Those are the sorts of issues that can be investigated through a survey of the fundamental elements of architecture, such as we provide here. But such an enterprise raises as many new questions as it answers old ones—which is how it should be. The writers of this book interpret their subject matter in their own terms, and you, the reader, should do the same.

You are probably already interested in design and style, but we hope you will now look at buildings in another context, and share our fascination with what has made them as they are. You will see that they result from the interaction of cultural influences and practical constraints. They encapsulate, on the one hand, the particular circumstances of time and place, and on the other, the universal concerns and the achievements of humankind.

Miles Lewis

Introduction

Stemming from the fundamental human need for a dwelling place, architecture has evolved over millennia into an artistic, highly sophisticated practice, combining a multitude of skills and technologies. Throughout its history, the role of the architect and the purpose of architecture have been continuously debated.

Architecture: An Overview

Architecture, much like art, is difficult to define, even though we may think we know it when we see it. We tend to elevate to the status of "architecture" grand and imposing buildings such as the Alhambra in Granada, Spain, or Machu Picchu in the Peruvian highlands. Yet we frequently overlook the residential districts, commercial structures, industrial landscapes, and agricultural buildings that comprise the majority of our physical surroundings. We know that architecture exists *somewhere*, but don't always recognize it where we happen to be.

For those who can afford to travel, architectural wonders offer a focal point around which a holiday might be organized. What would a trip to Egypt be, for example, without experiencing the monumental piles of stonework that comprise the Great Pyramids of Giza? How could one travel to Guatemala without confronting the perilously steep stairs marking the faces of Tikal's temple-tombs? Could an initial visit to Rome fail to include entering the Pantheon and lifting one's head to the oculus atop the perfect dome? Does not Chicago beg for visitor interaction with the legacy of the world's first steel-framed commercial skyscrapers? Is a trip to Barcelona, Spain, possible any longer without encountering the architecture, or at least the architectural influence, of Antoni Gaudí? Or, for that matter, can one visit Glasgow, Scotland, and avoid exposure to the work of Charles Rennie Mackintosh and Margaret Macdonald?

What is Architecture?

Architecture has forever stirred our imaginations, inspirations, and dreams, and it is no wonder we desire a firsthand encounter with its most extraordinary examples. Works such as those highlighted in this book, including the Hagia Sophia in Istanbul, the Parthenon in Athens, and the Castle of the White Heron in Himeji, Japan, reflect the highest levels of architectural achievement—whether for their proportional harmony, engineering precision, material treatment, detailed ornament, or for offering excellent examples of spanning, enclosure, circulation, or use of daylight. Any student or scholar of architecture should keep in mind, of course, that the construction of many of the world's most celebrated buildings required

The ruins of Machu Picchu in Peru, a mountaintop citadel built and used by the Incas between the mid-fifteenth and early sixteenth centuries CE, were only discovered by Westerners in 1911. They encompass residences, temples, fortifications, and steep terraces.

At New Gourna, near Luxor, in the 1940s, Egyptian architect Hassan Fathy demonstrated that Egypt could develop a modern building style using locally available materials—mainly mud brick—and traditional indigenous construction methods.

the conquest of large territories, the unbridled authority of particular leaders, and enormous financial outlay. Some works took whole generations to complete, required the often involuntary labor of thousands, and benefited only an elite few. Yet whatever the circumstances of their building process, there is little question that the finished products, even in ruin, constitute architecture.

But what of the less permanent, less ornate buildings that undoubtedly once enveloped these achievements? What of the outbuildings, storehouses, and workers' villages, the infrastructure of streets, walkways, and water supply systems? What of the physical spaces required for eating, drinking, sleeping, and other aspects of everyday life? These parts of the architectural context are typically designed and planned by somebody, but can often be assigned no specific authorship. Are these also considered architecture, whether in the past or the present? And, if so, what therefore *is* architecture?

Architectura *and Much Else*

That question is not so easily answered. The term "architecture" derives from the Latin *architectura* (which in turn comes from the Greek *architekton*) and refers specifically to a master builder in charge of construction. But this does not cover the numerous ways in which this most public of the arts is interpreted. Open 15 books discussing architecture, and one is confronted with at least 15 different definitions. Leaf through those books and one is likely to discover all sorts of buildings and other structures, from temples and towers to train stations and tipis. Examining any one project closely reveals numerous layers of meaning.

Take, for example, Hassan Fathy's New Gourna Village project, built near Luxor in Egypt, beginning in the mid 1940s. The construction of the village was commissioned by the Egyptian Department of Antiquities, which wished to resettle the inhabitants of the town of Gourna, who for many years had lived atop the pharaonic tombs and periodically raided them for a living. Constructing a new town, 5 miles (8 km) away but along a popular visitor route to the Valley of the Kings would remove the villagers from their proximity to the tombs yet

still allow them to capitalize economically on their location by selling crafts to passing tourists.

Although modern construction methods and materials, such as concrete, were available, Fathy envisioned New Gourna as a low-tech demonstration of ancient building practices. He rejected the use of expensive non-native materials and new machinery, considering them an imposition on Egyptian culture. Instead, he employed adobe bricks for walls, vaults, and domes, and mandated that all of the buildings be erected by hand. He turned to indigenous vernacular architecture and planning for inspiration, calling for individual dwellings of minimal decoration to surround courtyards featuring communal wells.

One can find beauty in these materials and geometries, and in the shadows they cast at the site. Yet this was not all that Fathy was aiming for: by practicing ancient techniques to create age-old forms, he hoped his efforts would train all residents to build for themselves, thus circumventing the need for costly, imported materials and outside influences. Fathy wanted New Gourna's architecture to work as a didactic exercise: encouraging residents to value their history and their community, and, perhaps most importantly, making them into better citizens.

But Fathy's architectural experiment ultimately backfired: the residents who moved to New Gourna did not wish to live in some romanticized version of the past. Extended families necessitated additions to existing dwellings, and soon some houses stretched into the communal courtyards, whose wells were soon discarded for running water. Residents also obtained concrete to expand their houses vertically. Fathy's master plan was eventually suspended, and so many alterations have been made over time that picturing the settlement's original appearance is a challenging task.

Fathy's work highlights architecture's myriad characteristics and raises a number of interesting questions about this dynamic field. Must architecture be created by a master builder or designed by a professionally trained architect, or can anyone do it? Should architecture respect tradition, or can it reject the past in favor of something new? Is the original design of a building, village, or city most crucial in considering architectural

The Castle of the White Heron, or Himeji Castle, in Hyogo Prefecture, Japan, was built in the first decade of the seventeenth century, incorporating a fourteenth-century fort on the site. The central tower has seven floors and rises to 150 ft (45 m).

Muller and Muller's Millennium Park Bicycle Shed in Chicago, opened in 2004, provides a vital service for commuters, and also serves the broader community by minimizing energy use and pollution.

worth, or should changes over time be taken into account? Should architecture affect behavior in profound ways, or can it be neutral? Must architecture be beautiful, or can it be mundane? Does architecture have inherent meaning, or is meaning provided by critics, historians, passersby, and users—in short, by culture?

Cathedrals and Bicycle Sheds

To a significant degree, our understanding of architecture remains crystallized in a dichotomy laid out by the British architectural historian Sir Nikolaus Pevsner in the first sentence of *An Outline of European Architecture* (1943). To distinguish between "architecture" and a "building," Pevsner declared, "A bicycle shed is a building; Lincoln Cathedral is a piece of architecture." Pevsner implied that a bicycle shed cannot be architecture because it lacks aesthetic appeal and its interior has no effect on human sensations. At the same time, he described Lincoln Cathedral (1192–1280) as being so important and influential that it helped define English national character; the arches of the cathedral's Angel Choir in particular, he claimed, were demonstrations of "supreme beauty" and "warmth and sweetness."

Today, however, we might reconsider this distinction. Lincoln Cathedral has not lost its power as architecture, but, as a building type, the bicycle

Renaissance architects saw ancient Greek buildings, such as the Temple of Concord, at Agrigento, Sicily, Italy (below), as successfully combining functionality, stability, and beauty. The Temple of Concord dates from around 430 BCE; from CE 597 it was used as a Christian church, which aided its preservation.

shed has gained supporters. A bicycle shed might be an unlikely candidate for defining national character, and if any sheds feature rib vaulting, stained-glass windows, trefoils, and sculpted angels—all features of Lincoln Cathedral—they are not well known. But in towns or cities where bicycles are crucial means of transportation, human engagement with a bicycle shed might be more valuable than with a cathedral or with other examples of monumental architecture. The shed may not offer obvious spiritual uplift, but as a functional building for bike parking, it has a cultural significance that belies a possible lack of aesthetic appeal. Does this not also make it significant as architecture?

In fact, it has already been demonstrated that a bicycle shed can be a work of architectural importance. The Millennium Park Bicycle Commuter Station in Chicago, designed by the architectural firm Muller and Muller and opened in 2004, does not have a particularly striking visual presence in the city. However, its 120 photovoltaic roof panels, natural ventilation system, and atrium with climbing plants make it a significant building as part of the city's

efforts to lower energy costs, encourage cycling, and reduce pollution. Insofar as lowering carbon emissions is today a global imperative, is not this glorified bicycle shed an important symbol of our time, and thus architecturally significant? In this respect, do its aesthetics even matter?

To discuss a bicycle shed in this fashion suggests a shift in our attitude toward the proper objectives of architecture and a willingness to recognize that aesthetic grandeur is not the only measure of architectural worth. Increasingly, too, we recognize the importance of spatial experience: unlike other arts, architecture is fundamentally three-dimensional, and permits human movement in space. Any building, even a plain box, can be culturally significant and allow for movement.

Utility, Stability, and Beauty

Yet not everyone agrees that simple, unornamented boxes merit architectural consideration. Popular wisdom still holds that a bicycle shed and its ilk—the water tower, the warehouse, the factory, the mobile home, and the fast-food restaurant, for example—are not architecture. They lack beauty. The roots of this attitude may date back to the first century BCE, when the Roman military engineer Marcus Vitruvius Pollio, usually known simply as Vitruvius, completed what is the only surviving treatise on architecture from antiquity: *De architectura libri decem*, or *Ten Books on Architecture*. In the treatise, Vitruvius carefully delineated three principal characteristics that all works of architecture must contain. Firstly, they must have *utilitas*, meaning "use," "commodity," or "function"—in other words, architecture must serve a purpose. Secondly, architecture also must demonstrate *firmitas*; that is, buildings must have firmness or structure, they must be stable. And finally, architecture must display *venustas*, which means

Lincoln Cathedral (1192–1280; right), in eastern England, was a yardstick of architectural beauty for the historian Sir Nikolaus Pevsner, and for Victorian critic John Ruskin, who called it "the most precious piece of architecture in the British Isles."

"delight" or "beauty." If buildings are to be more than functional and stable—if they are to rise to the level of art—they must embody the intangible characteristic of beauty. Vitruvius did not define beauty, but thought it could be discovered in ideal proportions following the natural laws determined by his predecessors, the Greeks.

In the fifteenth century, the Italian humanist Leon Battista Alberti codified Vitruvius's three-part architectural definition in his own work *De re aedificatoria libri decem*, or *Ten Books on Architecture* (1472). The title's echoing of

An Iconoclast?

Fusing uneven surfaces, outlandish colors, parabolic vaults, and an eclectic range of materials, the work of Catalan architect Antoni Gaudí defied categorization and challenged architectural conventions. Active in Barcelona, Spain, at the turn of the twentieth century, Gaudí drew inspiration from the Gothic tradition, Spain's Moorish past, the local natural landscape, the work of Barcelona-based artists and architects, and rational principles of structure prominent in nineteenth-century Europe. But upon closer inspection of his works, rationality and clarity seem to dissolve. Gaudí's eccentric designs blur the lines between sculpture, architecture, and nature, coming across as a physical realization of some surreal dream. Many of Gaudí's contemporaries saw them as shocking and hideous and a threat to the age-old standards established by Vitruvius. Nevertheless, Gaudí's work is today championed as the principal symbol of Barcelona and an icon of Spain, and is recognized across the globe.

In Gaudí's remodeling of the Casa Batlló in Barcelona, Spain, the only straight lines are those of the pre-existing windows.

Vitruvius's treatise was intentional, for Alberti wished to update Vitruvius's earlier work to meet the demands and ideals of his own age. Like Vitruvius, Alberti suggested that architects should turn to classical models for aesthetic inspiration. But to a greater extent than Vitruvius, he found it necessary to separate builders from architects. According to Alberti, builders should have manual skills, such as the ability to dress and lay stone, but architects should be well-read men of *ideas*. Thus, with the publication of Alberti's *Ten Books*, architecture became rhetorically established as an intellectual pursuit—one that extended well beyond the technical knowledge required for the building process. It also resulted in it becoming a profession dominated by educated men of the elite.

Because Alberti's and Vitruvius's works dealt exclusively with classical antiquity as the standard for architectural beauty, for centuries most writings on architecture treated the Western tradition—and classicism in particular—as the pinnacle of architectural achievement, with almost everything else existing on a sliding scale somewhere beneath it. Later scholars even treated monumental works of medieval architecture, despite their structural accomplishments and elaborate sculptural programs, as an aberration.

A World of Architecture
Using classical architecture as a barometer, not only would bicycle sheds never qualify as architecture, but most non-Western buildings also would struggle to measure up. And, indeed, that is what happened for a long period. Many early reports on non-Western architecture, whether in India, Mexico, Vietnam, or North Africa, for example, treated even the grandest buildings in these regions as, at best, inexplicable and mysterious, and, at worst, barbaric, unsophisticated, and primitive, with all the negative and racist connotations those terms imply. We must remember of course that many of these accounts

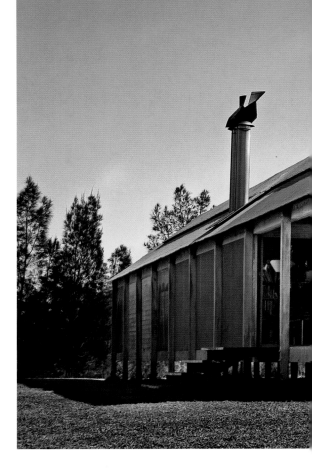

Glenn Murcutt's Marie Short House, near Kempsey, Australia, completed in 1975 (above), is typical of his work in its form and its use of locally available materials—the walls are of timber, the roof of corrugated metal, and the window louvers of enameled steel. At the same time, the design claims to be environmentally sensitive and energy efficient.

The temple complex of Angkor Wat in Cambodia (below) was constructed during the reign of King Suryavarman II (CE 1113–1150). French explorer Henri Mouhot, one of the first Westerners to view the complex, in the mid-nineteenth century, refused to believe the indigenous Khmer people had built it.

were written by European missionaries and colonizers to justify their attempts to "civilize," dominate, and exploit indigenous populations. Given the political situation, only under rare circumstances were outstanding examples of non-Western architecture given their due. Today, however, non-Western architecture is more often recognized on its own terms.

To understand the architecture of any culture and to assess its merit as architecture, one must attempt to understand the culture's traditions, practices, resources, and climate. To judge the architecture of Western antiquity as more monumental and sophisticated than, say, that of China or Japan, fails to acknowledge that, for example, many East Asian cultures typically place less importance on permanence in construction. To align with a variety of spiritual imperatives, the renewability of particular materials in Asia trumped their longevity. An inability to recognize these imperatives will lead only to a superficial and limited impression of architectural achievement.

Global Responsibility

The knowledge that buildings are the world's largest consumers of energy compels us to reconsider what counts as architecture, or at least what counts as *responsible* architecture. While buildings featuring technological advancements, fine craft, and exquisite detail continue to be executed worldwide, architects increasingly look to vernacular traditions and local materials in an effort to reduce waste, lower costs, and more effectively connect to the spirit of a place.

In recent years, recycled, non-toxic materials, passive solar technology, water-catchment systems, and sod roofs to prevent stormwater runoff have all established themselves within the conventional architectural lexicon. Such materials, technologies, and systems may be neither cheap nor lend themselves to aesthetic beauty. Yet with the desire to reduce the world's carbon emissions and reconnect with the natural environment, perhaps some of the best architectural examples today showcase the reused, recycled, and energy efficient.

In the words of the Australian architect Glenn Murcutt, drawing from an Australian Aboriginal proverb, such buildings will "touch the earth lightly." Murcutt has long designed in ways that pay homage to indigenous methods of building in form and material, while simultaneously having minimal impact on the natural environment. But his architecture still offers maximum natural light and ventilation and appears refreshing due to his inventive use of modern materials such as steel, corrugated metal, and glass. In an age of computer-aided design and digital modeling software, massive architectural firms, and splashy buildings regularly gracing the pages of architectural journals, Murcutt's work, nearly all of which is in the Australian state of New South Wales, seems modest, quiet, almost mundane. And yet Murcutt, who works in a tiny architectural firm consisting only of himself, received the profession's highest honor, the Pritzker Architectural Prize, in 2002.

Perhaps the future of architecture will be less about whether a building attains *utilitas, firmitas,* and *venustas,* but instead about whether it meets new goals for environmental responsibility and makes an effort to connect to the land, history, and local tradition. Such goals will only add to architecture's many facets, raising new questions as much as they answer old ones. In the pages that follow, the reader is invited to enter into this world of complexity and richness.

The Hearst Tower in New York, designed by Norman Foster and opened in 2006, was the first building in Manhattan to receive a Gold Rating from the US Green Building Council, the national authority on environmentally sensitive design. The tower sits on top of the original six-story Hearst headquarters.

The Evolution of Architecture

The earliest surviving works with an architectural intention are cave paintings in southern France and northern Spain, such as those of animals at Lascaux in the Dordogne, France which may be 16,000 years old. These create powerful spatial effects through their placement and combination, ranged overhead like sprawling constellations or painted in groups at eye level. How these spaces were used is only partly known; certainly they were not dwellings.

The early development of architecture is undocumented because the majority of prehistoric buildings were constructed of perishable materials and survive only as, for example, postholes in the ground. Ritual spaces were often built to last longer or maintained more scrupulously, so structures such as Stonehenge in southern England have outlived their makers' other constructions. Like Stonehenge, the earliest dwellings known in Britain are roughly circular and loosely grouped, for example the half-buried

homes at Skara Brae in the Orkney Islands of Scotland, which date from around 3000 BCE. Ten dwellings from the original settlement survive, linked by low tunnels, the nearest thing to a set of constructed caves.

Between a settlement like Skara Brae and the earliest cities lie many lost transitional stages. Recently, part of this story has been filled in with the discovery of ancient urban conglomerations in Anatolia, most notably at Çatal Hüyük. In later millennia, Mesopotamian cities were marked by huge central mounds called ziggurats, consisting of the remains of earlier structures and scaled by elaborate systems of stairs and crowned by temples, which entered folklore as the Tower of Babel. These were the setting for the exploits of Gilgamesh, following the emergence of writing at cities such as Eridu, Uruk, and Ur, (in modern Iraq) in the fourth millennium BCE. In a parallel but separate development in Egypt, a form of picture writing now known as hieroglyphics

permitted the administrative structures necessary for a unified state, sizable cities, and monumental architecture. At this stage, the greatest energy was poured into building tombs and the ritual sites attached to them. The first monumental stone buildings in the world were erected at Saqqara as the funerary complex of King Djoser, halfway through the third millennium BCE.

Patterns of the Pyramids

After Djoser, the development of Egyptian architecture was extremely rapid. Within a century, the stepped pyramid had been perfected to the familiar smooth-sided form, its slope symbolizing the spreading pattern of the sun's rays as well as the pharaoh's path to the heavens. The construction of Khufu's pyramid, the largest of the three main pyramids at Giza, has mystified the world ever since it was completed, probably in 20 years around 2650 BCE. It was the world's largest and tallest structure until surprisingly

The Stone Age village of Skara Brae (left) in the Orkney Islands off the north coast of Scotland, was entombed in sand for centuries before being exposed by powerful storms in 1850 and 1926.

The ziggurat of Ur (*c.* 2100 BCE) in Mesopotamia, now Iraq, has been reconstructed on the original site (above). Three stairways led to a small shrine on the summit, dedicated to the moon god Nanna.

recently, but contains the burial space for just one person, and his grave goods, contents long ago removed by tomb robbers, along with the outer coating of polished masonry. Speculation still surrounds the numbers, skills, and remuneration (if any) of the workforce, the kind of ramp (or its absence), and the means of lifting and transporting materials used to build the pyramid. The attention to detail was remarkable: the pyramid is oriented extremely accurately to the cardinal directions, is dimensioned carefully using multiples of *pi*, and incorporates "ventilation shafts" aligned with critical points in the heavens.

Nothing so impressive was built in the 3,000 years of Egyptian architecture that followed. Temples unconnected with tombs began to be built at Abydos in the next dynasty. The fulfillment of this development is the complex at Karnak, which was added to and developed, ruined by invaders, and rebuilt over 1,200 years, ultimately becoming the largest and most complex of Egyptian temples.

Classical Refinements

Egyptian objects have been discovered at Mycenae, and the earliest freestanding Greek figure sculpture is obviously dependent on

Egyptian precedent. Likewise, the post and beam, or post and lintel, structure of the majority of Greek temples probably springs from the architecture of Minoan Crete, which had trading connections with Egypt and constructed flat roofs in a similar way.

The earliest architectural sculpture in Greece appeared around 1250 BCE over an entrance in the defensive walls at Mycenae, in the form of a carving of two lions guarding a central column, a feature that was to become a crucial and distinctive element of Greek architecture. According to Vitruvius, the column was identified with the human figure, and the proportions of the body thus determined the proportions of architecture, resulting in buildings generally on a more modest scale than in Egypt.

Refinement of the column gave rise to what later became known as the classical orders. The Doric order became standardized over the whole Greek world except Ionia, as reflected in the temples at Paestum in southern Italy (mid-sixth and mid-fifth centuries BCE), the Temple of Zeus at Olympia, Greece (just previous to the Periclean Parthenon), and at the Parthenon in Athens (447–433/2 BCE). One of the other orders of ancient Greece, the Ionic, is seen in the enormous temples built at Ephesus in the sixth century BCE and at Didyma in Asia Minor.

Roman Discoveries Lost

Roman architecture generally survives more intact than Greek, partly through historical or geological accident. The eruption of Vesuvius in CE 79, for example, preserved an entire Roman town, including houses, shops, public spaces,

Elegant Ionic columns (below) are among the remnants of the elaborate temple built at Didyma, near Miletus in present-day Turkey, between 500 and 200 BCE. The temple was the home of an oracle of Apollo, considered the most important oracle in the Hellenic world after that of Delphi.

The original two-story buildings of Trajan's Market in Rome (left), used in ancient Roman times as shops and offices, are topped by medieval dwellings.

Magnificent mosaics in the Byzantine style (right) decorate the Church of San Vitale in Ravenna, Italy, built in CE 530–548. The church was begun under Ostrogothic rule and decorated after the Byzantine reconquest of the city.

and even the plants in Roman gardens. In the city of Rome itself, a great deal of early architecture remains, sometimes, as at the Pantheon (*c.* CE 118–128), because older buildings were given Christian functions, and sometimes, as at Trajan's Market (*c.* CE 100–112), because the site was so intractable. The market, a masterful piece of mixed-use planning, incorporates a vaulted hall on two levels (like a modern shopping mall), large vaulted spaces that might be lecture halls, and its own internal streets. The span of the Pantheon's dome remained the

greatest in the world until 1911. A shell of such size and thinness was only made possible by the Roman discovery of concrete, here used in varying consistencies, with large chunks of rubble incorporated lower down the structure and smaller chunks higher up. The cylinder of the dome contains brick relieving arches, which lightened the mass and made it possible to go on building while the concrete cured.

Concrete vaults and brick-clad concrete construction were the great Roman architectural discoveries, but the techniques were soon lost. Domes subsequently built in the Eastern Roman Empire, also known as the Byzantine Empire, were most often made of brick. The magnificent early-sixth-century church of Hagia Sophia in

Constantinople (now Istanbul) successfully hybridized various Roman spatial motifs on the grandest scale, combining a central domed structure with an elongated plan by means of semidomes, and galleries, which manage difficult transitions seamlessly. No later Byzantine building is nearly so ambitious as Hagia Sophia, but a variety of tall, dark, domed spaces, coated in mosaic, fresco or a combination of the two is found across a wide area that includes the Balkans (especially mainland Greece), Sicily, Armenia, southern Russia, and parts of Italy. Indeed, for historical reasons the Byzantine capital at Ravenna on the Italian Adriatic coast is perhaps a better place to sample Byzantine imagery than Constantinople itself, and San Marco in Venice remains a moving derivative of Byzantine architectural ideas.

Norman success in conquering extensive areas of Western Europe in the tenth and eleventh centuries led to some of the most ambitious building of this period, imposing consistency on regions that had previously built in more idiosyncratic forms, such as Anglo-Saxon England. The name "Romanesque" identifies the link between the new forms and Roman arched construction in stone. By comparison with the later Gothic style, Romanesque buildings are usually heavy and dark, but many of the most important innovations of the Gothic, including rib vaults and pointed arches, are present in potential in such Romanesque monuments as Durham Cathedral, begun in 1093.

The Writing on the Walls

The widely observed prohibition on animal or human figures in the decoration of sacred buildings led Islamic designers to the richest geometrical and calligraphic ornamentation in world architecture. The spiritual content of Koranic calligraphy is obvious; geometrical intricacy is also viewed as a form of divine revelation, mirroring the symmetry and harmony of reality. In the Friday Mosque at Isfahan, Iran, geometry and calligraphy are combined in the hypnotic mosaic of *iwan* vaults; the principal mihrab or prayer niche, 20 by 10 ft (6 by 3 m) of deep stucco relief, was designed by a calligrapher and incorporates long inscriptions in three different scripts all threaded into a bed of vegetation. In Samarkand and Turkestan, too, there are tombs and memorial complexes that are covered with glazed tiles carrying inscriptions in stylized scripts that turn entire buildings into writing.

Calligraphy and geometric patterns predominate in this *iwan* vault in the Friday Mosque, Isfahan, Iran.

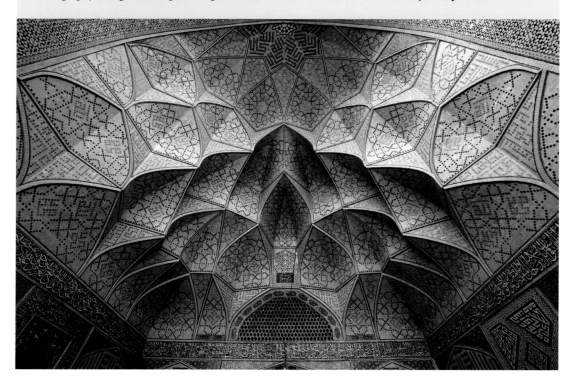

Islamic Architecture

In its earliest phases, Islamic architecture is marked by extreme simplicity. Mosques of the seventh to tenth centuries CE combine three elements: a high perimeter wall, repetitive arcades forming a rudimentary covered area, and a large open court, often with a fountain for ritual ablutions. From early times, a prominent tower was part of the complex, which is otherwise of markedly low profile. This tower or minaret functions as a marker in the urban fabric (or in the vastness of the desert), and had a practical function as a high point from which to call people to prayer.

Preexisting cultures on which Islam was overlaid contributed local forms that differentiate the buildings of particular regions, such as the rich tilework and onion domes of Persia, the stucco decoration (inherited from Rome) found over much of the Middle East, and the striped and joggled stonework of Egypt. Islamic decoration often plays over the surface obscuring the structure lurking beneath.

One of the finest examples of the early Gothic style that emerged in northern France, the cathedral of Laon, northeast of Paris, was begun in the mid-twelfth century and completed in 1235.

Beginning in the mid-eighth century, at Ellora, near Aurangabad, India, temples were hewn out of cliffs. The largest, the Kailasa Temple, represents Kailasa or Mount Kailash, the home of the Hindu deity Shiva.

Gothic Triumphs in Europe

One could almost say that the Gothic style of architecture has a single inventor, the French royal adviser Abbot Suger. His renovations of the church of Saint-Denis near Paris in 1136–1144 incorporated a range of innovations that were much copied and came to define the style. They included increasing the height of the central vessel and the amount of light let into the building through the use of ribbed vaults and external buttresses. After Suger, architectural development was extremely rapid in a small area of northern France. The cathedrals at Laon, Chartres, Reims and Amiens are the major landmarks in the process, each outdoing the other in simplifying internal elevations, and in raising the height of naves until the sense of soaring vertical movement becomes overpowering and windows seem to fill practically the whole wall. The end of the process was reached later at Beauvais, where the striving to externalize the structural frame in a skeletal system of flying buttresses in order to build ever lighter and higher overreached itself. In 1284, twelve years after the building was completed, the chancel vault collapsed, though it was quickly rebuilt over sturdier arcades.

The Gothic style quickly spread from northern France across the rest of northern Europe and Spain; only Italy remained relatively immune. Regional styles varied: in England, for example, large Gothic churches emphasized length as much as height and, in the fourteenth century, attention focused on the elaboration of vaulting ribs, often in defiance of structural logic. In German lands, too, extravagant variations on rib patterns became a striking feature. In fact, the late Gothic of the fourteenth and fifteenth centuries in most of Europe was a time of decorative exuberance, when the stone fabric of buildings was brought to life in ogee arches and thickets of carved creatures.

The Cosmos in Stone

The Middle Ages were also the great age of temple-building in India. From the beginning, ritual structures in India were based on cosmic symbolism: monumental buildings, such as the Buddhist stupa at Sanchi, constructed in the first century BCE in central India, were seen as mountains, unbreachable spherical mounds faced in stone and surrounded by fenced stone platforms circumambulated by devotees. At the cardinal points, these were marked by gateways exuberantly carved with scenes from the life of the Buddha and the natural world; in places such as Amaravati in southern India, built around CE 200, the stone fences and terraces were also covered with carved scenes.

By natural progression, Buddhist cave temples led to Hindu versions of the union between the building and the mountain, and to structures such as the Kailasa Temple at Ellora (CE 750–950), in western central India, where the temple-as-mountain was created by carving a tiered structure out of a basalt rock slope, which still flanks the freestanding building on three sides. At Khajuraho in central India, a cluster of temples, built from 950 to 1050, towers like

a chain of mountain peaks. In the largest examples, the marker over the inner shrine, reached after traversing a series of porches and low halls, is a many-tiered, solid mass of stone composed of a series of diminished replicas of the main tower, which narrows to an elaborate sculptural finial, rather than any sort of enterable space. A fascinating range of derivatives of such temples is spread across Southeast Asia, in Cambodia, Burma, and Indonesia.

Limits and Boundaries in the East

The pagoda or *ta*, one of the distinctive features of Chinese architecture from an early stage, is an expansion of the umbrella finial that crowns Indian stupas. The first examples were built over Buddhist relics, and at first formed the entire shrine. Early Chinese architecture was constrained by its typical material, wood, which limited most buildings to one story, so elaboration usually involved building along horizontal axes, with, typically, the most prestigious buildings at the center and important structures set apart on platforms, at the tops of stairways, and inside series of moats and gates. The ultimate form of this arrangement is the palace at the heart of the city, surviving in the plan of Beijing, where the Outer City leads to the Inner City, which contains the Imperial City and, inside it, the Forbidden City, most of which was out of bounds except to the imperial family.

Chinese gardens, however, seem to violate these principles of order in their asymmetry and irregularity, which extends from the shapes of ponds and rockeries to the layout of passageways

and sequencing of views. Japanese gardens go even further in pursuit of the rustic and of seemingly accidental effects. The explanation for this may lie in the indigenous Japanese Shinto cult, which, unlike Chinese animism, takes its own architectural form—the Ise Shrine, Uji-Yamada, Japan, completed in CE 690, is a notable example. In a quite different and much later building, the early-seventeenth-century Katsura Imperial Villa, the summer place of an idle aristocrat, now on the outskirts of the city of Kyoto, we also find the veneration of simple materials and shapes, along with a more sophisticated taste for rambling plans and an interfusion between nature and architecture.

The design of the Forbidden City in Beijing (1406–1420) reflects a highly ordered, hierarchical society. Only members of the imperial family or of the highest levels of government could enter the central compound through the major gateways, including the northern Shenwu Gate (above).

The seemingly haphazard but carefully planned estate of the Katsura Imperial Villa near Kyoto, Japan (below), was developed from 1590 by Prince Toshihito, brother of Emperor Go-Yozei, and finished by his son Prince Toshitada. It encompasses a number of residences, as well as four teahouses.

Completed in 1510, the Tempietto at San Pietro in Montorio in Rome, Italy, was commissioned by King Ferdinand and Queen Isabella of Spain and designed by Donato Bramante.

The Renaissance in Italy

In Italy, the classical past was always nearer at hand, and the climate made the pursuit of lighter interiors less urgent, so the Gothic never made significant inroads. Nonetheless, the Renaissance in Italy became one of the great watersheds in architectural history. From this point onward the names of individual architects are attached to buildings—part of the revival of the ancient idea of secular fame—and led to the proliferation of biographies of artists.

Filippo Brunelleschi first came to notice for a feat that was as much science or engineering as architecture: erecting a dome over the crossing of the cathedral in Florence. His next project, an ideal temple interior on a miniature scale,

in the Old Sacristy at San Lorenzo in Florence, perfected a much-copied geometric system. The key was the application of clear spatial logic, based on the circle and the square, and executed in starkly contrasting materials—gray local stone used sparingly for details, white plaster as a consistent background, the result nearly colorless, like an analytical drawing (except that in this case the sculptor Donatello added color and depth, which apparently displeased Brunelleschi).

One of Brunelleschi's main rivals, Leon Battista Alberti, was both a more erudite and more romantic classicist, applying the three principal classical orders (Doric, Ionic, Corinthian) to a single façade, on the Palazzo Rucellai in Florence, and dabbling in colored marbles of Byzantine opulence. Donato Bramante follows in this strand of classicism and his most perfect work, the Tempietto at San Pietro in Montorio in Rome (1502–1510), is intellectually and aesthetically among the most satisfying buildings in the history of architecture.

The architectural works of Michelangelo are among the most unclassifiable and influential in the history of architecture. In his design for the vestibule of the Laurentian Library in Florence (begun in 1524), the staircase fills the bottom half of the tall, narrow space uncomfortably while the surrounding walls upset a number of conventional ideas of function: windows are blind and gigantic columns appear to sit inside the walls. These disconcerting effects seem to spring from a deep rethinking of the elements of architecture, but their point is still obscure; and in the hands of Michelangelo's Mannerist successors such subversive play often feels more like an idle game.

Baroque Extravagance

Michelangelo is sometimes credited with providing the initial stimulus to the Baroque, an expression of impatience with Renaissance harmony and calm. Gian Lorenzo Bernini was another sculptor turned architect, who enjoyed blurring the boundaries between genres and materials. His earliest sculptural works at St. Peter's Basilica in Rome, the birthplace of the style, may be only quasi-architectural, but have overarching architectural intentions. The *Baldacchino* (1624–1633) is an altar canopy on a Herculean scale, and the *Throne of St. Peter* (1657–1666) converts tattered wooden relics into a staggering explosion of colored light, combining rich materials and complex forms into scenographic sequences. Later, Bernini added a huge oval colonnade to the front of the church, creating an outdoor space that more than doubles the total area of St. Peter's.

Baroque was the style of rulers, and used in orchestrations of whole territories, such as the vast gardens at Versailles. But there was another, more willful and mannered Baroque, exemplified by Bernini's assistant and subsequent rival Francesco Borromini and, a generation later, by Guarino Guarini, a mathematician and priest, who built mainly in Turin. At Sant'Ivo della Sapienza, the university church in Rome, Borromini put a dome of alternating concave and convex segments onto a plan based on a six-pointed Star of David.

Toward Naturalism

Dissatisfaction with the florid style of most Baroque architecture was expressed in France with a move in the early eighteenth century to smaller, more comfortable interiors in softer colors and more delicate forms. The style became known as Rococo, which suggests shells and grottos, being derived partly from the French word *rocaille* for "shell." When the style turned up in Bavarian church interiors, it transformed them into outdoor spaces, a pulpit, for example, becoming a gushing spring and a ceiling becoming a cloudscape where the architectural fabric frayed into nonexistence.

Oddly enough, the urge toward expansive naturalism had also emerged in Protestant

The Cult of the Momentary

In the pilgrimage church of Vierzehnheiligen, near Bamberg, Germany, designed by Balthasar Neumann and built between 1743 and 1772, a flimsy coach appears to have stopped temporarily in the center of the space, which embodies in its colors and materials a cult of the momentary, and which in turn feels unexpectedly secular. The "coach" is an elaborate altar, built over the spot where a local peasant saw repeated visions of 14 helper-saints. These saints (in stucco polished to resemble marble) are perched in ascending tiers on the pavilion-like structure. Around this complex sculptural piece swirl the curved spaces loved by Rococo architects, which are extended further by vaporous scenes frescoed onto the ceiling vaults.

In the lavish Rococo interior of Balthasar Neumann's church of Vierzehnheiligen, the oval shape of the central altar depicting the 14 helper-saints is echoed by the curved arcades and by the nave and apse.

England, at places like Stowe and Stourhead, from the 1740s onward, in a new form of garden that strove to blur into the wider landscape through devices such as sunken fences that hid boundaries, and artificial lakes of picturesque, indeterminate shape.

The rapid industrial expansion that transformed the functional and conceptual role of architecture started in England. For a time, however, this drastic change was masked by a series of revivals of styles originally conceived in quite different circumstances. Classical and Gothic revivalists were enemies in their day, but now seem almost equally regressive reponses to new conditions.

In the meantime, Victorian engineering was raising and meeting new challenges, such as the building of bridges and railways sheds. The results pay the merest lip service to traditional ornamental vocabularies. After the partial clearing away of Victorian clutter carried out by Art Nouveau and its offshoots in the late nineteenth century and early twentieth century, it was to such designs that Modernist innovators would turn.

Modernism and Beyond

Modernism occurs later in architecture than in other arts. Significant forerunners of the style are found in Austrian architect Adolf Loos's sugar cube houses, such as the Steiner house in Vienna (1910), and Walter Gropius and Adolf Meyer's model factory in Cologne (designed for an exhibition, not for industry) of 1914. But the breakthrough finally came in the 1920s with the houses that Le Corbusier designed for artists and collectors in Paris and its outskirts. These invert and transform traditional styles (and the lives of their inhabitants), raising the dwelling on stilts and moving the garden to the roof, dissolving interior walls through steel and concrete structures characterized by such trademarks as continuous strip windows on the periphery and ramps between levels.

Even bolder in their attack on the traditional room were designs by Mies van der Rohe, particularly the design for the Brick Country House (1924) and the Barcelona Pavilion (1929), where boundaries are formed by expanses of plate-glass, some of which can be raised and lowered electrically. The freed inhabitant could drift through this seemingly unlimited space like the newly discovered atom.

The history of architecture since the 1960s has been a series of reactions against the purer Modernism of the period between the two World Wars. Some have been jokily traditional (called Postmodernism), some more modern than Modernism (High Tech), and some, based on an earlier distortion of modernist geometry out of political conviction (Russian Constructivism) but now expressing terminal disillusionment (Deconstruction).

Frank Gehry's Guggenheim Museum in Bilbao, Spain completed in 1998, is symptomatic of many current trends. Its outline is easily recognizable, like a company logo; its architect, a Canadian practising in California, is a star, even outside the narrow world of architecture; it is coated in a material, titanium, whose use only became feasible after a dip in the international metals market suddenly made it a cheaper option; it would fit just as well anywhere else, if only someone else had commissioned it first. Like certain other features of the global economy, the Guggenheim in Bilbao, in a region formerly troubled by separatist terrorists, is exciting, rootless, and hard to assign a meaning to.

The massive titanium-clad forms of the Guggenheim Museum in Bilbao, Spain, have since become something of a signature in the work of its architect, Frank Gehry. At Bilbao, the shimmering surfaces echo and reflect, literally, the Nervión River, and can be seen to refer to the city's maritime heritage.

A Timeline of Architecture

The earliest-known dwelling at Ein Guev in Israel, is a round pit covered with skins and branches.

The oldest-known stone monuments created by hunter-gatherers are pillars carved with boars, foxes, lions, birds, snakes, and scorpions, in Gobekli, Turkey.

The oldest identifiable communal building is in the Neolithic rice-growing village of Banpo, in China. It measures 36 by 33 ft (11 by 10 m).

The first large interior space, interrupted only by slender columns, is built in the Hittite capital of Hattusas in modern Turkey.

The first ashlar, or finely dressed stone construction, is used at Saqqara, Egypt, immediately followed by the stepped pyramid, then the smooth-faced form of the Great Pyramid at Giza.

13,000 BCE   **10,000** BCE   **5,000** BCE   **2,000** BCE

Some of the earliest manufactured building materials, irregularly shaped baked clay bricks are used in Jericho, in the West Bank.

The oldest-known complex human settlement is at Çatal Hüyük in Turkey. The single-roomed houses have no door or windows and are entered through the roof.

Large dressed stones, including corbelled and trabeated stone roofing, are first used at the megalithic temples of Malta and Gozo.

The first planned complexes, with multiple stories, balconies, stairs, and corridors, occur at Knossos and other Minoan sites in Crete.

Stone barrel and groin vaulting is revived in the Romanesque Europe during the eleventh century.

Structural concrete developed by the Romans enables them to put solid roofs over large spaces, such as the great dome of the Pantheon in Rome.

The basilican church form, which will dominate for 2000 years, emerges from the precedents of the Roman secular basilica, the Christian burial hall, and the private cult chapel.

The Dark Ages in Europe see invasions of barbarian tribes with different architectural traditions, displacing Roman ones, and forming the basis of stylistic diversity amongst emerging European nations.

Visigothic Spain, Merovingian France, and Saxon England see the revival of dressed stonemasonry, which had been dead in Europe since the fourth century.

Following the birth of Islam, the mosque takes shape, initially as a courtyard, then as a columnar hall. Byzantine influences later lead to the domed mosque.

CE **100**   CE **300**   CE **600**   CE **1000**

Palmyra in Syria, flourishes as a Roman frontier town incorporating, exotic Mesopotamian and Parthian design elements into a grand Roman urban fabric with colonnaded streets.

Hagia Sophia in Istanbul, Turkey, marks a crossroads in design, as the last great engineered building in the Roman tradition with a giant dome, as well as the ancestor of centrally domed Byzantine churches and of the great domed mosques of Ottoman Turkey.

Tikal in Guatemala, the finest of the Mayan sites of Central America, is built. Its steep pyramidal forms ressemble the structures of ancient Egypt and Mesopotamia.

The Mezquita in Córdoba, Spain, becomes the greatest of the colonnaded hall mosques. A forest of columns carries banded lobed arches, influenced by earlier Visigothic architecture.

The Great Mosque of al-Mutawakkil in Iraq is one of the great courtyard mosques of early Islam, with a spiral minaret reflecting the tradition of the Mesopotamian ziggurat.

The present Great Wall of China (mainly Ming Dynasty) is constructed. It is one of several walls of different dates, which together constitute one of the greatest engineering achievements of mankind.

Isfahan in Iran represents the greatest decorative achievement of brick and tile architecture, combining semi-structural forms with a tradition of ceramic decoration using non-figurative Islamic ornamentation.

The Picturesque Style is created from the informal landscape movement of England, led by William Kent, Capability Brown, and Humphry Repton, and dominates in the nineteenth and twentieth centuries.

In the Industrial Revolution, coke smelting makes cast iron readily available in England. The first iron-framed mills appear, followed by other iron buildings.

1500   **1600**   **1700**   **1750**

The Château of Fontainebleau in Fontainebleau, France is one of the several sites in France where the Italian Renaissance confronts medieval traditions to create a lively French synthesis of styles.

The Taj Mahal in Agra, India demonstrates the achievements of Islamic designers. It is not only one of the most beautiful buildings in the world, but also the greatest ever material expression of love.

The Residenz in Würzburg, Germany, one of the culminating works of the central European Baroque is a flamboyant response to the classicizing Baroque style of Versailles in France.

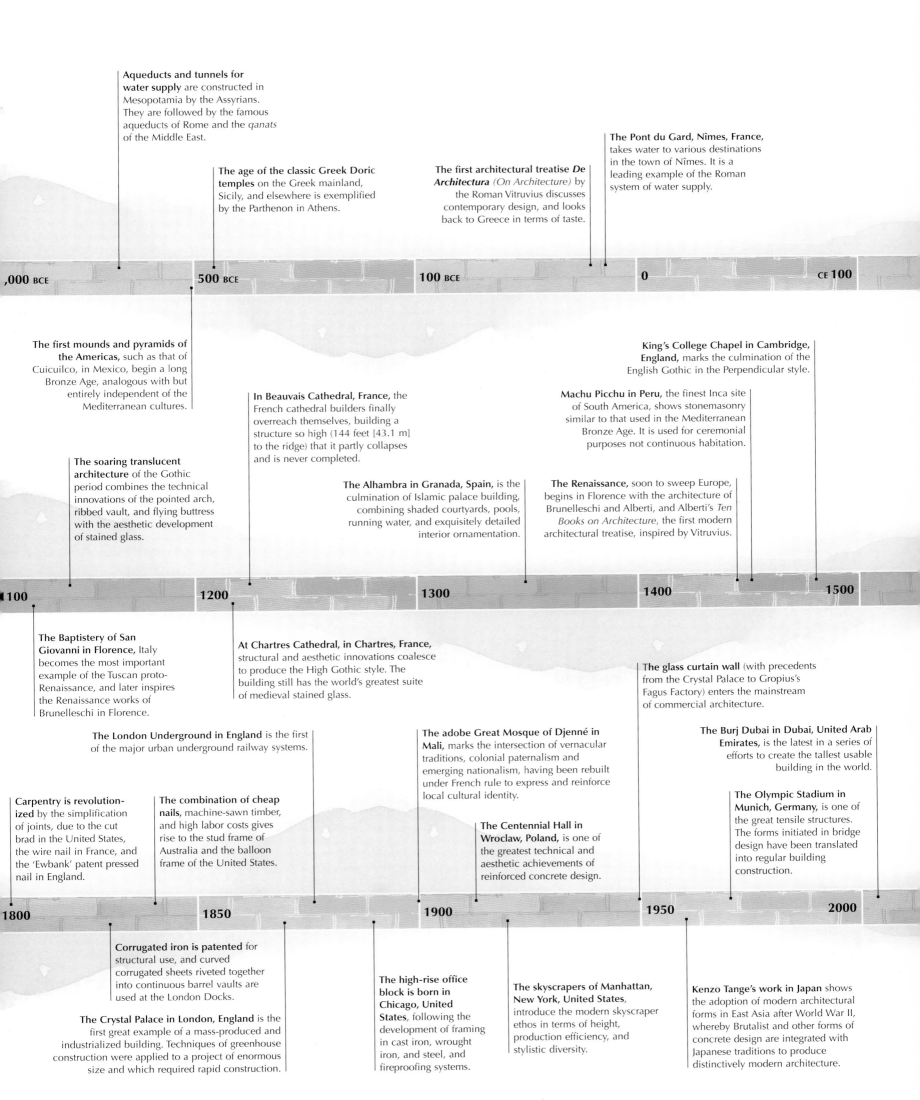

Aqueducts and tunnels for water supply are constructed in Mesopotamia by the Assyrians. They are followed by the famous aqueducts of Rome and the *qanats* of the Middle East.

The age of the classic Greek Doric temples on the Greek mainland, Sicily, and elsewhere is exemplified by the Parthenon in Athens.

The first architectural treatise *De Architectura* *(On Architecture)* by the Roman Vitruvius discusses contemporary design, and looks back to Greece in terms of taste.

The Pont du Gard, Nîmes, France, takes water to various destinations in the town of Nîmes. It is a leading example of the Roman system of water supply.

,000 BCE 500 BCE 100 BCE 0 CE 100

The first mounds and pyramids of the Americas, such as that of Cuicuilco, in Mexico, begin a long Bronze Age, analogous with but entirely independent of the Mediterranean cultures.

The soaring translucent architecture of the Gothic period combines the technical innovations of the pointed arch, ribbed vault, and flying buttress with the aesthetic development of stained glass.

In Beauvais Cathedral, France, the French cathedral builders finally overreach themselves, building a structure so high (144 feet [43.1 m] to the ridge) that it partly collapses and is never completed.

The Alhambra in Granada, Spain, is the culmination of Islamic palace building, combining shaded courtyards, pools, running water, and exquisitely detailed interior ornamentation.

King's College Chapel in Cambridge, England, marks the culmination of the English Gothic in the Perpendicular style.

Machu Picchu in Peru, the finest Inca site of South America, shows stonemasonry similar to that used in the Mediterranean Bronze Age. It is used for ceremonial purposes not continuous habitation.

The Renaissance, soon to sweep Europe, begins in Florence with the architecture of Brunelleschi and Alberti, and Alberti's *Ten Books on Architecture,* the first modern architectural treatise, inspired by Vitruvius.

100 1200 1300 1400 1500

The Baptistery of San Giovanni in Florence, Italy becomes the most important example of the Tuscan proto-Renaissance, and later inspires the Renaissance works of Brunelleschi in Florence.

At Chartres Cathedral, in Chartres, France, structural and aesthetic innovations coalesce to produce the High Gothic style. The building still has the world's greatest suite of medieval stained glass.

The glass curtain wall (with precedents from the Crystal Palace to Gropius's Fagus Factory) enters the mainstream of commercial architecture.

The London Underground in England is the first of the major urban underground railway systems.

The adobe Great Mosque of Djenné in Mali, marks the intersection of vernacular traditions, colonial paternalism and emerging nationalism, having been rebuilt under French rule to express and reinforce local cultural identity.

The Burj Dubai in Dubai, United Arab Emirates, is the latest in a series of efforts to create the tallest usable building in the world.

Carpentry is revolution-ized by the simplification of joints, due to the cut brad in the United States, the wire nail in France, and the 'Ewbank' patent pressed nail in England.

The combination of cheap nails, machine-sawn timber, and high labor costs gives rise to the stud frame of Australia and the balloon frame of the United States.

The Centennial Hall in Wroclaw, Poland, is one of the greatest technical and aesthetic achievements of reinforced concrete design.

The Olympic Stadium in Munich, Germany, is one of the great tensile structures. The forms initiated in bridge design have been translated into regular building construction.

1800 1850 1900 1950 2000

Corrugated iron is patented for structural use, and curved corrugated sheets riveted together into continuous barrel vaults are used at the London Docks.

The Crystal Palace in London, England is the first great example of a mass-produced and industrialized building. Techniques of greenhouse construction were applied to a project of enormous size and which required rapid construction.

The high-rise office block is born in Chicago, United States, following the development of framing in cast iron, wrought iron, and steel, and fireproofing systems.

The skyscrapers of Manhattan, New York, United States, introduce the modern skyscraper ethos in terms of height, production efficiency, and stylistic diversity.

Kenzo Tange's work in Japan shows the adoption of modern architectural forms in East Asia after World War II, whereby Brutalist and other forms of concrete design are integrated with Japanese traditions to produce distinctively modern architecture.

29

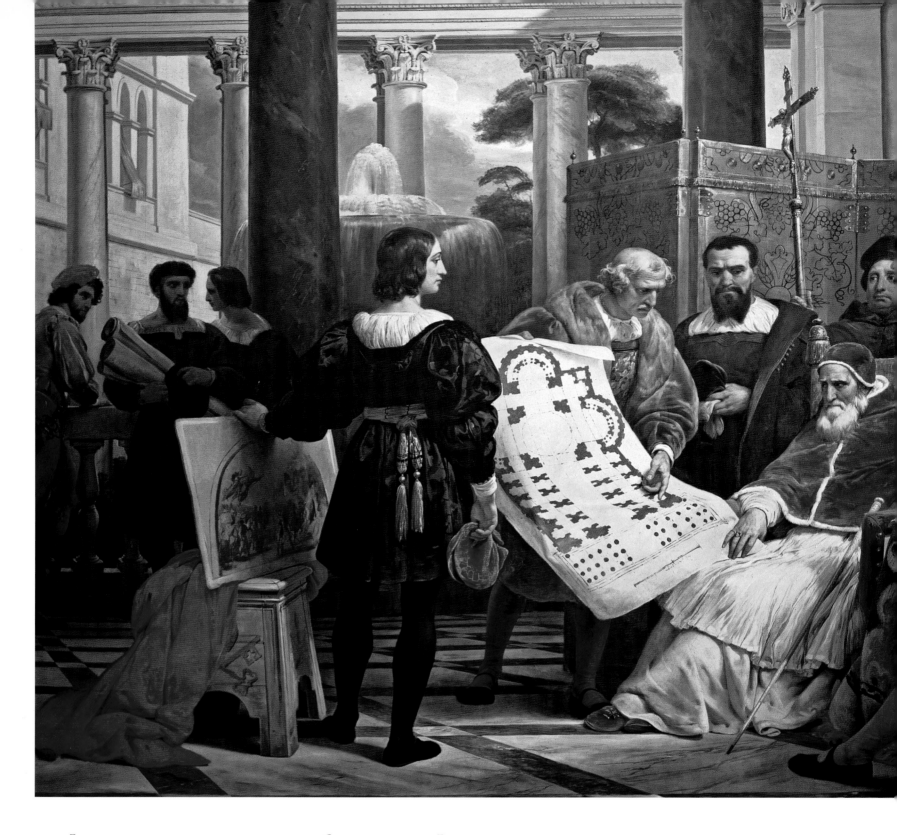

Elements of Architecture

The construction of a building is one of the most complex undertakings among human activities. It needs to take account of many conditions, including legal, economic, and societal concerns, as well as satisfy demands relating to beauty, structure, and utility. It is an act of balancing and synthesis. Because so many issues are involved and so much care is required, it is necessary to first conceive a building in the form

This image of architectural instruments is part of a carved relief made in Rome in the second century CE and now in the Museo Capitolino.

of a drawing or model. That way all the requirements and potential problems can be fully explored and adjustments and changes made before the building is actually constructed.

Thus, architecture is often understood as consisting of two main phases, design and execution. Other terms have been used for these phases, with variant nuances. Vitruvius, the author of the oldest surviving architectural treatise *De Architectura*, regarded architecture as consisting of *fabrica* (that which is made) and *ratiocinatione* (that which names it). The Renaissance architect and humanist Leon Battista Alberti contrasted the design process usually involves a series of decisions that proceed from the abstract toward the concrete. At the start of the process, the architect focuses on what is expected of the future building, and by the end of it he or she knows every component of the building, what each is made of, and how all the components will be assembled to create the building.

Architects often study existing buildings to analyze particular design issues that relate to a new project. They might look, for example, at buildings of the same type (other schools, city halls, railway stations, or churches), and also at how particular technical or cultural issues have been resolved in the past. By referring to such architectural precedents, the architect can foresee the consequences of certain design decisions prior to employing them. In this way the study of architectural history can shape the design of future buildings.

Many professional organizations recognize a definitive number of stages in the design process. For example, the American Institute of Architects (AIA) identifies four phases: programming, schematic (or preliminary) design, design development, and the construction document. For the American architect and educator Michael Graves, each stage of the architectural design carries a distinct nature and purpose and is characterized by a particular type of architectural drawing. The first stage is represented by what Graves calls a referential sketch, a shorthand record of an architect's discovery, which can later be recalled, elaborated, and combined with other referential sketches. The next stage, the preparatory study, poses questions or examines alternatives, and is capable of conveying the essence of the design. Finally, the definitive drawings indicate the dimensions and details more precisely and introduce quantifiable elements, such as the dimensions of treads on a staircase. They are the last step before the actual construction.

The Swiss architect Le Corbusier, one of the most influential contributors to Modern Architecture, stressed the importance of the referential sketch. He stated:

When one travels and works with visual things ... one uses one's eyes and draws, so as to fix deep down in one's experience what is seen. Once the impression has been recorded by a pencil, it stays for good, entered, registered, inscribed. The camera is a tool for idlers, who use a machine to do their seeing for them. To draw oneself, to trace the lines, handle the volumes, organize the surface ... all this means first to look, and then to observe and finally perhaps to discover ... and it is then that inspiration may come.

The importance of the architect's ability to transfer ideas onto a sheet of paper has long been recognized. In the seventeenth century André Félibien, Secretary of the French Academy of

Horace Vernet's oil painting (above), dating from 1827 and now in the Louvre, shows (center, left to right) Raphael, Bramante, and Michelangelo showing plans for the design of the Vatican to Pope Julius II.

lineamenta (deriving from the mind) and *materia* (deriving from nature). In order to stress the importance of design in the discipline of architecture, Alberti further compared the architect with the carpenter. According to Alberti, the carpenter is "but an instrument in the hands of the architect," who "knows both how to devise through his own mind and energy, and to realize by construction."

From Vision to Reality
Although there may be as many ways of designing a building as there are architects,

The Swiss architect Le Corbusier, seen here at his desk in 1934, drew incessantly, deriving information and inspiration for his pioneering Modernist designs from his often rapidly executed referential sketches.

Brunelleschi's Passion

Seeking to win the commission for the construction of the dome of the church of Santa Maria del Fiore in Florence, Italy, Brunelleschi built a model to demonstrate his method and design. According to Giorgio Vasari, when a meeting was held in 1407 to discuss the difficult task of constructing the dome, Brunelleschi explained his method but refused to show his model unless the commission was given solely to him. The authorities refused and the government held another meeting, in 1420, having called architects and engineers from France, Spain, and England as well as Tuscany. Here, Brunelleschi explained his method again. When the audience was not convinced, he grew increasingly passionate until attendants carried him away by force. Later, when no architect was found for the difficult task, Brunelleschi suggested that the commission be given to whoever could make an egg stand on a smooth surface of marble. After many tried without success, Brunelleschi struck the egg on the marble and let it stand on its crushed end. Others complained that they could have done the same. Brunelleschi's response was that if he had shown his model, other architects would have been able to copy it and build the dome. Finally, the commission was given to him.

Brunelleschi made these wooden models of the dome and apse of the cathedral of Santa Maria del Fiore in Florence, Italy, to accompany the proposal he submitted for the design of the new building.

Architecture under the French king Louis XIV, introduced the term *esquisse*. Derived from the Italian *schizzo*, meaning "sketch" in English, it referred to the first pencil marks the architect put down on paper, capturing his or her fleeting ideas as quickly as they appear in the mind of the architect. Even today, when computer-aided drawings help in many aspects of the architectural design process, it is important for architects to develop and maintain sketching skills. For sketches allow architects to put down their ideas quickly and any time and anywhere, without relying on any equipment.

Perspectives and Dimensions

Drawings are of course two-dimensional, and therefore never able to represent all aspects of a three-dimensional building. However, this limitation can be turned to the architect's advantage, for it forces the viewer to focus on particular aspects or features of a building. For example, floor plans allow an examination of spatial organization, while sections allow for study of the volumes of the planned spaces. A perspective drawing clarifies how a building will look from a particular viewpoint, which can be extremely important. When the architectural competition for the Houses of Parliament of England was held in 1835, after a fire a year earlier, the entrants were required to include in their submission perspective drawings from two specific viewpoints, one of which was from the Westminster Bridge over the River Thames. Considering how the view has become the iconic image not only of this governmental institution but also of the city and the nation, we realize the organizers' insightfulness at the time of the planning.

An axonometric or isometric drawing represents three-dimensional features and depicts a building as a three-dimensional object. However, it remains a two-dimensional drawing and allows the viewer to see the building from only one angle at a time. The limitations of drawings led many architects, even in early times, to construct detailed models of new projects to assist with the decision-making process and to show to prospective patrons. Leon Battista Alberti, for example, recommended the use of a model in addition to drawings.

With the development of sophisticated digital technologies it is certain that we will continue to generate new types of architectural representations and designs. Already, architects are able to create three-dimensional virtual models of buildings that allow clients to see, on screen, what it would be like to walk through the building, before it is even built. One technique, which

has been highlighted by the work of Frank Gehry, involves making a physical model then scanning it with laser equipment, which enters thousands of coordinates into a computer program. A three-dimensional model can then be viewed on the computer screen and translated into a format that is more easily understood by contractors and manufacturers of materials. This method has in turn allowed architects much greater freedom of form, enabling them to escape the bounds of conventional geometry.

The Elements of Form

We often recognize a building by its color, material, or use, but above all we recognize its form. For example, we would describe Henry Hobson Richardson's Billings Library at the University of Vermont as a library made of reddish stone with a large entry arch and a polygonal reading room. Many discussions

Frank Gehry's design process involves experimentation with paper and cardboard models, at a range of scales. At various stages, the models are digitized, so that the structures and forms can be further analyzed and quantified for contractors.

The prominent roofs or sails of the Opera House, Sydney, Australia, which were designed in 1957 by Jørn Utzon and completed in 1973, are its primary element, and are offset by the secondary element, the horizontal base.

on form evolve around a fundamental question: what determines the form of a building?

When analyzing the form of a building, it can help to think of it as being composed of a primary element, secondary element, tertiary element, and so on. The primary element is the most prominent part of the entire composition, and usually works as the organizing component of the other elements. For example, the most prominent feature of the Sydney Opera House, Australia, designed by the Danish architect Jørn Utzon and the English structural engineering firm Ove Arup & Partners, is unquestionably the roof (in fact a series of roofs), which consists of large pre-cast concrete panels in the form of partial spheres. The secondary element of any architectural composition relates to the primary element through repetition, transformation, or contrast. In the case of the Sydney Opera House, the podium under the roof creates a stark contrast by introducing the horizontal form, which echoes the surface of the water in Sydney Harbour. Once understood as a way to analyze a complex form of architecture, this same method can be used to help create a design.

The question of what determines form has always interested architects and architectural historians. In indigenous constructions, architectural form is often a natural synthesis of many conditions, including available materials and construction methods; topography and climate; and social conditions and religious beliefs. Indigenous buildings such as the *trulli* of Puglia, Italy (white-washed cylindrical houses with conical roofs); the distinctive houses, topped with a *badgir* (wind tower) of the Sind region of Pakistan; and men's clubhouses of bamboo and thatch in Maipua, Gulf of New Guinea—all are authentic answers to the materials, climate, and way of life of their particular regions.

When more recent architecture draws attention to its materials or structure, it is more often than not a result of a highly conscious design decision by the architect. For example, for the

Thorncrown Chapel in the Ozark Mountains of Arkansas, the American architect E. Fay Jones designed trusses in a form that expressed the slender, straight lines of pressure-treated pine timber; and the Alamillo Bridge over the Guadalquivir River in Seville, Spain, is a poetic expression of tension cable structure designed by the Spanish architect, sculptor, and structural engineer, Santiago Calatrava. Whereas indigenous forms are results of long traditions of building

Indigenous buildings, such as these *bories* in France, have provided inspiration for countless generations of architects. Characteristic of southeastern France and dating back to 600 BCE, *bories* are small huts made of local stone and built without mortar.

and therefore belong to the particular culture, the contemporary forms of these examples are, for the most part, the results of creative decisions made by individual architects.

The architect's synthesis of cultural and geographical influences, the materials available, and construction methods creates a style. The meaning of the term "style" changed during the nineteenth century. Prior to that time, a building's style was very much determined by the time and place to which the building belonged. After the Industrial Revolution, however, the development of construction technologies, the rapid expansion of transportation and communication, and the much wider dissemination of materials freed architectural style from regional constraints. Today, materials, technology, and ways of life are shared around the globe; as a result, an architectural style is more often associated with a set of formal traits that distinguish the works of an individual architect or the designs of a group of architects and designers who share a certain outlook or beliefs. Style is no longer bound to a specific geographical area and chronological period, but is the direct result of conscious design decisions made by the architect or architects.

The Pitfalls of Regionalism

The more the style, and therefore the form, of architecture is the result of the architect's independent aesthetic choices, the more it is important to ask what influences those choices. The answers could be many and varied but a number of broad historical and philosophical influences, or movements, have played an important part in determining many modern architectural styles.

Regionalism is the school of thought that holds that designs should reflect the natural or built forms of the region, and also evoke indigenous traditions. An example is Frank Lloyd Wright's Taliesin West, his winter home in Scottsdale, Arizona, built in 1937. Its reddish colors, thick walls of local stone, stepped floors, and roof forms all echo elements in the topography and landscape of the Arizona

desert. Similarly, the emphasis on horizontality in Wright's Robie House in Chicago (1910), expressed in the extended eaves and prominent layers of bricks, refer to the wide open spaces of the Great Plains.

For the contemporary Australian architect Glenn Murcutt also, horizontality, as expressed for example in his 1975 Marie Short House at Kempsey, Australia (seen earlier in this chapter), is a way for his architecture to become part of the Australian landscape:

Horizontal linearity is an enormous dimension of this country, and I want my buildings to feel part of that. Take the iron sheeting on outside walls, for example, generally it runs vertically, and I believe it should run horizontally … If it runs vertically, it competes with the trees. I don't want to compete with trees; let them complement the horizontality of the man-made iron sheets.

Borrowing the indigenous architectural forms of a region can raise problematic ethical questions when the set of conditions—including building materials, construction methods, and the local way of life—has changed. The Australian scholar Kim Dovey has argued that the quest for "authenticity" results in fakery, as exemplified in the kind of window shutters that appear on some residential buildings but are not operable and whose width does not even match the size of the window. Another example might be a building whose design refers to a traditional form but has nothing to do with the original building type in function or in method of construction. Two high-rise office buildings in Asia, the Petronas Twin Towers in Kuala Lumpur, Malaysia, designed by Cesar Pelli, and Taipei 101 designed by C. Y. Lee & Partners, both refer to Chinese pagoda structures in their overall forms; however, no other relationship exists between these skyscrapers and the pagoda, which in its original form was a Buddhist temple.

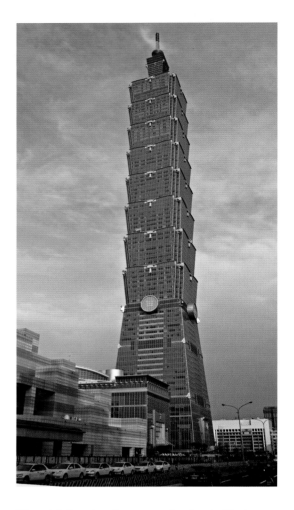

Though it has since been overtaken by the Burj Dubai in the United Arab Emirates, Taipei 101 in Taipei, was the world's highest building upon completion in 2004, rising 101 floors to a height of 1,667 ft (508 m), including its spire.

A classic example of Frank Lloyd Wright's so-called Prairie Style, the Robie House in Chicago was built in 1909–1910 for Frederick C. Robie, a bicycle manufacturer. Robie went bankrupt eighteen months after moving in and was forced to sell the house, which narrowly escaped demolition in the 1950s.

The search for a more sophisticated way to reconcile indigenous influences and the use of modern technologies and materials led the American architectural historian and critic Kenneth Frampton to argue in the 1980s for the adoption of what he termed "critical regionalism." An eloquent expression of this approach is the Italian architect Renzo Piano's design for the Jean-Marie Tjibaou Cultural Center in Nouméa, on the island of New Caledonia (1991–1998), in the South Pacific. Recognizing the project's "Promethean challenge," Piano invited the French anthropologist Alban Bensa, who had long been involved in the study of New Caledonian culture, to assist with the design process. The result celebrates New Caledonia's indigenous Kanak culture in its explicit reference to traditional men's club-houses made of bamboo, yet still embodies modern social attitudes in that it rejects the exclusivity of the traditional buildings, from which women and some other members of the community were excluded.

Determining Influences

The form of a building may be determined, at least in part, by the historical, political, and cultural context in which it is produced. In other words, if an architect makes decisions about a design based on knowledge of recent developments in architecture, he or she is practicing a form of historical determinism. Historical determinism has been a dominant force in architecture since the beginning of the twentieth century. For example, even though the major movements of that century, Modernism,

Postmodernism, and Deconstruction, produced buildings that are all quite distinct from each other, they were all similar in that they were primarily concerned with generating the kind of architectural form that its designers thought most appropriate to their time. In contrast, Thomas Jefferson, to take one notable example, was not bound by any ideology and freely went back into history, to the Roman Republic in particular, in his search for an appropriate architectural form for the public buildings of the new United States. Modern critics of the tendency to represent the zeitgeist point out the danger that such practice will turn into mere formalism without any philosophical basis.

It has long been claimed, too, that a building's form is determined by its function. The best-known proponent of this provocative view was the American architect, Louis H. Sullivan, who famously wrote, in "The Tall Office Building Artistically Considered" (1896), that "form ever follows function." This was already a well-traveled idea, dating back to the Italian architect Carlo Lodoli (1690–1761), likewise better known for his theories than his own largely unbuilt designs, but it was given a new lease of life by Modernists and pursued to its logical conclusion in buildings that simplified forms in allegiance to the direct-ness of their functions. Yet, to say that the form of a building is determined by its intended function is shortsighted, or "naïve," as Italian architect Aldo Rossi has put it. For the functions of Sullivan's buildings, or those of the majority of Modernist architects for that matter, would not explain all aspects of their forms.

The Tjibaou Cultural Center in Nouméa, New Caledonia, designed by Renzo Piano and opened in 1998, reflects indigenous Kanak architecture, with its "great houses," structures resembling traditional Kanak huts, linked by a long (covered) walkway, which echoes the central alleyway of a Kanak village.

One way to demonstrate the weakness of the argument for functional determinism is to point to examples of buildings that were built for one purpose but later used for another, and continued to serve their users perfectly well. Hagia Sophia in Istanbul, Turkey, was built as a Christian church by the Byzantine Emperor Justinian in the sixth century CE, but was turned into an Islamic mosque by Sultan Mehmed II of the Ottoman Empire in the fifteenth century, and since 1935 has been used as a secular museum. Other examples of this kind might include a tourist center that was once a church, a hotel that was originally a convent, and a railroad station converted to a restaurant. In such cases, the original form and organization of the building adequately serves its new role—the architectural form that, for instance, once supported the way of life of an order of nuns can be adapted to function as tourist accommodation, with, say, a chapel becoming a dining hall and nuns' cells serving as guest rooms.

Expressing Values

It is the case, however, that there is often a relationship between form and particular roles and human values. This can be seen in the design of major public buildings, such as libraries. The Reading Room of the former British Library in the British Museum in London, for example, is circular in plan and covered by a large dome. The circular form supports the notion that the reading room is the center of the entire institution and conveys a sense of the prime importance of intellectual pursuits within this community. In contrast, the Phillips Exeter Academy Library in Exeter, New Hampshire, United States, designed by Louis I. Kahn, has a square form. Inside the building, the central square space functions as a place where one orients oneself in relation to the books in the library. In relation to the campus as a whole, the square form of the library affirms the existing organizational axes that run through the campus grounds, and allows the library to belong to rather than to dominate the rest of the built and natural environments. Additionally, the square form affirms the academy's philosophy, which supports the diversity of the student community and is expressed in its unofficial motto "Youth from every quarter."

The Laurentian Library, in the church of San Lorenzo in Florence, Italy, designed by Michelangelo beginning in 1524, has a linear form. Here the repetitive bays articulated by pilasters and windows correspond to the ceiling beams and the two rows of wooden *plutei* (a *pluteus* is a combination of a bench and a lectern, behind which books and manuscripts were stored, lying flat). This architectural form supports the organization of the library, which is divided according to the subject matter—the side of each bench facing the central passage carries a panel that lists the topics.

Architectural forms can also reflect the different ways in which people congregate and relate to each other inside a building. Theaters offer excellent examples. The semicircular form of Greek and Roman theaters, the polygonal form of the Shakespearean theater, with its stage projecting into the center of the auditorium, and the U-shaped form of Christopher Wren's Sheldonian Theatre in Oxford, England, all suggest particular kinds of relationships between the performers and the audience, and between

Provoking a Response

The meaning of a work of architecture lies not simply in any message or information its design conveys, but also in the reaction or behavioral response of the visitor to the building. Tadao Ando's Water Temple on Awaji Island, Japan (1991), is a good example. Traditionally, the floors of Buddhist temples were raised above the ground, as a sign of reverence for the Buddhist deity housed within the temple and the religious activities held there. But at Awaji, Ando has placed the sanctuary below ground level. This obliges visitors to descend underground and thereby induces a sense of humility. And the still surface of the adjacent pools, highlighted themselves by water lilies, the symbols of the Buddhist paradise, draw attention to the surface of the earth, making the viewer even more aware of his or her descent into a subterranean realm.

various different groups within the audience. The horseshoe plan, seen in theater architecture like Charles Garnier's Paris Opera (also known as the Opéra Garnier or Palais Garnier), also supports a specific set of relationships between diffferent groups within the audience: at the Paris Opera the Emperor Napoleon III and Empress Eugenie, who sat in what we usually call the royal box, were supposed not only to see the performance but also to be seen by the rest of the audience.

A reconstruction of the Globe Theatre, one of the theaters in which Shakespeare's plays were performed in the early seventeenth century, opened in London in 1997, a short distance from the original site.

Everchanging Forms

The notion advanced by many Modernists and some earlier architects that "form ever follows function" can be a trap, because the category of *functions* comprises all manner of physical, economic, and semiotic activities. Signification, inspiration, and domination are functions of architecture no less than shelter or ventilation. Ornate Gothic cathedrals that send messages about reverence and social order are performing one function; palaces and mansions, with their accumulation of detail connoting the owners' capacity to command great reserves of skilled labor, are performing another. However, the effort to understand building forms by analyzing functions (and vice versa) can yield invaluable insights. And forms have followed and facilitated functions in an intricate dance throughout history.

Preurban Communities

The earliest permanent housing forms yet found, such as the Neolithic settlement at Çatal Hüyük, Turkey, suggest that much early construction was densely arranged well before recognizable cities developed. Historical contingencies affect the preservation and excavation of structures, and knowledge of them is necessarily fragmentary, but the idea of a house as a detached, private structure appears relatively modern. Ancient humanity appears to have understood the advantages of collective living for both social cohesion and defense.

Houses at Çatal Hüyük were built of mud brick, standardized in shape (rectangular), and aligned contiguously without spaces separating them, but with separate walls. Instead of doors and windows, these buildings had sheltered roof-top openings serving as a combination lighting source, entrance (via ladders), and chimney. However, instead of representing Neolithic building styles generally, Çatal Hüyük may be a singular case. In Cyprus, Egypt, the Jordan Valley, Mesopotamia, and elsewhere, rounded, oval, and beehive-shaped houses have been found at both older and younger sites. It may be that

Çatal Hüyük's form developed in response to a particular external threat—its close-packed rectilinear forms would certainly offer protective advantages against marauders.

Other informative features at Çatal Hüyük include the intermingling of shrines and graves among residences, the absence of public buildings, and limited structural variety, at least in areas uncovered to date. This implies that the settlement's socioeconomic structure was uncomplicated and preurban. Çatal Hüyük probably housed 5,000 to 10,000 people, and agricultural surpluses might have allowed some residents to pursue occupations other than food production, but the findings do not so far support this.

Neolithic communities elsewhere also built residences in close proximity, in scales and forms influenced by resources and climate. In Chinese urban formations such as Banpo (Ban-po-ts'un), an archaeological site in Shaanxi province east of Xian, which dates to around 4000 BCE, the houses were semisubterranean circular wattle and daub structures with wooden columns and beams supporting conical roofs. The recessed construction used the earth's insulating properties to stabilize temperatures, and the roof's cone included an opening for ventilation. A larger central rectangular building on a rammed-earth foundation probably served as a meeting space or the home of a tribal leader.

Village architecture at Banpo bears resemblance to those of some pre-Columbian Native American groups. The tipis of North American plains tribes, constructed of portable materials appropriate to nomadic life (sapling poles and animal hides), also used conical forms; smoke flaps create a chimney for an internal hearth. A related design in the American Southwest, the *wikiup,* is a single-room dome with a light skeleton of arched poles and coverings of bark, brush, and related materials. The hogan of the Navajos uses earth and wooden frames, either domed (the "female" hogans, which are larger and residential) or conical (the "male" hogans, which are smaller and chiefly ceremonial).

The Anasazi or Pueblo peoples of the American Southwest built both pit houses and cliff dwellings of adobe and sandstone, accessible only by rope or rock climbing. Some of these, like the Cliff Palace at Mesa Verde, Colorado, were two- or three-storied multiroom complexes intricate enough to resemble compact towns, with large underground ceremonial chambers *(kivas)* and assorted spaces for storage and work. Anasazi communities left evidence of unique accomplishments not limited to masonry; the relatively sudden abandonment of their constructions around CE 1300 remains one of archaeology's major mysteries.

The Shapes of Cities

Perhaps the world's first proper city was the Sumerian settlement of Uruk in southern Mesopotamia (Warka or the biblical Erech), and now in southern Iraq. Public structures occupied significant proportions of Uruk's civic space, and the White Temple (*c.* 3500–3000 BCE) offers an early model for the ziggurat or temple-tower. On a sloping-sided brick terrace formed by successive constructions on the same site and rising over 40 feet (12 m) from ground level, the rectangular temple to the sky god Anu

The hogan is the traditional form of dwelling among the Navajo people of southwestern North America. The walls and ceiling of the hogan are constructed with logs then covered with mud. The doorway always faces east, toward the rising sun.

At Mohenjo-Daro in the Indus Valley, Pakistan (2500–2000 BCE), hundreds of brick buildings surrounded a central citadel mound. The houses had plumbing, bathrooms, and drainage systems.

arose as a brightly plastered reminder of the social prominence of the priesthood.

Ziggurats at Ur, Babylon, Choqa Zanbil in Persia (Iran), and dozens of other sites were not public plazas but simulated mountains believed to be literal dwellings for the cities' patron gods; only priests entered a ziggurat. As primitive urban economies created the conditions allowing political and theological hierarchies to form, the elevation of the stepwise form offered a potent metaphor for secular domination. Ziggurat-like monuments throughout history, from ancient Mesopotamia to skyscrapers, signify humanity's linkage of height with power and prestige.

Egypt's Old and Middle Kingdoms feature *mastabas* or rectangular tombs with deep subterranean burial shafts. Temples resembling pyramids also appeared in Mesoamerican civilizations (Olmec, Mayan, Aztec, and others) between about 900 BCE and CE 1000, in a style distinguishing substructures—an architectural extension of the earth—from vaulted superstructures, sometimes featuring sculptured roof combs or twin extensions dedicated to different deities.

Residential construction steadily diversified as cities became more complex. Advancing societies developed multichambered, multistoried residences with access to streets. Two-story houses and public plumbing appeared at Mohenjo-Daro and Harappa in the Indus Valley, Pakistan, around 2500–2000 BCE. Akrotiri, a Bronze Age site on the Greek island of Santorini (or Thera) was buried by a cataclysmic volcanic eruption some time around 1650–1500 BCE. It was thus well preserved beneath deep deposits of ash and three-story mortared stone town houses with

At its peak in the thirteenth century CE, the Mesa Verde community of Colorado numbered around 5,000 people living in a range of cliff dwellings. The largest, the Cliff Palace, seen here, was inhabited by around 250 people, living in more than 200 rooms.

indoor plumbing and communal drainage. Houses with internal courtyards, providing light and ventilation, are found at Ur and Lagash in Mesopotamia, the early Greek city-state of Mycenae, and later classical Greece. Courtyards, in a sense, invert the structural principle of temples: if a temple was both a god's house and an offering, with its chief features arranged on the outside, construction around a courtyard creates effects visible from within, implying a new emphasis on human perspectives.

Another important structure from the late Bronze Age and afterward is the large corbel-vaulted tomb or *tholos,* cut into a hillside and lined with decorated masonry. The earliest such tombs appear in the Neolithic Tell Halaf culture of Syria and Turkey, in the fifth or possibly sixth millennium BCE; the technique recurs at multiple Mediterranean sites. The Treasury of Atreus or Tomb of Agamemnon at Mycenae, *c.* 1300 BCE, has a long approach passage *(dromos)* leading to its beehive-shaped burial chamber; the upper part of the tholos is covered with a mound, and the dromos was filled in with earth after the burial.

Greek city-states had distinct political forms (democratic in the case of Athens) and were frequently at war. They required specific building types to support the life of the state, or *polis.* Fortifications on city limits were common, and boundaries between interior and exterior were sharp; city plans, particularly in new colonial settlements, sometimes followed a grid, with stairways rather than lateral curvature around steep gradients. Along with the familiar orders, classical Greece developed the *agora,* a gathering place for trade and discussion, often bounded by stoas—colonnaded, sheltered walkways. Stoas would provide the model for Roman basilicas, timber-roofed halls for business and legal proceedings.

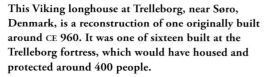

This Viking longhouse at Trelleborg, near Søro, Denmark, is a reconstruction of one originally built around CE 960. It was one of sixteen built at the Trelleborg fortress, which would have housed and protected around 400 people.

Additional public structures included gymnasia (sites of both athletics and education outside city walls), stadia, and theaters.

Rome's contributions to its inheritance from Greece include triumphal arches and a system of aqueducts, roads, and bridges throughout its empire. Bridge design involved large arches of precut stone, sometimes with ribbed vaults of travertine (a type of limestone) or travertine-faced concrete for added stability. Within the capital, some town houses had rooms grouped around a central court or atrium containing an *impluvium,* a pool collecting rainwater. Larger Roman houses incorporated second stories, shops, or other tenancies facing the street, an additional large colonnaded court or *peristyle* to the rear, and Greek-style ornamental gardens. High urban density made courtyards less practical; the *insula,* a four- or five-story structure sometimes including ground-floor shops, anticipated the mixed uses of the modern apartment block.

Communal Living

After the fall of Rome, nothing as sophisticated as the insula persisted in European housing. Earlier forms prevailed, and construction in northern areas reverted to nearly Neolithic standards. The Viking longhouses of Scandinavia were wooden-framed rectangular dwellings or meeting halls with convex outer walls and a profile resembling an inverted ship, sometimes with turf roofing in regions lacking ample timber, such as Iceland. Some archaeologists cite recurrence of this form in areas as remote as Newfoundland as evidence that Viking explorations reached the pre-Columbian New World.

Elsewhere in Europe, large rural homesteads were usually walled complexes, which could easily be defended. Feudal societies' castles and citadels,

elevated and fortified, represent regional variations on a common theme, from the *motte-and-bailey* mound and courtyard combinations of eleventh- and twelfth-century France, Britain, and Ireland to the borrowings from Byzantine and Islamic military engineering after the cultural contacts of the Crusades. East Asian feudalism shows comparable functions and structures, including the Japanese *shiro* (castle) and *maru* (bailey) from the fifteenth and sixteenth

centuries, though more commonly with wooden construction atop a stone base in the shiro.

For several centuries after Roman Emperor Constantine's recognition of Christianity, the most substantial new architecture in both the Western world and the Near East would serve religious functions: churches, cathedrals, and monasteries in the Christian realms, mosques after the rise of Islam. Large-scale churches would adapt structural principles from public halls like

A classic motte and bailey castle, the Château de Gisors, in northwestern France was built by the Normans in the late eleventh century as part of a chain of defenses against French aggression.

the Basilica Nova in Rome, begun by Maxentius and completed under Constantine. Evolving from stoas and from the central halls of *thermae* or late-Imperial public baths, the basilicas could accommodate large assemblies in the central nave.

Geometric Formalism

The classical Greek talent for mathematics, geometry, and visual harmony manifested itself in the golden mean (also known as the divine ratio or golden section), a proportion between two elements in which the ratio of the larger element to the smaller element is the same as the ratio of the sum of the two elements to the larger element. To three decimal places, the ratio is 1.618. Euclid first defined it, and the sculptor Phidias is believed to have used it in statues at the Parthenon—it is sometimes rendered as the Greek letter *phi* in his honor. Aesthetic and architectural theorists, such as Luca Pacioli in the fifteenth century and Le Corbusier in the twentieth, have discussed concepts of ideal proportion in terms of the golden mean.

Formalism also affected the way in which architectural elements were assembled. The classical language of architecture contains certain components, such as columns and capitals, which are analogous with the words in a spoken language. It has implied rules, like those of grammar, which say that a capital should go on top of a column rather than the reverse. And it contains idiomatic phrases, or ways of putting these things together, which come and go with fashion, such as the Roman triumphal arch form, or the aedicular window (one flanked by columns or pilasters and surmounted by a pediment, like a little temple front).

This relief by Andrea Pisano, *c.* 1334–1340 shows Euclid of Alexandria, the "Father of Geometry."

Set on a rocky islet separated from the mainland by tidal flats, the religious sanctuary of Mont Saint-Michel in Normandy, France, originated in the eighth century CE, and the first abbey was built by the Normans in the tenth century. It was substantially rebuilt in the thirteenth century.

The recessed (usually semicircular) apse at one end provided a conveniently authoritative focal point, originally for a magistrate on a raised dais, later for an altar. Regional variations and subsequent elaborations of the basilica concept would form the basis of national cathedral styles across the West through the Romanesque and Gothic periods and beyond.

A new type of collective residence, the monastery, convent, or abbey, appeared in connection with medieval churches as early as the fourth century CE, possibly influenced by Buddhist *vihara*, or monastic centers, which had arisen some seven centuries earlier. Doctrines promoting a secluded life called for structures supporting communal self-sustenance, often including agriculture and viticulture. While different Christian monastic orders' constructions reflected different levels of asceticism or enterprise, a typical monastery would be centered around a church, located near water, and equipped with a refectory, dormitory, and storage facilities. Some monasteries included infirmaries and hostels. The modern school and library can trace their lineage to the monastic *scriptorium*.

Secular Adaptations

During these centuries (referred to as the "Dark Ages" by those who followed Petrarch in comparing their culture unfavorably to Rome, but also known to us today as "dark" because few written records survive from the period), the Christian nations' preeminent structures were Romanesque cathedrals, which were sturdy and symmetrical and also characterized by prominent articulation, arches, groin vaults, and sculpture. At the same time the Islamic world was in its Golden Age. With representations of humans and animals banned as idolatry, Islam's domes, octagons, arches (often pointed or horseshoe), Persian-style *iwan* (vaults open at one end), hypostyle halls, and minarets were often decorated with calligraphy, foliage, and repeating patterns. Secular life in the Near East supported other distinctive forms. Along trade routes linking Asia, North Africa, and southeastern Europe, *caravanserais* offered rest to travelers. Entrances were large enough for beasts of burden; courtyards were open, usually rectangular or square, with baths, stalls, and shops. Modern hospitality architecture takes considerable inspiration, consciously or unconsciously, from these roadside havens.

A double arcade surrounds the courtyard of the Khan al-Umdan, an eighteenth-century hostel in the ancient port city of Acre, now Akko in Israel. It was used by merchants for accommodation and for storing their goods.

Hórreos are traditional granaries found in northern Spain; this one is at Cadavedo in Asturias. The wooden upper structure sits on stone pillars, each of which is capped with a wide stone slab to prevent rodents reaching the grain.

Later medieval Christian cathedrals, beginning in France, developed features including cruciform floor plans, tall spires, pointed ogival arches, flying buttresses, ribbed vaults, stone mullions, sizable windows with elaborate tracery, and sculptural detail intricate enough yet rational enough to suggest a microcosm of the universe. The description "Gothic" (unrelated to tribal Goths) originated as a pejorative, but the style permeated Europe from the twelfth to sixteenth centuries and enjoyed multiple revivals, particularly in England. Secular adaptations established it as a prevalent style for universities, government buildings, and other institutions.

The rediscovery of Tuscan Romanesque and classical Roman architecture during the Italian Renaissance did not so much vanquish Gothic elsewhere in Europe as challenge architects to fuse it with the architectural language of antiquity. This interaction produced eccentric versions of the Renaissance in France and Britain, and of Mannerism in the Low Countries. The subsequent Baroque style was expressed in classical forms, but was also a reaction against classical principles. In turn, it brought about another reaction, in the form of a revival of Andrea Palladio's principles by Colen Campbell and others in the early eighteenth century, and later by Thomas Jefferson.

A Need for Efficiency

As economic institutions gained power, rivaling those of religion and politics, humbler structures proliferated to address workplace needs. Agrarian life requires sturdy, inexpensive construction (arguably a precursor of industrial functionalism), such as simple gabled or gambrel-roofed Dutch barns and wooden silos, which were practical enough to spread widely through England and North America. Spain's rectangular wooden granaries *(hórreos)* and Sweden's older, similar *härbren,* ventilated with grooved walls and

elevated on pillars for safety from rodents, represent unpretentiously elegant solutions to a common storage problem. Industrial rationalism and economies of scale addressed a similar challenge in nineteenth-century America, yielding a revolutionary invention, the grain elevator. The massive concrete grain elevators at Buffalo inspired Le Corbusier to formulate a design philosophy appropriate to an age of mills, factories, and transportation technologies.

American variants on these European themes included the octagonal houses, schools, and churches advocated by Orson Squire Fowler (who, despite pseudoscientific enthusiasms— he promoted phrenology—accurately observed that octagons enclosed more space economically than comparably scaled rectangles or squares); the balloon frame house, with its light timber skeleton held together by mass-produced iron nails; and the Beaux-Arts derivations of Richard Morris Hunt and his successors, particularly the

Championed by Orson Squire Fowler, who argued that such buildings were more efficient and better ventilated and lighted, octagonal houses proliferated in the mid-nineteenth century United States. This example, the Hyde House, is in Mumford, New York State, not far from Fowler's birthplace.

Henry Hobson Richardson developed a rustic masonry style related to the Romanesque architecture of southern France, seen in his Ames Gate Lodge (1881) at North Easton, Massachussetts (above).

Curves, domes, and details such as tile and mosaic decorations tie Santiago Calatrava's City of Arts and Sciences in Valencia, Spain (right), to a tradition stemming from his compatriot Antoni Gaudí.

Romanesque public buildings of Henry Hobson Richardson and the City Beautiful movement led by the Richardson protégés who would found the influential firm of McKim, Mead & White.

The signature structural form of modernity is the commercial skyscraper, made possible by safe elevator technology and steel frameworks, and made popular with landowners by lucrative returns per square foot ("form follow[ing] finance," as noted by historian Carol Willis). Early skyscrapers by Daniel Burnham and others adhered to familiar styles (Renaissance, Gothic revival, Beaux-Arts) while extending their scale, whereas the work of Louis Sullivan departed more freely from these conventions. New York's 1916 zoning law, which stipulated that buildings had to be set back from the ground as they rose higher, to allow more light to reach the street, shaped the tapered towers typified by the Empire State Building and its Art Deco competitor, the Chrysler Building. Engineering advances yielded cable-suspension systems, supporting the Brooklyn Bridge and its successors worldwide.

Against the Modernist Grain

Modernism's smooth lines, glass walls, and reduction of ornament made it the de facto building mode of the twentieth-century corporation. Many of the utopian-futurist theorists associated with the Bauhaus, Russian Constructivism, *Congrès International d'Architecture Moderne,* the Japanese Metabolists, et al. might have seen dark irony in this outcome. Modernism has always attracted criticism and countermovements, and its dominance of much twentieth-century debate can obscure the persistence of more traditional forms, particularly in residential construction. Ranch homes derived from the low-slung Prairie and Japanese-influenced styles of Frank Lloyd

Wright's Usonian houses (perhaps more subtly influential than his cantilevered masterpieces) are practically the only Modernist designs to attain mass-market popularity. When occupants of Le Corbusier's Quartier Frugès workers' housing complex in Pessac, France, decorated their residences in ways that defied his rationalism, opponents saw a populist repudiation; later commentators and residents describe Pessac as evidence that Le Corbusier's forms are flexible and harmonious enough to accommodate unanticipated diversity.

Advances in theory and technology have led architects working after Modernism's peak to develop alternatives well outside the glass box. Antoni Gaudí's fusion of biomorphic and liquid forms with the spires and arches of Gothic established a modern variant that was irreconcilable with his contemporaries' mainstream Modernism. But Gaudí's affinity for nature's curves and asymmetries would find later echoes in works by Eero Saarinen, Oscar Niemeyer, Jørn Utzon, Greg Lynn, Zaha Hadid, Santiago Calatrava, Ben van Berkel, and others preferring wings, shells, waves, blobs, and intertwining strands to boxes; Utzon's Sydney Opera House singlehandedly raised an entire continent's architectural profile. The combination of reinforced concrete and computer-enhanced design allows the realization of forms inconceivable a few decades earlier. More aggressive angularity appears in the now-recognizable contours, playful fenestration, and titanium cladding of Frank Gehry; the deconstructivism of Peter Eisenman and Daniel Libeskind; and the hyperrational problem-solving of Rem Koolhaas and colleagues.

Conviction that design can answer practical challenges motivates many contemporary architects to address the environmental effects of the

industrial era's energy and resource consumption. The ascendance of sustainable architecture involves both simple practicality (non-toxic materials, natural light, low-waste construction, and so on) and formal innovations. Norman Foster draws on the radial geometries of his mentor Buckminster Fuller to bring both conservation and elegance to airports, towers, and other public buildings. Experiments with repurposed materials, as in the paper tube and shipping container constructions of Shigeru Ban, dovetail with the social mission of groups such as Architecture for Humanity. "Green" architects are coming full circle to rediscover the efficiency of ancient techniques like rammed earth *(pisé de terre)* construction. If the future calls for crisis-oriented architecture, its forms may be traceable to long-vanished communities that fostered cultural progress without unbalancing the mechanisms of the Earth.

The Architecture of Social Control

Modern functionalism's roots are broad, deep, and in some instances disturbing. The eighteenth century English philosopher Jeremy Bentham's *panopticon,* a radial prison with a central observation post from which all chambers are potentially visible, marks a singular point in the architectural rationalization of social control. Prisoners in a panopticon do not know when they are being watched; in theory, the impression of potential central omniscience fosters compliant behavior and less violence than in a conventional prison, and thereby reduces labor costs.

Despite spending much of his personal fortune on his efforts, Bentham was unable to persuade the British government to construct panopticons, but the design has influenced both prisons and hospitals, not to mention literature (Orwell's *1984* and other dystopias) and social theory (Foucault's *Discipline and Punish*). Few panoptical prisons exist today, a notable exception being the octagonal Chi Hoa in Ho Chi Minh City, Vietnam (built by the colonial French in the former capital Saigon), but many penal institutions worldwide use a design inspired by Bentham's theory.

Among the prisons built along the lines of Bentham's Panopticon was the Stateville Penitentiary in Illinois. From the central observation post or "roundhouse," guards were able to monitor all cells, each of which was sealed only with bars on the facing side and backlit by a small window.

45

Materials and Techniques

The process of building has gone through four stages: the use of materials like boulders or branches which could be collected from the ground; the use of materials cut and dressed with tools; the use of components mass-produced by sawmills, iron foundries, and factories; and finally the use of compounded materials like reinforced concrete, and of synthetics such as plastics.

Natural Resources

Almost every location can provide building materials, but whether these can be extracted and used depends upon technology. Some materials can be gathered from the ground or plucked from vegetation. Others need to be quarried, cut, or shaped. Others again need to be baked, refined, or processed. Today, some building materials are entirely synthetic, but these are generally expensive and therefore amount to a very small proportion of building construction. Most building still relies on traditional materials, even if at times in unfamiliar forms. But whereas such materials were once obtained on or close to the building site, today they can be shipped over long distances, and the place of origin is, in many cases, a minor consideration. Indeed, it may be cheaper to fabricate the complete building in another location, or even in another country.

Early Materials and Tools

Some of the earliest known dwellings, which date from about 10,000 BCE in Ukraine, were framed of mammoth bones or tusks, for these were the by-products of hunting, and therefore immediately available. Although the evidence does not survive, there is no doubt that humans would have regularly used animal hides where they could be spared, tree branches of suitable shape and size where they could easily be snapped off, whole boughs complete with foliage, or bundles of grass, rubble stone, mud, and clay. However, the use of cut timber, stone, and molded earth first required the development of tools.

The earliest tools were cumbersome and inefficient, typically flints or pieces of obsidian lashed to handles of wood or bone, and they would never have been used for the production of building materials. They were required for

more important tasks, such as cutting up animal flesh, fashioning garments, or carving sacred objects. But once cereal crops were cultivated there was automatically a by-product, straw, which was useful for building purposes. How people in Neolithic times were able to cut down a tree is unclear, but we do know something of early stoneworking techniques, which were incredibly labor intensive. Lack of good tools and the laborious processes explain why earth was so important in early building. It could be dug, mixed, and formed into cob or pug walling using only the most primitive of implements.

In the past, there was, of course, no sense that natural resources were finite, nor that any sort of care should be taken to avoid cutting down entire forests or exhausting supplies of a particular stone or mineral. However, if materials were scarce in one location, they would need to be transported considerable distances if required for building elsewhere. Given that spanning interior space was the major challenge of the early builder, it is not surprising that large timbers suitable for beams were the items most commonly transported.

Fuel, Water, and Other Resources

Two indirect resources required in building are fuel and water. Fuel was needed for the baking of bricks and tiles. In the Near East, given the limited supplies of wood for baking bricks, adobe (mud brick) was widespread, and baked bricks were often reserved for special buildings or locations. Northern Europe had no such shortage of fuel, and baked bricks were used prolifically.

Water is a building resource in three senses. Limited amounts of water were required in processes like brick manufacture and mixing plasters and cements, but supply on that scale was rarely

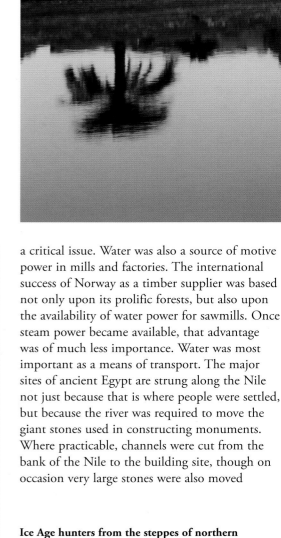

a critical issue. Water was also a source of motive power in mills and factories. The international success of Norway as a timber supplier was based not only upon its prolific forests, but also upon the availability of water power for sawmills. Once steam power became available, that advantage was of much less importance. Water was most important as a means of transport. The major sites of ancient Egypt are strung along the Nile not just because that is where people were settled, but because the river was required to move the giant stones used in constructing monuments. Where practicable, channels were cut from the bank of the Nile to the building site, though on occasion very large stones were also moved

Ice Age hunters from the steppes of northern Europe built shelters from the bones and tusks of the mammoths they pursued. Archaeologists have reconstructed one of their huts, shown on the left.

In ancient Egypt, boats or rafts transported huge blocks of building stone along the Nile to sites on the river such as Karnak, at Thebes (above).

In medieval Europe, skilled masons, like the ones shown in this manuscript illumination (right), were itinerant, traveling to wherever work was available.

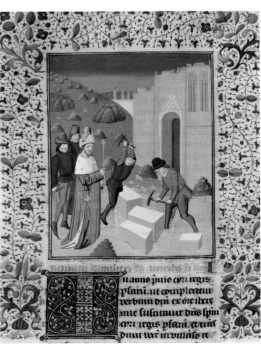

overland, though necessarily with an enormous expenditure of labor.

Of all natural resources it is labor, both animal and human, which is most important in the building process. At first, sheer brute force—such as that provided by beasts of burden—would have been needed, but the historical evidence does not suggest that animals played a big role. Human labor was cheap and easy to direct. Over time, as skill and craftsmanship became more important, the labor market became more specialized, and as mechanical aids like pulleys were developed, brute force became less significant. After the revival of stonemasonry in Europe in the seventh century, the demand for masons was such that teams regularly traveled between nations. Physical

resources also became increasingly specialized. Not only was timber transported great distances, but, by the Roman period, so were marble and ornamental stones, such as granite from Egypt. Still more so were metals and minerals.

Today, it is hard even to say what a building resource is. Significant components are made from hydrocarbons, and whether these have been made by recycling or by using up new resources of petroleum is something the user may never know. The use of energy is even more problematic. It is not possible, for example, to assess the net benefit of a solar collector without knowing how much energy went into its manufacture. The direct link between the builder and the natural resource has ceased to exist.

Grass and Timber

Local grasses provide the thatching material for this Tuareg hut in Mali. Ropes placed over the top of the hut help to keep the thatch in place.

Grass, reed, cane, bamboo, bark, and timber form a spectrum of materials of which our historical knowledge is limited because, unlike stone or brick, they all decay and burn. But they have a capacity to frame and cover a building which stone and brick do not have, and that makes them ubiquitous, and, in some parts of the world, the only building materials.

Shelters and Huts

Temporary shelters and windbreaks are most easily made of grassy materials, boughs, and foliage, and this is exemplified in the Australian Aboriginal *mia-mia*, which may be put up for shelter during a single night, and then abandoned. Other Aboriginal dwellings of a more permanent nature use woven canes, but it is in Africa that we find the greatest range of woven basketlike hut frames, some of them portable, and often covered with thatch. In Pacific cultures, rectangular frames and wall coverings of basketwork matting are more common. But buildings of both types are found both in Africa and the Pacific, and have been found, or still exist, in many other parts of the world.

Domed huts of thin saplings tied with bark strips are used by the Ituri Pygmies of the Congo, the Pygmies of Cameroon, and the Gabra of Kenya. A similar domed form with a thatch cladding is used by the Native American Wichitas in the United States, and Australian Aborigines built domes with palm cladding until late in the nineteenth century. The Kipsikis of Kenya use the dome on top of circular palisade walls as a roof, covered in leaves and then thatch. The Fulah of Mali build a semipermanent tent on a square-framed structure, with an arched roof, clad in matting. In fact, there is almost every gradation from the basket to the frame (this is covered in more detail in a later chapter, *Putting Up Walls*).

The lashed pole or bamboo frames of the Pacific and Southeast Asia are often clad in basketwork or matting using palm leaves and other plants. In the Gilbert Islands, part of Kiribati in the central Pacific Ocean, there is even a traditional coconut-leaf screen with horizontal slats, which operate like a venetian blind, pulled by a string.

A New Use for Bark

Pieces of bark have been used as roof shingles in many places, but only a few types of tree produce large sheets suitable for wall and roof cladding, notably the stringybark and box trees in Australia. The Australian Aborigines used bark for canoes and dwellings, but they did not face the problems which Australia's European settlers encountered in trying to make use of bark to clad conventional pitched roofs. Settlers found that bark sheets curled and shrank, and that if they were nailed into place with more than one nail, the sheet tore itself apart as it shrank. It was best, they discovered, to use one nail in the middle of the sheet, but this did not stop the sheet from curling and letting in the weather or being torn off by the wind.

The solution to the problem was in two parts. Firstly, the bark sheets were tied down rather than nailed, either using cords made from the bark itself or, better and more commonly, using greenhide, which can stretch to take up the shrinkage of the bark. Secondly, the whole bark layer was weighed down with timbers to prevent it curling or blowing off. The timber structure was not actually fixed to the building at all, but draped over it: saddle poles lashed together in pairs were slung across the ridge, then heavier timbers running longitudinally along the roof surface were tied onto them.

It is not clear whether this ingenious solution was the invention of the settlers, perhaps combining the ledgers and roof riders which they remembered from thatching, or whether they knew of those rare forms of thatching which already combined the two elements (in Estonia and Sumatra). But the novelty lay not just in the combination of the elements: rather it was

The Adaptable Yurt

The yurt, used by central Asian nomadic herdsmen, is the most sophisticated lashed structure, in that it is portable and has had to evolve into a form as light and flexible as possible. There are several different versions, from the Kyrgyz *boz oy*, through the Kalmyk, Mongolian, and Turkmen types, but essentially the roof is a shallow dome shape with curved rafters running in to a central post, and the wall is a diagonal lattice which can be folded up for transport and pulled open again to create the wall. A canopy of felt or animal skins is drawn over the surface.

A Mongolian family cover the lattice walls of their newly-erected yurt with felt, having already prepared the roof. Several such layers, perhaps topped by canvas, help to insulate and rainproof the dwelling.

These houses in Fiji (above) use traditional building materials, including woven bamboo for the walls and palm thatch for the roofs.

An Australian Aboriginal shelter (left), photographed in 1930, consists of a single piece of bark supported by stout branches. Aborigines built various types of dwellings—both temporary like this one, and more permanent—appropriate to the season and climate.

Circular depressions in the grass, each with four postholes, mark the locations of dwellings at a fourth- to fifth-century CE site at Toro, Japan. A reconstructed dwelling is in the background.

the creation of a frame that rested on the roof surface without penetrating it.

Pit Dwellings

Today, lighter materials, such as boughs, bamboo, foliage, basketwork, matting, animal skins, thatch, and bark are generally used in tropical and subtropical climates. However, in the past they were not only used in these area, but also in the colder regions of Europe and East Asia as roofing for pit dwellings. It appears that in both regions an early form of dwelling was a sunken pit covered with a pitched roof. Earthfast posts— timber poles or trunks stuck into the ground— came to be used as supports, and over time the pit became shallower and an above-ground vertical wall became standard.

The Chinese bag dwelling of about 10,000 BCE was a round pit with a narrow neck. It probably had a lid of an ephemeral material like thatch. A large Chinese building at Bando consisted of a shallow square pit containing four vertical timber posts to support what may have been a pyramidal roof, which descended to the ground, so there was still no visible vertical wall. A much smaller Japanese dwelling type, called a *tateeana*, similarly had a pit with four posts supporting a square of beams. The roof above was an odd combination of a horizontal ridge at the top with a conical shape below, while a related structure of the fourth to fifth centuries CE, now reconstructed at Toro, Japan, has the four posts in an oblong form and a simpler ridged cone shape externally. A house at Murabeyet, Syria, of about 8000 BCE, was an irregular oval shape, partly excavated into a hillside and partly walled in mud, but it had posts supporting a short horizontal ridge, and would thus have had a similar ridged cone shape.

The thatching of these structures would have depended upon the vegetation available and is

of no real consequence, but the use of the ridge is significant in the development of timber construction. At first sight it seems an unnecessary elaboration on these conical roofs, but it reflects the fact that unless they are extremely slender, timber poles or trunks cannot be satisfactorily gathered together at a single point.

Major timber members were not at first dressed to shape, though where it was essential to construction they would have been notched or halved together. Suitable timber could, however, be split, and this is what gives rise to the cruck in Europe. A section of oak tree, which is naturally curved, can be split in half to produce a symmetrical pair of bent timbers. These can be pinned together to the top and set in the ground at the base, creating a stable self-braced triangle. A series of such pairs is what constitutes a cruck building, and it has been surmised that crucks were first used in shallow pit dwellings, and were only later used fully above ground. The cruck is particularly associated with the Celts, who spread across Europe in pre-Roman

times and formed much of the base population of northern Italy, Cisalpine and Transalpine Gaul (in northern Italy and France), Galicia (in northern Spain), Britain, and Ireland.

The Beginnings of Carpentry

In the same way, pit dwellings incorporating earthfast posts must have evolved into above-ground buildings. A village near Gladbach, Germany, shows something of this evolution. (Though it dates from the seventh to eighth centuries CE, this merely reflects the fact that much of Europe reverted to a near-Neolithic state after the decline of Rome.) There are 40 pit dwellings and semipit dwellings that measure about 10 x 13 ft (3 x 4 m) on average, and are built with undressed earthfast timber posts. It has been suggested that these posts formed part of fully carpentered frames, with dressed timbers and appropriately formed joints, but there is no evidence of this, and it is more probable that the roof members, such as rafters, were either tied to an upright or supported in the cleft of an upright. Either way, these dwellings are making the transition from the pit to above-ground structures.

The log cabin is a natural form not only in central and northern Europe but in forested areas elsewhere, including Japan. Building a log cabin involves cutting down substantial trees, and was perhaps not a very early development because of the lack of good axes. The survival of a number of log-built tombs under artificial earth mounds, in Asia and Europe from approximately 700 BCE onward, suggests that the same

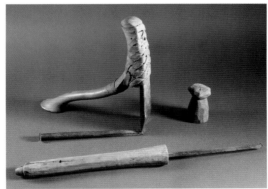

construction was used in regular building. The earlier uses of timber, ranging from single pillars and beams to complete log cabins, depended upon the development of cutting tools. Felling, splitting, and adzing were the basic procedures required for any effective use of timber. The axe and the adze were developed in a number of different cultures, but it was only when stone heads were replaced with metal ones that these became really effective.

Sawing timber into planks and other pieces of the required sizes is the next stage, and there is a surprising degree of uniformity in tools and procedures across cultures. The log is first broken down into smaller sizes with a large saw operating vertically, by one sawyer above and one below. In Europe, the log may be positioned over a pit, within which stands the lower sawyer; in Japan, it may be propped up at a steep angle to provide the necessary access from below. Lighter than this large saw, and used to cut smaller sizes, the frame

This medieval English tithe barn (above) uses a cruck frame of naturally bent oak, a form most commonly found in areas settled mainly by the Celts.

Among these Egyptian carpenters' tools of 1500 BCE (left) is an adze with a metal blade lashed to a wooden handle. It would have been reasonably functional.

saw is set within a frame to prevent it whipping and buckling, and again is used on an angled piece of timber in Japan and a horizontal piece over a pit in Europe, though it is also illustrated in the eighteenth century in Diderot's *Encyclopédie* being used to cut a horizontal piece raised on a trestle. The water-powered sawmill appeared in the medieval period, and the sketchbook kept by Villard de Honnecourt shows a cumbersome-looking example in which the flow of water turns a wheel, and the circular motion is then converted into reciprocating motion to operate the saw. The circular saw came much later.

Also needed for cutting and dressing timber are mortising axes and chisels, which are required for all sorts of purposes, but most of all for the construction of the mortise and tenon joint, so critical in the evolution of the timber frame. This joint was known in ancient Egypt long before it appeared in Europe. In the Egyptian Museum, Cairo, is a tomb model of a complete carpenter's shop, which shows adzes, men sawing wood, a carpenter cutting a tenon slot in a plank, and men re-tempering copper blades. The essentials of carpentry had developed even before the introduction of iron.

Earth and Brick

arth building covers a wide range of techniques, but the simplest form using soft mud, cob (or pug), must be one of the oldest building techniques in the world. Earth is also one of the least durable materials and the least distinctive, in that it is usually exactly the same as the natural ground nearby. Where we find evidence of early cob it is usually because it has been built up on a masonry base, because the building burned and in the process baked the cob, or because it was enhanced by the addition of materials such as lime or dung. An example

involving two or possibly three of these factors is the second palace of Mallia, Crete, of about 1700–1450 BCE.

Cob is durable in a dry climate, and one type, "layered construction," is used in African and Arab countries, but unknown elsewhere. Each layer has a sloping face and slightly overlaps the one below, and the layers follow around the building in an attractive plastic manner, quite unlike adobe or *pisé*. Cob is also used in regions with wet climates, including Britain, where it relies for its preservation upon wide eaves, an

This picturesque white-painted building in Somerset, England is of cob construction. The roof is thatched and the wide eaves help to keep the cob dry.

impervious surface treatment, and a masonry base. Earth is moistened, mixed, and piled onto the wall with a pitchfork in layers about 18 in (45 cm) high, each of which is left for perhaps two weeks to set before the next is placed, and the surface is finally pared off smooth. But there are drawbacks to this method: the walls often

Adobes, or mud bricks (above), lie drying in the sun in China, where this building material has been used for thousands of years. These adobes have had straw added to give greater strength; additional ingredients such as rice husks and manure may also be used.

Pisé de Terre Construction

Pisé de terre, or rammed earth, is an ancient, sophisticated, and very well documented method of construction. It uses a fairly dry, gravelly loam, rather than the clay preferred for adobe. It is rammed into place in thin layers between panels of boarding, which are then removed to reveal the dry wall, and depends upon a more advanced level of carpentry than does adobe. It can be traced back about 2,200 years in Carthage, in North Africa, and it appears independently in China and India. From Carthage it passed to Spain and central France, from Spain to Latin America, and from France to most of the world.

The Hakka people of Fujian province, China, built extraordinary circular communal dwellings, called *tulou*, of *pisé*. These multistory buildings, big enough to accommodate 100 people, as well as domestic animals, are built around a main courtyard, and have walls up to 6 ft (1.8 m) thick.

become damp, and the straw that is frequently included to bind the mixture not only decays but provides a haven for vermin. Cob buildings were therefore a major target of housing reformers in Britain in the nineteenth century.

Turf Construction

Building in turf cut from the ground can be done with primitive tools, so it must be almost as old a tradition as cob, but we can only guess this because little evidence remains. A typical method is to choose a grassy area that will have a good mat of roots, cut the grass as low as possible, and then chop out blocks from the ground to be used in the same ways as bricks. Even more simply, a plow can be used to turn up a continuous strip of sod, which is then chopped off in convenient lengths. In the nineteenth century, a specialized "grasshopper plow" was used for the purpose by settlers on the prairies of the United States.

Although pure turf construction normally leaves very little archaeological evidence, it may survive when combined with other materials, as in the stone corbeled tomb at Newgrange, Ireland, of about 3200 BCE, which was built in layers of turf with water-rounded stones between. When the material is used alone in walls, it is

built up like bricks, often to a thickness of more than 3 ft (0.9 m). Flatter strips than those used for the walls, rather like modern-day instant lawn, are used for roofing, laid longitudinally and overlapping up the slope like clapboard. A reconstructed Bronze Age house at Hjerl Hede, Denmark, is of log construction but is roofed with strips of turf in this way.

Bricks

Adobe, or sun-dried brick—made by mixing water and clay—is probably the oldest building material of which there are datable remains. A surviving brick from Jericho, in modern-day Israel, dated to at least 8000 BCE, measures about 12 x 3 x 3 in (30 x 8 x 8 cm), and looks like a loaf of bread because it was made by hand in the same way as bread. From about 6000 BCE onward, rectangular bricks begin to appear, but in Mesopotamia during the third millennium, in about 2800–2300 BCE, a crude form of adobe was used, the base being flat and the top curved, often with fingerprints left by the molder. These were typically 9 x 6 x 2½ in (23 x 15 x 6 cm) at the thickest part. They were often laid herringbone fashion—two or three courses leaning one way, two courses flat, then two or three sloping

the other way—and they were strong enough to be used for arches over the doorways of houses. Usually a mortar of the same basic mud was used, but sometimes they were laid dry.

The rectangular adobe arose later because it required skilled carpentry to make the rectangular mold. Molded slabs of earth, so large as to need two men to lift them, have been found in the remains of houses at Çatal Hüyük, southern Turkey, dating from about 5700 BCE. In the north of Mesopotamia, the first sun-dried bricks appear in about 5000 BCE, and by 3000 BCE rectangular molded bricks were in fairly wide use in the Middle East.

Baked brick arises from the same roots as adobe. It uses the same raw material, clay, and is molded in a similar way. It is not surprising, therefore, that it emerges in the same places as adobe arose, from Mesopotamia to China, where it was discovered that firing the brick in a kiln at high temperature produced a stronger material which also better resists weathering. In these places, too, baked brick is very commonly combined with adobe in the same structure, the baked brick being used on outer and more decorative surfaces and in places where the load is heavy or damp may be a problem.

Great Mosque of Djenné
Mali

The Great Mosque, or Friday Mosque, of Djenné, Mali, is one of the most remarkable earth buildings in the world, although one of the least authentic. There is a tradition of earthen mosques in North Africa, and at Djenné —the oldest known city of sub-Saharan Africa— there have been three: one of about the thirteenth century, a second of around 1834–1846, and the present structure of 1907.

African Crossroads

The nearby settlement of Djenné-djenno, or old Djenné, had been established by the third century BCE, and the present Djenné was a major center by CE 850. By the thirteenth century, Djenné was a cosmopolitan trading town, which had already given birth to the more famous Timbuktu. Also at this time, Koi Konboro, king of Djenné, converted to Islam. He built a very large mosque of mud brick, which, because it was constructed before his pilgrimage to Mecca, was of a local character. The earliest known West African mosques, in the

Arab-influenced Berber settlements of Kumbi (Koumbi Saleh) and Tegdaoust (both in what is today Mauritania), date from some time between the ninth and thirteenth centuries, and excavations have shown them to be simple combinations of courtyard, sanctuary, and square minaret. The Djenné mosque must have appeared very grandiose in comparison. Its influence was then spread by the Dyula people, who from the fourteenth century established settlements along trade routes from Djenné to the Akan goldfields (in modern-day Ghana), and built in the settlements pinnacled, buttressed, and trabeated (post and beam) mosques of the Djenné type.

The rise of Islam had meant not only the creation of new building types, notably the mosque and the *madrasah* (theological school), but the dissemination of what had been the fairly static building traditions of Mesopotamia and Syria throughout the Arab world, into North Africa, Spain, and then farther afield. It also meant the fusion of this new type of architecture with local

building traditions, and in some cases the adoption and rediffusion of regional forms, such as the Visigothic horseshoe arch from Spain. The original Djenné mosque was one of these regional Islamic buildings, blending the imported forms and technology with local traditions and characteristics.

Adobe originated in Mesopotamia, together with the corbeled dome form, which cannot be constructed in cob or *pisé de terre*. This building tradition had been long established in Syria and southern Turkey, and to some extent Arabia and Egypt, but it was now carried to North Africa, where the earliest earth building tradition was the *pisé* of Carthage. With adobe came the corbeled dome. As used on houses in Syria and Turkey, these corbeled domes are circular and pointed, and are commonly the sole roofing of the house, in whatever number is required by the plan. In Arabia and Africa, they are generally taller, are combined with flat roofing rather than being the sole roof form, and often, as at Djenné, are themselves square in plan rather than round.

The mosque's eastern wall (above left) has three towers, which taper to spires, each of which is crowned by an ostrich egg, a symbol of fertility.

A New Mosque Rises

In 1816, Shehu Ahmadu Lobbo came to power in Mali. As a fundamentalist Muslim, he was appalled by the lax religious practices of Djenné, launched a successful *jihad* (holy war) against the city, and began the construction of his own capital, Hamdallahi, with its own larger but less flamboyant mosque. Ahmadu closed the mosques of Djenné and Timbuktu, and, although the destruction of mosques was prohibited, he blocked their gutters to cause their demise. The Friday Mosque was given a reprieve but left uncared for, until in 1835 it received the same treatment. The gutters were plugged above and below, causing the rain to collect on the roof, which became waterlogged and collapsed, exposing the massive pillars to the weather. Meanwhile, Ahmadu built his own very large but low and austerely designed mosque on a different site to the east.

By the beginning of the twentieth century, the only substantial remains of the old mosque were parts of the east and north walls. These romantic ruins were finally replaced by a new building, completed in 1907, when Mali was under French administration. There is evidence to suggest that the new mosque was of a local African initiative and design rather than a French one, as has been commonly believed. The architect of the new building was Ismaila Traoré, head of Djenné's guild of masons, and the construction was done by forced labor. The design has been criticized in the past as being too massive and banal in character, but it has acquired the patina of age, and now seems an attractive building.

The present mosque makes use of the arch form—which is not believed to have been used in the area prior to the colonial period—and it uses both oval and rectangular bricks. Externally it is punctuated by the *toron*, protruding beams (originating in Syria) upon which a worker can stand while replastering the surface, which is done every spring. However, the *toron* are perhaps more ornamental than functional, as they occur on some vertical surfaces but not on others of a similar nature. The two spiral staircases are not traditional, and were the inspired contribution of a young mason, Madedeo Kossinentao, when it was realized that because of the great height of the building, traditional straight staircases would have to be too long for the plan. There are no loudspeakers, and the call to prayer is issued live five times a day by a *muezzin* standing at the northeast corner.

Seen from the air, the great size of the mosque becomes apparent (top). The building stands well above Djenné's main square on a raised platform, which gives protection from seasonal floods.

On the mosque's flat roof (above) are 104 ceramic lids, which are opened at night to allow hot air out.

Stone and Masonry

Natural rubble stone, laid dry or bound in mud, is an ancient building material that deteriorates easily, and can be almost as hard to recognize in archaeological remains as the various earth constructions. But cut and dressed stone (depending upon the type of stone) is extraordinarily durable, and has been used for many of the greatest monuments of history. How it was quarried and how it was shaped and dressed, even before the advent of iron tools, are major historical questions. How it was transported from quarry to site, and how it was raised into position, are equally major questions, but ones that can be answered with slightly more confidence.

Megalithic Structures

In the late Neolithic period, vast megalithic (giant stone) structures appear in many parts of Europe—simple dolmens (upright stones supporting large flat stones), menhirs (standing stones), chambered tombs, stone circles, and stone avenues. Their stones have usually been partly shaped, but they are a long way from ashlar, the perfectly squared, close-fitting stones used in formal architecture at later dates. But the megalithic structures of Malta and Gozo, dating from about 3500 BCE onward, are architecturally more complicated than those erected elsewhere, multi-lobed in plan, and with trabeated (post and beam) or corbeled roof construction.

The dolmens and cromlechs (stone enclosures) of Celtic France and Britain seem to have been built originally to form a burial chamber within a raised earth mound (barrow), which has often disappeared. These, and similar structures in Denmark and elsewhere, are basically trabeated structures—that is, the roof consists of one or more large slabs of stone spanning like beams.

Stonehenge, in England, is on a grander scale. It dates from approximately 2300 BCE and incorporates stones used in an earlier monument, of

There are 20 or so Neolithic temples scattered across Malta and neighboring Gozo. This one at Mnajdra, Malta, of 3500–2500 BCE, is believed to have been at least partly roofed with corbeled stone bocks.

around 2500 BCE. There is an outer ring of post and beam construction, and an inner arc or horseshoe of five trilithons (sets of three stones, each consisting of two uprights and a horizontal lintel). The outer ring and the trilithons are of sarsen, a local sandstone, from Marlborough Downs, 20 miles (32 km) away. Between the two is a smaller ring of freestanding upright stones ("bluestone") which date from the earlier monument and came from Wales, 150 miles (240 km) away, and could have been transported mainly by water. How the much larger sarsens were transported, without wheeled vehicles or modern roads, it is almost impossible to conceive, but probably by a combination of wooden sleds

The figure at left gives some idea of the massive size of the stone blocks used to build the walls of the acropolis at Mycenae, Greece, of about 1400 BCE. Masonry of this type is known as cyclopean.

and water transport. It was probably roofed in timber, for it was preceded by giant timber-columned circular structures, such as one at Stanton Drew, near Bristol, and has a framework suited for a conical roof with the rafters propped halfway on the inner arc of trilithons (probably with a central column, but possibly an opening).

Structures made of smaller stones sometimes survive in recognizable condition, and scholars have been able to reconstruct the form of a hut from Luni, in the Appennines of Italy. It has rubble walls, which differ from drystone walls in that they use mud or other mortar. During the Bronze Age (generally in the Mediterranean, 3500–1200 BCE), cyclopean masonry appears throughout the Mediterranean and Near East. The term "cyclopean" is a Greek one, and refers to the fact that later Greeks believed the blocks to be too large to have been positioned by men, and that the walls must have been built by the Cyclops, a giant. Commonly, cyclopean masonry makes up only the lower part—typically about 3ft (0.9 m)—of walls that are otherwise of mud-brick or half-timber construction. Some properly squared stones, called orthostats, are sometimes used in critical locations, for in the Bronze Age—using bronze implements—stone could be sawn.

The most striking features at Tiwanaku, Bolivia, are the large, finely made stone structures, such as the Kalasasaya Platform, shown here.

South American Masonry

One would expect the first complete dressed stone walls to be of rectangular blocks simply laid one upon the other, but some Egyptian and some later Greek stonemasonry is of a different character. All the stones have been quarried square, but they are not of uniform height, and did not automatically form horizontal courses. When they were laid, the existing courses were cut away to fit the new stones, possibly by some process of rubbing, achieving a very tight fit. This crotched, or quasi-coursed, masonry occurs in a number of different cultures, including those in South America that were totally unconnected with the Mediterranean world, such as the Incas of what is now Peru.

Some aspects of stone construction in South America are quite distinctive. It seems that dressed stone first appeared before 1000 BCE at Cerro Sechín, Peru, then well-jointed and cut stone between 900 and 400 BCE at Chavín de Huántar in the Peruvian Andes. The craft reached maturity in the hands of the people of Tiwanaku (Tiahuanaco), in modern Bolivia, between about 200 BCE and CE 1000. Not only did the masons at Tiwanaku dress the face of the stone smoothly, but they also cut the most ingenious decorative motifs, requiring great technical skill.

Greek Temple Construction

The classical Greek temple is testament to the ingenuity and craftsmanship of its architects and stonemasons, as well as to the wealth and power of the Greek city-states. Some of the principal temple construction techniques are shown below.

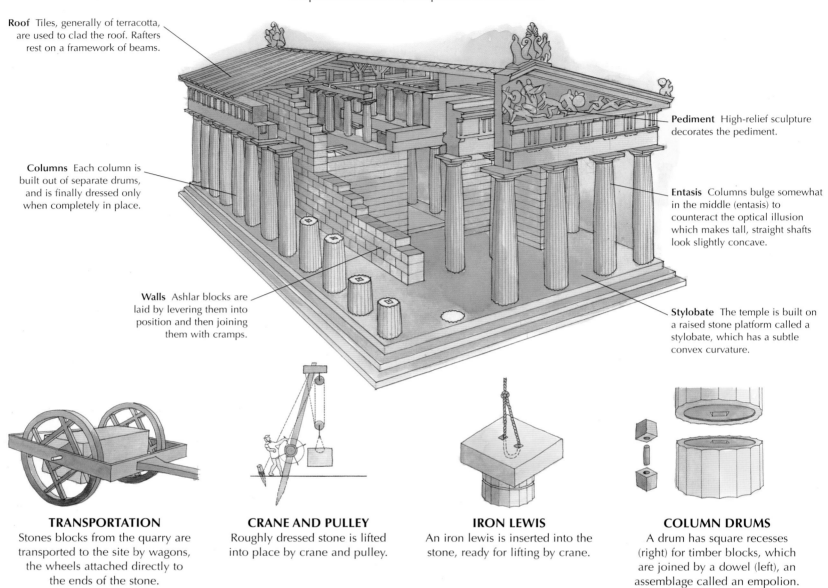

Roof Tiles, generally of terracotta, are used to clad the roof. Rafters rest on a framework of beams.

Columns Each column is built out of separate drums, and is finally dressed only when completely in place.

Walls Ashlar blocks are laid by levering them into position and then joining them with cramps.

Pediment High-relief sculpture decorates the pediment.

Entasis Columns bulge somewhat in the middle (entasis) to counteract the optical illusion which makes tall, straight shafts look slightly concave.

Stylobate The temple is built on a raised stone platform called a stylobate, which has a subtle convex curvature.

TRANSPORTATION
Stones blocks from the quarry are transported to the site by wagons, the wheels attached directly to the ends of the stone.

CRANE AND PULLEY
Roughly dressed stone is lifted into place by crane and pulley.

IRON LEWIS
An iron lewis is inserted into the stone, ready for lifting by crane.

COLUMN DRUMS
A drum has square recesses (right) for timber blocks, which are joined by a dowel (left), an assemblage called an empolion.

Although they may have been influenced by the Tiwanakans, the Incas, who had their capital at Cuzco, Peru, are thought to have developed stone dressing almost independently, and it is far cruder work, more like that of the Mediterranean cultures. Inca stonemasonry is best seen at Machu Picchu, a settlement established around CE 1450. The Incas and Tiwanakans were bronze cultures like those of the Mediterranean, and the similar technology and constraints produced similar results in the case of the Incas. But why the people of Tiwanaku became so much more sophisticated is impossible to say.

Quarrying Stone

The Egyptians quarried softer stone by cutting channels about 4½ in (11 cm) wide into it, probably with a mason's pick, and then using a line of wedges to split it. Otherwise, they might drill a line of holes rather than cut a channel.

Very similar techniques continued in use into the twentieth century, but there are variants such as using dry timber wedges, then wetting them so the expansion splits the stone. When the stone was harder, as in the granite quarries at Aswan, splitting stone was much more laborious, but wedges could still be used, and driven in by force. An unfinished obelisk at Aswan gives an insight into Egyptian practices (see the box opposite).

By the nineteenth century, the standard way of splitting stone was the plug and feathers. A hole was drilled, either using a chisel, which was turned 90 degrees between hammer blows, or a pneumatic rock drill (introduced late in the nineteenth century). The feathers—two prongs of iron, wider at the base than at the top—were driven into this hole. Then a wedge (the plug) was driven in between the two prongs, causing the base of the feathers to expand in the drill hole and split the stone.

In Mesopotamia, stone was generally much rarer than in Egypt, but where it was used the techniques seem to have been very similar. In the Assyrian Empire, of about 900 to 700 BCE, a form of gypsum now known as Mosul marble was quarried. It was soft enough to extract with a pick, and cut with great iron saws, examples of which have been excavated at Nimrud, in modern-day Iraq.

We understand a certain amount about the methods used by the classical Greeks to quarry and transport stone. These resembled those of ancient Egypt, but were much more sophisticated. In a quarry at Cave di Cusa, Sicily, Italy, we can see shafts in various stages of being cut out in much the same way as the obelisk at Aswan, except that they are vertical. A circular trench was cut, of the diameter of the column drum and just wide enough for a man to work in. This trench was steadily deepened until the whole drum was

In Athens, a column of the Temple of Olympian Zeus (the Olympieion), has collapsed, revealing the dozen or so column drums that make it up. The use of monolithic (single-piece) columns was rare.

exposed, and this was then undercut, snapped off, and removed. Elsewhere, separate sections of columns, or drums, were cut.

Moving and Positioning Stone

The ancient Egyptians commonly used earth or sand ramps to raise stones to the upper parts of a building. The column drums were put in place in a very rough state, and the earth packed around them as they rose. Stonemasons then carried out the final dressing of the column, starting from the top and working downward as the earth was removed. A column at Karnak has had the earth removed prematurely, before the dressing stage, illustrating the procedure.

The classical Greeks also used earth ramps, but unlike the Egyptians they had the pulley, and understood the principle of mechanical advantage: that when pulleys are used, the force exerted is less than the weight lifted. For the higher parts of the building, where constructing earth ramps would not be cost effective, a pulley and shear legs (three poles lashed together at the top) would be used to raise the blocks. The blocks would have bosses protruding from them to make it easier to tie ropes around them, and these protrusions would later be struck off the surface of the finished building. A different technique was used to lift stone at some of the temples at Agrigento, Sicily, Italy. At each end of a block (which would not be visible in the finished building) a U-shaped channel was cut to take a rope, and slightly undercut in the curve to stop the rope slipping off. The block could be suspended on the pulley until it was in the

exact position required, and then the rope at either end untied and pulled out.

Otherwise, in both Egypt and Greece, the final exact positioning of a block was done with bronze or iron levers. When the stone was in place, it would be secured to the next one with a cramp. Some early Egyptian cramps are double dovetails of timber, shaped like a bow tie, and some metal examples are the same shape, while others are simple bars with right-angled bends at either end. Where two blocks met, a Greek mason might dress the edges to a perfect fit, but roughly cut away the rest of the face to save on skilled work. This technique, where the dressed edge stood highest, is called raised band anathyrosis.

A Greek column is normally made up of separate pieces or drums, upon which raised band anathyrosis is used. At the centre of each circular face is a square recess into which a timber block is placed. A timber rod or dowel links the timber blocks above and below and holds the drums in correct alignment, and this assemblage of two blocks and a dowel is called an empolion. As well as holding the drums in alignment, the rod or dowel allows the upper drum to be rotated to grind the edge to an exact fit (probably with the aid of water and grit). An even more specialized aspect of Greek stonemasonry was the dressing of the column to its very subtle profile, which is discussed in a later chapter, *Putting Up Walls*.

The Unfinished Obelisk of Aswan

A giant obelisk which remains in a quarry at Aswan in Egypt, half-cut, would have been the largest single block ever handled in the world, but a crack appeared near the point, and it was abandoned by the quarrymen. The greatest mystery is the means of digging out the rock. Balls of dolerite (a coarse basaltic rock) have been found at the quarry, and it has been inferred that these were used to beat the stone. But the idea of quarrying stone by bashing it with a lump is patently ridiculous, and the theory can now be put to rest, because similar balls found at Malta were clearly used, like ball bearings, to move stones. How the cutting was actually done at Aswan has not been resolved.

The unfinished obelisk measures nearly 42 m (138 ft) and weighs more than 1,000 tons.

Pyramids of Giza
Egypt

The three pyramids of Giza, near modern-day Cairo, were constructed in the middle of the third millennium BCE. Together, they make up the oldest of the ancient wonders of the world, the only one that survives. Each pyramid is named after the pharaoh for whom it was built: Khufu (Cheops), Khafre (Chephren), and Menkaure (Mykerinus).

The pyramids are so well known and so symbolic of ancient Egyptian culture that it is hard to think of them as being the result of experiment. But the idea of a smooth-faced pyramid was a novel one, and the angle upon which to construct such a pyramid was a technical question. The stepped pyramid form had evolved almost fortuitously at Saqqara, but it was not continued elsewhere.

At Maydum (or Medum), in about 2680 BCE, the pharaoh Snefru first turned what was probably a stepped pyramid into a smooth-faced one. But it had a base angle of 51°52', and there are signs that it began to collapse during construction. Snefru then built the Bent Pyramid at Dahshur, which begins at 54°31' then bends in at 43°21', possibly because of the same problem. Finally, the North Pyramid at Dahshur is all at 43°. However, the Egyptian designers must have regained their confidence, because the pyramids of Giza resemble that at Maydum: the Great Pyramid of Khufu is 51°52', that of Khafre 53°10', and that of Menkaure 51°.

A Tomb Fit for a Pharaoh

The purpose of these pyramids was to securely house the body of the pharaoh, and to enable his soul to ascend to the heavens. It is thought that the pyramid itself was a solar symbol, and the Great Pyramid contains narrow tunnels that are aligned with great accuracy to astronomical features. Each of the three had a mortuary temple located next to it, linked by a causeway to a valley temple, though at the Great Pyramid the evidence has been largely destroyed.

The Great Pyramid was originally 480 ft (145 m) high, and 755 ft (230 m) square at the base, covering 14 acres (5.7 hectares), and used 2.3 million blocks of stone, varying from 2½ to 40 tons in weight. There are three burial chambers. The fact that there are three, rather than one, may be the result of changes in intention on the designers' part, but could also reflect the fact that no one could predict when the pharaoh would die, which meant an interim tomb had to be available before the final, ideal scheme could be completed. The first chamber was centrally placed below ground level, and reached by a descending ramp. The next, the Queen's Chamber, was constructed within the masonry mass, above ground.

The final burial place, the King's Chamber, was even higher up, and reached by a very tall and impressive ramped gallery, the sides of which gradually corbel inward.

The pyramids were built up of square blocks quarried nearby, and it is generally believed that the smooth facing was added at the end. Some of the original stone facing remains on the top of the Pyramid of Khafre. The Great Pyramid had a facing of white limestone from Tura, across the Nile, and used Aswan granite for the burial chamber. Other imported materials included copper from Sinai, alabaster from Hatnub in the Eastern Desert, and cedar from Byblos, in what is today Lebanon. The King's Chamber of the Great Pyramid measures approximately 17 x 35 ft (5 x 10 m) and is roofed with a series of five horizontal slabs, one above the other, with voids between them, and finally by pairs of stones leaning against each other to create a triangular archlike structure (the Egyptians did not use the true arch), which throws the weight from above to either side. The exterior entrance has a similar triangular-headed opening.

Building the Pyramids

In cross section, the Great Pyramid can be seen to be constructed in the same way as the earlier (but abortive) stepped pyramid of Sekhemkhet, with a large battered (sloping-sided) pylon at the center, and successive walls leant against it. But that does not indicate the sequence in which it was built.

A huge workforce was needed to build the pyramids (below) of Menkaure (left), Khafre (center), and the Great Pyramid (right), together with associated structures. Archaeologists estimate that the Great Pyramid alone required up to 25,000 workers.

It seems certain that ramps were used to raise the stone, and to be effective they must have been at a fairly shallow angle. Earth ramps used alone would have covered a huge area and contained an enormous volume of material, for every time the height is doubled, the ground area is quadrupled and the volume of earth multiplied eightfold. The most promising theory is that as much of the ramp as possible was built on the top of the masonry of the pyramid itself, ascending around the perimeter in a square spiral. This idea gains indirect support from the fact that some ziggurats in Mesopotamia were square spirals.

The pharaoh's body was transported on the Nile to a temple where it was embalmed, and from here a causeway led to the mortuary temple adjoining the pyramid itself. Enough evidence survives of the mortuary temple adjoining the Great Pyramid to know that it consisted of a great basalt-paved courtyard surrounded by a portico on granite pillars, the temple's outer limestone walls carrying superb relief carving under the shelter of the portico. At the back was a colonnaded vestibule leading into a space that probably contained statues in niches, as in the better preserved chapel of the Pyramid of Khafre. In the 1950s, archaeologists discovered parts of a large wooden boat in a pit next to the pyramid. This extraordinary vessel, probably designed to carry the body of the ruler, is made of large timbers, which are stitched together with rope rather than being joined with metal fixings.

The Pyramid of Khafre (top) retains some of the white limestone which once gave all three Giza pyramids smooth faces. The stone was stripped in the fourteenth century CE and used to build Cairo.

A nineteenth-century engraving (above) shows tomb robbers in one of the Great Pyramid's passageways.

Iron

Before the late eighteenth century, iron was an expensive material that was not used for primary building components. It did nonethless play a crucial role in the form of masonry cramps, reinforcing bars in stone lintels, and ties of various sorts, although most of the evidence for this has disappeared. In fact, the main cause of the destruction of classical buildings has been the value of the iron and bronze they contained, removed by later looters either by burrowing into the structure or by taking it apart.

Ancient Iron

Although iron can be used for nails, screws, and other fixings, this was not as common as might be supposed. The Romans had both nails and screws, but until the nineteenth century most timber frames were joined so far as practicable with much cheaper timber pegs and dowels. In the classical Greek world, the most interesting use of iron was to reinforce a beam, as in the Propylaea, the monumental gate to the Acropolis of Athens. Here columns spaced in the usual way would have been too close together for a formal or processional entrance, and the central spacing is therefore one and a half times the norm. To cover this greater span, the builders positioned an iron bar in a recess cut in each marble beam for about half the length. Each bar was so small that it would seem useless, but when structurally analyzed it proves to halve the stress on the stone beam (something which the designers could only have appreciated intuitively).

An iron bar was apparently used to reinforce the underside of the lintels in the fifth-century BCE Temple of Zeus Olympius at Agrigento, Sicily, Italy, the sheer size of which meant that it was difficult to span between the stone columns. Iron was then extensively used by the Romans, and iron ties were important in the sixth-century CE church of Hagia Sophia, Constantinople (now Istanbul, Turkey), but the metal largely went out of use during the medieval period. There is, however, one remarkable exception, Sainte-Chapelle in Paris, which is a very steeply proportioned Gothic church of the thirteenth century, lacking the flying buttresses normally required to contain the outward thrust of a High Gothic church roof. This is possible because there is an iron chain all around it at roof level. After the Renaissance, chains were commonly used in this way to contain the outward thrust of domes (though the word "chain" in this context can refer to a series of linked timbers or pieces of stone or timber).

The Age of Cast Iron

The Industrial Revolution brought about a sharp increase in the use of iron. In the eighteenth century, in England, Abraham Darby I developed coke smelting, in which coke replaced charcoal as the fuel, and was able to produce cast iron in quantities. For a long time, therefore, cast iron was far more readily available than wrought iron, far cheaper, and therefore much more commonly used in buildings. It was only in the 1840s that wrought iron was widely used in buildings.

Iron was used sparingly in ancient times. In the Propylaea of Athens, Greece, dating from the fifth century BCE, 6-ft (1.8-m) iron bars embedded in the marble beams are used as reinforcement.

In the later eighteenth century, cast-iron columns began to be used in churches in England, but their really important application was in the new mills for the spinning and weaving of cotton and flax. The typical cotton mill was a five- or six-story building with brick or stone walls and wooden floors. It was terribly susceptible to fire, because spinning, like flour-milling, produced a very fine dust, which in the presence of flame exploded like a gas. For this reason, William Strutt was especially concerned to devise a fire-proof structure when he built the Derby cotton mill in 1792–1793. Cast-iron columns were used more or less for the first time, and they carried timber beams approximately 12 in (30 cm) wide, spanning 9 ft (2.7 m), between which were brick arches spanning 8 ft (2.4 m). The underside of the arches was plastered and there was no combustible material exposed in the structure.

However, there was a weak point: horizontal wrought-iron tie-rods were used to contain the expansion of the arches, and these were accessible to fire. The problem was not that they would melt in the first instance, but they would expand in the heat, allowing the arched floor structure to spread and crack, giving the fire access to the timber beams.

Cast Iron

Cast iron is the impure iron obtained from smelting iron ore, and contains up to four percent of carbon or a total of ten percent of other elements alloyed with the iron. Cast iron is formed by pouring the molten metal into a mold. It withstands compression well, but it is not good in tension or bending, and is brittle under sudden changes of temperature—such as when water is played onto it in a fire—which can make it particularly dangerous. For most purposes, before the nineteenth century, cast iron was converted into wrought iron by burning or working out the impurities, to create as pure a material as possible. Wrought iron has quite different properties. It can be hammered and worked into shape, and this working gives it a fibrous texture: it is more resilient than cast iron and can take tension, though it is not as strong as cast iron in compression.

A nineteenth-century engraving shows workers in a foundry pouring molten iron into molds to produce cast iron.

In the late eighteenth and early nineteenth centuries, architects and engineers were quick to take advantage of the newly abundant building material: iron. They used cast iron, first in bridges, churches, and mills, and then in the new railway stations. Columns at Kettering Station, England, are shown here.

In 1796, Strutt's acquaintance Charles Bage designed the flax mill of Benyon, Bage, and Marshall at Shrewsbury, England, making the beams as well as the columns of cast iron. This mill, finished in 1797, is the first known example of a complete internal iron frame, although the external walls were, as usual, of load-bearing brickwork, and there were still brick arches with wrought-iron tie rods exposed below. In Strutt's mill at Belper North, of 1804, he made a significant improvement by raising the wrought-iron ties to a position above the soffit (underside) of the arch, embedded in masonry and not exposed to fire. This eliminated the major weak point in the system. Thus, over a period of about twelve years there had evolved a fireproof framing system that was to remain in use, almost unchanged, for more than a century.

Building Iron Bridges

Meanwhile, there were a number of developments in bridge design, beginning with the first complete cast-iron bridge at Coalbrookdale, England, constructed between 1775 and 1779. But this and most others were conceptually flawed, using curved cast-iron ribs which imitated the wooden ribs used in many bridges of the time, but which were structurally illogical. There were also iron circles in the spandrels between the arch and the deck, imitating the iron apertures in stone bridges, which lightened the masonry and relieved flood pressures. The engineer Thomas Telford eliminated these design flaws in the bridges he built, and also designed some of the first suspension bridges.

Railway bridges were of more relevance to the mainstream development of architecture. They were required to be stiff (unlike suspension bridges) so as to withstand the stress of a single large moving load. They also tended to be self-contained, like a beam, neither exerting outward thrust on the abutments like an arch, nor inward tension on the anchorage like a suspension bridge. The major early examples were by the railway engineers George Stephenson and his son Robert. It is almost certain that the father designed the small bridge at Gaunless on the Stockton and Darlington line (the first public locomotive railway) in 1834–1835, and also used some of the first solid-iron beams as bridges over streets. The son designed, in 1849, the High Level Bridge at Newcastle (a series of tied arches, which were also self-contained), and, one year later, the Britannia Bridge on the Menai Straits between the island of Anglesey and the mainland of Wales. This simple box beam was so large that the trains ran through the inside of it.

From the mid-century, parallel-chorded forms such as the Warren girder—in which the top and bottom members are parallel, with diagonal members between them—came into general use following the development of the necessary structural analytical techniques. This was a development of major importance not just to bridges but also to conventional buildings, because these girders, unlike earlier bridge forms, were suitable for use in buildings. A number of other forms of truss were to follow later. They were to find their fulfillment with the introduction of steel.

Although its design borrowed elements from stone and wooden bridges, the first iron bridge, at Coalbrookdale, England, was a dramatic demonstration of the potential for the structural use of iron.

in the form of square rods, from which he cut a section of the size required for the nail.

In about 1776, an American, Jeremiah Wilkinson of Rhode Island, invented a process for cutting tacks with shears, then holding them in a vice while forming the heads. A number of improvements followed. Before long, tacks and brads were being formed without a proper head at all. A strip of iron would be fed into cutters at a slight angle, which would snip off a piece, then the strip was turned over so that the next snip was at the opposite angle. This meant that the piece cut off was in the form of a long triangle, a shape that has been popular for glazing brads until recent times. Other shapes could be cut off in alternate directions, without waste, if the cutter was designed appropriately. But all would be of a uniform thickness, determined by the original nail plate, and the cutter created only the profile.

Machine-made Nails

One of these shapes was an elongated L, with a long, slightly tapering shaft, and a short head extending to one side only. This was to be the common cut brad used for purposes like flooring until about 1870. It could not be used for important structural joints, or for ledged and braced doors, because it lacked the resilience of a nail worked by a smith, and would snap if it was bent sharply. This meant that the carpenter was not able to clench it—that is, drive it right through timbers and bend the point sideways at right angles, preventing it from being pulled out.

There followed two important forms of machine-made nail that were capable of being clenched. One was the wire nail—so named

Nail-making was once a laborious process carried out by blacksmiths. The Romans made wide use of nails, and this stone relief carving of the first century CE depicts a Roman smith at the anvil.

because it was formed from wire—which would already have acquired some fibrous quality and resilience from the process of forming and drawing it. This type was developed mainly in France between about 1800 and 1840, and widely known as French nails or *pointes de Paris*. It was in wide use on the Continent around the middle of the century, but was accepted only slowly in Britain and North America. The other type was made by machinery that to some extent imitated the actions of the smith. It was developed in Britain in about 1835, but drawing to some degree upon US patents, and it became widely known as the Ewbank patent pressed nail. These developments greatly reduced the cost of nails.

Improving Nails

Iron played many other roles, for example in ornamental work, but another fundamental use was in nails. Since ancient times wrought-iron nails had been the product of an individual blacksmith, who would beat them into shape, and in the process improve their resilience. The mechanization of the process began with the introduction of the slitting mill, which could be used to cut sheet iron into nail rods—strips from which individual nails could then be cut. The circumstances of its invention are unknown, but a mill was exported from Liège (in present-day Belgium) to England toward the end of the sixteenth century. It spread to the United States within decades, and was in use by 1645 at Saugus, Massachusetts. The smith now received the iron

The earliest experiments in iron-frame construction occurred in textile mills, such as this flax mill in Leeds, England, pictured in the 1840s. Its owner, John Marshall, had been a partner in the mill in which an internal iron frame was used for the first time, in 1797.

Steel

In 1879, the Chicago & Alton Railroad company built this all-steel bridge over the Missouri River at Glasgow to connect Chicago and Kansas City.

Like cast iron, steel is an alloy of iron and carbon, but it has a much lower carbon content. There are several different types, each with specific properties, including corrosion-resistant stainless steel, and high-carbon steel, used when greater than normal strength is required. But it is mild steel—containing not more than 0.25 percent carbon, and with the ability to be worked easily—that is today the most widely used steel for construction purposes. Its tensile strength is better than iron's, but it is not so resistant to corrosion. Steel came into significant use in the 1870s following the development of the Bessemer converter and the open-hearth furnace, the improvements of Mushet, and then Siemens's open-hearth process. Mild steel has now superseded wrought iron, and where iron decorative work is sometimes referred to today as wrought iron, it is in fact made of mild steel.

Experimenting with Steel

In the United States, steel was first used for structural purposes in 1868–1870. The engineer James Eads was responsible for building a particularly difficult bridge over the Mississippi at St. Louis, Missouri, and decided to use steel instead of cast iron in the arches. Even so, he

could not get the properties he required, and work had to be suspended after the initial clearing and construction of the caissons in 1867. After tests using different types of steel, the work resumed in 1868, using expensive chrome steel for the first time. The first American bridge to be built entirely of steel was also in Missouri, over the Missouri River at Glasgow, in 1879. The structural members were tubes, 18 in (45 cm) in diameter and ¼ in (6 mm) thick.

In France, the engineer Gustave Eiffel, with one partial exception, made no use of steel, but an important aspect of Eiffel's work was the sophisticated graphic, analytic, and experimental techniques he used in his designs, as well as the high performance and precision he achieved in jointing and riveting, which set new standards for construction generally.

In Scotland, the Firth of Forth Bridge was constructed of steel in the late 1880s, and has a span of 1,710 ft (513 m). Here, the Scottish engineer William Arrol developed machines for hydraulic riveting at unprecedented pressure and speed, as well as machines for drilling the 12-ft (3.5-m) diameter tube sections while preassembled.

Steel was used for some of the beams of the Home Insurance Building, Chicago, of 1885, but

the Statue of Liberty, New York, completed in 1886, was the first building other than a bridge in which steel was used for the major load-bearing members. Although it was a sculpture—designed by Frédéric-Auguste Bartholdi—it was also a substantial building in its own right, measuring 150 ft (45 m) high, and in an exposed location that made wind bracing necessary, as was to be the case in later skyscrapers. The internal structure was designed by Gustave Eiffel, in conjunction with the Keystone Bridge Company, the fabricators. The four main posts are of steel, though the girders supporting the base, and no doubt the other members, are of wrought iron.

Steel had thus taken some time to make any impact on the building industry generally, and one reason was cost. In the early 1870s, steel was about twice as strong as wrought iron and twice as expensive, and therefore offered little or no cost benefit, unless perhaps in extreme spans where the weight of the structure itself was a significant issue. Until late in the century, the range of sizes rolled in steel was much smaller than in wrought iron, which was a further disadvantage, and its physical properties were less than ideal. Although steel was better for bending and shaping, it lacked the fibrous quality of wrought iron, until in the

An engraving shows the Statue of Liberty, New York (above), nearing completion in 1886. Beneath Liberty's skin of copper is a skeleton of iron straps, which are attached to a steel core strong enough to support the statue and resist the winds of its exposed harbor location.

Molten steel pours from a crucible at a modern rolling mill. Once rare and expensive, steel is now by far the most commonly used metal, thanks to a series of technological improvements starting with the Bessemer converter in the 1850s.

Stainless Steel

One of the biggest drawbacks of steel is its susceptibility to corrosion. The term "stainless steel" embraces a range of alloys containing iron and eleven percent or more of chromium, which were investigated early in the nineteenth century. So far as architectural purposes are concerned, its use developed from the work of Edward Maurer of Germany from 1909 to 1912 on austenitic stainless steel, which contains eighteen percent of chromium and eight percent of nickel. This was one of various white metals used for ornamental purposes in the Art Deco style, and one of the earliest major applications of it was in the Chrysler Building of 1930, New York.

A cladding of stainless steel is responsible for the gleam of the spire of the Chrysler Building in New York. It has been cleaned only twice (in 1961 and 1995), and remains in perfect condition.

1880s a fibrous steel was developed and patented by the British company Dorman, Long & Co. in association with R. Harrison.

Perfecting Steel Beams

As had been the case with wrought iron, larger structural sections could be built up from simpler pieces, initially by bolting, later by riveting, and finally by welding. Some special sections were invented, especially for columns, which were stronger than the slender, solid columns previously used. One was the Phoenix Column, an American invention in which curved segments with flanges pointing outward were assembled to form a cylinder, with fixings through the flanges. The common rolled joist, or I-beam, is so called because it has only short flanges at top and bottom, like the letter "I." But in beams it is often an advantage to have wide flanges—it is easier, for example, to connect such beams to other elements of a frame. Wide flanges can easily be formed in cast iron, but are much harder to roll in steel. Larger beams were always built up by bolting or riveting, and only later were systems developed for rolling "universal," or H-sections, with much wider flanges.

The traditional way of rolling a joist or I-beam was between two rollers that contained grooves corresponding to the flanges. The steel was squeezed into the grooves, but tended to be spongy and of poorer quality in this portion, so that the practicable depth of the grooves was quite small, and therefore the breadth of the flange was limited.

Henry Grey, an Englishman who had migrated to the United States, developed the Grey Mill. This used main rollers shaped to fit the side of the beam, and other rollers at right angles to form the flanges. There were no rollers at right angles within the section, and the mill still could not produce the universal section of more recent times, because a substantial taper was still needed across the flanges. Nevertheless, the effect was to make much broader flanges possible, and to reduce the need for sections built up by means of plating, or joining on additional pieces of steel, as described above. Grey developed his process at the Ironton Structural Steel Company of Duluth, Minnesota, and in 1902 installed the first mill at the Differdingen (Differdange) steelworks in Luxembourg. He soon after became manager of the Carnegie Company's works at Homestead, Pennsylvania, but the American rights to his process were acquired in 1908 by the Bethlehem Steel Co., which at first had difficulty finding a market for the beams.

Welding Steel

Traditional welding, dating back to ancient Egyptian times, had involved hammering or pressing together two pieces of heated metal, whereas modern welding involves the actual melting of the metal to produce a more or less homogeneous joint. It is heated either by the use of an electric current to melt and fuse the

A Vierendeel truss bridge is shown spanning the Albert Canal, Belgium, in 1935. The Vierendeel principle was the use of rigid joints, as had been done in the portal frames of some Chicago skyscrapers in the 1890s.

In 1949, the head of the Lustron Corporation, Carl Strandlund, posed with a model of one of his prefabricated steel houses. Buyers had a choice of four exterior colors: blue, gray, yellow, and tan.

two components, or with a flame which burns oxygen and acetylene (oxyacetylene) or oxygen and hydrogen (oxyhydrogen), with additional metal (weldmetal) melted into the joint. The first serviceable oxyacetylene torch was developed in England in 1900.

In arc welding, an electric arc is used to melt the weldmetal and the pieces being joined. It developed from the electric arc lamp, and had been introduced by N. V. Benardos of Russia in 1887, with variations by Zerener in 1888 and N. G. Slavianoff in 1890, at first using carbon rods, later replaced with metal wires. "Alumino-thermetical" welding was developed by Dr. H. Goldsmith of Germany, and seems to have been an ingenious means of producing small quantities of molten steel, but to have fallen short of welding in any rigorous engineering sense.

Steel Houses

After World War I, Britain constructed numerous all-steel dwellings on the Weir, Atholl, and Telford prefabrication systems as public housing. In the 1920s, Germany took up the idea, and in about 1928 the Vereinigte Stahlwerke, or German steel trust, began a serious attempt to exploit steel houses. One of the most promising systems was that of the Deutsche Stahlhausbau-Gesellschaft of Upper Silesia, which used external steel panels and internal insulation and plaster panels, set within a structural steel frame. However, in 1933, when the Nazi Party came to power, steel was

withdrawn from the housing market. In France, a building of panels faced in steel on both sides was designed for the Roland Garros Aviation Club at Buc, near Paris, by the architects Eugène Beaudouin and Marcel Lods. It used a panel edge shaped to facilitate site assembly, and asbestos insulation sprayed onto the faces of the steel sheeting inside the panels.

Meanwhile, the Americans, who had at first known nothing of the European work, began their own development of the All Steel house. A number of other US experiments followed, generally of a somewhat conservative nature, until the Lustron House was designed in 1947 by Carl Strandlund, of the Chicago Vitreous Products Co. (later Lustron Corporation), who sold the idea to high-ranking members of the Truman administration as an affordable solution to the postwar housing shortage. Manufacture was started with the aid of a $15.5 million loan from the Reconstruction Finance Corporation, and the first house came out of the Columbus, Ohio, plant in March 1948. These houses, however, were plagued by production problems and obstacles created by housing codes and deed restrictions, and production was discontinued after only a few years.

Joints and Sections

The idea of building with rigid joints, as in the portal frames of the early skyscrapers, was adopted by the Belgian constructor Arthur

Vierendeel, in a series of bridges that he designed to span the Albert Canal, between Liège and Antwerp, from 1933. The joints, where there would be no bending moment in a pin-jointed structure, are rigid and carry the maximum bending moment. The Vierendeel "truss" —not a true truss due to its rigid joints—was now applied to conventional buildings such as the International Agricultural Co. plant, at Chicago Heights, Illinois, of 1938, where it was useful in providing space for the overhead conveyor tracks. Rigid-jointed frames had already become the norm in reinforced concrete construction, where it is natural to have continuous joints, but in terms of steel, the Vierendeel truss and the portal frame were not widely used until after World War II, when they became standard elements in structural design.

Between the two world wars, there appeared structural sections made by deforming or bending cold-rolled steel strip or sheet. These were light in weight, neat and easy to handle, and could be assembled into larger sections by spot welding. In 1935, E. Mopin of France framed a complex of 1,200 apartments with these members. Generally, they came into use for lighter weight structures, such as warehouses and sheds, in which fireproofing was not required, and in forms such as standardized open-web girders and Z-purlins—relatively lightweight sections, shaped like the letter Z in cross section, suitable for roof framing.

Manhattan Skyscrapers
New York, United States

The skyscraper was conceived in Chicago, but it was in New York, and specifically on Manhattan Island, that it came to fruition. Since its rebuilding after the great fire of 1871, Chicago had had a robust and pragmatic building culture, and within that environment the essential development of the steel frame was completed in only a few years. In New York, by contrast, there was a less innovative and more eclectic architectural tradition, but there was an insatiable demand for high-rise office accommodation in Manhattan, which ensured that the steel frame was pushed higher and higher over a period of decades.

A Skyscraper Race
Richard Morris Hunt's Tribune Building, built in 1873, was only nine stories high, but the floor-to-ceiling heights were so great that it measured

Headquarters of the *World* newspaper, the 309-ft (94-m) Pulitzer Building was the world's tallest structure when completed in 1891.

260 ft (79 m). In 1883, the Mills Building, by G. B. Post, reached 11 stories, and has been claimed as the first modern office building, but the exterior design was rather stolid and uninspiring. Such buildings were not as high as those of Chicago and they were less innovative in construction. But New York seized the initiative with G. B. Post's Pulitzer (or World) Building of 1891, which was 20 stories high, and then with Kimball & Thompson's Empire Building on Broadway, finished in 1898, which used what was perhaps the first complete steel frame in New York.

In 1899, R. H. Robertson's Park Row Building reached 30 stories. Around the same time, in 1903, D. H. Burnham & Co. were responsible for the Fuller (or Flatiron) Building, not so high, but dramatically wedge shaped, on an isolated corner site. In 1908, the Singer Building, designed by Ernest Flagg, reached 47 stories and 612 ft (187 m). This achievement was immediately eclipsed by the Metropolitan Life Insurance

The instantly recognizable Manhattan skyline of today is the result of various technological and architectural developments beginning in the 1870s.

Building on Madison Square, by Napoleon Le Brun & Sons, in 1909, which reached a height of 700 ft (213 m).

But even in this hothouse environment the Woolworth Building of 1913 stood out. It rose to 55 stories and a height of 760 ft 6 in (232 m), which was to make it the highest building in the world until 1930, and it also had an area of about 30,000 sq ft (2,787 sq m), which gave it by far the largest usable floor areas of any office building so far built. It has been described as "the classic American skyscraper", not only due to its dimensions or its high cost ($7.5 million), but also for its structural design and for its stylistic treatment by the architect Cass Gilbert.

Woolworth Gothic

The New York skyscraper was nothing if not eclectic in exterior styling. While the Flatiron Building had an Italian Renaissance façade, the Metropolitan Life Insurance Building was an inflated version of the campanile of St. Mark's in Venice, Italy. The architect Gilbert devised an attenuated Gothic style for the exterior of the Woolworth Building. This later came to be seen by Modernist architects as the epitome of irrelevance, a meaningless historic veneer serving only to conceal a creative engineering achievement. The term "Woolworth Gothic" came to denote poor judgment and bad taste. But within its context it was done well, and the building receives more sympathetic attention today. It is still difficult, however, to see the application of historic styles as anything other than simplistic

and meretricious, particularly when Chicago had done so much better some decades earlier.

Chicago itself was to succumb to the vertical Gothic in Hood and Howells's Tribune Tower of 1925, but in New York two new nonhistorical approaches emerged. Completed in 1926, the New York Telephone Company Building, by Vorhees, Gmelin & Walker, was in a form of stripped Modernism that would become quite widespread. In contrast, William Van Alen's Chrysler Building of 1930 was in lavish Art Deco style, which has made it one of the most loved icons of New York. But though one or two others followed, notably the RCA (or General Electric) Building of 1931, which was in a sort of confused Art Deco, this was really a stylistic dead end.

The Empire State Building Guides the Way

The Empire State Building of 1931 was not only a megastructure, but also a clearer guide to the future of high-rise buildings. The building stands 102 stories and 1,250 ft (381 m) high. It was a commercial speculation, and size was crucial to the conception, but the design by William F. Lamb, of Shreve, Lamb & Harmon, was sensitive to the imperatives of skyscraper design. There are Art Deco touches to the crown of the building, but its body is a much more elegant vertical interpretation of the stripped design previously used in structures like the New York Telephone Company Building. The finishes are limestone, granite, aluminum, and nickel.

After the Empire State, the near-monopoly of New York in skyscraper construction ceased, but its role as the symbolic home of the skyscraper was sealed. The skyscraper fantasies which had begun with the publications of *King's Views of New York* in 1908, and were most advanced by

Hugh Ferriss's *The Metropolis of Tomorrow* of 1929, were firmly identified with New York, and crowned by King Kong's engagement with the Empire State in the 1933 movie.

There were to be other iconic skyscrapers in the city: the Rockefeller Center, with the RCA Building of 1933; the United Nations Building of 1950; Lever House of 1952; and the Seagram Building of 1958. But the World Trade Center, by Minoru Yamasaki and Emery Roth & Sons, completed in 1973, became the modern symbol of the New York skyscraper, and its destruction by terrorists in 2001 made it a symbol of much more significance to the free world. There were many who seriously predicted that this event spelled the end of the skyscraper—quite apart from its ecological undesirability, it was simply too vulnerable to attack. But they were wrong: there was hardly a pause before skyscraper building resumed, even in New York itself.

The spire of the Empire State Building (top) was originally designed as a mooring mast for zeppelins. A broadcast antenna was added to it in the 1950s.

The novelist H. G. Wells compared the Fuller (or Flatiron) Building (left) to a ship, "ploughing up through the traffic of Broadway and Fifth Avenue."

Fifth Avenue and Flat Iron Building, New York City.

Concrete

One of the great innovators of reinforced concrete design was Pier Luigi Nervi, who built this sports stadium in Rome (above) for the 1960 Olympics.

Concrete is an artificial stone, made by mixing lime or cement with particles of real stone and sand. It is a relatively primitive material, not sharply distinguished from some forms of earth construction, especially *pisé de terre*, to which lime might be added. Reinforced concrete is a totally different proposition. It is a sophisticated engineering material in which the structural role of the concrete can be clearly distinguished from that of the steel reinforcement enclosed within it.

Concrete, with added *pozzolana* (volcanic ash), was used extensively by the Romans. Medieval buildings often include concrete of a sort, for example within the thick walls and giant column

Roman Concrete

Historically, there are many materials that can loosely be called concrete, but it is the Roman version which deserves the most attention, for two reasons. The first is that by adding a volcanic ash called *pozzolana* the Romans were able to achieve improved properties, including hydraulicity—the capacity to set under water—which common lime lacks. The second is that they used concrete on an unprecedented scale for architectural and engineering works, and especially for vaulted and domed roofs. The dome of the Pantheon, in Rome, is the most striking example, but many other Roman structures that present the surface appearance of rubble, brickwork, or diagonal square blocks are, in fact, of solid concrete.

drums of Norman architecture, but it is really only an infill material. Only in the eighteenth century were attempts made, especially in France, to improve concrete to a standard that was suitable for engineering uses. The focus turned to the type of lime used.

The Quest for Artificial Cement

Lime is made by burning calcium carbonate, which is usually in the form of limestone, but may be another material such as marble, coral, or seashells. Carbon dioxide is driven off and the product is calcium oxide or quicklime, a corrosive and difficult material, which is usually slaked with water to produce calcium hydroxide, or slaked lime. Over time, this material reacts with the carbon dioxide in the atmosphere to give off water and become calcium carbonate, which is the process of setting.

If the raw material is not pure calcium carbonate, and contains some clay (aluminum silicate), it may, depending upon the temperature of the burning and the grinding of the product, produce a hydraulic lime or cement. Early experimenters added pozzolanic material (not *pozzolana* itself, but ashes, or Dutch trass) to common lime. They experimented with less pure limestones, until, in the late eighteenth century, the Englishman James Parker discovered nodules of septaria, containing a suitable mixture of lime and clay, at Sheppey on the lower River Thames. When burned, septaria produced a partly hydraulic natural cement, which Parker and his business partner James Wyatt sold as Roman cement, though it had nothing to do with the cement used by the Romans.

Early in the nineteenth century, the Frenchman L. J. Vicat reasoned that it should be possible by mixing similar ingredients to match, and probably to improve upon, the natural combinations of lime and clay found at places like Sheppey. Such a contrived mixture is an artificial cement, and a number of English manufacturers worked to produce their own versions. Also at this time, the British military engineer Major General C. W. Pasley conducted experiments at Chatham, England, which tended to support the practice of burning at a higher temperature and retaining and grinding the clinker (solid lumps) which early manufacturers had thrown away.

From the 1840s, artificial cement was marketed as portland cement, from a purported resemblance to the fashionable Portland stone, reflecting the fact that the principal use of the material was as a stucco render on the face of a building, to imitate such stones. Over the following decades its properties were improved enormously, and it came into general use as an important engineering material.

Designed by Kenzo Tange, the Yoyogi National Gymnasium complex, Tokyo, Japan (above), of 1964, has a rounded, almost sculptural exterior of exposed concrete topped by a sweeping steel-plate roof.

In the late eighteenth century, a natural cement was made in England from nodules of septaria such as this one (right). Known as cement stones, they contained just the right amounts of lime and clay.

Reinforced Concrete

Reinforcing concrete with metal is a hybrid idea that springs from two quite different sources. The first was the use of bonding in mass materials to prevent cracking. From the 1840s onward, in masonry construction, layers of bonding material, such as perforated hoop iron, might be put at intervals in the wall, and it was natural enough that small amounts of metal would be put into mass concrete. The other source of the idea is the problem of fireproofing metal frames, which could be done by encasing the iron or steel in plaster or concrete. The metal frame remains the structure, with the concrete only as a covering, just as in the case of metal used as a bonding material, the mass concrete was the structure with the metal only there to resist shrinkage and settlement cracks. True reinforced concrete appears only when designers combined the two concepts and used the concrete to take compression and the steel to take other stresses, especially tensile ones.

W. B. Wilkinson of Newcastle, England, seems to have been the first to really understand the principles of reinforced concrete. He took out a patent in 1854 for a method of building concrete floors reinforced either with flat iron bars placed on edge, or with wire rope. In his patent, Wilkinson states that the reinforcement must be placed in the concrete so as to take the tension, and he shows his ironwork bent down at the center of the span to resist the maximum bending moment, bent up at the top over supports to resist negative moment, and with provision for anchorage at the end. Wilkinson's patent was based upon practical experience, and he constructed a number of buildings in northern England of reinforced concrete, of which none survive. Outside England, Wilkinson's invention seems to have remained unknown.

Paris was the center of experiment. A French contractor may have built a small concrete boat in 1850. At the Paris Exposition of 1855, Joseph-Louis Lambot showed a flat-bottomed boat with 2-in (5-cm) thick sides of hydraulic lime concrete reinforced with a skeleton of iron rods. The first serious French patent was taken out in the same

Reinforced concrete is the main building material for Le Corbusier's Chapel of Notre-Dame-du-Haut, built in 1955 in Ronchamp, France.

year by Lambot's compatriot, François Coignet, who used concrete with criss-crossed rods. The Parisian gardener Joseph Monier had made plant tubs and tanks of concrete surrounding a wire skeleton, and in 1867 he patented a system in which two sets of parallel bars were placed at right angles, forming a mesh

There followed a period of trial and error development. In London, W. H. Lascelles built a number of cottages in 1877 with walls of concrete slabs reinforced with diagonal rods. In New York, W. E. Ward put up a complete building in 1871–1876 in which the walls, floor beams, and roof were all reinforced with iron rods and I-beams. Others in the United States experimented with metal reinforcement. Thaddeus Hyatt conducted experiments in 1870–1877, particularly in developing forms of anchorage. In 1883, J. F. Goldring developed expanded metal,

In 1904, François Hennebique built this house for himself in Bourg-la-Reine, Paris, using reinforced concrete. He used the same material for his own tomb.

in which a metal sheet is punctured with a staggered pattern of slits and then pulled sideways to create a diamond lattice pattern. This was first used as plaster lathing, but was applied as a reinforcement to concrete in 1890.

The American E. L. Ransome introduced twisted square reinforcing bars, for better bonding with the concrete, in 1884. Ransome was responsible for some important reinforced concrete structures, from a warehouse in 1884 or 1885, to the museum building at Leland Stanford Junior University, of 1889, which was reinforced throughout and had spans of nearly 45 ft (14 m). He also built the first reinforced concrete bridge in the United States, the Alvord Lake Bridge at Golden Gate Park, San Francisco in 1889. which he reinforced with his twisted iron bars bent around the curve of the arch.

The Monier System

So far, no one had clearly articulated the fundamental principle of reinforced concrete: that the concrete should take only compression, and the iron or steel all the tensile and other forces. But Monier followed his 1867 patent with others in 1873 and 1877, with an addition a year later in which the distinct function of the iron was for the first time made explicit. In 1879, he

Construction workers pouring concrete through a large hose into a reinforced structure. Today in industrialised countries most concrete used in construction is reinforced concrete.

displayed his inventions at the Antwerp Exhibition, where he came in contact with the German engineer G. A. Wayss, to whom he subsequently sold the German rights. Wayss began an experimental investigation of the Monier system, and in 1887 published *Das System Monier*, including in it valuable formulae and principles of design. In 1893, Wayss formed the partnership of Wayss & Freytag to market the Monier system.

Although Wayss had developed the Monier patents into the first coherent and scientific system of reinforced concrete, there were many experiments by others, and many other theoretical advances. In 1890, Paul Neumann published calculations that allowed for the difference in elasticity between concrete and steel. In Germany, regulations inhibited construction in reinforced concrete, but there was a great deal of activity in Austria, and the Austrian Joseph Melan developed his own system of reinforced concrete design in 1890, used mainly for bridges. In 1884, the Hungarian Robert Wunsch had developed another concrete bridge system, which was used across much of the world. Other systems and other patents, based upon different forms of reinforcement, were made use of by engineers wishing to avoid the Monier monopoly.

Meanwhile in France in 1892, Edmond Coignet (son of François Coignet) took out a patent which included the use of stirrups to resist shear, and in 1894 Coignet and Napoléon de Tedesco developed what has been called the first rational design theory for reinforced concrete. Among the hundreds of reinforced concrete systems— there were more than two hundred developed in Germany alone—the names of Edmond Coignet and François Hennebique, a French engineer, stand out. As time went on, it was Hennebique's system which became the more generally accepted. Hennebique is said to have been the first to use steel rather than wrought-

iron reinforcement. He took out his first patent in 1892, in which he developed earlier ideas on the use of stirrups to resist shear, and in 1897 he developed the use of multiple layers of cranked-up rods (rods bent up at an angle) for the purpose.

Developments since 1900

As systems of calculation developed, and as the first generation of patents expired, something like a common system for reinforced concrete emerged, based mostly upon the Monier system. In 1906, the first code of practice for reinforced concrete was promulgated in France. But there remained some distinctive strands. Armand-Gabriel Considère of France invented *béton fretté* or hooped concrete, in which the compression members were wound around with heavy helical reinforcement to improve the compressive strength of the concrete within.

Flat-plate construction, which is still used today, had its genesis in US patents granted in 1902 to O. W. Norcross. The slab is built as a flat plate, without any beams. But this creates enormous shear stresses at the point where the slab meets the column, and these must be resisted with extra reinforcement. A second problem is that the slab is shallower than the beams would have been, and proportionately more tensile reinforcement is required. The final problem is that all of this reinforcement must be brought into the column and linked with the vertical rods, and there is simply not enough room in the slab or the column to contain it. This is dealt with by using drop panels, or squares, around the column where the slab is deeper, and/or by expanding the head of the column itself in a conical or flared profile.

In the century since, concrete has been subject to many improvements, including the use of foams and carbon-fiber reinforcement rods. A recent development is carbon concrete, claimed to be an ecologically sound alternative.

Centennial Hall
Wroclaw, Poland

With its massive concrete dome, the Centennial Hall (now the People's Hall or Hala Ludowa) at Wroclaw, Poland, is one of the great structures of the twentieth century, but due to accidents of history it is an underappreciated one. It was built in 1913 as the Jahrhunderthalle (Centennial Hall) in what was then Breslau, Germany, but World War I broke out before it received much publicity. After World War II, Breslau became Wroclaw, Poland, in the Soviet bloc, where German national achievements were held in little regard and where visitors and researchers were few and far between. The building should be considered in two contexts, firstly as one of the great concrete roof spans of the world, and secondly as a creative exercise in Expressionist design.

Wroclaw had been ruled by Polish kings in the tenth century, but from the fourteenth century was largely occupied by Germans, and it was they who rebuilt the city after it was sacked by the Mongols. It prospered under Bohemian and Austrian rule, and was increasingly referred to by the German name until in 1741 Frederick the Great officially changed the name to Breslau. In World War II, Breslau was the last stronghold of the Third Reich in the struggle against the advancing Soviet forces, and after the war Stalin effectively moved Poland westward, absorbing existing Polish territory into the Soviet Union, and transferring German territory, including Breslau, into Poland in compensation.

The Architect

The architect Max Berg was born in Stettin in 1870, and studied architecture at the Berlin–Charlottenburg Technical University. In 1909, he was appointed the Municipal Architect (Stadtbaurat) of Breslau, and it was in this context that he was commissioned to design a memorial hall to commemorate the centenary of the war of liberation of 1813 (the victory by Prussian and other forces over Napoleon at

Leipzig), as well as a surrounding area for exhibitions. His contemporary, Hans Poelzig, who had also studied at Berlin–Charlottenburg, was responsible for some buildings within the complex, including the four-domed pavilion next to the Centennial Hall, of 1912.

After the end of World War I, Berg designed other prominent buildings in Breslau, including a nearby exhibition building roofed with timber arches and beams, the Messehall, in about 1924; two hydroelectric plants on the Oder in 1921 and 1924; and schools, hospitals, and housing developments of which little detail is known. He moved to Berlin in 1925, and nothing significant is known of his activities after this time. He died in 1947. Other distinguished architects who were active in the city were Erich Mendelsohn, Ernst May, and Hans Scharoun. The exhibition grounds themselves remained a venue for avant-garde architectural projects until the beginning of World War II.

The Dome

The 220-ft (67-m) span of the dome is a daring and remarkable achievement, almost doubling that of the previous record-holder, Melbourne Public Library (Australia), completed only slightly earlier. At the same time, the dome is only fifty percent greater than that of the Pantheon in Rome, the extraordinary achievement of which is only enhanced by the comparison, given that

A German postcard celebrates both the opening of the Centennial Hall and the battle of 1813 which the building was designed to commemorate.

the ancient monument was built of unreinforced mass concrete. The largest reinforced-concrete roof before the Centennial Hall was not a dome, but an extraordinarily ingenious sawtooth roof slung between hogback trusses, at the Dennys Lascelles Austin Wool Store, Geelong, Australia, by E. G. Stone.

Remarkably, for a pioneering exercise in reinforced concrete construction, no published information exists to indicate the reinforcement system. Günter Trauer is credited with the structural design, and the building was erected by Dyckerhoff & Widmann of Dresden, under the engineer Willy Gehler.

The Hall is a quatrefoil structure—a domed space out of which extend four semicircular apses—so that although the dome spans 220 ft (67 m), the distance from apse to apse is 318 ft (97 m). It occupies more than ten million cu ft (295,000 cu m) and stands 138 ft (42 m) high. The structure is in two parts: the cylindrical arcaded base, upon which are 32 brass bearings carrying the dome, which is surmounted by a lantern of steel and glass. It accommodates 6,000 people. The windows were prefabricated, and the concrete frames and floors were cast in molds and lifted into place by crane.

The plan is similar to those of the late antique Basilica of San Lorenzo, Milan, or the sixteenth-century Church of Santa Maria della Consolazione, Todi, by Cola da Caprarola. In each of these Italian churches, four conches (or half-domed apses) open out from a central domed space. But the interior space most closely resembles that of Hagia Sophia, Istanbul, Turkey, the main dome of which steps down to two, rather than four, subsidiary half domes, but then to another four smaller conches on the angles.

Externally, the Centennial Hall is a rather bald, gasometer-like building. Internally, it is fluid and Expressionistic, and totally without ornament, with the marks of the formwork exposed. Its interior is, however, finished with a sound-absorbent layer, described as being of concrete with wood or cork (but probably a magnesite compound). It was intended to have frescoes, stained-glass windows, and sculptures—although not so as to obscure the basic concrete forms—but these were never added.

A rather unprepossessing exterior (left) masks the building's great achievement: a huge dome (right) supported by 32 exposed, reinforced concrete ribs.

Glass

Glass is essentially melted sand, and when it was used for something like a bottle, it was cast in a mold. Flat pieces could be cast on a surface with raised edges like a tray, to make plate glass. In antiquity, small pieces of plain or colored glass, or thin slices of other materials such as alabaster, were sometimes used for windows, but historically the great bulk of windows have not been glazed. They were simple openings, which might be closed by wooden shutters, or they were covered in oiled or glazed fabric or paper.

A typical English Georgian house (left) has windows with numerous panes because of the high cost of manufacturing large glass sheets.

L'INDUSTRIE DU VERRE.—
La fabrication des verres à vitres.

Glass for Windows

Before the twentieth century, the majority of glass was manufactured either by the crown, cylinder (sheet), or plate processes. Crown glass was made in Roman times and, by the Middle Ages, in the Middle East, North Africa, and Europe. A lump of molten glass was attached to a blowpipe, and was blown up like a balloon. Then it was transferred to a rod called a punty. The punty was rapidly rotated and the bubble opened out to form a circular disc, or table, the worker reheating it as necessary to keep it soft. The table was finally allowed to cool off and harden, detached from the punty, and cut into pieces

This process produced panes of a very limited size. The table was between 40 and 60 in (100 and 150 cm) in diameter, with a lump or bullion at the center where it had been attached to the punty. The glass cutter had to avoid the bullion, and it was uneconomic to produce pieces much larger than 3 sq ft (0.3 sq m). This is the reason for the multiple-paned window sashes of the Georgian style in England, though it was possible to obtain much larger sheets of plate or other glass at a cost.

Cylinder or sheet glass is also known to have been used in Roman times, and by the nineteenth century it had became the dominant type on the Continent of Europe. The blower formed a bubble of glass in the same way as for crown glass, but then swung it around in a vertical plane (made possible by a trench in front of him) until it elongated into a cylinder with hemispherical ends. This was allowed to cool and harden. The ends were cut off with a hot wire, creating a plain cylinder, which was then slit along its length. The

cylinder was put into a furnace and softened until it flattened out into a rectangle, which could be up to 13 sq ft (1.2 sq m) in area. This process had been forgotten in England, but was reintroduced there in 1832.

Plate glass was simply cast by pouring it onto a table, and in Roman times pieces of 10 sq ft (nearly 1 sq m) were occasionally made. When the method was revived in France in the later seventeenth century, much larger pieces were made by using rollers to spread the glass over the table, after which it had to be ground and polished to a true finish. Pieces of up to 70 sq ft (6.5 sq m) became standard, and much larger ones were possible. The reason why large sizes of glass were not used in England before the mid-nineteenth century was that larger pieces had to be made thicker, and thick pieces of glass were uneconomic because the British Government

Glass cylinders, their ends already removed, are ready to be reheated and flattened in this late nineteenth-century French illustration of cylinder glass-making.

charged a high excise duty on glass, calculated by weight. This duty was removed in 1845, and so far as England was concerned, this was the most important reason for the rise of glass buildings, most notably the Crystal Palace of 1851.

During the later nineteenth and early twentieth centuries, there were improvements in glass manufacture, including making window glass by drawing the sheet directly out of the melt, developed in Belgium and the United States from about 1904. This type of glass was slightly irregular, a problem overcome in the 1950s by the introduction of float glass, in which the glass was drawn across the surface of a bath of molten metal until it was perfectly flat.

Other Glass Products

Of more architectural interest are the new glass products. From 1845 onward, Thaddeus Hyatt of New York developed a way of naturally lighting basements in urban areas by means of pavement lights consisting of glass cones and lenses glass set in a cast-iron frame, to capture and refract the light toward the rear of the room. The biggest

manufacturer of pavement lights was to be the Radiating Light Company of Chicago, formed in 1886, which later adopted the name Luxfer.

About the beginning of the twentieth century, the modern form of glass brick was invented in Germany, and, by the early 1920s, the decorative glass Vitrolite became generally available. This was a rolled opal glass with a brilliant finish, used in place of materials like ceramic tiles, at first in white and later in other colors, and it became an integral element of the Art Deco style. In the 1920s, F. E. Lamplough of England invented Vita Glass, designed to capture the beneficial properties of sunshine by allowing optimum transmission in the therapeutic range. Many types of light-sensitive glass have since been developed, including those which darken in bright sunlight to reduce the light penetration. Safety glasses began with the first process of toughening in the 1870s, but have been the subject of many improvements, including the alternative process of lamination. Double glazing first appeared in the 1920s, with two sheets of glass sealed into a metal frame, and an air space between to provide insulation from both heat and sound.

The Crystal Palace, (shown above) was erected in Hyde Park, London, to house the Great Exhibition of 1851, and had an iron framework clad with almost 300,000 panes of glass. It was taken down and re-erected at another site in London in 1852, but destroyed by fire in 1936.

New Materials

The Laban Dance Centre, London, of 2003, has an outer skin of semi-transparent colored polycarbonate over an inner one of glass. Daylight shining on the polycarbonate results in constantly changing colors.

M ost of the more recently discovered or invented materials are used in buildings in only very small volumes, though there are exceptions such as aluminum, Bakelite, and vinyl. And some of the most specialized materials are the by-products of other activities and industries rather than any program of development within the building industry.

Aluminum could be refined only with great difficulty from the natural bauxite (hydrated alumina) ore until, in 1886–1887, C. M. Hall of the United States and Paul Héroult of France simultaneously discovered an improved electrolytic process for the electrical reduction of alumina in a warmed bath. The metal suddenly became much more viable for commercial purposes. By 1888, Hall's reduction process was put into production by the Pittsburgh Reduction Company, (later the Aluminum Company of America or Alcoa). Aluminum was used in 1884 for the tip of the Washington Monument in Washington DC, weighing about 7 lb (3 kg). In 1893 aluminum elements were used in the Venetian, Isabella, and Monadnock buildings in Chicago, and the statue of *Eros* in Piccadilly Circus, London was cast in aluminum. Its use increased steadily from this point until in about 1912 more than 900 sand-cast aluminum spandrels were used in the Koppers Building, Pittsburgh, Pennsylvania. Later, the metal was put to a wide range of uses, especially for window frames, curtain wall systems, roofing, and siding.

The Age of Plastics

The plastics are the most characteristic materials of the twentieth century. Bakelite, or AG-4 phenolic resin, was the first plastic made from synthetic components. It was developed from 1907 to 1909 by the Belgian Leo Baekeland, by the reaction under heat and pressure of phenol (a toxic, colorless crystalline solid) and formaldehyde (a simple organic compound), generally with a wood flour filler. It was used in appliances for its electrically nonconductive and heat-resistant properties, and for architectural fittings such as knobs and door handles, but has today been superseded by other plastics.

Vinyl (strictly, polyvinyl chloride or PVC) was the first flooring material to seriously challenge linoleum (a material based upon natural substances, principally cured linseed oil). In 1926 in the United States, Waldo Semon and B. F. Goodrich developed a method to plasticize PVC by blending in various additives. Vinyl floor tiles were first produced in the United States in 1931, though not manufactured in significant quantities until after World War II. PVC also came to be used for coating metallic wiring, and for making water pipes, building siding, and other building components. More

than half the PVC manufactured in the world is now used for construction purposes.

World War II led to an acceleration of technical development in paints, as well as to shortages of traditional materials like linseed oil, and after the war a series of water-based synthetic emulsion or "plastic" paints was introduced, the most prominent being the acrylics, introduced in the 1950s. These dried fast and were easy for amateurs to use, but produced a thinner coat than oils and locked moisture into old walls.

Melamine (correctly, melamine resin) came into use for building purposes after 1912 with the invention of Formica, a laminate of melamine resin with paper or fabric (originally conceived as an insulating material substituting "for mica"). This durable, decorative surface, suitable for kitchen benches and furniture, began to be popular before World War II. Melamine resin is also the main constituent of laminate flooring.

Polystyrene is an aromatic polymer that is manufactured from petroleum. It is a colorless, hard substance with little flexibility, but cheap and easily molded, and is used in sheets for building purposes, including concrete shuttering, and expanded to produce styrofoam insulation.

Nylon, a generic term for the polyamides, was first produced in 1935 by the American chemist Wallace Carothers of the DuPont company. It is one of the most common polymers to be used as a fiber, first of all in women's stockings in about 1940, but because it is tough and resists abrasion, it is also used in solid form for a variety of building applications, including castors, and window and door fittings.

Polycarbonate is a thermoplastic polymer. This lightweight material is almost as transparent as glass, nearly unbreakable, and resists heat. Among many other applications, it is used to make safety helmets, CDs, and DVDs, and is used in sheet form as cladding and glazing.

Asbestos

Serious commercial exploitation of the fibrous mineral asbestos began in Canada in 1877, when mines were opened at Thetford and Coleraine. It came into use for purposes such as the lagging of steam pipes, and the H. W. Johns Manufacturing Company, of the United States, was then mainly responsible for developing other practical applications. By the 1870s, the company was known for its asbestos paints, and it later developed other products, including asbestos roofing fabric; a stove and furnace cement; a roof coating of ground asbestos and silica in coal tar; building felts; and a millboard. The main rationale behind these products was that the material was fireproof, but the fine fibers were also found effective in reinforcing cement. The Austrian Ludwig Hatschek hit upon the combination of the fiber

Looking like an alien spaceship, the Selfridges
department store, Birmingham, England, is clad in
15,000 aluminum disks, which completely obscure
the underlying concrete structure.

One of the the most commonly used insulation materials is fiberglass in the form of woolly batts. Manufactured in sizes to fit between ceiling joists, they are easy for amateurs to install.

with portland cement, and produced and patented the first asbestos cement sheets in 1900. These were found to be inexpensive and durable for roofing and cladding purposes.

Hatschek manufactured his material in the form of slates or shingles, which were commonly laid on the diagonal, and were soon made in Belgium under the brand Eternit. Sheet materials soon followed, including Uralite. By 1918, the material was manufactured in Britain by three or four companies. Asbestos in general and asbestos cement in particular were utterly discredited by the 1970s, when evidence of the role of inhaled asbestos fibers in mesothelioma and other lung conditions could no longer be denied. Manufacturers turned to cellulose and other substances to reinforce cement wallboards.

Mineral Wools

Other mineral fiber products were to become important for insulation. In the nineteenth century, slag or mineral wool was produced at blast furnaces in Osnabrück and Zwickau, Germany, by sending a blast of air or steam through the molten slag, producing a white material like spun glass. The material, known as *Schlackenwolle* (slag wool), was of a poor quality, and rapidly crumbled to powder. A somewhat similar material was produced in the United States as mineral wool, and used for purposes such as lagging pipes and insulating partitions (in the latter case in the form of cakes of "slag felt"). Meanwhile, the British believed that the wool produced in the Tees district by Charles Wood was far superior to the German or US types, for because of the special nature of the Cleveland slag it was tough, elastic, and retained its consistency. Slag wool was later made by mixing

particular types of stone with molten blast furnace slag, and forming it into fibers, and (at least in the United States) this was the most common type of mineral wool.

A second mineral product was rock wool. Made from granite heated to 3,000°F (1,650°C), it was totally free of sulfur, and claimed to be the only odorless type. It was said to be a mass of gossamer-fine filaments blasted from molten rock by high-pressure steam jets, so that 90 percent of the volume was air. Another mineral product, expanded shale, came into widespread use in South Africa and North America for various insulation and acoustic purposes, and as an additive in lightweight concrete.

Glass and Carbon Fibers

Fine fibers in general are efficient reinforcers of other substances. Glass fiber, consisting of extremely fine strands of glass, was developed in the United States from 1931 by R. G. Slayter, produced commercially as an insulation material in 1936, and then from 1938 by the Owens-Corning company. Glass fiber insulation was introduced in Britain by the Chance brothers in the early 1930s, and in 1938 they joined forces with Pilkington Brothers to form Glass Fibres Ltd. Subsequently, glass-reinforced plastic was developed, and in common usage this is what is meant by the word fiberglass. It was a popular material in applications such as translucent roof sheeting, but it proved to be less durable than expected and rather unsightly as it decayed.

In 1958, Roger Bacon of Cleveland, Ohio, created the first high-performance carbon fibers in the form of graphite whiskers, or sheets of graphite rolled into scrolls. Early work on carbon-fiber reinforced concrete conducted in

Building with Titanium

Titanium, discovered by the English chemist William Gregor in 1791, is a light, corrosion-resistant metal with the highest strength to weight ratio of any metal. It is used in tools and in some architectural applications. Commercially pure titanium has become especially popular as a construction material in Japan; the Fukuoka Dome, of 1993, is a prominent example. In Spain, the Guggenheim Museum, Bilbao, of 1997, is sheathed in titanium panels $\frac{1}{50}$ in (0.5 mm) thick. The first building in North America to be clad in titanium is the Cerritos Millennium Library, California, in 2002. The metal is also important as the source of titanium dioxide, a white pigment used in paints.

The Fukuoka Dome, Japan, is covered with titanium roofing, retractable for multi-role and all-weather applications.

Japan found that the use of two percent of carbon fibers (by volume) approximately doubled the flexural strength, and by 1999 engineers at Pennsylvania State University had developed a computer-controlled manufacturing process to make carbon-fiber concrete reinforcement grids more cost competitive. While carbon-fiber grids are more expensive than the equivalent steel reinforcing rods, they have several advantages: they can be handled easily without heavy equipment, they need no assembly on site, and they will not corrode like steel rods.

Sealants, Waxes, and Concretes

Synthetic rubbers, made from hydrocarbons, were developed largely to meet the requirements of the automobile industry, but proved important in the glazing of buildings, and especially the curtain wall. Neoprene and Butyl were developed in the United States during the 1930s, but were not used in the building industry until the 1950s. Other sealants included Thiokol, the first widely

used elastomeric (flexible) sealant based upon a synthetic polysulfide polymer or rubber, developed by the Thiokol Chemical Corporation in 1929 and monopolized by them until the 1950s. Silicone polymers had their origins in the nineteenth century, but the first building sealant based upon them was introduced by the Dow Corning company only in 1960. Acrylic sealants appeared at about the same time, and urethanes and latex at later dates.

Among the range of environmentally orientated products now available is phase-change wax. This is a paraffin wax which changes from a solid to a fluid at a specific temperature (predetermined by the manufacturer). In the process, it absorbs a large amount of energy (that is, latent heat), just as ice does when it melts, and subsequently releases the energy when the temperature drops again, typically at night. Incorporating small spheres filled with this wax into a plaster or concrete panel makes it behave like a much thicker material and a much better

Synthetic rubbers and silicone sealants are used to fix the glass of curtain walls securely into place, as in these buildings in New York.

insulator. This is most cost-effective in situations where thick and heavy panels are undesirable, as in high-rise office buildings.

Concrete has been subject to various improvements other than carbon reinforcing. These include lighter foam-based concretes which require less energy to produce, and products like CeramiCrete, which is twice as strong. But the greatest interest now is in ecologically desirable forms, such as a viable alternative to cement developed by the oil industry. C-Fix, or carbon concrete, is a thermoplastic heavy-duty binder developed by Shell and the University of Delft, and already in use on roads in the Netherlands. It is claimed to be suitable for replacing 90 percent of present concrete and asphalt applications. Moreover, 3½ tons of carbon dioxide emissions are said to be saved by using a ton of C-Fix in place of regular concrete.

From the Ground Up

The stability of a building depends on the ground or foundation upon which it rests; on the footings or lowest part of the structure itself; and on superstructures such as cellars and tunnels. For many of the world's oldest buildings, these elements are the only evidence that survives today.

Foundations

The more substantial buildings of the ancient world were built straight onto the ground, or into trenches excavated until they reached stable soil or bedrock. Some Greek temples were so carefully designed that the bedrock on which the stonemasonry would rest had been cut to fit the subtle curvature of the proposed building.

Such techniques were inadequate in situations where the ground was soft, or where the building was placed above a body of water. As early as in Neolithic times, some structures rested upon piles. These were usually simple tree trunks that were driven vertically into the ground. In Roman times, piles were widely used for harbor works, bridges, and other engineering purposes, though conventional buildings were generally constructed in a more conservative way upon stable ground.

Built on Earth

In the past, it was common practice for the floor of a building, especially of a house, to be laid directly onto the ground, and therefore to have no structure of its own. A recently discovered floor of about 3000 BCE in China consisted of a sort of concrete made of sand, stone, pottery, and bones. Earlier Mesolithic hut floors at Lepenski Vir on the Danube were made of red lime, gravel, and sand, which had been mixed with water. In almost all later cultures, there has been some sort of earth floor, varying from simple compacted soil or puddled clay, through a variety of more complicated recipes, that typically contained one or more of the following ingredients: animal dung, ashes, tallow or other fatty material, ochre or some other natural coloring matter, lime, and oxblood or other animal blood. Some types of floor required to be regularly watered, and often they could be polished to a very dense and durable surface. Another useful flooring material was antbed, or crushed-up ant hills, which was used in Africa—by the Khoekhoen in the Cape area, and, at the other end of the continent, by the Raik Dinka in the Sudan—in Sri Lanka, and elsewhere, and which was taken up by European settlers in these places and in Australia.

Types of Foundations

In the nineteenth century, as buildings got higher and loads consequently heavier, gravel or mass concrete (a very different thing from the later reinforced concrete) was sometimes placed in the foundation for greater stability. The distinction between the foundation and footings became important. The foundation is the ground upon which the building rests; the footings are the lowest part of the building itself, which rest on the foundation. The footings might be pads of stone, masses of brickwork, strips of reinforced concrete, grids of steel, or a series of stepped-in

This traditional Hausa house in northern Nigeria is built upon a foundation of dried earth laid directly on the ground. The walls and bed are constructed of the same material.

Foundation Stones

In many ancient and medieval buildings, it was customary to place animal or human sacrifices into the foundations to ensure the building's success. Later it became common to commemorate the patron and designer by incorporating a foundation stone. Contrary to common belief, this was not an inscribed stone visible from the outside, but an anonymous stone in the footings, under which might be an inscribed tablet and other objects. The fashion for an inscribed stone on the outside of the building dates from the nineteenth century.

This foundation brick of c. 1900 BCE is from the Temple of Shamash, Mari (Tell Hairiri, Syria).

courses of brickwork, which provide a large bearing surface on the foundation but then reduce to the thickness of the pier or wall above.

Where it was necessary to build upon softer ground, or where the sheer mass of the newer and larger building types, such as skyscrapers, was excessive, either piers or a raft might be employed to support the structure.

The raft can carry a heavy building upon quite soft ground, but only if the load is distributed effectively so that the raft itself does not break. For this to be achieved, the raft must be very thick if it is made only of masonry or concrete, or it must be constructed of a mass of criss-cross beams of timber, iron, or steel (called a grillage). Reinforced concrete can achieve the same effect in one homogeneous structure, but still needs to be of considerable depth; therefore it might be cellular, with large internal voids.

Inadequate foundations will, of course, sink or tilt a building, a prominent instance being the Campanile, or Leaning Tower, of Pisa. But with a raft foundation, some degree of subsidence over time is normal and acceptable, provided that it occurs evenly.

A problem arises when additions are made to the structure because, if they are matched up when first constructed, the building will crack as the additions subside. Even if a joint is provided to allow for this movement and to avoid any cracking, the new work will no longer match up to the original building correctly.

The famous "lean" on the Campanile in Pisa, Italy (above), is caused by the foundations subsiding. The inclination became obvious during construction and various efforts were made to halt it.

The Colosseum in Rome, of CE 70–80, had 40-ft (12-m) deep foundations made of mass concrete. The rooms immediately beneath the arena (below) were used to house gladiators and animals.

When a building is to be built over water or very moist soil, it may be necessary to use a coffer dam to keep the water out of the area, or caissons around the individual piers: these are boxes that are sufficiently watertight to be kept dry by pumping. In soft soil the caissons can, if necessary, be sunk further as the work proceeds. During the building of some major structures, a complete, pressurised chamber has been created underwater at the foundation level so that the workers can enter and leave in stages in order to avoid rapid changes in pressure and the risk of getting the bends.

In modern construction, it remains desirable to build upon bedrock, but in most cases this is not possible. In such situations, the load-bearing capacity of the ground must be assessed, and then an area of footings provided that is large enough to transmit the load of the building but does not exceed this capacity.

This may be done with a flat slab or a raft. It may also be done with pad footings, which are square bases laid beneath each column of the structure; the area of the bases varies according to the load—for example, it will be larger for a heavily loaded interior column than for a less loaded exterior column. In smaller buildings, there may be strip footings under each wall, and in this case their width will vary, according to whether they are supporting an exterior load-bearing wall, for example, or a single floor-height internal partition wall.

Protecting the Base

The building's base is commonly a battleground between humans and vermin. Great ingenuity has been expended in devising methods for keeping out rats, mice, snakes, termites, and other pests, particularly from granaries and food stores. Not a great deal can be done, however, unless the building is raised on stumps or piles. It is possible to prevent larger vermin from entering cavity or hollow walls by closing the bottom of the cavity with a horizontal piece of timber or vermin plate.

In nearly all cases, moisture is a critical issue. Water from the ground will always tend to climb up into the building structure by capillary action. Once there, it will make lower rooms and sub-floor spaces dank and unpleasant, and will foster the growth of molds, and of dry-rot in timber. Even more seriously, it may carry up natural salts from the ground, or leach out salts from the lower levels of mortar and concrete, then leave them behind when it evaporates above ground level. Often a spread of fine crystals (known as efflorescence) can be seen at this point, but it is even more dangerous when they cannot be seen, because if the salts crystallize just below the surface of the material (a process known as

crypto-efflorescence), their gradual expansion tends to split off the outermost layer, and then the next, and so on. Often the effects upon this wet and weakened stone are accelerated by wind erosion, especially by wind-born sand, or even by animals licking the surface for the salts.

Up to the middle of the nineteenth century, many damp-proofing measures were based upon asphalt or coal tar, but then new compounds began to be introduced. Asphalt had been used in the Middle East from Neolithic times. In Mesopotamia ziggurats and other structures had a layer of reed matting and tar in the lower levels to prevent the rise of moisture, and ponds and tanks might be lined in baked brick set in pitch to make a waterproof layer. Most of the asphalt in commercial use was gathered on the shores of the Dead Sea, but new deposits were discovered in Trinidad by Sir Walter Raleigh in 1595, and later rock asphalt was found in Germany, France, and Switzerland. A more recent development is coal tar, which was used to make an artificial asphalt for building purposes.

The rise of asphalt was a sudden phenomenon in Europe. Natural deposits were opened up in France, and asphalt footpaths were introduced in Paris by the 1830s. Artificial asphalts followed, and during 1838 there was said to be an asphalt mania on the London stock market, with some companies claiming exclusive rights to the only genuine asphalt "mines" in France, others that German asphalt was just as pure, and yet others asserting that perfectly good asphalt could be found in England. Claridge's, the type most used in the mid-nineteenth century, was made of the natural calcareous bitumen obtained at Pyrimont, Seyssel, in the French department of Ain: this contained nine parts of limestone to one part of bitumen, and the quality was improved by the addition of pitch or tar.

The design of moisture barriers had been less critical in major buildings in the past because the stronger building stones used in the bases of these buildings, such as granites and basalts, were largely impervious to moisture. But wide mortar joints, or the inside filling of a rubble wall, might still provide access. Good practice was to build a horizontal damp-proof course or moisture barrier into the wall. This could be made of overlapping layers of roofing slate, with the thinnest possible mortar joints, but any shift in the building's structure might crack this slate course and let the moisture through. A soft metal, especially lead, was more reliable in these circumstances. In the nineteenth century, a wide number of other types of flexible damp-proof courses were developed, from such materials as asbestos felt which was impregnated with bitumen.

Modern Damp-proofing

In a modern building, the problem is rarely so simple as running a few horizontal damp-proof courses through the walls. Basement rooms have to be tanked, or waterproofed, all around the walls and floor. Flat concrete slabs on the ground

From 1913, when it was completed, to 1930, the Woolworth Building in New York, designed by Cass Gilbert, was the world's tallest building. It was built on 69 concrete piers, some of them 20 ft (6 m) in diameter. Bedrock at the site is very deep, averaging 116 ft (35 m) below street level. Engineers sank metal caissons into the solid rock, then filled them with concrete. These concrete piers support a total weight of around 223,000 tons (202,000 tonnes).

are laid on a complete plastic membrane, which is folded upward at its edges—and there is always the risk that a builder's laborer may accidentally pierce the membrane, and that this may passed unnoticed when the concrete is laid.

If the location is very wet, it may be necessary to provide for continuous pumping-out of the groundwater during the life of the building. On sites that are polluted with industrial wastes, the groundwater may be acidic and dangerous to concrete and steel, and necessitate a complete protective layer around the substructure of the building. But, as the materials available for this purpose have a limited lifespan, this is only a temporary expedient.

The *rorbu*, traditional wood houses, in Moskenesøy, in the Lofoten Islands, northern Norway (right), have been built on stilts sunk down to the undersea bedrock. *Rorbu* is derived from the Norwegian words *ror* (to row) and *bu* (to live).

The Kornhaus of 1929–1930 (below), designed by Bauhaus architect Carl Fieger, is located on the Elbe River, Dessau, Germany. The building is still in use today as a restaurant.

Caves and Chambers

The Necropolis of Pantalica in Sicily, Italy, which dates from the thirteenth to the eighth centuries BCE, consists of an estimated 5,000 tombs in caves and rock-cut chambers cut into the limestone cliffs on either side of a narrow valley.

Natural caves have always been used by humans, although it is doubtful that the bulk of any population ever lived in caves for most of the time. It is truer to say that caves were used where they were available, especially for refuge against cold weather, but that most people lived in places where suitable caves did not exist. Caves were probably more important as places of religious significance, to which occasional pilgrimage was made, than as dwelling places. Some of the earliest constructed dwellings were partly underground, but there is no convincing evidence they related to caves.

However, in the absence of durable human-made structures, the cave must have had some special spiritual or other kind of significance, and especially connotations of womb-like protection and/or connections with the spiritual forces of the underworld. There is a considerable body of evidence that caves were used for sacred purposes, and much cave art appears to have been designed to invoke fertility within the tribe, fertility in the animals that the tribe hunted, success in the hunt, or success in battle. Australian Aborigines generally used rock shelters, which were open at the front, rather than true caves, and their art

served not only these purposes but, it seems, recorded notable events, including the arrival of the first Macassan fishing boats and, later, of European sailing ships. Other functions of the cave were for human burial and, from Neolithic times, for the storage and preservation of food or other valuables.

There is no sharp distinction between the natural cave, which might be expanded and improved, and the fully excavated space. The Hal Saflieni Hypogeum in Malta, which was constructed between about 3600 and 3000 BCE, is a multilevel complex of halls, chambers, and passages covering about 5,380 sq ft (500 sq m), excavated from solid rock. This would have contained about 7,000 bodies. The Necropolis of Pantalica in Sicily dates from the thirteenth to the eighth centuries BCE. It consists of thousands of individual caves and rock-cut chambers which open on either side of a complex of gullies.

Caves as Tombs

In ancient Egypt, some of the earliest tombs were *mastabas*, which were excavated into the ground beneath platform-like superstructures, and were reached by vertical shafts or staircases. Later, the

Living Underground

The multilevel settlement of Kaymakli in Cappadoccia, Turkey, may have been occupied as a refuge in time of trouble, vacated, and then reoccupied as required. It incorporated sophisticated provisions for defense and ventilation. Stone discs like millstones were set in grooves beside important doorways, so they could very simply be released to roll across and seal the opening in the face of attack. A central ventilation shaft, which could also be used for raising and lowering goods, opened at ground level at a considerable distance from the main entry, where it was doubtless hoped that an enemy would not find it, or would not recognize its purpose.

The façade of El Khazneh (The Treasury) at Petra, Jordan, is divided horizontally with a porch below and a turret dividing the broken pediment above. Cut into the rock, it is 92 ft (27 m) wide and 130 ft (39 m) high. Behind is a rectangular chamber. The buildings are thought to date from the second century BCE.

rock-cut tomb was an alternative to the pyramid for a pharoah, and would necessarily contain a mortuary chapel or temple and other subsidiary spaces, although little or no evidence has been found of any temples being built underground in their own right.

Two of the most dramatic rock-cut pharoah tombs, at Deir el-Bahari, were set in behind a cliff face and linked with above-ground structures in front. The earlier was that of Mentuhotep, the ruler who reunited Egypt and founded the Middle Kingdom; it dates from about 2100 BCE, and today it is entirely ruined. Nearby, the tomb complex of Hatshepsut—one of the ancient world's most innovative and important buildings —still stands with its structures in front. It dates from about 1500 BCE. However, the temples of Ramses II and Hathor at Abu Simbel, which date from the thirteenth century BCE, have no such structures in front, only a row of colossal seated figures flanking the entrance to each temple. These cave temples were excavated, dismantled, moved, and then reinstated in an artificial cliff face in the 1970s. Led by UNESCO, this massive international operation was designed to save the temples from submersion in the Aswan Dam.

Cave Ancestry

In Malta, as well as some notable underground burial complexes, there are megalithic structures dating back perhaps to 3000 or 3500 BCE. These are believed to be temples and, although they are built partly or wholly above ground, they seem to reflect a cave ancestry. In the ancient Greek world many sacred sites dedicated to local or chthonic deities, as at Akragas (present-day Agrigento) in Sicily, developed from caves. Others, notably at Delphi on mainland Greece, were defined by the presence of sulfurous springs arising from caves and crevasses. A priest or priestess would inhale the sulfurous fumes, and the incoherent words uttered by the intoxicated celebrant would be carefully interpreted and then handed out as oracular pronouncements.

The Phrygian temples at Midas Sehri, western Turkey, dating from around 700 BCE, present façades that evoke freestanding gabled temple structures, but they are really natural sanctuaries with only rudimentary chambers behind each façade. At Petra, in Jordan, the famous Nabatean and Roman rock-cut structures—believed to be tombs—are also mostly façades and have limited interior development. The major temples at Petra were freestanding in the conventional manner.

The substantial creation of underground temples (as opposed to the use and development of existing caves) is best seen in the Buddhist assembly halls at Bhaja, Nasik, Karli, Ellora, and Ajanta in India, which were constructed between about 250 BCE to CE 250. These simulate above-ground architecture in considerable detail, and at Karli actual wooden roof ribs are inserted.

Caves cut out of the soft yellow earth (*loess*) serve as homes for more than 40 million people in northern China. This type of loess pit dwelling in Shaanxi province, is built where there are no hills. After a courtyard is made, usually about 35 ft (10 m) deep, rooms are dug off it.

Cellars

For centuries, wines have been made in cellars of the vineyards of Europe and then stored there as they ferment in oak barrels. A cool, dark, slightly dank underground cellar (left) is the ideal place to keep wine at its best.

The cellar is one of the optional elements of a building, and is more often the by-product of the building technique than of any particular functional requirement. But where the cellar is specifically required, it is usually for the preparation and storage of food, oil, or wine. In the simplest instance, the cellar is produced by the excavation of stone or brick earth for use in constructing the building above.

Partially Excavated Cellars

The cellar is also found as a distinct structure without a building over it. Some early dwellings were of this type—typically, a pit covered with an insulated roof. Later, in the cooler climates of northern Europe and America, it was used for the root cellars, where root crops were stored, and sometimes for the ice houses, although these were often of more specialized designs. In more temperate climates, the pit cellar might be used for a meat house, coolroom, or dairy.

Such partially underground structures, known as *Grubenhäuser,* usually with a steep roof rising direct from the ground surface, have been found over much of Europe. They date from the earliest times up until about the fourteenth century. In England, they comprise the majority of known Anglo-Saxon buildings. At most European sites these underground rooms occur with a frequency which indicates that—rather than being cool-rooms or other specialized structures—they must have been dwellings.

Slavic cellars, from about the sixth century CE, include both storerooms and dwellings. Examples reconstructed at the Skanzen Brezno, near Louny in the Czech Republic, include a corn storage pit

in a deep bottle shape, with a conical roof of reeds on top, and a shallower cylindrical pit for the same purpose, sheltered by a ridged thatched roof. The cellar's interior was baked, presumably by setting a fire in it, and then lined with straw. When the cellar was full, it was sealed with a lid made of layers of wood, straw, clay, and sods. A dwelling hut of the same period was oblong with curved corners, only partly excavated, and the sides were reinforced with something resembling wattle and daub. Its gable roof was thatched and it had a ridge pole carried on two posts.

Dutch settlers introduced similar excavated structures to North America in 1650 as a type of dwelling that was suited to the cold New England regions. They would dig a square pit in the ground, 6 or 7 ft (1.8 or 2 m) deep, case the earth walls with timber, and line it with the bark of trees or other material to prevent it caving in. This cellar may be floored with planks and given a ceiling and a roof of spars covered with bark or green sods. It is known that settlers and their families lived satisfactorily in these pit-chambers for up to four years before they built themselves a conventional dwelling.

Cellars in History

Because the superstructure has been destroyed, our knowledge of many ancient buildings is virtually confined to the cellars. At Hattusas, the Hittite capital in Asia Minor (in the Black Sea region of present-day Turkey), underground rooms, dating from the fourteenth to the thirteenth centuries BCE, hold large terracotta pots for storing oil, but the precise forms of the larger rooms above are unknown. Other similar spaces,

The front basement area of the keeper's house at Somerset House, London (right), designed by Sir William Chambers between 1766 and 1786, extends under the public footpath. In most town houses such spaces contained bunkers for storing coal.

These generously vaulted cellars (below) are in the Alcázares Reales (Royal Alcazars), in Seville, Spain. The two-story Moorish palace dates from 1364. The cellars were used for the storage of food and wine.

narrow enough to be easily spanned by the main floor structure, are found in Mesopotamian sites and in the Minoan palace of Knossos, on Crete.

The Romans developed something quite different: a vaulted space which was known as a cryptoporticus. This might be found under a private house or a palace, and it often ran along the side of a forum or street, with small apertures letting in light at the kerb level, and was probably used as a storage space by the retailers above it. Good examples of cryptoportici are found at Arles in France, Bayrakli (just north of present-day Izmir) in Turkey, and Bosra in Syria.

Cellars beneath buildings were often used in medieval times for dungeons, the most extreme case being the oubliette, a narrow dungeon entered only from above by way of a trapdoor. The cellars might also be linked by tunnels to those of adjoining buildings, or to more distant locations. In a defensible building, they would often include large water tanks or cisterns.

In some cases, where houses were built against limestone or other easily excavated cliffs, as on the island of Santorini, and at Cappadocia in Turkey, cellars might be excavated a considerable way inward at the same level as the house, and were used to store primary produce. In northern Spain and other places, independent, horizontally accessed cellars not attached to any house were used for purposes such as food and wine storage.

By the eighteenth century, urban houses were often heavily dependent upon basements and cellars. In large London terrace houses, the front door might be reached by a bridge crossing a sunken area, which gave light to the basement rooms. On the street side, extending under the public footpath, would be bunkers for storing coal. Basement rooms within the house itself might include laundries, kitchens, and other functional spaces. Even in detached villas and country houses, it was not uncommon to place the kitchen in the basement level.

It was often difficult keeping these basement rooms watertight and dry. In cities, there was a particular sanitary problem due to overflowing cesspits. The cesspit was an underground tank into which the household sewage flowed, and it was supposed to be regularly pumped out by contractors. If the cesspit was badly constructed, however, it leaked into the surrounding ground, and if the contractors were lax it overflowed. It was not uncommon for cellars to be polluted with the resultant effluent. This contributed to serious outbreaks of disease, such as the London cholera epidemic of 1848–1849 and 1853, which killed 25,000 people.

The Catacombs
Rome, Italy

The catacombs of Rome are best known for their art and for their association with the early Christian Church. But, in fact, they were simply burial places of pre-Christian origin. Those in Rome were the most prominent examples of a type also found elsewhere, from Akragas, (present-day Agrigento), in Sicily to Lutetia (now Paris). The soft tufa found in the Latium region made this a practical and convenient method of disposing of the dead. The catacombs are narrow passages, which vary from head height to about 17 ft (5 m) high, usually in multiple levels, one above the another. They were not planned on any coherent system, but grew in an ad hoc fashion over time. In the Catacomb of Santi Marcellino e Pietro is an illustration of a *fossor*, or gravedigger,

who is doubtless one of the complex's creators. Some catacombs contained Christian martyrs, and there was great pressure to be buried near them. Some of those used for Christian burials were associated with a parish church or *titulus equitii*. After the fifth century CE, the catacombs went out of use.

On either side of each passage or gallery were recesses to accommodate the dead, usually in the form of *loculi* or *arcosolia*. The *loculus* was a long slot at right angles to the passage into which a body, wrapped in a sheet, could be slid as if in a filing cabinet. It would be closed by a brick or marble panel carrying the details of the deceased, although these tablets have nearly all been broken or looted. A more important corpse would be

placed in an *arcosolium*, an arched space in the side of the passage, which was large enough for a sarcophagus to be placed in parallel. Sometimes a small chamber, or *cubiculum*, opening off the side of the passage would contain a number of interments, probably those of a particular family, and even larger spaces were used as chapels or for funerary feasts. The decoration might refer to the occupation of the deceased, as with the anatomy lesson in the Catacomb of the Via Latina.

Christian Sanctuary

There was already a well-organized Christian community in Rome to welcome St. Paul when he arrived in CE 61 and, despite the persecutions of Emperor Nero, the community continued to

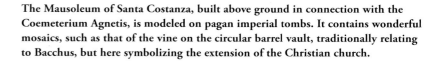

The Catacomb of San Callisto (St. Callixtus) was constructed in the reign of Pope Callixtus (CE 217–222). It contains a number of levels of steep passages with *loculi* or burial slots on either side. It is the oldest official cemetry of the Christian community of Rome and nine third-century popes are buried there.

The Mausoleum of Santa Costanza, built above ground in connection with the Coemeterium Agnetis, is modeled on pagan imperial tombs. It contains wonderful mosaics, such as that of the vine on the circular barrel vault, traditionally relating to Bacchus, but here symbolizing the extension of the Christian church.

expand. By around CE 200, there were numerous Christians, but Christianity was not recognized as legal within the Roman empire until the Edict of Milan of CE 313. In the meantime, Christians were intermittently subjected to persecution. It is no longer thought they lived in the catacombs for substantial periods, but they probably used them occasionally as places of refuge. The Catacomb of Santi Marcellino e Pietro was specifically for those martyred in the persecutions of Diocletian, and was named after the first saints killed.

Because the Christian religion was illegal, the art associated with burials had to conform to Roman norms. In the arched space at the back of an *arcosolium* would be a standing figure with hands raised in the attitude of prayer, known as an *orans* or *orante*, and representing the soul of the deceased. The vine, the pagan symbol of Bacchus, was appropriated to represent the spread of the Christian church. The fish was used as a cryptic symbol of Christianity because the Greek initials for "Jesus Christ, Son of God" spelled out *ichthus*, the word for fish. The fish symbol might be associated with a dove, a ship, or an anchor.

Pagans typically held a funeral feast, or *agape*, that symbolized loving union with the dead and early Christians did much the same. A banquet illustrated in the Catacomb of San Callisto was formerly taken to represent the Eucharist.

The principal catacombs are those of saints Callisto, Domitilla, Marcellino e Pietro, Priscilla, Commodilla, and Praetextatus, the Via Latina, the Giordani, Pamphilus, and the Coemeterium Maius (or greater cemetery, to distinguish it from the smaller cemetery in the Via Nomentana).

Originally, the catacomb of the Via Latina was commissioned privately by a few families and was not intended for Christians. Most of the other catacombs were founded philanthropically by the citizens whose names they bear, and only in the Catacomb of San Callisto is there evidence that it was initially owned by the church itself (most of the third-century popes were buried there).

It was the scholar Giovanni Battista de Rossi who rediscovered, explored, and wrote about the catacombs of Rome in the nineteenth century.

Associated Structures

Many of the catacombs are associated with other structures, the most important example being the complex of Sant'Agnese fuori le Mura, associated with the tomb of St. Agnes, who was martyred in the third century. Previously, the site had been occupied by a large shed-like cemetery basilica measuring 130 x 330 ft (100 x 40 m), of which there remains the Coemeterium Agnetis, which contains graves and is without flooring, as with some other structures built around CE 300.

The Columbarium of Pomponius Hylas, from the first century CE, is the best preserved *columbarium*, small chambers for funerary urns of those cremated. It is believed Pomponius built the tomb as a financial investment and sold off the vacant spaces.

Linked with this basilica is the mausoleum of Emperor Constantine's daughter, Constantina—now known as Santa Costanza. In form it is a typical pagan Roman circular mausoleum, or *heroum*, but its decoration contains Christian iconography. Under and around the basilica is a vast catacomb in three parts, one of which dates from the late second to the early third centuries, one from the third to early fourth centuries, and a third from the fourth and fifth centuries.

The tomb of Santa Costanza attracted other Christian burials, and was later celebrated by the construction of a shrine. This was replaced with an underground basilica that was constructed by Pope Honorius in the seventh century. Today, the mausoleum church of Santa Costanza, which dates from about CE 350, is the most prominent element remaining on the site, and it contains some of the finest mosaic decoration of their kind, including the Bacchic vine mosaic in the vault of the ambulatory, in which the art of the pagan and Christian worlds meet.

Tunnels

Tunneling has been associated principally with water supply, mining, and, more recently, road and rail traffic. In about 700 BCE King Hezekieh of Judah constructed a 1740-ft (530-m) S-shaped tunnel, which still exists, to take water from the Gihon spring to the Siloam pool within Jerusalem, to ensure a water supply to the town in time of siege. At about the same time, the Assyrians were using aqueducts, and probably tunnels as well, for the transfer of water to Nineveh from the northern foothills. The surviving Evpalinos tunnel on the island of Samos, which was designed by a Greek engineer in the sixth century BCE, brings water to the town through a mountain ridge. In fact, it actually consists of two tunnels: an upper one through which the engineers could walk, and the watercourse below, more accurately adjusted to minimum slope for the water flow.

Roman Tunnels

Tunneling was a technology that the Romans made their own. The aqueducts for which they are well known were necessarily linked with tunnels to take water through mountains and over high ground. The tunnels also required advanced surveying skills. In CE 148, a Roman engineer designed a tunnel at Saldae, in modern Algeria. He returned to Rome after construction began, but was called back a few years later because the teams digging from both ends had failed to meet.

One way to control the direction of a tunnel was to dig a series of shafts and then tunnel between them. Pliny the Elder refers to a tunnel constructed to drain Lake Fucino as being the greatest public work of the period, taking 30,000 labourers 11 years to construct. It was 3½ miles (5.6 km) long and passed under Monte Salviano,

requiring 40 shafts up to 400 ft (120 m) deep, and a number of *cuniculi*, or inclined galleries, up which the excavated material was drawn. Shafts also provided ventilation and access for maintenance. This system persisted after Roman times in the Middle Eastern *qanat*, a horizontal tunnel to carry water, punctuated at intervals with vertical shafts or stairs to the surface.

Tunneling Techniques

The technology for cutting a tunnel, and when necessary propping up the ground above, was no different from that employed in mining and quarrying. No significant developments, apart from the introduction of gunpowder, occurred until the nineteenth century. A demand arose then for shallow tunnels for railways and other purposes. They could be more easily built by

The *qanat* (above) is a tunnel to carry water, punctuated at intervals with vertical shafts to the surface. The one above is from Iran. They were widespread throughout the Middle East.

Marc Brunel's Thames Tunnel in London was an astonishing engineering feat and its long, eventful construction process was followed with great interest by the public. This coloured aquatint (below left) of cut-away views of the tunnel was one of many commemorative souvenirs produced.

The machine used for boring a tunnel during the development of the New York City subway system in the early 1930s (below) is sophisticated for its time, but would be dwarfed by modern tunneling machines with diameters of 50 ft (15 m) and more.

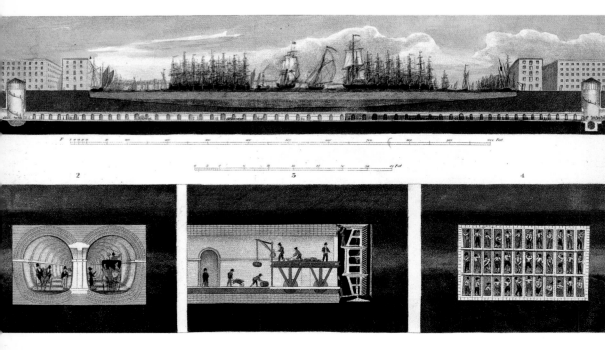

the cut-and-fill method—that is, by digging an open trench, constructing the tunnel, usually of brick, and filling over the top.

There were also demands for deep tunnels passing under rivers, the first major example of which was the Thames Tunnel, proposed in 1823 and begun in 1825 by the engineer Marc Brunel. A shaft was sunk, and horizontal tunneling—at times passing through liquid mud—started in 1826. By April the next year, 540 ft (162 m) of tunneling had been completed when the river broke in. Work then progressed slowly, and was abandoned completely when another influx of water occurred. Some government financial assistance was obtained in 1835, however, and a protective shield was installed, behind which the tunneling could proceed. By 1842, a double tunnel between Rotherhithe and Wapping was completed, the deepest part being 76 ft (22 m) below the high water line.

A tunnel dug under the Detroit River between Michigan, in the United States, and Canada, was begun in 1872 but it was abandoned because of the inflow of water. The 4½-mile (7-km) Severn Tunnel was begun in England the following year, and it was completed, only after considerable difficulties, some 13 years later.

Techniques for tunneling developed rapidly during the latter part of the nineteenth century.

Mont Cenis Tunnel, built through the Alps in the 1860s, made the first use of compressed air to drive rotary rock drills, the compression being achieved by a series of water rams. These rotary drills were then replaced by percussion drills, on Thomas Fowles's American patent, and the work continued using pneumatic drilling in the modern sense. The St. Gotthard Tunnel, which followed in 1872–1881, was far more advanced. It used air compressed by turbines to drive Ferroux drills, which struck about 180 blows per minute. The builders of the Croton Aqueduct Tunnel, New York, no less than 33¼ miles (52 km) long, achieved a tunneling rate of 1¼ miles (2 km) per month using Ingersoll drills.

The shield used by Brunel in the construction of the Thames Tunnel weighed 198 tons (180 tonnes) and was divided horizontally into three separated cells, within which the miners worked independently at the face of the excavation. This shield was improved upon by later engineers, notably by J. H. Greathead and Benjamin Baker. Baker's pneumatic shield was crossed at the front by horizontal plates with cutting edges, and each level was fitted with vertical plates that could be slid open or closed. When enough material had been removed from in front of it, the shield was pushed forward by hydraulic pressure, and arched brickwork was built to permanently secure the

tunnel behind. Greathead developed a shield that cut a circular hole 10¾ ft (3.2 m) in diameter, behind which cast iron segments were bolted together, creating what was literally a metal tube, designed to almost exactly fit railway carriages: the train operated like a piston, driving the air through the shaft and improving the ventilation. Greathead's system was first used from 1886 in the City and South London Railway, the first of the underground "tubes."

Tunneling technology further developed over the twentieth century, and what would have been spectacular engineering achievements in Baker's and Greathead's time now seem commonplace. The 31½-mile (50.5-km) Channel Tunnel, built between Britain and France, includes 23½ miles (38 km) beneath the sea, which is the longest undersea tunnel in the world. The largest of the modern tunnel-boring machines have diameters of over 50 ft (15 m) and have been used to bore the Chong Ming tunnels in Shanghai and the M30 ring road in Madrid.

Railway tunnels were cut through the European Alps in the nineteenth century, linking regions that were geographically close but cut off by mountains. A series of road tunnels was built in the twentieth century, the most famous being the Mont Blanc between France and Italy.

The Underground
London, England

There was intense interest in the development of London's underground rail system in other big cities around the world. The illustration (above) is from a 1898 edition of the French journal *La Nature*.

The development of London's underground railway system during the mid-nineteenth century was the result of economic pressures. Separate railway companies had built above-ground lines outward from London, with their own city terminals, which were not linked.

In the 1850s there were various proposals for a connecting system, not necessarily one that was fully underground but at least with the separation of railway trains, road vehicles, and pedestrians. In 1854, a bill was presented to Parliament to authorize a new underground line, which had been designed by the engineer John Fowler. After a number of changes, the proposal for the line, which was called the Metropolitan Railway, was finalized in 1858.

The Early Underground

Work on the line began in February 1860, and on January 9, 1863, the inaugural stretch of the London Underground was opened, a length of nearly 4 miles (6 km) between Bishop's Road, Paddington, and Farringdon Street in the central city. It was constructed using the early cut-and-cover method—by digging up streets, building a brick tunnel, and filling over the top. Until this

time, the two rail companies, the Metropolitan and the Metropolitan District, had placed their lines in open cuttings as far as possible, and only built tunnels where this was unavoidable. An example of this cut-and-cover construction is the stretch of tunnel between Paddington and Moorgate stations, which was built as an elliptical arch, 28½ ft (8.5 m) across and 17 ft (5 m) high, with seven "rings," or courses, of brick and three thicknesses of brick at the sides. The tunnel was spanned with iron beams where the depth was too shallow to permit a brick arch.

The first major hurdle that the engineers faced was caused by the smoke and steam emitted by the locomotives. Early commentators suggested that it was not a problem, or that it was possible to design a locomotive which would retain the combustion products, at least until it reached the open air (the line was not a fully self-contained underground system). An experimental engine produced by Robert Stephenson in 1861 still emitted steam from every opening, as well as becoming dangerously overheated, and the rail company rejected it in favor of tank engines, which released steam into a water tank below the boiler, but still belched out smoke.

The Metropolitan District Company then built an underground line between Westminster and South Kensington and linked it into the Metropolitan's branch line to Edgware Road. This was opened in 1868. Both companies then extended their lines eastward. The Circle Line was complete by 1884.

Before long, the theory that the underground lines should be approximately circular in plan was discredited, because the distance between any two stations was longer than a straight line would be, and the distance to reach a point within the circle, by foot or other means, was inconveniently long. Railway companies now came to favor radial lines, which provided a good service for a proportion of the population, rather than a poor service for everyone.

The underground system itself was challenged by the elevated rail system that was introduced in New York in 1871–1878, and then in other United States and European cities. There were many advantages to the "El," as it was known in New York, particularly that smoke and steam could disperse easily rather than building up in the tunnels. As the traffic increased in volume, this no doubt became a health problem as well as a potential safety issue. In 1898, one London

Banks of elevators are characteristic of underground systems—they are the fastest, most efficient method of carrying passengers to and from street level. These (left) are at Canary Wharf Station, built in 1999.

driver reported to a Board of Trade committee that the smoke was "very seldom" so thick as to prevent him from seeing the signals. From 1890, however, the problem was well on the way to being solved, by converting engines from steam to electric traction.

London persisted with the development of the underground network, but largely abandoned cut-and-cover construction. The method had a number of disadvantages: it confined the route to existing streets and other accessible land, making it difficult to achieve short routes and easy curves in the line; it could require an excessive depth of excavation if the surface level above varied; and it caused major disruption to surface traffic during the construction process.

Tunneling

The cut-and-cover method was superseded by tunneling, which allowed ideal routes to be planned at any depth and with little regard for the properties at ground level above, although there was often some risk of subsidence at a later date. The Thames Tunnel, between Rotherhithe and Wapping, had been built between 1825 and 1843 by Marc Brunel and his son Isambard. They had introduced tunneling behind a metal shield, as was done in mining works. Although it

was designed for horse traffic, the tunnel was converted for use as a railway tunnel on the East London Line in 1869. A second tunnel under the River Thames, between the Tower of London and Bermondsey, was opened in 1870, but it operated for only a short time before being converted to pedestrian use. The Circle Line included three tunnels: the Clerkenwell Tunnel, the "widening" tunnel that is parallel to Clerkenwell, and the Campden Hill Tunnel.

Further extensions to London's Underground were on a more or less ad hoc basis, and were relatively minor compared with the tunnels being built elsewhere, but they did embrace the new system of "tube" construction. This enabled the lines to go much deeper, through the blue clay substratum—about 70 ft (20 m) beneath the ground, although this varies substantially—and to avoid pipes and sewers, which were a major problem closer to the surface. It is this mode of tunneling that has given the system its colloquial name, the "Tube."

These incremental extensions to the Tube— the latest was the 1977 Jubilee Line, which was further extended in 1999—have created a system that now has 12 lines, over 250 miles (400 km) of railway lines and 275 stations, and supports three million passenger journeys each day.

This entrance to Bank Station (above) has changed little since it was opened in 1900. During the blitz of London in the Second World War, many of the underground stations were used as bomb shelters.

At rush hour, the platforms at underground stations (above left) are crowded with commuters—over three million people use the Tube every day. Around 40 stations are no longer used: these are referred to as "ghost stations."

Piles

Piles or posts are the main alternative to constructing a building with a continuous footing on or in the ground. They tend to be used where the building is above water or boggy ground, where it is necessary to drive deep to find a sound foundation, or where it has to be raised well above the ground surface.

The word "post" is used for a timber support of any length, but not one that has to be driven deep into the ground or be sawn into a square shape. "Pile" generally refers to a long piece of timber that is driven deep into the ground; it is often used for the sort of posts which support a building over water; and it is occasionally used for ordinary stumps. Stumps are short supports under a building, made of timber and usually sawn square, or of concrete; however, in some countries, other terms, including "blocks" or "piles," are used to describe these stumps.

The Uses of Piles

Buildings over water are known from Neolithic European remains, such as those which have been reconstructed at Unteruhldingen, Lake Constance in Germany. But the raising of buildings above the ground on piles or stumps is a widespread

phenomenon, particularly in tropical regions. A number of factors influence the practice: the fear of flooding, the need for good ventilation, the need to keep out vermin, the need to sleep above the level of low-flying insects such as mosquitoes, and the need for protection against enemies or wild animals.

In Europe, stumps were generally confined to specialised structures such as grain stores, where vermin were a particular problem. In the Rhineland and Scandinavia, there is evidence of Neolithic granaries built on posts. Raised log storehouses were later found in Scandinavia, one example being a Swedish *härbre*, dating from 1522. Similar storehouses and granaries were built in North America by Swedish settlers. Likewise, in Africa the granaries of the Nupe were raised high on monolithic stone piers.

Around the mid-nineteenth century, stumps rose to real popularity in colonial areas. In 1852, Elizabeth Fielden described her new house in Natal, South Africa, as "standing upon legs, or posts, we can see under it and might possibly creep under if we chose." This was regarded as a means of keeping out ants, snakes, and wind-blown sand, as well as keeping the house cooler.

A Sarawak longhouse, in Kuching, Malaysia, is raised on tall posts above the rainforest floor. Being high off the ground, the longhouse is protected from floods and cool air can circulate. The longhouse design is flexible: it may be built to house a community of a few dozen people or a group in the hundreds.

The Carysfort Reef lighthouse, completed in 1852, is a late example of the openwork lighthouse type introduced by James Walker. It is one of a series of offshore lighthouses marking the dangerous Florida reef in the Florida Keys and is still operational.

By 1859, in the United States, piers or posts were being used for barns and other farm outbuildings, although not for houses.

Stumps were not in themselves sufficient to keep out most vermin, unless some proportion of their height was clad in a material that could not be climbed. They were sometimes encased in sheet tin or other metal. In a barn at Celle, in France, the posts were clad around the lower part with overlapping slates, and the upper part with panes of window glass—all designed to prevent rats climbing up, and apparently with success.

Piling Technology

Piling—in the engineering sense, in which a large timber, usually a dressed tree trunk, is driven into the ground by hammering—is seen as a Roman invention, and certainly the key to many major Roman works, such as Julius Caesar's bridge over the Rhine in 55 BCE. It involved a pile-driving machine repeatedly raising a weight, by animal or other power, and dropping it on the head of the pile. Once the pile reached a solid base, or bedrock, its top would be sawn off at the correct height and the superstructure begun. But it did not necessarily have to reach a solid base, because even in soft ground a stage is reached where the pile can be driven no further, simply because of friction, and this is sufficient for it to carry load.

Roman piling technology was largely forgotten in Europe until after the Renaissance, and there were no really significant developments until the nineteenth century. Then a particular problem arose in the construction of some lighthouses: previously, most of these had been built of stone resting on bedrock, sometimes even below the water line. But this was not always possible, and a new form of lighthouse was developed by James Walker and others in the form of an openwork polygonal structure with slanting piles around the periphery. But securing these piles in sandy shoals was often impossible until Alexander Mitchell invented the screw pile in about 1833. This was a broad, flat archimidean screw, which was literally screwed into the sand, and provided a remarkably stable base. It was first used for the Maplin Sands light on the English south coast, completed in 1841.

Another nineteenth-century technological development was sheet piling. Previously, it had sometimes been necessary to drive a continuous row of piles to create something like a retaining wall. This could be done much more efficiently with iron or steel piles, which overlocked at the side and created a continuous diaphragm. Iron piles were also used in more conventional ways for major structures where higher performance was needed or where wood was not sufficiently durable. Reinforced concrete piles became available early in the twentieth century, then prestressed piles; they offered the tensile strength required for the construction of skyscrapers.

The Steddle

One way of keeping out animals and vermin was the steddle, a stubby stone shaft or timber log with a projecting flat cap, like a mushroom. The steddle is known in model buildings from China of the Eastern Han dynasty (CE 25–220) and in a relief at Borobudur, Indonesia, of the ninth century. It has been used in most European cultures for granaries and other buildings susceptible to vermin or predators, including the *hórreos*, or grain stores, of Spain. Pigeon houses were commonly raised on stone steddles in order to protect the birds from predators in the Pyrénées region of France.

In Galicia, Spain, the *hórreos* are monumental structures built of granite raised on mushroom-shaped steddles. Similar structures are found in Portugal and Scandinavia.

The Burj Dubai
Dubai, United Arab Emirates

The Burj Dubai, which is still under construction at the time of writing, is the world's tallest building and still rising. By July 2007 it had surpassed the 1,667 ft (508 m) of Taipei 101, the previous contender. Although the intended final height has not been officially revealed, it is thought to be 2,650 ft (808 m). The height is so great, that as the building grew, the walkie-talkie radios used by the construction workers ceased to be reliable, and a wireless mesh system had to be installed.

The tower is a commercial venture by Emaar Properties in the oil-rich Gulf state of Dubai, in the United Arab Emirates, which is known for the dramatic sail-like shape of the Burj al Arab. The estimated cost of the Burj Dubai project will be about US$800 million.

The Burj Dubai's structure is carried on a thick, reinforced concrete slab, which has an area of 80,000 sq ft (75,000 sq m) and rests on 192 bored reinforced concrete piles more than 165 ft (50 m) deep. The tower above is built mainly of reinforced concrete. Because the concrete had to withstand Gulf temperatures which can reach 122°F (50°C), ice was added to the mixture and it was poured at night when it is cooler. The need

The Burj Dubai towers above an associated, large-scale building development in Dubai. Here, two rows of sheet piling—a series of panels with interlocking connections—have been driven into the ground to form an impermeable barrier.

to pump liquid concrete to an unprecedented height was one of the main technical challenges for the architects, as the previous record for pumping concrete was 1,745 ft (532 m). The climbing formwork used to cast the concrete required 32 layout changes as it rose higher. The concrete part of the structure, 1,973 ft (601 m) high, was completed in November 2007.

The Building's Structure

The structure uses the "buttressed core" system, newly invented by American engineer Bill Baker, in which the lateral load is resisted by a central core and shear walls linked to the exterior columns, all of which are made of very strong, high-density reinforced concrete.

The tower has a triple-lobed footprint, with the three wings arranged around the buttressed central core, and as it rises setbacks occur in each wing in an upward spiralling pattern. At the top, the core emerges as a finishing spire. The tower's exterior cladding, which is designed to withstand Dubai's extreme summer temperatures, consists of reflective glazing with interlocking aluminium and textured stainless steel spandrel panels, up to two stories tall.

The building will have 56 of the fastest elevators in the world, with a speed of 40 miles (64.4 km) per hour, double-decked, and able to carry 21 people on each deck. The window-washing system consists of three track-mounted telescopic machines, each with a jib reaching

The Burj Dubai (third from right) will be over twice the height of Paris's Eiffel Tower, completed in 1889, and will far surpass the 1,667-ft (508-m) Taipei 101 (second from left) and the previous tallest structure, the CN Tower in Toronto, Canada (fourth from left).

118 ft (36 m). With all three operating, it will take three to four months to clean the exterior.

The architects are Skidmore, Owings & Merrill LLP, whose antecedents designed the pioneering glass-box skyscraper, Lever House in New York, in 1952, and who have since designed the Sears Tower in Chicago, and the Freedom Tower, New York. The contractors are Samsung Engineering & Construction of South Korea, who also built the Petronas Twin Towers in Kuala Lumpur, and Taipei 101 in Taiwan.

When it was announced in early 2003, the Burj Dubai's design was the same as the 1,840-ft (560-m) Grollo Tower design that was proposed for Melbourne, Australia. However, a new design was released in May 2003. In January 2004, work began on the foundations.

There will be up to 180 floors, with a hotel occupying the lower 37 floors, 700 apartments, corporate offices and suites, and an indoor/outdoor observation deck on the 124th floor. The spire will hold communications equipment and some habitable spaces.

The Burj Dubai has been built primarily by immigrant engineers and workers from Pakistan, India, Bangladesh, China, and the Philippines. Skilled carpenters were earning US$7.60 a day, and laborers US$4. In March 2006, the workers rioted, because of anger over low wages and poor working conditions, and caused approximately US$1m destruction. Workers building a new terminal at Dubai International Airport joined the strike action. An offer by the United Arab Emirates government in June 2007 to fly home illegal immigrant workers free of charge was met with overwhelming demand, jeopardising the supply of workers on the Burj Dubai and other construction projects. The government declined to prescribe a minimum wage, but the Burj Dubai contractors agreed a 20 percent increase.

Tallest Building

When finished, the Burj Dubai is expected to meet the four criteria of the Council on Tall Buildings and Urban Habitat—the height of the structural top, highest occupied floor, the roof's top, and the spire's highest point—to become the world's tallest structure. Previous recordholders include New York's Empire State Building at 1,250 ft (381 m); Shanghai's Jin Mao Building at 1,381 ft (421 m); Chicago's Sears Tower at 1,451 ft (442 m) and Malaysia's Petronas Towers at 1,483 ft (452 m). The CN Tower, in Toronto, Canada, is the tallest freestanding structure, at 1,815 ft (553 m). The Burj Dubai is unlikely to hold its crown for long. The proposed Crystal Island in Moscow is intended to be the tallest tower in the world, and will have seven times the floor area of the Burj Dubai.

An aerial view of the Burj Dubai under construction (right). By February 2008, its height had reached 1,985 ft (604.9 m) and 159 floors. Once construction of the main structure began, a floor was completed every three days.

Putting Up Walls

The wall may be the main structural support of a building, a source of security, or a way of keeping the weather out or the heat in. But equally it may be nothing more than a screen for privacy or a location for advertisement or decoration, for it is usually the part of the building with the greatest impact on the viewer.

Forces and Resistance

During the lifetime of any building or other structure, a variety of forces will affect it on a daily basis and others only once in a while. When a building is designed, in order for it to remain in a stable, intact condition, a structural engineer makes an analysis of the forces to ensure that each element of the structure will remain effective under all conceivable conditions. It is usual nowadays to include the method of erection for a structure within this approach, and also how it may be safely taken down at the end of its projected life of, normally, fifty years. There will continue to be important buildings that have longer life expectancies, but the lavish use of materials and labor of the past will not apply to the more utilitarian constructions of today.

Force and Loading

Force can be either positive or negative. Positive force causes compression, as in pressing down on a bed spring, and negative force causes tension, as in a tow rope. We commonly express force in kilograms or tonnes. Engineers mostly use the standard metric system and convert weight to mass as part of their computational methods. A force spread over a given area, say 1 sq m (about 11 sq ft), becomes a loading, which is a more convenient measure since the engineer must deal with floor and roof areas where loading is important.

Working from nationally recognized codes and known masses of materials, the structural engineer is able to break up the building into separate loaded elements. Some of these loads are obvious, such as the self weight, or dead load, of the building, and those transient forces generated as a result of people occupying the building—furniture, equipment, or people themselves—which are termed live loads.

Tying Down in Case of Disaster

In December 1974, tropical Cyclone Tracy devastated the northern Australian city of Darwin. Wind speeds reached 135 mph (217 km/h) before measuring instruments ceased functioning. About seventy percent of the city's buildings were destroyed, leaving more than 20,000 of Darwin's inhabitants homeless; seventy-seven people died. This disaster provoked a thorough overhaul of tie down requirements in cyclonic areas, since loss of roofs usually led to the walls exploding as lateral support disappeared. In Australia, and in some other countries, it is now obligatory to secure roofs in areas prone to cyclones or hurricanes with cyclone bolts, which are in effect one-story-high rods, linking the roof tie down to the floor below.

The ruins of a house in Darwin demonstrate the enormous forces at work when a very intense storm such as a cyclone or hurricane strikes an inhabited area. Cyclone Tracy damaged about ninety percent of the buildings in Darwin, many beyond repair. It took several years to rebuild the city.

Roofs have their own live loads, since they will need maintenance or repair at some time in their lives, and so will need to support people, and, in the case of flat roofs, occupants often make use of the roof surface, thereby creating heavier live loadings than on sloping roofs. All roofs in cold climates are subject to snow loadings, which can be heavy and persist for some months. In these climates, snow load is often the determining factor in vernacular design. Roofs may either be high pitched to

This house in Switzerland has the sturdy, low-pitched roof typical of Alpine regions, a design that can support heavy and prolonged snow loads. Additionally, the roof holds the snow in place, a feature traditionally used to insulate the roof, and the wide eaves shed melting snow well away from the walls.

shed snow, as in the Scandinavian countries, or be the heavy, weighed-down, low-pitched roofs typical of the Alpine regions. All buildings and structures, wherever they occur, are also subject to wind and to temperature effects throughout the changing seasons.

Less obvious forces are those due to movements within the ground itself, such as seismic tremors, settlement due to mine workings, and the movement of clay soils. Some sites may receive oscillating tremors through industrial or traffic vibration, and certain buildings, such as those specifically designed to be used in the wake of a disaster, are required to resist even greater forces. In regions where underground mining takes place, or has taken place in the past, surface movements may occur as a result of underground work, and additional forces due to settlement need to be assessed.

Taking into account all these forces, the structural engineer assembles the skeleton of the proposed building as a framework of distributed loads and point loads, and from the proposed use of the building, calculates the live loads which are likely to apply.

Suction and Pressure

The human body registers the effect of wind as a pressure, but only rarely records the corresponding suction effect of wind around the body. This is because we, as rounded shapes, are to a large degree streamlined. Most buildings are not, and will have four or more corners. The effect of a windstream being deflected around walls or roofs is to generate vortices at these corners. The suction developed by the rotational effect of a vortex is well demonstrated by whirlwinds, hurricanes, cyclones, and typhoons, which are able to lift substantial amounts of material. Hence, in any windstream, the side and rear walls will experience suction forces nearly as large as the pressure developed onto the wall facing into the wind. Being tension forces, these suctions on the walls try to pull the building apart and need to be resisted by the building frame.

Similar forces are at work on roofs, but these mostly present at an angle to the prevailing windstream, and it is the angle of the roof which determines the type and magnitude of the force developed. Steep roofs are subject to pressure on the upstream side and suction on the downstream side. Low angle roofs often present a nearly aerofoil effect in strong winds, and substantial uplift forces are developed. This effect causes incidents nearly every year in which houses and other buildings lose their roofs, and regulation changes in the last three decades have concentrated on adequate tie down for roofs.

Winds are slowed by friction with the Earth's surface and are greatest where the fetch of the windstream—the distance over which the wind blows—is exceptionally long, such as over large areas of water, or over flat plains. Because of the braking effect of the ground's surface, wind speed increases with altitude, and, approaching the stratosphere, winds may attain jet stream conditions, often exceeding 250 mph (400 km/h). This means that very tall buildings are subject to very much higher wind speeds at their tops than at their bases.

A worker stands on the 730-ton tuned mass damper inside the Taipei 101 building. At about 1,670 ft (509 m) high, Taipei 101 is extremely vulnerable to wind and other forces, in a location subject to typhoons and earthquakes. The damper acts like a huge pendulum to counteract the potentially disastrous swaying produced by these forces.

At Nôtre-Dame de Paris, ranks of graceful flying buttresses transfer the thrust of the roof from the upper wall to the ground. Each flying buttress is a half-arch connecting the wall of the building to a freestanding support.

Resistance and Restraint

Even in the simplest of buildings it is necessary to tie the walls against wind forces and rafter thrust. The roof rafters take the roof dead load, and any live loads resulting from maintenance or wind, but most rafters are laid at a slope. Because of the angle of the rafters, there is an outward force developed to the base analogous to the force developed at the foot of a ladder, acting as a constant outward thrust onto the external walls. In traditional construction, separate tie-beams were provided across buildings, at top-plate level (the top of the wall), to absorb the rafter thrust and any wind suction forces. In modern pitched-roof houses, these forces are absorbed by the ceiling joists nailed to the top plates of opposite walls, and in trussed roofs the forces are balanced out

within the truss itself. In some rare medieval instances, iron tie-rods were used, at prohibitive expense, but the normal solution was to adopt timber tie-beams. When iron became readily available in the first half of the nineteenth century, iron tie-rods became a common feature in chapels, churches, courthouses, and other buildings lacking separate ceilings.

Older buildings constructed without ties depended on the inertia of very thick walls to absorb the thrust, or on external support from wall buttresses. These sometimes grew to massive proportions like the buttresses of sixth-century Hagia Sophia, Istanbul, Turkey. The elegant solution of the Middle Ages was the flying buttress, used in many medieval cathedrals, with perhaps the best known being those of Chartres and of Nôtre-Dame de Paris. These carried the thrust of the roof framework to the ground. To do this without tension forces being developed, increased vertical forces at the outer pillars of the buttresses were needed, which were achieved by thickening the buttress roots, and adding tall pinnacles to them as extra mass.

Seismic Events and Earth Tremors

Seismic forces, generated by friction between abutting continental plates deep within the Earth, travel essentially horizontally along the ground surface as a pressure wave, displacing the ground itself in a horizontal direction, together with any buildings built on the affected area. Very lightweight structures made of wood or fabric suffer little damage as the wave displaces the building frame, first in the wave direction, immediately followed by a rebound to its original position. It follows that flexible structures of low mass are unlikely to experience serious damage, even in a severe earthquake. Conversely, solid masonry structures, having high mass and low flexibility, are at high risk and will inevitably experience some damage.

Around the Mediterranean basin, areas such as the Provence region of France, parts of Italy, and the Balkans experience only low-level tremors. In these places, there are some ingenious ways of incorporating flexible timber ties, which act as dampeners to the wave shock, within the walls. After the Great Lisbon Earthquake in Portugal

The church of São Nicolau, Lisbon, lies in ruins after an earthquake struck the Portuguese capital on November 1, 1755. Much of the city was destroyed, and 60,000 people are thought to have died. Better building codes resulted from the disaster.

In Italy in 1999, workers attach steel cables to Pisa Cathedral's campanile—the Leaning Tower—as part of an ultimately successful attempt to stabilize it. The tower leans because its foundations are inadequate for the sandy soil on which it was built.

in 1755, buildings with braced infill panels of timber subframes and brick were noted to have survived with the least damage. This form of construction was made standard in Portugal and was adopted in Spain and Sicily. The vernacular, light, flexible timber construction of Japan and parts of Indonesia reflects the need for flexibility in these earthquake-prone areas.

Ground Movements and Mining

Mining of seams of minerals such as coal below ground ultimately gives rise to a wavelike settlement as props left behind underground gradually decay and collapse. It is possible to design in advance for this process, either by providing sufficient articulation within buildings, or by ensuring that the foundations are rigid enough in themselves to ride out the progressive subsidence, rather like a raft on rapids.

Regular vertical ground surface movements occur in drier climates on clay soils which experience regular or occasional wet winters; the soils swell when damp, and shrink when they dry out, potentially causing damage to anything built on them. Soils with no clays, such as sands and gravels, do not swell or shrink, and not all clays exhibit this phenomenon to the same degree. The origins of the parent materials from which the clays are derived, as well as the method of deposition of the clays, both play decisive parts. The chemistry of the parent rock governs the potential water storage of the individual molecule, and basaltic clays, for example, exhibit a larger water storage capability than granitic clays. All clays are comprised of microscopic platelets, able to store water within the structure of the clay molecule. As the amount of water stored increases, each platelet itself increases in thickness, thereby causing surface heave. Using site investigation techniques the engineer is able to estimate the worst-case range for any individual type of clay and can use this information to design foundations to suit.

Ground Resistance

Ultimately, all forces developed in a building have to be absorbed by the foundations and resisted by the ground itself, and site investigations are carried out to determine the safe founding depth. The need to improve the bearing characteristics of soft ground is referred to in the Bible, and many practices used today have medieval parallels. In England, Ely Cathedral is founded on hard stone fill, and Winchester Cathedral on a grillage of oak logs. The failure to recognize and stiffen the irregular soft, silty sand lenses of Pisa, Italy, is to blame for the tilt of the town's famous campanile. Major improvements in foundation works have been developed in the last century, and ground stabilization by grout or chemical injection, freezing, ground anchors, or reinforced earth is now relatively common.

Timber Walls

Today, timber is increasingly scarce, and is being replaced even in domestic construction by other materials, such as steel wall studs and synthetic cladding. But it is a strong and versatile substance, which until recent times seemed almost inexhaustible. In one form or another it has been the main material used for building walls, despite the traditions in some areas for building in stone, earth, and brick.

The idea of timber construction today generally evokes the idea of frames made of sawn timber, but in the history of timber construction the sawn timber frame is a relatively late development. The first timber structures would certainly not have required cutting tools, and, apart from shelters of branches and twigs, we can take it for granted that for centuries the majority of shelters were built of such materials. Timber log walls come later and are traditionally found in heavily forested regions, especially in areas such as central to northeastern Europe, the northern United States and Canada, parts of Japan, and elsewhere in East Asia. Framed timber walls are even more dependent upon tools, and so appeared later still in history, but are yet more widespread geographically.

The Palisade

The earliest known solid timber wall type is the palisade, in which timbers (whether whole logs or split pieces) are stuck vertically into the ground in a continuous row. This appears at some Neolithic sites, though in the absence of metal tools the construction must have been very crude. Many early Neolithic villages were only semipermanent, and the Danubian settlement at Köln-Lindenthal in Germany was

abandoned after about ten years when the soil had been exhausted by cultivation. Even so, it consisted of gabled houses measuring as much as 20 x 100 ft (6 x 30 m), partly built using posts with a lighter infilling between, but partly of palisade. The late Neolithic (possibly Celtic) village of Aichbül, on the shore of the Federsee, southern Germany, seems to have had the same mixture. The palisade continued as a vernacular building technique, especially in Scandinavia, but always had the problem that the timber decayed where it was buried in the ground. As late as the nineteenth century it was a favored method for building forts and stockades in the United States and elsewhere.

Log Construction

In principle, the log cabin is simpler than the palisade, in that it relies upon the weight of the timber and requires no excavation, and, so far as the wall is concerned, no frames, ties, or braces. It is a pile of material in compression, like a stone wall. A rough structure of this sort could doubtless be made from dead tree trunks, but there is a major challenge in cutting down the large trees required for proper log construction, and in joining them securely at the corners, as both operations require tools of quite an advanced

The corners of this house of sawn logs are secured by means of dovetail joints. Though time-consuming to cut, this joint gives the tightest fit of all the ways in which logs can be connected at the corners, and no nails or timber pegs are needed. The gaps between the logs are chinked with clay.

Log Tombs

The main physical evidence for early log construction is from tombs, which often imitate the ordinary buildings of the same culture. A Phrygian tomb of about 696 BCE, under a large artificial mound at Gordion, Turkey, is of log construction surrounded by rubble, but many of the logs are partly sawn and those of the roof completely squared, so it is clear that it is a highly evolved example, and that there must have been much earlier, less-sophisticated log buildings. The tomb of a sixth-century BCE prince found at Hochdorf in Germany is very much like the tomb at Gordion, under a mound 200 ft (60 m) in diameter, and built of a double layer of halved logs with rubble between.

A skeleton lies inside the *c.* 696 BCE Phrygian tomb at Gordion. The log walls of the tomb can be seen in the background (the columns were erected by archaeologists to support the roof).

type. For this reason, log construction is not as early a form of timber wall as the palisade.

Log construction dates from the Iron Age, when it became widespread in central, northern, and northeastern Europe, as well as in the vicinity of the Black Sea. At a later date, the Roman architect Vitruvius wrote of the log houses of the Colchians in Pontus, and contrasted them with the Phrygians who lacked forests but still used logs to make roofs (both were in what is today Turkey, south of the Black Sea). This is interesting because the use of logs in a largely woodless country is a strong indication either that the inhabitants are immigrants, or that the country was once forested. In this case, the Phrygian territory had formerly been wooded, and there is specific evidence that Phrygian structures of seven or eight centuries before Vitruvius's time were built entirely of logs.

Later, the Slavs, who came into eastern Europe from the fifth century CE, are believed to have occupied semi-underground log cabins, partly buried in earth or sods. However, log construction had also developed in Scandinavia, and the Russian tradition of above-ground log buildings probably owes more to the Varangians, a people who entered Russia from Denmark and Sweden in the ninth century, than to the original Slavic house type.

Within these northern cultures there are some variations in how the logs are connected at the corners, which is the most important aspect of log construction, but it is not really possible to associate each technique with a particular race or date. The most obvious approach is to cut out

(or rebate) the top and bottom surfaces of the log, so that what remains is only half the original depth. Then a similarly rebated log can be placed across this, and so on. Another approach is to cut a semicircular channel from the top surface only, extending to half the depth. A transverse log will fit snugly into this channel, and it in turn will be cut to take the next. There are other forms (half dovetailed, fully dovetailed, or saddle notched), which cannot be described here. The logs are never entirely uniform, so there will always be spaces between them unless they are planed off carefully to give a smooth fit. Usually the joints are chinked (filled with mud or mortar), but in Russia at least they are sometimes caulked, as in shipbuilding, using old rags or rope impregnated with tar or resin.

Russia has a tradition of magnificent log-built churches with timber-shingled roofs, and often onion domes, as seen at Khizi Island and elsewhere. But it also has a tradition of ordinary log houses, which continued to be built into the early part of the twentieth century. Log buildings are found throughout Scandinavia, and in Estonia, Bavaria, Austria, Switzerland, the Czech Republic, Romania, and parts of China, Japan, and Mexico. In North America, despite being seen as the traditional rural form, log buildings were introduced only after more conventional timber frame construction, first by the Finnish settlers of New Sweden, Delaware Bay, in 1638, then by French settlers in Quebec before 1685, and then independently by German settlers in 1710. In Canada, from the late eighteenth until after the middle of the nineteenth century, the first house of a settler in Ontario was almost always of logs. The Russians, quite separately, brought log construction to Alaska, which was

The Church of the Transfiguration, of 1714, is on Kizhi Island, near St. Petersburg, Russia. It has a roof of twenty-two onion domes clad in aspen shingles. Today, the island has become a museum of Russian timber architecture.

St. Mary's Church, Auckland, New Zealand, was built between 1886 and 1898, using the vertical board-and-batten technique. At the time, stone was the preferred material for the building of churches, but timber was much more readily available.

Clapboards stained dark brown clad the House of the Seven Gables, in Salem, Massachusetts, which dates from around 1670 (with many later additions). This is an early, and very grand, version of a type of house that became common in the New England region, where timber was abundant.

at that time in their possession. The techniques of log construction in North America are as varied as in Europe.

Infill

The palisade is one form of earthfast construction, in which the timbers are supported by the fact that they are stuck into the ground. The use of posts with infill between them is another form. Although this creates something that could be loosely described as a frame, it is not a frame in the truest sense of the term—in that it is not self-contained, with diagonal timbers or braces to keep it in shape without external support. It has been and still is a widespread way of building, and it can be used with all sorts of infill materials such as adobe or brick, basketwork, wattle and daub, and *lehmwickel* (a German technique in which stakes of timber are wrapped in mud and straw). One of the earliest ways of filling in such a structure was with small poles or trunks placed horizontally between grooves in the posts.

Cladding

There are infinite variations in the ways in which a timber wall can be built and can be filled in, but another approach is to clad it—that is, to put a layer of material right over the surface. Historically, that has usually been done with one or another form of timber boarding. Here, there is a problem of terminology. In some countries, including Britain, the term weatherboard may be used for most of these cladding types; in the United States it tends to mean vertical board and batten; in Australia it means horizontal boards which overlap each other at the edge, giving a

sawtooth profile. In the United States this overlapping boarding is generally called clapboard, a term previously used in Britain for a board suitable for barrel-making, and deriving originally from the German *Klapholz* or *Klapperholz*, which means barrel staves. But the usage is not universal even in the United States, and in Virginia it is or was called weatherboard.

Overlapping boarding is almost certainly the oldest form of timber cladding, traceable to medieval Europe and probably very much older. It originally consisted of split boards of a very irregular character, but by the nineteenth century these had been almost entirely superseded by sawn boards of uniform size. These are normally thinner at the top edge, where they are nailed, and thicker at the bottom edge, where they are exposed to the weather, but two boards put together form a rectangular cross section, and this is how they were cut. That is, a rectangular section of timber (sometimes called a deal) was cut into two, four, six, or eight tapered boards.

It was possible to avoid the sawtooth profile by using boards with a section cut out of the top and end bottom edges, so that the projecting tongue of the upper board overlapped that of the lower one, leaving what was essentially a vertical surface, except that it was common to make the joint visible as a horizontal channel. This technique involved expensive carpenter's work in the shaping of the boards, and was therefore not common, but it became widely used in the nineteenth century when mechanically milled timber was available. It is generally known in Britain, rather oddly, as shiplap boarding, and in Queensland, Australia, a version of it is called chamferboard. Another system of cladding, particularly common in North America and New Zealand, is board and batten (or what might be simply called "weatherboard" in the United States), consisting of vertical boards, with small fillets of timber, or battens, covering the joints.

Shingles are another external facing, traditional in Europe but especially popular in the

The architects Charles and Henry Green made lavish use of timber in the Gamble House of 1909 in Pasadena, California. Teak, maple, cedar, redwood, and oak were used for the interior. The exterior is clad mainly in green-stained redwood shingles.

United States in the late nineteenth century, giving rise to the Shingle Style. In the colder areas of North America, these forms of timber cladding (boarding or shingles) are generally not attached directly to the building frame, but to a timber lining. This lining may be made of boards placed diagonally, or of a sheet material such as plywood, and faced with an insulating material such as building paper. Today, many timber-clad buildings, as they deteriorate or need repainting, are covered over in modern metal or plastic siding that imitates the appearance of boarding. This looks neater, but keeps in moisture and thus accelerates the decay and final destruction of the authentic building surface.

Stone by Stone

The Earth's molten interior erupts to the surface to form our basic building materials: the soils in which trees grow, mud from which bricks are made, and rocks. Rock is formed from minerals, of which quartz is the principal component. There are three types of rock. Igneous rocks, such as granite and basalt, have been forced up into or through the Earth's crust in a molten or plastic state. Sedimentary rocks, such as sandstone and limestone, have been formed by the compression and modification of deposited weathered rock debris or sediments, including the remains of plants and animals. Metamorphic rocks, such as marble and slate, are formed when sedimentary rocks become buried and subjected to forces of intense heat and pressure.

Irregular pieces of stone, in the form of rubble, are among the oldest construction materials known, and their use is discussed in the *Materials and Techniques* chapter. Some stones produce flattish pieces, which can be built into corbeled vaults or domes (or in fact pointed shapes rather than true domes). Corbeling is when one stone is projected out horizontally beyond the one below, and this is sometimes done from both sides of an opening or space until they meet at the center. Once metal tools were available, it was common to improve some of the natural stones by a certain

The Oratory of Gallerus, Dingle, Ireland, built in the early sixth or seventh century CE, uses dry stone corbel vaulting, and is said to be still weatherproof. Its only openings are a square-topped door on its west side and a single window on its east side.

amount of dressing or splitting, which means that few corbeled structures existing today are built of totally natural stonework.

Corbeled structures of this sort, usually circular, include the *nuraghi* (tower fortresses) in Sardinia, Italy, from about 1500 BCE onward; the so-called Treasury of Atreus (in fact, a tomb) at Mycenae, Greece, of about 1325 BCE; some Etruscan tombs in Italy, of about the seventh century BCE; Thracian tombs of about the third century BCE, in what is now Bulgaria; and the Oratory of Gallerus in Dingle, Ireland, which was built in about CE 600. The best known of these structures are the beehive-shaped *trulli* of southern Italy, which have prehistoric origins, and the *bories* of southern France, some of which are similar, while others are square in plan and finish in a cloister vault rather than a pointed dome. But our evidence of corbeled structures in brick and in large quarried blocks of stone is earlier than all of these, so it does not seem that corbeling was a fundamental way of using natural or partly dressed stones.

The *Trulli* of Puglia

The *trulli* (singular *trullo*) are traditional beehive-shaped stone buildings of Puglia, a region in southeastern Italy. They were built without mortar using limestone pieces gathered from the fields, and examples remain in a dozen or so towns in the region. Rising from vertical walls an average of 5 ft (1.5 m) in height, the roof of a *trullo* is a good example of corbeled construction, with each successive course narrowing to a single keystone. The dome is then faced with an outer layer of flat limestone slabs to shed water. *Trulli* are topped by a pinnacle, mostly of a unique design with symbolic meaning.

The conical roofs often have painted symbols such as crosses, stars, or crescents.

Although the dry stone construction technique dates back to prehistoric times, *trulli* building flourished in the fifteenth century, when there was a tax on buildings. A *trullo* could be partially demolished prior to an official inspection, so that it would appear to be unsuitable as a dwelling, and the tax would not have to be paid.

A row of *trulli* lines a street in Alberobello, Puglia, Italy. The town, a UNESCO World Heritage site, has more than a thousand of these buildings.

Rubble and Concrete Walling

Walls constructed from rubble stones merely fitted against each other are called random rubble, and those built from unhewn stones arranged into courses are called coursed rubble. Rubble is sometimes worked into roughly squared blocks which can be laid in completed courses, usually of varying heights. More frequently, however, squared rubble blocks are fitted together into discontinuous courses, also known as quasi-courses. The largest form of rubble, cyclopean masonry, is discussed in the *Materials and Techniques* chapter.

During the Roman period, builders used stone rubble as the coarse aggregate in mass concrete walls, and they developed a technique of bringing the larger and flatter surface blocks to the face. This technique, known as *opus incertum*, probably meant that the wall faces could be partly built ahead of the infill, and that less timber formwork was required to support the wall during construction. Next, the Romans developed a system of using long, square pyramidal blocks with the square face on the surface and the point extending into the wall to bond it into the rubble concrete. The square blocks on the surface were arranged on the diagonal and created a netlike appearance known as *opus reticulatum*. These pyramidal units were sometimes of tufa stone

(a type of igneous rock), but later more commonly of baked terracotta. *Opus reticulatum* gave way in turn to a system of facing the wall in flat bricks, called *opus testaceum*. At later dates, the French and Italians built walls which are essentially similar to their Roman predecessors, called *bocage* or *muraglia di getto* respectively, by loosely throwing rubble between boards and using mortar to bond the stones together.

Quarrying and Transport

Most of the oldest recognizable stone structures are megalithic, meaning made of very large stones, and the task of splitting these stones from the rock, before the development of iron tools, must have been incredibly difficult. So too must have been transporting them from the quarry and raising them into place in the building. Splitting was done by inserting wedges into a sawn groove, cut with a mason's pick, or into a series of holes laboriously drilled by striking and turning a bronze or iron chisel. The sawing of all but the softest stones was done with an untoothed metal

Corbeling was used to construct the Treasury of Atreus, a tomb at Mycenae, Greece, dating from c 1300 BCE. It measures 48 ft (14.5 m) in diameter, and is 44 ft (13.5 m) high.

117

A contemporary engraving shows the re-erection in 1586 of a 330-ton, 83-ft (25-m) high obelisk from Heliopolis, Egypt, that now stands in front of St. Peter's Basilica in Rome.

bar, which was continuously fed with grit and water, but in the Assyrian Empire (*c.* 900–700 BCE), where a soft stone known as Mosul marble was available, relief sculptures show masons with toothed iron saws, actual examples of which have been excavated at ancient Nimrud (Calah), in modern Iraq.

Technical advances in quarrying have been gradual, and many procedures used today are centuries old. Blasting is generally impracticable because it fractures the stone being extracted, but by the nineteenth century a series of advances, including improved saw blades, the application of steam power, and the pneumatic drill, reduced some of the labor involved in quarrying.

The Neolithic builders, and even the ancient Egyptians, seem to have shifted their enormous blocks without mechanical aids beyond ropes and levers. The classical and Hellenistic Greeks added the use of pulleys and shear legs, and the Romans used the crab winch. The Greeks sometimes transported blocks by road on wagons, or avoided the problem of broken axles by pulling a stone drum directly overland like a roller, or building wheels around a rectangular block so that it could be rolled. After the Roman era, there were no real technological advances, even in the Renaissance, but for very large blocks, where it was hard to bring enough force to

bear, a number of ropes or chains could be connected to separate capstans, each with its own crew of men. This was essentially how Domenico Fontana moved an Egyptian obelisk in 1586 from the site of the Circus Maximus in Rome (where it had been placed in the first century CE) and re-erected it in the forecourt of St. Peter's Basilica, where it stands today.

Shaping the Stones

The stonemason shapes rough pieces of rock into accurate geometrical shapes, mostly simple, but some of considerable complexity, and then arranges the resulting stones, often held together with mortar, into structures, buildings, and sculptures. Today, many of the traditional techniques handed down over millennia are still in use. Sawyers cut these rough blocks into slabs and billets of required size; banker masons carve stones into the required geometrical shapes in the workshop; stone carvers cross the blurred line between art and craft and use their artistic ability to carve intricate patterns representing foliage, figures, animals, or abstract designs into the stone; fixer masons specialize in placing stones onto buildings using all means of mechanical aids; and lastly, monumental masons carve memorials, gravestones, and inscriptions.

Ashlar is a term sometimes used for any facing stone. However, when applied to stonemasonry in formal architecture it is defined as stone with carefully worked beds, finely jointed (in most cases, no more than 3/16 in, or 5 mm, wide) and set in horizontal courses, and is described according to the surface finishes. In elevation, the stone should ideally be perfectly rectangular and the face must be bounded by neat, well-chiselled margins worked straight and square to the beds. Common ashlar finishes include plain or rubbed, boasted, punched, rock-faced, tooled or battered, rusticated, reticulated, and vermiculated.

The stones within each ashlar course are of the same height, although successive courses may be of differing heights. Course heights of ashlar have traditionally varied between 6 in and 18 in (15 cm and 45 cm), with blocks usually three to five times as long as they are high. However, modern equipment and machinery has enabled the used of larger stones.

Stereotomy

Stereotomy is the science and art of cutting solid blocks of stone into precise shapes for the construction of complicated geometrical forms, such as the treads of spiral staircases, wedge-shaped blocks (voussoirs) to form the curved parts of an arch or vault, corners of buildings (quoins), corbels, string courses, projecting cornices, and parapet walls. Frequently, these special-purpose blocks will have a different surface finish from the ashlar blocks forming the main body of the walls.

In the classical world, the finest efforts of the stonemason are exhibited in the *entasis*, or subtle profile of the Greek column, particularly in the Doric order. Like most columns, it tapers from the base to a narrower diameter at the top. But the taper is not uniform: at the bottom it is very slight—almost vertical—but it steadily increases. To look at the same thing another way, the profile of the column is a convex curve, but the diameter is at no point larger than that of the base. That is, it is not cigar-shaped.

To establish this profile the correct diameter was worked out and marked on the top and bottom of each drum or section of the column. But this was only the beginning of the stonemason's task, because the column is faced with twenty grooves or flutes with sharp arrises between then, which would easily be damaged if they were formed before the column was in place. So each drum was formed into a cylinder, then cut more exactly into a dodecagon, or twenty-sided polygon. Then it was cut down to the precise level at which the arrises would lie, and finally the flutes were hollowed out in between. And all of this work had to take account of the subtlety of the *entasis*.

During the medieval period, stereotomy was applied especially to spiral staircases, and it continued into the Renaissance, particularly in the work of the French architect Philibert de l'Orme, who came from a family of stonemasons and was himself an expert stereotomist. His finest work is the *jubé* or screen of the Church of St-Étienne-du-Mont in Paris, which dates from approximately 1545–1550. It is like a bridge across the church, reached by spiral stairs at either end, and flanked by perforated stone balustrades, all exquisitely carved.

A stonemason carefully shapes a voussoir of an arch. Despite the decline in the use of stone as a building material in the twentieth century, many of the traditional techniques, from quarrying to final placement and carving, are still practiced.

Intricate stereotomy characterizes the elaborate *jubé* or screen of the Church of St-Étienne-du-Mont in Paris (above). The screen dates from the mid-sixteenth century.

With their precise fluting and subtle entasis, the Doric columns of the Parthenon (447–432 BCE) in Athens, Greece (left), display the highly refined art of the Greek stonemasons.

Machu Picchu
Cuzco, Peru

To grow crops, and to halt erosion, the people of Machu Picchu terraced the steep terrain and watered their plants using an irrigation system. Some terraces were still being used by local people when Hiram Bingham reached the site in 1911.

Machu Picchu stands on an almost inaccessible ridge in the Peruvian Andes at a height of about 7,700 ft (2,350 m), some 50 miles (80 km) northwest of the old Inca capital, Cuzco. Built in the fifteenth century by the Incas, the settlement was abandoned perhaps a century later, and lay unknown to outsiders and overgrown by vegetation until its discovery in 1911 by Hiram Bingham, a Yale University archaeologist. The site's combination of spectacular mountain scenery and beautifully preserved architecture, with its intricate, close-fitting stonework, has made it one of the most popular tourist attractions in South America: the site receives more than 400,000 visitors a year. In 1983, Machu Picchu was added to the UNESCO World Heritage list.

Urban Planning and Civil Engineering

Rather than being a conventional town, Machu Picchu is generally believed to have been a royal estate and religious retreat, built at the behest of the Inca ruler Pachacuti Inca Yupanqui (reigned c. 1438–1471). The site, covering about 5 acres (2 ha), may have accommodated up to 1,000 people. The urban area contained a royal palace, various temples and other religious buildings, many houses, storehouses, baths, open squares, and a prison. Connected to one of the temples, and evidence of the religious nature of Machu

Picchu, is an astronomical clock (intihuatana), which consists of a large single stone column mounted on another single piece of stone the size of a small automobile. It has been shown to be a precise indicator of the date of the equinoxes and other significant celestial events.

The settlement's agricultural area consisted of stepped terraces, formed by stone retaining walls, which also stabilized the slopes and controlled erosion. An ingenious irrigation system of stone channels, some of which still function today, watered the maize and other crops. A 2,500-ft (760-m) long stone channel carried water from a spring through the agricultural terraces and into the town, where the water fed a series of sixteen fountains. Numerous stairways, some consisting of as many as ten steps carved from single blocks of stone, connect the terraces and buildings.

Stonemasonry Techniques

The Incas were masters of dry stone construction, and they employed a variety of stonemasonry techniques at Machu Picchu. Many of the agricultural terraces and the walls of the less important buildings were constructed from roughly shaped blocks in uncoursed rubble, or in rubble with quasi-courses ranging from a few inches (6–8 cm) to more than 18 in (45 cm) in height. More important buildings, such as the Temple of the Sun and the adjacent Royal Tomb, have perfectly worked ashlar blocks in regular courses, achieving a high architectural quality. The Incas also employed a technique of stonemasonry using huge blocks of stone, This was similar to the cyclopean walls of the Bronze Age Mediterranean. Blocks weighing fifty tons and more were shaped and precisely fitted together, with joints so fine that even a knife blade cannot be pushed between them. Some are polygonal in shape, with as many as thirty points or corners, and worked so that all angles fitted precisely with neighboring stones. The faces of the stones were given a smooth finish. The Temple of the Three Windows shows an interesting mixture of stonemasonry types. It has uncoursed, polygonally jointed, cyclopean blocks rising from the ground, topped by much smaller stones in lesser quality quasi-coursed, squared rubble.

Typical buildings have walls that are wider at their bases than at their tops, with trapezoidal-shaped openings for the doors and windows.

Royal astronomers recorded the movements of the sun at a circular tower known as the Temple of the Sun. A line inscribed in the rock points through a window to the rising sun on the June solstice. The stonework here is particularly fine, an indication of the temple's importance.

The mountain of Huayna Picchu towers over Machu Picchu (above). Although up to 1,000 people may have lived here on occasion, experts now believe that there were probably only about 300 permanent residents. The population swelled when the Inca ruler visited this royal estate and religious site.

The majority of walls and buildings at Machu Picchu are built using large polygonal blocks of granite (left). Masons shaped and fitted these together with great precision without the use of mortar.

These features, and the mortar-free construction, have given the buildings remarkable resistance to earthquake damage over the centuries.

Building Machu Picchu

The Incas cut their building blocks from the granite of the ridge on which the settlement stands. The remains of a quarry on the site are visible, as are partly shaped huge stones that were being readied for installation in the building known as the Principal Temple. No one knows what tools the Incas used to cut or work stone, but they had no knowledge of iron.

Rocks in the quarry with drill holes in them indicate how the Incas may have quarried the hard, unyielding granite. The technique, common to many cultures, involves first drilling holes in the bedrock and driving timber wedges into the holes. When the wedges are dampened, they expand, splitting the stone. Stone split in this manner is rough. To create a smooth finish, the Inca masons may have rubbed the blocks with sand.

Exactly how the Incas moved and placed the enormous blocks is not known for sure. They did not use the wheel in any practical manner, and had no beasts of burden apart from the llama. However, temporary sloping ramps can still be seen at Machu Picchu in uncompleted work, which suggests the builders used teams of laborers to push large stones up onto the walls. Each stone would then be levered into position. Some experts speculate a labor force of 5,000

would have been required to construct Machu Picchu. To feed and house this number of people in an isolated location would have presented formidable logistical challenges.

The Inca Empire was conquered by the Spanish in 1532, but Machu Picchu may have been abandoned before then. This was perhaps because it was too costly to maintain as a result of huge population losses in the 1520s due to smallpox, introduced by the Spanish and to which the Incas had no natural immunity. Whatever the reason, the existence of the site appears to have been quickly forgotten, and the conquistadores, who looted other Inca cities, never discovered Machu Picchu, allowing the preservation of the site and its highly crafted stonework.

Defensive Walls

A defensive wall is a fortified architectural element most commonly associated with the medieval castle. Walls of this type are planned and built primarily to protect the inhabitants of a settlement. The walls normally enclosed the settlement and therefore became the physical definition of its boundaries. The basic elements of a defensive wall, or fortification, are the wall enclosure, gate, and tower. Normally, the top of the walls was accessible to defenders. Artillery and other weapons could be launched at an invading army from there. In many cases, these walls linked towers and provided easy maneuverability from one tower to another. This kind of defensive wall is referred to as a screen or curtain wall.

Ancient Fortifications

Both literary and archaeological evidence show that defensive walls were commonly constructed during ancient times. The easiest walls to build were earthen embankments, timber forms, and those of adobe (mud brick). Walls of stone, however, became common among the advanced civilizations of the ancient Mediterranean. By about 7500 BCE, the settlement of Jericho was fortified by a stone wall and gate with a single round tower. In ancient Greece, the Mycenaeans incorporated defensive walls in the construction of their massive citadels at Mycenae and Tiryns. At Mycenae, the Lion Gate formed the main entrance to the fortifications, and at Tiryns a postern was incorporated into the western wall (opposite the entrance side). A postern is a small gate in a defensive wall, usually hidden and at the back of the complex, which allows for ease of escape during a siege.

Later, during the Greek Hellenistic age, defensive walls served to both protect and aesthetically enhance Greek city-states. The Acropolis of Athens was not only protected by its location on a hilltop, but also by its defensive walls. The only point of access to this sanctuary of Greek temples, including the Parthenon, was through a special gatehouse, the Propylaea.

The Roman Model

The Romans built defensive walls, towers, gates, and all forms of defensive outwork for their cities across the Mediterranean and western Europe. After the decline of the Roman Empire in the fourth and fifth centuries, many cities

The Aurelian Walls surrounding Rome, built in the third century CE of concrete faced with brick, were originally 13 ft (4 m) thick and 24 ft (7.2 m) high. Added to over the centuries, they remained a significant defensive barrier until the nineteenth century.

held on to their Roman layouts and support systems. They relied heavily on Roman-built fortifications for protection against invasion. During the early medieval period, and particularly under the reign of the Frankish monarch, Charlemagne (768–814), western Europe became the focal point of civic restoration. Towns in Spain, Germany, and France rebuilt

Homer and the Walls of Troy

One of the most famous fortified settlements of the ancient world is Troy in present-day Turkey. The Greek poet Homer tells us that this city of 50,000 was enclosed by mighty defensive walls, which included towers and a gate. The city, its occupants believed, was impenetrable. Homer tells us that the only way for the invading Greeks to breach the walls was to trick the Trojans into bringing a wooden horse (with Greek soldiers hiding inside) through the city gate. While Homer's account may not be entirely accurate, archaeological excavations have proven the existence of massive defensive walls, gates, and towers at Troy, the earliest of which date to 3000–2000 BCE.

This part of the walls of Troy dates from the period known as Troy VI (1800–1300 BCE). The walls were originally about 15 ft (4.5 m) thick at the base and more than 17 ft (5 m) high.

Medieval Defensive Walls

Roman defensive walls and transformed themselves into strongholds. The urbanization of Europe had begun, with the city and its defensive walls as the center of civilization.

Barcelona in Spain, was one city to benefit from Roman fortification and European growth. During the medieval period, it developed into an important center of trade. It retained its Roman street grid, with main thoroughfares connecting the gates of the city walls to the central plaza. If a hostile army laid siege to the city, the gates could be shut, preventing invasion.

Protection, however, was not the sole function of a medieval city's gate. In fact, the gate served a pivotal role in the local economy. During peacetime a great deal of wealth could be derived by the town, lord, or the church through the gate tolls charged to enter the city. Additionally, merchants would often set up shops just outside the city gates, the prime location for the exchange of goods and services. In some European cities, beyond the main gate was a secondary gatehouse known as a barbican. Normally, this standalone outwork was specifically designed to protect the main gate of a defensive wall.

It was during the height of the Middle Ages that defensive walls became standardized, taking on the Gothic-inspired forms now familiar to us from medieval castles. One such feature is the battlement, or parapet. At its top are alternating indentations called embrasures, from which archers could fire arrows, and raised portions called merlins, which protected the archers. This feature is more commonly referred to as crenellation. In the eighteenth and nineteenth centuries, crenellation came to be favored for its aesthetic qualities, and can be seen in many neo-Gothic buildings of this time. Arrow loops, or arrow slits, cut into the merlins, became common features. These slits allowed archers to fire their arrows while fully protected by the merlin. Closely related to the battlement is machicolation: a cantilevered gallery built on the outside of the defensive wall, with openings in the floor through which projectiles or boiling liquids could be dropped.

The development of the cannon, especially after the fifteenth century, required additions and improvements to the defensive wall, both

With its moat, towers, and thick, crenellated walls, Bodiam Castle, England, presents a formidable appearance. Originally built as a manor house, it was fortified in the fourteenth century because of the threat of French invasion.

to maximize use of the defenders' cannons and to protect against the attackers' missiles. A common addition was a half-circular tower, called a half-moon, as well as low bastions (also known as salients). An outward slope at the base of the wall, called a *glacis*, had previously been found effective in preventing scaling ladders from being placed and battering rams and siege engines brought to its base. Now this slope was sometimes continued right up to the battlements, to help deflect cannon balls.

Great Wall of China

The Great Wall of China, considered by many to be the greatest of all defensive walls, is one of the most remarkable architectural achievements in the world. This massive defensive system is universally admired as a statement of engineering genius.

There are several key features which make the Great Wall a significant example of fortification. First, it does not fully enclose a settlement, city, or territory. In fact, it is a series of walls interconnected by the natural terrain of northern China. It lies well outside of populated centers, although permanent colonies were eventually placed along its path to help keep the wall fully secured. Second, it is on a scale that is simply astonishing: the wall as we know it today stretches some 2,000 miles (3,200 km) across a rugged and mountainous landscape. Third, the wall showcases the technological capabilities, both in design and engineering, of early China as equal to that of its contemporary civilization, Rome.

Unlike the Romans, however, China's rulers did not build structures for the enjoyment or service of the people. There were no public theaters, baths, or forums in China. Thus, the Great Wall is an unprecedented statement of utilitarian public architecture in China.

The Qin Wall

The wall did not always resemble its present form. The first wall was constructed under the First Emperor of the Qin Dynasty, during the third century BCE. He had conquered rival territories in China, finally uniting all of them under his authority around 220 BCE. In order to protect his newly unified nation, he ordered that a defensive wall be constructed to protect it from invaders from the north. Unfortunately, we know little about this first wall because almost no evidence exists to reveal either its location or composition. Based on what is known, including contemporary construction techniques, we can

make educated guesses as to how the first wall was built. Without a doubt, the concept would have been simple: a series of earthen embankments and stone battlements. The earliest sections would most certainly have been of earthen embankments. As the wall progressed, builders could have used large stones for the foundations, with earth and rubble as infill. Smaller and more precisely cut stone would have been used to face the wall, again with earth and rubble as infill. This layering of materials would have given the wall great strength.

The Ming Wall

The Great Wall as we know it today is a series of walls, towers, and gates which extends across northern China, from the desert in Gansu Province to the Yellow Sea. It was constructed during much of the Ming Dynasty (CE 1368–1644) by hundreds of thousands of laborers and soldiers, an unknown number of whom died

Inside the Great Wall

The Great Wall of the Ming Dynasty was built of brick and stone, with a core of rubble and earth, and incorporated a range of defensive features, most obviously merlins and embrasures, and towers of various types.

Guardhouse This two-story structure serves as a dormitory for troops and a storehouse for weapons and food.

Inner side A low wall prevents troops and horses from falling.

Exterior layer The exterior is clad in brick or stone.

Base At its base, the wall is about 25 ft (8 ft) thick.

Roadway The paved surface on top of the wall forms a roadway, aiding communication.

Outer side Merlins and embrasures protect the defenders from attack and allow them to return fire.

Core The core of the wall is formed of compacted rubble and earth.

Inner layer Stone slabs form a layer between the infill and the facing.

from starvation, disease, and exhaustion in the process. Massive stone blocks were used for the foundations of the wall. Next, the builders would have faced the earthen and rubble infill with cut stone, then formed the top of the wall with both stone and brick. The brick would have been fired at the site in specially built kilns. The brick path on top of the wall created a roadway by which a communication and trade route was established through northern China. Like the gatehouses of medieval western European cities—in which merchants set up shop—this roadway had an important economic role beyond its defensive purpose, enhancing China's prominence in the hostile northern mountain regions of Asia.

The form of the Great Wall is what is known as battered. Its outer face is sloped inward as it rises, meaning that the wall is wider at its base than at its top, similar in shape to a trapezoid and making it extremely stable. In a typical section, the Great Wall stands 20–30 ft (6–9 m) high, 25 ft (8 m) wide at the base, and 15 ft (4.5 m) wide at the top. The top of the wall, much like a medieval European castle battlement, allowed for the easy maneuverability of defensive forces. The wall is crenellated, having at its top both embrasures and merlins. These features served to protect defensive troops while allowing them the advantage of firing down upon an invading army.

The wall had some 25,000 towers, which served as gates, guardhouses, watchtowers,

temples, and shrines. A beacon tower stood about every 11 miles (18 km), so that a fire or smoke signal could be set as a warning to troops on nearby towers in the event of an attack.

A Barrier Built to Last

The wall built during the Ming Dynasty was much stronger and more elaborate than the Qin wall. Similarly to the earlier one, however, the Ming wall used earth as the basis for its stability. The thick layers of brick and stone which covered the interior composition of earth, stone, and rubble gave the wall unprecedented strength. This layering of strong and durable materials is one reason the wall survives to this day. As invading armies continued to raid the northern boundaries of China, the Ming rulers devoted considerable resources to repairing and reinforcing the wall, with the sections nearest the capital, Beijing, being made exceptionally strong.

The irony of the Great Wall is that despite its size and the resources expended on its upkeep and defense, it ultimately failed to stop northern invaders from entering China. The end of the Ming Dynasty came in 1644, when the Manchu not only crossed the Great Wall from their homeland in Manchuria, but also entered Beijing and established the Qing Dynasty. Today, the wall is in a varied state of restoration and neglect, but it has always remained a source of great pride for the Chinese people.

Wherever they could, the builders of the Great Wall took advantage of the natural terrain, following the ridges across mountains, for example. The stretch of the wall (above) is near Badaling, north of Beijing.

Troops, weapons, and even horses could move with ease along the broad paved roadway on top of the wall (above), making it possible to quickly reinforce an area under threat of enemy attack.

Brick by Brick

The earliest bricks are from the Middle East—a region lacking in trees or plentiful stone suitable for building—and date from 7000–8000 BCE. Adobe, or sun-dried brick, a simple mixture of clay and water, developed first. Baked bricks probably arose when adobe buildings were found to harden when accidental fires caused any additional support structure to burn down, leaving exterior walls and chimneys in a superior state of durability. Similar developments in brick occurred in China where baked brick had appeared by the sixteenth century BCE.

Before the nineteenth century, wherever baked bricks were used, they were made as close as possible to the place of construction, as the transportation of bricks was expensive and slow. This limited their use and the spread of the technology. Brick nonetheless became an important building material in the ancient civilizations of Babylon and Egypt, and spread gradually out from the Middle East. However, it was in Rome that brick technology achieved a new level of sophistication.

The Impact of Rome

A popular perception of ancient Rome is that stone was its preeminent building material. The Emperor Augustus (reigned 27 BCE–14 CE) famously claimed to have transformed Rome from a city of brick to one of marble, and it is true that many impressive stone monuments were indeed built during his reign. However, despite this, brick was, in fact, very important. Excavations at Ostia and Pompeii show that it was the main material for the houses, shops, and taverns of the merchant and working classes. These structures clearly

Henry VIII's Hampton Court Palace (c. 1520), on the north bank of the River Thames, near London, made lavish use of red brick (right). During the Tudor period, brick emerged in England as a luxury building material to rival stone in prestige buildings.

illustrate the widespread use of brick in everyday building at this time.

The Romans developed a technique of facing both sides of a wall with brick, and filling the center with another material—earth, rubble, or, most commonly, concrete. This made higher and thicker walls possible. During the reign of the Emperor Tiberius (CE 14–37), the new method of construction called *opus testaceum*, saw square bricks cut into triangles, with their points into the concrete so that the two faces of a wall were bonded together, making for a stronger wall. The facing of walls with these specially designed triangular bricks allowed the development of different decorative methods of bricklaying and the incorporation of additional brick ornament.

The Romans gave their name to a scale of brick, still called the roman, longer and narrower than most subsequent bricks. This type of brick would be revived in the late nineteenth century by a number of key architects, including Frank Lloyd Wright and Stanford White.

The Romans spread brickmaking and brick construction technology throughout their European empire and into northern Europe and Britain. Although brickmaking fell from favor after the fall of Rome, it slowly reestablished itself, emerging as an important force in Europe

during the medieval period. The new Gothic style of building in brick appearing across northern Europe, from the Low Countries to Russia, again brought with it new decorative methods, which responded to the more expressive needs of Gothic churches and cathedrals. The revival of English brickmaking began in the first half of the sixteenth century under Henry VIII. Large parts of Hampton Court Palace, built around 1520, near London, were constructed in brick, and the craft flourished under the reign of Henry's daughter, Elizabeth I (1558–1603).

The Industrial Revolution

Over the centuries, bricks have gone in and out of fashion among architects. The Renaissance and Baroque periods saw the use of exposed

The Casa Diana (House of Diana) in Ostia, Italy, was a brick apartment building *(insula)* of three or four floors, with its rooms arranged around an inner courtyard. Shops took up the ground floor. It dates from the mid-second century CE, when this port city had a population of more than 50,000.

Brick Bonds

The patterning of a brick wall is determined by the bond, the way in which each line or course of bricks overlaps. A number of different bonds have developed, including English, Flemish, basket, garden, and herringbone. In the nineteenth century, a preference developed for the use of the English bond for industrial buildings and the Flemish for domestic work. The English bond (below) consists of a course of stretchers (bricks laid parallel to the face of the wall) followed by a course of headers (bricks laid with their short ends showing). The Flemish bond (above) has alternating headers and stretchers within each course, with each header centered over the stretcher below it. Today, the most commonly used bond is the stretcher, which shows only the long side of the brick and in which each new brick is placed at the midway point of the brick on the course below.

Flemish bond (top) and English bond (below) were the two most popular brick bonds until the twentieth century, when they were eclipsed by the stretcher bond, which can be laid more rapidly, reducing labor costs.

brick walls fall from fashion. Roman and Greek revival styles of the eighteenth and early nineteenth centuries largely rejected exposed brick, although some Georgian architects used red brick to considerable effect on domestic projects. But the Industrial Revolution of the nineteenth century saw bricks become more widely available and cheaper to transport, and by the middle of the nineteenth century bricks had regained popularity in the Gothic Revival style. Also increasing the attraction of brick for architects was the variety of finishes and the speed with which a brick building could be built, which suited the fast-paced development of the mid-nineteenth century.

Before the nineteenth century, bricks had been made by hand, by pressing clay into wooden or metal molds, before they were fired. Hand-molding produced bricks with variations in size and shape. However, new machine manufacturing methods both made consistency more readily achievable and improved economies of scale and rapidity of production. The development of extruded bricks—in which wet clay containing up to twenty-five percent water is extruded through a die and cut by wire to the desired length—was significant. This allowed for the first hollow extruded brick to be developed in France in 1843 and in England in 1844. This, and the later development of a method to make bricks with a series of round holes through the center, further reduced cost, improved thermal qualities, and made lighter, more easily handled bricks.

Kiln Technology

The simplest kind of kiln is a clamp, a pile of bricks in the middle of which a fire is set. Updraft and downdraft kilns consist of two chambers, a lower one containing a heat source, and one above it containing the bricks to be fired. In an updraft kiln, the heat from the lower chamber rises directly into the upper chamber, baking the bricks. But this produced overburnt bricks, or clinkers, close to the heat, and underburnt ones, or doughboys, further away. A downdraft kiln has an elongated shape, with the fire at one end and the chimney at the other. Instead of rising directly upward, the heat passes around the bricks and then downward off the kiln wall. This gives a more even heat, and improves brick quality.

In these kilns, the firing process ends when the heat source is extinguished. In 1857, the Austrian F. E. Hoffmann invented the continuous brick kiln, consisting of an arched tunnel surrounding a central chimney, in which the heat moved past chambers of bricks, firing each chamber one at a time, without the need for the fire ever to be extinguished. In 1876, an English engineer developed the Bull's Trench Kiln—in which the fire moved along a trench recessed in the ground—which combined a low capital investment with high capacity. These kilns are still widely used in India, Pakistan, Bangladesh, and Myanmar. In 1927, the German Alois Habla invented the Habla kiln, a highly automated, labor-saving tunnel kiln which proved very popular in Germany, the United States, and England in the prewar period.

Throughout this time of technological change, molding bricks by hand continued, as the process was useful in order to manufacture bricks with unique shapes or to create decorated bricks.

The best-known building designed by Willem Dudok in Hilversum in the Netherlands, and one of the most influential of all twentieth-century brick buildings, is Hilversum Town Hall, completed in 1934. In 1915, Dudok became the municipal architect for the town, and designed a large number of buildings there.

Bricks in Modern Architecture

Modernism on the whole tended to reject the use of brick on the grounds that it was a traditional building material. Modernist architects instead favored a combination of steel, concrete, and glass. Despite this, most of the twentieth century's leading Modernist architects do have brick buildings to their credit, including, in Germany, Walter Gropius and Adolf Meyer's Fagus Factory of 1913 and Mies van der Rohe's monument to Karl Liebknecht and Rosa Luxemburg of 1926, and, in France, Le Corbusier's Maisons Jaoul of 1956. The US architect Frank Lloyd Wright was unusual for his continuing commitment to brick; he was also influential in the reintroduction of the roman brick. Among his significant brick buildings are the Larkin Building, Buffalo, New York State, of 1904, the Robie House, Chicago, of 1910, and the Imperial Hotel, Tokyo, Japan, of 1920. Influenced by Wright's work, the Dutch architect Willem Dudok used brick with dramatic asymmetrical massing of geometrical forms in such influential buildings as the Hilversum Town Hall of 1934 and the Utrecht Municipal Theater of 1937, both in the Netherlands.

In Scandinavia, the Finnish architect Alvar Aalto was important in the reintroduction of brick to modern architecture. Aalto drew on the historical traditions of the brick architecture of northern Europe and Scandinavia to create a Modernism with regional leanings, as opposed to the International style, during the 1930s.

With further development in cavity walls and brick veneer technologies, architects in the postwar period were able to again innovate in brick. In the United States, Louis Kahn brought new attention to the material in works such as the Richards Medical Research Building, Philadelphia, Pennsylvania, of 1961, and the Exeter Library, Exeter, New Hampshire, of 1972. He was aided by new technologies that improved the load-bearing properties of the brick wall.

The Postmodern generation of architects used brick ironically or to tell or build jokes about bricks. This is perhaps most clearly articulated in the works of SITE's Peeling Project Showroom of 1971 for the BEST Products Company in Richmond, Virginia, which features a wall of brick veneer that appears to be peeling away from the rest of the building. Other architects, such as Philip Johnson, Robert Venturi, Mario Botta, and Aldo Rossi, used bricks in a way that heavily referenced historical forms—some of which, like the Art Deco style skyscrapers of the 1920s and 1930s, had always sat outside the mainstream of twentieth-century Modernism, but which had made effective decorative use of brick.

Alongside architectural decorations made in clay, these decorated bricks were in great demand by nineteenth-century architects and builders. In London, major landmark buildings, such as the Victoria and Albert Museum of 1866 and onward, and the Royal Albert Hall of 1871, (which featured terracotta ornament on an allegorical theme), ensured that brick, and its close relative, terracotta ornament, became immensely popular. Like the Romans before them, the British spread the use of bricks throughout their empire, and the major colonial cities of South Africa, Australia, and New Zealand used the material to great effect.

The nineteenth century also witnessed the introduction of the cavity brick wall—in which two layers of brick are separated by a void—to reduce the passage of moisture from the exterior to the interior. Today, the cavity is often filled with insulating material. In the twentieth century, as labor and materials costs rose, brick veneer construction became very popular. A single outer layer of brick is tied to a timber or metal frame, giving the external appearance of a full-brick building, but at much less cost.

In US cities of the late nineteenth century, the escalating cost of land saw the development of high-rise structures. The use of brick in such buildings presented technical problems. To bear the load of high-rise buildings, brick walls had to be of a great size, as illustrated in the 16-story Monadnock Building, built in Chicago in 1891. The walls were 6-ft (1.8-m) thick at their base, significantly reducing the percentage of floor area available for rent. In the early twentieth century, brick began to wane in popularity. This was the result of more than just technical problems; the dominant architectural philosophy, Modernism, preferred other materials.

The Royal Albert Hall, London, was built from 1867 to 1871 to a design by Colonel Henry Scott and Captain Francis Fowke. Oval in shape, the hall has a façade of red brick, which is encircled by a terracotta frieze depicting "The Triumph of Arts and Sciences."

Isfahan

Iran

Perhaps nowhere else in the world is the decorative and structural potential of brick architecture as clearly articulated as it is at Isfahan, also called Esfahan, Iran's third-largest city. Here, Middle Eastern brickwork achieved a high point, in part because of the scale of the building project—almost all of which is achieved through the engineering of brick—and also because the use of brick, in combination with tiles, produced patterns of great beauty.

Located 210 miles (340 km) south of Tehran on important overland trade routes, Isfahan grew in size and wealth under the Seljuks during the eleventh and twelfth centuries. However, the city's golden age occurred under the Safavid dynasty, from 1598 to 1722, when it was the capital of the Persian Empire. Most of its key buildings were commissioned by the Safavid ruler Shah 'Abbas I (reigned 1571–1629), who, once he had secured his empire's borders, turned his attention to the development of the arts. 'Abbas I significantly rebuilt the city as a showpiece for his empire. Without access to building stone or plentiful supplies of timber, the royal architects turned to brick as the main building material.

'Abbas I ordered a brick vault built to enclose the Bazaar Qaisarieh, which runs from the Maidan to the Masjid-i-Jamis in the old part of Isfahan. The bazaar is still used for its original purpose, the buying and selling of all manner of goods.

The Maidan, Center of an Empire

'Abbas created a new town center to the south of Isfahan's old city. The heart of this new city— and the symbolic heart of the Safavid empire— was the Maidan, or Naghsh-e Jahan Square, which measures 1,640 x 520 ft (500 x 160 m), and is surrounded on all sides by two-story walls of brick featuring arcades set with shops. The Maidan impressed many visiting foreigners in the seventeenth century both for its size and homogeneity, which was brought about by the even tones and clear rhythms of the brickwork. Military displays, polo matches, and festivals took place in the center of the square, which was lit at night by thousands of earthenware lamps.

A major building is located on each side of the Maidan: the Bazaar Qaisarieh, the Ali Qapu Palace, the Masjid-i-Shah, and the Mosque of

Sheikh Lotfollah. On the northern side is the entrance to the Bazaar Qaisarieh (Great Bazaar), consisting of a high *iwan* (a vaulted doorway opening onto a courtyard) flanked by two stories of vaulted galleries. The covered streets of the bazaar wind for 1¼ miles (2 km) back to the old city's Masjid-i-Jamis, or Friday Mosque. Although built in 771, the mosque contains many additions from later periods, the most notable being the eleventh-century North Dome Chamber, a masterpiece of Persian brickwork.

On the Maidan's western side is the Ali Qapu Palace. The name means "Magnificent Gate," a reference to its role as the first and most visible building of the palace precinct that lies behind. Unlike the other major buildings on the square, it lacks a large public entrance in its lower brick façade. However, it makes up for its rather restrained ground-level structure with a towering, open first-floor space, the ceiling of which is supported by enormous timber columns cut from single chenar trees.

The Maidan's Mosques

Isfahan's two major mosques, the Masjid-i-Shah (Imperial Mosque, now called Imam Mosque) and the smaller Mosque of Sheikh Lotfollah, are the jewels in the city's crown. The grand Masjid-i-Shah, located on the square's western side, was begun in 1611, but was not completed until 1638. More than 18 million bricks are estimated to have been used in its construction and the portal minarets reach a height of 158 ft (48 m) with the central dome reaching 170 ft (52 m).

The foreground of this aerial view of the Maidan is dominated by the Masjid-i-Shah, which was built out of alignment with the square so that it faces Mecca. About midway along the Maidan's right-hand side is the Mosque of Sheikh Lotfollah; the Ali Qapu Palace stands directly opposite.

The Masjid-i-Shah is a considerable achievement in seventeenth-century brick engineering. Nevertheless, the bricks themselves are completely overshadowed by the visual contribution made by the 472,000 brightly colored glazed tiles that cover the mosque, inside and out.

Facing the palace complex is the Mosque of Sheikh Lotfollah. Constructed between 1602 and 1619 to the designs of the architect Muhammad Riza, it is smaller than the Masjid-i-Shah, as befits its role as a place of private prayer. It lacks the usual courtyards, side galleries, and, most noticeably, minarets, and this has led a number of scholars to believe that it may have been intended as a mausoleum, although it was never used as one. Arcades of exposed brick flank the entrance to the mosque. Above, on the roof terraces surrounding the dome, the sophistication of the brickwork becomes more apparent as the complex patterns required to support the decorative vaulted ceilings below are revealed. However, visitors are likely to have their attention captured by the beautiful exterior tiles of the dome, which range in color from cream through pink to brown, depending on the lighting. Similarly, inside it is the exquisite blue tilework that leaves the most lasting impression on the visitor.

The Si-o-Se Pol and Khwaju Bridges

Some distance from the Maidan, brick was also used to construct bridges across the Zayandeh River. The Si-o-se Pol ("Bridge of Thirty-three Arches") was erected by Allahverdi Khan, one of 'Abbas's generals, in 1602. An impressive 1,000 ft (300 m) in length, it is on two levels, one for pedestrians and one for animal traffic. A teahouse was incorporated into it, beginning at the Chahar Bahn, Isfahan's main street, of which the Si-o-se Pol is an extension. More complex is the Khwaju Bridge, built in 1650, which essentially has three levels—a base of stone and two levels of brick—focused around a large central pavilion. Traders and their animal-drawn carts traveled on an interior road, while pedestrians strolled along exterior arcades with open river views. Flood gates on one side of the bridge allowed the level of the river to be controlled.

'Abbas I died in 1629. His successors also made their mark on the architecture of Isfahan—notably, 'Abbas II, who built the Hakim Mosque of 1656—but none had either the money or the passion for building possessed by their predecessor. Much of the later story of Isfahan has been one of alteration and restoration.

The Khwaju Bridge is more than just a river crossing. On its upstream side are flood gates for controlling the river's flow; on its downstream side, steps leading down to the water make for a popular and restful meeting place with views of river and city.

Frameworks

Broadly speaking, buildings are of either mass or framed construction. In mass construction, such as brick, stone, or logs, the same material creates the wall and carries the load. In framed construction it is the frame which carries the load, and other materials are used to clad or cover the frame, and/or to fill in its gaps. But in reality it is not quite as simple as that. The same building may combine mass and framed construction, or the infill and cladding of a frame may come to carry part of the load.

It is worth clarifying these principles because modern building is heavily dependent upon the frame. Mass construction is now only infrequently used in high-rise or large-span structures, or any really large or important buildings. The development of the frame has been a major theme of technical history. Many huts have been built of light materials woven together like a basket, but this is a continuous surface like a diaphragm, whereas in a pure frame every member (every vertical column, horizontal beam, diagonal brace or rafter) has a specific function, to take compression, tension, or bending, or to brace the structure.

Early frames were of timber or related materials such as bamboo, and were found in areas where timber was plentiful. The earliest of them would have been earthfast, with the columns set into the ground and supported by it, so that they required little or no support from the other timbers. But this is a primitive way of building. It can be used only for fairly small structures, and because the wood in the ground tends to rot, the building collapses within months or years. The cruck frame, discussed in the *Materials and Techniques* chapter, is more durable because it is made of large timbers.

The Ground Sill

The next phase of development involves the ground sill. This is a large piece of timber which rests on the ground, or better still can be raised slightly on a brick or stone wall to keep it clear of moisture. The frame of the building is built on top of it, and this has important implications.

The joints need to be better made, and because the columns or vertical members are not held upright by the ground, they need to be braced.

No one can say when the ground sill was invented, and it is not universal even today. Archaeologists find much evidence of earthfast construction because it leaves postholes, sometimes containing the remains of timber or the ash from its burning. But a frame built on a ground sill leaves no postholes, so it is likely that there were many more and many earlier examples than are known. But so far as evidence goes, it seems that the ground sill had appeared in northern Europe by the Iron Age, perhaps by 200 BCE. It was presumably known much earlier in Mediterranean cultures, where timber construction was less widespread, and earthfast construction was certainly also known, as in the House of Romulus, Rome. At Valkenburg, in the Netherlands, remains have

Many woodworking techniques were perfected by the ancient Egyptians. In the center of this model of a carpenter's workshop, from a tomb of *c.* 2160 BCE, a man saws a plank of wood, while another, on the right, uses a mallet and chisel to cut out a mortise.

A band of !Kung set up the frame of a new hut in Botswana, its columns of pliable sticks set firmly into the ground. The frame will be covered in grass.

been found of framed and wattled structures (that is, filled with basketwork) of the Roman period, both with and without ground sills. The Germanic tribes who invaded Europe after the Roman period seemed not to have used the ground sill, and it had to be rediscovered, which in Britain occurred in the Saxon period.

Because construction on a ground sill calls for better joints it is not surprising that our evidence for the most important of these, the mortise and tenon, is of the same date, appearing first in the Iron Age. The mortise is a rectangular slot cut through a piece of timber. The tenon is a narrowed piece or tongue formed on the end of another piece of timber, of a size which can be inserted into the mortise. Once this joint is formed it is best wedged, pegged, or otherwise fixed so that the tenon cannot be withdrawn again. The early ground sills contain mortises, corresponding to the locations of the vertical members which were tenoned into them.

Bracing

The other requirement brought into being by construction on a ground sill was bracing. To understand the principle, picture a structure like a carport or shelter with four columns, set in a square arrangement and connected by four horizontal beams. Unless the joints are strong and perfectly rigid the posts can simultaneously lean to one side until the whole frame folds down onto the ground. A small table can be built so that the joints are rigid enough to avoid this collapse, but at the scale of a full-size building that has not really been possible until the twentieth century.

In the absence of rigid joints, it is possible to brace our frame with a diagonal piece of timber in one of the square sides. This divides the face into triangles, and makes it impossible to distort it (until it actually breaks), so the frame cannot collapse in that direction. Put a similar brace in a panel at right angles, and it cannot collapse in that direction either. It is now a stable structure.

A diagonal right across the panel is the most obvious form of bracing, but not the only one. Diagonals merely cutting across one or more corners will also work, but are subject to greater stress and need to be better constructed. Where these are exposed to view they are called angle braces. A piece of more or less L-shaped timber fixed right into the corner will also work, but it needs to be even more carefully made. This is used in furniture and shipbuilding, as well as in some ordinary buildings from the medieval period onward, and is known as a knee brace.

The framework of an old barn is stabilized by angle braces between the columns and tie-beams.

A three-story box-framed house is under construction in this illumination from the medieval manuscript known as the *Bedford Hours*, although ostensibly the building of Noah's Ark is depicted. Most houses in the Middle Ages were built using either the box frame or the cruck frame.

framing timbers can be seen externally. The panels are filled with a material such as brick, or wattle and daub (plaster on basketwork), with a plastered and whitewashed surface. The structural timbers are left visible, and often stained a dark color. Framing filled in this way is known as half timbering, or *fachwerk* in German.

In a half-timbered building it is important to distinguish the main framing members from any timber which is used within the panels, such as the vertical members in wattle and daub. Vertical timbers within the panels, which are there merely to support the infill or the cladding, are smaller than the framing members, and are called studs. But in rare cases these studs become large and numerous, and begin to assume a structural role. This is called close studding, and appears in Normandy, and especially in Flanders. It was imported to England from Flanders in the eighteenth century.

Modern Timber Frames

In 1776, Nathaniel Kent published a book in England including illustrations of what he called "studd work cottages," based upon experience in the Lowlands. This was in principle a revolutionary development. His buildings were not frames in the normal sense, in which each piece of timber had a specific function. They were made of rows of uniform vertical studs, and though these mainly took compression, no individual stud was essential. You could make a door or window opening through them wherever you wished. Thus the wall was more like a diaphragm than a frame, and in fact comparable with the earlier systems of basketwork construction.

The stud frame, and the American balloon frame which derives from it, are now common throughout most of the world. The story of their development is controversial, but what we can confidently say is they became important in the nineteenth century as a result of three practical considerations. Rising costs of labor made it desirable to simplify the building process. The development of mechanical sawmilling meant that it was cheaper to produce a large number of uniform-sized pieces of timber than a smaller number of large and specially shaped pieces, such as were used in traditional frames. And the production of nails by machine enormously reduced their cost and made it practicable to use them in place of the complicated wooden joints of the past.

In the 1830s and 1840s, these simpler frames appeared in New Zealand and eastern Australia, but they were generally seen as makeshifts, for use when speed was essential or labor was scarce. It was another fifty years before they began to be regarded as options in serious building work. In this region, two-story timber buildings were rare, but where they occurred the tendency was to complete the lowest level of stud framing and start a new stud frame in the story (rather in the way that traditional box frames had been stacked on top of each other).

A different approach is to fill the panel with a solid material such as brickwork, which cannot be compressed and therefore equally prevents the panel from distorting.

The Box Frame and Half Timbering

A frame built on a sill, and braced to prevent it distorting, is like a box, and indeed could in theory be picked up and put down in a new location. In medieval Europe, it was common for an upper floor to be placed on top like another box, but somewhat larger in plan, so that it jettied out or overhung on the outside. There are many varieties of box frame in Europe, and often the

The Balloon Frame

In the United States, the form known as the balloon frame developed. The term seems to refer to the fact that the vertical studs were continuous through more than one story, creating a continuous building envelope, though other origins for the word have been suggested. Otherwise the balloon frame is much the same as the stud frame, with uniformly sized timbers and simple nailed joints. George W. Snow has been claimed to have built the first balloon frame in Chicago in 1833, but in fact nobody knows exactly what it was that he built. The more important fact is that the system had become fairly widely known by the 1850s, and was published in a book, *Bell's Carpentry Made Easy*, in 1857.

The seventeenth- and eighteenth-century core of Freudenberg, Germany, consists of half-timbered *(fachwerk)* houses with slate roofs. The builders have made good use of the decorative possibilities of this framework technique by emphasizing the contrast between the dark wood and the whitewashed infill.

Iron and Concrete Frames

In the United States, writers tend to regard the development of the iron and steel framed skyscraper as being in some way a development from the balloon frame, but it is difficult to see how this could be so. The iron frame had been developed in English cotton and flax mills in the late eighteenth century, as discussed in the *Materials and Techniques* chapter. By the 1840s, building prefabricators working in Glasgow and elsewhere were making iron frames which stood alone, without having a load-bearing masonry wall on the outside, so that the cladding materials hung off the structural frame. Soon afterward, James Bogardus of New York was doing the same thing. The seeds of the curtain wall had been planted.

In the iron or steel frame, the basic principles, such as the need for bracing, are the same as in the timber frame. But a major difference is that the joints can be made rigid, whereas in timber (with a partial exception where the knee brace is used) this is impracticable. Until the late nineteenth century, engineers had designed joints as if they were fixed with pins, and no bending stresses were transferred across the joint. With riveted and especially with welded joints, the joint can be just as strong as any other part of the structure. Bending moments are transferred through the joint, so the frame does not need to be braced. This is the principle of the portal frame, first used in Chicago skyscrapers in about 1890, and in the so-called Vierendeel truss, used for railroad bridges by the Belgian engineer Arthur Vierendeel, from the 1930s. In reinforced concrete the rigid joint comes naturally, and is the rule rather than the exception. Quite complicated trusses with rigid joints were being made by about 1900, especially by the French engineer Armand-Gabriel Considère.

Steel-framed High-rise Buildings
Chicago, United States

Steel-framed high-rise construction was pioneered and perfected in Chicago during the late nineteenth century. Its development, in only a few decades, is one of the greatest achievements of American architects.

Masonry Gives Way to Iron and Steel

The first high-rise buildings were constructed of masonry, and required extremely thick load-bearing walls, as in Chicago's 16-story Monadnock Building of 1891, designed by Daniel Burnham and John Root. This type of construction posed special problems at ground level, where prime rental space was lost to enormous load-bearing interior and exterior walls. The walls of the Monadnock Building are a full 6 ft (1.8 m) thick at ground level. The materials and specialized labor needed for such large masonry buildings added to the expense and time needed to construct them. Additionally, masonry buildings did not allow for expansive windows, often making their interiors dark and cavelike.

Iron and steel would prove to be the answer to masonry's limitations. By 1850, iron had become a staple commodity in the United States. It was first used in bridges, and later in buildings. By the end of the nineteenth century, Americans had shed their dependence on iron for an even better material, steel. Like iron, structural steel was first used in bridges, but soon found favor among Chicago architects for high-rise construction. The transition from iron to steel, however, was gradual, with many early Chicago high rises using

The structural form of the Reliance Building was based not on historic ideas of ornamentation, but on the grid of the building's steel frame. Additionally, it used large glass windows between the spaces of the frame, and serves as an early example of the modern glass box building type.

a combination of steel and wrought iron for their frames. In Chicago, in 1885, William Le Baron Jenney became the first to use steel in the frame of a high rise, the Home Insurance Building. The building's structural system consisted of cast- and wrought-iron supports in the lower levels with steel in the upper stories. The entire frame is concealed by a stone veneer or curtain wall, giving the illusion that the building is constructed entirely of masonry. With this new method, the weight of the building was carried by the frame and not the walls. The building's framework, because of its rigidity, light weight, and ability to carry great loads, allowed for large enclosed spaces. The thinness of the iron and steel members also allowed for expanses of large windows in the exterior curtain walls.

The Steel Frame Takes Shape

The advancements in steel-framed construction in Chicago were partly the result of the city's obsession with fireproof architecture. During the last half of the nineteenth century, cast iron was seen as the modern architectural replacement for combustible wood. In Chicago, cast-iron vaulting, floor systems, columns, façades, and entire iron buildings were constructed. But in 1871, a massive fire consumed a great deal of Chicago, and the so-called fireproof iron buildings failed under the intense heat. Architects soon learned that while cast iron did not burn, it must be shielded from heat to prevent the breakdown of the cast-iron members and collapse of the building. Soon after, however, steel became far more common. Not only was it superior to cast iron as a building material—being stronger, more durable, and with a higher melting point—but in a fire it held its form far longer. Nonetheless, architects in Chicago experimented with a variety of protective coverings for the steel frames of high-rise buildings. By the beginning of the twentieth century, a standard method of fireproof

encasement for steel framing had been developed in Chicago. Floor systems were normally made up of hollow clay tiles between the steel girders. A layer of concrete was used on top of the tiles, while clay was used to insulate the steel columns.

The Rand McNally Building, completed in 1890 to a design by John Root, was the first high-rise building with an all-steel frame. In association with Daniel Burnham, Root designed dozens of steel-framed high rises in Chicago. By the end of the nineteenth century, steel-framed construction had become the standard for high-rise buildings in the United States.

The Chicago School

The architects who developed the high rise in Chicago are known collectively as the Chicago School, although they did not necessarily have a unified belief or architectural manifesto which

The Chicago architect Louis Sullivan pioneered the high rise in designs such as this, the Carson Pirie Scott & Co. Building, built between 1899 and 1904. The lower two stories are highly ornamented with Art Nouveau cast-iron grillwork; above these levels, the sober façade, of plain white terracotta, follows the framework of steel girders.

Bruno Taut and the Glashaus

The Deutscher Werkbund (German Association of Craftsmen), a group of artists, architects, and designers, held an exhibition in 1914 in Cologne. Among the buildings exhibited was the Glashaus, a pleasure dome of color-tinted glass panes in curved metal sashes designed, in an Expressionist vein, by Bruno Taut. The writer Paul Scheerbart, who contributed aphorisms displayed on the Glashaus such as "colored glass destroys hatred," later inspired Taut to publish his sketches for *Alpine Architektur*—fantastic glass curtain projects for mountaintop communities. Taut also belonged to the avant-garde art and architecture association Novembergruppe, whose members included both Walter Gropius and Mies van der Rohe. Taut left Germany in 1932, and lived abroad until his death in 1938.

The truncated cone form of the Thompson Center in Chicago, 1985, designed by Helmut Jahn, fully exploits advanced glass curtain technology. A variety of colors and transparencies, from clear to opaque, sheath the dynamic curved form and filter the light entering the multistory central atrium.

The Rise of the Skyscraper

The architectural aesthetic of the glass curtain was given impetus during the development of the skyscraper in Chicago in the late nineteenth century. The ten-story Home Insurance Building of 1885 by William Le Baron Jenney introduced steel members into the skeleton frame in part. He added L-section metal shelves to the beam edges to support the external wall of masonry and glass sheets, transferring this load to the inner skeleton frame. Because the external masonry cladding could be reduced in dimensions and weight, Jenney was able to make windows larger than in previous high-rise buildings. Curtain wall construction gained favor with Chicago architects, engineers, and clients, as more rentable space per floor was achieved with the thinner glass curtain wall sheaths. And with the reduced building weight per floor, even taller office blocks were feasible. Jenney's metal shelf device thereafter became the standard for skyscraper construction.

The climax to this trend is Daniel Burnham and John Root's steel-framed Reliance Building of 1890 (extended in 1894). A curtain of non-load-bearing wall is divided, following the lines of its generous window areas, narrow piers, thin spandrels, and elegant mullions. Abstract geometry dominates the form, but Tudor Gothic quatrefoil patterns appear on the building's pale yellow ocher terracotta tile spandrels, piers, and mullions. The windows are the Chicago Type, consisting of a large rectangular fixed pane in the center and smaller flanking panes mounted in movable sashes.

The Twentieth Century

Architects continued to make innovations in glass curtain architecture in the early twentieth century, particularly in Germany. The Fagus Factory, built in Alfeld an der Leine in 1913, was a collaboration between the architects Walter Gropius and Adolf Meyer. Metal and glass panels are hung between the flat brick pillars, protecting the building's structural frame. Glass curtain wraps around the corners without visible vertical supports. For the glazing to the upper floor of the Model Factory for the 1914 Deutscher Werkbund Exhibition, in Cologne, Gropius and Meyer further developed the glass curtain aesthetic. The structural columns were set back from the outer wall plane, and the glazing system was suspended on the cantilevered concrete floor edges. This aesthetic also informed Gropius's buildings for the Bauhaus at Dessau, completed in 1926. Also active at this time was Mies van der Rohe, who created plans for spectacular glass curtain skyscrapers, a multifaceted form in 1919, and an organic freeform in 1920–1921.

In the United States in 1952, the firm of Skidmore Owings & Merrill used a glass curtain wall construction all around Lever House, New York, with tinted glass mounted in aluminum glazing bars, setting a worldwide standard for glass curtain office towers. Mies, in the 1951 Lake Shore Drive apartments, Chicago, and the 1958 Seagram Building offices, New York, sought a more powerful image of verticality, applying substantial steel and bronze joists respectively to the glass curtains of these soaring rectilinear blocks. More recently, the German-born US architect Helmut Jahn, who had studied with Mies at the Illinois Institute of Technology, Chicago, has forged a new glass curtain aesthetic in numerous buildings around the world, including the Thompson Center, Chicago, of 1985.

Cladding

The external walls of buildings are often finished with a non-load-bearing applied surface, that is, a cladding, which can be made from a diverse range of materials. The exposed surfaces of structural masonry or concrete walls are not called cladding, even though they may have been decoratively treated in profile and texture. Cladding is a material added to the basic construction. It may insulate, waterproof, fireproof, or otherwise protect a building's underlying construction, and its effect is most commonly aesthetic.

Renders, stuccos, veneers, and tiling are traditional cladding techniques variously applied to constructions of stone or brick. Similarly, boards and sheeting of various kinds are the cladding fixed to timber frames. Glass curtains are a modern form of cladding to frame constructions of iron, steel, concrete, or wood.

From the 1830s, iron-framed buildings were clad in flat sheet or corrugated iron (later galvanized, or coated with zinc). By the mid-1840s,

Louis Sullivan used terracotta tiles to sheath the entire framework of his Guaranty Building, Buffalo, New York State, of 1895. The intricate, low-relief designs were inspired by the shapes of seedpods, leaves, and flowers.

Scottish makers were finishing iron-framed buildings with ornamental cast-iron panels, and soon afterward James Bogardus of New York was doing the same. In France, Jules Saulnier pioneered the use of colored brick and tile panels set decoratively within the panels of an iron frame, and the English architect James Edmeston followed him in this. During the later nineteenth century, manufacturers in the United States began producing pressed and rolled sheet-iron cladding, which sometimes imitated weatherboard, brick, stone, or more complicated architectural schemes. More recently developed cladding materials include plastics, and sheet metals such as aluminum, zinc, and titanium.

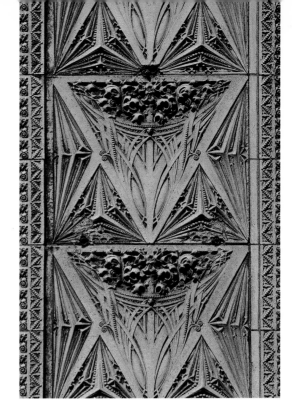

Stucco and Stone Veneers

At ancient Greek temple sites in Sicily and on the Italian mainland, marble was not available. Here marble-dust stucco was applied to structures of inferior local limestone, to create the smooth surface and precise edges required by Greek architects. The smoothness and precision of stucco has led to its widespread use in subsequent architecture across the ages. In the modern era, for example, stucco has often been applied to represent the imagined plasticity of reinforced concrete forms, for few designers had succeeded in exposing the concrete itself to good effect. At the University of California, Westwood campus, in 1927 however, the formwork marks were carefully preserved under a dash coat of stucco. Most of the Modernist architects were less scrupulous. In the Netherlands, the Schröder House of 1924, in Utrecht, is a cubistic construct, which was conceived by the Dutch architect Gerrit Rietveld as an assembly of interlocking slabs of reinforced concrete, but in reality it was made of brickwork clad in stucco. Similar measures were resorted to by Walter Gropius in his Bauhaus, at Dessau, of 1926, and Le Corbusier in the Villa Savoye, at Poissy, France, of 1931.

In the Roman period, load-bearing brickwork or concrete constructions were clad in veneers of marble and other stones. The Pantheon in Rome, built of concrete in the second century CE, once had a marble veneer cladding the exterior and bronze rosette panels fitted to the concrete dome coffering inside. There have been many subsequent examples of stone veneer cladding, and remarkably, in 1988, the US architect Helmut Jahn used laser-cut stone sheets instead of glass for a curtain-wall skyscraper on Wilshire Boulevard in Westwood, Los Angeles.

Jules Saulnier designed the Menier Chocolate Factory at Noisiel-sur-Marne, France, in 1872. Brightly colored brick panels fill the spaces between the building's external diagonal iron bracing.

Terracotta

Terracotta tiles laid on timber-framed walls in overlapping patterns were a tradition in Europe, and in England a version known as the mathematical tile was ingeniously shaped so that the exposed foot of the tile presented a vertical face in the shape of a brick. The development of extrusion machinery in the nineteenth century encouraged the development of cheap forms of terracotta for cladding, but the Arts and Crafts movement encouraged individually molded terracotta facings, a notable use of which was Alfred Waterhouse's Natural History Museum, of 1880 in London. In the United States, terracotta cladding, more commonly glazed and colored like stone, played a role in the Chicago School at the end of the nineteenth century. A good example is the Reliance Building, designed in 1890 by Daniel Burnham and John Root, in which an armature of iron struts supports a creamy glazed terracotta façade of a slightly Gothic character.

Also in the late nineteenth century, the Chicago architect Louis Sullivan developed an idiosyncratic expression for the skyscraper form, enhanced by cladding the piers, spandrels, and arched cornices with terracotta tiles, complete with his own system of ornament. The Guaranty Building, Buffalo, New York State, completed in 1895, characterizes Sullivan's style. The façades facing the site's street intersection have a two-story base with cutout horizontal window shapes,

Le Corbusier's Villa Savoye at Poissy, France, is thoroughly Modernist in its rejection of ornament, but its reinforced concrete structure is nevertheless clad in white stucco.

a multi-story shaft of offices with vertical piers arched at the top, narrow setback spandrels marking each floor level, and a projecting cornice above an attic of ocular windows. Every exposed solid member is sheathed in modular terracotta tiles ornamented with sinuous vegetal forms.

Timber Cladding

The various traditions of cladding timber frames with weatherboards, clapboards, shingles, or ship-lap are discussed earlier in this chapter. Ship's carpentry and rude rural framing were industrialized during the mid-nineteenth century, with mass-produced nails used in the framing and for fixing the timber cladding. In the United States at this time, timber was plentiful, and this abundance led to the emergence of the Stick Style (1830s–1870s) in domestic architecture, which was later eclipsed by the Shingle Style (1870s–1890s). In the Stick Style, the vertical, horizontal, and diagonal bracing members of the frame were visibly expressed in the wall. In contrast, the Shingle Style expressed the inner volume, with the shingle cladding attached in continuous sweeps masking the structure immediately

Vertical timber boards, weathered by sun, rain, and wind, clad one of the buildings of the Sea Ranch, (1966) a planned coastal community 100 miles (160 km) north of San Francisco, California.

beneath, as exemplified in the Stoughton House, Cambridge, Massachusetts, of 1883, by Henry Hobson Richardson.

The expression of volume is to be seen in the composition of simple barn forms, clad in vertical clapboards, cascading down the slope at the Sea Ranch, Sonoma County, California, designed by the firm of Moore Lyndon Turnbull and Whitaker in 1966. This design has revived interest worldwide in the sustainable architecture of timber frame and cladding.

Frank Gehry

Best known for his Guggenheim Museum in Bilbao, with its sinuous, titanium-clad walls, Frank Gehry is one of the very few architects whose names are widely recognized outside their own profession. His adventurous and experimental forms and surfaces, and his fanciful exploitation of the properties of frames and cladding materials, clearly appeal to a broad range of tastes.

Born Ephraim Owen Goldberg in Toronto, Canada, in 1929, Gehry, together with his family, migrated to Los Angeles, United States, in 1947. He studied architecture at the University of Southern California and then city planning at Harvard, opening his own practice in 1962 after gaining experience in several architectural firms.

In his work, Gehry treats each building as a unique sculptural object within which airy, usable, flowing spaces are contained, lit by the sun's traverse during the day and theatrically illuminated by night. Each project is conceived in the context of Gehry's admiration for Abstract Expressionist painting and sculpture. In architecture, he seeks to emulate the freedom and impulsiveness of this art movement's theory and practice. The spontaneous sketch, rapid model-building, experimental juxtapositions of shapes and materials—all are means that allow Gehry to determine or discover spiritual significance, however fleeting. The resultant rhythms and forms of each of his pieces are given a compelling, picturesque force with a variety of cladding materials, including glass curtains. An extensive palette of colors and textures is applied.

Gehry's Houses

Although widely known for his large buildings, Gehry also has designed a number of houses. For his own house, built in 1978 in Santa Monica, California (and extended in 1992), Gehry began with the purchase of "a dumb little house with charm," as he called it—a speculative builder's stud-frame house finished in clapboard cladding externally and interior plaster sheeting internally. He transformed it inside by removing internal walls and stripping the plaster sheeting back to the timber construction beneath. Outside, he added teetering glazed cubes. An additional enclosure set new house boundaries, blandly sheathed in galvanized corrugated iron sheet, chain-link screens, or oiled marine plywood. A low cement blockwork wall to the front garden edge was painted a pale yet vivid green. Ad hoc process and immediacy are strongly conveyed in an unfamiliar sculptural expression for a dwelling, which successfully challenges and disrupts a sedate suburban streetscape.

According to Gehry, pictured (left) outside his Bilbao Guggenheim Museum, "Life is chaotic, dangerous, and surprising. Buildings should reflect it."

The Nationale-Nederlanden Building in Prague, Czech Republic, has been nicknamed "The Dancing Building" and "Fred and Ginger" for obvious reasons.

The informal juxtaposition of walls of different color and texture occurred again in the Norton House in Venice Beach, California, built in 1984, but the whole is rhythmically unified because of the terracing of the roofs for views of the ocean. The repetition of horizontals is suitably counterpointed by the boxed writer's retreat thrust up on a pillar at the beach end of the split-level site. Gehry has variously clad the many small wall areas of the house in plywood sheeting and stucco, ceramic tile, copper sheet, cement boards, or glass curtain over internal timber framing. In this instance there is an urban design fit between the scale and variegation of Gehry's building fragments with the endlessly various roof and wall shapes and material finishes found in the curiously high residential building density of Venice Beach.

In contrast, the 1987 Winton Guest House, Wayzata, Minnesota, is set in a spacious garden. The house is highly picturesque and sculptural, an informally balanced composition. Four differently shaped forms are attached like limbs to a tall central body, with a connecting spatial flow between each inside. The central pyramidal form and each of its uniquely shaped corner rooms is sheathed in a distinctive material, for example, painted plywood sheets set in metal framing or oiled, butt-jointed plywood, and zinc or galvanized steel sheeting. One of the attached rooms is a red-brick inglenook and fireplace pavilion, the only visual clue to domestic habitation within the complex. Refinement of detail accords with an elegance of expression not seen in the two California houses.

Major Commissions

Gehry now has an international practice, with buildings to his credit in many countries. The first overseas commission was in Germany, at Weil am Rhein, in 1989, for the Vitra International Manufacturing Facility and Design Museum. The museum was to house the firm's collection of furniture pieces. (Gehry himself had gained international recognition for folded and stacked cardboard sheet furniture, and fish lamps with scales of fractured plastic sheets.) Curves partially introduced in the Winton House dominate the Vitra building design of interlocking tilted rectilinear, rounded, and spiral solids entirely finished in white stucco cladding and zinc sheet rooftops.

The Guggenheim Museum, Bilbao, Spain (left), displays the free-form sculptural style that has become its architect's trademark. The design of the museum involved the first large-scale use of the CATIA program by Gehry's practice.

With the design of the Fish Sculpture at Vila Olimpica, Barcelona, Spain, in 1992, Gehry's firm began using a computer program called CATIA (Computer-Aided Three-Dimensional Interactive Application). The software, developed for the French aerospace industry, digitizes physical models for the engineering and fabrication of complex curved building shapes. Gehry could now use naturalistic gestures in his sketches, plus curved card and folded cloth in quickly conceived models, digitize them by scanning, and work up a design in three dimensions on a computer. The model for the Experience Music Project, Seattle, Washington State, completed in 2000, was a smashed electric guitar. The building's fabricated steel frame is clad in concrete and in reflective sheet metal panels in contrasting vivid colors.

For the Nationale-Nederlanden Building, Prague, Czech Republic, of 1996, Gehry leaned a stack of conference rooms within a curved glass curtain wall beside a corbeled stucco-clad tower and office block. Looking like partners in a dance, these two lurching towers agreeably enliven the corner of a row of nineteenth-century office façades. In 1997 came the Guggenheim Museum, Bilbao, Spain, in which creative flourishes are organically combined in the piling up of curvilinear shapes clad in titanium sheeting. The building handsomely reflects the river bend where it is located. Back in the United States, the Walt Disney Concert Hall, Los Angeles, completed in 2003, proclaims curvaceous fun in its intermingling trapezoids clad in shiny metal sheeting above a base clad in limestone.

Resembling a lifeguard's tower, the writer's retreat of the Norton House (left) overlooks the boardwalk and oceanfront at Venice Beach, California.

Entranceways

The entrance to a building is not only functionally important, but is commonly the architectural focus of the façade, contributing significantly to a visitor's first impression of the whole structure. It is also critical to security and to defense, and often the location of sophisticated technology, in the form of hardware, locks, bells, and intercom systems.

Doorways

The Oratory of Gallerus, a Christian chapel of the sixth or seventh century CE, in Dingle, Ireland, had a door that swung on pintles rather than hinges.

We know very little about the doors on the earliest buildings, but it seems likely that few were lockable in the modern sense. Humbler dwellings probably had no real security, and greater ones relied upon the physical presence of guards. Most buildings, however, would have had curtains or hangings of some sort over their doorways, often for climatic reasons, and there is indeed some physical evidence of this. At Tarxien, Malta, is a complex of four megalithic structures, believed to have been temples. At the entrance to the central temple, built around 3100 BCE, the stone jambs on either side of the door each contain a pair of holes,

one above another and angled so that they meet internally, forming a "V" shape. It has been reasonably inferred that these were designed for a cord to pass through, and that the cords would have been used to tie back curtains on either side of the door. In addition, on the interior face of each of the same stones are two similar V-shaped holes, perhaps used to tie a solid panel across the doorway. This panel was probably secured by a heavy crossbar, for in adjoining stones there are large cylindrical holes, one deeper than the other so that a bar could be slid into place.

In Egypt, there is evidence that a mat was often rolled up to the top of a doorway and let

The original massive bronze doors of the Pantheon in Rome still admit visitors to the 2000-year-old structure. Since CE 609, the building has also been known as the church of Santa Maria ad Martyres.

In this doorway at the temple of Tarxien in Malta (3100 BCE), the holes on the left probably held cords to tie back curtains. The holes in the center may have held a panel that sealed the door and was secured by a crossbar running into the large hole on the right.

An underground chamber (above) at the tomb of Djoser, Egypt, c. 2600 BCE, is lined in faience tiles imitating reed mats. The cylinder faced with tiles at the head of the doorway shows how a mat would have been hung here and rolled up to permit access.

down when required. A subterranean chamber in the Djoser complex at Saqqara, dating from around 2600 BCE, is finished in bright faience tiles that simulate reed matting on the walls as well as a rolled reed mat over the doorway. This rolled mat becomes an abstract motif in later Egyptian doors.

It is also in Egypt that one finds the first evidence of swinging doors. In cultures that did not work metal, hinges, in the modern sense, were impossible to create. The normal alternative in ancient times was the pintle. At the top and bottom corner on one side, the door leaf was shaped into an extended cylindrical pin; one fitted into a socket in the lintel, the other into a socket in the threshold. Often these doors were made of heavy timber, sometimes ornamentally sheathed in bronze or other metal; others were of solid stone, carved in one piece, pintles and all. As well as in Egypt, pintle sockets can be found in the remains of Hittite, classical Greek and Roman structures, and in the post-Roman buildings of the Hauran in Syria, built mostly in the fifth and sixth centuries CE, in which are found remarkable numbers of solid basalt pintle doors, some of them still in place in buildings and in use today. In the Hauran, stone doors were perhaps used mainly on tombs, while commoner buildings had wooden doors of similar form. Evidence of pintles is also found in the remarkable Oratory of Gallerus in Dingle, Ireland, a Christian chapel of the sixth or seventh century CE.

Timber Doors

A timber door is commonly framed with vertical members or stiles, and horizontal members or rails, which divide it into four or six panels. The joints are traditionally mortised and tenoned. A simpler door can be made up of parallel vertical boards, connected to two or three crosspieces (at head, foot and handle height). This is called a ledged door. Typically, such a door will tend to sink at the outer edge as the timbers shrink and the joints loosen, and to avoid this happening diagonal pieces, or braces, are attached between the ledges. This is a ledged and braced door.

A pair of the earliest surviving hinged wooden doors of a much grander type was found at the church of Santa Sabina in Rome, and are now on display inside the church. They are of cypress, with carved panels showing biblical subjects, and date in part from the early fifth century CE. There were originally twenty-eight panels, showing historic and symbolic subjects and scenes from the Old Testament, inspired by classical art, sarcophagi, and the paintings of the catacombs. The Near Eastern influences are so strong, specifically Syrian ones, that the doors may have been carved by Syrian artists in Rome, if not actually imported from Syria.

Timber doors were often clad in metal, and at the fourth-century Basilica of St. Peter in Rome, also known as Old St. Peter's, the doors were covered with embossed silver plates. The surviving twelfth-century doors of the Cathedral of San Pantaleone at Ravello, Italy, are of wood clad in bronze. Solid metal doors were common in Rome, but most have since disappeared because of the value of the metal. However, examples exist at the Pantheon (c. CE 125) and San Giovanni in Laterano (CE 330). Surviving medieval examples include the solid metal west entrance doors of the Rozhdestvensky (Nativity of the Virgin) Cathedral, Suzdal, Russia, of 1222–1225 and later. Now preserved inside the building, they incorporate damascene work— gold inlay on bronze—which was fairly widespread in the East and originated in Damascus, Syria, as the name suggests. This type of panelled metal door is the ancestor of the great bronze doors of the Baptistery in Florence.

Hinges and Bolts

The Romans used both pintles and hinges, but in the later medieval period metal hinges became widespread, at least in grander buildings. Often they extend as horizontal straps on the face of the doors or create even more ornamental curvilinear forms. In Ottoman Turkey, the door was commonly enhanced by a decorative central knob—similar knobs at Xian, in China, suggest that this was one of the cultural connections fostered by the Silk Road.

In Europe by the seventeenth century, the *espagnolet* or *espagnolette* was widely used, particularly on double doors. As its name suggests, this device may have originated in Spain. It consists of a rod that runs vertically up the inside face of the door; when it is rotated, using a handle or lever at hand height, tongues at the top and bottom simultaneously rotate and lock into sockets. The espagnolet was generally replaced in the nineteenth century by a new device, the *crémone* (also spelled *cremon* or *cremorne*), made up of two separate vertical rods. When a handle was turned, it engaged with teeth on the rods, and the upper rod rose into a socket, like a bolt, while the lower one simultaneously fell into another socket. This is the ancestor of some forms of panic bolt used in modern fire escapes.

It is impossible to summarize all the later developments in door hinges and furniture, but the biggest changes were those of the nineteenth century. Early in the century there were two standard hinge types, the wrought-iron and the pressed-riveted; from the 1840s onward these were replaced by the patent wrought-iron hinge, invented in the United States and perhaps independently reinvented in Britain. The two halves of this hinge were formed with pieces of the knuckle projecting as tongues, and these were forced into dies to bend them over, so as to hold a pin. Thus the strength of the finished hinge no longer depended on welding or riveting. One ingenious hinge type, the rising butt, which is still used today, had the knuckle pieces cut on an angle, so that as the door opened it rose slightly. If it were not then held in place, it would tend to fall again and automatically close.

In the medieval period, metal hinges were often extended and elaborated to form a decorative element in the design of a door. The example above is from the fifteenth-century clifftop Sanctuary of the Blessed Virgin Mary in Rocamadour, Lot, France.

This ornate silver handle (right) on a door in Telouet, Morocco, is part of an *espagnolet* locking system. When the handle was pulled horizontally, away from the door, it released hooks at the top and bottom of the attached rod from their sockets.

Sliding, Revolving, Disappearing

Other types of door include sliding ones, which are reported to have been used on tombs in Asia Minor. Modern examples tend to use some sort of low friction track, or to be hung on wheels moving in a track above. Fire doors on this principle are generally metal-clad and have a sloping track, so that when they are released from the open position (for example by the fire melting a fusible link) they roll down the track and close automatically.

French doors, also called French windows, are glazed, and come in pairs like casement windows, but extend right down to the floor. They became fashionable in Britain early in the nineteenth century, and are characteristic of the Regency style. They commonly open onto the verandahs and balconies, which were also a distinctive feature of the Regency style.

In the nineteenth century the pneumatic or revolving door was invented to provide access, mainly to public buildings, without also admitting a draft. In the twentieth century, architects often tried to eliminate the visual impact of the door entirely, making it out of unframed toughened glass and setting it within a glass wall. This gave rise to the classic scene in Jacques Tati's 1958 film comedy *Mon Oncle*, in which the protagonist desperately fumbles along the wall of a Modernist building, trying to work out which segment is the door. The ultimate step in the elimination of the door was perhaps the air curtain, in which a blower at the top or bottom of the opening blasts out a sheet of air, which acts as a barrier to draughts while also keeping heat within the building. It is most often used at the entrance of department stores to give customers unimpeded access.

A modern revolving door may be manual or automatic, and will usually incorporate some form of braking system to prevent people rotating the door too quickly and injuring other users.

Lock and Key

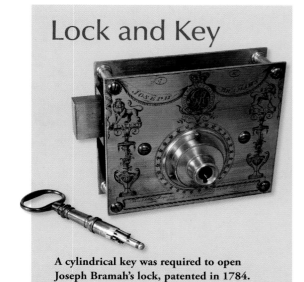

A cylindrical key was required to open Joseph Bramah's lock, patented in 1784.

Locks are known from ancient Egypt onward, and there are many beautiful and ingenious medieval examples surviving, but none were really effective until 1774, when Robert Barron patented his double-action tumbler lock in England. A tumbler is the latch inside the lock, which has to be raised to allow the bolt to move. Barron's lock had two tumblers kept in place with a spring, and a key cut with steps that would raise the tumblers to the right heights to allow the key to turn. In 1784, also in England, Joseph Bramah patented an even more intricate lock, in which a small cylindrical key with notches in its end pushed metal slides down to particular heights to allow the key to turn. Another Englishman, Jeremiah Chubb, invented a lock in 1818 that recorded attempts to pick it by trapping with a spring any tumblers raised beyond the correct level. Important advances were then made in the United States, where in 1848, Linus Yale developed the pin-tumbler lock, in which a serrated key raises a row of pins to varying heights to turn a bolt at the end of the cylinder. Modern versions of this lock are used for doors around the world today.

Baptistery of San Giovanni
Florence, Italy

The Baptistery of San Giovanni in Florence, Italy may incorporate the remains of a Roman structure. Its medieval decoration is surprisingly clasical in spirit.

In terms of their fame and of their impact on architecture and art, the doors of the Baptistery of San Giovanni in Florence, Italy, especially the northern ones designed by Lorenzo Ghiberti, could be said to be the most important doors that the world has ever seen.

The great south doors of the baptistery were designed by Andrea Pisano, beginning in 1329. Cast and gilded in bronze, they were placed on the east side of the baptistery in 1336 and later moved to their present location. The competition for the commission to design the northern doors was announced in 1401, and attracted entries from leading artists of the day, including Filippo Brunelleschi. The finalists were Brunelleschi and Ghiberti, both of whose entries were radically novel in their treatment of three-dimensional space. Ghiberti eventually triumphed, and executed his doors in 1403–1424. Cast in bronze and gilded, they incorporate 28 panels depicting the saints, and scenes from the Bible, framed by intricate modeled foliage and busts of prophets. Ghiberti was then commissioned to provide new eastern doors (replacing Pisano's) and worked on those from 1425 to 1452. Known as the Gates of Paradise, they feature ten panels showing scenes from the Old Testament. Both sets of doors not only won the acclaim of Ghiberti's contemporaries, but also had a profound influence on later artists, sculptors, and designers working in a range of media.

Antique Origins

In other respects, the Baptistery of San Giovanni is one of the most underappreciated buildings of the medieval period. Although everything externally visible dates from the eleventh or twelfth century (except for the Gothic—probably thirteenth-century—zebra striping at the corners), it is built directly onto the remains of an antique Roman building, and some scholars believe that part of the structure itself is of antique date, for the main body of the walls is rather like a Roman aqueduct in construction. In Dante's time the Florentines believed it to be an antique temple, probably dedicated to Mars, and it may well be that the Renaissance architect Brunelleschi shared this view, for he certainly saw it as a valid classical source and made use of it in forging his distinctive style. As a result of this, the building, together with the church of San Miniato in the same city, is sometimes referred to as belonging to the Tuscan Proto-Renaissance.

Consistent with the theory of an antique origin is the fact that the internal volume is massive and not typical of the medieval period. Indeed, the baptistery has more in common with the Pantheon in Rome or perhaps the Orthodox Baptistery in Ravenna than with the general run of early Christian baptisteries, which tend to be compact polygonal spaces surrounded by niches. The baptistery is roofed with a cloister vault rather than a true dome, and there can be no doubt that this was the inspiration for the dome on the cathedral of Santa Maria del Fiore next door, which Brunelleschi would design.

Classical Ancestry

The baptistery was consecrated in 1059. At that time, it incorporated the rectangular sanctuary that had replaced an earlier apse, but not its marble paneling or the cloister-vaulted roof.

There can be no doubt that the baptistery's interior decorative scheme was based upon the Pantheon. Although the Pantheon is round rather than octagonal, both buildings have colonnades at the lower level and their apses are treated in the same way. The use of colonnades carrying flat lintels is a classicizing feature that had scarcely been seen in Italy since the fifth century.

The baptistery has a continuous gallery at the upper level, the equivalent of the *matroneum*, or women's gallery, of churches in the East, and perhaps an indication of Byzantine influence. This gallery has flat pilasters, like those on the front of the church of San Miniato, and they seem to be derived from late antique prototypes (such as examples from Aquileia, at the head of the Adriatic, and in the Conservatori Museum in Rome). Clearly, there was a very specific antique revival taking place in Florence at the time.

Externally, one has to distinguish two main stages. The lower portion of the exterior (except for the striped corners) dates from the consecration of 1059. The arcade is comparable with the lower façade of San Miniato, built just afterward. It includes a projecting section of entablature to carry the arch, which only had to be released and made freestanding to become the impost block used by Brunelleschi in his more serious works. The attic level dates from about 1090–1128 and has marble paneling and flat pilasters like those of the gallery inside, but even more like those flanking the apse of San Miniato. Contrary to classical principles, the mouldings of the lintel turn down the sides to frame the whole panel. Brunelleschi said that this was the one thing wrong with the building—and unfortunately another architect copied this very detail onto his Ospedale degli Innocenti (Foundling Hospital) during his absence.

One important legacy of the baptistery was its impact on Leon Battista Alberti. He transposed the whole exterior scheme to his new façade on the church of Santa Maria Novella in Florence (1456–1470). Like Brunelleschi, Alberti probably believed the baptistery was an antique building and he certainly thought it was a homogeneous one, for he indiscriminately copied the lower pre-1059 part, the post-1090 upper treatment, and even the Gothic striping on the corners. Thus, this medieval building had an extraordinary and lasting impact on the first two masters of the Italian Renaissance.

The so-called Gates of Paradise, created by Ghiberti between 1425 and 1452, include ten Old Testament scenes framed by an ornate border incorporating 24 small busts—including one of the artist.

Gates and Gateways

Carvings of captives on the front of the Porta Nuova in Palermo, Sicily, Italy (above), celebrated the victories of Emperor Charles V in Tunisia, in 1535.

This gatehouse, or *gopuram* (right), was one of the main entrances to the Eastern Mebon Hindu temple, built during the reign of King Rajendravarman in Angkor, Cambodia, around CE 952.

Gates in some form must have been developed in Neolithic times when it became necessary to keep livestock either inside pens or outside cultivated ground, but they certainly would not have been hinged. We can surmise that they were in the form of the hurdle, still used by farmers into the nineteenth century—a moveable rectangular fence panel, usually framed in light timber, and often filled with basketwork or wattling. It could be used to close an opening, or a number of hurdles could be assembled together to create a temporary pen.

While hinged gateways do not appear until much later, there is plenty of evidence of monumental gateways in early periods. In Egypt, the gate to a temple was usually between two pylons, which were tall blocks of masonry with tapered sides; as temple complexes were often extended outward in stages, the visitor might pass through a succession of these pylon gates. The stone gateway, or *torana,* of the Buddhist shrine of the Great Stupa, at Sanchi, India (250 BCE–CE 250), consists of two stone pillars surmounted by three slightly curved crossbeams, spaced apart. In central India from ancient times onward, the *gopuram,* a massive towered gatehouse between courtyards was a distinctive feature of Hindu temple complexes. In Japan, the *torii,* a type of gateway found at Shinto shrines, is like the torana, but made of timber—an austere and elegant entrance consisting of two uprights and two crosspieces. The Chinese *pai-lou* is a heavier and more elaborate bracketed structure, often built as a memorial. Falling into the same category, and discussed in more detail elsewhere, is the Roman triumphal arch.

The triple-arched gatehouse of the Abbey of Lorsch in southwestern Germany (left) is one of the few intact parts of the eighth-century abbey. Nevertheless, the complex remains a vital source of information on the architecture of the so-called Dark Ages.

In 1701, French designer Jean Tijou installed a series of ironwork gates, now known as the Tijou screens (below), at Hampton Court Palace, Surrey, England. The intricacy of the designs is clear in this closeup.

In the fourth-century Basilica of St. Peter in Rome (Old St. Peter's), triple-arched openings through a two-story gatehouse formed an entranceway to an atrium in front of the church proper. This design was to be interestingly imitated in what is now a detached structure, the gateway to the Abbey of Lorsch, near Worms in southwestern Germany, constructed around CE 800. The strident patterning and zigzag arcading of this building, also known as the Königshalle (King's Hall), derive from its barbarian connections, and tend to conceal its derivation from the Roman prototype.

One of the most distinctive gate types is the medieval lych-gate, used especially in Britain at the entrance to churchyards. It incorporates a small roofed area where a coffin can be left under shelter prior to burial.

The Mannerist Mode

After the Renaissance, gates are important elements of private estates, but generally less important in the public realm. An exception is the Porta Nuova in Palermo, Sicily, Italy, built to celebrate the arrival of Holy Roman Emperor Charles V, then ruler of Sicily, in Palermo in 1535, following a military triumph in Tunisia. It is a wonderful rusticated Mannerist structure decorated with figures of the subjugated Arabs

and Negroes. The pyramid-roofed pavilion on top is an inapposite addition dating from the rebuilding overseen by Gaspare Guercio after the gate was struck by lightning in 1667. Another extraordinary Mannerist example is Salomon de Caus's gateway for the Garden of the Palatinate in Heidelberg Castle, Germany, built in the early seventeenth century. It has a dropped flat-arch lintel flanked by rusticated niches and obelisks, and a complicated pedimental composition incorporating a lion, deer, monkey, and other creatures, reflecting the fact that it was originally designed for the menagerie.

Three English gates can be seen as part of this European Mannerist tradition. One, at the Wilton Estate in Wiltshire, probably designed by Isaac de Caus, the younger brother of Salomon, in the early seventeenth century, is among the first whose integrated design encompasses metal gate leaves as well as rusticated masonry piers. The York Water Gate of 1626–1627, now in Victoria Embankment Gardens, London, was designed by Sir Balthazar Gerbier, a Dutch-born Huguenot, in imitation of Salomon de Brosse's wonderful Fontaine Médicis in Paris. Much later, toward 1660, Gerbier designed a highly flamboyant gateway for Hampstead Marshall, an estate in Berkshire, England, completed after his death by William Winde, another

man with Dutch connections. In this gate, too, the masonry piers and metal leaves were designed as a single scheme.

Leaves of Iron and Steel

Many monumental gateways did not contain a swinging gate leaf or pair of leaves, but most gates to private property did so. Wrought-iron gates were often elaborately decorated, and incorporated gilded elements. Those of the forecourt in front of the Palace of Versailles, southwest of Paris, made in the late seventeenth century, were particularly prominent and influential. They were highly ornate, gilded, and surmounted by the royal coat of arms.

In the nineteenth century, humbler gates were often made of cast iron, or of rolled wrought-iron rods combined with cast-iron elements. But there was also a revival of timber and combined metal and timber gates, and highly picturesque patterns for these were illustrated in publications such as those of J. C. Loudon in Britain in 1833 and Calvert Vaux in the United States in 1857. In the twentieth century, mild steel was often used to imitate the earlier forms of wrought iron. Woven wire and rolled steel might be used on their own or in combination. Later, pipe frames were used with chain-link wire mesh. The metal gate had descended from the sublime to the banal.

Drawbridges and Defenses

The drawbridge so beloved of swashbuckling adventure films has a very limited connection with reality. It did exist, but it was a late arrival in the science of fortification, and used at only a small minority of sites. A drawbridge might be useful in those few cases where the castle or town was surrounded by a moat filled with water, but it was of little use in the more common case where there was a dry ditch, and it was of no use at all where a citadel was built on a hill and the walls were directly accessible to an attacker.

Ditches and Moats

In ancient fortifications built of adobe or other earth construction, the dry ditch was a common feature, as the excavated material could be used to build the wall. An early example is the south wall of the Hittite capital, Hattusas, (in modern Turkey), which dates from around the thirteenth century BCE, where the material from the ditch was mounded up and then the wall proper built on top. But the ditch here was not filled, because water was scarce, and because it was raised above the level of the surrounding terrain. The late

Roman defenses of Constantinople also used a dry ditch, though their walls were of baked brick and stone. Moats filled with water were rare before the late medieval period, and very few survive today, one of the most prominent being at Bodiam Castle in Sussex, England (1385).

Generally the drawbridge formed only a part of the entrance defenses. In front of the gate there might be a forecourt, perhaps lightly defended but sufficient to delay an attacker while the next line of defense was readied. Otherwise there might be an independent fortified structure, or barbican, straddling the entrance axis in front of the gate, preferably connected to the main walls to allow its defenders an avenue of retreat. An early form of barbican, attached directly to the wall, was used at Khorsabad, near Mosul in modern-day Iraq, in about 720 BCE. A clearer, detached example, built in the early thirteenth century, survives at Aleppo, Syria, where it is on a ramped causeway traversing the dry ditch.

The drawbridge is mainly a feature of the later medieval period. At Bodiam there is a very wide moat, and the approach was first by way of a permanent bridge terminating on an octagonal

outwork set in the water. At this outwork the visitor had to turn hard right onto a drawbridge, which led to a barbican. This barbican was also on an island, and a second drawbridge had to be crossed to reach the castle entrance.

The archetypal drawbridge raised by chains to close the doorway was used at Conway Castle in Wales, but this type was only one among a number. Some, as at the Burg Ez-Zefer, Cairo, Egypt, were simply pulled back horizontally onto a platform in front of the gate. In another type, which architectural historian Sidney Toy dates to about the beginning of the fourteenth century, two long timbers projecting outward from the top of the castle entrance were attached by chains to the outer end of the drawbridge below; when the timbers were raised vertically, they raised the bridge, too, to a vertical position, in front of the

The citadel of Aleppo, Syria (below), first became a stronghold in the tenth century CE. The major works of fortification, including this barbican or entrance block, date from the reign of the Ayyubid Sultan al-Zahir al-Ghazi, who ruled from 1186 to 1216.

Drawbridge Design

One type of drawbridge widely used in medieval and Renaissance western Europe used wooden beams bearing long chains to pull the bridge up against the door of the castle.

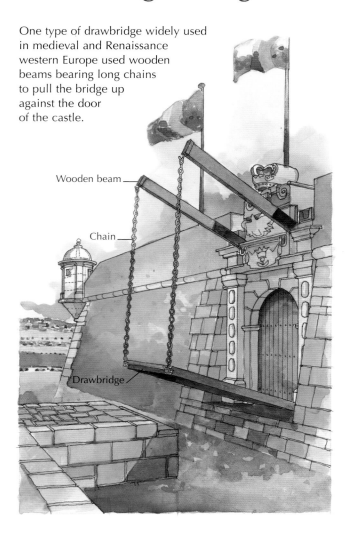

Wooden beam

Chain

Drawbridge

The Château d'Harcourt, a well-preserved medieval castle in Normandy, France, originally had a drawbridge that was retracted horizontally when the castle was under threat. The portcullis at the end of the drawbridge provided further protection.

opening. This type was much used in Italy and France in the fourteenth and fifteenth centuries.

Even if a castle entrance could be sealed by raising a drawbridge, it might also have a portcullis or grille, which slid down grooves at the sides of the opening. This was more convenient for day-to-day use, and it could be dropped instantaneously, whereas raising the bridge took time and effort. It was usually of timber, with points shod in iron.

The Defender's Last Resorts

Even if an attacker managed to penetrate a door, he would not necessarily have gained ready access to the interior. Often he found himself in a confined space, sometimes blocked by another door, where missiles or molten liquid could be launched at him from above. This was a much older device than the drawbridge; excavations have shown that the second city of Troy, around 2000 BCE, had such a space inside its gate, though whether there was a second gate here is unclear. The three surviving gates of the Hittite capital of Hattusas (the Royal, Lion, and Sphinx gates), of about 1400 BCE, are all double gates, within which an attacker could be penned.

At Medinet Habu in Egypt (c. 1200 BCE), there was an outer wall and gate, and then an inner wall whose only opening led into a constricted passage which led to another gate that was itself double. Beyond such chambers, access passages often sloped upward and doglegged, so that they presented no direct line of fire and could be readily defended. Something of this is seen in the ancient city of Tiryns in Greece, which flourished around 1300 BCE, and in the most complete of the crusader castles, Krak des Chevaliers in Syria, built in the early thirteenth century CE, which has a system of such passages.

Place of Refuge

In the small town of Steinsburg, close to Baden in southern Germany, a drawbridge was used in an unusual way to defend a late Romanesque octagonal tower, which stood in a walled enclosure with ordinary houses outside. The bottom floor of the tower was a large arched room that was normally used to store provisions, and probably at times as a dungeon for prisoners, but it had no access to the upper levels. The entrance to the tower was located on the second story, which was connected by a drawbridge to the neighboring houses. In times of trouble, the citizens would cross into the tower and quickly pull up the drawbridge. Isolated there, they might hold out for a considerable time, depending upon the amount of provisions they had with them, and could defend themselves even if the enemy occupied the ground floor.

Portals

The portal is the architectural elaboration of a major entrance to a building, and often the element that most defines its character and image. The Egyptian pylon gate is in some sense a portal, but the first really specialized examples are those of Mesopotamia, in which the arch is introduced into formal architecture. The arch was never recognized by the Egyptians or by the classical Greeks, for these were masonry cultures in which post and beam construction had defined the norms for serious architecture. In Mesopotamia, however, where there was little or no stone or timber (depending upon the exact location), construction was necessarily in adobe or baked brick; and the only way to span a large opening using small units such as bricks is with an arch. By around 700 BCE (and perhaps much earlier), the arch had become an architecturally

The triple portal of the cathedral of Reims, France (below), of the late thirteenth century, has over five hundred statues and a rose window in each archway.

acceptable form for a major entrance. The gateway to the Palace of Sargon at Khorsabad, Iraq (706 BCE), was a large archway set between two massive pavilions. Similarly, a plaque from a gateway at Balawat (the ancient Ingur-Bel), Iraq, of about 700 BCE, shows the castle of the King of Tyre with a large arched entrance; and a bronze model of an Urartu fortress, found at Toprakkale in Asia Minor, has a similar doorway.

Without some sort of projecting structure around it, an arched or other entrance barely

San Juan Bautista, Baños de Cerrato, Spain (above), was built in CE 661 by King Recceswinth and is said to be the oldest surviving Visigothic church in Spain.

qualifies as a portal, and in that sense the portal is not really a standard element in the Near East, and nor is it in Europe until the medieval period. It is much harder to be precise about other cultures. There are certainly Indian and Chinese entrance structures that can be regarded as por-

tals, but they are so varied as to make the term almost useless. It is more interesting to consider why the portal did not develop in the classical world, and the answer is simply the use of columns. A structure of freestanding columns, or portico, is the main alternative to a portal, and this was the classical norm.

Medieval Elaborations

The origins of the medieval portal can in part be traced back to late Roman city gates. At the Palace of Diocletian, Spalato, in present-day Croatia, of about CE 300), the main gate, the Porta Aurea, is a fortified entrance and has no freestanding columns at the front. But it does have architectural pretensions and is part of a family. A similar but cruder form of the same design is used at Resafe in Syria, a little later in date, while across the Adriatic at Ravenna in Italy it is loosely reflected in the so-called Palace of the Exarchs, or Calchi Palace, which dates possibly from the sixth century CE.

Ravenna played an important role in medieval architecture because it influenced the brick architecture of the Lombards nearby, and they in turn created the so-called First Romanesque style, which spread across southern France and into Spanish Catalonia. Meanwhile, there were some other experiments in elaborating the entrance. The seventh-century church of Santa Maria Foris Portas, at Castelseprio in northern Italy, has a very large gabled porch, or exonarthex, with an arched opening extending almost to roof height. The Visigothic church of San Juan Bautista at Baños de Cerrato in Spain, of CE 661, has a square projecting porch with a lobed arch doorway, grand by the standards of the time, which was originally set into a colonnade or arcade extending across the façade and returning at either side.

It is when these experiments begin to coalesce in the Carolingian period with the triple-arched form of the gatehouse to the Abbey of Lorsch in Germany, described earlier in this chapter, that the triple portal of the Romanesque and Gothic church is invented. The church of Saint-Riquier, at Centula in France, built around CE 800 and long since demolished, had a triple-arched entrance at the west end, and so did the derivative Corvey Abbey in Germany (CE 822–824), though both were rather plainly treated.

Multiple Archways

The elaboration of the entrance arch is a separate development. In the Romanesque period, doors and windows were often framed by multiple arches, supported by colonettes, with each one set a little smaller than the one outside it. The pairing of arch and colonettes is known as an order (a usage that has little connection with the word as used in relation to classical architecture). This multiple-order form springs in part from structural issues involved in the creation of an arch in a very thick wall, and in part from the Romanesque urge to articulate all volumes and surfaces. A Romanesque doorway can easily

The Portico de la Gloria (1168–1188) in the cathedral of Santiago de Compostela, Spain, is adorned with carvings of the Last Judgment by sculptor Maestro Mateo.

have five or more concentric orders, and the more there are the farther the door itself is set in from the outer wall surface. A classic example is the door of Sainte-Marie-des-Dames, Saintes, France, of the mid-twelfth century CE, which has four orders.

The façade of the abbey church of Saint-Denis, outside Paris, as remodeled in about 1135–1140, has three arches, and the central portal, of about 1137, is of the classic Romanesque form. It has three orders, a *trumeau* or central doorjamb, and sculpture in the tympanum (the area below the arch) representing the Last Judgment. At the great pilgrimage church of Santiago de Compostela in Spain, the façade, as remodeled in 1168–1211, also contained three arches, and set within the center of one was the wonderful main doorway, the Portico de la Gloria, which survives today behind a later façade treatment. All that now remained to arrive at the great Gothic portals of churches like Chartres Cathedral and Notre-Dame, Paris, was to change from the semicircular arch to the pointed arch and to unite the three openings into a single composition.

Porticoes

A portico is a columnar structure attached to the front of a building, an idea that first emerges in the Urartu culture of northern and eastern Anatolia around 700 BCE. At the Tesheban (Erebuni) Citadel in Armenia, of about 728 BCE, Soviet and Armenian archaeologists have reconstructed a large portico two columns deep with the rear wall stuccoed and decorated in an Assyrian manner. It is remarkably similar to what is believed to be the form of the Stoa at Samos, Greece, of the sixth century BCE—a stoa is a long verandah-like structure carried on one or two rows of columns, open on one side to the street or the *agora* (public space) and with shops or other buildings along the back.

Classical Styles

In classical Greece, only some smaller temples had porticoes in the form of a small projecting columned structure, and more had columns all around the outside. To understand the range of temple plans, it is necessary to refer back to the development of the *megaron* in Mycenean and Luwian times. The megaron was the basic house or temple form, consisting of a single room with a central door at one end and the side walls projecting out to form a small porch. As such structures grew in size, some gained a row of columns along the axis of the interior, and by the eighth century BCE buildings with a row of columns all around the outside began to appear.

The Romans tended to prefer axial buildings with one clearly designated point of entry, so many of their temples were prostyle, often with an axial flight of steps leading up to the porch. A similar portico could be used on a non-rectangular building, as was the case with the Pantheon. This is a particularly interesting example because it looks as if the portico doesn't fit properly: a pedimental shape higher up on the body of the building appears to indicate that a taller portico was meant to be attached. It is now believed that the Pantheon was designed to have columns with shafts measuring 50 Roman feet in height, or an overall height of 60 ft (18 m) including the base and capital, but that somehow—whether through a mistake or because of the difficulty of moving such large monoliths —the builders subsequently settled for 40-foot (12-m) shafts and a height of 48 ft (14.6 m).

"Temple Beauties"

The columnar portico is rare in medieval buildings, though in the cathedral at Palermo, Sicily, Italy, one of the three arches of the portico (1480) is carried on columns between side walls (in classical terms, distyle in antis). Florence has more important examples of this sort. The Loggia dei Lanzi or Loggia dei Priori, of 1376–1381, on the Palazzo della Signoria in Florence, consists of three semicircular arches under a horizontal roof rather than a pediment, and was the inspiration not only for the arcade of Brunelleschi's famous Ospedale degli Innocenti, or Foundling Hospital (1421–1445), but also for Alberti's Loggia Rucellai (1460), not far away. Subsequently, Andrea Palladio seems to have believed that ordinary Roman villas had been like temples, though less elaborate, and he gave many of his villas

Temple Terminology

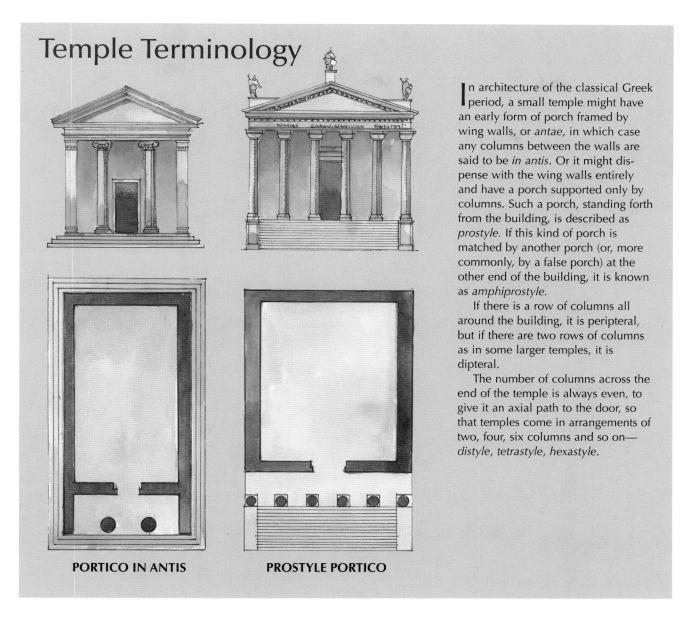

PORTICO IN ANTIS

PROSTYLE PORTICO

In architecture of the classical Greek period, a small temple might have an early form of porch framed by wing walls, or *antae,* in which case any columns between the walls are said to be *in antis.* Or it might dispense with the wing walls entirely and have a porch supported only by columns. Such a porch, standing forth from the building, is described as *prostyle.* If this kind of porch is matched by another porch (or, more commonly, by a false porch) at the other end of the building, it is known as *amphiprostyle.*

If there is a row of columns all around the building, it is peripteral, but if there are two rows of columns as in some larger temples, it is dipteral.

The number of columns across the end of the temple is always even, to give it an axial path to the door, so that temples come in arrangements of two, four, six columns and so on—*distyle, tetrastyle, hexastyle.*

The extra pedimental shape above the portico of the Pantheon, Rome (right), suggests that the structure was originally intended to be significantly higher.

pedimented porticoes resembling temple fronts; these are now seen as characteristic of his work.

Later porticoes almost all derive directly or indirectly from Roman architecture, and are so numerous as to defy description and so common as to perhaps seem uninteresting. But they always created a stir when they first appeared. In Britain, the first pedimented portico of the temple type was created by Inigo Jones at St. Paul's Church, Covent Garden, from 1631; Jones also designed the first with a horizontal entablature, on the west front of the old St. Paul's Cathedral, from 1633. At Covent Garden, the patron, the Earl of Bedford, complained that he could scarcely afford a barn, let alone a church: to which Jones replied "Then, my lord, you shall have the handsomest barn in England." He achieved this by using a sort of Etruscan style requiring less elaborate carving than the Corinthian, or even the Doric. Only in the early eighteenth century did Colen Campbell follow Palladio in putting temple porticoes onto private houses or, as he said, introducing "the Temple beauties in a private building."

159

Façades

The term "façade" is used for the main or front face of a building, or sometimes for any face that has been given a formal architectural treatment. The façade can broadly be said to be an invention of the Romans. There are many pre-Roman examples of course, but most earlier major buildings, such as those of the ancient Near East, tended to be plain externally, apart from some architectural elaboration at the main entrance, and ordinary housing tended to be built cheek by jowl on very narrow streets and to look inward to a courtyard, leaving the exterior unadorned. In any case, it was certainly the Romans who first created some sort of system for façade design.

Designing around the Arch

A classical building tends to be defined by its columns—for example, whether they are Doric, Ionic, or Corinthian, how big they are, and how they are arranged—and the nature of this arrangement can be described as the ordonnance. A less formal building may not have columns, and is therefore astylar (the term means "without columns," not "without a style"). In this case, it is defined more by the arrangement of doors and windows, also known as fenestration (from the Latin *fenestra,* meaning "window").

The Romans were the first to grapple with serious issues of principle involved in architectural ordonnance. Classical Greek architecture was generally single storied and trabeated—that is, based on the post and beam principle—and did not incorporate arches. Although the Romans had great respect for the Greek tradition, especially in religious or civic buildings, their buildings were usually multistoried and based upon the structural principle of the arch, or arcuated. Thus they faced two significant challenges—what was the correct way to design a multistory façade, and how was the arch to be used in the exterior of a building?

The solution to multistory design—which seems obvious enough to us today—was to stack up one more or less identical story on another, as at the Colosseum in Rome. The designers of the Colosseum solved the other problem in a subtler manner. The body of the building was made of concrete with barrel (or semicircular) vaults running both radially and circumferentially, and these arches are expressed externally, appearing to rest on solid rectangular piers of

One of the stone male figures that once supported the entablature on the Temple of Olympian Zeus, at Agrigento, Sicily, Italy, (above) was rebuilt on site.

The Colosseum in Rome (below), is faced in a complete system of columns and entablatures which has little to do with the actual arched structure.

stone. However, across the face of this arcuated system is constructed a trabeated system of classical columns carrying horizontal beams. This was a gesture of respect for the Greek tradition, but only that. The columns carry no load, and the whole apparatus has been introduced merely to satisfy architectural propriety. This specific device, a system of beams on columns overlying a system of arches on piers, was to be copied again and again in the Renaissance. Moreover, the general idea of a *represented* structure drawn across the face of the building was to be used even in the interiors of medieval churches.

Sculptural Elements

The introduction of sculpture, especially of human figures, was another important development in the evolution of the façade. Many early cultures had walls decorated with faience or shallow reliefs, and placed ceremonial creatures on either side of major doorways, but it was the Greeks who made the human figure an integral part of architecture. Perhaps the most famous example is the porch of the Erechtheion in Athens (421–405 BCE), which is supported by female figures, or *caryatids*, but an earlier and more interesting one is the Temple of Zeus Olympieon at Agrigento, Sicily (510–409 BCE), now a ruin, where sculptures of giant male figures or *atlantes* (*telamones* in Latin), with their hands crossed over their heads, originally helped support the entablature.

Sculpture never played such an integral role in Roman buildings, but in Romanesque and Gothic architecture the porch was often carved with great intricacy, and this often included lateral figures corresponding to each order of arches and purporting to support the structure. The most beautiful sculpted porches are those of Saint-Trophîme at Arles (1150) and Saint-Gilles-du-Gard (1135–95), both in Provence, France. Such sculpture was not used in the Renaissance, but it reappeared in Mannerism, and *atlantes* and other such figures were particularly favored in Germany.

The Palazzo Type

The Renaissance palazzo introduced a simple façade type that was to prove extraordinarily adaptable and popular. The palazzo of fifteenth century Florence was still as much medieval as Renaissance in character. Although the building was to some degree introverted, and at times fortified, it was also designed to express the owners' prestige and taste externally. The ground floor tended to be treated as massive masonry (often referred to, confusingly, as "rusticated"), and normally there were two more floors treated as smooth-dressed masonry, and an overhanging cornice at the top. The second level was that of the main reception rooms, the *piano nobile*, and

The magnificent Romanesque portal of the church of Saint-Trophîme in Arles, France (1150), combines columns and an entablature reflecting the strong classical tradition of Provence with the multiple sacred sculptures that would subsequently become the norm in the Gothic style.

tended to be the tallest. In the early period, the lower windows were sometimes arched, in the medieval tradition, but increasingly all the windows came to be treated with classically molded surrounds, and the most important of them with triangular or segmental pediments, as if each were a little building—a composition known as an aedicule. With or without these extravagances, the palazzo façade was found to be highly adaptable for use in the design of offices, factories, clubs (famously in Pall Mall, London), department stores, and even some early skyscrapers.

An unfortunate consequence of concentrating upon the façade has emerged in the last half century. Under development pressures, buildings of importance are often partly demolished, with the exception of the original façade, which is left as the veneer for a new structure. The phenomenon is known as façadism. To the serious conservationist, it is on a par with having your dead mother stuffed and then keeping her in the living room.

This example of façadism in Valparaiso, Chile, shows how a building's façade may be not only preserved but also incorporated in a new structure.

Paris Opera
Paris, France

Construction of the Paris Opera (also known as the Opéra Garnier or Palais Garnier, after the architect) was delayed by mishaps and political turmoil such as the Franco-Prussian War of 1870–1871. The building was finally opened on January 15, 1875.

In the design of the Paris Opera, begun in 1862, the building's architect Jean-Louis-Charles Garnier challenged the academic orthodoxy of French architecture, and the assumption that design should be based upon the authority of either classical or medieval precedent. Rampant and unprincipled eclecticism was to be the order of the day. This is vividly expressed in the building's façade, which is richly decorated and gilded and enormously impressive, though perhaps somewhat facile in its theatricality.

The centre of the façade is recessed between projecting pavilions in the reverse of the normal order of things (notwithstanding the precedent of the original park front of the Palace of Versailles), and surprisingly becomes more imposing as a result. The crowning sculpture is Hellenistic in conception, while the elaborately sculpted attic story below is without precedent but has Baroque overtones. The segmental pediments are Roman, though more prominent than any in Rome itself. The colonnade, though ultimately Greek, was a motif which had been favored in France since Claude Perrault's work on the Louvre in the seventeenth century, and the *oeil-de-boeuf* (bull's-eye) windows within it are fairly distinctively French. The scheme of a colonnade with

The sumptuous foyer incorporates gilded carvings, mirrors and ceiling frescoes, by Paul Baudry, depicting themes from the history of music.

pavilions at either end was to be widely imitated, though usually with much less success. Giuseppe Sacconi's Monument to Victor Emmanuel II in Rome (1885–1911) is one universally reprehended example.

The Evolution of a Theatrical Style
Garnier's approach to the design of the Paris Opéra was not entirely novel, for the flamboyant Second Empire Style had already been created at the Louvre. There, since 1853, H.-M. Lefuel had piled sculpture and ornament onto the work of his predecessor, T.-T.-J. Visconti, who had been working in the spirit of Pierre Lescot, the first designer of the building. This lavish French eclecticism soon had a major impact throughout Europe and its dependencies. But if Garnier's work had a dominant source, it was the Baroque, as might be expected, for the Baroque was the most theatrical of styles.

Theater design had evolved rapidly since the Italian Renaissance. Early examples imitated the semicircular *cavea* of the Roman theatre, but gradually the auditorium was lengthened to a shape more like a U, and some theaters were given tiers of boxes. By the seventeenth century, theaters such as the Opera on the Cortina in Vienna (1665–1666), and the Residenztheater in Bayreuth (1744–1808), by Giuseppe and Carlo Bibiena, had three tiers of boxes running continuously around the sides and back of the auditorium; in Italy, La Scala in Milan (1776–1778),

had no less than eight. The aim was to cram a many seats as possible into the auditorium or, rather, to position as many seats as possible within seeing and hearing distance of the stage. In general, however, little thought was given to the use of spaces outside the auditorium.

Directing a Spectacle
The design of the opera house had for two years been in the hands of Charles Rouhault de Fleury, under the direction of Napoleon III, when in 1860 the architect was abruptly dismissed and a competition was initiated. Garnier came fifth in the first stage but won the second stage, infuriating the Empress Eugenie, who had herself entered the competition. Garnier's design was not in any style, in her opinion, not Louis XIV, Louis XV, or Louis XVI. "Madame," responded Garnier, "c'est du Napoléon III"—"it's in the style of Napoleon III." Whether it was in his style or not, however, Napoleon III did not greatly admire it, and the only visit he made was to lay the foundation stone in 1862.

Garnier believed that opera was an expression of humankind's primitive instinct to gather together, share thoughts and dreams, and see and be seen. The spectacle was not confined to the stage, but contributed to by the spectators as well. The Opera was to reflect the entire society of the Second Empire, and whether members of the audience paid more or less, arrived by carriage or foot, their experience would be orchestrated for them. Even queuing was a part of the ritual, and details were considered such as mirrors in the foyer so that the women (not, apparently, the men) could make last-minute adjustments to their appearance before entering the great stair hall. Here, passing up and down the stairs, the wealthy displayed themselves to each other and to the lower orders who looked down from above. Though the staircase was copied from the one designed by Victor Louis at Bordeaux, G. A. Sala called it "the finest arrangement of curvilinear perspective that I have ever seen."

The auditorium seated over two thousand people and was of the traditional horseshoe shape, with four tiers of boxes. It was not aesthetically exciting, for Garnier argued (or rationalised) that attention was to be directed to the stage. These subsidiary spaces, however, were more generous than in almost any previous theater, including smoking rooms for the men and ice-cream parlors for the women, all richly colored and sumptuously decorated. Garnier also designed his own heating, ventilating, and stage machinery, which did much to establish an approach to theatre design as an exercise in technical as much as aesthetic virtuosity.

Taking the Strain

Every building must support the weight of its roof, whether the means to do that is a wall, a pier, or a column. The combination of a vertical post or column and a horizontal beam—known as trabeation—was the first structural system used in monumental architecture.

Post and Beam

It is easy for us to imagine how our ancient forebears might have placed one stick between two trees and thus invented the sheltering potential of the simple span. Every time a child plays with blocks and discovers how three blocks can create an opening, the invention is recapitulated. In architecture, the combination of vertical posts and horizontal beams, or lintels, is known as trabeation. Place a series of these three-part configurations in some geometric arrangement, and you will have what is known as a basic structural "bay." Assemble a series of bays, stack the arrangement, and multistory architecture is born.

In the post and beam system, the posts are in compression. The beam is in bending. This involves a combination of compression forces, which in a simple beam are towards the upper surface, and tension forces, which are toward the bottom. As with all spanning problems, both gravity and lateral forces act upon the system, which is actually much more sophisticated than its simple intuitive form suggests. Forces are transferred along the beam to the posts, and thence into the ground or foundation. Both horizontal and vertical members of the system must be appropriately sized, depending on the material used, to do the job of spanning without collapse.

Inspired by Nature

For our ancestors, nature provided many examples of sheltering spans, in the form of caves, natural arches, trees, and groves. Trees, in various combinations, perhaps offered the strongest suggestion of post and beam structures, and it is no surprise that wood was and is an excellent material for any trabeated architecture. Wood has the property of behaving well in both compression and tension, in part due to its directional grain: forces acting parallel to the grain in posts encounter good compressive resistance. It can also resist the combination of tension and compression forces which occur in a loaded beam. However, wood also has its drawbacks—it decays and weathers, burns easily, and can only span so far—and the builders of early wooden buildings had to find ways to counter these problems.

A particularly strong tradition of wooden post and beam architecture developed in East Asia, where wood was plentiful and wooden post and beam systems complemented a deeply traditional way of life. Early builders in China and Japan tended to extend the roof beyond the walls below, to provide protection from rain. This resulted in the wooden trabeated architecture being explicit and highly visible, and gave rise to distinctive features, such as elaborate bracketing at the corners of buildings to support a massive, overhanging roof. In the great Sakyamuni Pagoda of the Fogong Temple, a Buddhist complex in Yingxian, China (CE 1056), the bracketing also supports continuous balconies at each story, becoming a decorative motif for the entire five-level tower.

With the spread of rice cultivation across the East, raised floor buildings were required to keep surplus rice away from damp and vermin, and the wooden post and beam system was well suited to this type of structure. In Japan in particular, the raised floor building became the standard form for granary, shrine, and house. At the Great Shrine of Ise, Japan, built in 690 CE, in a form reminiscent of an early granary, the Shinto custodians of the temple found a unique way to deal with the decay of the wooden shrine of the sun goddess. Every 20 years, right up to the present day, the shrine is entirely rebuilt by specially trained carpenters.

In Japan, the upper classes adopted the raised floor building, using it for similar practical purposes but also as an ordering device for the hierarchical social space of the house. The joinery of

A teahouse in the grounds of the seventeenth-century Katsura Imperial Villa, near Kyoto, Japan. This type of structure, with its prominent posts and beams is typical of early Japanese trabeated architecture.

Lanyon Quoit (left) is a Stone Age dolmen near Madron, Cornwall, England. One of the simplest forms of post and beam structure, dolmens were used as burial chambers, and after construction were normally covered with a large mound of earth.

the beam to the post (for example the mortise and tenon joints seen at the seventeenth-century Katsura Imperial Villa outside Kyoto) provided a minimalist decorative expression in harmony with the prevailing Zen Buddhism of the Japanese upper classes. The span was limited by the material and technology, yet the Japanese architects used that limitation to full advantage. The basic structural bay was repeated, and was thus modular. The modularity extended to the other surfaces, such as the floor, which was usually covered with interlocking tatami mats.

From Wood to Stone

The oldest surviving trabeated structures are of stone, but their span is necessarily limited. Stone behaves extremely well in compression, but in tension it is weak and tends to split apart. Different kinds of stone offer builders different properties. Sandstone and limestone are easy to carve but often too porous or friable. Granite is hard and durable but difficult to carve. Marble, if close-grained, can be near to ideal: strong and durable yet workable. Without exception, all stone has high density and is therefore heavy and difficult to maneuver in large blocks. This makes it all the more remarkable that many of the most impressive buildings of the prehistoric era consist of post and beam structures made using enormous stone blocks, known as megaliths.

The earliest megalithic architecture dates from the fourth millennium BCE. Much of it seems to have been motivated by religious observances, including ritual burials, fertility rites, and even sacrifices. Some megalithic structures may have been a way to claim territory. Others may have had an astronomical function. Stones were sometimes erected singly (often called a menhir), as found at Filitosa in Corsica, where menhirs carved with human faces and forms were erected around 1500 BCE; or in rows and circles, as at the large, well-preserved stone circle of Callanish

on the Outer Hebridean island of Lewis in Scotland, which dates from around 2000 BCE.

Three large stones were often combined to form a trilithon: two uprights capped by a horizontal lintel. Among the most common megalithic structures were tombs known as dolmens. These took the most basic post and beam form: several crude uprights supporting an enormous tablelike beam or slab. After construction, dolmens were usually covered with earth; in many cases, over millennia, the earth has since been eroded, exposing the distinctive stone structure. Other forms of megalithic architecture include corbelled tombs, like those found at Carnac in Brittany, France, and passage tombs, among the most magnificent of which is the one at Newgrange, Ireland.

On the Mediterranean islands of Malta and Gozo are some of the oldest surviving examples of stone post and beam construction. A series of temple enclosures dating from 3500–2500 BCE

Threshold of the Sacred

A distinctive feature of Japanese Shinto shrines is the *torii*, a traditional gateway. Frequently built of wood, but sometimes of stone, and often painted red, a torii usually frames a landscape view of special quality. Passing through the torii marks the transition from the profane (the outside world) to the sacred (the inside of the shrine). Some shrines have multiple torii; for example, at the Fushimi Inari shrine in Kyoto, thousands of torii are set close together. The origin of the torii is shrouded in legend; however, its form is one of the clearest and simplest expressions of post and beam architecture.

At Itsuku Island, Hiroshima Prefecture, Japan, this *torii* stands at the entrance to a sixth-century shrine. Built on tidal flats, the torii is partially submerged at high tide, making it appear to float on the sea.

Greek Temple Plans

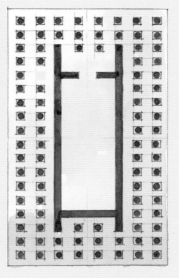

PERIPTERAL TEMPLE
In a peripteral temple, a single line of columns, or *peripteros*, runs around the outside of the building, supporting the roof.

DIPTERAL TEMPLE
A dipteral temple has two rows of columns, usually parallel and equally spaced, around the outside of the building.

has been found at sites including Ggantija, Hagar Qim, Mnajdra, and Tarxien. Half-oval spaces alternate with narrow passageways made with monolithic jambs and lintels. Figurines found at these sites suggest that they were places where people worshipped the Mother Goddess through sacrifice and other, unknown rituals.

At one of the oldest surviving Buddhist monuments, the Great Stupa at Sanchi, India, built between 250 BCE and CE 250, we can see a trabeated stone construction that mimics wooden gates and fencing. The stupa itself, a dome-shaped shrine, lies within a circular sacred enclosure, or *harmika*, consisting of posts and lintels containing three continuous horizontal members with a roundish profile. Cut stone techniques were brought to India from Persia a few centuries after Buddha (*c.* 563–*c.* 483 BCE), and they can be seen in the stupa gates *(torana)* at Sanchi, which are elaborately carved with figures from Buddhist legend, including lions and elephants.

How did humans 5,000 years ago lift stones as big as houses? The difficulty would seem prohibitive, yet this is what people did, over and over. The exact methods are unclear, but we can say with some certainty that accomplishing this took a fairly sophisticated system of cooperative effort.

A section of the forecourt of the Temple of Amon at Luxor in Egypt (above), constructed during the reign of Amenhotep III (1390–1353 BCE). The columns bounding the forecourt are carved in the form of bundled papyrus reeds.

The Temple of Hera I (below), also known as the Basilica, at Paestum, near Salerno, Italy, was part of a settlement established by Greek colonists in the sixth century BCE. The peripteral temple has a broad plan, with eight columns.

Cutting the enormous stones would have presented another challenge at a time when metallurgy was still at a primitive stage, and widely used metals such as copper, or even hardened copper in the form of bronze, were too soft for stone cutting. Apparently, most megalith builders did not use metal at all, but a stone-headed hammer or maul. A similar technique was used by the Hittites of Central Anatolia, until *c.* 1200 BCE.

The Triumph of the Stone Span

Under the Egyptians, who did not have many timber resources, stone construction flourished. Cut-stone masonry was first used at Saqqara around 2700 BCE. In Egyptian architecture, there was a clear botanical metaphor for the column, which could be a stylized papyrus plant or lotus. The bundling of the papyrus reeds suggests fluting, as seen in abundance at the New Kingdom temple complex at Luxor (*c.* 1360 BCE). It is known that bundled reeds were in fact used in the construction of lesser Egyptian buildings, as for example in Iraq until recently.

One of the most magnificent examples of the Egyptan stonemasons' work is the mortuary temple of Queen Hatshepsut at Deir el-Bahari (*c.* 1520 BCE). Here we find an austere and impressive array of piers and lintels, arranged on monumentally scaled terraces in strict symmetry. Every aspect of a project like this one, which even had a built-in irrigation system, had to be carefully planned, from quarrying the stone to the final touches with the finishing chisel.

There is some evidence that the Greeks learned the art of masonry from the Egyptians. But they also innovated, creating their own special building type, the peripteral temple, which was based upon the stone post and beam system. A peripteral temple was usually rectangular with a gable roof of wood and tiles and a continuous line of columns, or *peripteros*, wrapping the building and engaging the roof edge. Many different theories have been put forth as to the conceptual origin of the peripteros. It may be that the roof overhang allowed and supported by the line of columns at the perimeter was designed to protect the inner wall that enclosed the cult statue, which was often made of simple mud brick.

At the ancient site of Paestum, near the city of Salerno in southern Italy we can see some of the best-preserved peripteral temples. Here, as in the Egyptian buildings mentioned above, the stone cannot span very far, and so there must be many columns arranged in rows or grids. At the Temple of Hera I at Paestum (*c.* 530 BCE), the columns have an almost figural presence. They exhibit two features that became essential for all monumental Greek architecture: the top of the column, or capital, splays out to take the weight of the beam; and the shaft of the column is tapered, gently curving inward as it rises—a form called *entasis*. This shaping of the Greek column is an almost animated expression of the compressive resistance to gravity.

Stonehenge
Wiltshire, England

The most famous Megalithic site of all is visible for miles across a chalky-soiled plain near Salisbury, England: Stonehenge. The brooding presence of its massive standing trilithons has fascinated people for centuries. Some believed, erroneously, that the stones had been erected by druids; others that the builders were Egyptians, Mycenaeans, Romans—even Martians! An association with dark forces has persisted: in the nineteenth-century Thomas Hardy set the final downfall of the tragic heroine of his novel *Tess of the d'Urbervilles* among the monoliths of Stonehenge.

The true builders of Stonehenge were simply the early inhabitants of the area. Megalithic culture appeared in the British Isles some 6,000 years ago and gave rise to numerous standing stones and earthworks. The emergence of the culture coincided with the shift from hunting and gathering to agriculture. The oldest surviving built remains are mainly burial mounds surrounded by circular earthworks. Mapping the distribution of these early burial mounds in southern England indicates the probability of equal small territories, each with some identity, surrounding each burial center. Some time around 3000 BCE, the simple clusters of burial mounds gave way to major ritual enclosures

called henges. The henge builders belonged to much larger communities, and the complexes they built, including Stonehenge, would have required a fairly sophisticated organization, perhaps with greater top-down leadership.

The earliest phase of building at Stonehenge, *c*. 2900 BCE, involved the creation of a circular ditch and bank with 56 holes at various points, of uncertain use. Some 400 years later, 82 grey-blue dolerite stones quarried in the mountains of Wales were erected in a double-ring of 38 free-standing pairs; the six remaining stones defined the northeastern approach axis. These so-called bluestones were repositioned several times, despite the fact that each weighed approximately 2 tons (1.8 tonnes). At some point, a massive standing monolith, known as the Heel Stone, was installed to the northeast. Finally, around the year 2300 BCE, 75 massive stone lintels and standing stones (called sarsen stones), some weighing about 20 tons (18 tonnes), were hauled to the site from a quarry almost 20 mi (32 km) distant (exactly how remains a mystery, although levers, drag ropes, and supporting wedges may have been used). The trilithons visible today were part of that ensemble. Stonehenge remained an active cult place for another 12 centuries, and then religious activity there ceased.

Stonehenge and the Cosmos

Contemporary archaeo-astronomers have studied Stonehenge intensely and can show that the placement of the standing stones indicated not only the solstices but also solar and lunar eclipses. This is credible on several levels. Solar movements were of utmost importance to farming peoples everywhere in the temperate latitudes, who were at the mercy of the seasonal cycle. Also, most cosmologies worldwide recognized the moon, too, as the second largest celestial body, as having importance almost equal to that of the sun and therefore being well worth tracking. For example, at present-day Newark, Ohio, in the United States, between 200 BCE and CE 500, the early Native American Hopewell people built a huge octagonal earthwork (known as the Octagon) and associated features, which spread out over a large area and indicated the northernmost moonrise, an event with a periodicity of 18.6 years. It is not too big of a leap to suppose that the Hopewell, and the henge builders, believed in some metanarrative surrounding the celestial bodies and their interventions in human affairs.

At Stonehenge the choice of site would almost certainly have been highly significant in this respect, too. The wide surrounding plain facilitates observation of the horizon. It also

enhances an appreciation of the patterns inherent in astronomical cycles. It is an unforgettable place in both manmade and natural aspects.

New Evidence, New Controversy

The use of advanced archaeological techniques, such as aerial radar, has led to a new understanding of the activities that took place at Stonehenge and of how it might have been linked to other, similar sites across the south of England. Most archaeologists now agree that festivals, possibly involving ritual procession, took place concurrently at these sites. Recently, excavations at Durrington Walls, 2 mi (3.2 km) north of Stonehenge, have also revealed a village settlement, which may have been the home of the Stonehenge builders, since the dating coincides. Questions still to be answered involve the exact relationship between the village and Stonehenge, the relation of both to the River Avon, the temporality of village and henge, and the functions of certain of the village buildings.

Another new theory, still very controversial among researchers, is that the bluestones were believed in prehistoric times to have healing powers. If this were true, then Stonehenge would also have been a sort of prehistoric Lourdes as well as an astronomical observatory.

Debate also surrounds the preservation of Stonehenge, which is a World Heritage Site. A busy highway passes near the outer ditch of Stonehenge and providing visitor facilities, including parking, is difficult. The most extreme remedy proposed involves building a tunnel for the highway, which could be prohibitively expensive. At any rate, the expanding regional understanding of Stonehenge and related

monuments suggests that the ever-high curiosity about the site, combined with the popularity of walking, cycling, and horseback riding, would make a system of trails connecting Stonehenge, Durrington Walls, the Avon, and other sites, most appropriate and welcome.

A considerable amount of cooperation, pulling power, and leverage would have been required to erect the standing stones and maneuver the lintels into place.

This aerial view of the site today clearly shows the horseshoe of trilithons within the sarsen circle.

A carving of a column flanked by lions caps the entrance to Mycenae, the city that dominated the Greek mainland in the period 1600–1100 BCE.

Trajan's Column in Rome was originally surrounded by a series of high colonnaded galleries from which its reliefs could be closely examined.

Columns

Although it is an intrinsic part of the post and beam construction, the post or column can, of course, stand up on its own. Throughout history, the column has been regarded as sacred in certain cultures, and freestanding columns as monuments abound in the history of architecture. Roughly speaking, the column can be seen as a stand-in for the human figure in that most human of positions: upright. But many additional metaphors can also apply: the column stands for human construction, for human power, or as an antenna opening up communication between humans and gods—on an abstract level, the vertical column is the *axis mundi*, the point of connection between Earth and the heavens.

Sacred Stones
One of the earliest signs of the significance of the column in the ancient Greek world is the famous

Lion Gate of Mycenae. Built around 1250 BCE, this entranceway to the Mycenaean citadel is capped by a low-relief stone carving, roughly triangular in shape, which sits directly above the massive 16-ft (5-m) wide stone lintel of the gateway, and below the corbelled wall above, which acts as a sort of relieving arch for the lintel. The carving shows a stone column flanked by two lions. The column is of a style (with reverse tapering and pillow-shaped capital) seen in the architecture of the Minoans of Crete, whom the Mycenaeans eclipsed as a power in the Aegean Sea and from whom they borrowed many architectural forms.

In ancient Egypt, there was another supposedly magical, much-revered form, the obelisk, which was almost always a granite monolith. The top of the obelisk usually had a pyramidal shape, and the obelisk was considered to be an object linking the worldly leader of the Egyptians, the

pharaoh, with the god of the sun and chief creator, Ra. The sides of the obelisk were usually inscribed with elaborate hieroglyphics. Often obelisks were reused, and even reinscribed.

Classical Column-monuments
In ancient Greece, as in Egypt and elsewhere, sacred or honorific columns tended to adorn the most holy places. Delphi, between Mount Parnassus and the north coast of the Gulf of Corinth, was sacred to Apollo, was considered to be the navel of the world (they actually built a navel here out of stone), and was also the headquarters of the most famous oracle in Greece, the Pythia. Pilgrims traveled to Delphi from all parts of the Greek world and many built column-monuments in tribute to the gods. One of the oldest surviving is the charming Naxian Sphinx, donated by the island of Naxos. Its sphinx perches, cat-like, on a large, fluted (grooved) column with an early Ionic capital.

The Romans were great admirers of Greek culture and appropriated many of its artistic and architectural forms, but they also had their own creative energy and traditions. They synthesized Greek architecture in innovative and unique ways. For example, the Emperor Trajan and his architects created a completely new type of column-monument, built in CE 113. Trajan's Column, as the monument is known, still stands today in the partially excavated Forum of Trajan in Rome. The marble column is 125 ft (38 m) high, and has a spiral staircase, also of cut stone, running up its hollow center. As famous as the column itself is the spiral frieze, carved with a continuous narrative, that winds around the entire shaft and tells the story of the two Dacian Wars in 155 scenes. It is valued for its intrinsic artistic qualities, but also for the wealth of detail about Roman warfare, building, towns, and infrastructure shown in the panels. The frieze was probably added by Trajan's successor, Hadrian, but it clearly celebrates Trajan's skill as head of the Roman legions.

Trajan's Column, which subsequently provided the model for the Column of Marcus Aurelius in CE 180, was such a beloved monument that it never suffered the dilapidation of much of Rome's monumental center. By the early Middle Ages, however, it had been appropriated as a belfry for the tiny church of San Nicola de Columna. It was the first ancient monument claimed by the popes (in the 1550s) and the fact that they were willing to demolish a church in order to show off a pagan monument demonstrates how deeply embedded humanistic concerns were in the Italian Peninsula at the time. Nonetheless, in 1588, a bronze statue of St. Peter was placed at the very top of the column, and St Paul was placed at the top of Marcus Aurelius's column in 1589 by Pope Sixtus V, the pope who set up so many obelisks all over Rome.

To Honor and Commemorate

Roman frieze columns provided inspiration for later architects. In the Baroque period, a young Austrian stonemason, Johann Bernhard Fischer von Erlach trained in Rome in the studio of Carlo Fontana, an eminent Italian architect, and

Rome's Obelisks

After the Romans conquered Egypt and made it a province of their empire, all things Egyptian suddenly became the rage in Rome. Dozens of obelisks, despite their weight and risk of breakage, were dismantled and shipped to Rome, where they were reerected in important public places. The Roman Emperor Augustus even used one as the needle for a gigantic sundial that he had built just north of Rome's civic center. In the early Middle Ages, as the remnants of the empire crumbled away, the obelisks were largely forgotten. That all changed in the Renaissance, when the obelisks were appropriated by the popes, starting with Pope Sixtus V, and positioned all over Rome as an expression of papal temporal power.

Pope Clement XI had this obelisk erected in the Piazza della Rotonda in Rome in 1711.

soaked up knowledge about both contemporary and ancient monuments. Returning to the Hapsburg court in Vienna, his knowledge and talents gained him favor with his imperial patrons, who appreciated his talent and rewarded him with elevation to the nobility. His most successful work in Vienna, the Karlskirche

J.B Fischer von Gerlach's Karlskirche in Vienna, Austria, aimed to combine elements from great buildings of the past, including Trajan's Column, the Pantheon, St. Peter's, and Istanbul's Hagia Sophia.

(St. Charles's Church; 1716–1737), incorporated not one but two spiral frieze column-monuments in its spectacular ceremonial façade.

The column-monument continued to be a popular choice for memorializing momentous events, such as the Great Fire of London of 1666, which was commemorated by the construction of a column designed by Sir Christopher Wren and Robert Hooke and completed in 1677, which still stands at the end of Monument Street near London Bridge. Nonetheless, an association with victory remained strong. Nelson's Column in Trafalgar Square, London, a Corinthian column topped by a statue of Admiral Horatio Nelson, was designed by William Railton and built in the early 1840s to commemorate Nelson's victories over France, including the battle of Trafalgar, at which he died. The Berlin Victory Column, or Siegessaüle, capped with a golden statue of Victory personified, marked Prussian triumphs over Denmark, Austria, and France in the wars of the 1860s and 1870s.

Roman Innovations

In ancient Greek architecture there was usually a very direct expression of the post and beam system, which was an authentic structural system. The Romans allowed themselves much greater freedom in the use of columns because they made the almost revolutionary discovery of concrete. This allowed them to create massive spanning forms of great plasticity, including various types of vaults and domes, and in turn liberated them from the limitations of trabeated architecture.

In the twenty-first century, we would suppose that having made the innovative move to an entirely new structural system, we would thoroughly discard the old system. But the Romans did not think this way. Instead, they found a way to integrate trabeation and the use of concrete. However, they did not try to hide the new with the old. They exploited the potential of the synthesis, and played with columns and entablature in a way that made the relationship clear. Thus in some of their favorite building types, such as the theater stage façade or the public fountain *(nymphaeum)*, pairs of columns pop out of the wall, forming small structures within the larger building. These column pairs, together with their entablatures, are called aedicules, a word derived from a Latin term meaning "little buildings," or "temples."

One of the best-preserved aediculated façades is that of the Library of Celsus, built by the Romans at Ephesus, in modern-day Turkey, in CE 114–117, where column pairs on the upper story straddle those on the ground floor. The upper-story pairs are capped by pediments, some

Designed by Heinrich Strack, the Victory Column in Berlin was built to honor Prussian triumphs in mid-nineteenth-century wars. The main column is made of sandstone blocks bearing cannon barrels captured from vanquished foes. The golden statue at the top was the work of sculptor Friedrich Drake.

On the magnificent two-story façade of the Library of Celsus at Ephesus in Turkey (CE 114–117), named for its sponsor, Tiberius Celsus, statues representing Wisdom, Reason, Virtue, and Knowledge adorn niches inside the lower-floor column pairs.

triangular and some segmental—the idea of the "little temple" complete unto itself is reinforced by the pediment, no matter what form it takes. The aedicule proved so successful that it reappeared in the medieval period, especially in Gothic architecture, often embellishing the exterior buttresses or as finials terminating the vertical elements.

Display Purposes

Very long, straight sections of masonry must either be overly massive, or periodically braced in order to stand up. A simple buttress will do the trick, but the Romans liked to brace important walls with rows of columns tied back to the wall with beams. In such cases, the entablature springs forward in what is called a *ressaut*. Beautiful examples of Roman column-braced walls can be seen in the Library of Hadrian (*c.* CE 131) near the Agora in Athens, and on the northeastern face of the Severan Basilica (CE 216) at the site of Lepsis Magna in North Africa.

Around the same time that the Roman architectural revolution took place the expanding empire took ownership of diverse stone quarries. The emperors liked to display beautiful colored granites, marbles, porphyries, and breccias, and their preferred medium for this was the monolithic column. Granites came in a limited range, from red to gray to violet. But the other stones came in wild color combinations and patterns. From the tip of Euboa in Greece came a pale green striped stone called *cipollino* because it looks like a slice through an onion (*cipollino* is Italian for "little onion"). Serpentine came from several places and was often dark green with little confetti-like flecks. Deep red marbles came from the Pyrenees and parts of Greece.

After the Roman Empire dissolved, the quarries were closed. But the colorful columns, particularly if they formed a matching set, were often salvaged for use in churches. Columns were especially needed in basilica churches, such as Old St. Peter's in Rome (CE 318–322), though it required so many columns that a complete matching set could not be found. The architects of Old St. Peter's resolved this dilemma by arranging a series of different-colored columns in a repeating pattern.

Architectural elements that are reused in this way are called *spolia*, whether or not they perform their original function. In some Crusader-era castles, defense walls were built using old columns as through stones to tie the masonry—you can see their ends sticking out of walls at places such as the Ayasuluk Fortress at Selçuk in Turkey, or on the island of Kos in Greece. That is surely one of the most surprising places to see a column, because it is so divorced from its traditional function within a post and beam system.

The Classical Orders

Polychromy

When we think of a Doric temple, we think quite correctly of the Parthenon in Athens; and when we think of the Parthenon, we think of brilliant white marble everywhere. But both ancient literary sources and archaeology show that this is incorrect. The Greeks considered their temples naked unless the entablature and pediments were painted in bright colors: red, blue and yellow predominated. The metope sculptures were meant to tell a story and make it look real. We might find this surprising, even disappointing, given that we today admire the beauty of the underlying material. But for the Greeks, form (and moral content) always trumped material. The narrative of the metopes had the utmost importance; the intrinsic quality of the marble (which was a plentiful material) was not as important, as long as it was durable.

The columns and beams in the tombs at Beni Hasan, Egypt (2130–1785 BCE), were hewn out of solid rock.

For a long time our ideas about the classical orders were based almost entirely on one book: *De architectura libri decem (Ten Books on Architecture)*, written by Marcus Vitruvius Pollio in the first century BCE. We know from contemporary accounts that architectural treatises had also been produced in ancient Greece, but none survived. Vitruvius based much of his work on these lost writings. His own book not only survives intact, but also had an immense impact on fifteenth-century Italian humanist thinkers.

In Books Three and Four of his work, Vitruvius gives detailed descriptions of the four post and beam systems thought appropriate for temples and other important buildings, which he names Doric, Ionic, Corinthian, and Tuscan. Each of these is defined as much by the proportional relationship of its parts, as by particular features of the column or of the entablature—the horizontal beam component. Renaissance architects embraced the idea of these "orders," and wrote their own treatises, which greatly influenced later architects. Understanding the orders allowed architects to employ them in their buildings, and we can trace an adherence to the Vitruvian ideal in Renaissance, Baroque, and Neoclassical architecture of all types.

Since the nineteenth century, however, with the emergence of modern archaeology, we have direct evidence of ancient practice with regard to the orders, and the resultant picture is more nuanced, interesting, and mysterious than the Renaissance legacy would lead us to believe.

The Doric Order

In the Greek world, the column shaft of the Doric order had no base and was always grooved, or fluted. The Doric flute always took the form of a simple concave arc segment that met adjacent flutes along a sharp edge, or arris. Much has been written about the origin of this shallow-groove fluting. Some see it as clear evidence that the marble architecture in the Doric style was a simple replacement of a Greek wooden tradition going back to the Bronze Age. But it is more likely that Greek architects derived the feature from the Egyptian "bundle of reeds" style of column. We can see a style that is close to the Greek Doric at the mortuary complex of Queen Hatshepsut, Deir el-Bahari, Egypt (1520 BCE), and in the rock-cut tombs at Beni Hasan, Egypt.

The capital of the Doric column was multi-laterally symmetrical and therefore quite stable. It went through a development from the bulging

Types of Columns

EGYPTIAN
In ancient Egypt, massive stone columns were used to support wide beams. Column shafts can be polygonal, circular, or ribbed. Capitals are often shaped like the flower buds of plants such as the lotus, palm, and papyrus.

MINOAN
Unlike most other classical columns, Minoan columns were made of wood, specifically cypress, which was widely available. They typically have a wide, pillow-like capital and taper toward the bottom.

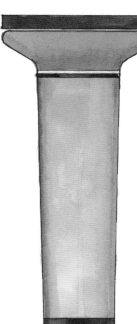

DORIC
The Greek Doric has no base, 20 shallow flutes divided by sharp arrises, and a very subtle profile known as *entasis*, which combines upward taper and convex curvature. The Roman version is slenderer and may have a simple base.

AEOLIC
The Aeolic is a predecessor of the Ionic found in Syria, the Eastern Mediterranean, and especially Aeolus, off Asia Minor. Unlike the Ionic, the volutes branch out from the centre. The timber columns do not survive. They were slender in proportion to the capitals.

ACHAEMENID
Columns in buildings of the Achaemenid dynasty of Persia (559–330 BCE) are capped by a ring of foliage, a series of scrolls, and a two-faced capital, such as a pair of bulls' heads and forelegs facing outwards, with a recess to take a timber beam.

IONIC
An Ionic column has a narrower shaft than the Doric, 24 flutes separated by narrow, flat fillets rather than sharp arrises, a base with convex mouldings (in either the 'Attic' or the 'Asiatic' form, and a capital consisting of two scrolls, or volutes linked horizontally.

CORINTHIAN
The Corinthian column base and shaft are exactly like the Ionic, and the entablature above may be also, but the capital consists of a double row of acanthus leaves, with small volutes at the corners.

TUSCAN
Notionally deriving from Etruscan architecture, the Tuscan order is characterized by a lack of ornamentation, a wide, smooth shaft, and a simple capital and base. It normally looks short and broad compared to the other orders.

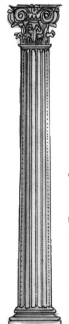

COMPOSITE
Developed by the Romans, the Composite has a base and shaft like those of the Ionic or Corinthian, with flat fillets between the flutes. The capital is a hybrid of the two, with a double row of acanthus leaves and Ionic volutes above.

On the portico of the Temple of Athena Nike in Athens, Greece, the central pillars have conventional double-fronted Ionic capitals. On the outer columns, in order to present the volutes on both facades, they are bent out together at forty five degrees, at the corner where they would have intersected.

metopes, broader panels that could be seen to suggest the space between the joists. Reinforcing this idea is the fact that the triglyphs are centered over each column and over each intercolumniation. In early Doric temples, it is possible that the metope was covered with a terracotta plaque, but in the full-blown Doric the metope became a place for bas-reliefs and sculpture.

The entablature and column spacing of the Doric order created a design problem that had few satisfactory solutions, known as the "corner triglyph problem." Consider a square Doric building with six columns on each side, equally spaced. The corner triglyph would have to be set outward from the column centerline in order to correctly place the whole line of the entablature as it turned the corner. This necessitated either two metopes larger than the inner metopes, or a first inner triglyph off-center from the intercolumniation. The latter, which we can see at the Temple of Zeus at Olympia (c. 460 BCE), was probably the more elegant solution.

During the Hellenistic period, architects got a bit more creative with the Doric order, and multiplied the number of triglyphs while lowering the height of the frieze. Literary sources refer to some Hellenistic architectural theorists who thought the Doric order should never be used. Nonetheless, sources also mention a faction that rallied around the Doric, thus possibly ensuring its survival.

form found in buildings such as the Temple of Hera I at Paestum (c. 530 BCE) to a tight, conical flaring, as at the Doric Stoa of the Asklepieion at Pergamon (third to second century BCE).

The Doric entablature had some features that may have derived from wooden trabeated archi-

tecture. The lower part of the entablature, the architrave, is simple in profile. Directly above, in the frieze section, the canonical Doric had a pattern of alternating triglyphs—panels with three vertical bands—that appears to simulate the ends of joists resting on the main beam below, and

Styles of Entablature

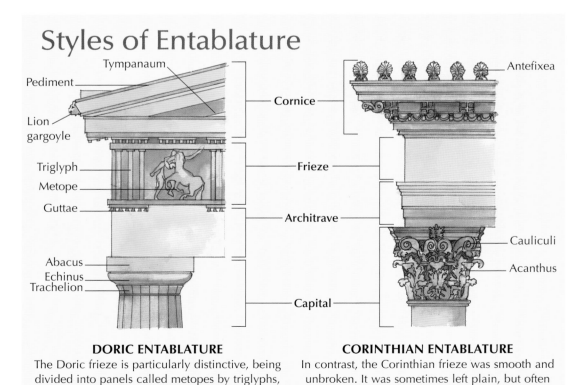

DORIC ENTABLATURE

The Doric frieze is particularly distinctive, being divided into panels called metopes by triglyphs, narrower panels bearing three vertical bands.

CORINTHIAN ENTABLATURE

In contrast, the Corinthian frieze was smooth and unbroken. It was sometimes left plain, but often decorated with carvings or used for inscriptions.

The Ionic and Aeolic Orders

The Ionic order, which emerged in the Late Archaic period, went through several experimental phases, yet at all times its capital could be recognized by its symmetrically arranged volutes, where the "stem" of the volutes was more or less horizontal.

Archaeological excavations have revealed an earlier voluted capital in which the stems began in a vertical position. This variation was first discovered in a part of western Turkey colonized by Greeks speaking the Aeolic dialect, so this order is called the Aeolic; since then, however, other examples have been found not only up and down the Aegean coast of Turkey, but also in the Levant. The early examples of the Aeolic style or order from the Levant were usually not freestanding column capitals but rather engaged-column or pilaster capitals. That aspect of the Aeolic tended to reemerge elsewhere: recently, at the site of Troy, archaeologists found an Aeolic engaged-column capital.

The disadvantages of the freestanding Aeolic capital were numerous. First, the style was essentially an extrusion of a two-dimensional motif into the "picture plane," to borrow a term from perspective theory, so the sculptural potential of the form was underutilized. Second, the Aeolic capital had structural problems, not unrelated to its formal problems. Every capital must take not only compressive but also shear forces. Because the volutes on the Aeolic capital were massive and projected far beyond the capital base, they tended to break off under shear forces. Because of this, the Aeolic represented an architectural dead-end and was not mentioned in ancient literature.

The structural problems of the Aeolic capital were solved in the Ionic by having smaller, more horizontal volutes. The Ionic frieze was a plain band, which eliminated the corner triglyph problem. Nonetheless, the classic Ionic also had a corner problem: seeing the scrolls of the volutes end on was the preferred view, but at a corner this was obviously only the case when looking from one side. The clever solution, seen in the Temple of Athena Nike, in Athens, was to create a special corner capital whose volutes splayed out at a forty five degree angle, thus creating a new axis of symmetry that allowed the preferred view to turn the corner.

The columns of the Ionic order were almost always fluted, but in a more sophisticated way than in the Doric: the concave grooves were deeper and met each other in a fillet, or band, rather than an arris. Aside from the visual effect of this kind of fluting, it may also have been more damage-resistant than that of the Doric flute. For these practical advantages as well as its more graceful proportions, the Greeks came to favor the Ionic.

The Corinthian Order

The corner problems were fully resolved with the Corinthian Order, which emerged in the fifth century BCE in the Peloponnese (south mainland Greece) and was named after Corinth, the gateway to the region. The Corinthian style is similar to the Ionic; its distinctive features include its capitals with acanthus-leaf carvings and more slender proportions. The Greeks were, however, generally reluctant to adopt the Corinthian for building exteriors, perhaps because its capitals seemed too fragile, and indeed many elegant, apparently more robust, variations on the Corinthian capital (including the Alexandrian and the Pergamene) were developed during the Hellenistic period. The Romans, on the other hand, embraced the Corinthian order wholeheartedly and made it their own. One of the finest examples of its use in the Roman world can be seen at the Maison Carrée in Nîmes, France (16 BCE). The Romans would also customize the Corinthian capital, as needed. At a temple of Demeter and Persephone in Sicily, they inserted beautiful portrait busts of the goddess and her demigod daughter on alternate sides of the capital, framed by reverse-scrolling cornucopia (horns of plenty, a symbol of Demeter), with acanthus leaves below. The temple was destroyed, but the capitals were reused (as spolia) in the nave of the lovely twelfth-century Cathedral of Monreale, in the town of the same name in Sicily.

The Tuscan and Composite Orders

The Romans had mysterious neighbors, the Etruscans, who left behind their own variation on the Doric, called the Tuscan. In the Tuscan order, the columns are never fluted. Its capital and base are similar and resemble the base of the Ionic and Corinthian orders. The Romans often used the Tuscan, and they also invented an order that added small, splayed Ionic volutes to the lower part of the Corinthian capital—this invention served their purposes well because it combined the stateliness of the Ionic with the versatility of the Corinthian. However, the High Renaissance architect Andrea Palladio was the first to give it a lasting name: he called it the Composite order.

The Maison Carrée (16 BCE) in Nîmes, France, has a hexastyle portico of Corinthian columns and 20 engaged columns on its side and end walls.

The Parthenon
Athens, Greece

The most famous Greek temple, and the epitome of the Doric style, is undoubtedly the Parthenon in Athens (447–432 BCE). It was an octastyle, peripteral Doric temple built of Pentelic marble. Its proper name is the Temple of Athena Parthenos—Athena was the guardian and eponymous deity of the city of Athens.

Like most Greek temples, the Parthenon was a religious space whose primary function was to house the cult image of the deity. Worshippers did not occupy the space inside, nor did sacrifices take place inside; instead the sacrificial altar lay outside, on an axis with the east entrance of the temple—sacrifice always took place facing the sunrise. Some of the secondary functions of Greek temples included housing the treasury and, sometimes, an oracle. The Parthenon had no oracle, but it did function as a treasury.

The Parthenon was built as part of a massive reworking of the Acropolis, the sacred center of Athens, following the destruction of the war with the Persians. The project was managed by one of the most skillful leaders Athens had ever had, Pericles, ably assisted by the architects, Iktinos and Kallikrates, and the sculptor Phidias, who was the artistic coordinator along with Pericles.

To pay for such an ambitious undertaking, Pericles expropriated funds amassed for the defense of Greece during the war, which should have been returned to their contributors after the war ended. The project was approved in a public referendum (once Pericles had removed the opposition). The city-state of Athens was at the peak of its power and that power was made explicit in the buildings of the Acropolis, which included, as well as the Parthenon, the Propylaia, the Temple of Athena Nike, and the Erechtheion.

Subtle Refinements

Much has been written about the refinements incorporated in the design of the Parthenon. Though some skeptics doubt that all of these effects were intended, Vitruvius attests to this

A detail of the inner frieze of the Parthenon, showing young men and their horses participating in the Panathenaia festival. The frieze would originally have been painted in rich, bright colors.

The Parthenon (below, at the top of the photo) crowns the Acropolis of Athens, site of the city's chief religious and municipal buildings. The site, which rises to 500 ft (150 m) above sea level, has been occupied by humans since the sixth millennium BCE.

aspect of the Parthenon and modern studies seem to confirm they were deliberately planned.

The first level of refinement is irrefutable. The dimensions of the plan, section, and column module all work on a ratio of four to nine, which indicates a deliberate methodology. Eight columns were used at the end of the building, rather than the traditional six, making the temple appear larger than it really was. Incorporating 16 bays along the sides, instead of the usual 12 to 14, allowed the full development of inner porches at both front and back. The porches permit a transition from Doric detailing on the exterior to Ionic detailing in the porch interior, the two styles providing stylistic links to, respectively, the Doric Propylaia, or gateway building, and the Ionic Erechtheion. In the larger, western chamber, the internal Doric colonnade was three-sided, an innovation that allowed the statue of Athena to be seen within a dramatic architectural frame. The smaller eastern chamber was quite different, with four Ionic columns supporting the intermediate beams.

The next level of refinement is the controversial part. The stylobate, or three-stepped podium, is not level, but curves slightly upward at the

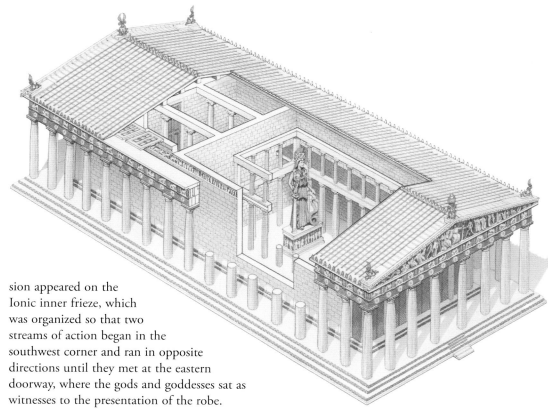

An artist's impression of the Parthenon soon after completion, showing the two interior chambers with their colonnades; the statue of Athena in the western chamber; and the richly coloured friezes.

center of each side. The entasis of the columns is more subtly curved than normal. The corner columns are slightly bigger and shift slightly inward. All the long axes of the columns tilt slightly toward the center.

The purpose of these refinements is still not clear, but they may have been intended to heighten the sense of grandeur. The Doric order could be static, but it could with subtle effects be quite dynamic. The Parthenon is undeniably grand and dynamic.

A Procession in Stone

The most important day for both city and goddess was the celebration of Athena's birthday in mid-August, once every four years. On this day, the festival of the Panathenaia took place. The main action of the festival was a formal procession through the lower city, wending its way up to the Acropolis, where a newly woven robe was presented to the cult image. Sheep and bulls would be sacrificed. The elite young women of Athens made their way up on foot, bearing baskets of garlands and other offerings; the elite young men showed off on horseback. Musicians accompanied the parade. An image of the procession appeared on the Ionic inner frieze, which was organized so that two streams of action began in the southwest corner and ran in opposite directions until they met at the eastern doorway, where the gods and goddesses sat as witnesses to the presentation of the robe.

The outer metopes do not have the continuous action of the inner frieze; instead, each is a scene from four thematically linked stories (one on each side). The Greeks fight different adversaries (usually interpreted as stand-ins for the Persians) on each of the three sides: the Trojans on the north, Amazons on the west, and centaurs on the south. At the eastern end, gods fight giants. The message of victory is quite clear. On the western pediment, the sculptors showed the birth of Athena, and on the eastern they depicted the victory of Athena over Poseidon in a contest to name the patron deity of the city. With this integration of sculpture and architecture, Phidias and Pericles created a triumphant masterpiece.

Colonnades

Detailed carvings adorn the columns in the Hypostyle Hall in the Temple of Amon at Luxor, Egypt (1312–1301 BCE). A hypostyle arrangement permitted the construction of very large, tall rooms; however, the columns often had to be so enormous that they took up most of the floor space.

The post and beam system, especially when translated into stone architecture, had limited space-defining options. The only way that large spaces could be enclosed was by multiplying the basic structural bay or set of spanning members. This could be done in two directions to create a forest of columns that could support a wide roof. This kind of structure, known as a hypostyle hall, was used in monumental Egyptian architecture, for example in the Hypostyle Hall in the Temple of Amon at Luxor (1312–1301 BCE), and is also found in Greek architecture, for instance in the Telesterion at Eleusis, northwest of Athens.

But a much more effective spatial type was created when the columns and beams were arranged along a single line to form a colonnade. The virtues of the colonnade are several: it can set a direction, either of movement or view; it creates a visual rhythm that offsets other patterns; it can provide shade in hot, dry climate conditions; and, finally, it can be either intimate or monumental relative to human scale.

The Romans used the colonnade in an innovative way, realizing that if one adjusted the positions of the post and beam units to create a curve, the structure could be used to define space effectively. A fine example is the oval plaza in the ancient Roman city of Gerasa, now Jerash in Jordan, where the colonnades follow the curve to create a sense of enclosure at an important node in the city's circulation system. Round columns with Corinthian capitals of some sort, rather than rectilinear piers, were essential for this kind of flowing space definition, because such columns are multilaterally directional.

Tricks of Perspective

In late antiquity, the colonnade was eclipsed by the arcade, a situation that endured until the Renaissance. In this period, with his design for the Pazzi Chapel, Florence, Italy, built in 1429–1446, Brunelleschi showed how both forms could be successfully combined. Subsequently, and particularly in the Baroque period, architects used their thorough study of classical architecture and a new understanding of optics and perspective to exploit the potential of classical forms like the colonnade beyond anything imagined in the ancient world and to engage their modern audience.

One device they used was forced perspective. By steadily decreasing the size of the colonnade bays, the architect could make a shallow space appear much deeper than it really was. For example, in the Teatro Olimpico at Vicenza in northern Italy, by Andrea Palladio, completed by his pupil Vincenzo Scamozzi (1580–1584), the stage has a permanent architectural backdrop from which three passageways recede, one on the central axis and two others angling away

Colonnades and Arcades

COLONNADE

An extension of the basic post and beam system, the colonnade consists of a line of columns supporting a series of horizontal beams. The colonnade may be straight or curved, and be an independent structure or part of a larger building.

ARCADE

An arcade consists of a row of columns surmounted by a series of arches. The arches' lateral distribution of forces helps them carry greater weight. Both the arcade and colonnade are often used to form a covered walkway.

to the sides, each treated in forced perspective, so as to create the impression of urban streets.

One of the most remarkable examples of the use of forced perspective in colonnades is Francesco Borromini's design for the side courtyard of the Palazzo Spada in Rome (1653), which makes a colonnaded gallery appear more than four times its actual length. Similarly, Gian Lorenzo Bernini's remodeling of the Scala Regia (Royal Staircase) in the Vatican (1663–1666) ingeniously made an existing cramped, converging space appear grand and expansive. In this case, the device of the coffered barrel vault (also used by Bramante at San Satiro), together with the spacing of the columns on either side—columns with dynamic composite capitals—makes the optical trick work exceedingly well.

Intuition and Meaning

All of the effects described above work because the post and beam system is such a simple and intuitive structural device. With a small amount of elaboration, it could also be a device promoting a sense of monumental unity, linking disparate parts. Thomas Jefferson used it for exactly those reasons when he designed the University of Virginia (1817–1825).

With the emergence of Modernism in the twentieth century, certain classical elements, including colonnades, were incorporated for their monumentality but stripped of their decorations—a style that is sometimes called stripped classical. Many architects working in Italy under Mussolini and for the Third Reich in Germany were proponents of the style, but it was not exclusive to Fascist regimes. It also appears during the 1930s in democracies—for example, in the interior detailing of the Empire State Building in New York City.

Contemporary architects have further reduced the colonnade to its essence, while still retaining the sense of dignity that it imparts. For example, Michael Graves has used heavy repetitive piers in his design for the Public Library of San Juan Capistrano in California (1981–1983) to give his work a sense of timelessness and weight. In a very different way, Sir Norman Foster uses a strong metal and glass frame for the façade of his Carré D'Art in Nîmes, France (1984–1993), in a way that clearly refers to and complements the classical colonnade of the nearby Maison Carrée, a first-century Roman temple.

Built to connect the papal apartments in the Vatican to St. Peter's Basilica in Rome, the Scala Regia (Royal Staircase) was originally constructed by Antonio da Sangallo the Younger. Bernini's redesign of 1663–1666 used colonnades to make the passageway look wider and more imposing than it really was.

The Piazza of St. Peter's

When in 1655 Pope Alexander VII needed to improve the area in front of St. Peter's Basilica in Rome, he turned to one of the city's most successful architects, Gian Lorenzo Bernini. To create a space worthy of the mass celebrations of the Roman Catholic Church, Bernini planned a symmetrical colonnade that would enclose a huge oval, and then lead directly to the façade of the basilica. Bernini was careful to keep his colonnade from being too high and thereby overwhelming the façade; for the columns, he chose to use a massive form of the Tuscan order—plainer than the Corinthian of the façade—but combined it with an Ionic entablature to avoid fussy triglyphs. The two centers of the smaller end radii of the oval piazza are each marked with a fountain, and the center of the oval, where the latitudinal and longitudinal axes cross, is marked with an obelisk. The ensemble is one of the world's most successful architectural achievements.

The colonnade around Bernini's Piazza of St. Peter incorporates 284 columns.

Palmyra
Syria

The Roman Empire was able to remain in control of a vast territory for as long as it did by empowering local elites to cooperate in tithing the local agricultural surplus. The elites were rewarded, and encouraged to build and live in cities—Roman cities. Every Roman city had certain common features, although of course there were a few regional differences. In Roman North Africa, Syria, as well as Asia, cities usually had public fountains and baths, theaters and market places, all connected by series of colonnaded avenues, which also led to the main civic and religious buildings.

Located in the Syrian Desert northeast of Damascus, Palmyra, known in the Bible as Tadmor, was an ancient city, a rest stop on the Silk Road. The Palmyrans kept a rumor going (it was picked up by Roman historians) that they only pretended to be "Romanized," but to look at their city and its architecture, that must only have been wishful thinking, for Palmyra is a very typical Roman provincial city of the east. Most of the Roman-style construction took place in the second and third centuries CE.

Palmyra makes a wonderful case study for the use of trabeation in urban embellishment. Columns appear in almost every combination, except freestanding. The variations include peristyles, propylons, peripteral temples, porches, exedrae, fountains, and colonnades, most notably the Grand Colonnade along the main street.

Columns on all Sides

A peristyle is simply a colonnaded outdoor space, and in Roman architecture the term usually refers to a colonnade running around the inside of a courtyard. In Palmyra, the peristyle was a common feature in all types of building, in much the same way that the patio is in Andalusia, Spain. The largest example belonged to the *agora*, or market, and had four sides, as is typical. The senate house had a very small peristyle as a kind of lobby. The baths had two adjacent colonnaded courts, one of which might have been used for lounging and the other for exercising.

The only three-sided colonnade surrounds the peripteral temple in the Sanctuary of Nebo.

The grand tetrakionion, or tetrapylon gateway, which marked a major intersection with the Grand Colonnade and the center of the city. The tetrakionion was reconstructed by the Syrian Department of Antiquities in 1963.

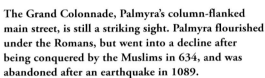

The Grand Colonnade, Palmyra's column-flanked main street, is still a striking sight. Palmyra flourished under the Romans, but went into a decline after being conquered by the Muslims in 634, and was abandoned after an earthquake in 1089.

This is actually a *temenos*, or temple precinct, not a peristyle. The temenos is quite interesting. There are only two entrances, at the north and at the south. The northern entrance is the convenient entrance from the main street, and has a small lobby nestled between the small shops facing the street. But it was the south entrance that was the ceremonial one, and it has a large tetrastyle propylon, or four-columned gateway. The reason for this was that the temple itself faced south and the architects wanted the visitor to enter from the south and be greeted by the imposing view of the temple on its podium. It was a typical Roman gesture.

The baths building had a tetrastyle porch that projected out into the colonnaded street, as if to advertise the presence of a large public building. Four columns also project in front of the colonnade at the *exedra* along the eastern end of the main east–west thoroughfare. An exedra is any concave side room, but in the context of a Hellenistic or Roman street it took the form of a marble semicircular bench, often bearing inscriptions of dedication. The fountain across the main street from the theater was housed in a similar structure, with the basin for the water replacing the bench of the exedra.

Thoroughfares and Boundaries

The columns of the Grand Colonnade along Palmyra's main street did not match perfectly, but were similar. They were about two stories high and had projecting brackets two-thirds of the way up the shaft to carry statues of notables. It is possible that awnings were stretched across the street to provide additional shade, as is currently done in the centre of Seville in Spain.

The large triple arch that straddles the street at its eastern end was a very clever device for redirecting the street slightly to the southeast. From either direction, the arch appears frontally; all the rotation occurs inside the arch. Toward the western end of the street, two large columns mark the entrance to a side street that runs off to the north. We can assume that an entablature probably connected the two columns, but we can only imagine what designs or statements it bore. It is vaguely reminiscent of Hadrian's Arch in Athens, which highlighted a territorial transition with an inscription on one side that said, "You are entering the city of Theseus," and another on the other side that read, "You are entering the city of Hadrian."

The colonnaded street of Palmyra extended westward to a piazza in the form of a truncated oval. In the middle of the piazza there was a large monument called a tetrakionion. Imagine a four-faced triumphal arch (which exists and is called a quadrifrons arch); then imagine that instead of four solid piers it has four piers each made up of four columns—that is the tetrakionion, or tetrapylon. It is not certain what the superstructure was like. Tetrakionions were usually placed at the intersection of colonnaded streets, and indeed, this oval piazza occurs at a T-junction of colonnaded streets.

The monumental arch at the end of the Grand Colonnade was the main eastern entrance to Palmyra. The columns on the right marked the entrance to another street. To the left, or south, lay the Sanctuary of Nebo.

Entablature

On the Doric east façade of the Parthenon in Athens, Greece, detailed statuary adorns the tympanum and bas-reliefs decorate the metopes on the frieze.

Although it later became increasingly decorative, the form of the entablature in Greek architecture derived from practical requirements, some of which possibly reflected the original use of wood rather than stone in trabeated buildings.

The classical entablature traditionally consists of three main horizontal elements: the architrave, frieze, and cornice. The lowest section, the architrave, had a vital job to do, in wood or stone: span from column to column. The cornice, too, had a very important practical function: that of throwing water away from the perimeter of the building. It did this in three ways. First, it

overhung the lower parts of the entablature, extending out as far as the column base below. Second, its profile was an agglomeration of what are called "drip molds"—the bottom of the piece is slightly undercut, so that water will drip off due to gravity. The third way water was shed by the cornice was via gargoyles, spouts penetrating through the upper part of the cornice, where the run-off from the roof collected. In Greek buildings, gargoyles almost always took the form of a lion's head. Later, in the Gothic period, however, gargoyles were inventively carved in the form of all kinds of monsters and demons.

The middle section of the entablature, the frieze, could be seen to represent the place where, in wooden trabeated architecture, the rafters would rest on the beam or architrave—the ends of the rafters are perhaps suggested by the triglyphs in the Doric frieze. In early stone architecture, there is some evidence that the frieze was first used as a convenient place to hang things,

such as weapons, shields, or bounty from a hunt. Perhaps it was taboo to bring things with blood on them into the house, or perhaps it was a way of displaying such trophies. (Alexander the Great did not get it quite right when he had gilded metal shields hung on the eastern side of the Parthenon—on the architrave, rather than on the frieze. To be fair to the great conqueror, there was no space left on the Parthenon frieze, and so he made do with what space was available.)

Increasingly, however, the frieze was used for decorations, painted on or carved in stone or terracotta. In the Archaic period, figural compositions, usually with mythical subject matter, appeared in the metopes of the Doric style, and in the Classical period continuous figural compositions were added to Ionic friezes—as at the Erechtheion in Athens. In some later Roman buildings such as the Forum of Nerva in Rome (CE 97), this was a deliberate "classicizing" motif. Otherwise in the Ionic and Corinthian orders, the decoration might consist of a simple vine motif.

During the Romanesque period there was a revival of the kind of frieze sculptures with figural narratives that had been used in the Ionic and Corinthian orders. In the twelfth-century church of Saint-Gilles-du-Gard in southern France, New Testament scenes appear at the west portal—the kiss of Judas scene is especially dramatic. Writers such as Victor Hugo made much of how this kind of decoration was intended to address illiterates, providing them with edifying stories in pictures instead of words. But this is a Romantic notion of questionable value, given that it is likely that such ornamentation derived from

Jain Temples

In India, one of the minority religions is Jainism. The Jain have a remarkable temple-building tradition, and luckily some of their early temples have survived. At the Dilwara temple complex, near Mount Abu, Rajasthan, (CE 1031–1300), every surface of the entirely stone buildings is richly carved. In one temple is an octagonal domed room. The beams that define the octagon are freeflying—the wall above them is open—and the space above the beam is filled in with a corbelled arch, also freeflying. The effect is dazzling, as a hard, dense material (marble) is treated as if it were lighter-than-air lace. It is uncertain whether this style refers back to wooden brackets, or to the rock-cut origins of many Indian temples, but the effect is clear: to inspire amazement.

The assembly hall of the Vimala Vasahi temple at Dilwara, Rajasthan, in northern India, dates from the mid-twelfth century CE.

buildings such as the Parthenon, whose frieze was about and for the elite of the community, who were literate.

Bending the Rules

In the Renaissance classical style, the entablature remained fairly conventional, usually appearing as a continuous band over columns arranged in simple squares, rectangles, and circles. But subsequently architects became fascinated by more complex shapes, such as the oval, or composite shapes, such as stars, and began building colonnades in these forms. Although the entablature usually followed the outlines of these shapes, it soon began to take off on its own.

In Michelangelo's design for the vestibule of the Laurentian Library in Florence (1525), we

see an artist beginning to bend the conventional rules of entablature: here, pairs of columns are recessed, and held up by brackets, whereas the wall between bulges forward, bringing the entablature forward with it. Cornices below pediments are truncated. Pilasters are thinner at the bottom than the top. Tuscan capitals have a Corinthian abacus, but with a bat face in place of a flower.

The façade designed in 1575 by Giacomo della Porta for the Gesù, the mother church of the Jesuit order in Rome, shows how architects started to play with the elements of the entablature and façade. First, there is a very clear organization of two stories, but the lower one is one bay wider to each side than the upper—a reflection of the nave and side aisles beyond. Giant volutes fill in the gap in width at the second

Giacomo della Porta's façade was added to the church of the Gesù in Rome in 1575, after the architect of the rest of the building, Giacomo da Vignola, died. Its design, while based on classical tradition, was innovative and became influential.

story. The columns are mostly pilasters and are almost always doubled up at the hypothetical structural line. Above the inner column pairs, the entablature pops out; above the main entrance it projects even farther, and above this is a triangular pediment nested inside a segmental pediment. The window surround at the second story has a broken (truncated) pediment. This formula was so successful that it was repeated in many church façades thereafter.

A Baroque Hallmark

The manipulation of the entablature, to heighten the dramatic effect, or create a sense of almost infinite depth, became one of the hallmarks of the Baroque period. In Rome, the style began with the works of two rival architects, Gian Lorenzo Bernini and Francesco Borromini. Each produced a small masterpiece, based on the oval, and located along the Viale Quirinale. Inside Borromini's church, San Carlo alle Quattro Fontane (1638–1641), he aligned the long axis of the oval with the main liturgical axis. In his church, Sant Andrea al Quirinale (1658–1670), Bernini did the opposite.

Both architects did interesting things with the entablature, on the façade and inside. Borromini's façade to San Carlo is a two-story arrangement, with no narrowing of the upper story width. The entablature of the first story is concave at the sides and convex in the middle, and the curves

The crest of Cardinal Camillo Pamphilj, the church's benefactor, crowns the portico of Sant'Andrea al Quirinale in Rome (1658–1670; left). Gian Lorenzo Bernini's design resolved the problem of a narrow site and street frontage most ingeniously.

In the interior of Sant Ivo della Sapienza in Rome (1642–1650; below), designed by Francesco Borromini, Corinthian pilasters rise to an entablature that is simple in form but follows a complex plan of alternate semicircles and half hexagons.

blend in a smooth transition. The upper entablature, including the cornice, is broken at the center to accommodate a strangely tilted oval medallion, known as a tondo. Inside the church, Borromini used nearly freestanding round columns, despite the limited space available. The entablature follows a complex geometry, incorporating alternating concave and straight sections, and very delicate transitions.

For his entrance façade, Bernini chose a single pedimented bay with a very subtle break in it. What really captures the attention, however, is the semicircular entablature surmounted by an arch; if one flipped the entablature up it would fit into the arch. The arch and entablature are echoed by the semicircular steps that lead up to the door. Pietro da Cortona had recently explored a similar combination at Santa Maria della Pace

(1656–1667), also in Rome, but Bernini's version is ultraelegant. Inside Sant'Andrea, Bernini created a variation on the Pantheon, with two fewer niches, and an oval rather than a circular plan. The entablature is interrupted only at the entrance, and projects forward only at the altar.

Borromini created another masterpiece in Rome, Sant Ivo della Sapienza (1642–1650). Its plan is based upon two equilateral triangles overlaid head to toe, but with alternating lobed and convex terminations designed to evoke a flying bee, the crest of the Barberini family (the family of the reigning pope, Urban VIII, and of Cardinal Francesco Borromini, who was responsible for Borromini's appointment as architect). Borromini may have got the idea for such a fluid plan, through not this specific form, from the Piazza d'Oro of Hadrian's villa at Tivoli. Large pilasters support an entablature that sweeps around this complex shape and ties it together; above, the pumpkin dome draws it inward to a central lantern.

Modern Reflections of the Ancient

Architecture that pushed and pulled the entablature continued until the Neoclassical movements of the eighteenth century, which rejected the emotionalism of the Baroque and imposed a new austerity. Benjamin Henry Latrobe, perhaps best known as an architect of the US Capitol, exemplifies the rationalism of the enlightenment. He attempted to update classical elements, as seen in his tobacco leaf and corncob capitals in the Senate rotunda, but at times also directly copied features from ancient buildings, as in the Paestum-style capitals of the Supreme Court. At the Baltimore Roman Catholic Cathedral, or Basilica of the National Shrine of the Assumption of the Virgin Mary, Latrobe's restrained classicism can be seen at work in the entablature supporting the dome: it is flattened in a proto-modern manner, yet the striking continuous inscription in the frieze band refers back to monuments of classicism such as St. Peter's.

Even following the advent of the skyscraper, architects continued to attempt to incorporate columns and entablature into modern buildings. Louis Sullivan, regarded by many as the creator of the modern skyscraper, set a new architectural standard in his 1896 essay "The Tall Building Artistically Considered" by proposing a new form for the skyscraper based on the elements of the classical column. As can be seen in his Wainwright Building in St. Louis, Missouri, (1890–1891) and his Guaranty (Prudential) Building in Buffalo, New York, (1894–1895), both produced with his partner Dankmar Adler, there was a clear composition of base, shaft, and entablature. At the top a deep cornice was used to hide the space for machinery that the new skyscraper type demanded. The vestiges of the classical frieze were seen in the uppermost story of round windows, contained among exuberant tendril designs, executed in terracotta panels—as in ancient times.

On the upper façade of Louis Sullivan's ten-story, steel-frame Wainwright Building (1890–1891) in St. Louis, Missouri (top), an ornate frieze references classical entablature.

In Bernini's Sant Andrea al Quirinale, Rome, (above), 1658–1670, the simple entablature follows the oval plan, becoming more elaborate above the altar.

Kenzo Tange

The history of architectural techniques in general is the history of man's struggle to develop the span, which is the basic instrument for enclosing space. Until the nineteenth century Japanese architects depended entirely on a simple wooden span composed of posts and beams.
—Kenzo Tange

A prolific builder and writer, Japanese architect Kenzo Tange (1913–2005) was one of the twentieth century's most influential architects. Best known for his large public buildings and urban designs, he never stopped investigating form and never settled on a formula, but his ideas were potent enough that he had no trouble finding clients.

Tange was extremely knowledgeable about the architecture of his native land. He wrote a book on the Katsura Imperial Villa near Kyoto that has influenced architects worldwide and designed a house for himself that was clearly in the Japanese tradition and influenced by his study of Katsura. When it came to nonresidential buildings, however, there was no direct quotation of historic structures; instead, Tange continually sought a synthesis of Japanese forms, including the tradition of wooden trabeated architecture, and the Modernism of Le Corbusier.

Tange's approach to public buildings was unified by a recognition that the limited scale of traditional Japanese architecture and its focus on fine detail did not satisfy the needs of the postwar period. Following Le Corbusier, his structural material of choice was reinforced concrete, which allowed for longer spans and much larger structures, even in the traditional post and beam style. Unlike some less successful Modernists, however, Tange recognized that every project needed a gradation of scales, in order to reconnect the megascale (what Tange called the "mass-human" scale) with the scale of the individual. Here his close study of traditional Japanese architecture probably proved most useful, for he understood, for example, how the use of the same material at both the structural scale (in a beam, for instance) and the craft scale (a window louver) could modulate scale for the entire design.

Synthesized Forms

The Kurashiki City Hall, built in 1960, gave form to this thinking. The reinforced concrete building is designed to eliminate both perimeter and interior columns, with the exception of a dozen massive and prominent piers on the ground floor. Tange achieved this by having other parts of the structure take some of its weight: the massive core elements (stairwells, lift shafts, shear walls), the closely spaced floor beams, and the horizontal beam-like sections of concrete skin that interlock at the exterior corners.

After the city hall was finished, some observers pointed out that the interlocking corners of the building reminded them of traditional Japanese "log-cabin" style warehouses. Tange protested that it was an unintended consequence of his investigations. It was not the first time that he had had to defend himself against these evocations. After the completion in 1958 of the Kagawa Prefectural Government Office, where the post and beam approach was more obvious, he had been told that the eight-story part of the complex resembled a pagoda. Then, too, Tange had had to explain that it had not been his intention. Kinder critics claimed that Tange had simply absorbed Japanese tradition so deeply into his thinking that it was unconsciously translated. At any rate, the more robust aspects of the Japanese tradition were the ones he evoked, and he himself was critical of a tendency in Japanese tradition toward *furyu*, a word that means "kitsch," or "meaningless prettiness." Tange's creations were never meaningless, and he did not aspire to prettiness.

Everyone has held Tange and his body of work in such high regard that critiques are often overlooked among the praise. Yet there were a few points on which Tange could be criticized during his "trabeated" phase (typified by Kagawa) and his "primitive" phase (typified by Kurashiki). His contemporaries, especially Italians such as Bruno Zevi, pointed out that he used reinforced concrete as if it were steel or wood, and did not take advantage of the special properties of the material. But by the time these types of comments were voiced, the ever-restless Tange had moved on.

Gradation of Scale

In 1960, the same year that the Kurashiki City Hall was completed, the already celebrated Tange was asked to deliver the keynote address at the World Design Conference in Tokyo. His short speech, published soon after under the title "Technology and Humanity" and widely disseminated, laid out his new directions. Tange identified vital issues that architects working in major urban areas needed to consider, such as mobility, mass communications, building life cycles, potential for further growth, and scale clashes. In further explaining his gradation of scale from the mass-human to the individual, he used a biological analogy, equating the individual scale to the living cell, which constantly renews itself, and using the word "metabolic" to describe his approach. This in turn gave rise to a highly influential architectural movement, Metabolism.

Kenzo Tange (top) in front of his Musée des Arts Asiatiques (Museum of Asian Arts) in Nice, France, in 1999. Modest in scale, the museum's design is based on basic geometric forms—the square and the circle—that have sacred significance in Asian culture.

In Kurashiki City Hall (above), Tange sought to blend traditional Japanese architecture and Modernism. Cast in concrete, the lines and forms of the building echo the prominent posts and beams, and broad eaves of early Japanese buildings.

The Fuji Building in Odaiba, Japan, completed in 1996, embodied many of Tange's "metabolist" ideas as well as his vision for the expansion of Tokyo— Odaiba lies just outside the city on reclaimed land.

Trusses

Designed by one master carpenter, William Etheridge, and built by another, James Essex the Younger, in 1749, the Mathematical Bridge at Queens College, Cambridge, England, is based on a type of truss known as a tangent-and-radius truss. Due to decay, it was rebuilt in 1860 and 1905.

There must have been times in the ancient world when a long span was desirable, but only limited lengths of timber were available. The answer to this problem was the truss. A simple triangular truss consists of three members: two sloped rafters and one horizontal (tie-)beam that pins them together, so that each member is either in tension or compression without bending. The truss behaves more or less like a deep, long, shaped beam. It can be easily integrated with a pitched roof, is relatively simple to build, and is relatively affordable. Various forms of truss evolved over the years, incorporating different combinations of horizontal, vertical, and diagonal members.

It is unclear when the truss was first used. Most simple utilitarian buildings, in which a primitive truss might have been employed, have disappeared from the historical record. However, if we consider that timber shipbuilding began in the Minoan period, it must be assumed that the Greeks had both the skill and understanding of principles required to build a wooden truss. The council chambers of Miletus, Priene, and Troy (Ilion) all had significant central spans where a primitive tie-beam truss might have been used.

Clearer signs of the use of the truss date from the period when the Romans began exploiting the concrete vault, which required truss-like timber centering that is still visible in the form of putlog holes. It is likely that the Romans used the truss fairly widely for roofing and centering, and eventually for bridges.

After Constantine the Great made Christianity the official religion of the Roman Empire, there was a sudden need for very large churches. Rather than invent totally new forms, Roman architects adapted existing structures. Some churches explored the round or polygonal form, but the obvious form to borrow was the basilica—a long, narrow, double-aisled public hall, often with a mezzanine or clerestory. The basilical form, if it was not vaulted with masonry, was best spanned by a series of trusses: one full triangle above the clerestory, over the nave, and two half-trusses over each side aisle. One example of this type of construction was Old St. Peter's Church in Rome, since replaced by St. Peter's Basilica; another, still extant, is Sant'Apollinare in Classe, in Ravenna, Italy, built around CE 532–549.

Toward Structural Analysis

During the medieval period, particularly in Northern Europe, general understanding of the true truss waned. In monumental buildings, especially after the Gothic style instigated steeply pitched roofs, a truncated tie-beam, called a hammer beam, was often used to form a high-pitched ceiling. The hammer beams projected horizontally from the wall and were supported by vertical beams and curved brackets. The hammer-beam ceiling worked on the principles of bending and the cantilever, rather than balanced compression and tension, so it was not a true truss. In many cases, the ends of the hammer beams were carved and painted, as in the fourteenth-century church of St. Agnes at Cawston, Norfolk, England, where the exposed ends of the beams are in the form of angels.

In the Renaissance, the true truss was revived by Andrea Palladio for use in bridges. A truss bridge designed by Palladio still stands in Bassano, Italy; he also published drawings of at least five different wooden bridges (and several stone ones as well). For the Sheldonian Theater at Oxford, England, built in 1664–1668, Sir Christopher Wren adopted a modern (for his time) timber truss proposed by a mathematician, John Wallis, and used it to span 70 feet (21 m).

Following the investigations of Sir Isaac Newton in the early eighteenth century into a branch of physics known as statics, engineers and architects gradually became able to use mathematical formulae to work out the ideal design for any structure. This is the basis for all modern structural analysis. Nevertheless, master craftsmen, rather than engineers, continued to use true trusses in roofs and build some very beautiful truss bridges, such as the famous Mathematical Bridge at Queens College, Cambridge, England, built in 1749.

Trajan's Bridge

A spectacular use of the wooden truss in antiquity was the bridge built over the Danube by the Roman Emperor, Trajan, in CE 105. Trajan needed to build a bridge to supply his legions, which were attempting to subjugate the region of Dacia, but the Danube was almost 900 yards (800 m) wide at the point he wanted to cross. His architect, Apollodorus of Damascus, solved the problem by building 20 masonry piers spanned by wooden truss-arches. Each span was approximately 42 yards (38 m) wide, in itself a remarkable feat. Today only the piers on the embankments remain, although the rest were visible in the river until the mid-nineteenth century.

Modern Ways to Span

In the Industrial Age, the development of timber, cast iron, and then steel trusses was spurred by the proliferation of railways, which required bridges and viaducts. Some consider the Firth of Forth Bridge (built in 1890) in Scotland to be the world's longest truss bridge. Today, trusses are everywhere and are usually made of steel, although they are occasionally made of reinforced concrete. In many countries, prefabricated wooden trusses with metal gusset plates are not uncommon in domestic architecture.

If you take the planar truss and expand it three-dimensionally, you obtain a structure called a space frame. Developed in the 1970s, the space frame is often seen in airport terminals or convention center roofs. Recently, however, it seems to have been eclipsed by paraboloid structures (which also can be made up from straight members positioned along a curve), and in bridge design by high-strength steel suspension. Trusses, however, will always have a use in spanning.

The distinctive undulating roof of Southern Cross Station in Melbourne, Australia, designed by Sir Nicholas Grimshaw and opened in 2006, is held up by steel trusses.

Types of Trusses

KING POST

Long used in roofing, the King Post has a vertical central member, sloped top chords, a horizontal bottom chord, and two diagonals.

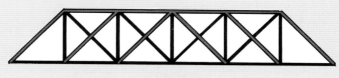

HOWE

William Howe, a bridge builder in New England in the United States in the early nineteenth century, designed the Howe Truss Warren trusses for bridge construction. It has timber diagonals and iron verticals.

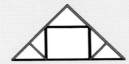

QUEEN POST

In a Queen Post Truss, the vertical member of the King Post is replaced by two shorter verticals and a horizontal beam.

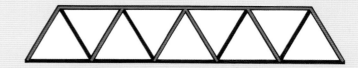

WARREN

The Warren Truss has no vertical members, only horizontal and diagonal members under central load. Only every second diagonal member is under compression; the others are under tension.

 Under compression   Under tension

Bridging the Gaps

Enclosed spaces need roofs, and humans discovered a long time ago that the curving form of an arch can sometimes do this job very well. In a formal sense, it is the geometry of the circle and the sphere that comes into play with this spanning task, producing an endless variety of curving arches, vaults, and domes.

Constructing an Arch

In masonry construction, bricks and stone (either exclusively or in some combination) are arranged in piers and walls. These are usually held in place with mortar between the units—although some very precise types of stone masonry are assembled dry, using no mortar at all. Whether with or without mortar, masonry is excellent in compression and can easily carry the loads from the roof and upper parts of a building downward to the foundations. But what happens when you place an opening in a masonry wall? Even when it is an infill wall (a non load-bearing wall), the masonry units above the opening need extra help to span the opening safely, without collapsing. The arch solves this challenge, keeping the masonry units in compression while resolving the forces to the sides, and thus allowing a clear opening below.

In a true arch, the wedge-shaped pieces, called "voussoirs," that make up the arch are of equal size and shape. These voussoirs have a rectangular aspect ratio, so that their depth is always greater

than their width. There is one center of curvature, and both the arch intrados (inner curve) and the arch extrados (outer curve) are concentric semicircles around that point. The keystone is centered directly above it, and all the joints between individual voussoirs align with radial projections from it. This set of rules generates a half-circular arch. The two blocks on which the arch is set are called the "impost blocks" and the first two voussoirs (one on either side) are called the "springers."

Of course there are many variations on this basic arch form. But if these rules are ignored too much, the arch may develop bending and shear forces, and it will no longer exist in pure compression. This may occur, for example, if the aspect ratio of the voussoirs is reversed (so that the width exceeds the depth). In addition, arches and vaults made of brick do not behave in such a straightforward manner because of the mortared joints used in brick construction. When these set, they change the forces in an arch.

THE ARCH

The wedge-shaped blocks (voussoirs) that make up an arch are in compression. The base of the arch pushes outward against the adjoining masonry in a form something like a parabola (depending on the exact loading conditions).

A – Keystone
B – Arch extrados
C – Arch intrados
D – Voussoir
E – Springer
F – Impost

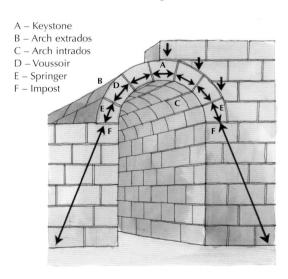

Building the new Library of Congress in Washington DC in 1892, (left) workers maneuver the keystone of the southwest rotunda's clerestory arch into place. Arches are rarely used today; the use of reinforced concrete and steel for lintels has made them obsolete.

Centering

Every true arch requires a type of formwork, called "centering," during the construction phase. Traditionally, wood was used. A trusslike timber fabrication was set to span from one impost to the other, and if no bracket was built into the masonry to support this, then it was supported from the sill below. The outer and upper edge of the centering had to trace the outline of the arch intrados. Then the springers were set in place, followed by the voussoirs in balanced pairs, and finally the keystone. In a construction that didn't use mortar, the centering was removed once the keystone was in place. The radial joints between the voussoirs send the forces around the arch in something similar to a parabolic route, pushing outward against the masonry at either side. In a building that did use mortar, the mortar had to dry before the centering could be removed. The resulting arch would have a tendency to behave monolithically, with a more complex array of actions and reactions, as explained above.

The need for centering may seem a major disadvantage of the arch. But in a rationally planned building, the centering is used over and over, so the time and material spent on it eventually balances out. A building with a series of parallel arches, such as the second-century CE Roman market at Smyrna (now Izmir in Turkey), does not need any major (timber) roof girders, and door and window openings using arches do not need large timber lintels. In both instances, the resulting masonry building has greater fire resistance. Finally, the façade of a building with arches has enormous aesthetic potential, although it is curious that the decorative possibilities of the arch were barely explored before Roman times.

Cutting Corners

During the Roman Empire, concrete arches and vaults were used to maximum advantage by architects and builders to create dynamic spaces with long spans. The Roman masons had a whole set of "rules of thumb" for knowing the limits of their construction methods. These were conservative enough to make structural failures uncommon—so long as the rules were followed. Some Roman slumlords must have cut corners, however, because injury, even death, in a building collapse was a common fate for the poor tenement dwellers of ancient Rome.

The Arch and Ornament

The arch has elements and geometry that integrate well with architectural ornamentation. For example, it became customary to alternate the coloring of voussoirs in some cultures, as seen in the Islamic medieval buildings of Spain and the Romanesque churches in certain parts of France and Germany. The dramatically contrasting hues of the adjacent units would thus draw attention to the radial nature of the arch. Many arches had a specially carved keystone, often a face, which may have been emblematic but may also have been designed to keep evil spirits at bay. Indeed, one of the oldest uses of the arch is the city gate, and a protective keystone would have been entirely suitable in that context. In some architectural traditions, most notably the Byzantine, the arch was combined with the lintel to form a relieving arch, known thus because the arch directs the compressive forces away from the lintel. The space between lintel and arch is called a "lunette" or "tympanum," and like the classical frieze, it was an opportunity to use more fragile, decorative materials, such as carved plaster, terracotta, painted sculpture, or mosaic.

Rows of arches in alternating dark and light stone line the nave of the basilica of Sainte-Madeleine at Vézelay in eastern France. This Romanesque church begun in 1104 housed relics of, so monks claimed, Mary Magdalene, and was a popular pilgrimage site.

Pont du Gard
Nîmes, France

Almost 2,000 years ago, the aqueduct that included this magnificent bridging span (right) endowed the Roman city of Nemausus with a constant flow of fresh water. Every stone of the Pont du Gard was precisely cut to fit—the structure uses no mortar.

Travelers to southern France throughout the centuries have marveled at the Pont du Gard. This massive limestone arched construction just outside the modern city of Nîmes is not a bridge at all, but the bridging span of an aqueduct. It was built by the ancient Romans at the point where the aqueduct's water-bearing channel had to cross the Gard River.

The Romans were not the first people to find a way to bring water to a settlement, but they truly excelled at feats of hydraulic engineering. Picky about water quality, they would first find a suitable source of water, usually in the hills—the entire water channel system had to be gravity-fed, so a source downhill from the city was never an option. The water would be collected at the point of origin in some kind of catchment basin, then directed to the channel. The channel could be underground, at ground level, or high above the ground, depending on the topography. Where the ground level changed drastically because of hills or valleys, the aqueduct planners had to make a classic cost–benefit analysis: invest labor and materials in diverting the channel for long distances around the obstacle, or instead opt for tunneling or bridging. Sometimes, they could overcome the problem of a valley by using the reverse siphon effect: as long as the rise that the water had to make on the far side of the valley was less than the height of its origin, it could be done. But siphons could be a maintenance problem, and so bridging was often a better solution to a deep, long, but narrow valley such as the gorge through which the Gard River ran.

Getting over the Gard

The Nîmes aqueduct was planned during the time of the emperor Augustus, just over 2,000 years ago, to supply the Roman city of Nemausus (now Nîmes). Augustus intended the city as a place to settle many of the veterans of his war in Egypt, and indeed, the legions supplied the manpower to build the aqueduct. Since labor was plentiful and well organized, limestone quarries abounded, and time was pressing, the supervisor of the aqueduct project decided, when they got to the Gard River, to bridge over the valley with a triple-tiered series of arches.

The Pont du Gard's simple, utilitarian structure has been much admired for its beauty. The setting is very picturesque, with natural exposed limestone embankments, the usually clear, trout-flecked water of the Gard River, and forests of holm oak on the slopes. The particular limestone used for the aqueduct has an even graininess and a beautiful golden color. The masonry is also exceptionally fine for a utilitarian structure. It was built entirely without mortar, and each block had to be skillfully cut.

It is the form of the aqueduct, however, that is its most awe-inspiring feature. The river's low-water channel was spanned in one central arch (no caissons and pumps were therefore needed).

From the air, the perfect alignment and symmetry of the Pont du Gard is clear. The three tiers of arches rise almost 165 ft (50 m) above the deep gorge of the Gard River. The central arch of the bottom tier crosses the river in a single span of 80 ft (24 m).

The arches on either side were slightly narrower than the central arch but equal to each other, so the arrangement was symmetrical. The second-tier arches had the same spacing, so the vertical piers aligned. The arches' two different radii were accommodated by lowering the springing point of the larger central arch, so that the keystones of all the arches were at the same height. The ratio of the two different radii was 3:4. This became very significant on the top tier, which carried the water channel. The top series of arches were much smaller, and their spacing was modular: three arches sat over the second-tier side arches, while four arches sat over the second-tier middle arch. Thus the vertical forces were gathered symmetrically and aligned as they were directed down through the construction. To either side of the valley, the arches continued until they met the bedrock slopes of the gorge. In all, there were 17 arches in the lower two tiers and 38 arches in the top tier.

Another feature of the Pont du Gard is its structural clarity of expression. Each voussoir is clearly visible. The arch spring points and the top edge of each tier are marked by a projecting cyma recta molding, which no doubt also served as a ledge for the arch centering as the structure went up. Other remnants of the building process, such as pole set-holes and projecting blocks (to hold scaffolding and formwork), were not filled in or chiseled away after the aqueduct was finished. Whether or not these served later maintenance purposes is not clear; the decision to leave them may have been to save time.

Bringing Water to the City

Once the aqueduct was completed, its water channel would have been lined with a hydraulic cement and prepared to take water. All Roman aqueducts were equipped with clean-out drop-boxes and manholes at regular intervals. Once the 31-mile (50-km) long aqueduct reached Nemausus, the water which was flowing at 105 gallons (400 l) a second, was redistributed in the city. Amazingly, the total vertical drop along the entire run of the aqueduct was less than 50 ft (15 m)! This is a testament to the skill of the Roman topographers and engineers.

And how was the water used? Certainly the city would have had at least one public bath. Nemausus had a sizable amphitheater but was a relatively unostentatious Roman city—street fountains would have been utilitarian rather than dramatic. The water ran continuously and would have drained into the street sewers, helping to flush them out. Every citizen of Nemausus was guaranteed fresh drinking water and clean streets thanks to the aqueduct.

Arches

True arches were first used—indeed, they were plentiful—in ancient Mesopotamia. The builders in this arid region quickly developed a brick tradition because neither large timbers nor good building stone was readily available. Initially, they used sun-dried bricks, but these have limited uses, producing very massive walls with few openings. When they discovered that kiln-fired bricks were both hard and stable, builders had found a suitable material for many methods of building, including arches.

The soldiers of Alexander the Great brought the concept of the arch back to Greece in the early fourth century BCE, after their contact with Eastern cultures, especially Babylon. Certainly, one application in the first generation of arch use was military: fortress gates. There is no evidence of an experimental phase in Greek arch building; rather, it appears that the idea was transmitted fully formed. The Bronze Age predecessors of the Greeks, the Myceneans, created corbeled forms similar to true arches and vaults, but these were not the ancestors of the Greek arch because of the use of corbels, not voussoirs.

Greek architects did not think the arch an acceptable form for monumental buildings such as temples. Instead, it was relegated to utilitarian settings such as water storage tanks, underground passageways, retaining walls, and stairwells. Their attitude remained very conservative toward the spanning capacity of the arch, and they mostly failed to exploit its potential.

Roman Developments

The Greeks did, however, pass on the arch to the Romans, through military contact in southern Italy in the third century BCE. The idea took hold very quickly, although without major innovations until the first century BCE.

Types of Arches

ROMAN ARCH

The ancient Romans made full use of the true, semicircular arch, so much so that it is often called the "Roman arch." But it was often built of concrete and functioned more like a monolith than a true arch.

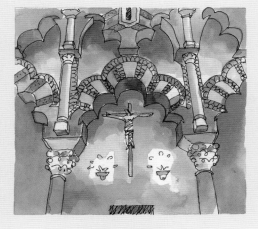

LOBED ARCH

A lobed arch has three or more lobes or foils. It may also be called a "foiled arch" or, more descriptively, a "clover arch." The three-lobed or trefoil arch has three lobes, the five-lobed or cinquefoil has five, as shown here. Beyond this, there is the multifoil arch.

HORSESHOE ARCH

This arch extends the ends of the semicircular arch past the halfway point until they start to converge, creating a shape like a horseshoe. It was introduced by the Visigoths in Spain, and became characteristic of Moorish architecture.

LANCET ARCH

A lancet, or pointed, arch was more flexible than the Roman arch. It was a feature of Islamic architecture and, later, of Gothic architecture.

OGEE ARCH

The ogee arch is made up of two curves, both concave then convex, like two S shapes with vertical ends. It first appeared in the Middle East, and later became an element in European Gothic architecture. It is particularly associated with Venice, Italy, so much so that it is also called the "Venetian arch."

MONOLITHIC ARCH

This is a lintel (a horizontal block across a space) with an arch carved into it. This is purely decorative, as cutting out an arch weakens the lintel considerably.

Then the Romans developed a very sophisticated arcuated plus trabeated architectonic language of curves combined with horizontal lines. The Colosseum in Rome (CE 80) is the culmination of this Roman invention: the tiered structure stands three stories high, and continuous arches run around its elliptical perimeter. Also continuous are the engaged classical orders: the Corinthian order above the Ionic above the Tuscan. The projecting impost of each arch has a proportionally pleasing relationship to the two columns that frame it. This formula was so successful that it can be found residually in every basilical church of the Middle Ages. It also reemerged in clear, studied imitation during the Renaissance.

Variations on the Arch

By the early Middle Ages, several other distinctive types of arch had appeared, which is consistent with the seismic cultural shifts of that period. Some of these, such as the lancet arch, can be more effective than the Roman arch.

An arch takes vertical forces and directs them to the side; in doing so, it creates large horizontal forces, called "thrust." One possible way to counteract thrust is by placing sheer mass in the area to either side of the arch (the spandrel) or by at least creating an abutment at the impost block. If thrust is not counteracted, the arch will fail through outward deflection. The other way to counteract thrust is to change the shape of the arch: if the shape is attenuated vertically, the thrust vector acts more vertically than horizontally, and there is less of a tendency for the arch to move outward. The lancet arch is just such a shape. The radii of the arcs in a lancet arch are greater than the span of the arch. The two arcs meet at an angle, without tangency (that is, the two arcs have a single point of contact but no implied crossing). It is also called a "pointed arch."

Other distinctive arch types evolved in Spain, North Africa, and the Middle East. The earliest was the horseshoe arch, brought to Spain by the migration of the Visigoths in the fifth century. It extends for more than half a circle, so its base is narrower than its diameter. After the Arabs defeated the Visigoths in 711, it continued to be used in Christian work created under Arab rule (known as "Mozarabic"), such as the church of San Miguel de Escalada (913). It was also taken

Semicircular stilted arches, outlined in marble and supported on marble pillars, spiral up the staircase and along the balconies of the fifteenth-century Palazzo Contarini del Bovolo in Venice, Italy.

up in Moorish architecture, and from Spain it then spread to North Africa and elsewhere.

Three other arch types, the lobed, the four-centered, and the ogee, evolved in both Islamic and Christian communities during the Middle Ages. The lobed arch has three or more concave sections on each side, purely for dramatic effect. Its other name, the cloverleaf, is more descriptive of its appearance. It had its roots in the Moorish Iberian Peninsula. The four-centered arch has more than one radius, as suggested by its name, but the different segments meet at a point of tangency (except for at the top). It is a slightly flattened version of the lancet. The ogee is yet another variation of the lancet. Here, the curves are in an S shape that meet at the top in a point. It was much favored by builders in Venice, Italy.

It is for this reason that the ogee arch was sometimes called the "Venetian arch."

Some variations on the arch have no voussoirs; these are often made of one stone (similar to a lintel) and are known as monolithic arches. They are not free of bending and shear stresses, and thus are not true arches.

The Arcade

The Romans applied their formula for arcuated–trabeated architecture to many building types apart from amphitheaters and theaters. Basilicas, archives, libraries, and fountains all used the arch but the façade was "ennobled" with the orders superimposed. In the second century CE, a subtle shift occurred, as evidenced at the Emperor Hadrian's Villa at Tivoli, Italy (CE 118–134)—the Emperor was himself an enthusiastic amateur architect. In this purely nonfunctional piece of architecture, a single line of columns supported alternating entablatures and arches. It is an early example of the arch spanning between two columns as opposed to two piers, and it sets up the conditions for the arcade as it was to develop.

Under the Emperor Diocletian, the arcade came into its own, especially at the Palace of Diocletian at Spalato (c. CE 300–306) (modern Split, Croatia), where true column-supported arcades flanked the monumental forecourt. When the double-aisled Old St. Peter's Basilica in Rome was built two decades later, in c. CE 320–330, the architects had it both ways: the nave was colonnaded with a straight entablature, but the inner aisle was arcaded, with the arches being supported by columns on pedestals. A very innovative form of the arcade was used one generation later for the Mausoleum of Constantina in Rome (CE 350). Constantina was the daughter of the Emperor Constantine the Great and her tomb became the church of Santa Costanza. Here, an annular vault surrounded an arcaded drum; the twelve pairs of columns of the arcade were arranged radially, and all sense of trabeation is gone.

In medieval Christian architecture, the arcade and the basilica (which has an aisled nave) were combined for a lasting system of spanning and fenestration. Because of the thrust problem that is inherent to arches, these church arcades were to develop several tendencies over the centuries: a thickening of the column into a pier; an attenuation of the rounded arch into a pointed form; and an integration of the arcade with the ceiling vaults. The development of the Gothic vault was very much a part of this.

Return of the Semicircular Arch

During the Italian Renaissance the semicircular arch (or Roman arch) enjoyed a revival. In some

ways, the classical tradition had never died out in Tuscan cities such as Florence. Nevertheless, the new breed of architects, such as Leon Battista Alberti, Filippo Brunelleschi, Luciano Laurana, were humanists with humanist patrons. The Roman arched arcade was used for churches, loggias, and courtyards. It provided both design regularity and a reference to antiquity, ideas that this age of humanism found sympathetic. The Renaissance arcaded court was more open and less inward-turning than the medieval cloister.

In his loggia for the Ospedale degli Innocenti (Foundling Hospital) in Florence, Italy (1419–1444), Brunelleschi collaborated with the artist Donatello to provide round terracotta panels called *tondi*, one per spandrel, each decorated with the figure of a baby in swaddling clothes.

The medieval cloister was an arcaded space. One of the finest is at Monreale Cathedral in Sicily, Italy (1189) (above). Arches rest on marble columns that are plain or patterned in gold and colored glass.

The spandrel tondo was perfected, in terms of its size and position, by Laurana in the courtyard of the Palazzo Ducale at Urbino, Italy (1472). This harmonious arcade was used many centuries later in some of the work of Beaux Arts architects such as McKim, Mead, & White, for example, in their Boston Public Library (1895).

End of the Arch

Since the Industrial Revolution, new materials, mostly steel and plate glass, have virtually made the arch obsolete and archaic. Even the Marshall

Field Wholesale Warehouse in Chicago (1887), designed by H. H. Richardson, which resembled some of the extraordinary Roman aqueducts on the outside, hid an iron skeleton that was the real structure for the whole interior. The massive wall of masonry only had to support itself. The next generation of large city buildings stripped away the masonry, leaving the lighter true structure to become the modern curtain wall.

One architect who persisted in using masonry, and in a very organic way, was the idiosyncratic Catalan Antoni Gaudí. With his grandiose and as yet unfinished masterpiece, the Church of La Sagrada Familia (the Holy Family) in Barcelona, Spain (1882–), his desire was to build a towering work in true structural masonry—an ambition that is proving impossible. Nonetheless, in the arches and tracery of the completed transept, we can see how completely Gaudí and his craftsmen understood the Gothic systems of building, but interpreted them in an updated way.

After the rise of Modernism in the twentieth century, the traditional arcade disappears. There are new interpretations of the arcade from a few architects who either had a strong rationale (such as the Italian traditionalist Giovanni Guerrini with his Palazzo della Civiltá Italiana in Rome (1943) or who appeared to welcome a change from the rigid orthogonal quality of the Modern movement. Edward Durrell Stone, the architect

of the Kennedy Center in Washington, DC, was just such a noncomformist. His design for the Library (1968) of the State University of New York in Albany, New York, is a significant update on the arcade idea. For the Metropolitan Opera House (1966) at the Lincoln Center, New York City, Wallace K. Harrison created five great arches for the façade, which frame an asymmetrical glass wall with giant murals painted by the artist Marc Chagall behind.

Lights inside the Metropolitan Opera House in New York City (1966) sculpt its five arches and illuminate a wall of giant murals by Marc Chagall. Wallace K. Harrison's design is an urbane and witty updating of the opera house type, radically transparent but suggestive of tradition through his use of the arcade.

The central nave of the Church of La Sagrada Familia (the Holy Family) in Barcelona, Spain (left), begun in 1882, was completed in 2000. The columns of the arches branch to support their load. Where Antoni Gaudí used scale models, computer modeling is used today to realize the complex columns and arches.

The Alhambra

At the Alhambra (1338–1390), the palace and fortress built by the Muslim rulers of Granada, Spain, the Moorish use of arch and arcade reached its zenith. In the Court of the Lions, many slender columns support stilted, multi-lobed arches of intricately carved plaster. The patterned intricacy at ceiling level is in marked contrast to the floor, with its simple marble paving and axial, recessed water feature. You can wander from one arcaded court to the next in the palace, in what is not unlike the experience of a dream.

Monumental Arches

From early times onward, the single arch often denoted extraordinary passage—passage from one realm to another. For example, cities often had defensive walls that made a very hard edge; the arch in the gate marked the transition from an uncontrolled to a controlled area. The arch thus embodied the notion of engaging with an ordered environment.

Rulers also used the arch at the entrance to their palaces or throne rooms to show that the individual holding power also exerted control over the surrounding area. At one of the palaces in the Assyrian city of Nimrud in modern Iraq (ninth century BCE), a mighty brick arch was flanked by two guardian figures, both of which had the body of a bull and a human head. At the Ishtar Gate (c. 575 BCE) in the ancient city of Babylon (now in Iraq), 42 guardian beasts (bulls, dragons, and lions) were depicted in glazed brick reliefs. The blue glaze of the background bricks is startlingly vivid, and the brick voussoirs are clearly defined. Ishtar was a Babylonian moon goddess and it is likely that the Ishtar Gate was a point along an important processional route.

The Triumphal Arch

The Greeks came to the arch form belatedly, and there are only a few examples of arches used to glorify passage in the ancient Greek world. In the Hellenic city of Priene in Asia Minor (now southwest Turkey), a simple arch with a profile similar to an Ionic architrave marked the entry to the agora, or marketplace. The arch did not support any other construction—it was purely emblematic of passage.

The Romans, however, adopted the arch and turned it into one of the most enduring forms in Western monumental architecture: the triumphal arch. This form had its roots deep in Roman ritual. When a victorious general returned to the capital, Rome, he had to be purified before he could reenter the city. As part of this process the general and his retinue would proceed along the Via Sacra (Sacred Way) and through a specially created arch. It is believed that on the actual occasion a wooden arch, decorated with painted panels and garlands, was erected. This was later replaced with a more permanent stone construction, rich in sculpted relief panels.

By the mid-Empire there were innumerable triumphal arches throughout the city, but today only a few remain. Some earlier important arches, such as the Arch of Augustus (29 BCE) in the Forum, are known only from their foundation stones and depiction on coins.

The Forum today houses two of the best preserved arches: the Arch of Titus and the Arch of Septimius Severus. The Arch of Titus (after CE 81) celebrated the Roman victory over Jerusalem in the first century CE. It has a single opening: the sack of the Temple of Jerusalem is depicted on the inside walls (you can see soldiers dragging off the sacred menorah), while the arch's peak depicts the dead but deified Titus carried aloft to the heavens by an eagle. The Arch of Septimius Severus (CE 203) is a great deal more grandiose, its large central arch flanked by two smaller ones. The keystone of the central arch is carved with the head of Mars, God of War. The entire arch is covered in rich carvings illustrating personifications of Victory, prisoners, trophies of war, and reliefs of key scenes from the military campaign against the Parthians. It is equipped with stairs and can be occupied—in the Middle Ages it was used as a fortress.

The third well-preserved arch in the old civic center of Rome is the Arch of Constantine (CE 315). It, too, has three openings. But it has a new development, the reuse of older panels from other monuments, which results in a mixing of styles. At first glance this appears slapdash, but Constantine may have wanted to refer to former emperors with his sculptural program. Clearly, this arch marked a shift in aesthetic sensibility from a sense of unity to a sense of multiplicity.

The Romans built their triumphal arches in provinces throughout the Empire. Some very well known examples can still be seen in Benevento, Italy, and also in Orange and Autun, France.

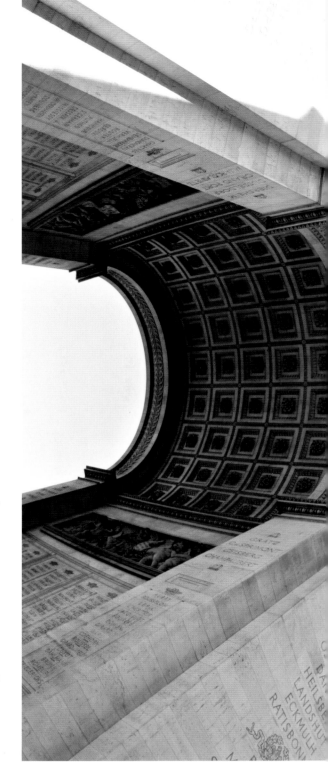

From beneath the Arc de Triomphe in Paris (1806–) (above), the vast scale of the largest triumphal arch in the world becomes clear. It commemorates those who fought for France. The names of French generals are engraved on the inside walls, and the Tomb of the Unknown Soldier lies at its base.

This model of the Ishtar Gate (left) stands at the entrance of the archaeological site of the ancient city of Babylon in modern Iraq. The original, with its rich blue and brown glazed tiles, was excavated by the German archaeologist Robert Koldewey and is now in the Pergamon Museum in Berlin, Germany.

Those built in the province of Gaul (now France) are thought to have contributed greatly to the knowledge of medieval builders centuries later.

There was another type of ceremonial arch built in the provinces of Gaul and Iberia (Spain): the bridge arch. The road network was key to the success of the Roman Empire. Where roads went, bridges were needed, and sometimes, arches were erected at either one or both ends of a bridge to symbolize the protection of Rome. In the town of Saint-Chamas, in southern France, arches at either end of the Pont Flavien can still be seen. They are articulated with Corinthian pilasters, and carry an inscription dated to about 12 BCE.

A French Interpretation

The triumphal arches and bridge arches of the Gallo-Roman world seem to have made a deep impression on the French psyche, judging from some examples built in Paris in much later

The Arch of Constantine in Rome (left) celebrates Constantine's victory over Marcus Aurelius Valerius Maxentius, at the Battle of Milvian Bridge in CE 312, in a power struggle to decide who would be Emperor.

periods. When architect Claude-Nicolas Ledoux, a dedicated exponent of Neoclassical ideas, built the luxurious urban villa, the Hôtel de Thelluson, in Paris (1783), he placed a bridge and rusticated arch at the carriageway entrance, and designed the symmetrical house and garden as a world apart. Unfortunately, the bridge and arch were demolished during the nineteenth century to clear the way for one of Baron Georges Eugène Haussmann's avenue projects. A triumphal arch on a scale that Haussmann would have no doubt found acceptable is the Arc de Triomphe (1806–) in Paris, commissioned by Napoleon Bonaparte, which dominates the Place Charles de Gaulle at the western end of the Champs-Elysées.

Barrel and Cross Vaults

A complex of interconnecting barrel vaults lies beneath the arena floor of the Flavian Amphitheater in Pozzuoli, near Naples in Italy (first century CE). It was the third largest amphitheater in Italy.

An arch can be extruded horizontally in a tunnel-like way to completely span a rectangular area. The resulting structure is called a barrel vault. This type of vault usually requires centering, although not always for the entire space. Rather, since the profile of the barrel vault typically does not change, the centering can be moved along from one end of the vault to the other as it is constructed. Roman builders in Asia Minor (modern Turkey) invented a clever way to do this without constantly having to reposition the centering. They inserted narrow terracotta pipes vertically at regular intervals along the vault crown. Instead of resting on the floor, the heavy wooden centering hung from, and was controlled by, ropes passing through the pipes. This saved time during construction.

One problem with the barrel vault is thrust. The semicircular construction exerts a horizontal force that needs massive side walls to counteract it. However, if a series of barrel vaults are placed side-by-side parallel to each other, they counterbalance the thrust—only at the edges parallel to the entire group of vaults is an abutment needed.

The Romans exploited this system for utilitarian buildings such as their huge granaries.

Brick and Concrete

The Romans did not invent the barrel vault, however. The Greeks used it for some utilitarian structures and had probably seen much older examples in Mesopotamia. On rare occasions they even built concrete barrel vaults; an example was found covering a cistern at Acrocorinth, on mainland Greece. The Romans created a technological revolution, however, with their concrete formula. They added pozzolana, a volcanic ash,

to their concrete mix. This gave their concrete vaults exceptional strength, water-resistance, and cohesion. But Roman concrete was very different from modern concrete. For one thing it was not poured but, rather, laid up in courses. The Romans used their distinctive tile-like bricks as both formwork and facing with concrete for this type of construction in vaults of all shapes. If the building was an important one, they would finish it with plaster or cut marble revetments.

For relatively simple barrel vaults made of brick and concrete mortar, they sometimes built pitched, or canted, vaults, using canted courses, a method that eliminated the need for centering. The technique has been observed at the Assyrian city of Dur Sharrukin (modern Khorsabad in Iraq) (c. 720 BCE), where it was used for drain covers. The Nubians of southern Egypt still build mud-brick vaults in this way, without using any centering; this is perhaps best known as the Nubian vault. If the corbels are tilted out of the vertical plane, they are held in place during construction by a combination of the cohesive strength of the mortar and gravity.

Eventually, the barrel vault became more respectable; it was used widely in the medieval period for church construction. For example, the nave of the Romanesque church of Saint-Philibert at Tournus, France (950–1120), uses a series of parallel transverse barrel vaults that are supported by perpendicular arches.

Lighter, Stronger

The barrel vault is dark. If openings are cut in the vault to let in light, they weaken it. Even so,

A Modern Interpretation

The American architect Louis I. Kahn sometimes drew inspiration from the past, especially from examples of Roman vaulting that he sketched during his travels. For the Kimbell Art Museum in Fort Worth, Texas (1972), he used parallel "butterfly" canopies that suggest barrel vaults but that allow a continuous light baffle at the crown. The particular curve that he used in the profile is called a "centroid." For materials, he used modern reinforced concrete together with travertine, a light-colored, porous stone quarried near Rome. This combination was one of his signatures.

some architects used it for its very strong, space-defining aspect, such as Étienne-Louis Boullée's Project for the Library for the King of France (1785). But the builders of ancient times had a solution to the dark barrel vault—the cross vault, also known as the groin vault. The advantages of this type of vault were not completely lost on the Greeks—there are several examples, such as at the Terrace of Attalos I at Delphi (third century BCE). The complex cuttings of the intersecting stones at this site show that the Greeks understood the form well. Here again, it was the Romans who went much further with cross vaulting, especially after the concrete revolution allowed a seemingly unlimited number of vault combinations.

As with the arch, where the lancet or pointed form performs better than the semicircle form, so it is with the barrel and cross vaults. If the crown of the vault is raised, the horizontal thrust is reduced. Medieval masons understood this well, which is one reason why the pointed vault, like the pointed arch, appeared in the Gothic style. In addition, if the lower part of the vault is steep enough, centering is not needed until a certain angle is reached. In Catalonia, Spain, a special tradition allowed this type of self-supporting vaults: the builders layered terracotta tiles and mortar in alternating herringbone patterns to create vaults with no need for centering. The family that is best known for this technique, the Guastavinos, emigrated to New York City in the nineteenth century. Their distinctive vaults can be seen in places such as the Great Hall on Ellis Island and Grand Central Railroad Terminal.

Guastavino tiles form the barrel vault of the City Hall Subway Station platform in New York (1904) (bottom). The station was closed in 1946, but was reopened for the subway's centennial in 2004.

Types of Vaults

A barrel vault (right) is achieved by extending a single semicircular arch horizontally. This creates a beautifully simple, tunnel-like space, but one that tends to be dark—one of several constraints of the barrel vault is the difficulty in allowing light in. One solution is the cross vault, or groin vault (far right). This vault form is created by intersecting two barrel vaults at right angles so that they meet with diagonal seams crossing in the center. The cross vault distributes loads in more directions, which allows for a less linear building and also a more spacious one. There are more opportunities for lunette openings at the barrel ends to let in more light. It is not much more difficult to build than a barrel vault.

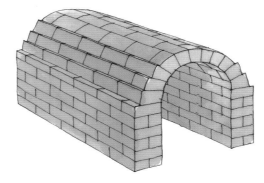 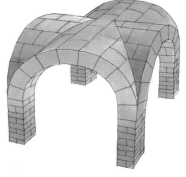

BARREL VAULT   **CROSS (GROIN) VAULT**

Hassan Fathy

The *khan* (right) was a public building—a hostel with workshops where master craftsmen could live, work, teach their trade, and sell goods. These new trades were to be the basis of the village's economy.

The architect Hassan Fathy (1900–1989) was already recognized in his own country, Egypt, when he published *Architecture for the Poor: An Experiment in Rural Egypt* (1969; the original title was *Gourna: A Tale of Two Villages*) and suddenly gained international acclaim as a pioneer in solving the problem of affordable housing in developing nations. His solution was to return to traditional building materials (mud brick) and traditional building forms (the vault). He also believed in a partnership between the architect and the intended occupants.

Old Vault for a New Village

The village of New Gourna arose because of the Egyptian government's desire to relocate a community of peasants, who were squatting over the ancient necropolis of Luxor, making an uncertain living from looted antiquities and forgeries. The Egyptian government confiscated the land, but also took on the responsibility of rehousing the evicted peasants.

That was when the experiments of Hassan Fathy attracted their attention. Here was an eminent architect, professor at the University of Cairo, who had built several vaulted houses from mud brick while investigating solutions for low-cost housing. For Fathy, the Gourna project was a dream come true: a chance to finally test his ideas about affordable, locally built housing.

Fathy had been investigating how to build using mud bricks. This was after World War II had broken out, when imported steel and timber for building had disappeared. He wanted a brick vaulting technique that did not need centering, because the good materials and skilled carpenters that centering demanded were also in very short supply. His first attempts were dismal failures. Then came the breakthrough. His older brother, who was helping direct the Aswan Dam project in southern Egypt, told him about the Nubian peasants in the south who made mud-brick vaults with no centering. Fathy traveled to Aswan early in 1941 to learn the secrets of an ancient, traditional architecture.

The Nubians built their vaults by using the principle of canted courses, just as in ancient Mesopotamia millennia before. As they used the pitched, or canted, vault technique, the Nubians's repertoire of forms included domes as well as parabolic barrel vaults. Fathy found masons who were adept at the technique and could thus train others. He invited several to journey north and begin work on experimental housing at Bahtim (1941). Fathy was enchanted by other traditional techniques preserved in southern Egypt, such as decorative mud-brick latticework that allowed screening without blocking air flow, and stairs supported on brick arches. He was to use all these features at New Gourna.

Consultation and Sustainability

The Egyptian government purchased a 50-acre (20-hectare) site for the new settlement, and the Department of Antiquities sponsored the project. The first season of building the village of New Gourna started in 1945. It was to house a total of 900 families who had to move in by 1948. The entire village had to be built in three years.

Rather than arbitrarily design a complete settlement and then spend three years supervising its construction, Fathy took a different approach. In principle, he set aside plenty of time to consult with each family and learn their requirements, and this allowed a briefer period for building.

The theater was an unroofed space with seating and a simple stone stage (below). Fathy's idea was that it be used for performances by musicians and dancers, and for competitive quarterstaff fights with long poles— entertainment that was a part of village ceremonies.

He believed that as the techniques and materials would always be the same and require few tools, each house could be built very quickly. But in practice, the special relationship he developed was with the master masons, who could produce the mud-brick constructions from very simple diagrams. The future occupants showed more concern for stabling their animals than housing their families, for complicated cultural reasons. So Fathy built about twenty model houses to show the future occupants the possibilities. The peasants still could not articulate their needs.

Fathy resorted to careful observation of the villagers in order to understand how to build for them. For example, he looked at their social structure. Groups of about ten to twenty families would typically group together in a kind of allegiance called a *badana*. Common *badana* activities such as festivals and weddings needed an outdoor space, and so New Gourna was laid out with clusters of ten to twenty houses around open squares. Each *badana* square had its own cafe, bakery, barber, and grocer.

Hassan Fathy's housing experiments, his creative problem-solving, and consultative approach have been an inspiration to many architects, from the current work by Habitat for Humanity, to the Rural Studio of the late Sam Mockbee, and even film star Brad Pitt's involvement in the rebuilding of New Orleans.

And whatever the problematic features of the New Gourna approach in the twenty-first century, there is one aspect that ought to bring it renewed interest. The traditional mud-brick architecture of Egypt, and Hassan Fathy's slightly updated versions, is ideally suited to the climate. Thick masonry walls are ideal in a hot, desert climate because heat transmission through the wall is delayed until the chill desert night, when the heat is appreciated. Air-conditioning, a technology that plays a key negative role in global warming, is not so necessary. The natural size limitations of the domes and vaults also ensure that the houses have good cross-ventilation. Remarkably, Hassan Fathy wrote about these environmental factors long before the terms "green" and "sustainable" were household words.

Thick walls and courtyards (above) help interiors to remain cool as the day heats up. By the time the heat has penetrated, evening has come, with a big temperature drop—the radiating heat may actually be welcome during the coolest hours of the night. By morning, the interior has cooled off again.

A balcony is decorated with mud-brick latticework. A system of main and secondary vaults meant there was no need for heavy filling between the vault curve of the ground story and the flat floor above. Thus the mud-brick buildings could have two stories.

Ribbed Vaults

Over the centuries, masons of both stone and brick experimented with ways of making vaults less heavy and unmanageable. One technique was ribbing. By building vaults with thickenings, which were called "ribs," they could concentrate the vault forces at regular, controllable intervals. The ancient Roman market buildings of the second century CE at Smyrna in Asia Minor (modern Izmir in Turkey) used rather clunky cut stone ribs to support flat roofing slabs. However, the aesthetics of the rib were apparently unpalatable to the Romans, and in their brick-faced concrete domes, such as the dome of the so-called Temple of Minerva Medica in Rome (mid-third century CE), bricks were stacked up in ribs that were eventually "buried" in the fabric so that they didn't protrude. By the late fourth century CE, however, the Romans had begun to accept the simple ribbed cross vault—one is still standing in the vestibule of Santa Sabina in Rome (CE 422–432).

The Triumph of the Rib

The distinctively Gothic style of vaulting arose as a result of medieval masons grappling with the problem of defining the seam of intersection, called the "arris," in the cross, or the groin, vault. In northern France and Lombardy, Italy, in particular, they found that the geometry could be sharper if the vault had ribs that followed the line of intersection. The next step, which happened in and around Paris, was to understand the ribs as a system: the diagonal ribs were along the arris; the wall ribs and arcade ribs defined the wall elevation; the transverse rib spanned from arcade pier to arcade pier; and (if used) the longitudinal rib connected the boss at the crown to the next boss. As the ribs merged together at the wall and arcade piers, structural logic dictated that they continue down to the foundation. Thus the piers became big bundles of articulated ribs, often with a residual column and capital buried somewhere in the center. The wall elevation was divided into a series of horizontal zones (from bottom to top: arcade, gallery, triforium, and clerestory) and was made up of repetitive bays. If the columns of the arcade were interspersed with smaller, intermediate columns, then an alternating bay system with an A–B–A–B–A–B rhythm was generated. The resulting vault was called a "sexpartite" vault, and it became quite complicated, with an intricate beauty that was typical of the Early Gothic style. Laon Cathedral in France (*c.* 1160–*c.* 1230), with its four horizontal zones and an alternating bay system, is an exquisite example of this period.

The quadripartite vault helped give the great High Gothic cathedrals, such as Reims Cathedral in northern France (right), their harmonious quality. The kings of France were crowned here until 1825.

Intersecting Geometries

In the early medieval period, Islamic centers such as Córdoba, in Spain, started exploiting ceiling forms derived from free-flying, interlacing arches. At the Mezquita (Great Mosque) of Córdoba, Spain, *c.* 786, special points, such as in front of the *mihrab* (prayer niche) are marked by ingeniously lobed domes. These small domes are held up by eight interlacing arches, which begin to act like ribs, resulting in a lancet form. Many aspects of the Moorish culture were spread throughout southern Europe, including this type of interlacing arch/rib, as can be seen at the Cattedrale di Sant'Evasio at Casale Monferrato (*c.* 1106), near Milan, Italy.

Interlacing arches at the Mezquita in Spain start to function like ribs.

The medieval builders of Chartres Cathedral (1194–c. 1224) simplified the wall elevation to an A–A–A rhythm (that is, only one column or bay type) with only three horizontal zones (the arcade, triforium, and clerestory). The resulting vaults at Chartres (called "quadripartite") were much simpler and more elegant, and became the standard formula for the High Gothic style.

This style, as exemplified by great cathedrals such as Reims (begun 1211), still retained in a very residual fashion the classical elements of architecture, which dictated a series of horizontal subdivisions: base, impost, capital, frieze, cornice, second story pedestal, base, etc. With all the real stress on the vertical ribs, the wall surface came to seem as though it were "woven" together. In a late stage of the Gothic, called the *Rayonnant*, the horizontal remnants of the classical wall were jettisoned. The architecture became unabashedly vertical, and the emphasis was on plastic form. Ribs had already taken on a plantlike organic energy—this was now unleashed fully, while elements such as the base became mere bulblike thickenings without any horizontal breaks. In Rouen, France, examples include the churches of Saint-Ouen (begun 1318) and Saint-Maclou (1434–1521). In Central Europe, too, the rib took on a life of its own. At Freiburg Münster in Germany (thirteenth century), ribs are carved as if piercing other ribs (such as where a diagonal meets a wall). Previously, the intersection would have been absorbed into the capital, but in this style there is no capital.

Elaborate Patterning

English builders broke free from the French tradition and introduced new, more elaborate elements to the ribbed vault during the Late Gothic. They placed a ridge rib at the center along the longitudinal axis. Then they introduced extra ribs, called "tiercerons," which were diagonals connecting to intermediate points on the ridge rib. In the nave at Lincoln Cathedral (1192–1280) tierceron vaults are very much in evidence. With a growing tendency to flatten the center of the vaults and multiply tiercerons, it is not hard to see how the fan vault developed. The concentration of the tierceron ribs at the pier drew attention away from the crown, however. Seeing this as an aesthetic flaw, architects in the early fourteenth century introduced a new structural element, the lierne rib. The lierne was a short secondary rib that created a mesh pattern closer to the crown. The lierne rib did have a structural role as well as a visual one—it helped distribute loading on the vault web.

In Germany and Bohemia the mesh pattern reached an ultimate profusion of forms. "Free" rib patterns became completely independent of the vault shell shape: "flying ribs" arched through space and lierne ribs connected only at one end. Some outstanding Bohemian examples are found at the church of St. Barbara at Kutná Hora (1481–1548) and Vladislav Hall (1493–1502) in the Old Royal Palace at Prague Castle.

Ribbed Vaults

Vaults were initially reinforced with masonry ribs to stop them collapsing. The aesthetic possibilities suggested by these ribs saw ribbed vaults evolve, until the ribs were purely, and wildly, decorative.

SEXPARTITE VAULT

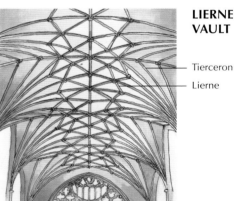

LIERNE VAULT

Tierceron

Lierne

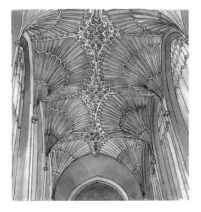

FAN VAULT

FREE VAULT

King's College Chapel
Cambridge, England

In England the development of medieval architecture had its own particular trajectory. It was influenced by French developments at times, such as when William of Sens, the French master mason, worked at Canterbury Cathedral in the Early Gothic style during the 1170s. But for the most part, English medieval architecture solved the problems of vaulting and unity of form in an independent, English way. By the late medieval period a distinctive style, known as the Perpendicular, had emerged. The feature that best represents this style is the fan vault. And the building that represents its stylistic culmination is King's College Chapel at Cambridge (built in three phases between 1446 and 1515), which is renowned for its graceful fan vaults designed by John Wastell.

The Perpendicular style emerged at Gloucester Cathedral during remodeling work carried out in the fourteenth century, more than 50 years before work started on King's College Chapel. As the name Perpendicular suggests, an emphasis on

King Henry VI founded King's College as a college of the University of Cambridge for students from Eton, a private boys school that he also founded. The Chapel (below) was part of this lavish patronage.

verticality was a hallmark. But much more than that was at the core of its approach. The notions of quaint irregularity and contrasting decorative elements on all surfaces—which had become a feature of Gothic architecture—was rejected at Gloucester in favor of an immediate clarity and unity. The Perpendicular style favored absolute clarity of form, achieved with the use of repetitive bays and a reduction of decoration, whereby only the tracery (the patternwork in stone filling the upper windows) retained the articulated frenzy of earlier, more exuberant forms. Only in the choir vaults were the Gloucester architects not entirely successful in achieving their ideals: these vaults have more lierne ribs than any other vault built in England, and the bays are an uneasy combination of quadripartite and sexpartite systems. The architects moved toward a solution in the cloister of Gloucester Cathedral, however. There, they employed the fan vault, which multiplied and equalized the tiercerons of the vault in a way that was compatible with the wall treatment of the Perpendicular style.

The Greatest Perpendicular Interior

The king who founded King's College at the University of Cambridge was Henry VI, who was known and venerated by many for his exceptional piety. Much of his reign was bogged down in the Hundred Years' War with the French, and this was then immediately followed by the War of the Roses, a civil war that saw the king imprisoned in the Tower of London in 1461 and then finally murdered there ten years later. If we accept the characterization of Shakespeare's Henry VI, the unlucky monarch escaped somewhat from the harsh realities of his time through his religiosity and charity. For the chapel of the college, he apparently took as his model the cathedral choir rather than the typical collegiate chapel. The chapel remained unfinished at the time of his death, and was finished by Henry VII.

The first striking thing about the interior of King's College Chapel is its strong spatial unity. There are no side aisles. The entire structure is built of a light beige, fine-grained limestone. The only element that interrupts the continuous sense of space is an elaborate carved wood choir screen that doubles as an organ loft, which separates the area reserved for the townspeople from the area for the students.

Each bay of King's College Chapel is exactly the same as the next, so you are not distracted by any sudden changes. The transverse ribs are heavier than any others, which gives further emphasis to the repetitive bay system. Large pendent bosses mark the central point of each bay, each equidistant from the transverse ribs.

The fan vaults are all the same. Each vault is the perfect culmination of the piers, and each subdivides into many smaller panels of equal size which remain entirely subservient to the vertically linear expression of the whole. Diagonal liernes, which make starlike patterns not at all in keeping with the verticality, are completely absent. Rather, the configuration of the fan ribs is generated as though the window tracery were simply applied to the curving shell of the vault itself, with the

necessary displacement of the ribs following the three-dimensional geometry of the shell.

The walls of the chapel are formed by enormous glazed panels of stained glass, which fill the building with light. The windows that the visitor sees at King's College Chapel are the originals, thus sealing the experience with an exceptional authenticity seldom found in the architecture of the medieval period.

Other Royal Foundations

Two other projects benefited from the generosity of Henry VII and fulfilled the promise of unity that the Perpendicular style represented. At St. George's Chapel at Windsor (1474–1528), near London, the sense of the cathedral model for a chapel is also very strong; the chapel even has side aisles and a crossing, which make it a little darker, but also much grander. The vaults used at St. George's are lierne vaults rather than fan vaults, but all the arcades and vaults follow the line of a flattened, four-centered arch. This gives a sense of expansive space.

The second project was the Henry VII Chapel (1503–1519) at Westminster Abbey in London. It is quite a contrast to the classic dignity of King's College Chapel. A typically Gothic density of decoration reemerges, along with very complex plan geometries. The vaults seem to attempt to do in stone what was more commonly done in wood: truncated, bracing arches; deeply hung and carved pendants; and fan "cones" tying the pendants back to the vault. It is as if the austerity of King's College Chapel never happened.

The fan vault ceiling was the third and final phase in the construction of King's College Chapel. The vault was originally planned as a lierne design. But a later decision to change to fan vaulting was ideal for the grand scale of this single-chambered chapel.

Buttresses

The load-bearing walls of any vaulted structure must resist the outward thrust exerted by the vault, whether it is a barrel vault or a cross. There are many different ways of doing this, and all profoundly affect a building's appearance. The Romans used a series of vaults leaning on each other to counteract each vault's thrust. But this ended at the edge of the building, and the thrust was frequently counteracted by the sheer massiveness of the outer wall. As a result, Roman vaulted buildings, including basilicas, palaces, libraries, and temples, had a tendency to be inward-turning, since the perimeter was often a massive wall with few openings.

This started to change during the reign of the Byzantine Emperor Justinian (sixth century CE), thanks to the buttress. Introducing light effects into a church to create a sublime atmosphere was important to Justinian. He also wanted certain churches to hold a large number of people and be relatively fire-resistant. But how did you build long spans in masonry and still let in some light? The answer was to vastly thicken the parts of the outer wall where the thrust forces were concentrated, thus allowing the wall area in between to be thinner and have larger openings. The thickenings could even appear as massive walls perpendicular to the outer wall. That, in essence, is a buttress.

The quadrant arches came out from under the gallery roof at churches such as Sainte-Madeleine at Vézelay in eastern France during the twelfth century. These were among the first flying buttresses.

Breakthrough at Durham

The most common vault form of Romanesque architecture was the barrel, a form that did not help to bring light into a basilica. The walls remained massive, with small windows, and were so effective at supporting the aisle vaulting that quite often the simple exterior buttressing did not even align with the piers inside. This suited the hot Mediterranean regions of Europe, but was not so pleasant in the darker, damp, and cool northern areas. It is therefore hardly surprising that experiments in new forms occurred in the northern regions of France such as Burgundy and Normandy and in England. At Durham Cathedral in northern England (1093–1133), the nave was vaulted with a ribbed groin that allowed for clerestory windows, because the gathered forces of the vault (at the pier) could be resisted by semicircular arches spanning the side aisle below (similar to St. John's at Ephesus in Turkey). It was an experimental phase, however, and the arched buttresses failed, mostly because the arch was inefficient in counteracting the bursting forces of the groin vault haunch. In the end, the

walls and piers at Durham were still so massive that it did not matter. However, when the nave vaulting was extended twenty years later, the masons used properly placed quadrant arches (arches that are just a quarter of a circle) for buttressing, and that worked.

The Flying Buttress Revealed

With the arrival of the buttress, the way was now clear to build cathedrals with vaults ever higher, clerestories ever larger, and buttresses ever more graceful. The next important step was to take the roof off the buttressing quadrant arches, thus allowing more light into the interior. At Sainte-Madeleine at Vézelay in eastern France (1120–1138) and Saint-Denis near Paris (1137–1140), masons moved the quadrant arches up above the gallery roof and exposed them to the elements. This innovation was the true flying buttress.

This buttress opened up myriad possibilities for the Gothic cathedral builders, particularly for the nave elevation (that is, the horizontal arrangement of the nave wall inside the building, which was intricately tied up with the combined issue of thrust, light, and vaulting). During the Early Gothic period in northern France, builders tended toward a more complex nave elevation in combination with flying buttresses. For example, Laon Cathedral (c 1160–c. 1230) has four major horizontal zones (from bottom to top): side-aisle arcade, gallery, triforium, and nave clerestory. At Durham, there were only three horizontal zones: side-aisle arcade, gallery, and nave clerestory. The only zone that had no windows was the Laon triforium, and that is because it was the zone of the gallery roof.

There was quite a lot of structural redundancy in the Laon solution, however. For example, the diagonal and transverse ribs used in the nave vault could have ended at bracketed corbels;

Types of Buttresses

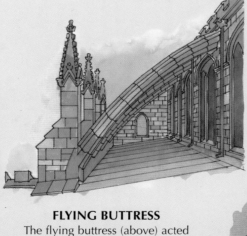

FLYING BUTTRESS
The flying buttress (above) acted with an equal and opposite force on an upper-story wall, to counteract the force from the vault roof inside that was pushing the upper-story wall outward.

BUTTRESS
The earliest buttresses (above) were thickened piers set at right angles against the wall that needed support to offset the sideways forces from the internal spanning structure.

SCROLL BUTTRESS
The scroll buttress (right) took the shape of a scroll. It appeared in examples of Baroque architecture from the seventeenth century, and was as much a decorative motif as a structural necessity.

Chartres Cathedral has so much exquisite stained glass that it has been described as "almost designed around its windows." This was possibly due to its flying buttresses with triple flyers (right). The lowest arch braces the arch above it with radiating spokes.

It took most of the thirteenth century to build Reims Cathedral, one of the most important High Gothic cathedrals. In the flying buttresses of the *chevet* (the radiating chapel at the rear), each span is decorated with an frilly, crucifix-tipped pinnacle.

the structure would not have been weakened. However, the builders thought it desirable to express the ribs down the piers for aesthetic reasons. Likewise, the four elevation divisions gave more than enough bracing for the vaults.

Chartres Cathedral (1194–c. 1224) simplified the Laon-type nave elevation by eliminating the gallery. Thus, in a sense, the Durham elevation is recapitulated, but with two important differences learned from the Early Gothic experiments. The architects at Chartres used true flying buttresses, and they kept the triforium in the place of the gallery, to allow more light for the clerestory. This formula for the nave elevation became standard for the High Gothic, as did the simplification of quadripartite over sexpartite vaulting, also found at Chartres (as described earlier in this chapter). All this was made possible by the flying buttress.

Further Refinements
By the thirteenth century the Gothic builders had refined their art to a level unprecedented in

the history of architecture. Features of the Gothic style that might seem to be mere sculptural whimsy often had a structural role to play. For example, the lacy, crocketed pinnacles that top the tower part of the flying buttresses add vertical loading, which helps divert downward the thrust of the arches. The skill of the builders allowed the nave vault to be placed higher and higher, although doing so subjected the upper part of the cathedral or church to heavier wind loads. At Amiens Cathedral (1220–1270) the architects added an extra tier of flyers to brace the upper part of the building. The builders also realized which parts of their flying arches were doing the work, so that at Amiens the spandrel of the arch became hollow tracery. At Chartres (which had triple flyers), the lowest arch braces the next one up through a little colonnade of radiating columns. At Narbonne Cathedral (begun 1272) in southwestern France, the flying buttresses of the choir end are braced laterally by a set of perpendicular full arches.

In central France, the Gothic builders came up with an alternative version of the very large, double-aisled cathedral at Bourges Cathedral (1195–1250). What was radically different was the general shape of the transverse section. At Bourges it was generally triangular, whereas at

Nôtre-Dame de Paris on the Ile de la Cité in the middle of the Seine in Paris is famous for its flying buttresses (above). Those that support the nave are double-span, and differ from those of the *chevet*. This was one of the earliest Gothic cathedrals.

a cathedral such as Amiens, it was an inverted T-shape (with the very tall nave being the stem of the T). This meant that Bourges's inner aisle vault height was approximately halfway between the outer aisle vault and the nave. The inner aisle thus had an elevation that recapitulated that of the traditional High Gothic nave: arcade (of the outer aisle), triforium (roof of the outer aisle), and clerestory (of the inner aisle). As a result, the structure was sounder. The intermediate flying buttress at Bourges was braced by the inner aisle, whereas at Amiens the intermediate buttress had less bracing.

Modern Engineering Studies
Recently, engineers interested in the structural problems of the large Gothic building have tried some innovative modeling techniques. If photoelastic material is cut out in the shape of the transverse section of a particular cathedral and placed in a wind tunnel in the laboratory, the lines of stress become visible under polarized

The Church of St. John

The church of St. John at Ephesus, in Turkey (CE 527–565) is a ruin, but the foundations clearly show that the domed building had buttresses at key positions. In some reconstructions, those buttresses rise up to end in large brick-haunched arches— a primitive version of the flying buttress. The sixth-century architects certainly had the technology and theory to create such buttresses. In their building tradition, counterposed arches and vaults had long been a staple of multi-aisled or multi-bayed structures. Bringing the building envelope one bay or aisle inward (and essentially making it a nonstructural wall) had the same effect as placing arched buttresses outside the perimeter.

Post-Gothic Uses

The buttress is essential to any compression masonry construction, but it need not take on the extreme aesthetic of the Gothic. Indeed, the Gothic buttress was at complete odds with the classical tradition as it came down from ancient Greek architecture. As a result, during the late Renaissance and the Baroque periods, buttressing was carefully embedded or concealed. On the two-story basilica façade of the Early Baroque, as exemplified by the church of Santa Susanna in Rome (1603), designed by Carlo Maderno, there is a "scroll" buttress. This negotiates the change in width of the two stories, and functions as much visually as structurally. During the Late Baroque in Venice, Italy, a bolder structural use of the scroll buttress can be seen in the drum of the domed church of Santa Maria della Salute (1631–1687) designed by Baldassare Longhena.

In the twentieth century, reinforced concrete, with its tensile strength, completely eclipsed traditional load-bearing masonry, and since the beginning of Modernism it is difficult to find architects willing to take on a combination of the two. Louis I. Kahn is an exception, especially at his Library at Phillips Exeter Academy (1972) in Exeter, New Hampshire. Kahn was intrigued by the remains of Roman brick-faced concrete that he had seen and sketched during his travels. He made the brick exterior walls of the library load bearing, rather than being just a veneer, and the openings therefore get larger as they go up in the five-story building. At the ground floor the brick wall takes the form of a four-sided arcade; the piers are buttressed on the inside by perpendicular brick flat arches. The interior structure of the building is reinforced concrete. Right at the top, below the large central skylight, large diagonal beams converge over an atrium. The diagonals are something like flying buttresses turned inside the building, and the enormous circular cutouts in the reinforced concrete box that forms the atrium are something like arches.

light as "oilcanning" patterns on the material. Some models have shown that when subjected to high wind loading, the original flying buttresses of the cathedral of Nôtre-Dame de Paris (c. 1163–1250) would crack where they meet the wall. Without modern techniques, the Paris builders apparently recognized this problem and worked to fix it in the 1220s. Some additional corrections were made in the nineteenth century by the architect who understood more about Gothic structures than anyone else at that time: Eugène Emmanuel Viollet-le-Duc.

An analysis of Chartres Cathedral that used the wind-tunnel method has revealed that the uppermost flyer, which was positioned so high on the nave wall that it could not have contributed anything to the support of the nave vaults, did in fact help protect the building from "pier distress." This is the cracking of buttresses and piers caused by lateral forces (that is, thrust and wind). This uppermost flyer at Chartres had long been controversial, as it seemed to serve no purpose.

In the atrium of the Library at the Phillips Exeter Academy (1972) (left), Louis I. Kahn used modern concrete elements in a structurally expressive way that is reminiscent of the structuralism of the Gothic builders.

Beauvais Cathedral
France

As the High Gothic style developed in the great medieval cathedrals of France, the height of the nave vault steadily increased. Reims Cathedral, at 123 ft (37 m) from the floor, was higher than Chartres, at 118 ft (35 m), and Amiens Cathedral, at 137 ft (42 m), was higher than Reims. The cathedral builders continued the trend with Beauvais Cathedral, also known as Cathédrale Saint-Pierre de Beauvais, in northern France (c. 1220–1272). But they went even further in their quest for

what may be the defining features of the Gothic period—height and light. The nave vault crown was planned to be 157 ft (48 m) from the floor. The triforium was glazed—what is solid stone at Amiens is open at Beauvais and it is filled with stained glass panels. This daring design produced an interior that was soaringly high, resembling a glass cage. Beauvais would have been the ultimate triumph of the High Gothic, had not the east-end vaults collapsed in 1284, only 12 years after their completion in 1272.

Audacity, Failure, Repair

The builders of Beauvais appear to have been aware of the risks they took, yet they pushed the structure to its limits. By adding the extra height to the central aisle wall, they also added weight. Indeed, glazing the triforium could be seen as an acknowledgment of the problem—in reducing the weight of the triforium area, the overall wall could be made taller. But it proved insufficient. In trying to keep the proportions of the nave arcade similar to that of Amiens, the arcade piers were spaced relatively far apart. So all that weight came down on relatively few piers. The failure at Beauvais in 1284 most likely started with the foundations. The pier foundations could not carry the weight and settled, so that the vaults were thrown out of balance and collapsed.

If the flying buttresses at Beauvais could have taken more weight, the failure might have been averted. But they were the typical High Gothic flying buttress, configured to withstand the lateral forces of wind and thrust but not to carry weight. To do the latter, their profile would have needed to be very different.

The builders at Beauvais seem to have fully understood what had gone wrong: the foundations had not received the necessary attention. They doubled the number of piers of the central arcade so that the upper wall's weight would be distributed over many more supports. To be able to add piers in what was a finished interior, they had to rebuild the aisle vaults, changing them from quadripartite to sexpartite. The minor ribs of the sexpartite vaults rested on these new piers with their new foundations, which were added exactly in the center of each original arcade, equidistant between each original pier. This of course affected the proportions of the central arcade elevation. Even though the aisle vaults were set lower than the original vaults, the arcade arches had to be severely stilted in order to reach the necessary height. The result is a rather odd elevation, but one that is still acceptable.

Understandably nervous, the builders added some backup reinforcements. For example, they added a layer of tracery stiffeners to cross-brace the aisle vaults, as well as a hidden membrane wall to these vaults. They placed wrought iron tie-bars between the flying buttresses of the choir. Interestingly, this was a similar element to the masonry arches of Narbonne Cathedral's choir buttresses, though they are even more resistant to deformations because wrought iron behaves well in both compression and tension.

The Impact of Beauvais

Beauvais's dramatic collapse overshadows some of the true achievements of the Beauvais masters.

As it was, the cathedral was never completed, and it instead became the culmination of the High Gothic. The collapse in 1284 showed where the technical limits were, and one could say that the Beauvais experience stopped the urge toward "heightism" in French Gothic architecture. There were to be some great masterworks of medieval building during the later thirteenth and the early fourteenth centuries. But none attempted the exaggerated height of the nave in combination with the deconstruction of the wall that had been the trend since Reims. Rather, reasonable size was combined with spatial clarity as well as decorative innovation. In southern France, where windows had always remained smaller, this formula was quite successful. One example is the choir and transepts of Saint-Nazaire at Carcassonne (1270–1325), with its life-size pier-figure sculptures. The brick cathedral of Albi (1282–1390) is another, with its generous open space between massive buttresses; chapels between the buttresses replace the side aisles. And these are not flying buttresses. Instead, an extraordinary shaping of the wall with thickenings and roundings helps strengthen the building envelope.

Inside the cathedral, its improbably lofty height is clear in the choir and its radiating *chevet* (above). Despite the building's projected design never being realized, it is still a very beautiful Gothic space, due in part to the elongated bays and piers, and the glazed triforium.

These Gothic architects were in some ways able to combine the success of the Chartres–Reims model with that of the Bourges model. When they decided to further integrate the section of nave wall that included the triforium and clerestory, they were continuing an investigation that had begun at Chartres and ended at Amiens. The treatment of the inner aisle at Beauvais also took something from Bourges, however. At Beauvais, the choir and ambulatory chapels take the place of the outer aisle at Bourges, and their vaults are a further step down in height, allowing an outer, lower clerestory. If only they had designed the foundations properly, Beauvais might have led the way to another generation of new, and even larger, Gothic cathedrals.

Often, as at Beauvais (above), Gothic builders started at the east, or choir, end, and worked toward the west, or nave, end until funds ran out. When its choir vaults collapsed, Beauvais's projected nave was never built. The towering width of the choir and transept are attached to the old tenth-century nave.

Domes

A dome can be thought of as a true arch rotating 360 degrees around its center-point. The hemispherical dome that results (and even a rough approximation of it) is a very rigid structure because it has a double curvature. It also contains the maximum possible volume for the minimum surface area. Vernacular architecture from all over the world reflects this understanding, from the *trulli* houses of southern Italy to the igloo of the Inuit, although most of these structures are not based on the true arch. Specifically, they do not have voussoirs in the exact sense. Rather, they use corbeling or, in the case of the igloo, a continuous spiral formation.

Challenges

A perfectly hemispherical dome will have all its parts in compression. However, humans have long devised attenuated masonry membranes for spanning, and these involve bending and shear stresses. Engineers today call these as thin-shell structures and fully comprehend their theoretical underpinnings. Until the recent past, however, builders only understood thin-shell structures empirically; even so, they were able to build vaults and domes that have stood for centuries.

The dome has other problems, the same as those of the arch and vault. It must overcome the bursting failure at the haunch, where diagonal thrust is greatest, and saddle failure at the crown. In a corbeled dome, each course of masonry forms a stable compression ring, but it can frequently be convenient to close the top with radial masonry as in a true dome. In a true dome, each horizontal ring of masonry is likewise a stable compression ring. Each ring has to be supported

Types of Domes

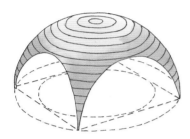

SIMPLE DOME
A simple dome is a hemispherical shape. In theory, it is achieved by rotating a true arch 360 degrees around its vertical axis.

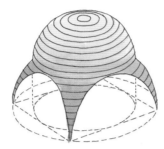

COMPOUND DOME
A dome is supported on pendentives, the curve of which would create a sphere with a greater radius than the dome's.

CLOISTER VAULT
A cloister vault is made up of cylindrical surfaces (like a cloth cap), and may resemble a true dome in appearance.

DOME AND DRUM
A dome sits on a drum, a cylindrical wall with the same diameter as the dome. The drum allows light in.

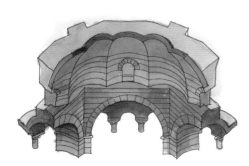

CONVOLUTED DOME
The convoluted, or pumpkin, dome is made of concave sections. From outside, it has an appearance like a pumpkin.

ONION DOME
The onion dome is an external form rather than a structural one. It swells beyond the base, then narrows to a pointed top.

until it is complete, although a circular opening can be left in the top if required.

So why go to all the trouble? The reason is that the dome is exceptionally rigid. It is also aesthetically unparalleled. It has been used to span extraordinarily wide spaces, creating remarkable buildings that are the product of enormous ingenuity. Its formal and aesthetic variations have allowed great creativity in many types of architecture in many parts of the world. The most basic dome of all is the simple, hemispherical dome.

The reading room of the Bibliothèque Nationale in Paris (below), designed by P. F. H. Labrouste (1867), has a roof of nine pendentive domes of glazed terracotta carried on slender cast iron columns. Light is admitted through a glazed oculus in each dome.

The Taj Mahal in Agra, India (1653), is the finest example of Mughal architecture, with an onion dome of white marble from Makrana, surrounded by four kiosks, or *chhatris,* with hemispherical domes.

It can be supported on a drum (cylindrical wall) of equal diameter to its base, like the Pantheon of ancient Rome, or on pendentives (curved triangular segments). In the compound dome, which is very common, the dome's curvature is not continuous with the pendentive, as in Hagia Sophia in Istanbul, Turkey. A cloister dome is segmented, and each segment has single as opposed to double curvature. More elaborate convoluted domes take the form of a pumpkin or melon, even an onion.

Convoluted Domes

Once the Romans discovered how strong walls and barrel vaults made of their special concrete could be, they were soon using it for domes. The most famous of all, which is still in use today, is the Pantheon in Rome. But they also produced some striking convoluted, or pumpkin, domes. To understand the convoluted dome, think of a pumpkin that has been sliced through its equator and hollowed out. Looking up, you see a series of concave, fluted segments that meet at obtuse angles. The arrises, where the segments meet, begin to act like the ribs in a ribbed vault, carrying some of the forces to points where buttresses can resist the thrust. Each concave section also has extra rigidity.

The Emperor Hadrian was greatly interested in this dome's potential, as evidenced by several variants that can be seen today, in a half-ruined state, at his Villa at Tivoli, Italy (CE 118–134). Plan forms that can generate a convoluted dome without using transitional geometries such as pendentives may have also fascinated him and his architects. At the large axial pavilion of the Piazza d'Oro, the plan is similar to a Greek cross, with apsidal ends. In fact, the wall of the pavilion undulates as concave apse becomes convex intrusion and then, at a point of tangency, starts to become concave again, and so on, around the eight sides to close at the point of origin. The dome thus springs directly from an undulating entablature. The sections narrow up to the top, where they may have converged at a round opening, or oculus.

In the sixteenth and seventeenth centuries many architects from Rome and Tuscany traveled the short distance to Tivoli to study the famous Hadrianic ruins. Francesco Borromini certainly made the trip, and then built his own superb version at his church of Sant'Ivo della Sapienza, Rome (1642–1650). Here, Borromini used two interlocking triangles to form a six-pointed star.

Islamic Domes

The convoluted dome was often used in the Islamic building tradition. At the Mezquita (the Great Mosque) of Córdoba, Spain (c. 786), the Lantern of Al-Hakam II (part of tenth-century extensions) has eight lobes alternating with small folded arrises. It resembles an inverted golden vessel, and rests on an octagon supported by interlocking arches. In Central Asia another tradition flourished, based on brick building techniques. At buildings such as the Gur-e Amir (Tomb of Timur) in Samarkand, Uzbekistan (1404), and the Abu Nasr Parsa Mosque at Balkh, Afghanistan (c. 1460), the typical melon-shaped dome has an outer surface of turquoise blue glazed bricks, making the effect all the more startling.

This was instead of Hadrian's four- to eight-sided figure. The dramatically convoluted dome rises from the entablature, and the alternating concave and convex sections meet at an oculus covered by a lantern, which, astonishingly, is in the form of a spiral. The tinted plaster decoration designed by Borromini for inside the dome accentuates the ribs and the diminution toward the top. In San Carlo alle Quattro Fontane (1634–1682), yet another church that Borromini built in Rome, he used the unique Composite order of the Piazza d'Oro, with its inverted volutes, but he exploited another Roman doming technique: the coffered dome. Coffering lightened the weight of a vault or dome by removing material (in a highly patterned, geometric fashion) from where it was not needed. Originally developed for flat ceiling slabs in solid stone, coffering made even more sense in a vault or dome.

Medieval Dome Bays

During the medieval period, builders relied on the "additive" design principal. Buildings tended to have a modular bay system, and if one needed more space, one simply added more bays. These were often vaulted, but could be domed. Two outstanding examples are the Basilica di San Marco (St. Mark's Cathedral) in Venice, Italy (c. 1063–1073), and the Cathedral of Saint-Front

in Périgueux, France (1120–). Superficially, there is a resemblance, as both these churches are essentially Greek crosses with five hemispherical domes—one over each arm of the cross and one over the center. To overcome the thrust problems, each dome has its own four massive pier supports cleverly worked into the plan. The domes of San Marco, following Hagia Sophia, have many more windows than the French version. There are other examples of domed bays in the same region of central-west France from the same Romanesque period. The darkness of these churches, together with the obvious conservativism of their builders, may have been what doomed this construction type to obscurity, especially given the imminent success of the early Gothic architects.

Exterior Versus Interior

In the late medieval period, the dome's exterior profile became more important, thanks to the breakthrough realization that the interior and exterior surfaces could be somewhat independent

The twelfth century Cathedral of Saint-Front (below) in Périgueux, central-west France, used the archetypal Byzantine style of domed bays in a uniquely local way. Outside, the five cupolas and colonnaded turrets are rendered in carefully cut stone. Inside, the domes on pendentives create a severe geometric space.

of each other. There were many different ways to structure such a dome, and European builders exhibited great ingenuity, especially when they attempted to span extra-large diameters. Perhaps the most notable is Filippo Brunelleschi's dome (1420–1434) for the cathedral in Florence, Italy (1296–). Since the late thirteenth century, the ambitious Florentines had been determined that their cathedral would have the largest dome in Tuscany. The project took several generations, and several architects, to complete, and it was Brunelleschi who solved the problem of how to build a dome above the vast octagonal crossing of the nave and its huge drum—a span of almost 150 feet (45 m) in diameter. The dome that Brunelleschi designed was an eight-sided cloister dome. But he realized that without some internal tension members, the dome would burst the drum. His solution was to build a double shell of radial and concentric ribs, locked into the drum by means of octagonal tension rings made from interlocking cut stones. The exact size of these stones was critical, and he may have learned some fastening techniques from his careful observations of Roman ruins. He expedited the unprecedented construction job by designing special bricks that interlocked and therefore reduced the amount of centering needed, and by designing a special reversible cam gear for the main ox-driven hoist.

The Chuch of the Transfiguration (above) stands on Kizhi Island, in the densely forested regions of far northern Russia. With axes and chisels, and no nails, the builders created a church 100 ft (30 m) tall, with 22 onion domes, made entirely of wood.

After the Great Fire of London in 1666, Christopher Wren was put in charge of rebuilding 51 churches, including St. Paul's Cathedral. Three designs were rejected before the domed octagonal crossing design, the dome having three shells and a lantern (above).

This eliminated the time-wasting step of having to reverse the animal's position in the harness. The result of Brunelleschi's gifts was a building that still stands today, one that the Renaissance critic Giorgio Vasari called "heaven ordained."

In Russia, experiments with double domes resulted in the complex curves of the onion dome. The origins of this dome are disputed, but certainly in a part of the world where snowfall is heavy, such a form, which sheds snow and ice efficiently, makes a good deal of sense. The Russian builders had an abundant supply of wood and built many all-wood domed churches. The Church of the Transfiguration (1714) at Kizhi Island, northern Russia, has an astonishing 22 domes, each one shingled in aspen. The best

known of all Russian churches, the Cathedral of St. Basil the Blessed in Moscow (1555–1561), is a masonry building. Each one of its eight onion domes is deliberately different, creating a picturesque composition using extraordinary polygonal drums with varied arching and sloping sections, all exaggerated vertically.

Conical Cored Domes

Italian masons showed great inventiveness and skill in dome building. The builder of the Pisa Baptistery (1153–1265) achieved a feeling of interior height by using a 12-sided pyramid, which, through plastering, appears conical. The full weight of the dome is carried down through a drum and arches to a mere 12 columns. This unlikely construction stands because it is braced by a lower, outer annular vault, which is itself braced by 12 diaphragm walls, and by periodic stiffeners within the vault. The very top of the pyramid is crowned with a little dome. This very ingenious structure is wrapped in a lacy system of Pisan Romanesque arcading, which plays on the ratio of 3:5 also present in the structure.

When Christopher Wren designed the dome for St. Paul's Cathedral, London (1675–1710), he used a structural brick cone which had no precedent except for the Pisa Baptistery. But he concealed it from view with an inner dome of self-supporting masonry and an outer lead-clad dome supported off the cone by timber framing. This arrangement contrasts with the triple dome form pioneered by Jules Hardouin Mansart in the church of Les Invalides in Paris (c. 1677–1691), which was almost contemporary with St. Paul's.

The Pantheon
Rome, Italy

The interior (above) is a vast, geometrically exact space, less ornate than in the second century CE, but the best preserved of all ancient Roman buildings.

The most famous dome to survive from antiquity is the vast, gravity-defying dome of the Pantheon (CE 118–c. 128). This iconic ancient Roman building was rededicated as a church in the early seventh century CE and thus escaped demolition. This is extremely fortunate because the experience of entering the vast domed space, with its colonnaded niches and ceiling coffers lit from the central oculus, has no equal—even in a city such as Rome, filled with monumental architecture.

For many centuries there was much justifiable confusion about the date of the building, but in recent decades an examination of the stamps that the Romans customarily placed on their bricks shows that the Pantheon was built during the Emperor Hadrian's rule. This certainly makes sense, given Hadrian's evident fascination with

domes and his tendency to not attach his name to monuments built during his reign. The kind of brick-faced concrete used for major parts of the Pantheon was also not seen much until the latter half of the first century CE.

A Brilliant Structure

The Pantheon represents a magnificent resolution of the problem of the dome, and it might have withstood the destructive forces of nature even without the care that came with its continuous use. There are four major components of the building: a pedimented portico with a total of 16 monolithic granite columns; an enormous Roman concrete drum spanning 142 ft (43.2 m), to remain the largest dome in the world until the dome of the cathedral in Florence was built from 1420–1434; a transitional block with an attic

between the portico and drum; and finally, the coffered concrete dome. The masonry used in the transitional block is not bonded into the masonry of the drum and so they function independently in terms of structure. Together, the drum and dome are often referred to as the "rotunda."

The secret of the structure lies in the drum. Its walls are, in effective dimension, 20 ft (6 m) thick. However, if this were all filled solid with material for the more than 72½ ft (22 m) of the drum's height, the drum would fail, crushed under its own weight—that is assuming that the concrete ever dried. Even as it is, the foundations of the Pantheon are 15 ft (4.5 m) deep! Instead of being filled, the drum walls are honeycombed with numerous voids at several levels. The eight major niches at ground level (one forms the entry from the portico) are the only visible result of

Rows of coffers converge on the oculus (right), 30 ft (9 m) wide, a compression ring for the dome and the main source of light for the interior. Pantheon means "temple of all the gods." In 609 it was converted into a Christian church and has been used as a tomb since the Renaissance. Masses are still celebrated here.

this lightening of the structure. Another eight voids are accessible only from the exterior in most cases. In addition, the entire drum wall is a system of piled-up relieving arches, both concentric and radial relative to the center. All these features are geometrically exact and exactly placed. The interior surface of the drum was covered with multicolored marble revetments of great refinement and balanced design. Some of these original finishes survive and were avidly studied by later architects such as Bernini and Raphael (whose tomb, with its moving epitaph, can be found inside the Pantheon).

The concrete dome was neither covered with marble panels nor faced with brick. This would only have added unnecessary weight. Instead, the dome uses some very clever tricks to reduce mass, especially where it was least needed, toward the crown. Coffers, which are recessed panels, cover the dome surface. The springing of the dome and the top of the drum's cylinder overlap for the first few courses of coffers, thus redirecting the thrust to the drum with its bracing radial piers. The coffers themselves have two structural functions: to lighten the dome and to define ribs that can direct the dome's forces to the solid parts of the drum. The crown was made even lighter by using pumice (a volcanic stone so porous that it floats in water) as the concrete aggregate rather than a denser stone. The oculus itself acts as a compression ring.

In the hands of a lesser architect (sadly, we do not know who designed the Pantheon), the coffered dome might have appeared clunky. But this is not the case. Each coffer has four tiers of insets, the exposed faces of which are simple bands without any further molding or profile. There are 140 coffers in five rows. There is no offsetting, so all the resultant ribs are strictly horizontal or vertical. However, because the coffers adhere to a spherical form and the vertical ribs converge at the dome's zenith, each coffer is trapezoidal in shape. The vertical banding of each coffer is subtly tapered so that their lines also converge at the zenith, while the horizontal bands remain parallel to the horizon. Only five different formworks would have been needed— the absolute minimum number, and yet the geometries are in perfect balance.

Temple or Audience Hall?

The Pantheon's exact function is not known. It was probably not a typical Roman temple dedicated to a deity or a group of deities. The deep portico with its massive granite columns defines spaces on either side of the entry to the rotunda. The large, deep niches set within the transitional block accentuate the spaces. The niches may have held cult statues that some believe were of the Emperor Augustus and General Agrippa, his friend. The first version of the building, which burned down in CE 80, was built by Agrippa to honor Augustus. Others believe Mars and Venus (two deities with strong ties to the Julio-Claudian dynasty) were associated with the porch. At any rate, the building had a clear association with the imperial cult, and living emperors may have held court under its spectacular dome.

From the air, the exterior of the Pantheon's dome is a shallow, stepped profile, typical of the domes made using Roman concrete and building techniques. The dome was originally covered in bronze tiles. The brick walls would have been faced in marble and in stucco. Today, the exterior is comparatively dull.

Pendentives

Domes, with their spherical sections and two-way curvature, have great structural rigidity. But what if the function of the building below demands a plan form other than the circle? How do you make the transition from a round dome to a square plan, especially if the square is so big that the circle of the dome can be inscribed within? Or from an oval dome to a rectangular plan? Four similar elements would be needed to fill the gap at the square's corners. Furthermore, those elements might need to take advantage of the principles of both vaulting and arching to direct some of the forces of the dome down to support points below. One of the most elegant solutions is the pendentive.

Roman Invention

The pendentive appears in a number of quite minor buildings in the region around Rome from the second century CE, as well as in the baths at Gerasa (modern Jerash in Jordan). But it is not until the Early Byzantine period that the pendentive is adopted on a monumental scale. At the church of San Vitale at Ravenna, Italy (CE 538–548), a shallow dome is supported on an octagonal drum, which in turn is held up by eight arches. The spaces between the different geometries are filled with vertical masonry in the lower section between the arches and octagonal drum, and little vaulted sections between the drum and the dome.

At Hagia Sophia in Istanbul, Turkey, built just before San Vitale in 532–537, the pendentive proper appears—a curving triangular surface that forms a transition between the circular dome and the square base below. The dome is supported by a ring-shaped cornice of lesser diameter, which is supported in turn on four huge arches of equal size (which define the square). The curved surface of the pendentives makes the transition between the arches and the cornice. Conceptually, the pendentives all belong to one hemisphere, which is cut vertically by the arches and then horizontally by the cornice (like lopping off the top of a soft-boiled egg). The solution became a standard Byzantine feature.

At St. Sophia Cathedral in Kiev in modern-day Ukraine (1037–1061), the four arch and pendentive solution is used with an additional verticality, which is a typical feature of Russian churches. At St. Mark's Cathedral in Venice, Italy (c. 1063–1073), you can see the classical four arch solution, whereas the monastery church of Hosios Loukas in Greece (early eleventh century) has an eight-sided set of pendentives. As with Hagia Sophia, the lower part of the dome was punctured with multiple windows, so that light flooded down from a semiconcealed source.

In the remote valleys of Armenia, a distinctive regional variation of the dome on pendentives developed from the seventh century. The drum of the dome tended to emphasize verticality, as in Russia (although these traditions were unrelated.)

This vividly colored tiled *muqarnas* (below) is from the Masjid-i Shah, or Imam Mosque, just one of the magnificent buildings of the Safavid dynasty that surrounds the main square of Isfahan in Iran.

Precision Cut in the Charente

The dome bays of the Romanesque churches of central-west France rested on pendentives of proportions that were archetypally Byzantine. The Charente masonry style used finely jointed ashlar blocks throughout—including for the pendentives and dome. Every block was carefully cut to exact dimensions, with a large number of special pieces. This was quite unlike most other masonry styles in France at that time, which tended to use small, rough-cut stones as if they were a kind of brick. So even though the dome on pendentives was something of a dead-end in French medieval architecture, the emerging Gothic builders might have learned a great deal, technically at least, from the architecture of the Charente.

The pendentives took the form of a folded plate, and could only be seen inside the building, while the pendentive zone was supported by squarish haunches on the outside. Thus the exterior expression of the typical Armenian church was stronger and simpler than that of the typical Byzantine construction, with its multiplicity of buttresses necessitated by the many dome windows and lighter interior. (Indeed, one could say that the Armenian church is to the Byzantine church as

The dome of the Katholikon of Hosios Loukas, the eleventh-century walled monastery in central Greece (left), sits on eight pendentives. Light from the dome's windows reveal rich mosaics and murals of saints and of Christ as Pantokrator, Ruler of All.

the Romanesque is to the Gothic.) The trade-off for the geometric simplicity of form was smaller windows and a darker interior. The Armenian churches' strong geometry had several variants, such as a tall cylindrical or octagonal drum above the cubic crossing, often topped by a dome with a pyramidal outer surface.

The Squinch

The pendentive was not the only solution to the dome-geometry problem. Another way to negotiate the transition from the circle or octagon of the dome to the square or rectangle of the room below was to use an element called a squinch. It was common in the Greco-Sicilian

tradition, for example, at San Giovanni degli Eremiti at Palermo, Italy (1132). Sometimes, a very small half-dome, called a "trompe," was placed beneath the squinch arch.

Sicily was a melting pot for the cultures of the Mediterranean: Greek, Roman, Norman, and Arab. When the traditional squinch and trompe builders met Arab builders, a very elaborate type of vault, called a "stalactite," evolved. If there are multiple small trompes and these are "stilted" (i.e., the vertical below the impost is attenuated) and the stilted sections are corbeled out, they begin to resemble natural cave formations. In the Islamic building tradition this technique reached a level of high refinement. The vaults, known as *muqarnas*, received the same elaborate decorative treatment as the wall surfaces around them. At the Masjid-i Shah (Imam Mosque) at Isfahan, Iran (1612–1638), the decoration was glazed tile. The Alhambra in Granada, Spain (1338–1390), had *muqarnas* made of carved plaster.

Pendentives

PENDENTIVE

A pendentive is a triangle cut from a spherical surface. Pendentives make the transition from circular dome to square or rectangular base, taking the weight of the dome, concentrating it, and transmitting it to the piers below.

SQUINCH

A squinch is an element that spans a corner. It often takes the form of an arch or half dome, but can sometimes be a cone, beam, or stepped corbel. It is another way of making the transition from circular dome to square or rectangular base.

Hagia Sophia
Istanbul, Turkey

Hagia Sophia's vast interior (right) was the largest enclosed space in the world for almost 1,000 years. The arcaded upper galleries and the half dome where the main altar stood are visible. The black disks are inscribed with the names of Allah and Muhammed.

When the Byzantine Emperor Justinian came to power in Constantinople (Istanbul in modern Turkey) in the early sixth century CE, he inherited an unstable situation, both temporally and spiritually. But he was determined not only to stabilize his world but also to forge a closer partnership between the secular and the sacred. During his long reign he was quite successful in this synthesizing mission, and also took on a much more ambitious military mission: to reconquer the Western Empire of the former Rome, which had fallen to various barbarian powers. He succeeded in the reconquest but only at great cost to the Eastern Empire, and it proved unsustainable. But Justinian's efforts to shape the form of Byzantine power and belief were long-lasting, not the least in that he erected a great work of architecture, which was a direct expression of that synthesis. This was the Church of the Holy Wisdom, Hagia Sophia (532–537), which would remain the wonder of Christendom for many centuries.

Centralized Versus Basilical

Justinian's Hagia Sophia was not the first church on the site, next to the imperial palace complex. His predecessor, Theodosios II, had erected a large basilical church with nave and side aisles, roofed with timber trusses. During the troubles leading up to Justinian's reign, the church burned to its foundations. Rebuilding the church gave Justinian the perfect opportunity to effect his synthesizing goals. Apparently, he also had more practical concerns—he wanted to avoid using a wooden roof to make the church fire-resistant. There were already clear options available with masonry vaulting and domes in various combinations. Justinian also had experience as the patron of centralized churches such as the octagonal

Hagia Sophia's exterior (below) evokes its varied history. It was desecrated in 1204 by the Crusaders, and converted into a mosque when the Ottomans took Constantinople in 1453, with four minarets added. Since the 1930s it has been a museum.

church of Sts. Sergius and Bacchus (which was begun c. 527) not far from the palace complex. Given his ideas about unity, it seems likely that Justinian wanted his new Church of the Holy Wisdom to have a centralized form, or at least a very large dome to express this unity.

Justinian selected two mathematicians to design his new church. Anthemius of Tralles was a professor of geometry and an architect with engineering skills who had repaired flood defences in Mesopotamia. Isidorus of Miletus was a mathematician who had taught physics at Alexandria. The two designed a truly innovative building. They combined a huge dome with two half domes, all of equal radius, arranged along the longitudinal axis. This yielded a clear span along the axis of nearly 250 ft (76 m) from the entry to the main altar. Along the latitudinal axis, the central dome was supported by huge arches (infilled with lunette walls) with the same radius as the dome, braced by the arcaded galleries over the side aisles. The half dome at the altar end was

supported by three smaller half domes with pendentives. The central dome is thus supported on four pendentives supported on four giant arches and their massive piers. The result was a vast and spectacular space. The dome and the half domes were decorated with gilding, which would have interacted with the ethereal light sources in otherworldly ways. Even today, although much of the original decoration is gone, Hagia Sophia never fails to inspire awe.

Every care went into the design of the interior. The walls to the top of the galleries (above which are only arches, pendentives, lunettes, half domes, and the dome) were covered with colored marble revetment. Two stories of gallery columns were colored marble monoliths with white marble capitals. They were made especially for Hagia Sofia. They are an elaborately stylized rendering of the Corinthian order, with the monograms of the Emperor Justinian and his Empress Theodora interwoven among the acanthus leaves. As we know from the official court historian Procopius, Theodora came from a very lowly background (her father was a circus performer, her mother a prostitute), and she was an actress before she was Justinian's mistress, then wife. She was not readily accepted as Empress, so having her monogram set in stone in such an important building, especially a church, was a bold move by Justinian.

Four pendentives, gilded and decorated in images of Seraphim, hold up the central dome (above). The base of the dome is pierced with windows, and the resulting light and soaring height make the dome appear to be hovering in defiance of gravity.

In this way, Justinian left his mark. Yet in the elaborate procession that took place inside Hagia Sophia, only the Patriarch was allowed to occupy the area around the altar. Before the Patriarch took his place at the altar, however, there was a moment when he and the Emperor would meet under the central dome. They would exchange salutations and the Emperor would present an offering—all of this witnessed by the respective imperial and ecclesiastical retinues occupying their specified locations in the galleries and under the half domes. At the moment when the Patriarch approached the altar, it seems that the Emperor occupied a throne set under the right-hand gallery.

Failure and Adjustment

Justinian's architects were clearly innovative. However, it seems that they underestimated the thrust and gravity forces of the combination of domes. The half domes probably contribute little to solving the problem. Because of the architects' miscalculations, the dome collapsed 21 years after the church's consecration and had to be rebuilt. It collapsed twice more in the following centuries. Eventually, huge buttresses were added on the outside to resolve this.

There is some evidence that the foundations of the original basilica on the site were reused in the initial building of Justinian's Hagia Sophia. These older foundations were probably not completely suitable for the new church, and this may have contributed to some of the problems.

229

Geodesic Domes

Imagine a salesman coming up to you and telling you that, although the dome of the Pantheon and the dome of St. Peter's, Rome, each weighed 15,000 tonnes, he could provide a ready-made dome of the same diameter that weighed 1/1000th of that! It sounds ridiculous, but that is exactly what an American inventor called R. Buckminster Fuller said, and did, in 1949 when he formed a company that was called Geodesics Inc., which produced geodesic domes.

The weight of the masonry domes of the past came from the compressive materials used, the brick, the stone, or concrete. A great deal of this heavy material was not really contributing to the spanning effort, no matter how clever the design. The challenge with any dome is to put the least amount of material in the most effective place. Fuller understood this, and he used geometric principles to create the geodesic dome, with its exceptional lightness. He began his investigations by placing the ribs of the dome along the "great

circle" lines of a sphere—the lines concentric to the center of the sphere that represent the shortest distance between any two given points on the surface of the sphere. Eventually, the structure of his geodesic dome was based on adjacent polyhedrons. (A polyhedron is a three-dimensional version of a polygon. A cube, for example, is a polyhedron, specifically, a three-dimensional version of a square.) This gave the dome that Fuller created a depth of construction that made it incredibly stiff, strong, and stable. He investigated the prismatic shapes of Plato and Archimedes for suitability and determined that the truncated icosahedron (think of a soccer ball) was one of the most efficient forms. In any case, Geodesics Inc. produced this shape as well as a range of combinations of polyhedrons.

First Attempts
Fuller had experience designing aircraft and automobiles, and ready-made housing that

was so light that one person could lift each part into place with just one hand. He was a 50-year-old failed businessman the year he "discovered" the geodesic dome, almost 30 years after Walther Bauersfeld designed and built a dome that was geodesic for a planetarium in Jena, Germany (opened 1922). For lack of any other productive activity, Fuller had accepted an invitation to teach a summer design studio at Black Mountain College, the unorthodox school in the mountains near Asheville, North Carolina, that was a beacon to many twentieth-century intellects. The invitation came from Josef Albers, the famous painter and Bauhaus refugee. The College community looked somewhat skeptically at Fuller and his failed enterprises. They may have looked even more skeptically after the student project from Fuller's studio—a dome made from Venetian shade slats—collapsed.

But Fuller, perhaps accustomed to failure, was not so easily discouraged. For one thing, he had

The US Pavilion at Expo 67 in Montreal, Canada, R. Buckminster Fuller's geodesic dome (left), had 9 million visitors. When lit up inside at night, the acrylic skin became transparent.

talented students at Black Mountain, such as Kenneth Snelson, who early on in the studio built small, abstract, kinetic sculptures with discontinuous compression members. Fuller made note of this and developed the idea in later years as the "tensegrity" structure. (This was to cause a rift with Snelson, who had a successful career with his signature sculptures.) At any rate, Albers must have believed in Fuller, because he not only invited him back for a second summer (1949) but also asked him to direct the entire summer program. Fuller went back to North Carolina better prepared—this time he brought the metal and plastic parts he would need to build a new geodesic dome with a diameter of 47½ ft (14.5 m). This second attempt was not without problems, but it had structural integrity and it was the right idea at the right time, finally, for Fuller.

Expo 67 and Beyond

By 1951, Fuller had founded his company and applied for a patent (awarded in 1954), and he was teaching at the prestigious Massachusetts Institute of Technology. The project that was Fuller's breakthrough was the Ford Rotunda in Dearborn, Michigan (1953). The dome spanned 92 ft (28 m), with a weight of 4.25 tons. It was a series of tetrahedrons, each made of 16 prefabricated aluminum tetrahedrons. The following year Fuller found a new collaborator in a former student, Japanese-American Shoji Sadao. Fuller

La Géode (below), built in Paris in 1985, is a perfect sphere of polished stainless steel triangles. The movie theater inside its geodesic supporting structure has a huge hemispheric screen with images ten times bigger than those of a traditional movie screen.

and Sadao formed a second dome company, Synergetics Inc., in 1954. The culmination of their work together was without doubt the US Pavilion for Expo 67 at Montreal, Canada. It was, of course, a geodesic dome, acrylic-glazed, with a diameter of 250 ft (76 m). The dome geometry was a so-called "star" tensegrity truss made of steel; the glazing was hexagonal. It was a huge success and was retained as a permanent structure after the fair ended. Unfortunately, the acrylic-glazed surface was destroyed in a fire in 1976, but the steel structure still stands and houses the Montreal Biosphère.

Many of Fuller's domes were used for Arctic and Antarctic expeditions, for they were very effective in withstanding extreme weather. Others were used for military buildings, planetariums,

The Eden Project's geodesic domes (below) in Cornwall, England made of tubular steel frames and thermoplastic hexagons, house a humid tropics and a warm temperate biome, full of plant species.

exhibition spaces, and aviation hangars. A few were quite large, and so were significant in terms of structural research. Materials such as fiberglass and magnesium were developed for the frames. Other versions were small and made of humble materials, such as cardboard.

The geodesic dome never became a part of the mainstream—its aesthetic was too rigid and its spherical volume is not easily used. Its glory days were the 1950s and 1960s, but it has not disappeared. Rather, it has retained an association with futuristic, entertainment, and high-tech projects. Hence its use in the Amundsen–Scott South Pole Station Dome (1975); La Géode cinema-sphere at the Parc de la Villette, Paris (1985); the Eden Project at Cornwall, England (2001), a biosphere center designed by Nicholas Grimshaw with others. And in 1995, the Itsuko Hasegawa Atelier designed a geodesic sphere to enclose part of the Sumida Culture Factory at Tokyo, Japan (1995). In this way, the geodesic dome has perhaps finally entered permanent mainstream architecture.

Tensile Structures

If you take an arch, which acts in compression, turn it upside down, and then hang weights on it, it will act in tension to resist gravity. If the arch is made of conventional masonry units, it will probably fail. But if it is made of a material that acts well in tension, such as modern rein-forced concrete, it will do better, although this would not be the best use of the material. But what about taking a steel cable and then hanging weights on it? As suspension bridges demonstrate, a material that is superlative in tension, such as steel cable, can carry a massive amount of weight. If the weight is applied uniformly to the cable, the cable tends to form an ideal tensile shape. This is called a "catenary." Catenaries only have tensile strength; they only act in tension. In com-pression, they simply give way. They also have no resistance to lateral forces unless a bracing cross-catenary is applied (think of a tent). The great Catalan architect Antoni Gaudí recognized the connection between the two forms, the tensile and the compressive, and derived the shape of the parabolic nave of the Church of La Sagrada Familia (the Sacred Family) in Barcelona, Spain (1882–), by inverting the shape of model caten-aries that he created in the studio.

From Premodern to Modern

The principles of tensile architecture are as fol-lows: pneumatic form, elements in tension, and compressive support. We tend to think of tensile structures as either prehistoric and vernacular or ultra-modern and sophisticated. But in fact there are several examples from premodern times. The Romans created vast sunshades out of fabric and ropes, called *vela,* for use in amphitheaters such as the Colosseum. Still visible at the Colosseum in Rome are the multiple stone armatures for the masts from which the *vela* were stretched. And when the English King Henry VIII wanted a large, temporary, roofed banqueting hall erected in Calais, France, his Office of Revel produced a circular structure, 123 ft (37 m) in diameter, with a central wooden mast 130 ft (40 m) high. The mast supported a canvas roof, which was stretched over three-story-high perimeter walls made of timber. The structure was destroyed, like a ship, in a violent summer storm.

The sudden and rapid development of tensile structures occurred after World War II. This was the heyday of the pneumatic tensile structure, which stands up because, like a balloon, the air pressure inside it is greater than the air pressure outside. In addition, new, very airtight synthetic materials became available after the war, as did

the mechanical systems needed to keep the air pressurized inside an entire building. The US Pavilion at Expo 70 in Osaka, Japan, had an influential air-supported roof in a form called a "super ellipse," which is an efficient combination of both elliptical and rectangular forms. But the popularity of pneumatic structures was to decline because of some well-publicized failures. As a result, they came to be used only for particular activities—usually recreational.

Tension's Partner: Compression

In the classic tensile structure there must be at least one compression member, usually in the form of a mast. The most basic form is called the "anticlastic geodesic surface," more simply known as the four point saddle. It is generated from a square of fabric or netting. Two diagonal corners are held up with compression masts; the other two diagonal corners are stretched downward and pinned to a counterweight. The resultant shape is a saddle. Geometrically, the form is a series of intersecting parabolas whose nodal points can be connected by straight lines. A series of saddle structures can be combined in an almost infinite number of ways to create a large building, such as the Jeppesen Terminal at Denver International Airport, Colorado (1994).

Engineers and architects have experimented with tensile structures because they want to

Tensegrity elements of bright blue steel rise from the glass roof of the Waterloo International Terminal in London. The overlapping sheets of glass can flex and expand to accommodate the 440 yd (400 m) curve.

The Millennium Dome (1999) (above), now a sports and entertainment complex called the O2, is one of London's most visible landmarks. The masts reach 330 ft (100 m) high; the canopy is of durable plastic.

exploit the lightness and slenderness of this type of architecture. They also want to create maximum effect for minimal material investment. Their concern for slenderness extended to the compression members, or masts, as well as the tension members. The development of the tall television antenna showed that the main compression members could be very slender if braced by tensioned intermediate struts and guy-wires. The glass curtain wall of the Jeppesen Terminal is stiffened by such a tension system.

The ultimate continuous tension structure was pioneered by R. Buckminster Fuller. It is called the tensegrity structure. Esssentially, it is a tetrahedron with rigid joints. There are six struts in all: the structure has no integrity until the last strut is added, and the members generate only "islands" of compression, whereas the tension is continuous. Tensegrity elements have been used in projects such as Nicholas Grimshaw's Waterloo International Terminal at London (1993), the Georgia Dome at Atlanta, USA (1994), and the protective roof over part of the archaeological site at Ephesus, Turkey (2001).

Tents, Ships, Spiders

The technology of tensile structures has been exploited by humans for millennia in the form of tent structures made from stretched skins and in sailing ships. The sailing ship uses all the principles of tensile architecture: pneumatic form in the sails, tensile elements in the rigging, and compressive support in the masts. Nature also provides an ideal model for tensile structure in the spider's web. Pound for pound, a spider's silk is one of the strongest materials ever made—it is the subject of current materials research. By instinct, a spider knows exactly how to hang and reinforce its web, and engineers have observed it with awe and appreciation.

Ten miles (16 km) of steel cable and 34 masts hold up the Jeppesen Terminal roof at Denver, Colorado.

Olympic Stadium
Munich, Germany

The most iconic tensile structure from the second half of the twentieth century is without doubt the Olympic Stadium at Munich, Germany (1972). The lead designers, Behnisch & Partner and Frei Otto, were both important figures in architecture and engineering. They were based in Stuttgart, but already widely known. Behnisch & Partner won the competition for the new stadium design for the 1972 Munich Olympics. Their competition entry proposed the type of cable-net tensile structure that Otto—an engineer and expert in tension-based structures—had designed with Rolf Gutbrod for the German Pavilion at the Montreal Expo 67. It was a foregone conclusion that Otto would play a major role in the design of the stadium. For no one else had done as much research as he had on so many aspects of tensile structures, in part through his

Institute for Light Surface Structures (IL) based at Stuttgart and founded in 1964. He had also proven the research results through many built projects beginning in the mid-1950s.

The plan for the Munich Summer Olympics included two tensile-structure stadiums next to each other for the main venue. The larger of the two, the main stadium, attracts most attention—the smaller stadium uses the same materials and similar forms but in a different configuration. The basic form of the main stadium's roof is a

The two stadiums spread out across Munich Olympic Park. The main stadium is in the background. Since the 1972 Summer Olympics, it has been used as the home ground of two German soccer teams. It has also hosted major sporting events, even cross-country skiing and snowboarding, plus open-air concerts.

series of extensive surfaces hung from canted and guyed masts of tubular steel. The interior edge of the roof is a catenary form, with a length along the entire curve of 1,445 ft (440 m). Nine secondary suspension cables loop from the main masts to the main catenary. Tertiary "flying" masts (which do not touch the ground but are instead supported on suspension cables) hang from the secondary suspension cables and in turn support a cable-net surface. The flying masts define high points in the surfaces, and result in an undulating vaulted volume that has no vertical supports to interfere with sight lines or air circulation. The maximum roof height is 190 ft (58 m) and the overall roof area is 40,660 sq yd (34,000 sq m). The main catenary and mast guy-lines required massive abutments to counter the forces that are placed upon them.

Frei Otto used rigid acrylic panels (above), held by clamps to the cable net, for a transparent roof. You can now do a roof climb, a guided tour with rope and carabiners, high up on the roof of the stadium.

Steel cable guy-lines are connected to massive tubular steel abutments (above), which help to hold the structure taut by countering its enormous tensile and compressive forces. They are like the tent pegs of a giant tent—the pegs hold the guy-lines taut, which keep the tent poles standing upright.

points from multiple camera positions, and Otto and the IL pioneered its use in sophisticated engineering problems.

Since the mid 1960s Otto had also been experimenting with cable fittings, including developing a "self-climbing" grip to be used in retractable roof membranes. The roof at the Munich Stadium is not retractable; nevertheless, Otto's thorough understanding of the issues of the cable connections helped ensure its success.

Impact of the Stadium

In some ways the work of Frei Otto at Munich was ahead of its time. The more subtle aspects of tensile structures—such as strut-braced walls, post-tensioned lattice domes, tensegrity, asymmetrical solutions, and other hybrids—have emerged in the last two decades in an exciting explosion of long-span and other daring structures. The Munich stadiums are the lodestone for both these investigations, even if they are not directly imitated. In addition, it must be remembered that, through his teaching at the IL, his publications, and his exhibitions, Frei Otto has had an enormous impact. Many of the leading designers of cutting-edge structures today have had some contact with the IL.

An area of current research that is unthinkable without the Munich stadiums is self-regulating tensile structures. The active elements in such a structure can respond to applied loads on tension members and thus prevent overall deflection of a structure. Traditionally, tension members (of trusses, for example) have intermediate turn-buckles that can be manipulated to stiffen or to soften the member and thus the overall behavior of the truss. Self-regulating structures have active elements made of elastic materials with "shape memory," such as carbon fiber components, and they respond to forces by returning to an original geometry. Optic fibers can sense stress and strain in a structure and trigger control movements. This may seem trivial, but in fact it allows some very long-span structures with very slender forms.

The cable-net surface was finished with rigid acrylic panels, somewhat against the designers' wishes. Frei Otto typically used a membrane roof, but the subdued light under such a roof was not acceptable to the Games' organizers, especially as televising the events and advertising revenue were driving forces behind the Olympics. So the designers had to choose a material that brought more daylight into the space. It also covered spectators without greatly affecting their view.

Sophisticated Methodology

During the design phase, Otto and his colleagues at the IL were continuing their research into new ways of analyzing tensile structures. In addition to building conventional scale models of the overall design, they found new ways to calculate the behavior of the structure, especially under conditions such as snow-loading. This was prescient, as during the construction of the Munich stadiums, a very heavy snowfall caused the Montreal Pavilion to fail. The calculations they developed at the IL for the Munich structures were more accurate for several reasons. First, they continued working to refine "strain gauges," measuring devices that they had developed during the Montreal project for reading the actual tensile forces in wires. They also subjected a scale model to projected forces, and they used before-and-after photogrammetry documentation to show how the structure changed under those forces. Photogrammetry is a method of taking accurate three-dimensional measurements by triangulating

An example of a smaller project that probably has the Munich Olympic Stadium in its genealogy is Shoei Yoh's award-winning Glass Station (1993), a glass canopy created for a gas station in Kumamoto, Japan. The major structure consists of four prestressed asymmetrical concrete arches, which throw the glass roof into an undulating form. The glass panels are completely supported on pairs of prestressed tension wires. The result is an exciting form that covers the maximum area with minimal material—something that always informed the efforts to create tensile structures. The Olympic Stadium at Munich pushed such concerns to the fore.

Across the Rooftops

If a building is, by definition, some sort of shelter, then it is defined by its roof, and the technology of the roof's construction is essential to its success. The form of a roof can vary enormously, so it also serves as a cultural indicator. However, roofs are most exposed to damage, and we therefore tend to know little about early examples.

Flat Roofs

The flat roof seems to have been universal in the early cultures of the Middle East, where the climate is dry and often hot, and where sleeping on the roof at night is still a widespread practice. When found in other parts of the world, the flat roof has been imported or has evolved later, as in parts of Mexico and New Mexico in the United States. Its appearance in Europe is very late, and is the result of the stylistic demands of Modernism and the enabling technology of the reinforced concrete slab.

All of this must be qualified by the fact that we know very little about ancient roofing. When looking at imaginative reconstructions of ancient buildings, it is easy to forget that, while we may understand the foundations in great scientific detail, we know only a limited amount about the lower walls, very little about upper stories, and usually nothing at all about the roofing. However, illustrations of buildings found in some frescoes and reliefs and models of buildings that are found in tombs and elsewhere can provide some information. Useful literary references are very scarce, however, and drawing analogies from modern vernacular practice, although very tempting, can rarely be justified.

The Earliest Evidence

Çatal Hüyük in modern Turkey is the oldest settlement about which we have substantive knowledge, dating from about 6800–5700 BCE. It is a solid mass of houses, with some courtyards but with no streets or spaces between, and it is certain that access was through the roof of each house, and that the roofs were trafficable and therefore flat. It is unclear whether this settlement pattern was normal or the result of some threat. In the twentieth century at least, one example is known of an African village of detached houses being abandoned, in the face of a threat to its security, in favor of something like the form of Çatal Hüyük. What this means is that even if the roofs at Çatal Hüyük and the similar, later settlement of Hacilar were flat, we cannot be sure that this was normal practice.

Our next solid information comes from Malta, where a tiny model carved from Globigerina limestone has been found at Ta' Hagrat near Mgarr. It represents one of the Maltese megalithic buildings and it may date from any time in the Temple Period (c. 4000–2500 BCE). The roof is shown as being made of seven large horizontal stone slabs. This would have been the natural outcome of megalithic stone construction technology, not necessarily because of any functional requirement to make use of the roof space.

Palm Trunks and Plaster

It is in Egypt that we get our first information on what became the standard flat roof construction.

Timber other than palm trunks was very scarce in Egypt; large beams had to be imported by sea from Lebanon and elsewhere. The flat roofs were made with a continuous layer of parallel palm trunks that were plastered over the top, as seen in the stone representations of this construction technique found at Saqqara, described later in this chapter. The situation in Mesopotamia must have been similar. Certainly, the many reliefs of this region that show buildings never feature a roof projecting up above the parapet or stepped battlements (except for a few examples of what may be corbeled mud-brick domes). Around the Mediterranean, a Middle Helladic house at Eutresis, Greece (*c.* 2000–1600 BCE) has been reconstructed (on the basis of what evidence is not clear) with large tree logs serving as beams, across which is laid a complete layer of small logs 2½–3 in (6–8 cm) in diameter, then a 3-in (8-cm) layer of clay, a layer of reeds, and finally another 2¾ in (7 cm) of clay. At the Palace of Knossos, Crete (seventeenth century BCE), the roof edges (reconstructed) show a series of discs that symbolically reflect a similar layer of logs.

Flat roof construction continues around the Mediterranean today, and indeed the deforestation of Turkey has to some extent forced builders back to the ancient method of using lighter logs or saplings. In the New World a Mexican mission church of the seventeenth century has been interpreted as having rather similar roofing, and an ancient Puebloan house in Chaco Canyon, in New Mexico, has roof construction that is fairly similar to that at Eutresis. There is no suggestion

Malta is renowned for its megalithic stone temples. During excavation of the Ta' Hagrat Temple (3600–3200 BCE) near the village of Mgarr, a tiny limestone model of a megalithic building, possibly a temple, was found (above). As well as the entrance and walls, it shows the roof as made of seven horizontal slabs.

The Palace of Knossos was built by the Minoans on Crete—the legendary Minotaur roamed the labyrinth below. The reconstruction of the Palace's North Entrance (below) by British archaeologist Sir Arthur Evans shows a row of white circles, representing log ends laid side by side to form a flat roof.

of any influence here: it is rather that similar climatic conditions and material constraints have inexorably produced similar results.

Large, square-columned halls were developed by the Hittites by the thirteenth century BCE, and continued in the Urartu and other cultures in Anatolia, where timber was plentiful (and palm trees were not). It appears that these were roofed on a structure of large timber beams, though we can only speculate as to how the roof surface was finished and sealed. These halls had their descendants in the Achaemenid capital of Persepolis in Persia (begun 518 BCE), which is remarkable because there was very little timber near Persepolis and the beams would have been imported from huge distances. We do know that the beams were very large because the column capitals designed to fit them survive.

European Developments

In medieval Europe, trafficable flat roofs were required on castles and fortifications, and if they were built only of stonemasonry, they probably leaked extensively. Some French châteaux and many English Elizabethan houses had flat roofs, topped with belvederes or pavilions in which one might feast or enjoy the evening air. They used sheet lead to seal the roof, seamed together at the edges to create a continuous membrane. To "walk the leads" meant to take a stroll on the roof.

A nineteenth-century solution was invented by Lord Stanhope—a fireproof "composition for flat roofs," which was first used in about 1797 for stables at Broomfield Lodge, in Surrey, England.

It consisted of a layer of tar mixed with chalk, which remained flexible, then a layer of tar and sand, which hardened and cracked but provided a firm base for slate flagstones, which were placed while the tar–sand layer was still boiling hot. It was then smoothed out with large flat irons. The architect John Nash used this system in a number of buildings from 1807 onward, including the roof of Buckingham Palace. It failed and he was subsequently dismissed.

The English writer J. C. Loudon discussed the use of "tiles covered with Roman cement in three coats and courses" that could be laid perfectly flat and form "one of the most efficient and durable of roofs," as well as "terrace roofs" carried on tile arches that spanned between cast-iron joists. The architect Charles Fowler similarly used courses of tiles embedded in pure cement and carried on iron beams, both at the Hungerford Markets in London and at his own house (a system probably not invented by Fowler, as commonly supposed, but by a man called Smart).

Fire and Water

At Cape Town in South Africa, the flat roof began to be preferred in the Dutch East India Company's buildings because it was less susceptible to fire, and by 1732 private settlers were using it as well. It was used extensively by British settlers in the Western Cape and at Port Elizabeth in the early nineteenth century. In 1835 Jeremiah Goldswain's house near Bathurst had a "flat rufe maid with Stone and Lime and ... wood" on the kitchen and associated rooms, and it was there

that the family retreated when they feared the local Xhosa people would torch the house.

The South African roofs were built with heavy beams, then layered with 1–1½ in (25–35 mm) of "yellowwood" or deal boarding, a crushed brick aggregate, and three coats of shell lime and seashells (which strongly suggests chunam). When the roof leaked, it was repaired with tar or paint. If it was to be walked on, it was paved with red "Italian" tiles or with the local Robben Island slate. At Port Elizabeth in about 1815, such roofs were made of brick, lime mortar, and large flat tiles or Robben Island slate. The last recorded use of lime-based roofing for government work was on the prison at Rondebosch in 1832, for by then it had been established quite conclusively that tarred canvas was cheaper and more readily repaired. Timber roofs finished in tarred felt or in tarred or painted canvas were now becoming more common.

By the 1820s, flat roofs were being denigrated in South Africa as less thermally effective than conventional thatched roofs, liable to leakage, and lacking the storage space of a pitched roof. However, they retained the advantage of being fireproof, and in 1834, during the Cape Frontier Wars, the inhabitants of Grahamstown were glad to be able to take shelter in the surviving flat-roofed buildings.

Flat roofs were very well known in California by the mid-nineteenth century, and much as in South Africa, they were made of wooden boards covered in pitch or tar. Buildings were thus very susceptible to fire, and in one case it was reported that water barrels were kept standing around the perimeter against this eventuality. Other roofs were covered in a layer of sand and then of metal screenings, which made them both trafficable and less combustible. The roof of the Cooper Union Building in New York, built from 1853–1859,

Longleat House (below) in Wiltshire, England (1567–1580), is an Elizabethan country house designed by Robert Smythson. It has a symmetrical exterior, and the flat lead roof around the perimeter encloses roof pavilions and two inner courtyards.

to the design of the architect F. A. Peterson, was described as being of "tin, painted then slate bedded in asphaltum and gravel upon that." It was probably an example of the roof based on felt (presumably bitumenized or tarred) with gravel on top that was developed in 1854 either by W. H. H. Childs or by his corporate predecessor. Such materials were widely accepted in both Britain and the United States, especially for small areas of flat roofing such as porches, bay windows, and belvederes.

The Concrete Slab

The development of reinforced concrete between 1890 and 1910 made it increasingly practicable to roof a building in a flat slab, and this appealed greatly to the abstract aesthetic of the Modern movement. In Britain especially, pitched roofs of traditional construction were concealed behind parapets so as not to mar the cubist elegance of the new style. Where the roofs really were flat, they had to maintain a seal that would survive both movement in the concrete and the weather. Commonly, the seal was some combination of tarred felt and molten tar or a similar material, and the surface was gravel, as in Childs's roof, or concrete tiles laid in tar, as in Stanhope's system.

A Mughal Variation

In India the flat roof made of chunam plaster (a soil, cement, and crushed-shell or shell-lime mixture) had been used in Mughal architecture. European colonists and entrepreneurs had adopted it in the buildings for their trading posts by the seventeenth century. In the nineteenth century it became common in the houses of East India Company officials, when the classic bungalow evolved as a separate type. In Indian flat roofing, as described early in the nineteenth century, teak joists supported arched brick vaulting which was then leveled up with mortar, and finally finished in fine mortar, chunam, or stone cement, polished while it was drying.

The concrete slab has been the roof of choice for architects throughout the world designing modern housing complexes, such as this one in Mexico City. The flat concrete roof has also been put to effective use by architects such as Le Corbusier.

Saqqara
Egypt

Viewed in retrospect, Egyptian architecture seems extraordinarily static over 3,000 years. A detailed examination modifies this picture, but it is true that most innovation took place in the earlier phases of this civilization, and is concentrated in one place, Saqqara, and one brief time period, around 2750–2600 BCE. This vast burial ground of the ancient Egyptians contains representations in stone of architectural forms previously built in perishable materials, including our first and only detailed information on ancient flat roof construction.

The Egyptians had no strong, durable timber, so they imported large beams from overseas for their most important architecture. For lesser buildings they used close-set rows of palm logs, with earth or other materials on top to create a flat surface. We know this because there are stone versions of the palm log roof at Saqqara, in the Entrance Hall and in the House of the South. We also have some confirmation of it because in Crete, which had some contact with Egypt, the Palace of Knossos has rows of discs along the eaves, according to reconstructions. These seem to show logs being used in much the same way, although a millennium later and probably in timbers other than palm.

This undoubtedly continued in Egypt. However, there is no later evidence to compare with that of Saqqara. This is because it was here that monumental stone architecture was first created, and the architect had only the precedent of the existing mud and timber buildings to draw upon. Later Egyptian architecture is much more rigid and conventional, and rarely refers to these ephemeral prototypes.

Stairway Tombs to Pyramids

The 4-mile (7-km) spread of Saqqara is equally important for the evolution of the pyramid form. Simple tombs of the Archaic Period, before

The stepped pyramid of Djoser stands at Saqqara (below), with the spur walls of the Entrance Hall in the foreground. The complex included chapels, temples, a causeway, and a surrounding wall.

3000 BCE, were capped above ground by a sort of slab of mud or rubble, probably intended to both monumentalize and protect the burial. The tombs of the pharaohs, as discovered at nearby Abydos, were on a much larger scale, inside giant platformlike mounds of dirt and rubble and sloping sides. This form is known as a "mastaba."

At Saqqara there are mastabas measuring as much as 200 x 100 ft (60 x 30 m), and all sorts of variations in design. One mastaba had brick steps around three sides, which may have been concealed by additional construction, while the other side was a flat façade containing the tomb entrance. In the same area the remains of a large stone enclosure contain the tomb of the pharaoh Khasekhemwy. Both the enclosing wall and the use of stone are significant developments.

The tomb complex built for Khasekhemwy's stepson and successor, Djoser, in c. 2630 BCE, combines the four ideas: the mastaba, the stepped form, the walled enclosure, and the use of stone for building. An enclosing wall contains various buildings, including a stepped pyramid, which is

(so far as we know) the first large monument in the world to be built of stone. It began as a large mastaba, and only during building were three extensions made to the mastaba platform, then three steps built on top, then considerable extensions made all around, and the final two stages built—to make six steps in all and create the first pyramid. The skill of the architect, Imhotep, was much admired, and he was subsequently elevated to the status of a god.

While the stepped form of Djoser's pyramid seems to have evolved almost fortuitously, later designers created the shape deliberately. Over a relatively short period the stepped pyramid evolved into the classic smooth-faced pyramids of ancient Egypt, like those at Giza.

Natural Forms in Stone

The Djoser complex is entered via the Entrance Hall, which contains spur walls running in at right angles from the walls on either side. The ends are finished like columns, and they have a novel and highly distinctive characteristic, convex fluting, which is thought to be derived from the appearance of bundles of tied reeds. So we see in this experimental context something like the formal orders of architecture in the making, partly based upon natural plant forms.

The south building of the complex, according to reconstructions, was extraordinarily elegant,

With carefully cut stone blocks, Djoser's stepped pyramid was constructed, one platform on top of another. The later smooth-sided pyramids were built by leaning successive walls against a central pile.

The now largely reconstructed Entrance Hall is lined with spur walls, which end in fluted columns, thought to be suggestive of bundles of tied reeds. The columns are relatively squat.

and, just as in the case of the palm-log roof form, looks as if it were derived from a much lighter timber or other architecture. It has some engaged columns (columns that are set half into the face of the wall), but they have concave fluted faces, reminiscent of the columns of the classical Greek Doric order. The question is whether the bundle reed form of the column was simply a decorative conceit, or whether it was a reflection in stone of actual reed construction. The latter seems to be the case. Reed construction was used in Egypt from Neolithic times (7000–4500 BCE). It was also used in ancient Mesopotamia, and was still used into modern times by the Ma'dan, or Marsh Arabs, of Iraq.

In fact the Djoser complex contains further reflections of ephemeral architecture. A subterranean chamber is finished in imitation of rush matting walls, with a mat rolled up to the head of a doorway to permit access. A cylinder appears in this location in many later Egyptian doors, but without the evidence from Saqqara, it would be difficult to guess its origin.

This is what makes the complex so innovative, for it is the place where sophisticated stone construction was invented, and where, therefore, the conventions of stone architecture had to be created. This was done in part by copying forms developed in vernacular construction using mud brick, reeds, and palm logs.

Sloping Roofs

The pitched roof has two sides that slope up to meet at a horizontal ridge, usually creating a gable or pediment at either end (known as a gable roof). It is, for practical purposes, an invention, and one that can be traced with some confidence to the late eighth century BCE in Mesopotamia and Anatolia. Of course it is not an invention in the strictest sense of the word, because it is the most common and most natural roof type used in a primitive hut, but the idea that it should be used in serious monumental architecture, as opposed to the flat roof, was a radical one.

A Monumental Element

In the Middle East and Mediterranean, the flat roof enabled some cultures, such as the Arzawan in Anatolia and more notably the Minoan in Crete, to develop complex and at times informal planning. It also enabled the Hittites and their successors to create the first large interior spaces,

This terracotta model from the Greek city state of Argos dates from about 700 BCE and is dedicated to the goddess Hera. It represents a megaron house or temple with a sloping roof, which would probably have been made of thatch and clay.

the sort of interior spaces that would be required for holding community gatherings and political assemblies, and it is therefore fundamental to the evolution of Western culture. It is striking that related cultures in the same regions, such as the Mycenaeans of mainland Greece (and less clearly the Luwians of Anatolia), built exclusively in the megaron form, which is a single oblong chamber with a door at one end, entered through a rudimentary porch. The reason must be that they used the simple pitched roof (made of crude materials such as thatch and clay), which allowed only a simple rectangular outline.

The distinction is partly cultural, partly climatic, and partly resource-dependent (on the availability of timber). The use of flat roofs in Crete as opposed to megarons on the mainland is clearly demarcated. In the Greek legend of the Minotaur, Theseus saw King Minos's palace on Crete as a labyrinth. This is because he came from mainland Greece, where a palace was only an agglomeration of simple megarons. Long corridors, doglegs, rooms opening in enfilade, and staircases were all alien to him. But in Asia Minor, the traditions mingle. The Hittites and Arzawans, for example, seem to have used the flat roof. The pitched roof seems to have been more

Sloping Roof Types

GABLE ROOF
A gable roof has two sloping sides that join at the top, creating a triangle shape at either end. That is the gable, known as a pediment in classical architecture.

HIPPED ROOF
A simple hipped roof is shaped like a pyramid. It has four sloping surfaces, which intersect at right angles and join in a single point at the top of the roof.

JERKIN-HEAD ROOF
The jerkin-head roof is a pitched or gabled roof that has the upper part of the gable sliced off at an angle to create a small section of hipped roof. It is often used in farm buildings.

MANSARD ROOF
A mansard roof is a hip roof with two slopes. The lower slope is very steep, in contrast to the upper slope, which is much flatter. The roof thus has extra space for an attic or even rooms.

The square nave of the Mausoleum of Galla Placidia in Ravenna, Italy (*c.* CE 425), has a hipped roof which was imitated by important monuments in the Dark Ages. It was built for the tombs of the Empress, her husband Constantius, and her son Valentinian III.

important in the north, toward the wooded areas around the Black Sea, and farther to the east. The megaron form was found farther south in Syria.

The pitched roof as used on the megaron was, so far as we know, still a primitive hutlike construction. In approximately 700 BCE, it was transformed into an element of monumental architecture, and the pediment was born. The evidence includes a relief at the Assyrian city of Dur Sharrukin in Mesopotamia, (Khorsabad in modern Iraq) which shows an attack by King Sargon's troops, in the eighth year of his reign (*c.* 714 BCE) on an Urartu temple at Musasir in Asia Minor. The pillars and triangular pediment of the temple are clearly visible. Also, the tomb of the Phrygian King Midas at Gordium (*c.* 696 BCE), west of modern Ankara in Turkey (which may be the actual tomb of the King Midas whose touch reputedly turned everything to gold), is a sort of log cabin underneath a giant burial mound, or tumulus. Not only does it have a pitched roof of well-squared and fitted logs, it is thought that at least one building in the neighboring township had a similar roof. Finally, in the seventh century, Greek temples such as the Temple of Apollo at Thermon (*c.* 620 BCE), show evidence of having

a monumentally treated entablature and pediment, often of timber clad in decorative terracotta panels.

Complex Roofs

There was little further development for the next six centuries. It must have been a hurdle for a carpenter, accustomed to the simple framing of a pitched roof on a rectangular plan, to first construct a hip, where two slopes intersect at right angles. A greater hurdle would have been to construct a valley where two slopes meet internally. Of course, in a culture that had the skills to build ships, such things were theoretically possible. But it was not only the carpenter who was challenged. The roof tiler would have had to cut tiles on an angle to fit the junctions, provide some sort of ridging tile to cover the hip, and find a way of waterproofing the valleys.

It is not known when these steps were taken and where, but these more complex roof forms

were in use by Roman times. Indeed, the atrium of a larger Roman house typically had four roof surfaces sloping in to the rectangular opening (*compluvium*) that admitted rain to fill the pool (*impluvium*) below, and hence there were four valleys at the corners. Unlike certain aspects of Roman technology, the hip roof was never forgotten. During the Dark Ages, the hip roof of the Mausoleum of Galla Placidia at Ravenna, Italy (*c.* 425 BCE), was imitated in seventh-century Visigothic buildings such as the Baptistery of San Miguel at Tarrasa near Barcelona, Spain, and São Frutuoso de Montélios, near Braga, Portugal.

The vernacular pitched roof was converted into stone and terracotta in many other cultures. The Mayan village hut, which can still be seen in Guatemala, has a steep pitched roof with crossbeams or collar ties a little above midheight, and visible from the space below. The great Mayan stone monuments have chambers similarly roofed in an inverted V shape; some even had timber

Why All the Brackets?

The Chinese roof is the most perplexing sloping roof of all. It is supported on a system of timber brackets growing outward from the heads of the columns—which is labor-intensive, structurally inefficient, and counterintuitive. Structurally, it is more like the principle of corbeling found in stone construction, and that may have been a source of influence. What it does do, however, is to create a wonderfully complex visual effect from below and facilitate the construction of a sweeping curved profile in the tiled roof above.

The Triangular Lodge near Rushton, England (above) was built by a devout Catholic, Sir Thomas Tresham, in 1597, when that faith was persecuted. Based on an equilateral triangle, with three sides, stories, roofs, gables, it symbolized the Holy Trinity and the Mass.

crossbeams, whose function must have been symbolic only, reflecting the vernacular tradition.

Steeper Versus Flatter

By the end of the eighth century there was a new spirit in European architecture. Buildings of the Carolingian period tended to be steeper in proportion, made up of simple blocky or cylindrical shapes, with steep roofs, including pyramids and cones where appropriate to the shape below. The Abbey of Saint-Riquier in France (c. 790 and known only from illustrations) exemplified this. These characteristics remained particularly strong in the German Rhineland. The source of these tendencies toward verticality, abstract shapes, and articulated volumes may well have been the now lost timber building traditions of the Germanic tribes that swept into Europe and overran the Roman Empire. The verticality was to be taken to its extreme in French Gothic architecture, as at Beauvais Cathedral and the Sainte-Chapelle (Holy Chapel) in Paris.

In 1642 François Mansart was commissioned to build the Château de Maisons (above) on a very rich financier's country estate, just northwest of Paris, at Maisons-Laffitte. This château, with its symmetrical façade and mansard roof, is seen as his finest work.

The pitch, or the angle of slope, became very important in Europe. The Italian Renaissance palazzo normally had a fairly low-pitched hipped roof, and by the time of Andrea Palladio in the mid-sixteenth century, this was freqently hidden behind a parapet. The idea was an interesting one, later revived in Modernism—that it was desirable for the roof to appear to be flat even if it was not. But in France especially, the roof tended to be steep and highly visible, following the Gothic tradition. Moreover, French buildings were often broken up into linked blocks or pavilions, each clearly defined by its steep roof, a principle known as "pavilion planning." When this tradition was revived by François Mansart in around 1635, his name was given to the mansard roof, a steep roof, sometimes with a convex or concave profile, that contains habitable rooms which might be lit by dormer windows through the roof surface. Barns and other farm buildings commonly have steep, mansard-type roofs, or related forms such as the gambrel or jerkin-head roof.

British roofs before the seventeenth century were likewise steep, and the hipped roof hardly existed, so that when it was reintroduced it was referred to as the "Italian roof." Inigo Jones, the English architect, stated, "The pich of Roofe ar maad according to the Region high or low," and "In Ittali a low Pich is beast," but this did not stop him from using the Italian low-pitched roof on the Banqueting House, Whitehall, in central London, and elsewhere. Technical innovations in English construction practices were required in order to produce such low-pitched roofs, and the perception that the hip rafter was likely to spread and sink seems to have given rise to the invention of the dragon beam.

More complex roof forms now developed. Two roofs placed side by side (sometimes called an "M roof") create an internal valley, and the resultant problem of getting rid of the water. It becomes possible to roof almost any shape, but the risk of leakage increases markedly. Sometimes, the valley is totally surrounded by roofs and it is necessary to take a gutter through the roof space to the exterior. The observer may not always see that, however complex the roof, the angle of each slope is, if possible, the same. That simplifies matters for the carpenter, and means that every intersection of roofs is at 45 degrees in plan.

Roofing Vast Spaces

The importance of the pitched roof declined by the late nineteenth century except in domestic buildings, with one countervailing tendency. The construction of large-span markets, exhibition halls, and railroad stations resulted in some fine roofs, and some buildings that consist of little else but the roof. After the Great Exhibition of 1851 in London, it became increasingly common for such events to have a distinct machinery hall with a large span to accommodate the equipment on display. At the Paris Exposition of 1855, the Galerie des Machines designed by F.-A. Cendrier and J.-M.-V. Viel spanned 157 ft (48 m) with a series of openwork arches.

Early railroad stations tended to consist of platforms with canopies to shelter the public, leaving the train in the open air. However, it was soon necessary, at least in the major termini, to shelter passengers, platforms, and trains under a single overarching structure. The first really great example was St. Pancras Station, London (1868), by engineers W. H. Barlow and R. M. Ordish.

St. Pancras Station train shed in London (1868) is an awe-inspiring span of wrought iron and glass, a testament to Victorian Britain's railroad age. Bombed in World War II and underused from the 1980s, a fully restored St. Pancras International opened in 2007.

Its span of 243 ft (74 m) was the largest in the world for a quarter century, and it remained the largest in Britain until the late twentieth century. The form is that of a three-hinged arch—a hinge at each side of the base and one at the peak of the roof—which is efficient in engineering terms. The two components joined by the hinges are elbows, comprising a section of vertical wall and a section of sloping roof.

This shape was repeated in the Galerie des Machines at the Paris Exposition of 1889, by the architect Ferdinand Dutert and the engineers Contamin, Pierron & Charton. The entire shape was determined by the simple engineering form, and it is hard to see what the architect's role was beyond designing the patterns in the glass screen covering the end of the building. The Alameda Station at Santiago, Chile (c. 1897), takes this one step further. Designed by Gustave Eiffel and prefabricated by the Schneider Company, France, it is the same three-hinged arch form, but totally open at the ends. In other words, it is essentially one large roof.

Eaves

The Temple of Concord at Agrigento, Sicily, Italy (*c.* 430 BCE) shows subtle variations in the spacing of the columns, triglyphs, and metopes.

The eave is the part of the roof that projects out beyond the wall, and its importance depends upon the dampness of the local climate. While it can be a protection from the sun, in hot, dry climates throughout the world there is usually no eave at all. In a wet climate, however, it is often critical for keeping rainwater away from the wall surface. Water will directly erode the wall, especially if this is made of earth, such as cob, adobe, or *pisé*. If it enters the wall, it may make the interior damp and moldy, and it may cause crypto-efflorescence, which destroys the exterior surface as the water evaporates. Often more important, and less appreciated, is the damage that is done from splashback, when the water hits the ground and then splashes back against the building. This in turn may be aggravated by wind erosion.

Where the roof has adequate spouting or guttering, the problem of water damage is avoided. Another option, which is traditional in Japan, is to allow the water to fall to the ground, where a trench filled with gravel runs directly under the eave line, ready to absorb the falling water and prevent splashback. This will only work if the weather conditions are fairly still and the water is not being moved sideways by wind gusts. But even that can be largely dealt with by discharging the water from the roof at points where there are chains hanging down. The water will run down the chain almost as effectively as it would run through a downpipe.

The Classical Entablature

The eave became important in formal architecture when it evolved into the classical entablature. The entablature in a classical building is all that part between the columns and the pediment. It includes the beam (also known as the lintel), the frieze, the cornice, the fascia, and the cyma. In the Doric order especially, it contains a number of elements that have become conventional, and that seem to have evolved from existing timber prototypes. Typically, the Archaic Greek temple was a mud brick or similar building on a rubble foundation, with timber columns and a timber roof structure. Between the eighth and the sixth centuries BCE, it became common to face the timber structure in baked terracotta panels and moldings, that were often highly colored. These were, in turn, replaced with marble.

What had been the ends of timber beams, held in place with pins driven up from below, became—so the argument goes—triglyphs with guttae at the bottom. What had been infill panels between these became metopes, the site first for painted decoration and then for relief sculpture. The whole level of the triglyphs and metopes was the frieze. In the Ionic and Corinthian orders this was simply a decorative band, for those orders have no triglyphs or metopes.

The Doric frieze presents an aesthetic problem which has had far-reaching consequences. The Greeks apparently felt that the Doric order ought to conform to certain conventions. The columns should be spaced at equal distances, as should the triglyphs—one directly over the center of each column, and one at midspan. The triglyphs and the metopes should be of uniform size, and the frieze should finish with a triglyph at the corner. But these rules are geometrically incompatible. A normal-sized triglyph, located on the center line of the column, would result in a leftover piece of metope on the corner. If you moved the triglyph out to the corner, it would leave an inordinately large metope behind.

Bending the Rules

The solution was to fudge it. The triglyph was moved off the center of the column and out to the corner. In addition, or alternatively, the column was moved inward to shorten the entablature and leave the triglyph at the corner. Either way, the triglyph was no longer on the axis of the column. The Temple of Concord at Agrigento in Sicily, Italy (*c.* 430 BCE), presents what is possibly the most refined solution of any surviving Greek temple. It combines these two solutions (moving the triglyph outward and also moving the column inward) with some others. Not only is the corner column shifted in slightly, making the outermost intercolumniation (the interval between columns) smaller than average, but the second intercolumniation occurs somewhere in between, so that there are three different column spacings. Moreover, this variation was so carefully preplanned that it is reflected in the jointing of the stones of the

High snowfall is another good reason to build wide eaves, preferrably on a steeply sloping roof. Such eaves are a feature of the vernacular architecture of alpine villages in Switzerland, as seen in these houses in the municipality of Trachselwald (above).

stylobate (the flat platform that supports the columns) down to the fourth course of the concealed foundations.

Furthermore, at the Temple of Concord the corner column slopes inward slightly, which helps to bring the top inward without reducing the spacing in the stylobate. Finally, not only is the outermost metope enlarged to take up the extra space, so is the second metope, thus making the difference less conspicuous. On the other hand the third and fourth actually have to be smaller than normal, because of the closer spacing of the columns below. So there are metopes of four different sizes, and intercolumniations of three different sizes, all on the one façade.

This solution is, at best, an unsatisfactory compromise only, and the formal problem of composition was to be the death of the Doric order. The Roman writer Vitruvius tells us that Greek architects were so concerned about the problem that some of them—namely, Arcesius, Pytheos, and Hermogenes—declared the Doric unsuitable for temples. He proposed a solution of spacing the triglyphs regularly and leaving half a metope on the corner. No actual examples of this are known from Roman times, but it became common in the Renaissance.

Wide, upswept eaves with ornately decorated timber "arms" were a feature of important buildings in South Korea. This pavilion (left) is part of Gyeongbok Palace (1394), a complex of more than 100 buildings in Seoul. Some burned down during the Japanese invasion of the 1590s. They were restored from 1867.

Guttering

Historically, roof guttering has been the exception rather than the rule, the outcome either of luxurious building or acute scarcity of water. In classical buildings it was used not to collect rainwater but to gather it and throw it outward. The first examples were probably made of timber, and then of terracotta, but there are surviving marble gutters from the Tholos (*c.* 580 BCE) and from the Treasury of the Syphnians (*c.* 525 BCE), both at Delphi, in Greece. They are generally an L shape in section, positioned on the same slope as the roof, so that the water runs along the angle of the L and out through holes, some in lions' mouths. Very large sections of this sort, with richly carved lion faces, survive from the Temple of Victory at Himera, in Sicily, Italy (after 480 BCE)—each lion's tongue forms a semicircular channel for the water.

Timber and Iron

We can only surmise what earlier timber gutters were like, but the obvious form, believed to have been used in medieval Russia, is a solid half-log hollowed out to create a semicircular channel. Later, squared pieces of timber were hollowed out in the same way, so they looked from below like conventional beams. Another alternative was to fasten two timber boards together in a V shape or, in a really sophisticated building, build a complete rectangular channel of boards, preferably tongued and grooved together. This rectangular form was also used as a box gutter, concealed behind the roof eave. All timber gutters are best finished with a substance such as tar to improve watertightness and reduce decay, and those built up of boards should really be lined with metal such as lead, zinc, or copper.

Surprisingly, perhaps, most of these forms of timber gutter were used into the twentieth century. Even the solid, hollowed-out type was still used in England during the early nineteenth century. Hertfordshire architect William Wilds described one made of a solid piece of seasoned fir that was generally about 4 in (10 cm) square; the trough cut into it was sloped on a fall, so that the gutter as a whole could still be placed on the building horizontally. In the eighteenth-century houses of Tidewater in Virginia, the eaves had gutters hewn from solid logs, or formed from two boards joined in a V shape. In Cape Town, South Africa, wooden gutters either built up of boards or "cut out of beams" were a tradition. Originally, they were pitched and tarred inside to waterproof them, but after the British occupation, a lining of lead or zinc became the norm. Philip Knobloch's *Good Practice in Construction,* published in New York, illustrated wood gutters cut from solid timber, with one rectangular gutter shown in external profile and one with a cyma recta face (concave above, convex below) as late as 1925.

A timber gutter (right) is held in place under timber-shingled eaves by a simple forked branch. The building is a village water mill, built in the early nineteenth century in Slovakia. The gutter is a solid half-log hollowed out to form a semicircular canal.

In the nineteenth century cast-iron gutters were commonly used in expensive buildings, and often ornamented with lions' faces that served no function. As galvanized iron became more readily available in around 1850, it was used in a half-round section for guttering. Later, a more elegant ogee profile, which resembled a classical cornice, was preferred for galvanized gutters, while in the twentieth century cruder square and bullnose forms appeared.

Technical Difficulties

There are a number of technical issues involved in roof gutters. Firstly, it is hard to join the separate pieces together at the ends so they stay watertight, particularly if they are timber. Metal gutters can more readily be provided with a large overlap and sealed with tar. Secondly, they must slope if they are to function properly, and this can look very bad, especially if designed to be part of the classical entablature of a building. Here, a gutter hollowed out of solid timber has the advantage because the slope can be created internally and remain invisible, as described by Wilds. Thirdly, they can get squashed if a ladder is leaned against them. Fourthly, they are hard to fix in place. If only the inner edge is attached to the roof or the fascia board, the gutter may sag over time, or even break. It is therefore best to support it from below with a shaped metal bracket. Alternatively, a fixing may cross the top of the gutter, but this risks obstructing floating material, such as leaves, and causing a blockage. A standard form developed in the nineteenth century was a long screw that extended from the outer face through and across the top of the galvanized gutter and into the timber face. It passed through a thin metal roll like a pipe as it crossed the gutter. This roll also served as a spacer to prevent the gutter from being crushed.

The Philadelphia Gutter

Aparticularly American form is the Philadelphia gutter, which is placed farther up the slope of the roof, often directly over the outer wall face. A sophisticated form of this occurred at the Octagon Building in Washington DC, as reroofed in 1818. The roof was shingled, but a balustrade stood on it some way in from the eave, apparently for architectural effect, although it may also have kept debris or snow from sliding down into the gutter. The gutter was on the down-slope side of the balustrade. It was a flat tray of cast lead, tilted to follow the slope of the rafters, and the shingled surface was simply interrupted to accommodate it. A similar gutter was used at Thomas Jefferson's estate house Monticello, in Virginia.

Monticello (above) was the home of Thomas Jefferson near Charlotteville, Virginia (1770–1808). Jefferson designed it himself. The first balustrade on the roof is part of the Philadelphia gutter.

The Art Nouveau entrance to the Porte Dauphine station of the Paris Metro from 1900 (below) has a radiating glass roof and metal gutter with downpipes. The architect Hector Guimard was commissioned to design the Metro entrances.

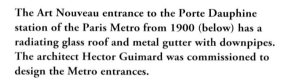

Gables

The gable is the vertical surface at the end of a pitched roof and is usually triangular in shape. The classical pediment is the most important type, and is usually defined by a fascia molding horizontally across the base and cyma moldings up the sloping sides. The recessed space within is the tympanum, and in ancient Greece it was often the site of major sculptural decoration. On the peak of the pediment and at the two side corners, decorative elements called *acroteria* might be carved, usually based on vegetable forms but occasionally statues. Interestingly, vestiges of these sometimes survive on the corners of modern galvanized-iron gutters in the form of small pieces of sheet iron folded at the angle and cut in a decorative scroll profile.

Dramatic Asian Examples

Gables of a much more flamboyant nature are found in many Asian cultures. The Toraja people of Sulawesi, in Indonesia, build house roofs that curve up at the ends, with the peaks projecting out at a sharp angle to create overhanging gables of enormous size; the wall continues as a vertical surface within. Even more dramatic buildings occur in the Sepik River region of New Guinea. The *haus tambaran*, a sacred or spirit house, has a roof like a Toraja roof except that it starts directly from the ground with no walls underneath, and is about 30 ft (9 m) wide and 66 ft (20 m) high.

The tympanum within the gable is not vertical; rather, it slants outward. Its woven basketwork and sewn sago-palm bark sheets are painted in dramatic colors and patterns.

In the houses of some Thai cultures and the Minangkabau of Sumatra, Indonesia, roofs overlap each other as they recede, so close together that only the lowest and outermost roof shows a substantial area of gable. In Japanese castles, the multiplication of roofs is vertical, making the successive gables a major component of their appearance. Japanese gables with a concave roof profile on either side are called "plover gables" *(chidori-hafu),* because the shape resembles the outstretched wings of a plover. Another Japanese type is known as the "cusped gable" *(kara-hafu);* it has a shallow arch with the curvature reversing at either side. In Malaysia the houses of Kelantan and Terengganu States often have a small area of roof that slopes outward and downward from within the gable end. In what is a very common ornamental motif, the beams forming the gable continue upward to cross each other. It is widespread from Shinto shrines in Japan to log houses

The ornate gables of guild houses from the 1690s overlook the market square in Brussels, Belgium (below). Each guild represented a particular type of artisan, and used an array of Baroque detailing and statuary to differentiate its house from its neighbors'.

in Estonia, with religious or symbolic meanings often ascribed to it. Elsewhere, the peak of the gable ridge may be decorated with a terminal ornament (similar to the *acroterion* in function). In China, this is often a dragon.

The European Tradition

In Europe, gables may appear at the base of a church tower, while small gables (gablets) may be let into the face of a sloping roof or placed below the end of the ridge in a hipped roof, where they can act as ventilators for the roof space. Steep ornamental gables are common in Holland, northern Germany, and around the Baltic, and they are frequently treated in a formal Renaissance manner. The crow-stepped gable, where the sloping edges step upward, dates from at least the fourteenth century in Bruges, and occurs later in Germany, Flanders, France, and Scotland. The term "Dutch gable" tends to be reserved for a gable with a profile formed of convex or concave quadrants or other large curves, possibly under Baroque influence. It is found in Holland; in Dutch-influenced British buildings such as the Dutch House in Kew Gardens; in Dutch colonial buildings, such as the Stadthuys in Malacca; in Boer homesteads in South Africa; and in the British red-brick revival style known as Pont Street Dutch.

The *rumah gadang* (big house) of the Minangkabau of western Sumatra, Indonesia, has multiple gables with upswept ridges (above). This is a matrilineal culture. A woman, her sisters, and their children live in the house, which passes from mother to daughter.

The Curved Pediment

The curved pediment developed later, in general, than the triangular pediment in the ancient world, although a curved gable end has been discovered at Saqqara, Egypt (c. 2800 BCE), shown earlier in this chapter. During Hellenistic and Roman times, small structures with curved roofs were used as pergolas and garden pavilions; these are now known only from fresco and mosaic decorations. The curved pediment passed into the classical vocabulary from these structures, becoming a form to be used in niches and aedicular window surrounds.

In the nineteenth century many houses in Britain and the United States were designed in a supposedly Gothic style (which, in reality, was usually more Elizabethan), with looping ornamental barge boards or verge boards running up the slopes of the gables and pointed finials at the peak. A major source for these details was a book published in 1831 by Augustus Pugin (father of the noted Gothic revivalist of the same name), *A Series of Ornamental Timber Gables, from Existing Examples in England and France of the Sixteenth Century.* Gothic house designs with these barge boards appeared in British pattern books such as S. H. Brooks's *Designs for Cottage and Villa Architecture,* and in the works of A. J. Downing and Calvert Vaux in the United States.

In Britain, a gable was sometimes clad in tiles or slates, particularly where it projected beyond the wall below, and this stopped the wall from continuing upward. The feature was revived in houses of the Arts and Crafts movement. The equivalent in US colonial architecture was the shingle-hung gable of the Shingle Style, but this was less distinctive because the complete walls were often clad in the same material as the gable. Even so, in an example like McKim, Mead, & White's W. G. Low House, in Bristol, Rhode Island (1887), the wonderful spreading gable is the dominant feature of the house.

Castle of the White Heron
Himeji, Japan

In East Asia an ascending pile of hip and gable roofs can be a major architectural theme, and this is exemplified by the Castle of the White Heron at Himeji, Japan. Japanese castles of the late sixteenth and the early seventeenth centuries were built by the daimyo, or territorial lords, who emerged from the samurai class after more than a century of civil war. Castles such as Himeji were not simply functioning fortresses. They were also instruments of propaganda designed to express authority. They achieved this with their size and height, their multiple stories and ornamental roof shapes, and most of all their stone bases, usually made of beautifully laid polygonal rubble, often with an elegantly flared profile.

A Power Base
During the long period of civil unrest, warlords built thousands of fortifications, mainly out of timber. With central power reestablished at the end of that period, a daimyo had to obtain the emperor's permission to build. The result was far fewer castles, but those that were built were of much greater substance and prestige, constructed mainly between 1575 and 1615. With the Portuguese introduction of the musket to Japan in 1543, firepower rather than swordsmanship became the key to military success, and this inevitably affected castle design.

The ruler Toyotomi Hideyoshi made Himeji, on the Harima Plain, the base for his campaign to subdue the daimyo in western Japan in 1577–1582. A fort had been built here in 1333 by Norimura Akamatsu, ruler of Harima Province, and consolidated by his son Sadanori in 1346. Hideyoshi incorporated the fort's remains into a three-story castle that he built on the site in 1581. After his death in 1598, Tokugawa Ieyasu seized the leadership, then sought to reward his followers while undermining the power of the *tozama,* or "outside" daimyo, who were still a threat to him. It was in this context that Himeji Castle was rebuilt on a grander scale by Ikeda Terumasa, on Ieyasu's orders, in about 1601.

Design and Materials
The castle's layout is complex. It has multiple gates and walls; four main wards including the

Himeji is also known as the Castle of the White Heron, or Shirasagijo, because its white-plastered gable walls with the concave roof profile resemble a white heron ready for flight. It is a classic example, and the best preserved, of a Japanese medieval castle.

inner, or *bizen,* compound; a main tower, or keep; and three smaller towers. The outer walls have rectangular, circular, and triangular embrasures from which to fire upon attackers. Access was deliberately complex and indirect, by a route passing through a whole series of gates. One of the smallest openings is the *Ru-no-mon,* through which you are forced to make a hard-left turn uphill. Ultimately, you must pass through a small roofed gate, the *Chi-no-mon,* into a courtyard surrounded by guardhouses, before making a 180-degree turn to go through the *Bizen-mon* into the main enclosure. The *bizen* had enough space to accommodate several hundred soldiers. It also had access to a well, which provided water, in the basement and a long, narrow storehouse (*koshi-kuruwa*), which held a supply of rice and salt in case of siege.

On the ends of some of the tiled roofs are finials in the form of a *shachihoko* (right). This is a mythical creature with a tiger's head and a fish's body, its raised tail symbolizing the creature throwing up the waves and causing the rain to fall.

The main tower, known as the *tenshu,* is five stories high externally, although inside there are six stories and a basement. It was built around two timber pillars nearly 3⅓ ft (1 m) in diameter (both replaced), and it is furnished at the corners with *isho-otoshi-mado* (windows from which to drop stones, the equivalent of European machicolations). At the very top is the Osakabe Shinto shrine, which was installed because it was felt that a curse had been incurred when an existing shrine had to be removed from the crest of the hill so the castle could be built.

The base of such a castle was commonly a mound of earth with a stone facing wall added. Sometimes, this wall was simply angled. Sometimes, it had the concave profile used at Himeji and known in Japan as a "fan curve." The ruler would require the daimyo to provide stones and labor in proportion to their income, but where stones were in short supply, the builders would sometimes include recycled materials: at Himeji, lantern bases, gravestones, and coffins, mainly of Buddhist origin, are all incorporated into the walls. The wall surfaces above are mostly of white

plaster laid on cane laths, and the walls of the main tower are 20 in (50 cm) thick. But the *abura-kabe* (oil wall) has a smooth, brown, glossy finish, having been made of clay and sand mixed with boiled rice water, and it has survived for more than four centuries. The nailheads in the timber gates are concealed with decorative bosses, and the *Bizen-mon* gate leading into the main enclosure is fully sheeted in iron to reinforce it and protect it from fire. Japanese roof tiling uses a shallow concave tile to cover the surface area and a roll profile tile to seal the joints between. The roll tile is covered at the eave with a disc *(maru-gawra),* and each intermediate tile *(oni-gawra)* has an apronlike pendant; these surfaces carry the crests of daimyo who built or repaired the structure. One is the "spear points around wood sorrel" crest of Sakai Tadazumi, whose family lived at Himeji from 1747.

Himeji Castle was never attacked, nor were its defenses put to the test. Of course, that might simply indicate that its strength was so evident as to deter attackers, which is itself a measure of success. But the reality is that Himeji was built as much for prestige as for military purposes.

The ascending piles of roofs that make up the one main tower and three lesser towers of the castle are either hipped or gabled. Elongated eaves and upward-curving ceramic ridge tiles and finials give the roofs their distinctive flared shape (below).

Thatching

Thatch is almost certainly the oldest roofing material in the world. Before the development of effective cutting tools, the only materials that could produce a reasonably waterproof roof were animal skins, which would have been at a premium for clothing, and grasses or reeds. Even bark requires cutting tools, and not very many types of bark are suitable for roofing. Thatch, on the other hand, can be made from a very wide range of raw materials, and some types can be executed without sophisticated tools. As a consequence, thatching is found in traditional architecture almost everywhere.

Historical evidence is hard to come by because thatch decays rapidly and leaves no trace behind. Nor does a thatched roof have a very distinctive appearance in illustrations. Three-dimensional representations can be more helpful. The Lycian Harpy Tomb at Xanthos in modern southern Turkey (late fifth century BCE) is in the shape of a small building with what certainly seems to be a thatched roof. Other similar examples are found at Aperlae and Kekova (also in Turkey). Archaeologists surmise that many or most of the early Greek megaron structures were thatched, up to and including the Heraeum on the island of Samos, dating from the seventh century BCE.

Materials Worldwide

There are quite different traditions of thatching all over the world. The Chol Indians of Mexico use palm foliage, while the nike palm is used in Indonesia and Malaysia, and pandanus and coconut palms in the Gilbert Islands. Reeds and other plants are used from Cameroon to Fiji. In New Zealand, indigenous plants such as nikau palm, raupo, and "snow grass" were used for thatched roofing; raupo was also used for walls both by the Maoris and by the later European settlers. In Australia there is some evidence of Aboriginal mia-mias (temporary shelters) being made from

Buildings in the village of Djiri in Burkina Faso, in West Africa, are made of mud bricks with straw-thatched roofs. The large circular building is a house, while the thinner circular buildings raised on mud-brick stilts are granaries, for storing the harvest of millet away from rodents and insects.

reeds, and of European settlers speaking of their own grass huts as mia-mias, a rare occasion when Aboriginal culture influenced Europeans. There are also indications that the Aboriginal people used porcupine grass in central Australia and a local tussock grass in eastern Victoria, but only after European settlement gave them access to cutting tools. The European settlers used grass tree (Xanthorrhoea) where it was available, and cane grass later.

In agricultural societies, including Japan and China, the stems of wheat, rye, and barley are used. Similarly, the picture-postcard thatched roofs of Europe tend to be a by-product of the cultivation of cereal crops, and they require sharp cutting instruments and considerable manual skill. In England, rye straw was thought the best, but wheat, barley, oats, and natural grasses were all used. Thatching with reed was common to East Anglia and north Wales, although references to "reed" in thatching can be misleading, since in the west of England this was the technical term for combed wheat straw, which is the stiff, unbroken stalks that were used for thatching.

A Basic Method

The roof is first prepared with timber battens or rafters. Bundles of reed are laid on the roof in courses (layers) of horizontal strips. Sways (steel or hazel timber rods) are fastened to the rafters with a steel spike—the spike's hook end holds the sway over the course of reed, thus holding it in tension against the rafters, while the spike's pointed end goes into the rafter. Each course is fastened on top of the preceding layer until the thatch is a minimum thickness of 12–15 in (30–38 cm). The ridge and any gables, valleys, hips, and saddles are also thatched. The ridge, eaves, and gables are trimmed and dressed (shaped to a desired pattern); the main roof surface is made even. Liggers (long hazel timbers) may be laid over the surface of the ridge, and down to the eaves, in a decorative pattern.

A cottage in Ludham in Norfolk, England, has been thatched so that the gables are covered and each ridge edge capped in an ornamental shape (above). Norfolk reed grows in the marshy fens of East Anglia and is traditionally used in this part of England. Cereal straw tends to be used elsewhere.

The thatchers would carefully separate it from the fodder straw. Europeans took their own distinctive thatching traditions to their colonies and settlements (such as Ukrainian houses and barns in Canada). In the Australasian colonies, settlers mostly used wheat or other straw.

Methods

In most parts of the world the thatching material was tied in bundles and these were then tied to the roof battens. In Britain, however, a roof was often rethatched by twisting the strands around a sharpened piece of timber, called a "broach," which was then driven into the existing thatch. In Europe, the finished roof would be trimmed smooth then measures taken to prevent it being peeled off by wind—a process that usually began at the eave or, less commonly, at the ridge. The thatch could be stitched over with thin twigs near the eave, often creating decorative patterns. Long timbers, called "liggers," could be laid horizontally near the eave and at intervals above, usually supported by broaches driven into the roof. At the ridge, short pieces of timber could be pegged or lashed together in pairs, or larger pieces, called "roof riders," might extend right down the slope on either side.

Thatch could also be combined with a layer of sod or turf. In northern England and Scotland, it was common to make a roof with a layer of sods (also called "scraws" in England) and then thatch over the top of this layer, securing each bundle of thatch by pushing the top through or between the sods. In Aberdeenshire and Banffshire, in Scotland, the thrusting tool was called a "stob," in Peeblesshire a "sting." The method was known as "stob thatch" in Scotland. In Northumberland, in England, thatchers used a different method, laying the straw across the turf and holding this in place with rods laid across it, which were held by broaches driven into the turf.

In European countries including Germany, Czechoslovakia, and Romania, there was also a tradition of less formal thatching for farm sheds. A shed might be built with timbers in the round, often using trunks that had natural forks as posts to support the main beams, and with a very shallow sloping roof. Leafy boughs were laid on the roof frame as a substrate, then the straw thatch was piled on top rather than being stitched in place. A rope net, weighted at the eaves, might be put across the entire roof to prevent the thatch blowing off. Sheds of this sort reached Canada and Australia, and by the late nineteenth century wire netting was being used instead of rope to keep thatch in place.

Roofing Tiles

Polychrome roof tiles are part of the riot of color and detail found on every surface of the Church of the Savior on Spilled Blood in St. Petersburg, Russia. It was built in 1883–1907 on the site where Czar Alexander II was assassinated—hence the name.

Terracotta roofing tiles must be almost as ancient a building material as baked brick, but because of their vulnerability and fragility, we know much less about early examples. The basic form is a flat rectangle, possibly modified in some way to help in fixing it to the roof, and these were important in northern Europe. But the majority of tiles found elsewhere in the world have a variety of shapes, and it is important to understand why.

Flat tiles (also known as shingle tiles or crown tiles), must have the side joint between each tile covered by another tile to prevent leakage, much like slates. Successive courses of tiles must also overlap each other considerably in the direction of the roof slope to stop rain from being driven up between them by the wind. Moreover, terracotta tiles tend to be slightly distorted by the firing process. This makes them fit together less tightly than slates, which are invariably flat, so that the problem of weather penetration is even greater and they may have to overlap even more. It is not uncommon to have three thickness of tile at any one place on the roof, which is very heavy, and is also expensive.

Simple Tile Designs

With traditional methods of tile manufacture, there is little that can be done to avoid the overlap in the direction of the roof slope. However, the sideways overlap can be reduced greatly by shaping the tile. A tile is formed in much the same way as a handmade brick. A shallow timber frame is placed on a flat surface and filled with clay. The upper surface is scraped off smooth and the frame removed, leaving a flat tile that simply needs to be dried, then fired (baked in a kiln). A shaped tile is made by using exactly the same method, except that it is removed from the flat surface while still soft and draped over a timber form of the required profile.

The simplest tile to be made in this way is semicircular in section. It is laid on the roof in a concave position, then the joints on either side are covered with tiles of exactly the same shape, placed the other way up. This is often known as "Spanish tiling," or "Cordoba tiling," and it is indeed used in Spain, as well as Italy and other parts of Europe, and right across Latin America. The tiles are not half cylinders. Because they must be able to overlap each other in the direction of the roof slope, they are slightly conical, so that the large end of one fits over the small end of the next.

Another tile is the "pantile," widely used in the Netherlands and elsewhere (and also known as the "Flemish tile"). This tile, in effect, combines a concave tile and a convex tile into one; it is an asymmetrical S in cross-section, so that the small arc of the S of one tile is overlapped by the large

Like village buildings throughout Europe, this small church in the Peloponnese in Greece is roofed with simple semicircular tiles that overlap in the method called "Spanish tiling." The circular roof is achieved with conical tiles and by reducing the overlap.

arc of the S of the next tile. Because these tiles tend to be used in harsher, more northerly climates and on steeper roofs, more attention must be paid to fixing them to the roof. The tilemaker commonly attaches a small knob of clay to the tile's underside. This hooks over the small timber member, or batten, that is fixed to the rafters and that supports it from below.

After the Tile Press

A revolutionary change took place when the tile press was invented. It allowed tilemakers to create tiles of any shape—within reason—that did not need to be of uniform thickness. The side joint did not simply overlap; rather, it overlocked in a watertight joint with a bead fitting into a groove.

The end joint could also lock together, further reducing the amount of overlap needed. The tile could be pressed with a central ridge that would reinforce it, and would thus allow the remainder of the tile to be lighter. Finally, a much drier clay could be used in a press. This greatly reduced the amount of time it took for the tile to cure and become dry enough to be ready for firing in the kiln—this curing phase was the riskiest time of all in a tile's manufacture. It also reduced the amount of distortion of the tile during curing and firing.

The machine-made single-lap interlocking tile was developed by the brothers Joseph and Xavier Gilardoni of Altkirch, in the Alsace region of France, during the 1840s. This was patented

in Britain in 1855. A number of designs then evolved in France. Some were to be laid on the roof in a rectangular grid, while others were to be laid in staggered rows, but all were the same in principle. They are often known as "French tiles." The particular model made in Marseille, France and widely exported is known as the "Marseilles tile" (the English spelling, Marseilles, is used). Each tile is fixed to the timber roof batten with a wire tie, a hole for which is formed on the underside as soon as the tile leaves the mold. There are other modern patterns, and indeed materials, such as concrete and plastics, but whatever form they take, they are overwhelmingly pressed tiles with a very small overlap, generally fixed to the roof framework in the same way.

Sets of Two

Classical Greek and Roman tiles come in sets of two: a flat or flattish tile (*tegula* in Latin) that does the main job of covering the roof surface, and a narrow convex tile *(imbrex)* that covers the side joint between the *tegulae*. In Greece the Corinthian tile was the commonest of this type of tile. The *tegula* was flat apart from its slightly raised edges, while the *imbrex* was like an inverted V, but in the Laconian tile the *tegula* was a shallow concave curve and the *imbrex* a smaller convex curve in section. Roman tiles were generally similar, although their design was much more varied.

Terracotta roof tiles (above) are arranged in the same way that classical Greek and Roman tiles would have been laid. Terracotta tiles would have been more expensive and labor-intensive for the Greeks and Romans to produce than thatch, but they were readily adopted because they were also more fire-resistant.

Sydney Opera House
Sydney, Australia

The Sydney Opera House is the happy outcome of a compromise: a design that was impossible to build was simplified to create the billowing form that is one of the iconic forms of the twentieth century. It is also one of the great flukes of architecture, for the choice of the design was largely a matter of chance. And it was carried through to completion despite the fact that it proved far more expensive than had been envisaged, and that it failed to provide the accommodation for which it was intended.

The History

In an international design competition for a large performing arts center for Sydney, the Danish architect Jørn Utzon's entry had been relegated to the discards pile. But it was rescued by one of the jurors, the American architect Eero Saarinen, and ultimately awarded the prize. The judges described the submitted drawings as "simple to the point of being diagrammatic," but they found themselves returning again and again to a concept that they recognized as having the potential to be one of the great buildings of the world. This

proved to be a perceptive assessment, although the jurors did not realize that they were dealing with an architect who had never supervised a large building from start to finish, nor with forms that were beyond the capacity of modern engineering to construct.

Utzon had envisaged the main roofs as a set of shells. But he had drawn freehand shapes that could not function as such, and that had central ridges across which it would not be possible to transmit forces smoothly. Ove Arup, the engineer, could not solve the problem of how to construct these shapes until Utzon proposed a radical simplification in 1961: all of the roof surfaces would be cut from a single sphere. The "shells" were—strictly speaking, and as actually built—spherically profiled concrete panels supported on precast ribs of triangular section.

Preliminary work got underway at the site at Bennelong Point, on Sydney Harbour, in May 1958. The foundations were designed before the roof form had been finalized, and when it was finalized, its weight had increased well beyond the original estimate. As a result, the foundations

had to be redesigned repeatedly. At times, parts of the structure were actually demolished because of these and other changes.

Costs were rising and delays were adding up. In addition, at one meeting, a representative of the Australian Broadcasting Commission—the intended major user of the building—stated that the Opera House would be of no use for concerts by symphony orchestras. The main hall would not hold enough seats to make concerts a paying proposition, nor would it be large enough to give the reverberation time required by the Sydney Symphony Orchestra. On February 28, 1966, Utzon resigned from the project under pressure from the New South Wales Minister for Public Works, Davis Hughes. There were national and international protests.

Peter Hall, a member of the building's executive committee, effectively took over Utzon's role. And Utzon's proposal of a combined concert hall and opera theatre was ultimately abandoned due to problems with acoustics, seating design, and management. The seating in the main hall, the Concert Hall, was increased, and the minor hall,

The Sydney Opera House (left) was formally opened by Queen Elizabeth II on October 20, 1973, with a helicopter fly-past, fireboats spouting water, flares, 60,000 balloons, and 2,000 small watercraft hooting. Jørn Utzon, the architect, was not present.

the Opera Theatre, was allocated to opera and ballet; this has constrained the size of productions ever since. The stage tower and proscenium of the Concert Hall were demolished and the stage was concreted over in an attempt to improve the acoustics. And only after the Opera Theatre's completion was it discovered that 100 seats had no view of the stage.

The cost estimate was revised to $85 million, and it was ultimately to reach $102 million. But this increase of almost 1,500 percent on the original estimate of £3.5 million ($7 million) proved to be not quite as serious a problem as it might have been, because an Opera House Lottery was instituted to pay for it. Thus the building's cost was largely removed from the realm of government annual budgeting.

The Building
The Sydney Opera House is raised on a podium on Bennelong Point, and is defined by its three groups of interlocking vaulted roofs, which cover, respectively, the Concert Hall, the Opera Theatre, and a much smaller restaurant. The building

Close up, the patterning of matte and glazed tiles is etched out by the dazzle of sunlight. The chevron shape of the panels is also evident. When the tiles were laid, they were placed face down on a tray so the concrete could be run over them from the back.

contains the Concert Hall, which has 2,679 seats; the Opera Theatre, which has 1,547 seats; three additional theaters; five rehearsal studios; two main halls; four restaurants; six bars; and various souvenir shops.

Though a technically complex building, only the roofs are really remarkable, and the "shells," which cover almost 5 acres (2 hectares), are one of the most famous roofs in the world. They are faced in off-white matte and glazed ceramic tiles manufactured in Sweden, 1.189 sq in x 0.457 in thick (30.2 mm² x 11.6 mm thick), which take up the changing colors of the sea and the sky. The change of the roof's form to spherical surfaces of uniform radius had a big impact on the roofing because it meant that these tiles could be prepared in standard panels, rather than having to be laid individually and cut to size. The panels are in a chevron form, which is like an oblong with one end extended out to a point and the other end cut in to a corresponding point. This means that they fit together in rows, with the largest panel measuring nearly 35 x 8 ft (10 x 2.5 m). The tiles are laid diagonally at 45 degrees, which is also the angle of each sail's point.

The practical defects of the building have not been forgotten, but a great deal of the bitterness surrounding its construction has. The Sydney Opera House's dominating feature, its sail-like roofs, were perhaps improved by the change from free form to spherical profile, for the design has lost none of its poetry. A degree of reconciliation with Utzon has been achieved, and in 2004, the first interior space rebuilt to match the architect's original design was opened, and renamed the Utzon Room in his honor. Throughout the world the building stands for Sydney, if not Australia. It was added to Australia's National Heritage List in 2005, and became a UNESCO World Heritage site in 2007.

The Concert Hall is used mostly for acoustic performances. It is lined with radial segments of brush box and birch timber. Its high vaulted ceiling has acoustic limitations—perspex rings, called "acoustic clouds," were added to improve the reverberation time.

Slates

Slate was perhaps the first really durable roofing material available to humans. It could be extracted with simple tools and, unlike tiles, did not need to be molded or fired. True slate is a sedimentary rock formed by the decomposed materials of older rocks or clay beds, deposited by water in regular strata and subjected to geological pressure. It is laminar and more or less easily split, depending largely upon the amount of mica present. A good slate will be hard, fine-grained, and impervious, and will split into thin sheets with a slightly glossy, smooth surface. This is the material commonly used as roofing slate, although there are other materials, such as some limestones, that can be split and so are also used for roofing. These are known as stone slates, and are normally much thicker.

Metal tools are needed to split slate out of the quarry. Sometimes, this is done in a very rough way, and in many parts of the world there is a vernacular roofing tradition, which uses irregular pieces of slate, usually with the larger pieces close to the eaves and the gable ends. A common detail in these roofs is that the slates at the ridge, rising from each side alternately, are notched into each other at the edges, so that they rest in place by their own weight. The technical challenge with slate roofing is how to fix the slates to the wooden roof structure. In a vernacular roof they may be held only with mud or lime mortar, which can work if the slope is shallow. But for a durable roof on a steeper slope, each slate must be fixed with nails.

In Cold Climates

There is not much evidence of the ancient use of slate roofing, simply because there is not much evidence of early roofs in general. Roman houses at Viroconium, near modern Shrewsbury, England, were covered in thick slabs of micaceous slate from Wales. Slate roofing is most commonly used in colder climates and on steeper roofs, especially in the northern parts of Europe, but is also used in alpine villages in Spain, the Balkans, and other places where the material was readily available. There are medieval references to slating in Britain and in France, where slate was quarried in both Normandy and Anjou. Only in Europe was slate distributed far from quarries, and it was not until the nineteenth century that significant quantities of roofing slate were traded internationally. Late in that century it became fashionable to lay slates of different origins and colors in patterns. The commonest slates were Welsh slates, generally of a blue-gray color, from Bangor, Caernarfon, Portmadog, and Penrhyn (the largest slate quarry in the world). Others included blue slates from Cornwall, in England, and Ireland; green from Westmoreland, in England; and both colors from Scotland. American slates from Vermont and elsewhere, which became prominent a little later, were mostly green.

Working with Slate

British slates were sold in an elaborate sequence of about 12 standard slate sizes, from a single, 12 x 8 in (300 x 200 mm), through duchesses, 24 x 12 in (600 x 300 mm) to queens, 36 x 24 in (900 x 600 mm). The larger sizes were thicker due to necessity. The slater would trim the edges on site, using a zax, or chopper. The holes for nails had to be carefully positioned to correspond with the location of the supporting roof batten, and were "pecked out" using the pointed end of the zax. In the nineteenth century, machinery for dressing slates and punching holes became available, but many slaters eschewed it. The slates were commonly fixed with composition nails cast

Stone Slates

Although some true slates are thicker than others, the very thick stone slates are a distinct category. They are not slate at all, but other materials, such as certain types of limestone, that can be split. They are essentially preindustrial, and detailed information exists only in England, where the Romans used stone slates fixed with iron nails. Famous quarries at Stonesfield, in Oxfordshire, produced three sizes during the Middle Ages. Other types were later quarried in Derbyshire, West Yorkshire, and in the limestone belt extending from the Cotswolds to Northamptonshire—an outlier of this region is Horsham in the south, the best-known location of such roofing today.

A brick and board house near Horsham in England has a roof of stone slates (below).

from an alloy of copper and tin; they were stiff and tough, with a yellow, brassy appearance.

The ridges and hips are of critical importance in any roof. It is possible to miter slates neatly at these junctions, but normal practice was to cover the joint with a tile or metal capping. One patented slate roofing system had a ridge formed with a cylindrical ridge roll of solid slate, with an ordinary-sized slate projecting from one side (all in one piece), and a groove on the other side to receive the top slate of the opposite slope.

The use of slate on flat roofs is very unusual, although Robben Island slate was used in this way in Port Elizabeth, South Africa, in the early nineteenth century. Slate was also used for other purposes than roofing, most notably in building systems where slate was set within iron frames for walls. The first system was developed by the English ironfounder John Cragg, and can be seen in churches in and around Liverpool, England, designed by the architect Thomas Rickman from *c.* 1820 onward. A similar system patented by Joseph George in 1846 was shown at the Great Exhibition of 1851 in London, and was used in some houses that were exported from Britain in the 1850s. In about 1841 a process of enameling slate was developed in London, and enameled slate became a popular material, particularly for decorative chimneypieces. Since the early twentieth century, slate has been used very little for new roofing. However, a wider range of slates sourced from countries such as Korea are very popular as flooring materials.

After the port town of Ålesund, in Norway, burnt down in 1904, its houses—previously of timber, the usual Norwegian building material at the time—were rebuilt in stone, brick, and mortar, in the Jugendstil (Art Nouveau) style. The steep roofs (above) were covered in dark gray, diamond-shaped slates.

In parts of rural France, including the uplands of the Dordogne and Corrèze, and the mountains of Savoie and Hautes Alpes, houses often have slate roofs. Rough-shaped slates of different sizes overlap thickly on the steep roof (left), with an even thicker covering of slates along the ridgeline.

Metal Roofing

Metal roofing comes in five main types: flat sheeting, metal tiles, corrugated iron, pressed sheeting, and decking. The tradition from at least medieval times was to lay sheets of lead over a boarded or other flat surface. Other metals, such as zinc and copper, have been used in a similar way, although most of these are more rigid than lead and have to be preformed (that is, shaped for the purpose). They are produced in pieces of a limited size or in rolls of a limited width, so there are numerous joints to be made watertight.

The standard practice was, and to some extent still is, to place parallel strips of timber with a rounded upper surface (rolls) on the roof, laying them in the direction of the slope, and spaced apart to suit the width of the metal sheet. The edge of the sheet was bent upward over the top of the roll. The edge of the adjacent sheet was also bent over, giving two layers of metal on top of the roll. A screw through the top secured both. The advantages were, firstly, that the overlap was raised above the roof surface, so that even if water lay on the surface or was blown back by the wind, it could not penetrate the joint. Secondly, there were no screw holes through the flat part of the sheet, where they would be likely to cause leaking.

This system was much the same as that used for fabric materials, such as canvas and oilcloth.

Tiles Made of Metal

Tinsmiths could always make tiles of tinplate (iron coated in tin), ternplate (iron coated in a mixture of lead and tin), or other stiff metal sheets. But it was the appearance of galvanized iron around the mid-nineteenth century that made metal roofing tiles popular.

Galvanizing is the coating of iron or steel with zinc. It was developed commercially between 1839 and 1843 while putative inventors battled over the patent rights. One of these contenders, Morewood & Rogers of East London, had a system of first coating the iron in tin and then in zinc. It was this company that developed the first galvanized tiles, which were exported throughout much of the world. The tiles were shaped much like preformed metal roofing sheets, curved up on either side to fit over timber rolls. However, they

Preformed metal roofing sheets cover the roofs of the Gare de l'Est (below), one of the major railroad terminals of Paris. Metal roofing, zinc in particular, features in views of Paris rooftops. About eighty percent of the city's roofing is made of metal.

The rise of galvanizing had been due largely to improvements in processing, which reduced the market cost of zinc enormously in the late 1830s. Zinc itself came to be used in other roofing forms as well as the flat sheet. Zinc sheet was pressed into shapes to imitate tiles, and the leading producer, the Vieille Montagne Company of Belgium, also exploited the fashion for the high mansard roof by making ornamental ridging, finials, roof vents, and dormers in zinc.

Pressed metal roofing on a large scale occurred mainly in the United States, using iron rather than zinc. By 1872, the Architectural Iron Works of Philadelphia had developed a complete range of classical entablatures, consoles, dormers, and complete mansard roofs in galvanized sheet iron. Late in the 1880s, the Canton Steel Roofing Company and others were making simpler forms of stamped steel roofing, as well as siding and other products. Other companies made individual metal shingles in Gothic or other ornamental forms, although the lead manufacturer was possibly Levi Montross of Toronto, Canada.

In 1844, John Woolley of Manchester, England, invented a roofing system in which strips of tin, with the edges turned up, were fixed along the top of each rafter, then the roofing sheets were placed in between, with their edges turned down over the strips. The development of preformed metal tray decking, as it was known, happened mainly in the United States, beginning with a system patented in 1876 and manufactured by N. A. Haldeman & Co. of Philadelphia. This consisted of flat iron sheets painted on both sides with iron oxide paint, with edges formed together into seams using special tools. Businesses such as the Garry Iron and Steel Roofing Company and the Porter Iron Roofing Company, both of Ohio, quickly followed. By the twentieth century, Sears, Roebuck & Co. was selling decking by mail order catalog, and it had become established as a standard US roofing material.

did not need the support of a boarded or flat surface, so the rolls could be fixed directly to the rafters or purlins (sloping or transverse members) of the roof.

New Types of Sheeting

Corrugated iron was developed and patented for structural purposes in 1829, by H. R. Palmer, the engineer of the London Docks. The corrugation of the sheet increases its strength and rigidity greatly, and if the sheet is curved lengthways, it becomes even stronger. This is what Palmer did, and although the sheets were quite small, he was able to rivet sheets together in both directions to make an arched roof so strong that it only needed slender horizontal tie rods to complete it. The arched roofs of the London Docks were to be the prototype for the many arched roofs of industrial buildings built during the nineteenth century. Palmer sold the patent rights to Richard Walker, who manufactured the iron but charged so much for it that it was rarely used before 1853, when the patent rights expired and other manufacturers entered the field. Most manufacturers galvanized the material, and it was galvanized corrugated iron that became well known.

Syre Kirk in northern Scotland (above) is built entirely of galvanized corrugated iron. Prefabricated buildings, from simple houses to churches and dance halls, were common in the Scottish Highlands and Hebrides from the 1850s. They withstood wild weather and were quick and quite cheap to assemble.

The Primera Zona Naval (Naval Headquarters) in the main square in Valparaíso, Chile (above), has a high mansard roof with elaborate metal ridging, finials, and dormers. Valparaíso is famous for its vernacular architecture, especially its corrugated iron houses.

Glenn Murcutt

Glenn Murcutt is an Australian architect who has acquired a special mystique as a lone practitioner, reviver of corrugated iron, and designer of environmentally sensitive buildings. He was born in London but lived in New Guinea until 1941, when his family settled in Sydney, Australia. After graduating from Sydney Technical College in 1961, Murcutt spent two years in Europe, working in London, traveling, and visiting buildings by Willem Marinus Dudok, Gerrit Rietveld, Le Corbusier, and most of all Alvar Aalto. After returning to Sydney in 1964, he was employed by Ancher, Mortlock, Murray, & Woolley, where he was responsible for major works including new buildings for the University of Newcastle in eastern Australia.

Murcutt founded his own practice in 1969, and has worked mainly on private houses and almost entirely alone ever since. His early works were based upon the Modernism of Ludwig Mies van der Rohe, but in about 1974, after a second overseas trip, the distinctive Murcutt house began to crystallize. This is most clearly evident in the confident, coherent simplicity of the Marie Short Farmhouse at Kempsey (1975).

The Murcutt Style

The Marie Short Farmhouse illustrates all the major features of the emergent Murcutt style. His houses consist either of one gabled unit or, as in this case, two, running in parallel, generally differing in length or staggered in their placement, but never with a hipped roof or an intersecting gable. The juxtaposition of a pair of parallel but staggered rectangles can be traced to a Mies van der Rohe prototype, the Farnsworth House at Plano, Illinois (1950). Most of the farmhouse's wall area is glass or glass louvers, and there are no verandahs. The building is raised on stumps and this gives the impression of minimal interference with the ground below, like a mosquito that has just landed.

The Murcutt roof is usually steep and made of corrugated iron. At the Marie Short Farmhouse, it continues in a curve over the ridge, so that no separate ridging is required. The curved sheets are raised slightly above the sloping roof surface on either side along most of the length of the ridge. This allows educt (extraction) ventilation from under the curved sheets' edges. It is possible that this may have been inspired by a similar device that was illustrated in J. D. Moore's *Home Again!*, published in Australia in 1944.

Murcutt's work during the seventies struck a deep chord with the Australian public, although he denied any interest in developing an Australian style and argued that the best architecture simply responds to the surrounding conditions.

But it is clear that his acknowledged interest in old barns has influenced his gabled, rectangular, verandahless forms.

Murcutt has encouraged the perception that his buildings are environmentally friendly. However, he has been challenged about the thermal properties of these structures, with their open subfloor space and extensive glazed areas.

Over time, the timber framing and cladding used in the Marie Short Farmhouse were replaced with elegant steel members and corrugated iron walls, while the forms became more capricious, as in the Henric Nicholas Farmhouse at Mt. Irvine (1980). The last of the gabled barn forms was the Fredericks House at Jamberoo (1982), an elegant reworking of the Marie Short model at a time when the architect's other works had left that mode behind.

Murcutt's reputation has overwhelmingly been based on the detached houses in spacious rural settings executed during this period. The prominence of these country projects is due to the fact that so many of his urban projects of that same period did not proceed. For in reality, Murcutt is an urban architect, most of whose work is in Sydney. Partly due to site constraints and compromises with neighbors and councils, the urban projects were less distinctive, and few had the characteristic steep iron roof.

The Magney House (1984) overlooks the Pacific at Bingie Bingie (left). The larger sweep of curved roof extends out over the north side, giving shade in summer. The louvers allow for cooling sea breezes.

Simplifying the Barn

From the mid-1980s, Murcutt's work becomes harder to characterize, for it no longer employed his unique vocabulary. He used increasingly elegant steel detailing, bringing him close at times to the work of his contemporaries such as Philip Cox. One of his best-known buildings, the Magney House at Bingie Bingie (1984), is in the single long barn form, but the roof is in two curved segments rising from an off-centre valley, as if a low barrel vault had been cut into two unequal sections, which were then transposed. Angled braces make an elegant structuralist play along the larger roof edge, and the rainwater head detailing is famously refined. Similarly elegant detailing was to be used elsewhere, for example, at the Done House in Sydney (1991).

In the late 1980s, Murcutt developed a concept even more basic than the earlier barn type. The Meagher House at Bowral (1992)

was essentially a simple long rectangle roofed with a simple lean-to detailed to a thin edge, almost like a piece of stiff card casually placed over the plan. At the Simpson-Lee House at Mt. Wilson (1994) the form was simplified into two plain rectangular plates, one on each of the linked pavilions. These houses were integrated with substructures and landscaping rather than delicately perched above the ground, but Murcutt revived that idea in the Marika-Alderton House (1994) for the Yirrkala Community in Arnhem Land in northern Australia. While the planning was intended to relate to Aboriginal traditions and sensibilities, the overall form, of a rectangle with a simple gable roof and very broad eaves, had much more to do with European architectural traditions in the tropical north.

In the 1990s, Murcutt's work became very varied and included a number of large projects, sometimes in conjunction with other architects, but these did not supersede the domestic practice that continued to be his main focus. He has won many Australian and international awards, including most importantly of all the "Nobel Prize of Architecture," the Pritzker Prize, in 2002.

The Arthur and Yvonne Boyd Art Centre on the Shoalhaven River (1999) at Riversdale, has accommodation and studios (right) for artists and students. This is one of Murcutt's larger projects, in collaboration with architects Reg Lark and Wendy Lewin.

The two parallel units of the Marie Short Farmhouse of 1974 at Kempsey (left) are roofed in corrugated iron—a ubiquitous feature of rural Australia's vernacular buildings. The farmhouse's living areas are raised off the ground because of seasonal floods.

Coatings

The coating of roof surfaces in tar or bituminous materials has a long but somewhat problematic history. Asphalt was used in the Middle East from Neolithic times, and up until the early nineteenth century most of the asphalt in commercial use was gathered on the shores of the Dead Sea. The English explorer Sir Walter Raleigh discovered new deposits while in Trinidad in 1595, and in the eighteenth century, rock asphalt was found in Switzerland, Germany, and France. In 1681, the method for making pitch and tar from pit coal was discovered, and then in 1690, deposits of coal tar were found in Norway. However, this material only become significant for roofing after the gas industry was established in the nineteenth century, creating coal tar as a by-product.

Asphalt and Tar

Asphalt and tar materials were used for paving, roadmaking, cellars, and industrial floors. They were also used for roofing, but as both these substances are vulnerable to sun and weather, they were laid with gravel or tiles on top, or in combination with felts or impregnated papers. In the eighteenth century both tarred felt and tarred paper were introduced in Sweden. A combination of cardboard and asphalt, which became known as either *carton pierre, steinpappe,* or stone pasteboard, was developed by the Swedish Navy, and became a common material for roofing houses in Norway, Sweden, and Russia. After a disastrous fire at Uleåborg in Finland in 1822, the houses in the town were rebuilt with roofs made of paper that had been drenched in a tar with rosin and red ocher added. The surface was then covered with a mixture of brick dust, smithy dross, and sand, and trodden into place, and this surface was renewed every year or two.

Tarred paper was manufactured in England from at least 1770, and was used in the British West Indies when shingles were hard to obtain during the American Revolutionary War. Early in the nineteenth century, a Prussian engineer called Büsscher studied *steinpappe* roofing in Sweden and Finland and established a factory in Germany. Sheets of his material were placed over boards onto which triangular fillets of timber had been nailed in parallel; they were spaced the width of one sheet apart (much like the rolls used in metal roofing). Sheets of the material were placed in between, narrow strips were fixed over the top of the fillets to give a slight lap, and then fluid asphalt was spread over the whole. In 1859, a Belgian paper manufacturer developed a system of saturating "slabs" of paper with tar, and it appears these were used there and in Greece for roofing railway stations and powder magazines. In France there were at least three tar products: *toiles cartonnées et bitumées* (that is, papered and bitumenized cloth); Didier-Letacq roofing, which seems to have been a bitumenized and sanded cloth or paper; and a non-combustible English roofing felt, presumably made under license.

Bitumenized felt roofing is believed to have been used in the 1840s in the American cities of Boston and Newark. The roofing product of W. H. Childs—gravel over bitumenized felt—followed in 1854. Five main types of bitumenized felt now evolved. The first type was impregnated bitumen felts. Sanded bitumen felts had enough weather-resistance to be used in a single layer to roof temporary shelters; they were also used in multiple layers for more permanent roofs. Self-finished bitumen felts were coated with fine talc or mica, while mineralized bitumen felts had this coating on the underside but were covered with slate or some other type of mineral granules on the exposed face. Both could be used for single-layer roofing or as part of a system of multiple layers. Reinforced bitumen felts were self-finished bitumen felts into which an additional layer of burlap was incorporated to prevent tearing.

Built-up bitumen roofing is usually used on flat surfaces, which present the most acute problems of waterproofing. To make this kind of roof, felt is nailed to the roof surface, then mopped with bitumen, then a further layer of felt applied, and so on. Gravel and bitumen are deposited on the roof in separate piles and then worked with wooden pushers to mix them and spread them across the surface.

Brightly painted walls compensate for the dark gray ashphalt roofs of a row of houses in Almere (above), one of the newest cities in the Netherlands. Created to deal with rapid population growth, the first houses were built here on reclaimed land in 1976.

Paint

Paint is a quite different form of surfacing, and various types were applied to iron and other roofing materials. As well as their purely decorative effect, some paints claimed to resist or repair corrosion, resist fire, or, perhaps most remarkably, insulate the building from heat. For example, "refrigerating paints" such as "Indian Dyphoor" and "Patent Vesuvius Refrigerated Paint" claimed to reduce the interior temperature by as much as 15°F (8°C). Other substances made even more remarkable claims. "Arabic cooling composition" was supplied as a "dry mineral powder" ready to be mixed with water, and when applied, even to the underside of the roof, was supposed to reduce the temperature inside by 15°F (8°C). Another roof-cooling product called "Antarctica" claimed to reduce the temperature by as much as 30°F (16.5°C). Such claims were, of course, entirely spurious, although a lighter-colored paint might have had some marginal effect.

A crofter's house on the isle of Tiree in the Scottish Hebrides has an asphalt roof. A crofter was a tenant farmer, and traditionally, the roof would have been thatched or, elsewhere in Scotland, layered with peat.

The Pentagon in Arlington, Virginia (right), is home to the US Defense Department. Its roof is covered in coal-tar built-up roofing. Many large US commercial buildings, and many apartment blocks in cities like Boston and New York, have this type of roofing.

What Exactly is Bitumen?

Bitumen is a generic term that covers coal tar, asphalt, and pitch—all are used. Pitch has the lowest melting point, which can be an advantage because it melts in the heat of the sun and flows into and seals any small punctures in the roof. But it also makes surfacing the roof with gravel or some other protective material essential. Both pitch and asphalt are affected by the sun, but areas in constant shade can last almost indefinitely.

Turrets

Turrets are small towers on a building, added mostly for defense or ornament. They are particularly associated with medieval architecture and with the picturesque pseudo-medieval architecture of the nineteenth century.

In general, the Romans did not attach a great deal of importance to vertical elements in design. However, they commonly placed turrets on either side of a city gate for defense, and in many cases they also placed turrets or towers at intervals all around the city walls. But these were functional, allowing the defenders to fire arrows sideways at an attacker approaching the wall or gate. It was only during and after the decline of Rome that an aesthetic impulse to create vertical elements emerged in Western Europe, and this is linked with the development of bell towers and spires. A square tower is shown on a fourth-century CE ivory casket from Brescia, Italy, and round towers appear on a casket from Werden, Germany, as well as on the fifth-century doors of the church of Santa Sabina in Rome. There were also four small turrets on the sixth-century church of San Vitale in Ravenna, Italy.

The Ornamental Turret

A new spirit of verticality appeared during the Carolingian period, most notably at the abbey church of Centula, also known as Saint-Riquier, in northwest France (c. 790). This church had a total of nine towers of one sort or another, and must be regarded as the source of the medieval turret. Though the building no longer survives, and is known only from a seventeenth-century engraving, it is thought that just the tower bases were of stonemasonry where they rose above the roofline. The balance was of wood. Few other churches had so many towers, but many built in France, Switzerland, and Germany adopted another aspect of Saint-Riquier—the westwerk. The west, or entrance, end of the church became a high slab, dominating the whole composition. It could be quite plain or it could incorporate a pair of slender towers.

The church of Sankt Cyriakus at Gernrode, Germany, has had later modifications, but the westwerk belongs to the original church of 961 and is flanked by round towers similar to those of Saint-Riquier. One has a ring of decorative

arcading, while the other has a primitive zigzag motif that dates from the Dark Ages.

The medieval castle had towers for defensive purposes, much like those of the Romans, but the Crusades and the age of chivalry resulted in castles becoming more ornamental, especially in France, their purpose being more to display the wealth and taste of the owner than to be defensible. The thirteenth-century gate of the Castillo de los Templarios at Ponferrada, Spain, for example, is flanked by turrets and crowned with machicolation for defense but seems to be consciously designed for picturesque effect.

With the fifteenth-century Château de Saumur in the Loire Valley, France, as illustrated in the *Très Riches Heures du Duc de Berry* (an illustrated medieval book of hours), all equivocation was left behind. This castle has more in common with the picturesque of the nineteenth century than with the grim defensive works of the past. Castles had ceased to be built in England by this time. There is very little evidence of purely ornamental castle turrets in that country, although during the reign of King Henry III in the thirteenth century,

Pilgrims on the Pilgrim Route through northwest Spain to Santiago de Compostela would have passed the turreted thirteenth-century gate of the Castillo de los Templarios (Templar Castle) at Ponferrada.

The westwerk was a western entrance area, almost fortresslike in appearance, with upper stories often flanked by towers. Churches such as Sankt Cyriakus in Germany (top left) incorporated this innovation.

with John Nash. He used it at Killymoon Castle (1802) and Shanbally Castle (1812) in Ireland, and his East Cowes Castle (1798) on the Isle of Wight. J. G. Graham also used the combination at Dunninald, Scotland (1819). The more picturesque turret cantilevering from the corner of a castle or house was a Scottish tradition, revived by William Atkinson in his design for Sir Walter Scott's house, Abbotsford (1819).

Abbotsford was enormously influential. Many Americans visited, including James Fenimore Cooper in 1834. He immediately returned to the United States to Gothicize the family home at Cooperstown, New York. Few American designs at this stage could match the size and complexity of Abbotsford, but turrets of one sort or another appeared regularly in the designs of architects such as A. J. Davis and A. J. Downing. During the remainder of the nineteenth century, turrets were regularly used in grander houses of picturesque medieval design throughout Europe and North America. Perhaps most memorably, they are a feature of the fantasy castles of the mad King Ludwig II of Bavaria, Germany, such as Schloss Neuschwanstein (1886).

Horace Walpole's Strawberry Hill near London (below) is the first house to have been designed in a deliberately asymmetrical form, with a slender turret next to a squat castellated tower.

Sir William Champney of London was said to be "the first man in England who ever built a turret on top of his house, that he might better overlook his neighbors." Soon after its completion (whether as a consequence or not), he was struck blind. The ornamental turret did occur in Scotland, because of that country's connections with France, but more often on steep fortified houses than on castles proper.

A Revival

Although England contributed so little to the original development of the ornamental turret, it was almost solely responsible for its revival. In the mid-eighteenth century, Horace Walpole began redeveloping his small house, Strawberry Hill, at Twickenham near London, in a deliberately picturesque manner. Walpole began work on the small house in 1747, and in 1749 took a crucial decision, announcing that "I am going to build a little Gothic castle." Ten years later a larger round tower was built at one end. Later still, a slender but taller turret—the Beauclerc Tower—was built next to it.

Whilst Strawberry Hill influenced many buildings by architects such as James Wyatt, and set a fashion for castellated architecture, the picturesque combination of the squat tower and the slender turret was to strike a special chord

271

Bell Towers

The church bell tower may have its origins in the mid-fifth century CE. Traditionally, it is said that Paulinus, Bishop of Nola in Campania, Italy, introduced the use of bells in about CE 420, and it is because of this that bells were anciently called *nolae* and *campanae*. But it is possible that this story was merely fabricated to explain the words.

Bells are not much mentioned until the writings of St. Gregory of Tours in about CE 585, but they had been installed at his church of Saint-Martin in Tours, western France, before the end of the sixth century. Bells were also used in Scotland and Ireland from the sixth century—a famous bell of St. Patrick is preserved in Dublin. They appeared in England by the seventh century, and by the eighth century were generally widespread in the churches of Western Europe. In the Eastern Church, a suspended *simantron* (a board of stone or wood) was struck with a bar.

Although no tower was purpose built for the bells, the church of Saint-Martin at Tours is believed to have had a defensive tower at the western, or entrance, end and a tower to admit light at the crossing (the intersection of the nave and transept), and the bells were installed in one or the other. It was later common in northern Europe to provide only a bell-cote, a section of wall projecting above the roof that contained an arched opening within which one or two bells were suspended. Although full peals of bells such as that at Crowland Abbey, England, in the ninth century, must have had proper towers (because bell-ringing imposes considerable structural strain on a building), we know little about any explicit architectural provision for bells until the campanile appears in Italy.

The Square Campanile

The earliest towers specifically built to carry bells are thought to have been the tower of the old Basilica of St. Peter's, Rome, built under the popes Stephen II and Hadrian I, between 752 and 795; the tower of the Lateran Basilica in Rome (about 750); and the circular campanile of Sant'Apollinare Nuovo at Ravenna (850–878). Subsequent campaniles at Ravenna were circular in plan, like Sant'Apollinare's, but Ravenna was an outpost of the Byzantine Empire, surrounded by the territory of the Lombards, where a square form of campanile developed.

The Lombard campanile was divided into stories, with an open bell loggia at the top of the tower and a diminishing series of openings in the lower levels. The oldest example is that of San Satiro, Milan (876), but the most beautiful is that of the Pomposa Abbey, near Ferrara. It is almost 157 ft (47 m) high and beautifully decorated with corbel tables dividing the stories and vertical pilaster strips and engaged shafts formed in the brickwork. The Lombards had an international reputation as builders, and so they carried their style (sometimes known as the Premier Art Roman or First Romanesque), including their style

The Benedictine Abbey of Pomposa, near Ferrara, Italy, was a very wealthy and culturally important monastery in the eleventh century. The very fine Romanesque campanile (left) was built during that period. It towers over the surrounding plains of the Po River.

of campanile, across southern France and into Spanish Catalonia. Meanwhile, still in Italy, a variant form developed in Venice, which still had the open loggia at the top, but the lower levels had small openings and no diminishing series. It can be seen at Torcello, an island in the Venetian Lagoon, and later in Venice itself, in the Campanile of San Marco, which is a replica of the thirteenth- to fourteenth-century structure that fell down in 1902.

The square campanile of Rome also appears to have been derived from the Lombard type, but differs considerably: it has more openings; the stories are more clearly defined by cornices supported on white stone brackets; and the use of brick gives it a warm hue, set off by the marble colonettes and the faience let into the walls. Because the liturgical reform of Pope Gregory VII required the clergy to celebrate mass at the traditional times, bell towers were needed in Rome from the eleventh century onward in order to summon the faithful. Some examples are those of Santa Pudenziana, Santa Francesca Romana, and also San Giorgio al Velabro (all twelfth century); Santa Prassede (twelfth or thirteenth century); and Santa Maria Maggiore (1377). In Rome more than elsewhere, the campanile tends to be attached to the body of the church, though it is still not integrated into the building as in the north European manner.

Other Purposes

The church bell towers of northern Europe are fully integrated with the building, unlike the freestanding or semi-freestanding campaniles of Italy, and even when built specifically for the purpose, they are not architecturally distinctive.

The Notorious Leaning Tower

Probably the most famous of all campaniles is the Leaning Tower of Pisa, built between 1174 and 1271, although the bell chamber on top was not added until about 1350 by Tommaso di Andrea da Pontedera. Although the arcading gives it a totally different effect, the cylindrical form, which is not common, relates to the earlier campaniles of Ravenna. Due to inadequate foundations, it began to settle unevenly during construction, and the attempts to build it back toward the vertical have given the shaft the shape of a banana. It is nearly 177 ft (54 m) high and more than 13 ft (4 m) out of plumb.

The campanile stands behind the Pisa Cathedral. It contains seven bells tuned to the muscial scale. They were removed during stabilization work in the 1990s to lighten the tower's weight a little.

However, there are other sorts of bell towers, such as those that carry alarm bells, fire bells, or ceremonial bells. Most of these are small structures or, in the case of fire bells, integrated with what is principally a lookout tower. An exceptional example is a 165-ft (50-m) tower built to house a carillon (a mechanical set of bells controlled from a keyboard) at Canberra, Australia, opened in 1970. In East Asia, gong enclosures are built, rather than towers; inside these enclosures, a suspended disc of bronze or other metal is struck with a bar.

An example of a bell tower that is not associated with a church is the 165-ft (50-m) tower built to house a carillon. This elegant structure stands on a small island, and the sound of bells peals out over the lake in Canberra, Australia. It was opened in 1970.

Spires

The spire is the steep, pointed roof of a tower, normally found on a Christian church. Although the distinction is not always clear, the word "steeple" usually refers to an architectural tower composition that may or may not terminate in a spire. The spire marks the location of a church and expresses its status, but it has no liturgical role or connection with Christian doctrine. Any symbolic significance that may be ascribed to it is after the fact. It is therefore almost pure architecture.

The Desire for Height

The spire first developed, along with several other vertical elements, as part of a spontaneous urge toward verticality during the Carolingian period, which probably arose in some way from the ethos of the Franks. The new Carolingian forms were like building blocks—tall rectangular prisms and cylinders, roofed with pyramids and cones. These roofs were distinctive but not particularly steep at first. The pyramidal roof, or *helmhaus,* became common in the Carolingian Empire and later in Germany. From it developed the helm roof, as at Speyer Cathedral, Germany (1030–1061), in which the pyramid is steeper and is rotated so that the angles fall over the centers of the tower walls below and thus create triangular gables. Steeper versions followed in France. The church of Saint-Étienne of the Abbaye-aux-Hommes, Caen (1066–1086), which was influenced by Speyer, has nine spires. The western ones are octagonal (with pinnacles added later). This was a new form, although some German churches (and later Speyer itself) had a squat octagonal roof over the crossing tower. The southwest tower of Chartres Cathedral in France (1194–c. 1224) also carries an octagonal spire.

The octagonal spire is a more subtle form than the square pyramid spire, but it presents a design problem when it rests on a square base, leaving gaps at the corners. To overcome this, the broach spire was introduced in Britain some time during the thirteenth century, with small hipped roofs running in from the corners of the tower to the faces of the spire. These broaches were sometimes built over squinch arches, which were visible underneath. Later, corner pinnacles were often placed at the corners, connected by a decorative parapet. The pinnacle, which is a small, ancillary pointed element, should be distinguished from the flèche, which is also a spike without a base

Caen in northern France is called the "city of spires" because of the church of Saint-Étienne (1066–1086). The choir end, viewed from the east, has four square spires with helm roofs (above). The west façade's twin octagonal spires were added in the thirteenth century.

of its own, but which occurs singly and usually rises out of the roof ridge. While the flèche is normally small, the one at Amiens Cathedral, in northern France, is a magnificent timber structure rising 177 ft (54 m) above the roof.

In England few spires of any sort were built in the Decorated Gothic period (1377–1485), but at St. Nicholas, Newcastle, a dramatic example of

Spires

The spire began as a tall square tower topped with a helm roof, a steeply pitched hip roof rising to a spiked point. From this, it developed its more typical appearance of a steep tower rising from a square or rectangular base in a continuously conical or pyramidal shape to a spike. Multiple stories and ornate decoration followed, but it was still a spire if it retained the basic overall outline of a long, slender spiked tower.

SQUARE SPIRE

OCTAGONAL SPIRE

WREN STEEPLE

GIBBS STEEPLE

1474 rests on the top of open arches, like flying buttresses, rising from the corners of the tower. A similar structure was added to St. Giles's Cathedral, Edinburgh, in 1496. These exercises in structural virtuosity were not confined to Britain. The west spires of Burgos Cathedral, Spain (fifteenth to sixteenth centuries), have the overall form of a conventional octagonal spire on a square base with corner pinnacles, but the spire itself is an open structure of lacy stonemasonry. Freiburg Cathedral in Germany was completed in 1513 with a similar openwork spire.

The Renaissance steeple was a multi-story composition of arcading and other classically derived elements, which developed most strongly in the Netherlands, and sometimes, as at the Nieuwe Kerk (New Church) in Haarlem (1649), it tapered sharply toward the top to form something like a spire. This was the tradition inherited by Sir Christopher Wren, whose city churches in London in the later seventeenth century have a wonderful range of steeples, some of which terminate in spires. However, it was Wren's follower, Nicholas Hawksmoor, who reinterpreted the spire most creatively. He was probably responsible for the spire of St. Vedast, London (1697), done by Wren's office, which is an interpretation of the ancient obelisk form in the Baroque manner of Borromini. Hawksmoor's works independent of Wren include two notable examples: at Christ Church, Spitalfields (1729), a literal broach spire, and at St George's Church, Bloomsbury (1730), an extraordinary stepped spire, which was inspired by Pliny's account of the Mausoleum at Halicarnassus, Asia Minor, with four pedimented temple fronts as a base and a statue of King George III on top. James Gibbs built steeples in the Wren tradition at his London churches of St. Mary le Strand (1717) and St. Martin in the Fields (1726), and added one to Wren's church of St. Clement Danes (1719). But more important than these were the alternative designs prepared for these steeples, which Gibbs was to publish in his *Book of Architecture* (1739) and which were then copied over much of the world.

Fantastically Modern

Antoni Gaudí was to create extraordinary spires at his Church of La Sagrada Familia (the Holy Family) in Barcelona, Spain. They are even more remarkable for not having been inspired by medieval precedents. He had visited Tangier, Morocco, in 1883 and been struck by the mud-built towers of the African tradition. When commissioned ten years later to design a Franciscan mission there, he gave it several circular spires with a convex curve, or entasis, in profile. Although the mission was never built, the form remained in his stylistic repertoire, and he used it again in 1908 in a proposal for a hotel in New York, also unbuilt.

La Sagrada Familia started as a fairly conventional Gothic design, but as it occupied most of Gaudí's career and evolved remarkably over time. Apart from the Gothic apse, the south transept façade was virtually all Gaudí was able to build.

Antoni Gaudí's design for his Church of La Sagrada Familia (The Holy Family) in Barcelona, Spain, was was designed with three portals, each with four spires about 330 ft (100 m) tall, to symbolize the twelve apostles. The four spires of the Nativity portal (below) mark the entrance to the south transept.

It began in the form of a Gothic triple portal with sculpture of a rather cloying religiosity, but as it rose the design began to sprout fantastic forms, seemingly based upon shapes in nature. The overall design of the spires was established by 1910, using the Tangier model, and they were relatively plain, with open vertical strips that contained stone louvers. At the top, however, they broke out into fantastic pinnacles, which continually changed shape as they rose. The fact that they were fully worked out and drawn by Gaudí in the days before computers is a remarkable testament to his skill.

Minarets

The minaret is the most visually arresting part of a mosque, yet like the spire of the Christian church, it is, in liturgical terms, the least essential. A mosque for prayer can be established almost anywhere—early Muslim armies would simply trace an outline in the desert sand and thrust a spear haft down into the ground to indicate the direction of Mecca. In the *masjid* (the mosque for daily prayer), a *mihrab* (prayer niche that points toward Mecca) became standard from the early eighth century. It is usually placed in a *qiblah,* a wall appropriately oriented at right angles to the Mecca axis. A *jāmi,* a Friday mosque for prayer and preaching on the sabbath, is often grander, and has the additional requirement of a *minbar* (pulpit).

The Call to Prayer

The minaret is, in a sense, a secondary development. Muhammad disliked the sounds made by the Jewish *shofar* (ram's horn) and the *simantron* (clappers) of the Christians, used to summon their worshippers. One of his companions recollected having a dream in which he saw a man chanting a summons to prayer, and this led Muhammad to turn to his Abyssinian freedman, Bilāl al-Habashī, and say, "Mount up, Bilāl, and call the people to prayer." Thus Bilāl, who was known for his sweet voice, became the first muezzin, charged with chanting the *adhān,* or summons to prayer. The higher the muezzin stood, the farther the sound of his calls would travel. When the church of St. John the Baptist in Damascus, in Syria, was redeveloped as the Umayyad Mosque (Great Mosque) of Damascus, from 712 onward, the already existing corner towers were used for this purpose. These towers, which were from the earlier pagan temple on the site and essentially pre-Christian, became the main model for subsequent minarets.

They were not unique. There was a tradition of square Syrian towers from both pagan and Christian times, and early minarets based upon these were also square and their proportions were

The tall, slender, fluted minarets of the Blue Mosque (1616) in Istanbul, Turkey (above), are typical of the Ottoman minaret. The fact that there were six caused a scandal, as this was the same number as the mosque at Mecca. To resolve this, Ottoman Sultan Ahmed I funded the building of a seventh minaret at Mecca.

The vast open courtyard of the Umayyad Mosque in Damascus, Syria, (begun in the early eighth century) is enclosed with an arcade. The Arus Minaret (known as the Minaret of the Bride) stands near the northern gate. This mosque is the oldest stone mosque in the world, and one of the largest.

Decoration

The Islamic tradition of decorating wall surfaces with calligraphy was especially used for minarets. Inscriptions were applied in bands, often separated by other bands of geometric or floral decoration, with the inscriptions themselves differing in style and scale. An impressive example is the twelfth-century octagonal minaret at Meskine, in northern Syria, on which Kufic script is ingeniously formed by the pattern of the bricklaying. During the 1970s, this splendid minaret was sliced into pieces and moved to a new site to avoid being flooded by a new dam on the Euphrates.

All 215 ft (65 m) of the twelfth-century Minaret of Jam (top) in Afghanistan is covered in delicate stucco and glazed-tile patterns and calligraphy.

often comparatively stumpy. The original ninth-century minaret of the Shibam Mosque in Yemen was this squat, square type.

When Islamic architects came to design taller minarets, these tended to step inward as they rose, as in the minaret of the Great Mosque at al-Qayrawān, in Tunisia (836–). In some areas, Christian bell towers and Sassanid fire towers have been suggested as prototypes for the minaret, and one of the oldest surviving minarets seems to relate to the Mesopotamian ziggurat. The Abbasid rulers of the Muslim Empire built a number of enormous buildings in their capital, Samarra (in modern Iraq), including the two largest mosques in the Islamic world. The Great Mosque (848–852) is no more, but the surrounding high wall with 44 semicircular towers largely survives, and measures about 790 x 525 ft (240 x 160 m). Its minaret, which also still stands, is a broad-based, tapering brick tower ascended by a spiral ramp like that of a ziggurat. It is known as al-Malwiya, or snail shell, because of its shape.

What finally emerged as the common form of the minaret had a square base, then a polygonal story, and a cylindrical shaft. At the top was a balcony of light wood or cantilevered masonry, and above this a conical or domed roof. In the early examples, such as the minaret of the Great Mosque, Harran, Turkey (eighth century), of which little stands today, the ground floor only was of stone and the upper floors were of brick, which is consistent with building traditions in the area from at least the second millennium BCE. Standard minaret construction consisted of a solid core surrounded by a spiral staircase, the treads of which, if they were of stone, served to tie the outer wall to the core. By this means the Ottomans constructed minarets more than 230 ft (70 m) high.

Changes in Status

One of the grandest minarets—though not the most elegant—is La Giralda (1156–1158) in Seville, Spain, built by the Almohads. It is so big that the core is a tower of square rooms, around which passes the spiral staircase. The outer wall is paneled with geometric brick designs. A lantern and belfry at the top were added by the Christians in 1520–1568, when they took it over as the tower of Seville Cathedral.

A conversion in the reverse direction is more common. After their conquest of Constantinople (Istanbul in modern Turkey) in 1453, the Ottomans converted all the Christian churches to mosques, often doing little more than obliterating the internal decoration and replacing the apse with a *qiblah* wall and a *mihrab* oriented toward Mecca. The change of function was more clearly marked by the construction of minarets, particularly the four that surround the great Hagia Sophia.

Some examples, such as the twelfth-century Minaret of Jam, Afghanistan, and the thirteenth-century Qutb Minar in Delhi, India, are technically minarets, but they were really built more as a proclamation of power than for the call to prayer. In other instances the minaret form was used for totally secular purposes, such as for lighthouses, sentry posts, commemorative columns, and towers for fire signals. A number of single minarets on the Khurasan Road in western Iran, which still survive from the eleventh and twelfth centuries, have staircases leading not just to the muezzin's balcony but right to the very top, where a signal beacon could be lit.

Scaling the Heights

Over time, people have devised various ways of moving between levels. The earliest ramps, steps, and ladders were simple, functional structures. In some cultures, people built high to get closer to the gods. Everywhere, the march of civilization and technology has seen us climbing farther upward—and contriving more elaborate elevators as required.

Ramps

Ramps play an important architectural role as a way of gaining elevation when neither space nor cost is a consideration—and the monumental temples and tombs of antiquity are a prime example of this. Simply a slope that connects two different levels, the ramp can be an integral part of the exterior or the interior of a building, as well as a type of outdoor pathway.

If a ramp is too steep, people may slip and fall. It is then necessary to make supplementary low steps that provide a more level footing for pedestrians. Examples of this can be seen in some of the ramp/step combinations at Frank Gehry's Guggenheim Museum in Bilbao, Spain, in the roadway on top of sections of the Great Wall of China, and in the stepped ramp winding up the Spiral Minaret of the Great Mosque of al-Mutawakkil in Samarra, Iraq.

Ramps in Antiquity

The ramps of ancient Egypt served ceremonial and constructional purposes. In the absence of engines, cranes, wheels, and pulleys, how exactly the pyramids were built in the third millennium BCE is still unclear, but it is assumed that each huge block of stone used in their construction was raised into position by being dragged up an increasingly long temporary ramp made of earth and stone. Some scholars think that the ramp may have wound around the outside of the pyramid as it was built. Others visualise an immense wedge-shaped ramp rising up from the nearby plain. Both methods would have entailed major engineering challenges.

Architectural ramps as a primarily aesthetic feature also make an early appearance in Egypt— at the Temple of Hatshepsut, at Deir el-Bahari, Thebes, near the Valley of the Kings. With its lines of columns reminding one of Athens, yet predating the Parthenon by a thousand years (Hatshepsut was queen from 1479 to 1458 BCE), the building known as Djeser-Djeseru, or "Holy of Holies," comprises three colonnaded terraces sited at the foot of towering natural cliffs, and has been described as one of the "incomparable monuments of Ancient Egypt." Designed by the queen's royal steward, Senmut, and constructed entirely of limestone, the porticoed terraces at the Temple of Hatshepsut are nearly 100 ft (30 m) high. Five substantial ramps, which were once surrounded by great gardens, connect the lower terraces to the upper levels. The two broad and dominating central ramps form a processional way leading upward from the valley floor, and have a narrow row of steps in the center to give pedestrians a more secure footing.

Other monumental ramps of the ancient world were found in ziggurats. In Assyrian, the word *ziggurat* meant "pinnacle," and was applied to a kind of pyramidal stepped tower.

The Ziggurat of Ur (top), by the Euphrates River in Iraq, was already old when it was extensively remodeled in *c.* 2125 BCE. It had a solid core of mud bricks, faced with kiln-fired bricks.

In his influential Villa Savoye, near Paris (above), Le Corbusier connected the ground to the roof with a continuous sweeping ramp that zigzagged through the cantilevered concrete structure up to the roof.

The Palace of Khorsabad complex, in north Iraq, built for Sargon II in the eighth century BCE, included a ziggurat associated with the palace temples. The steps of the seven-tiered ziggurat formed a single, continuous ramp winding around the square structure from base to summit. The much earlier Ziggurat of Ur, in southern Iraq, had a massive entrance, with a central stepped ramp extending out into the surrounding precinct and two equally imposing adjacent side ramps abutting the front elevation.

Contemporary Ramps

The use of ramps as dynamic transitional structures was revived by Le Corbusier and Frank Lloyd Wright in the twentieth century. In his Villa Savoye of 1929–1931 at Poissy near Paris, Le Corbusier connected the floors with a continuous central ramp, from the service areas at the ground level, through the living areas, up to the roof garden and solarium. Some three decades later, Le Corbusier was to design an S-shaped curvilinear ramp for the Carpenter Visual Arts Center, in Cambridge, Massachusetts. The ramp rises from one street and descends to another, and has glass walls on either side. This walkway bisects the building's structure and connects with the main stairs and the exhibition space.

Spectacular spiraling ramps were created by Frank Lloyd Wright, first in the Morris Gift Shop in San Francisco and later, and most notably, at the Guggenheim Museum in New York. Although the shop was constructed before the museum, the designs for the Guggenheim Museum were begun in 1943 and actually predate the shop. The construction of the Morris Gift Shop allowed Wright an opportunity to experiment with building a spiral ramp before tackling the Guggenheim.

The Guggenheim Museum, completed in 1959, is a large, open, upturned bowl with a sweeping, interior ramp that runs around the sides of the curving walls, which function as the exhibition spaces. Asked why he chose a ramp of this kind, Wright explained that it was for the convenience of visitors. They could take an elevator to the top of the building, and then make a leisurely descent to the exit. Perversely, most wander up the ramp rather than down it.

At about the same time, Eero Saarinen's TWA terminal building at Kennedy Airport used gently rising and falling ramp-tunnels through which travelers walked from the main building to the departure lounges.

The spaciousness of outdoor ramps has always been appealing. In 1994, to provide a more open view for students at Columbia University, who might otherwise have been confined to stairs and elevators, architect Bernard Tschumi produced

The Finnish architect Eero Saarinen exploited the plastic qualities of concrete and steel in many of his buildings, notably in the bold sculptural forms of the TWA terminal at Kennedy Airport, New York, where he tied the interior together with curving ramps.

sketches resembling the Khorsabad ziggurat of antiquity. But the executed design for Columbia's new student center, Lerner Hall, on the Upper West Side in New York, did not quite follow the plan. To fit into the nineteenth-century campus, which was designed by the neoclassical architects McKim, Mead & White, Tschumi constructed two cubes that followed the Flemish-bond brick pattern of the historic buildings and joined them together with hanging ramps that are encased in a glass-walled structure.

The open-sided, multi-story spiral ramp of the Guggenheim Museum, New York, is the heart of the building. Not just a means of access, the ramp is the exhibition space. Some have criticized Frank Lloyd Wright's unorthodox design for being too dominant and overshadowing the works of art displayed there.

Great Mosque of al-Mutawakkil
Samarra, Iraq

The Great Mosque, or Malwiya, of al-Mutawakkil, begun in CE 847, is located in the city of Samarra on the east bank of the Tigris, 78 miles (125 km) north of Baghdad.

The largest mosque ever to have been built, much of its massive outer brick walls remains, as does the external structure of the Spiral Minaret, but the interior of the complex has long since disappeared. The Malwiya has been described as one of the most striking constructions in the history of Islamic architecture.

The Hypostyle Mosque

Over the centuries, mosques have had different forms. Most familiar today are those that have massive central domes, which were introduced by the Ottoman Turks in the fifteenth century, but they are a comparatively late development.

In the days of the Umayyad and 'Abbasid dynasties, which ruled the Islamic world from CE 660 to 1055, the favored mosque design was the "hypostyle" or congregational type. These were either square or rectangular complexes, with massive outer walls and an inner covered courtyard for prayer.

The Malwiya

Samarra's Great Mosque of al-Mutawakkil was of the hypostyle type. It consisted of an immense rectangular courtyard, measuring about 780 by 510 ft (238 by 155 m)—a ratio of about two to three—enclosed in high, bastioned walls of fired brick that were 8 ft (2.4 m) thick.

Integrated into the walls were 44 half-round towers, including a tower at each of the corners, 28 windows, and 16 gateways. Running along the upper course of the buttressed walls was a series of large-paneled decorative friezes. These walls were themselves enclosed by an extensive *ziyada*, or outer courtyard, which was around 42 acres (17 ha) in area.

Although the supporting brickwork collapsed long ago, it is clear that the flat, timber-roofed porticoes surrounding the inner courtyard were supported on mud-brick piers, nine rows deep on the *qibla* side at the south (the mosque's prayer chamber), three rows deep on the *riwaq*, or cloister, side opposite, and four rows deep on the two sides. As is the Islamic custom, the rectangular *mihrab* with two marble columns on each side was situated in the southern wall.

The immense, buttressed brick walls that encircle the Great Mosque of al-Mutawakkil in Samarra appear to have been built for defensive purposes. On the inside, they would probably have been richly decorated with fields of glass mosaics, pieces of which have been found on the site.

The Spiral Minaret is centered on the mosque's north side, 89 ft (26.5 m) from the walls.

The Malwiya's solid, brick, buttressed walls reflect the divisions that were raging within and outside the 'Abbasid dynasty in the middle of the ninth century. Al-Mutawakkil commissioned the mosque upon succeeding to the 'Abbasid caliphate. Military impregnability, an idea current at the time, seems to have influenced the design. The form is repeated in the nearby Mosque of Abu Dulaf, built by al-Mutawakkil in Samarra a decade later. This later mosque also included the Malwiya's distinctive helical ramp built around an immense core.

Glass mosaics are common at the site. For this reason, and clear evidence of its plan, it has been claimed that the Malwiya may be stylistically

At the top of the Spiral Minaret is a round, flat-topped pavilion, which contains eight long niches with pointed arches. The top part of the minaret was damaged by a bomb in April, 2005, during the Iraq War.

It is not known how the Spiral Minaret's interior was configured. Although archaeologists have driven some exploratory tunnels through various Mayan and Toltec pyramids in Mexico, to undertake any similar investigations in the mosque in Samarra would be likely to encounter strong religious opposition.

It is believed that the first mosques lacked minarets. Initially, the *adhān*, or call to prayer, was chanted from the roof or the top of the city walls. Then, early in the eighth century, at Medina, four corner towers were introduced to the mosque. Some historians have speculated that these were related to a form of lighthouse tower with a lantern on top, but most believe that the ramped cone minaret seen at Samarra derives its shape from the ziggurats of ancient Mesopotamia and, specifically, that the ramp winding around the Spiral Minaret owes its configuration to the form of the ziggurat in the Palace of Khorsabad complex in northern Iraq, which was constructed about 17 centuries earlier.

The unusual form of the cone-shaped minaret seems to have lodged deep in the European imagination. Pieter Brueghel the Elder's 1563 painting of the *Tower of Babel* has been described as an elaborate architectural interpretation of the Spiral Minaret. It is notable, however, that in his painting Brueghel has imposed on the tower a detailed arched façade and a most complicated interior structure—like a honeycomb—of rooms and what appears to be the skeleton of an earlier structure that has been built over.

compared with the Great Mosque of Damascus, completed in CE 715—the oldest extant hypostyle mosque. It is also thought that the inner arcades of the Samarra mosque were repeated by the architects of the Mosque of Ahmed ibn Tulun in Cairo, built between CE 876 and 879.

The Spiral Minaret

The massive cone-shaped minaret, about 165 ft (50 m) high, is encircled by a long external spiral ramp, with shallow steps, that winds five times around the structure counterclockwise. They begin on the side that is closest to the mosque itself. The diminishing circuits of the tower are equidistant, so that the ramp rises more sharply as it ascends to the sky.

The Spiral Minaret (above) is placed centrally on the northern side of the mosque, a tradition that was introduced by the Umayyad, the first dynasty of the Muslim caliphate, at the Great Mosque of Damascus 150 years earlier.

The stepped, spiral outer ramp (right) that encircles the Spiral Minaret at Samarra is reminiscent of those of the ancient Assyrian ziggurats. The square base of the minaret measures 355 sq ft (33 sq m) and is almost 10 ft (3 m) high.

Steps

steps climb to entrances; indeed, they are often the most important element in an entranceway. They give visual emphasis and are used to mark the boundaries between public and private spaces and between different areas within a building. They also provide vantage points for viewing the surroundings. But most of all they elevate, getting people and buildings off the ground.

The horizontal surface of a step is called a tread; the vertical surface is known as the riser. A well-constructed set of steps, with the risers of uniform height and treads of equal depth, should be installed on a comfortable gradient. Shapes range from the simplest—a single squared step— to complex spirals and U-shaped entranceways.

Types of Steps

A log cut with deep notches, as used as entrance steps up to a Dayak longhouse in Borneo, or a ladder in a stone farmhouse in Europe are the simplest types of steps.

Architecturally, it might seem an enormous distance from such constructions to the steps on the face of a Mayan pyramid or the massive and imposing approach to the Sydney Opera House. Yet the notched log and the stepped ascent to the Opera House both serve a similar function: using less space but more effort than a ramp, they enable pedestrians, one foot after another, to get where they need to go.

The Minoan palaces of Phaestos and Knossos, in Crete, prominently feature steps. Phaestos,

placed high on a hill, is the most dramatically— and strategically—situated of the Cretan palaces. Archaeologists have determined that an original structure was rebuilt in *c.* 1700 BCE. Excavations of the west courtyard have exposed some of the ancient exterior and they show broad converging flights of unprotected steps that lead down to a paved area below.

The internal flights of shallow steps at Knossos wind up and down what are in effect light wells. One of these open-sided flights of steps, added after earthquake damage around 1600 BCE, is monumental in scale. Throughout the palace, steps are used to accentuate the importance of spaces and rooms: for example, the throne room is set a few steps above its anteroom.

By the time of Periclean Greece in the mid-fifth century BCE, steps were being employed in a variety of ways in the eastern Mediterranean region. Athenians visiting the Agora, or market, used steps leading from one level to another, and on up to the Acropolis above. The traditional long, narrow Greek temples are famous for their ornate friezes and pediments, and for the various orders of their columns—principally the Doric and Ionic. The columns gained some of their effect by resting directly on a "crepidoma," which consists of three horizontal stone steps, as can be seen in the Parthenon. Likewise, the Romans typically grounded their temples on a stepped base or confined the steps to the front elevation.

The Aegean structures that utilized the step to the greatest advantage were the open-air theaters and the stadia used for athletic contests. Initially, the seating was of wood, but by the middle of the fourth century BCE these theaters were regularly constructed with integrated stone seating, as can be seen at the Colosseum in Rome and at the amphitheater at Epidarus in Greece.

The genius of Antonio Palladio can be seen in the Villa Rotonda, outside Vicenza, Italy. Completed in 1569, the villa has a remarkable symmetrical plan. On each of the four façades, flights of steps rise to an identical pedimented portico leading to a domed circular hall.

The Maison Carrée, at Nîmes in southern France (below), is the most complete remaining example of Roman temple architecture of the Augustan period. Built in 16 BCE, it is approached by steps to the deep porch.

Vitruvius on Temple Steps

The Roman architect, Marcus Vitruvius Pollio, in *Ten Books on Architecture*, written in the first century BCE and greatly influential during the Renaissance years, lays out the specifications for the steps of a temple: "The steps in front must be arranged so that there shall always be an odd number of them; for thus the right foot, with which one mounts the first step, will also be the first to reach the level of the temple itself. The rise of such steps should, I think, be limited to not more than ten nor less than nine inches [25 nor less than 22.5 cm]; for then the ascent will not be difficult. The treads of the steps ought to be made not less than a foot and a half [45 cm], and not more then two feet deep [60 cm]. If there are to be steps running all round the temple, they should be built of the same size."

Giacomo Vignola created an extensive, impressive series of sweeping steps and terraces at the Villa Farnese in Caprarola, central Italy (below). Water ripples down a curved pool in the middle of steps leading to the *casino*, a separate garden lodge.

The south façade of Kedleston Hall in Derbyshire, England (above), was designed by Robert Adam around 1765; the house was the work of several architects. Adam emphasized the entrance to the saloon with four freestanding columns and a pair of curving flights of steps down to the garden.

The Renaissance and Later

Nearly two millennia later, the Italian architects of the Renaissance built a variety of structures using steps for quasi-theatrical effect. Antonio Palladio's Villa Rotonda outside Vicenza is an unusual bi-axially symmetrical edifice with four identical Ionic façades approached by imposing, matching flights of steps. More dramatically, Palladio later used stone seating in his Teatro Olimpico, completed in Vicenza in 1580.

At Caprarola, Giacomo Vignola used a series of elaborately shaped steps and terraces—the pair of curved flights at the bottom stretch up to a terrace, from which two symmetrical zigzags lead to the main entrance—as a dramatic approach to the Villa Farnese, completed in 1573. A century later, when the church of Santa Maria della Pace in Rome was given a baroque restoration by Pietro da Cortona, he altered the church's façade by adding a protruding semi-oval porch with matching semi-oval steps to visually emphasize the elaborate entranceway.

Such spectacular entranceways were matched by later architects—for instance, in eighteenth-century Britain by Lord Burlington at Chiswick House, London, and Robert Adam at Kedleston Hall in Derbyshire—who incorporated multiple sets of matching flights of steps into the front elevations of large houses and used the terraced landings and balustrading as integral ornamental features to dramatic effect.

Tikal
Petén Province, Guatemala

Scaling the heights, both as a physical fact and as a sacred gesture, mainly inspired the monumental buildings of pre-Columbian Mexico: steps and stairs were everywhere. Just north of modern Mexico City is the early city of Teotihuacan (CE 100–650). There, a variety of pyramidal structures line the Avenue of the Dead, leading from the Pyramid of the Moon past the Pyramid of the Sun, most of them having flights of steps on more than one face.

The Aztecs, and the Maya in Yucatan and Guatemala, carried the pyramid to extremes. At the Mayan site of Chich'en Itza, from about CE 600, the stepped pyramid of the Temple of Kukulcan has stairways on all four sides, whereas at Tikal stepped and gently graded forecourts cover large areas of the total site.

The City of Tikal

Along with the rest of Mayan civilization, the city of Tikal flourished between the years CE 250 and 910. By the eighth century, its population was believed to have been around 50,000, with five temple pyramids up to 235 ft (70 m) tall.

Tikal, the largest city of the Mayans, was built on lowland rainforest. There are no rivers, lakes or springs in the immediate vicinity: it had no water and had to rely on what seasonal rainwater was collected and stored in reservoir basins and underground storage facilities. It was also reliant on intensive agricultural techniques.

Although only a small proportion have been excavated, thousands of structures were built at Tikal. Temple complexes comprised pyramids, ball courts, temples, and palaces, all of which were linked by broad causeways.

It is in the classic period after CE 550 when the pyramids of Tikal reached their soaring climax, topped with elevated temples. Each of the temples had two or three separate vaulted rooms; above the thickened rear wall of the temple was a high, tapering structure of sculptured masonry called a "roofcomb." Providing an architectural flourish, rather like a Mayan warrior's head-dress, these carved ornaments raised the total building height markedly. Pyramid I at Tikal is topped by the Temple of the Jaguar (known as Temple I) and rises to 148 ft (45 m). To its west and facing it is Pyramid II, standing 138 ft (42 m) high and supporting the Temple of the Masks. Pyramid III is 180 ft (55 m) high. Close to the Plaza of the Seven Temples stands Pyramid V, which is 187 ft (57 m) high. The highest of these monumental edifices is Pyramid IV at 213 ft (65 m), the westernmost of the major ruins and also the site of the Temple of the Two-Headed Serpent.

The upper steps leading to the temples on top of a pyramid might be fairly steep, with around

From the pyramid temple above the Central Acropolis high up in the Guatemalan rainforest the roofcombs of other Mayan pyramids can be seen. Uncovering the ruins is slow: at Tikal, it took 13 years to excavate about 10 sq miles (26 sq km) of buildings, plazas, and causeways.

Tikal was abandoned about a thousand years ago and soon was hidden in overgrown jungle. An Indian legend told of a lost city, but the Mayan ruins were not discovered until 1853, when a gumdigger caught sight of the temple roofcombs in the distance.

50 degrees of slope. In addition, there are shallow terraced stairways of considerable length, which lead from the base of individual pyramids to the plazas stretching before them. One of these is almost 240 ft (72 m) long, with a standing row of carved altars and stelae marking the boundary at the foot of the steps along the plaza's edge.

Tikal Uncovered

To archaeologists, the function of the Mayan pyramids was unclear at first. For many years it was supposed they were mainly for religious rituals associated with human sacrifice. It is known that Mayan captives, for example, might be taken to the top of the steps, bound tightly, and thrown down to their deaths. Something similar was observed by the earliest visitors to Mexico City in 1520: they described sacrificial victims being killed on the upper platform before the temple, the steep steps providing a kind of chute to the ground below.

In 1952, archaeologist Alberto Ruz Lhullier was excavating beneath a Mayan classic period structure at Palenque, a site to the west of Tikal. There he uncovered a burial chamber comparable to the Egyptian tombs, with a crypt 30 ft long and 13 ft wide (10 x 4 m), a high vaulted ceiling, and a monolithic and elaborately ornamented sarcophagus. Seven years later, archaeologist Aubrey S. Trik drove a series of tunnels through Temple I at Tikal. The tunnels made through the higher levels of the structure yielded little information. But the base of the pyramid was found to contain a vaulted burial chamber with a single male body, which was richly adorned with pearls, jade necklaces, bracelets, and anklets.

Also nearby were a variety of pottery vessels, an alabaster vase, and the decomposed remains of ocelot and jaguar pelts.

Tikal is the most impressive Mayan city found to date—and the largest excavated site in the Americas. Its central area covers about 6 sq miles (15.5 sq km) and, as well as the five major temple pyramids, it contains some 2,745 other structures, 2,200 of them small stone platforms. It is thought these were the foundations of family homes made of pole and thatch.

A major archaeological project undertaken by the University of Pennsylvania between 1956 and 1969 restored much of Temples I and II, along with most of the Central Acropolis in which they stand. Excavation and restoration work has been continued by a Guatemalan government project.

Beyond the Pyramid of El Mundo Perdido (the Lost World), in the foreground, is Temple IV, the highest building in Tikal. Two carved lintels found over the doorway leading into Temple IV on its pyramid's summit recorded a date that corresponds to CE 741.

Jared Diamond, in *Collapse*, his study of the causes of civilizational decline and fall, discusses some theories about the collapse of the Mayan civilization. Agriculture appears to have exhausted the available land and caused deforestation and erosion, aggravated by repeated droughts. Long-standing hostilities between Mayan tribal groups was another factor: "competition among kings and nobles ... led to a chronic emphasis on war and erecting monuments rather than on solving underlying problems."

stone balustrades without columns—solid walls of stone—were made by Nicola Pisano for the pulpits of the Pisa Baptistry and Siena Cathedral. A similarly massive style of early balustrade may be seen fronting the external pulpit by Donatello and Michelozzo for Prato Cathedral in 1428.

Renaissance Balustrades

The waisted or urn-shaped baluster which is commonly associated with the architecture of the Renaissance was unknown to the Romans, but isolated examples appeared in Donatello's sculptures, possibly derived from cabinetwork. The full-blown balustrade appeared in about 1480 in Florence and northern Italy, and was promoted by the architect Giuliano da Sangallo.

Michele Sanmicheli crowned the façade of Palazzo Canossa, built in the middle of the sixteenth century, with a boldly projecting cornice, and a striking balustrade surmounted by a skyline of eight sculptured figures, all taller than the balustrade itself. For sheer length, the balustrades on the rusticated façade of the Pitti Palace in Florence are exceptional. Designed by Brunelleschi around 1440, and purchased by the Medicis in 1550, the Pitti Palace has a balcony crossing the entire façade, linking the windows.

The extensive formal gardens which were attached to the villas of the Renaissance nobility in Italy made wide use of balustrades—flanking flights of steps, around the margins of artificial ponds and lakes, framing fountains, and defining terraces. Some of these various uses can be seen at Frascati, on the Alban Hills overlooking Rome,

Balustrades

A balustrade is a low protective barrier to stop people falling over the edge—externally, of a roof, a balcony, a long window, a garden terrace, an ornamental pool; and, internally, of a landing or a staircase. The "see-through" aspect of the balustrade is very important. It provides two planes for the eye to dwell on: near and far.

The vertical pillars are called balusters. There is usually a substantial molded rail along the top, and the whole structure is called a balustrade. There is almost no ornamental shape that has not been tried with balusters, including bulbs, upright vases, inverted vases, double bulbs, barley twists—which are separated and spaced by torus (a convex, semicircular profile)—and varieties of foliate additions as well. The architects of the Modern Movement favoured simple posts, often of extruded metal.

Externally, balustrades may form a parapet fronting balconies and terraces, and in this role are used as the crowning features of high façades.

These unsafe locations remind us of the original purpose of balustrades: on buildings such as Hardwick Hall in Derbyshire, England, or the Libreria Sansoviniana in St. Mark's Square in Venice, a substantial barrier around the roofline would have reassured those repairing the roof.

The earliest example of a balustrade may be Assyrian: there are window balustrades on ancient Mesopotamian reliefs. But neither the Greeks nor Romans allowed them to interfere with the severe lines of buildings in antiquity.

On rare occasions, the term balustrade may denote merely an internal division within a church. For example, in San Clemente in Rome, which was rebuilt in the early twelfth century on the ruins of a basilica, the barrier used to separate the nave and choir from the altar is described as a balustrade. In some Romanesque and Gothic churchs, the triforium—arcaded wall—above the nave was wide enough to accommodate a gallery or passage and was fronted by a balustrade. Later, in Italy at the end of the medieval period, carved

In the Library of the Cistercian Monastery of Fuerstenzell, in Lower Bavaria, Germany (above), which was built in the eighteenth century, the sculptures on the balustrade gallery are allegorical figures on the theme of honest and dishonest discourse.

Extravagant iron balustrades edge the undulating balconies of Casa Milà in Barcelona, Spain (below), by Antoni Gaudí. Gaudí grew up around metal—his father was a coppersmith—and many of his eccentric buildings are enriched with freely interpreted Gothic and Art Nouveau motifs in iron.

especially in the gardens of the Villa Torlonia and the Villa Aldobrandini, and in the Teatro delle Acque at the Villa Lancellotti.

Renaissance architects differed greatly as to the importance they gave balustrades as a design feature. In Michele Sanmicheli's Madonna di Campagna in Verona the low balustrade around the top of the drum seems trivial, out of scale, superfluous, and an afterthought. On the other hand, in Donato Bramante's Tempietto in the Cloister of San Pietro in Montorio, Rome—which is widely recognized as a masterly study in proportion—the balustrade is an essential element that harmonizes the architectural composition as a whole.

Balustrades beyond Italy

The balustrades which were introduced by the Italian Renaissance soon spread throughout Europe. The Antwerp Town Hall, dating from the mid-sixteenth century, shows both Flemish and Italian influences. It employs a number of small balcony-type balustrades for individual windows on the second and third floors, and a long continuous balustrade separating the third and fourth floors that provides a horizontal emphasis, anticipating the roofline above.

In France, the small, graceful, neoclassical château of the Petit Trianon, which was built in the grounds of the Palace of Versailles by Ange-Jacques Gabriel and completed in 1768, has façades dominated by Corinthian columns and pilasters, with crowning balustrades in a darker finish than the stone walls below to create a high and commanding effect.

Impressive examples of balustrades from Elizabethan England include Longleat House in Wiltshire (1572), designed by Robert Smythson, and the same architect's Hardwick Hall (1590–1597) in Derbyshire. A fine work by Inigo Jones from the early seventeenth century, the Banqueting House in Whitehall, showed that by then England had fully assimilated the principles of Palladio.

In the early twentieth century, balustrades developed in markedly different directions. Casa Milà in Barcelona, designed by Antoni Gaudí and built between 1905 and 1910, has the surfaces of its façade sculptured in fleshy organic contours, with a profusion of Art Nouveau vines and leaves of ironwork barricading its balconies. Even Charles Rennie Macintosh, on his Glasgow School of Art, added an ironwork flourish to his simple and austere modernism. Walter Gropius and the other Bauhaus architects were more streamlined, preferring rounded metal railings and banisters, unadorned with ornamentation, for interiors and exteriors alike.

Staircases

Although stairs may appear to be much the same as steps, there are a number of differences. Stairs are usually "encased" by balustrades and walls—hence the word "staircase"—whereas steps of any architectural significance are more usually unconfined and are often open to the weather, at least on one side.

In contrast, staircases are interior. The one in London's Ritz Hotel, completed in 1905, shows something closed and exclusive, securely balustraded to prevent falls, and as safe, private, warm, and waterproof as the hotel's wealthy patrons expected. Staircases may be straight or curved, spiral or dog-legged. They may also be grandiose and theatrical, like the wide, sweeping marble stairs that curve from auditorium to the entrance in the Paris Opera. Or they may be as mean as the stairwell of a tenement.

Staircases always have a sense of containment, which contrasts markedly with the sense of truly public space that is conveyed by external flights of steps in the open air.

Types of Staircases

The precursor of the staircase would have been the simple ladder. In the ancient world, staircases were generally straight and a key feature that we know appears to have been missing—there's little evidence of banisters and balustrades. In the Great Temple of Ammon at Karnak is found a staircase with a "dog-leg" turn, which consists of two flights of stairs, the upper set at 180 degrees from the lower flight, that are separated by a landing—this is known as a "quarter-turn" staircase. But the building of antiquity which made use of staircases on a scale seldom seen before or since was the Colosseum in Rome. With endless passages leading up and down to allow the free movement of around 50,000 spectators, it has been described as "a veritable palace of stairs and vestibules."

Early Italian Renaissance architecture of the kind represented by Filippo Brunelleschi and Leon Battista Alberti tended to regard staircases as utilitarian necessities that were to be hidden

The two spiral staircases at the Château of Chambord (above) cross and recross—but do not meet—as they climb to an equally elaborate 100 ft (30 m) lantern crowning the *terrasses*, or terraces, which were used as a promenade. The helical staircase is a great feat of design and engineering.

In contrast to the complexity of the double spiral at the Château of Chambord, the simple beauty of this narrow staircase in Cairo (left) is in the utilitarian way the materials have been shaped and fixed.

away between solid walls, accommodated in a separate "staircase room."

The privacy available with interior staircases—and even the possibility of romantic or political intrigue—is spectacularly displayed by the great double-spiral, or helical, design at the Château of Chambord, which was built in the Loire Valley between 1519 and 1547 as a hunting lodge for François I. Derived from an idea of Leonardo da Vinci's, the helical staircase features two spirals, each traveling opposite the other, but separated by a stone cylindrical wall in which occasional window openings have been cut. It was said that the double staircase enabled the king's visitors, when leaving, to avoid meeting their rivals on the way out—the multiple entries and exits on the three-story staircase are not in sight of each other.

At the Château of Chambord, the helical staircase is treated as an ornamental element in its own right, and it dominates the space around it. Situated at the intersection of two spacious corridors forming a cross, it is right in the center of the château. The stonework and balustrades are superb, and the cylindrical form is carried up even above the roofline, where a domed lantern rises over a variety of towers and chimney stacks to become the building's highest visible feature.

Once the staircase had emerged from being a minor interior utility, it rapidly turned into a spectacular architectural feature. For example, it might start in one flight, then at a landing split into two, or run up multiple flights around an open well. François I also commissioned the exuberant Renaissance architecture at the Château of Blois, where an open, cylindrical staircase appears as a nearly freestanding tower attached to the outer walls.

Parts of a Staircase

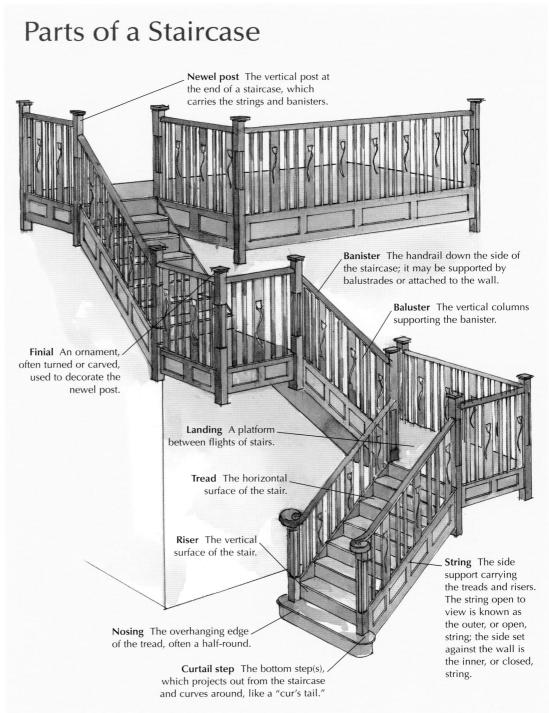

Newel post The vertical post at the end of a staircase, which carries the strings and banisters.

Banister The handrail down the side of the staircase; it may be supported by balustrades or attached to the wall.

Baluster The vertical columns supporting the banister.

Finial An ornament, often turned or carved, used to decorate the newel post.

Landing A platform between flights of stairs.

Tread The horizontal surface of the stair.

Riser The vertical surface of the stair.

Nosing The overhanging edge of the tread, often a half-round.

Curtail step The bottom step(s), which projects out from the staircase and curves around, like a "cur's tail."

String The side support carrying the treads and risers. The string open to view is known as the outer, or open, string; the side set against the wall is the inner, or closed, string.

Later Instances

Breaking with convention, in 1843 the neo-Gothic architect, Augustus Pugin, planned his house at Ramsgate, England, with a combined staircase room, hall, and living area. This was an arrangement that became a regular feature of Arts and Crafts homes. Henry Hobson Richardson's Watts Sherman House in Newport, Rhode Island, for example, is centered around a large stair hall, as is McKim, Mead & White's Isaac Bell House, also in Newport.

Other adventurous designs may be theatrical in flavor and monumental in scale. Staircases such as those in the Paris Opera of 1861–1874 were intended to show off the splendors of the audience as much as anything else. Designed by Charles Garnier, the staircase competed in size and architectural attention with the main auditorium, being a theater-sized space with its own balconies and foyers. The same concept—that a staircase is the perfect place for fashionable people to see and be seen—found commercial expression at the new nineteenth-century Parisian department stores, notably the Bon Marché and Les Galeries Lafayette.

The exit staircase for the Vatican Museum, built in the 1930s, represents an elegant modern treatment of the spiral form, as do the stairs at the Jencks House of 1986 in London. Materials like steel and aluminium allow great variety in staircase design. This can be seen in the delicate treatment of verticals and rails in the basement staircase in the Aarhus City Hall and the curved flight at Roche Chemicals, Welwyn Garden City in England. New materials and techniques allow such variations as staircases without risers (with treads knitted into the fabric of the wall) and flying staircases secured at the top and bottom.

Laurentian Library
Florence, Italy

When Michelangelo Buonarroti (1475–1564) was asked to design a staircase, the prevailing view of stairs was utilitarian, an architectural element that was better kept out of sight. The sculptor-architect bent the usual straight edges into more attractive forms, and quite literally thought outside the box. In the case of staircases, the sides of the box are the balustrades. One of Michelangelo's most startling innovations at the Laurentian Library was to put the two lateral flights of the staircase outside the balusters.

The Library Building

Florence's Biblioteca Medicea Laurenziana, also known as the Laurentian or Medici Library, is the repository of nearly 11,000 rare manuscripts and early printed books. The library owes its existence to the patronage of the Medici pope, Clement VII, and the task of its design and construction was entrusted to Michelangelo. He began designs for the library in 1524, at the same time as he was working on his scheme for the Medici tombs, also in Florence. Built in the precinct of the San Lorenzo monastery, the library was accommodated by adding a story above the refectory, with access at one end through a vestibule in a cloister adjoining the church.

The reading room of the library is a long, harmonious space lit by windows placed in bays between pilasters that match the spacing of the ceiling beams above. Between two matching series of *plutei*, wooden benches that incorporate desks and lecterns, which extend the full length of the room, the red and white terracotta floor is decorated with designs that are echoed in the delicately carved ceiling.

The three-story-high entrance vestibule is the library's most original and striking feature. The walls are divided into three bays by pairs of columns that rise from the second-floor level with scroll-shaped corbels below. Within the bays are large tabernacle windows with fluted pilasters and heavy pediments above. The well-defined gray stone columns and windows against the light plaster walls create an effect that is rather like an external façade.

The Staircase

By the time Michelangelo left Florence for good in 1534, the vestibule and the reading room had been constructed but the library still lacked a staircase. A full 21 years later, in a letter dated September 28, 1555, Michelangelo wrote to the painter and biographer, Giorgio Vasari, from Rome—where he was engaged in the design of St. Peter's Basilica—describing his idea for the stairs. "A certain staircase comes to my mind just like a dream ... it seems so awkward," he wrote. "The central flight from the beginning of the stairs to half-way up should be reserved for the master. The ends of the two wings should face the walls and, with the entire staircase, come about three spans from the wall," Michelangelo instructed Vasari. He later sent a clay model of his design to Florence.

Using the same gray sandstone, *pietra serena*, as the columns, corbels, and windows of the vestibule walls (left), Michelangelo sculpted a massive staircase for a remarkably small floor area. Originally, he had wanted the staircase to be of walnut, which would have been more in harmony with the library above.

The work was executed in *pietra serena*, the same gray sandstone used on the vestibule walls, by the sculptor-architect Bartolomeo Ammanati with assistance from Vasari in 1559. The organic and naturalistic forms—the curving central steps—almost reverse the normal direction of pedestrian movement. In contrast to temple steps that lead the worshippers upward to an exclusive sanctuary, these stairs flowing out and down suggest the dissemination of knowledge from the library to the world beyond.

Michelangelo's remarkable ideas disturbed even his greatest admirers. His innovations—the flanking lateral flights of stairs that some said were hardly usable, with their extended corner platforms and protruding moldings; the central flight with each curved stair curling into a horizontal volute as it reaches the balustrade; the gabled niches in the walls—were a long way from the classicism of his architectural predecessors.

Michelangelo's Architectural Genius

One of the three projects at San Lorenzo that Michelangelo had committed himself to for the Medicis, the library took a long time to complete and was not finished until 1571, under the rule of Cosimo I. Michelangelo, who had gone to Florence in 1516, had undertaken the library and the design and construction of San Lorenzo's New Sacristy, but was dismayed by the political and military chaos in Florence under the Medicis. The death of the Medici pope, Clement VII, in 1534 freed him, enabling him to quit the city, and he left for Rome.

Vasari wrote later that, in the New Sacristy of San Lorenzo and the Laurentian Library, the ornamentation Michelangelo employed was "in a style more varied and more original than any other master, ancient or modern, has ever been able to achieve." The cornices and capitals, bases and doors, tabernacles and tombs, were extremely novel, "and in them he departed a great deal from the kind of architecture regulated by proportion, order, and rule which other artists did according to common usage."

Of the Laurentian Library, Vasari wrote that in its staircase Michelangelo "made such strange breaks in the design of the steps, and he departed in so many details and so widely from normal practice, that everyone was amazed."

It is hard to realize just how original the Laurentian stairs were, especially in the Italian context. Constrained by the expectation that a staircase should be put in its own enclosed and limited space, Michelangelo made the enclosing vestibule into a richly ornamented room with a roofline higher than the library itself. His clients

may have assumed that a few small steps were all that were needed to provide access to the books in the reading room. Michelangelo made them into an enduring work of art.

Every internal detail of the library—one of Michelangelo's first architectural projects—has survived intact, from the inlaid wooden desks and painted glass of the windows in the reading room to the monumental entrance vestibule with its massive stone steps flowing down to the herringbone-patterned floor. The outside of the vestibule, with strip buttresses and a series of pedimented blind windows, was completed in the early twentieth century to the architect's design.

The reading room of the Laurentian Library (above) was completed 47 years before the staircase, in 1524. Every detail of Michelangelo's design has remained intact. Vasari noted "the beautiful distribution of the windows, the pattern of the ceiling …"

In the central flight, each of the steps is curved into a graceful oval shape and ends in a curlicue of stone at the balustrade. This subtle ornamentation repeats the massive scrolls at the head of the two lateral flights.

Elevators

nce the elevator was perfected, in the mid-nineteenth century, tall, multi-story buildings became inevitable. Cities leapt skywards and the density of urban occupation grew radically. Steel construction had made skyscrapers possible as an engineering project, but without safe and efficient ways of getting aloft they were hardly practical. Soon thousands of people were able to live and work comfortably above small patches of ground.

History and Operation

For millennia, people had dreamed of lifting machinery, and a number of muscle-powered devices were tried. Archimedes experimented in ancient Greece and developed a hoist using ropes, pulleys, and a capstan. In CE 100, at the Colosseum in Rome, gladiators and wild animals rode manually operated elevators up from the basement area to the arena level when fights were ready to begin. Medieval records show men and supplies being lifted by hoist up to monasteries in baskets or nets, and at the Palace of Versailles

in France, Louis XV installed a personal elevator, operating on a rope-and-pulley system in 1743. Far from the glamorous precincts of Versailles, thousands of coalminers were riding perilously up and down mineshafts in tiny cages.

In 1853, Elisha Otis exhibited a passenger elevator for general use. He essentially obtained a US patent for two inventions that resembled similar applications for mine cages. The first was a ratchet rail in the side of the shaft to prevent slippage, which had been used by 1838 in Jones's Ascending and Descending Machine. The second was a mechanism that applies a brake when the suspension rope or chain is broken and had been used by Fourdrinier's Patent Safety Apparatus for mines before 1851. Otis held a demonstration of the new elevator before a large audience at the 1854 New York Crystal Palace Exposition. Going up in an open-sided elevator, he had an associate cut the rope holding the car with an axe. The platform held fast and the crowd roared; Otis cried, "All safe, gentlemen, all safe." The elevator industry was born—and so was the skyscraper.

Parts of an elevator

The car is raised and lowered on traction steel ropes that are rolled around a deeply grooved wheel, called a sheave. The weight of the car is balanced with a counterweight. Buffers are sprung safety devices designed to stop a descending car or counterweight beyond its normal limit.

Sheave

Traction steel ropes

Car

Counterweight

Buffers

Initially, elevator shafts and cars were made of open ironwork, like this decorative one at the *Daily Mail*'s offices in Fleet Street, London (left), integrated into the design of the staircase's balustrades.

Other inventors and engineers contributed to the development of the modern elevator: a hydraulic system was developed by William Armstrong; the electric elevators that began to appear in late nineteenth-century Europe were invented by the German, Werner von Siemens, in 1880. But it was Elisha Otis who made the breakthrough needed to persuade people that a machine could take them to dangerous heights safely. In 1889, elevators at the Eiffel Tower in Paris began providing reliable transport for the 200 million visitors who have been there since.

In modern elevators, the car is raised and lowered by traction steel ropes. Several steel-wire cables are looped around a sheave, which is a driven wheel with concave grooves in the circumference exactly fitting the convex strands of the cable. When an electric motor turns the sheave in either direction, the car is raised or lowered. An important additional feature is the counterweight hung on the opposite end of the cables; this weighs as much as the car when at forty five percent of capacity. As the car moves up and down the elevator shaft, the counterweight moves in the opposite direction. Computerized elevators are fast: those at the Taipei Financial Center move at 37.6 mph (60.5 kph).

Rooms with Views

The earliest elevators were regarded as wonders, and decorated as such. The design solution to the strange and suffocating atmosphere "nervous riders" experienced was to open up the cage compartment and make it into a room with a view. Open-cage elevators like those in the 1893 Bradbury Building in Los Angeles—which had a five-story staired atrium with ornate, exposed elevator towers in the center—pointed the way. By the 1920s, the elevator lobby had reached new heights of elegance, with elaborately ornamented metalwork doors in Art Deco style, such as those

The elevator of today is streamlined, fast, and, most of all, visible. Riders of the glass cars at the Grand Hyatt in Santiago, Chile (above), can look down into the hotel's atrium as they speed up 24 stories to the top of the tower—watched by those in the atrium.

Art Deco architects and designers embraced the elevator, seeing it as the embodiment of the machine age. The decorative metalwork on these elevator doors in the entrance lobby of 275 Madison Avenue, New York (left), are restrained compared with some of the extravagant designs of Edgar Brandt, then the leading maker of decorative ironwork.

in Cross & Cross's City Bank Farmers Trust Building in New York, or in Holabird & Root's Daily News Building in Chicago. The sparkling elevator lobby in the Daily Express Building in Fleet Street, London, designed by E. Owen Williams and completed in 1932, was faced in chromium steel. It is a masterpiece of Art Deco.

After nearly four decades of elevators being widely treated as utilitarian, in the modernist manner, the architect John Portman began to take a more show-business approach. He placed elevators in a central position so they dominated an architectural space. At the Hyatt Regency, Atlanta, USA, completed in 1967, then at the Embarcadero Center in San Francisco, Portman put his ideas to work, with visually arresting results. First, his hotels were to have vast, multi-story internal atrium spaces instead of cramped corridors; next, he pulled "the elevators out of the wall and [made] them like moving seats in a theater." He designed sparkling space capsules that would shoot up and down "like kinetic sculpture for those sitting and watching."

Escalators

There was no doubt about the benefits of escalators to the engineer who installed them in the London Underground around 1911: "The moving staircase is not merely an ineffable blessing to weary legs," he said, "it is perpetual motion itself, and should be treated with reverence and respect."

History of Escalators

The inventor of the modern escalator, a power-driven, continuous moving staircase with self-levelling horizontal steps, was Charles Seeberger, who also coined the name "escalator"—from *scala*, Latin for "steps" and "elevator." Drawing on a patent registered by G. A. Wheeler in 1892, and teaming with the Otis Elevator Company in 1899, Seeberger produced and displayed the first true escalator at the Paris Exposition Universelle in 1900. Before then, a number of designs had been patented for what were called "revolving stairs," "endless conveyors," or "magic stairways." All of these were really moving belts or ramps: an issue of *Scientific American* from 1900 that dealt with all the moving ramps exhibited at the Paris Exposition listed no fewer than 31 of them.

The most immediately successful of these was patented and built by Jesse W. Reno in 1892. It consisted of an inclined belt with cleats attached. The first of Reno's climbing ramps was installed as a novelty ride at Coney Island, New York, in 1896, followed by another at Bloomingdale's department store at Third Avenue in Manhattan two years later. A variation of Reno's design was still in use in the Boston subway until 1985. But genuine moving stairs were being developed and manufactured on both sides of the Atlantic by 1900. The Seeberger/Otis machine eventually won commercial acceptance.

Specifications and Operations

Escalators are mainly installed in public transport systems—at airports, and at entrances and exits from underground rail stations—and department stores and shopping malls, as well as hotels and other public buildings.

As a system of moving pedestrians efficiently, escalators have many advantages. They take up little space. They can be very long, they can move diagonally, and they can be weatherproofed for outside use. Another advantage over elevators is their high loading rate. An escalator moving at average speed can shift more than 10,000 people an hour—much more than a standard elevator. They are often installed in pairs, with one going up and the other going down.

Elevators vary a lot in the speed at which they travel, but most escalators move at a constant pace—between 90 and 180 ft (27 and 55 m) per minute. Anything slower makes one impatient; anything faster makes it hard to get on and off.

When the Pompidou Center in Paris, by Richard Rogers and Renzo Piano, was opened in 1977, it was widely critcized. The building's workings are exposed to view, most prominently the tubular escalator that rises in stages across the northwest elevation.

Parts of an Escalator

The drive mechanism of an escalator is powered by a motor. The steps are on tracks that are pulled through an endless loop by sprocket systems at the top and bottom of the escalator. The handrails move on separate tracks.

Handrail drive

Handrail

Step

Motor

Comb plate

Bottom sprocket assembly

The hidden machinery of the escalator itself consists of a pair of chains, one on each side of the stairs, that are looped around matching pairs of gears. A one-floor escalator would have the drive mechanism at the top or bottom with the power coming from a single 100-horsepower electric motor. By the ingenious use of two sets of wheels per step, which roll along separate tracks, the orientation of the steps changes at the top and the bottom of their travel, where they level out to make it easy for users to mount and dismount.

Combined with this ingenious mechanism is the "comb plate," an inconspicuous but necessary element. With fine, matching longitudinal cleats on the moving stairs and the stationary landings, the gap between stairs and landing at the comb is minimized, ensuring that objects do not get stuck between.

Modern Developments

Terminal 1 of Charles de Gaulle Airport, designed by Paul Andreu and opened in Paris in 1975, has an aerial labyrinth of transparent-topped escalators zigzagging above the main lobby. At the Pompidou Center in Paris, by architects Richard Rogers and Renzo Piano, the services and workings of the building are exposed: among the numerous external service ducts, the most prominent is the tubular escalator that rises in stages, from ground left to top right, across the building's northwest elevation.

"Spiral" elevators—which, in fact, are curved rather than true spirals—have been installed in a number of buildings since Mitsubishi finally developed one that worked in 1985. Earlier designers had patented spiral designs, and Reno and Seeberger developed versions for the London Underground, which were never operational.

A Useful Conveyor

When Jesse W. Reno patented his machine in 1892 he described it as "a new and useful conveyor or elevator." This was an understatement. Today, some say that escalators and moving sidewalks are central to modern urban life—and this seems to be the view of Harvard University. In its *Design School Guide to Shopping*, the university gives the machine 30 pages, claiming that "No invention has had the importance for and impact on shopping as the escalator. As an instrument of smoothness, the escalator triggered a vast new domain of construction, which—through the very smoothness of connection—we now inhabit almost without thought, and without any sense of its true scale or radicality."

From its earliest days, the escalator was embraced by the department store. This central system links floors of a big store in Birmingham, England, whisking shoppers from purchase to purchase.

Aesthetically, spiral escalators are a great improvement on longitudinal designs. They are space efficient, increase useable floor space, and give an impression of opulence and grandeur. Striking American installations can be seen at the Forum Shops at Caesar's Palace in Las Vegas, Nevada, and at the San Francisco Shopping Center. They are also found in a number of Japanese buildings: for example, an assortment of spiral and straight escalators work in combination at the Landmark Tower, in Yokohama Minato Mirai 21, and the Yamako Department Store in Kofu City has paired curved escalators.

The two 40-story towers of the Umeda Sky Building in Osaka, Japan, are linked on their uppermost floors by bridges and an escalator crossing the wide void in between. The 568-ft (173-m) high twin buildings, by architect Hiroshi Hara, were originally conceived as a four-tower "city of air" project.

Comfort and Light

According to the architect Le Corbusier, "the history of architecture is the history of the struggle for light, the struggle for the window." Humans have endeavored to improve the illumination, temperature, and humidity of buildings by designing different types of windows, and defying limitations of construction methods, and building materials.

Natural Light

The daily and seasonal variations in the movement of the sun, with their varying light and heat effects—which differ from one geographic region to another—have shaped architecture as much as they have the lives and habits of people. The sun's benefits have long been recognized as an opportunity and utilized.

Until the widespread introduction of artificial lighting, heating, and cooling, daylight dictated the rhythm of getting up and going to bed. It set up work and rest schedules; defined the types of clothing worn and food eaten; decided the size, shape, and orientation of openings in buildings; and formed the typology of architecture.

Daylighting in Architecture

Daylighting is the practice of providing effective natural light from the sun as the main source of illumination in internal spaces. This is achieved by the careful design and placement of buildings, rooms, and windows.

Daylight offers many benefits. It provides for healthy environments, comfortable room temperatures and illumination levels, enhances the sense of spaciousness, adds aesthetic quality, and helps energy efficiency by reducing demand for electrical lights and air conditioning. It does have some disadvantages, however: because it is closely related to weather conditions, the time of the day, and the orientation of the building, it is unpredictable. Shading by nearby buildings, hills, and vegetation also affects the amount of light that penetrates into a room. Windows that allow too much direct sunlight may create unpleasant glare and excessive brightness.

For most of history, architects aimed to orient a building and design windows large enough to distribute daylight into interior spaces, without jeopardizing the thermal comfort by any excessive heat gain or loss. In his *Memorabilia*, written around 400 BCE, Xenophon mentions Socrates teaching that in "houses with a south aspect, the sun's rays penetrate into the porticoes in winter, but in summer the path of the sun is right over our heads and above the roof, so that there is shade … we should build the south side loftier

The glass dome of the Reichstag, Berlin, Germany, contains a mirrored cone that draws daylight down into the parliamentary chamber below. At night, the reverse is true: artificial light from the chamber strikes the mirrors and illuminates the dome.

to get the winter sun and the north side lower to keep out the cold winds." Socrates was referring to the Northern Hemisphere, of course.

In the twentieth century, however, innovations in the use of gas, electricity, and oil, as well as the development of new building materials and construction techniques, led to climatic factors and daylighting being largely neglected as design criteria. By the 1960s, most office buildings were air-conditioned, artificially lit, and completely sealed—and a growing number of people were affected by "sick building syndrome," with acute physical symptoms that appeared to be linked to occupancy of a particular building.

Nowadays, the overall architectural design of a building is influenced by efficient artificial light sources, improved glazing, new materials and processes, as well as by environmental health issues. Particular attention is given to daylighting to maximize visual comfort and productivity, and to reduce energy consumption.

Bringing Daylight into Interiors

There are many ways in which daylight can be brought into an interior: through a wall-mounted window (sidelight), a skylight on the roof, a roof monitor (toplight), and an atrium.

The simplest way of directing daylight into deeper parts of interiors is by the use of internal glazed doors or windows, and of grilles or screens in partition walls. However, these are not very efficient since daylight coming from a vertical window can only efficiently illuminate an area of up to 17 to 25 ft (5 to 8 m) from the source.

Taking the daylight from the top of a building through skylights, clerestory windows, and light scoops is useful; however, these mainly illuminate the top floors. The glass cupola of the Reichstag, the German Parliament Building in Berlin which was restored by Norman Foster in 1999, serves natural ventilation and daylighting functions. Its huge "light sculpture" or "daylight chandelier" is a 75-ft (23-m) tall inverted cone that is fitted with hundreds of mirrors: the daylight is filtered through a moveable screen, before it strikes the mirrors—thus reducing solar gain and glare—and then is directed downward to illuminate the parliamentary chamber below.

A number of devices have been invented to redirect sunlight inside a building efficiently. They either reflect daylight towards ceilings and walls, which in turn act as diffusers and provide soft and even lighting to the room, or directly diffuse the light themselves. The light shelf is mounted on the upper part of a side window and is protected by a shading device. The shelf projects beyond the shadow that is created by the shading device and reflects sunlight inside, towards the ceiling, from where it bounces off into the room. The light shelf dates back to the ancient Egyptians, as do light pipes and light tubes. These light-capturing systems are placed on the rooftop or the façade and redirect light down into the building through highly reflective cylinders. Recent developments include laser-cut panels and heliostats employing mirrors and sun-directing glass.

Atriums and light wells allow daylight to reach multiple levels. Atriums open up the internal space to the outdoors, usually with a glazed roof and/or large windows. The wealthy Roman town houses at Pompeii abutted each other and had no windows on the street façades. Inside, however, was a central atrium that provided daylight to the rooms that opened onto it. Similarly, the inward-looking house in hot-arid regions, such as Iraq, Egypt, Algeria, Spain, and Mexico, has very few external openings but possesses a small oasis of shaded courtyard, cooled by a pool or fountain, surrounded by rooms and/or high walls. The world's tallest atrium is the 600-ft (180-m) high Burj Al Arab in Dubai, completed in 1999.

Light and Shadow

Sunlight creates sharp contrasts with a play of light and shadow on architectural surfaces, which enhances the visual impact of the details. The shallow carvings on Hellenistic period columns or Roman reliefs in the sunny Mediterranean region do not have the same visual impact when replicated in countries with different daylight conditions. At the Alhambra, in Granada, Spain, for example, the sunlight catches the elaborately detailed carved stucco walls. In contrast, in regions where overcast conditions prevail, traditionally interiors were designed to admit a vast quantity of soft light, as in the great medieval cathedrals of Europe.

In a traditional Japanese house (above), sliding *shoji* screens, made of paper mounted on a wooden lattice, are used to close off rooms. The screen's translucence allows daylight into the house's interior.

The atrium in the House of the Vettii, at Pompeii, Italy (below), from before CE 79, allowed daylight into the rooms that opened onto it. This design was typical of elegant Roman town houses of the time.

Types of Windows

The word window comes from the Old Norse, *vindauga*, combining "wind" and "eye." Windows are significant façade elements that convey important information about the building—its historical context, its type of construction, technical developments, and availability of materials—through the rhythm created by their position, spacing, size, materials, style, and decoration. The use of large window openings with a thin skeleton on the façade may give a building an open, inviting appearance, whereas the sparing use of small windows tends to make a closed and protected impression. The design and placement of the windows through the façade also help identify and interpret the building's climatic region and cultural context.

A window is usually composed of a frame, which is divided into three parts: the architrave, or head, is the horizontal member at the top; the sill is the horizontal ledge at the bottom, which extends beyond the wall to direct water away from the wall under the window; and the jamb, or side post, at each side of the frame. Mullions are the vertical bars that divide the glass panels. Transom bars divide the window horizontally, and transom lights, or fan lights, are separate windows above a window or door. Lintel, flat arch, and platband are the terms used for a wood, steel, or stone horizontal member that is placed

over a window (or door) opening to support the weight of the wall above.

The Function of Windows

Windows control the passage of daylight, air, and sound into a building, keep the weather out, and frame the view from the inside. They are normally glazed with single or double layers of glass, depending on the harshness of the climate.

In ancient times, windows were simple holes in stone walls. These holes were covered with animal hide, fabric, or wood to shield the interior from the weather. A later development was the use of shutters that could be opened and closed. In the earliest glass windows, the panes (called lights) were either fixed or set into side-hung casements. By 1700, vertical sash windows had became popular and remained in fashion until the early twentieth century, when manufactured metal and wood casements became cheaper.

If the purpose of windows is only to admit daylight, they are usually sited high above floor level, so that the light can penetrate deep into the interior. The glazing may be translucent, which allows the daylight to be diffused and illuminate all parts of the room. There is no leakage of air because the glass is permanently sealed to the window frame. Windows designed solely for the view may be fixed and therefore have no hinges,

counterweights, or locks. The edges can be sealed with caulking materials. They are easy to build on site and are glazed with transparent sheets of glass. They can be further protected by inside shutters, operated manually. For most effective ventilation, windows should be installed at near-ceiling height and close to the floor: when they are open, cooler air enters the room via the lower vents and warmer air escapes via the upper ones.

Window Styles

Until the seventeenth century, window openings were wide, low, and divided by mullions, as larger panes of glass were still difficult to produce. The mullions, along with the lintel, sill, and jambs, were chamfered inside-out. After 1730, windows had fewer mullions and the proportions changed: they were squarer and taller. In the early 1800s, windows had no side casing, only a top lintel and a bottom sill.

No major changes occurred for window types until the end of the nineteenth century, when the Art Nouveau designers introduced a wide range of decorative windows. The twentieth century brought a range of innovations, among which were curtain walls (in the Seagram Building in New York, for example) and Le Corbusier's strip windows (that stretched along an entire wall of a building, as in his Villa Savoye at Poissy, France).

in the sky, and to heat loss during cold periods. Dormer windows, which are placed vertically in a sloping roof and have a roof of their own, deliver less light, and also have the heating and cooling problems of other rooflights.

Clerestory windows are placed at the upper level of walls, often above the main roofline, allowing light into a space. They originated in Egyptian temples, and are commonly found in Roman basilicas and Gothic cathedrals. The use of row upon row of sawtooth-shaped windows was widely used in factories, particularly in the nineteenth and early twentieth centuries. These windows are useful ways of providing daylight in an interior without the distractions of a view or compromising the privacy of the inhabitants.

Decorative Window Styles

Bay windows are often associated with Victorian architecture. They project out from the exterior wall of a building and may extend to the ground. They create a rectangular or polygonal space inside the building, forming a bay. The glazed, projecting bay area has at least three glass panels set at different angles, the most commonly used angles being 90, 135, and 150 degrees. These windows give the illusion that the room is larger, increase the amount of daylight in the space, provide natural ventilation by capturing breezes,

Clerestory windows high up in the dome spread diffuse light through the richly decorated interior of the Süleymaniye Mosque in Istanbul, Turkey, which was designed by the chief imperial architect, Sinan, and completed in 1575.

In the twenty-first century, windows have evolved into elements which can be easily controlled to protect the inhabitants from the weather and to domesticate daylight.

High Windows

Roof windows, which are installed on sloping surfaces, are more exposed to the weather than other types of windows, and therefore are more complicated to construct, and more expensive. Skylights are built into the roof structure, facing the sky. A roof lantern, also called a cupola or a roof monitor, is a multi-paned glass structure, that is built onto a roof to capture daylight or moonlight. These types of windows allow light into interiors, especially into dark central areas, where there are no possibilities for a vertical window. They also admit more light than vertical windows do, and they distribute it uniformly in the space. Although they do provide effective natural ventilation in warm seasons (if they can be opened), these types of windows are also prone to excessive heat gain when the sun is high

One of the masterpieces of modernist architecture, Mies van der Rohe's 1958 Seagram Building on Park Avenue, New York, is sheathed in curtain walls of bronze glass. The perfectly proportioned building has been widely imitated, but never surpassed.

Window Openings

There are various types of window openings: the kind used depends on the style of the building and the function of the window—whether it is to provide daylight or ventilation, frame the views, or keep the weather out.

CASEMENT WINDOW

This swings open, generally to the outside, on hinges like a door. The hinges may be hung at the side, top, or bottom.

DOUBLE-HUNG WINDOW

Also called a guillotine window due to its tendency to fall down. Recessed within the wall thickness, the window is in two separate parts (or sashes), one upper and one lower. Each sash slides up and down, one in front of the other, in a separate channel, supported at the sides by a cord, metal band, or chain, attached to a heavy counterweight.

LOUVER OR JALOUSIE WINDOW

A louver or jalousie window is made up of a number of slats of glass fitted into side frames; these are hinged to a fixed runner at the sides. The window can be opened and closed in the same way as a Venetian blind.

AWNING WINDOW

A top-hung hinged casement window. Awning windows are commonly used above, below, or next to a fixed glass section for ventilation.

SLIDING WINDOW

Sliding on horizontal runners at top and bottom, these windows can accommodate large panels of glass and may extend from floor to ceiling. Construction of a sliding window is relatively complex, making it more expensive than most other types of windows.

BAY WINDOW

Bay windows project out from an elevation. Inside the building they create a rectangular or polygonal space. The projecting glazed area has at least three glass panels set at different angles, the most commonly used angles being 90, 135 and 150 degrees. Bow and oriel windows are types of bay windows.

and offer better exterior views. Bay windows make it possible to increase the glass area in a wall opening without increasing the size of the opening itself.

Bow and oriel windows project out from the building, too. Also called a compass or radial bay window, a bow window is a rounded bay window in the shape of an arc and usually has five sashes. The oriel is a form of bay window projecting from the upper story of a building, supported on brackets, cantilevered arms, or decorative corbels.

Originally, the metal or wooden overlapping criss-crossed pattern, either diamond- or square-shaped, in lattice windows was made by glazing bars holding the pieces of glass together. Modern lattices do not hold the glass, but are decorative devices, and can pop in and out of the frame or are embedded between two insulating glass panes.

French windows, or French doors, consist of pairs of glazed, floor-length casement doors with multiple window lights. They usually open onto a balcony or garden, or are used between rooms.

One of the defining features of modernist architecture is the glazed curtain wall, an exterior wall, mainly composed of large glass panels, that does not carry any vertical load but must resist the wind load. The glass panes are hung on metal frames. The panels between the windows, called spandrel panels, are made of metal, thin slabs of concrete, stone veneers, acrylics, or opaque glass.

Church Lights

The windows of Gothic cathedrals were at first lancets, slender openings with a pointed head, sometimes paired or grouped beneath a circular window, which in England and northern Italy might be divided by radial spokes, called a wheel window. In France, the larger and more delicately

Lattice Windows

Unglazed lattice windows have ornate panels—carved out of wood, marble or stone, or made of timber strips—for ensuring privacy, shading, and letting in breeze. Many beautiful examples can be seen in India, Japan, Yemen and other parts of the Middle East, and at the Alhambra in Granada, Spain. In Chinese and Japanese houses, internal lattice windows covered with paper are economical and very widely used. Paper is translucent and softens and diffuses the natural light entering the room, creating a serene and peaceful atmosphere and a delicate scene of light and shadow patterns reflecting on the wooden floors and against the adjacent paper windows and sliding doors. Traditionally, the window paper was changed on the last day of the lunar calendar year, signifying a clean new start.

Four rows of different latticework used in the windows of this house in Muharraq, Bahrain, create complex patterned shadows inside.

divided circular rose window was common, in the west or entrance front of a church.

In the Decorated Gothic period in England, the simple lancet opening coalesced into larger windows divided by ingeniously cut stone bars, or tracery, based upon straight lines and arcs of a circle (Geometric), or more complicated flowing shapes, including ogee or S-curves (Curvilinear). France saw a similar progression, in what are known as the Rayonnant and Flamboyant styles. England returned to largely rectangular window divisions in the last, or Perpendicular, phase of the Gothic, from around 1330.

These pivoting windows are part of the curtain wall at the Bauhaus, in Dessau, Germany, designed by Walter Gropius in 1919. The windows are attached to the frame at the top and bottom, and rotate on the horizontal plane; pivot windows attached at the sides rotate on the vertical plane.

Glass Windows

The story of the glass window is closely related to the story of the domestication of glass as an architectural material. It is also about perfecting industrial glass-making processes and about finding the best production techniques to achieve the best results in architecture, all at a reasonable cost.

The first natural glass used to craft objects, such as utensils, weapons, and decorative items, was black obsidian stone, which is formed from quickly cooled volcanic lava. The core elements of obsidian, which are also found in glass today, are silica (quartz sand), soda, and lime. Window glass is made of sand, sodium carbonate (or sulphate), and calcium carbonate (limestone).

Early Glass Windows

Cuneiform tablets dating from 3,000 BCE contain glass-making recipes, indicating that glass was being manufactured in ancient Mesopotamia and Babylonia. The Phoenicians and the Egyptians are believed to be the first to have realized the plasticity of glass when melted. Both civilizations made beautiful glass objects, such as teardrop-shaped containers for perfumed oil, jewelry, and other luxury items. Four major manufacturing methods were used to produce glass: rod-and-core forming around a shape made out of sand; casting with open and closed molds; blowing into molds and forms; and free blowing.

The Romans began blowing glass around 50 BCE. Numerous furnaces were constructed and glass was used extensively to create a wide variety of objects that were blown and cast, cut, engraved, and painted. There is evidence that small glazed windows, only ½ in (12 mm) thick, made by the casting method, were being used by CE 100. These windows were translucent, not transparent, and, being expensive, were only found in the homes of the wealthy. A 32 x 44 in (81 x 112 cm) piece of window has been found at Pompeii. But glass did not replace window shutters in Roman houses: although the Romans tried to cast transparent, flat glass panes, they failed because they did not know that cast glass had to be ground and polished in order to make it transparent. Some Romans had their windows enclosed with thin, translucent sheets of gypsum or calcite alabaster, a mineral translucent enough to be used for small windows.

After the collapse of the Roman empire, in the fifth century CE, there was a decline in glass-making in Europe, although it continued to flourish in Iran, Iraq, and Egypt. But in the early twelfth century, the craft of glass-making was revived in Europe with the demand for stained-glass windows for cathedrals and monasteries. In the Middle Ages, the main developments in glass production techniques were colored glass windows, and the glazing of windows with small, round pieces of glass, called rondels, set in lead channels, which were common in private homes as well as in church and public buildings.

The small diamond panes, or lights, divided by lead mullions in this half-timbered Tudor house in Suffolk, England (below), are typical of their time. It was not economically viable to glaze a window with a single pane until the nineteenth century.

The Italians call the rondel windows at the medieval Doge's Palace in Venice (above) *rulli piombati*, literally "rolls of lead." The thick knots (that look like bottle bottoms) in the center of the glass plates show where the rod on which the glass was spun has been detached, and are surrounded by lead.

The stained glass skylight and windows on the Palau de la Música Catalana (Palace of Catalan Music), Barcelona, Spain, by Lluís Domènech i Montaner and completed in 1908, give the concert hall a feeling of openness and transparency.

in ordinary homes. The manufacture of flat glass was improved significantly in the nineteenth century using compressed air technology, which allowed for much larger and more regular pieces of glass to be produced and led to much greater freedom in window designs. It become possible to glaze a sash with one single sheet of glass.

The Modern Era

The famous Crystal Palace, designed by the gardener-architect Joseph Paxton for the 1851 Great Exhibition in London and constructed in Hyde Park, was only possible because of the advances in sheet-glass manufacturing. Built on the same principles as conservatories, the Crystal Palace had a prefabricated structure made of cast and wrought iron, covered with over 293,000 panes of glass. At the time, it was the largest enclosed, transparent structure in the world. It was also a precursor of the glass curtain wall. The Crystal Palace, which had been moved to South London, was destroyed by fire in 1936.

As the grinding and polishing of heavy glass plates became easier and faster with the use of water and steam power and then of electricity, the 1860s saw the rise of plate glass covering sparkling stores and office buildings in the cities of Europe and North America.

By 1890, Chance Brothers, the company that had manufactured the glass for the Crystal Palace, developed the drawn glass process. This involved pouring molten glass onto a tilted table, then feeding it through rollers into flat plates, which were cooled, then ground, and polished on both sides. In 1905, the Belgian engineer, Fourcault, developed an innovative process to manufacture sheet glass by vertically drawing a continuous sheet of consistent width. Around 1918, another Belgian, Bicheroux, came up with the technique of pouring molten glass directly through two rollers, a process employed in patterned figure and cast-glass production. By 1910, in an effort to strengthen flat glass, the lamination process Triplex was invented by the French scientist, Benedictus. It involved inserting a celluloid material layer between two glass sheets.

The twentieth century introduced some more revolutionary technological developments, which allowed endless sheets of window glass to be produced and the mechanisation of sheet glass manufacturing. In 1917, Colburn developed yet another method, the Colburn or Libbey-Owens process: this is similar to that of Fourcault, except that the glass is bent horizontally at a certain height and rolled into a very long sheet of around 200 ft (60 m). The Pittsburgh process, developed in 1928 by an American, Pennvernon, and the Pittsburgh Plate Glass Company, improved the combined Fourcault and Libbey-Owens methods.

Manufacturing Sheet Glass

Early glass windows were made of small panes of glass, due to manufacturing limitations. The crown glass technique, was seen in Roman times, developed in the eleventh century by German artisans and then further expanded by Venetian craftsmen in the thirteenth century. Crown glass was produced by blowing a glass sphere and opening it outward, then spinning the half-molten material, causing it to flatten out into a smooth round plate and increase in size, up to a diameter of about 36 in (90 cm). This process was called flashing. The glass disk was thicker at its center compared with the edges, and it contained air bubbles and a pattern of concentric circles. The round plate was then cut into small squares or diamond panes, which were joined with lead strips and fitted into mullioned frames; this is where the expression "lead lights" comes from. The thick knot—also called bull's-eye pattern—in the center of the plate where the spinning rod or punty was detached was a feature of medieval windows.

The hand-blown cylinder window-glass technique, which was introduced in the twelfth or thirteenth century, involved blowing a large cylinder out of molten glass. It was slit along its length while hot, allowed to cool, softened in a furnace, then flattened and cut into sheets.

By the end of the seventeenth century, the French had developed techniques for grinding and polishing cast glass to produce flat glass, but this was still expensive and only the wealthy could afford it. Later on, in the eighteenth century, when the blown-glass process was improved, glass windows became more common

In 1959 the British firm, Pilkington Brothers, introduced the float-glass process. This integrates the shiny finish of sheet glass with the optical qualities of plate glass: molten glass is poured across the surface of a bed of molten tin, before being pulled out in a continuous ribbon into the annealing kiln. This is now the standard method for producing sheet glass.

Recent Advances

By the early years of the twenty-first century, substantial technological advances had been made in the development and refinement of the flat glass for windows. They include: the addition of tints to reduce heat transmission and glare; strengthening processes by thermal and chemical tempering; and the coating with transparent films (using metal and metal oxide) to reflect heat or conduct electricity. Consequently, glass windows now significantly increase the safety, the comfort levels, and the aesthetic appeal of buildings.

Among the most interesting advances are solar windows, passive solar heating windows mainly used in cold climatic regions. In climates with an average winter temperature of between 19.4°F and 30.2°F (−7°C and −1°C), a solar window requires double glazing and a window area of approximately twenty to thirty five percent of the total floor area of the interior space for the effective solar heating of that space. In milder climates, single glazing is suitable and the glass area can be reduced to about fifteen percent of the total floor area.

The quality and design of solar windows, as well as their method of installation, affect their overall efficiency as heat-collecting elements; for example, if they have wooden frames rather than

Renaissance Windows

The two-light window divided by a column as at the Palazzo Strozzi in Florence, was a medieval type which persisted into the early Renaissance. It was superseded by the single-light rectangular window framed with pilasters and a cornice, or pedimented like a small temple front (or *aedicule*). Variations included the thermal or Diocletian window, (from its earlier use in Roman baths or *thermae*, such as the Baths of Diocletian in Rome), which was sometimes used by Andrea Palladio. Another was the Venetian window, consisting of an arched central light, flanked by two lower rectangular ones. Where the openings extend down to floor level, this is known as a Serliana (from its publication in Serlio's *Architettura* of 1537). This was used by Palladio to completely encase the Basilica at Vicenza (1549).

The two-light Renaissance windows of the 1489 Palazzo Strozzi were later superseded.

metal ones, the double-glazed windows provide twenty percent more insulation.

The generic term "smart window," which was introduced for architectural use in the middle of the 1980s, refers to the ability to control the optical and reflective elements of a glass window in order to alter the amount of sunlight that it allows into the building or to provide privacy: the technology allows the user to block some or all of the light coming inside. The glass goes from clear to translucent or opaque in an instant, at

the press of a button. Significant energy savings on heating, air conditioning, and lighting can be achieved and, moreover, the windows can be used as privacy screens. With liquid-crystal technology, for example, the glass can provide instant privacy: sensitive particles inserted between two panes of glass become active and allow the light to pass through the glass when the window is switched "on," giving a clear view to the outside; when it is switched "off," the glass becomes opaque and visual access is blocked.

Borrowing the techniques used in the 1840s by British prefabricators, New York builders constructed whole districts of commercial buildings with glass and cast-iron façades from 1860 to 1890. The iron structure allowed larger window areas than before. The landmark Haughwout Building was designed as a showroom for a china and glassware business.

The Maison de Verre (1928–1932), in Saint Germain des Prés, Paris, has a façade glazed with opaque glass bricks occasionally intersected by vertical panels of flat glass, inset in a steel frame. The architects Pierre Chareau and Bernard Bijvoet used various industrial materials such as steel beams, perforated sheet metal, and rubber flooring to construct the three-story box.

Philip Johnson, who worked with Mies van der Rohe on the Seagram Building, designed the Glass House, in New Canaan, Connecticut (below), for his own use. Built in 1949, it is a glass box hung on a slender steel skeleton. The fireplaces and bathroom are contained in off-center, round brick core.

Stained and Decorated Glass

Although it is widely claimed that stained glass originated in twelfth-century France as a form of Christian art, some pieces of stained glass have been found in Pompeii, where it was used in the villas and palaces of wealthy Romans in the first century CE.

Stained glass has been closely associated with religious buildings for over a thousand years. From medieval times, most religious windows have been gorgeously executed in stained glass, embellishing churches and cathedrals across the Christian world. An example of early English ecclesiastical stained glass was found in St. Paul's, a seventh-century church in Jarrow. Another early example is the Face of Christ, dating from the late tenth century, in the Lorsch Abbey in Hesse, Germany. The finest later examples are the great stained-glass windows of Chartres and Canterbury cathedrals, from the thirteenth and fourteenth centuries. Most of the flat glass for ecclesiastical windows was made in France.

Stained glass is most commonly associated with elaborately decorated church and cathedral windows and other religious buildings, and also with sculptures and art objects using colored glass. The pieces of stained glass are normally set between lead binding strips, or *cames*. However, the term "lead light" is more often used when describing the decorated glass windows of secular architecture (domestic and commercial), which have non-complex designs.

Stained glass is made of small pieces of flat glass, either colored or clear, which are specially cut and arranged into decorative patterns and designs; traditionally, they are joined by lead strips and held together by a rigid frame. Stained glass is also used to describe windows in which the glass parts have been painted with a brush. In the early medieval period, artists discovered that a paste formed with iron filings (black enamel paint) mixed with ground glass could be painted onto glass—applied in thick layers as black, or as a thin gray or gray-brown wash—with a brush to draw details and enhance the design. "Grisaille" is a term referring to black enamel painting on glass, which was widely used to create patterns on clear glass; it became increasingly common and almost replaced stained glass in the seventeenth and eighteenth centuries.

The term "stained glass" actually refers to the silver color painted onto the glass with a paint mixture that was referred to as silver stain (also called yellow-silver or yellow-gold). This color was mainly employed to paint jewelry, crowns, hair, and architectural elements in the scenes depicted. The painted parts were then placed in a kiln and annealed, a process in which the glass was heated—fired at a temperature close to the melting point of glass, which is approximately 1,112°F (600°C), to allow the pigments to fuse permanently into the glass, and to prevent the colors fading—then slowly cooled to release internal stresses.

Medieval and Gothic Stained Glass

In medieval times, stained glass had three main purposes. The first was functional: to enclose the building and isolate it from the weather while allowing light into the space. The second was to act as a purely decorative element, painting the interior space with sunlight and color. Unlike domestic windows, the stained glass in religious buildings is not intended to allow people to see out of the building, or even to let the daylight in, but its aim is to create a spiritual ambience, and encourage meditation and prayer. The diffused and color-washed light filtering through stained-glass windows is perfect to enhance this effect—which is the reason stained glass is so prevalent in ecclesiastical architecture. The third function is iconographic. Stained glass is a good medium to depict scenes and tell stories, and hence to convey the religion and messages from the Bible to a largely illiterate population.

The Gothic style, which developed in Europe in the twelfth century and lasted for about 400 years, was characterized by pointed arches, ornate tracery, and complex ribbed vaulting, and its magnificent stained-glass windows.

Renaissance Painted Glass

By the mid-fifteenth century, Renaissance glass painters, utilizing improved enamel paints, began to reproduce the bright, colorful scenes of fresco and easel painting. They depicted figures using delicate shading rather than the bold lead-lined and strong-figured style that was characteristic of Gothic work. Eventually, their paintings masked the translucency of the glass.

In an attempt to introduce a more humanistic approach—a reaction to the sheer scale of Gothic cathedral architecture—secular scenes became more prominent on painted glass. Glass painting was then slowly abandoned, as paint on glass had lost its original appeal and artists wanted to use

In the Sainte-Chapelle (Holy Chapel) in Paris, completed by Pierre de Montreuil in 1248, is an exceptional suite of stained glass, including the fifteenth century *flamboyant* style west rose window which depicts the Apocalypse.

This Flemish glass panel dates from about 1450. The design was drawn with a brown-black pigment made of iron filings and ground glass. The yellow-orange areas were highlighted with a silver compound. Once fired, the compound changed color, its density depending on the thickness of the yellow-silver.

more fashionable media. The decline in the use of painted glass was influenced by the fact that the painted interiors and sumptuous decorations of the new Baroque style, originating in Rome in the seventeenth century, required the use of more clear glass to allow in the daylight.

The Stained-Glass Revival

In the mid-nineteenth century, as Gothic Revival architecture became more popular, glass painters rediscovered the high quality of the enamel paints used in medieval glass. However, they were still under the influence of the Renaissance style of realism, retaining the modes of representation of figures, scenery, and decoration, as well as its enamel-painting techniques on clear glass.

Gradually, the Gothic Revival movement produced a wholly new art form by combining the medieval stained-glass technique of working with small, colored glass pieces with enamel-painting techniques, which they used as shading. At the same time, they were merging medieval motifs, Renaissance, and contemporary ideals. William Morris, one of the founders of the Arts and Crafts Movement, who is best known for his designs of wallpaper and patterned fabrics, believed that machine production was destroying everyday life by making inferior goods that were devoid of craftsmanship. Morris, together with the painter Edward Burne-Jones, created some of the finest examples of Gothic Revival stained glass. Later works by Charles Rennie Mackintosh, Frank Lloyd Wright, and other Arts and Crafts exponents, who were followed by the Art Nouveau architects, domesticated stained glass, making it an integral part of exterior and interior windows in houses and public buildings.

In the 1908 Gamble House, in Pasadena, California, architects Charles and Henry Greene combined fine cabinetwork—made in their own workshops—with fragments of Tiffany stained glass assembled into a "tree of life" pattern for the entrance doors.

Chartres Cathedral
Chartres, France

Chartres Cathedral is unparalleled for its architectural innovations and for its great sculptures. But, above all, the cathedral is known for its windows, which are regarded as the most harmonious and vivacious collections of stained glass ever assembled.

Nôtre-Dame de Chartres is recognized as one of the three masterpieces of the French Gothic style—alongside the cathedrals of Amiens and Reims. The cathedral is a key building, which represents the culmination of the Early Gothic style combined with the previous Romanesque architecture, and is on UNESCO's list of World Heritage Sites.

Situated about 50 miles (80 km) from Paris and constructed on the remains of an earlier Romanesque church, which burned down in 1194, the cathedral retains the crypt, the western façade, and the bases of the two towers of the earlier church. The main portion of Chartres was constructed between 1194 and 1220, at a period when the ribbed vault, made of masonry, was developed in France. Unlike the Roman vault, which was solid, it allowed walls to be broken up into pillars and bays, which could hold rows of tall clerestory windows through which sunlight streamed down into the body of the building. Cruciform in plan, Chartres Cathedral includes many of the innovative architectural elements of the Early Gothic period. These include flying buttresses to resist the lateral stress of the vaults and arches; the pointed arches; the vaulting; and the detailed ornamental treatment of stone.

The cathedral has two contrasting bell towers. The South Tower is a pyramid, 350 ft (105 m) high, from the twelfth century; the other is 375 ft (113 m) high and is Late Gothic (also known as Flamboyant) in style and dates from the early sixteenth century; both were built on the bases of the towers from the earlier church. Chartres Cathedral has an extensive cycle of sculpture in the portals, notably on the west front, which includes the Royal Portal, carved in the 1140s in a revolutionary funnel shape which later became a common feature of the Gothic style; its recesses are decorated with elongated, stylized statues of French kings and queens, and figures from the Old and New Testaments.

Inside Chartres

The Gothic vault uses pointed arches, rather than round arches over a square bay, as in the earlier Romanesque examples. This system of stone ribs spanning the space was lighter, with more clearly defined thrusts, and it was a great deal more flexible, making possible rectangular as well as irregularly shaped bays. Combined with flying buttresses, the construction was able to carry a great deal of weight, including that of vast areas of stained glass.

In Chartres, the internal space is breathtaking, with an unbroken line of vision down the 427-ft (128-m) long nave, from the western entrance through the wide choir to the rounded double ambulatory with radiating chapels at the eastern end. The broad transept, with aisles projecting to north and south, is close to the center of the cathedral. The nave arcade, 112 ft (34 m) high, is the widest in France. The cathedral has a three-story vertical arrangement—the nave arcades and aisles; the five-arch triforium (the shallow gallery backed by the outer wall thickness); and the clerestory—and shafts of stone run from the floor to the vault. The walls and the theatrical skeletal system supporting the vaults are slender, allowing space for the large stained glass windows.

Gothic cathedrals often took several centuries to complete. Nowhere is this more obvious than in the towers of Chartres, both built on the remains of the previous church. The South Tower (on the right) was completed in 1170. The Flamboyant style North spire was not added until the early sixteenth century.

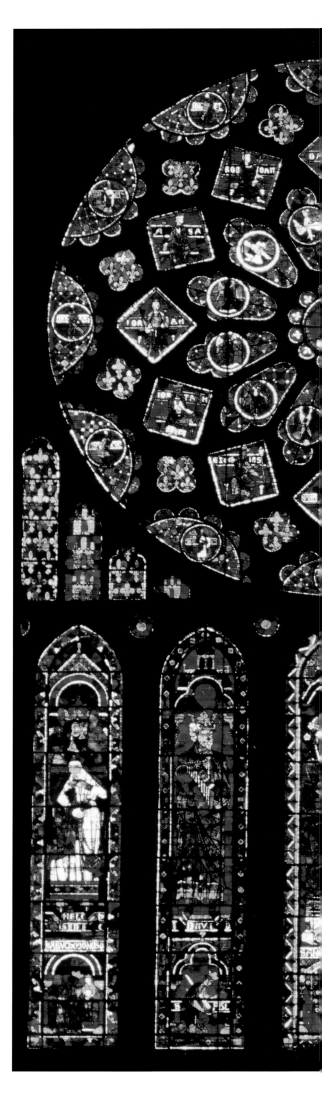

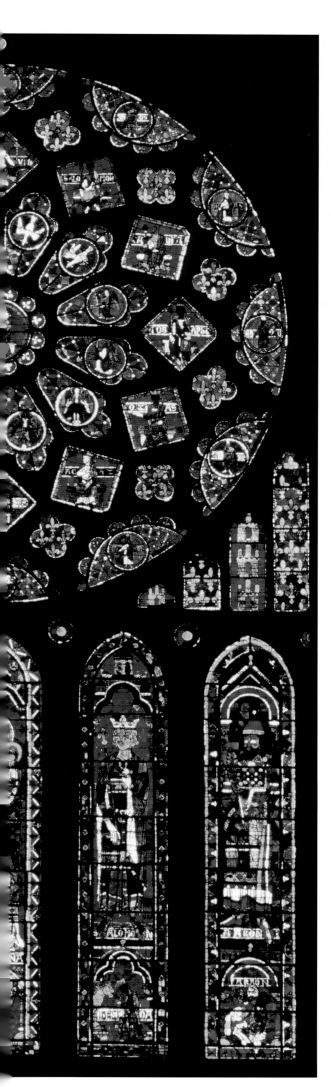

The north rose window, with five lancet windows (left), is known as the Rose of France and depicts the glorification of the Virgin. The set was donated by Blanche of Castille, wife of Louis VIII, in 1230. Spandrels above the lancet windows are decorated with her coats of arms and castles, and fleurs-de-lis.

A detail from the Tree of Jesse (above), one of the three west lancet windows depicting the genealogy, life, and resurrection of Christ. These are considered the finest extant group of Early Gothic windows. The pale blue "sapphire" glass is rich in soda and therefore more stable than the usual potash glass.

The Windows

By 1240, Chartres was filled with stained glass—it retains one of the most complete collections of medieval stained glass in the world, in spite of a modernization campaign in 1753 when some of the windows were renewed. Of the cathedral's original 186 windows, 152 remain. The windows cover more than 21,500 sq ft (2,000 sq m).

The stained glass adds the dimension of color to the light in the cathedral and is also a medium for figurative and narrative art, depicting scenes from biblical history and from the lives of Christ and the saints, glorifying God and the Virgin Mary, and representing the heavens.

The vividly colored windows of Chartres are most famous for their rich blues and their reds. The innovative Chartres Blue, composed of blue tones enhanced with traces of red, was first used on the three Romanesque lancet windows on the west front, saved from the 1194 fire. One of these, the rose window above the central entrance portal, depicts the Last Judgment, a reminder of the transitory nature of life on Earth and the dangers of succumbing to temptation. Rose windows are characteristic of the Gothic style. They are large circular wheel windows, divided into sections by stone mullions and tracery. It is believed the name comes from the Old French roué, meaning wheel.

Massive rose windows also decorate the two transept façades at Chartres. The one in the south, with five lancets, is to the glorification of Christ. The rose window in the North Transept is one of the oldest: known as the Rose of France, it has five lancets and a series of spandrels (set in the triangular space between the curve of the rose and the top of the lancets).

Chartres's clerestory which features an oculus, or rosette, set above pairs of large lancet windows, also includes magnificent stained glass. The Blue Virgin Window, which depicts the Madonna and Child, is an excellent example of stylized, two-dimensional imagery, with lead lines used boldly and the blue background receding. In addition to the religious motifs and scenes, some windows include symbols of royal influence, in the form of royal yellow fleurs-de-lis on blue and yellow castles against red backgrounds.

Lighting

In the Paris Opera, designed by Charles Garnier and completed in 1874, candelabra, chandeliers, and sconces powered by gas originally provided the light in the grand staircase, the enormous foyer, and the upper passageways. After the opening, Garnier experimented with various forms of electric lighting becoming available, mostly the carbon arc light.

Lighting is a very powerful tool for architects and designers: it affects our perception of colors and form, and ultimately our mood. Lighting is a "form giver," able to transform objects and spaces from being simply visible to being visually interesting. People's perceptions, and thus their responses, change as the quality and patterns of light change. Lighting can create varying ambiences and can add a sense of magic to a space. It can illuminate routes or attract attention by focusing on particular points. It can make a building, a room, or an object look soft and pleasing, monotonous and boring, dark and depressing, or radiant and exciting.

Throughout history, humans have strived to bring light into interiors in various ways and forms. The most obvious is sunlight through window and door openings—this is known as natural light. All other forms of lighting—from fire- and candlelight to the most sophisticated forms of electric lights—are called artificial.

Early Lighting

The first artificial lights were blazing torches and campfires. From ancient times, fire was used for light, warmth, and cooking. The earliest hearths go back to prehistoric campsites. The remains of fires have been dated to *c.* 400,000 BCE. The famous network of caves at Lascaux in southwest France are extensively decorated with paintings and engravings; executed around 15,000 BCE, these painted chambers are far from natural light sources and must have been illuminated with torches and primitive lamps. These would have been made of shell, horn, or stone, and filled with animal fat or vegetable oil. The addition of a wick improved their performance, allowing them to burn more evenly and for longer. The Sumerians of 2,600 BCE made lamps of alabaster and the inhabitants of Palestine before 2,000 BCE used hand-fabricated lamps.

Oil reservoir lamps were messy and their design remained virtually unchanged for several

As depicted by the advertising industry of 1900, the perfect French family living in a comfortable middle-class home enjoyed their evenings reading together in the glow of table lamps. Lamps were mostly fueled by whale oil and kerosene, but were superceded first by gas and later by electricity.

millennia. The Greeks were making terracotta lamps with handles from around the seventh century BCE: the word "lamp" comes from the Greek *lampas*, meaning torch. The main fuel used in the Mediterranean region was probably olive oil. Other types of oils used for lamps included sesame oil, palm oil, nut oil, fish oil, and castor oil. In the first century CE, Pliny the Elder described translucent lanterns made of cattle horn; it is likely that these lanterns would have been easily portable.

A number of civilizations were making tallow or beeswax into candles with internal wicks as far back as 3,000 BCE. Along with firelight and oil reservoir lamps, these were the principal means of lighting the interiors of buildings until the late eighteenth century. Rooms were enveloped in gloom, relieved only by pools of flickering light from candles and lamps, with some additional illumination from firelight in the cold months.

Candles were wall-mounted (in niches and sconces), ceiling-mounted (as chandeliers), or freestanding (in candlesticks and candelabras). Beeswax candles were expensive and therefore relatively rare; tallow ones were fast-burning and very smelly. The commonest candlesticks were wooden or brass. Sconces, which might have several projecting arms, or "branches," were often backed with tin plate, brass, or mirrored glass to increase the reflected light (and to lessen the likelihood of the building burning down). The earliest chandeliers were made of drops of rock crystal and beads; those composed of glass date from the seventeenth century.

Fireplaces—the main source of light and heat in interiors—were often the central decorative feature in a room. The chimney-breast, hood, and the opening surround were obvious sites for ornamentation, and they rivaled the ceiling as the most eye-catching feature. By the 1630s, designs for chimneypieces being published in Paris had projecting chimney-breasts heavy with carved and architectural ornament. Less elaborate were the Dutch versions, which had smaller openings and tiled surrounds. Where there was no fireplace, heat and light might be provided by a brazier, sometimes tiled. In the colder Scandinavian and central European countries, faience stoves rather than fireplaces provided the heat.

The introduction of the Argand lamp in the 1780s changed the way interiors looked at night. It had a circular meshed wick surrounded by a glass chimney, which drew up air more efficiently. It produced a light which was much stronger and more even than candlelight, with less smoke and smell. The lamp, along with a subsequent series of improved designs, was mainly fueled by whale oil, which created high demand and drove some whale species almost to extinction. In the 1850s, lamps using kerosene—a petroleum derivative also known as paraffin—with a flat wick in a cup and a bellied chimney were introduced.

After the architect John Soane's death in 1837, his London house was made a museum by an Act of Parliament. Electricity was installed in 1897 without disturbing the original decoration. In the Breakfast Parlour, the lamp hangs from Soane's domed lantern.

Gas and Electricity

In the 1790s, the introduction of gas lighting, which utilized coal gas, made it possible to light a room from several sources at the turn of a tap. Gaslight had a profound effect on the appearance of interiors—for the first time, it was possible to see properly at night—and the harsh light it produced made some colors appear sickly. By the middle of the nineteenth century, gas lighting had been installed in cities all over the Western world. Light fittings for gas were wall-mounted or hung on central pendants.

No less revolutionary was the invention of the incandescent electric lamp. This was considerably improved by J. A. Swan and Thomas Edison in 1879, when they perfected light bulbs that used carbonized filaments and burned for over 40 hours. By 1900, the electric light was becoming more common. The American novelist, Edith Wharton, complained that electric light, "with its harsh white glare, which no expedients have as yet overcome, has taken from our drawing rooms all air of privacy and distinction."

But improvements there were. The fluorescent lamp was patented in 1901 (although it was not produced commercially until the late 1930s). Ten years later, the Frenchman, Georges Claude, invented the neon lamp, in which an electric current is passed through a minute amount of the inert gas, neon, to produce a bright, orange-red glow. This became widely used for all types of

Chandeliers illuminate the interior of the Cathedral of the Archangel Michael, in the Kremlin, Moscow, Russia. Commissioned by Ivan III, the cathedral was built by Alovisio Novo in 1505–1508 as a mausoleum for the czars. Originally the frescoes, from the mid-seventeenth century, would have been lit by candles.

signs, and transformed streetscapes throughout the world. From 1915, more efficient tungsten filaments began replacing carbon in bulbs and in 1925 the first frosted light bulbs came onto the market. The 1960s saw the introduction of light bulbs using halogen, sometimes combined with tungsten, and, in 1991, a bulb using magnetic induction which could last 60,000 hours was invented by Philips.

The Use of Artificial Lighting

Light is essential for seeing. Contrast is necessary for distinguishing objects. The difference between the reflection of the background and the object creates contrast, which is the ratio of reflected light. If there is no contrast between two items, it is not possible to differentiate them.

However, high contrasts create glare, which has two distinct negative effects: psychological (discomfort glare) and physiological (disability glare). The greatest sources of glare are windows; among others are inappropriate artificial lights and reflections from shiny internal or external surfaces. Discomfort glare can interfere with visual efficiency or cause eye fatigue. Disability

In the Aula Magna auditorium at Ciudad University, Caracas, Venezuela, designed by Carlos Raul Villaneuva in the 1950s, the ceiling and concrete ribbed walls are pierced with spotlights among the acoustic *Clouds* sculpture by Alexander Calder.

The lighting in a stairway in the National Diet, the Japanese Parliament, Tokyo, is subdued but it serves its purpose of illuminating the route. The architect, Watanabe Fukuzo, won a public design competition for the building in 1918.

Atmospheric yet functional, the series of sconces in the entranceway of this house in Tortola, British Virgin Islands, direct the light down, washing the walls and floor with soft light and, at the same time, illuminating the steps and path.

glare impedes the visibility of objects, which can lead to accidents.

The activity carried out in a space dictates the type and quality of light required. The quality, level, and type of light needed in a living room is different from the lighting requirements of a storeroom. In the former, the aim is to create a pleasant, comfortable atmosphere in which to relax, spend more time and carry out specific tasks, whereas simply providing visibility is sufficient in the storeroom. In a bedroom, side lights are convenient for reading. Lighting the work area in kitchens for the preparation of food needs special attention for safe working; similarly, an office desk or the benchtop of a watch repairer requires focused lighting.

Artificial light also plays an important role in safety and security. The lighting of entrances or corridors can reduce the risk of facing unexpected intruders. In dark spaces, such as cinemas, stairs can be emphasized by light, or low light may be used to show direction.

Lighting Interiors

When choosing lights for interiors, the key considerations are visual performance and quality. Lighting can be directed toward the walls and the ceiling for creating spacious effects; to a corner for reading or carrying out other activities; to an eye-catching point such as a painting, sculpture, or a plant; and to a bas-relief or textured surface to emphasize three-dimensionality.

Artificial lighting can reveal or conceal details, accentuate or subdue, produce an atmosphere of gaiety or dignity, and can create a space that is cold and impersonal or warm and friendly. The quality of artificial light is as much about shadow as it is about illumination. Interior lighting can be divided into three basic categories, related to different visual requirements.

The purpose of general, or ambient, lighting is to throw light on a wide area, either from a central source, from which light spreads out, or by using a variety of sources. The intention is to achieve a comfortable level of brightness that allows occupants to see and walk around safely. But general lighting can create an uninteresting effect and may be inflexible. By fitting fixed lights with dimmer switches, lighting levels can be adjusted to suit the mood and activity.

Concentrated lighting focussing on specific areas has two main purposes. Task lighting is directed onto an area—such as a kitchen bench, a desk, a sewing table, or a reading chair—where certain tasks are performed. Accent lighting may be used to highlight particular features or objects, such as paintings or architectural features, mainly for decorative purposes.

Atmospheric lighting is for effect, to create atmosphere through subtle illumination and shadow. It can be created using lights placed low in the room, such as table lamps, with soft lights washing the walls and ceilings to give a feeling of spaciousness, and by directing light upward to bounce off the ceiling in a diffuse form.

External Lighting

The lighting of outdoor spaces, such as gardens, paths, entrances, and streets, as well as building façades, may be for safety and security purposes, or decorative, for highlighting the architectural features or art objects. Such security lighting is a uniform, high-intensity lighting. It may increase the feeling of safety, but does not necessarily make the streets safer. In the seventeenth century, when the streets of Paris were lit by lanterns, the French aristocrat Madame de Sévigné reflected that, "We found pleasure in giving Madame Scarron a lift, at midnight, to the deep end of the Saint-Germain suburb … We went back happily thanks to the lanterns, safe from robbers."

Ventilation and Cooling

People live in environments that are shaped by different climatic forces. The human body produces and dissipates heat, and the rate of these two must be the same in order to maintain a thermal balance with the immediate environment. Factors affecting thermal comfort are dry-bulb temperature (that is, the ambient temperature without the effects of radiation and moisture), relative humidity, relative wind speed, mean radiant temperature, activity level, and the clothing level.

Ventilation allows the circulation of air in interiors, by letting in fresh air and taking away stale air, and it can be achieved by either natural ventilation or artificial systems. The invention of mechanical systems in the early twentieth century led to a reliance on artificial ventilation and buildings became hermetically sealed spaces with permanently fixed windows. However, some recent studies have shown that the lack of fresh air, individual control over the environment, and visual connection to the outside seem to produce negative physical and psychological effects.

Natural ventilation—when air and heat flow into or out of a space—can occur intentionally, in the form of cross ventilation, or incidentally, through cracks and gaps. When windows and doors are open, the wind will blow air in through the windward side and suck it out on the leeward side and/or the roof. Although natural ventilation is not effective at reducing the humidity in the air, it helps dissipate moisture in enclosed spaces.

Different Climatic Regions

In humid climates, where day- and night-time temperatures do not fluctuate much, buildings should be shaded with wide porches, loggias, and verandas to encourage cooling air movements and to protect the interior from the sun. Walls have less importance here than in other regions. Besides being used for screening, jalousies and grilles, sliding or folding doors and windows are practical elements because they give access to air flow and provide solar protection.

The Australian Queenslander house, adapted to the climate, faces outward more than inward. It is a light, one-story, timber-framed structure elevated on piles, which allow it to catch the prevailing breezes and provide a cool air pool beneath the floor. Roofed with a steep pitch, its floor plan is symmetrical, with a central corridor which provides cross ventilation. Wide verandas with large overhangs are an integral part of the typical Queenslander: these offer a refuge from the intense sun and rain, as well as acting as wind scoops. Breezes, which otherwise would flow over the house, are thus directed toward it. These verandas are also utilized as an extension of the house's living spaces—as places to eat, socialize, read, and even sleep.

In hot-arid regions, where the night-time temperature drops considerably, keeping the doors and windows closed during the day and opening them after sunset cools the building at night and helps keep the indoor temperatures

The two square wind-catchers on a fort at al-'Ain, in Abu Dhabi, United Arab Emirates (right), have long, vertical slits to catch passing breezes. The basic principles of wind-catchers—which have been in use for centuries, particularly in Egypt, the Middle East, and Pakistan—are now being applied to architecture throughout the world.

A contemporary version of a Queenslander, this Australian building in the Daintree rainforest, northern Queensland, is raised on piles, albeit extremely high ones, and has the wide, roofed verandas of its antecedents that extend the living space into the outdoors.

lower the following day. In arid regions, houses with thick, closed external walls and inward-looking central courtyards surrounded by shaded porches are the best arrangement. Letting the breezes flow over natural elements, such as water bodies and shaded lawns, improves the cooling aspect. The fountains, pools, running water, and canopies of trees, as seen at Fontana Pretoria in Palermo, Italy, and at the Alhambra in Granada, Spain, are designed to cool the air as well as to inspire feelings of relaxation.

The courtyard-level floors of houses in regions such as Iraq, southeast Turkey, Egypt, Tunisia, Spain, and Mexico, are usually paved with stone, which provides a comfortable, cool surface to walk on and evaporative cooling when sprinkled with water. The thickness of the exterior walls—which may vary from about 20 to 45 in (50 to 110 cm)—absorbs the heat and there are few, if any, window openings to the outside. Windows and doors opening onto an internal courtyard, which behaves somewhat like a cool air reservoir or pool, provide cooling by natural ventilation. In addition, windows set high on the exterior help to decrease the amount of reflected light and excessive heat gain.

Houses in Harran, Turkey, have a striking beehive form, resembling the *trulli* of Apulia in southern Italy. The increased internal volume of the conical roof has space for hot air to rise, as well as providing good ventilation through the top opening. Walls and roof are of baked bricks, which have high thermal storage capacity.

Shutting out the Heat

Shutters, awnings, timber lattice panels, canopies, and slatted sun louvers help to provide privacy and cut down the intensity of the summer solar radiation, while letting the breezes pass through.

Window hoods made of timber or sheet metal are other ways to provide shade, and they divert rain away from timber window frames and sills.

These hoods may have side fins with punctured decorations for letting out rising hot air, which otherwise would stay trapped and stagnant. It is more efficient to use horizontally pivoted louvers to direct the moving air than sliding panels.

Using the Heat and Wind

Solar chimneys (which create a chimney, or stack, effect) are used in arid climates and wind-catchers (which use the pressure effect of the winds) in humid climates to draw fresh air into buildings.

Solar chimneys, also called thermal chimneys, improve the natural ventilation by employing heated air convection in a vertical shaft through a building. The air is heated in a separate part of the complex, isolated so that the heat does not have an adverse effect on the thermal comfort of the building. This hot air then rises in the vertical shaft and is released from the building at higher

The Torre Agbar (Agbar Tower), Barcelona, Spain, designed by French architect Jean Nouvel, opened in 2005. Temperature sensors regulate the opening and closing of blinds—made of nearly 60,000 sheets of glass—that cover the 466-ft (142-m) high façade, reducing energy consumption for air conditioning.

levels and, as it does so, it draws in fresh air from the lower openings.

Wind-catchers and wind-scoops, on the other hand, utilize the wind that would otherwise pass the building. The wind-catcher, a high structure set on the roof, is covered, and has openings on its side elevations. The pressure of the funneled, incoming fresh air pushes the stagnant interior air from openings. When the incoming air is warmer than the interior air, it can be cooled by passing through cooler underground spaces and evaporative cooling elements.

The Art of Ornamentation

Ornamentation is the decorative embellishment of an object, adding beauty, meaning, and emphasis. It may enhance the structural and protective components which are essential elements of architecture, for it can transmit meaning and culture and can convey a narrative or instill curiosity and delight.

Carvings

Carving can be used to emphasize or hide the structure of architectural surfaces, and if desired be completely integrated into the building components through the act of carving directly into the supports and connectors. Carved columns and beams are examples of this ornamental strategy. Alternatively, carvings can be completely independent of structure, applied as a surface or screen, hiding, instead of expressing the structure.

There are several types of carving. Sculptural reliefs protrude slightly from the overall surface (low relief or bas-relief); high-relief carvings are undercut sufficiently to free them from the background material; freestanding carvings have no background; and incised carvings have grooves that can be filled with paint, or inlaid with other materials for contrast, creating multicolored surface ornament. Carving can also be used to make a screen that both creates a division (between outside and inside, for example) and allows a certain amount of light through. Craftsmen make use of many different carving techniques and varieties of materials and finishes—ranging from smooth to rough—that can give the designs and forms additional character.

The material can affect the nature of the work. For example, a soft stone, such as soapstone, may not last as long as harder stones, but it is easy to

Roman senators take part in a procession depicted on the Ara Pacis (Altar of Peace), Rome, which was dedicated on January 30, 9 BCE, at the behest of Emperor Augustus. Appearing in other scenes from the procession are the emperor, members of the imperial family, priests, and magistrates.

carve, allowing form and texture to be expressed without difficulty. Color, veining (in stone), and grain (in wood) can become part of the design. Wood, while it is less durable than stone, is readily available in most places, can be used for furniture, is light in weight, and has interesting graining. Stucco has a neutral finish that can be painted to suit many conditions, can be formed into any shape the designer needs, and is light and relatively inexpensive.

Stone Carving

Ancient civilizations carved in stone, despite the lack of good tools to enable stone to be worked easily. The advent of iron tools made the job easier, and increased the possibilities for variation and intricacy in carving. The long history of stone relief ornament includes impressive examples from the ancient Near East and Egypt consisting of geometric patterns, figures, writing, and symbols. One motif, the depiction of people in naturalistic poses, was used by stone carvers in those regions for many centuries. Among

the many examples of these carvings are those found at the palace in Nineveh, Iraq, c. 647 BCE, the Audience Hall of Darius in Persepolis, Iran, c. 500 BCE, and at the burial ground of Saqqara, Egypt, of the third millennium BCE.

The architecture of the Greeks and Romans included superficially similar relief carving, but there are big differences between the two in style and meaning. Greek temples depict burial rites, hunting scenes, the various gods, and recurrent events, such as festivals. A prime example is the Parthenon in Athens, built and ornamented between 447 and 432 BCE. Here, the Greeks used marble carvings of various types, not just for ornamental purposes but as a key method of imparting meaning, adding to this temple's already impressive siting and massing. The building's ornamentation relates important historical events and also depicts gods that were important to the people of Athens. On the outer Doric frieze, metopes contain figures of warriors carved in high relief. On the temple's inner entablature an Ionic frieze is carved in bas-relief and depicts the Panathenaic festival—in which a procession makes its way to the Acropolis to honor the goddess Athena—a contrast with the much larger, fully three-dimensional sculptures of Greek gods carved for the two pediments. The deep shadows of the pediment sculptures, as well as the size of

Much valuable information about ancient civilizations comes from the carvings they made. This painted low-relief panel from the Mastaba of Mereruka (c. 2300 BCE) at Saqqara, Egypt, depicts people harvesting crops and plowing fields with oxen.

the sculpted gods placed far above the smaller carvings of the citizens of Athens, emphasize the importance of the gods.

By contrast, many Roman monuments used bas-relief to explain and commemorate imperial triumphs. Commissioned to celebrate battle victories in Gaul and Spain, the Ara Pacis (Altar of Peace), completed in Rome in 9 BCE, has low-relief vines and birds on the lower half as well as a low-relief procession depicted on the top. Trajan's Column, erected around 113 CE in Rome, is carved from marble in a bas-relief frieze that winds around the slender, 125-ft (38-m) monument. It depicts the Roman army's victories in the Dacian wars in what is now Romania.

Throughout Scandinavia, bas-relief rune stones, produced from the third to the eleventh century can be found. They were intended to be memorials and self-advertisements, and reflect Germanic pagan traditions as well as announcing a person's conversion to Christianity. Some are totally covered with incised text, while others have elaborate patterns—depicted in a flat, stylized manner—which include linked geometric patterned borders, and illustrations of beasts, valkyries, and warriors on ships rising to enter Valhalla. These patterns are echoed later in Scandinavia, in architecture, illuminated manuscripts, and other crafts, including wood carving.

Wood Carving

From the intricate woodwork of choir stalls, doors, and ceilings in medieval European churches to the joinery of Japanese temple architecture, wood carving has contributed to the beauty as well as the meaning, structure and function of architecture in many cultures. Islamic architecture incorporates a great deal of wood carving, using intricate geometric and other patterns for doorways, furnishings, and screens. Some mosques use a carved wood screen to define the *maqsura,* a separate prayer area for the ruler. Ornamental wood screens are also used in windows for privacy and filtered light, helping buildings stay cool and shady.

There are many regional wood-carving traditions. In Kashmir, for example, an intricate but unique tradition has created distinctive wood geometric interlace patterns that decorate the ceilings of houses and religious monuments. Similar patterns in latticework provide shade for windows and doorways.

A door in the largely eighteenth-century Djuma Mosque of Khiva in Uzbekistan is carved with a complex, interlocking design. In general, Islam rejects figurative art, and ornamentation in Islamic architecture takes the form of geometric patterning, calligraphy, or, as seen here, stylized floral motifs.

Colored Stone

Colored stone is both a surfacing material and part of structural strategies. During the Roman era, the variety of colors and patterns provided by marble and granite surfaces added to the overall architectural richness. The Romans perfected earlier attempts at covering less expensive but strong structural masonry, such as concrete, with cut stone, and these techniques were further developed in the early Christian and Byzantine period as designers exploited the natural colors and designs within stone.

In the Victorian era, the importance of color in architecture was underscored by the English art and architecture critic John Ruskin in *The Stones of Venice*, in which he explained the delight that color brought to medieval architecture. Victorian architects reinterpreted the medieval polychromy of Italian, Islamic, and Byzantine architecture, which used the various stone textures and colors as structural and decorative elements. One of the earliest such works was Christ Church built in Streatham, London, in 1840, and designed by James Wild. Brick, in three colors, decorates the exterior.

Patterning in Brick and Stone

In ancient civilizations, stone and brick, in varied colors and glazes, were used in polychromatic decoration. From the eighth century BCE, in Khorsabad, in modern-day Iraq, the Assyrians used a protective and brightly glazed brick on their buildings. One of the best-known glazed brick structures from antiquity is perhaps the Ishtar Gate of 575 BCE, in Babylon, Iraq, with a blue glaze, gold, blue, and white geometric and floral trim, and relief animal imagery.

Polychromy was achieved in ancient Greek architecture with paint on stone, using tempera (a water-based paint), encaustic (a wax paint), and frescoes to produce a multicolored stone surface. The Parthenon in Athens, Greece, for example, was once a colorful sight, rather than

The Venetian Palazzo Ducale (Doge's Palace), Italy, was largely built between 1309 and 1424, and has an upper story faced in pink and white marble, which contrasts with the white, open arcades below.

A detail from the Assyrian Ishtar Gate, Iraq, depicts a bull, symbol of the god Adad. The gate of glazed brick, built in the sixth century BCE, was part of a processional way leading into the city of Babylon.

the monochromatic one of today. In the Roman period, however, architects perfected the craft of using the natural colors of beautiful stone as surface material to cover structural stone and bricks in grand villas, baths, and temples. They used decorative stone for flooring as well. In Rome, the Pantheon, although somewhat altered from its original condition, still displays the polychromy in non structural stone that gave this temple of the second century CE a sumptuous interior.

Color in the Byzantine Era

In the early Christian and Byzantine periods, architects developed construction techniques based on Roman building practices. They continued to employ the Roman technique called *opus mixtum*, the practice of placing bands of brick through the width of a stone wall for stability and strength, resulting in colored stripes and patterns. They also continued the use of decorative stone as an ornamental facing. The Byzantine church of Hagia Sophia, built in Constantinople (Istanbul in modern Turkey) in

the sixth century, is one such example. Large panels of marble were trimmed with contrasting stone, and marble slabs were used almost like paintings. Stones in a variety of colors and patterns were carefully placed to feature their beautiful veining. Some were split in half and book-matched side by side to create symmetrical designs. With its colored stonework, ornate frescoes, and glittering mosaics, the church was a feast of color.

Italian and Islamic Polychromy

In medieval Italy, colored bricks, along with stone, contributed to the effect of both structural and non structural polychromy. The thirteenth-century Siena Cathedral, with its alternating dark green and cream stone stripes in the campanile, and the wider spaced stripes of the exterior nave walls, provided a model for later Victorian structural polychromy. This was true of many other medieval Italian monuments, including Orvieto Cathedral, begun in 1290, the eleventh-century baptistery in Florence, and, in Pisa, the cathedral,

In Pisa, Italy, the ornamentation of the Romanesque cathedral (on the left) is enhanced by bands of dark- and light-colored marble. The famous leaning campanile or tower (right) of the cathedral has a more muted color scheme.

campanile, and baptistery, built from the eleventh to the thirteenth centuries. Pisan buildings were also banded with courses of dark marble, which offset the lighter marble both inside and out. The floor of Pisa's baptistery, which has concentric marble stripes surrounding the central baptismal font, emphasizes the purpose of the building.

In the fourteenth and fifteenth centuries, Italian use of decorative stone continued. The Palazzo Ducale (Doge's Palace), once the seat of power in Venice, was designed with bricklike pink and white marble laid in a diamond pattern on the upper stories. Below, stone arches and walls contrast with the marble in both color and texture. The stone arcade paving is another strong contrast, with a cream geometric pattern against a dark gray field.

Islamic architecture extensively used structural polychromy. In Moorish Spain, notably at the Mezquita in Córdoba, the horseshoe arches are of red brick alternating with white stone, carried by exquisite salvaged columns in many different stones, resulting in a striking effect. In the Taj Mahal in Agra, India, stone flooring is treated with bold geometric patterns, contrasting with the floral decor on wall and screen surfaces.

Color in the Pantheon

The Pantheon, built in Rome in CE 125, was designed to be a temple to all the Roman gods. Although alterations were made in the third, seventh (when it was converted to a church), and eighteenth centuries, the building is essentially intact. The colorful, bold interior of a huge hemispherical dome sitting on a drum contrasts with the basically monochromatic concrete exterior, with its gray Egyptian granite columns. Interior surfaces are faced with pink-veined marble, trimmed with dark green, dividing the walls into smaller-scaled units. The flooring consists of large fields of stone sourced from various parts of the Roman world, including porphyry from Egypt, and a gray granite that may have been quarried in the Alps. The base of the drum is faced with several types of marble, and book-matched panels of alternating gray and pink marble create a band at the height of the capitals of six pairs of colossal pink marble Corinthian columns.

Mezquita
Córdoba, Spain

The Mezquita (Great Mosque) of Córdoba, which dates from about CE 786, is a magnificent example of early Islamic architecture. It was built at the behest of the Umayyad ruler of Córdoba, Abd ar-Rahman I, who had moved to the city from Damascus, Syria. The great size of this structure is testimony to the success of the spread of Islam in the West, while its ornamentation reflects the increase in contact between cultures at that time.

Influences

The design incorporates aspects of Syrian Umayyad mosques, which contained dazzling ornamentation, and the Dome of the Rock in Jerusalem (begun in CE 688). It also shows the influence of Byzantine architecture, which developed elaborately ornamented interiors during the same period. Byzantine architecture, notably the sixth-century church of San Vitale in Ravenna, Italy, was filled with complex patterns of mosaics made from *tesserae* (small tiles) in rich colors, many kinds of stone, carvings, and inlay applied to the interior surfaces. The style and patterns of the geometric designs found in these buildings were also used in the design of small, portable objects, such as religious artworks and textiles. It was the export of these Byzantine works that spread the motifs as far as Russia, the Balkans, and Spain.

Other influences include existing structures nearby, including a Roman bridge constructed with sixteen stone arches. The same technology was used in the famous double-tiered horseshoe arches of the mosque, striking for the height this creates and for the polychromy of alternating red-brick and white-stone voussoir blocks which form each arch. A hypostyle hall such as this, in which the roof rests on columns, was a common form for mosques in Spain, Arabia, and Africa, but this forest of bicolored columns supporting piers and a vaulted ceiling is unique. The vast two-tiered construction has the effect of making the interior seem almost infinite, with arches and columns interrupting the view. The variety of columns is also quite remarkable. Some are made of smooth marble, some are twisted, and, taken together, the columns display a great range of reused Corinthian and Corinthian-inspired capitals from Roman, Byzantine, and Visigothic buildings.

The Layout

At first, the mosque was twelve bays wide, but it was expanded several times to accommodate a burgeoning Muslim population, reflecting the city's growing prosperity. The original building, or at least the foundations, may predate the Islamic presence in the region. This may explain why the mosque was constructed with a southern orientation, and not built directly facing Mecca, which was and still is the practice in mosque design. As a result, the *mihrab*, a niche marking the *quibla* (the direction toward Mecca) is not centered in the prayer hall. In 832, Abd al-Rahman II began a program to increase the size of the building. The minaret, 111 ft (34 m) tall, was built in 951, when Abd al-Rahman III enlarged the mosque again.

Between 987 and 990, the mosque was again enlarged. Eight bays were added to the east side of the mosque, and Al-Mansur, the vizier of Hisham II, also enlarged the *sahn* (courtyard), filling the space with orange trees to give shade

The prayer hall of the mosque is a forest of two-tiered, horseshoe arches, each with distinctive voussoirs of red and white. They are mainly carried by columns taken from Roman buildings.

for the faithful as they washed before praying. By the end of its growth, the mosque was 19 aisles and over 30 bays wide—about 425 ft (130 m)—with a length of about 590 ft (180 m).

The Mihrab and Maqsura

When the existing minaret was erected in the tenth century, it was placed directly opposite the *mihrab*. To give emphasis to this axis, four domes that are not functionally necessary were added at the same time. These domes are subdivided with purely ornamental, non structural ribs, obscuring any hint of the actual structure. The purely decorative flourishes continue, with delicate geometric and organic ornamentation that dematerializes the surroundings of the *mihrab* domes even further.

The *mihrab* is a remarkable feature of this mosque. It is situated within a particularly ornate sector of the building, and is not just a niche but an entire octagonal vault, which is part of a bay of eleven aisles. Its entrance is a keyhole arch with large marble blocks supporting the ornately

decorated voussoirs carved with stylized vegetal ornament. Trilobed arches in the *mihrab* octagon support a dome carved to look like flower petals. The dome above the *mihrab* bay is even more ornate, with a scalloped dome inscribed in an octagon. This is braced by eight arches forming a star pattern beneath the octagon, and supported by pilasters with Corinthian capitals.

In addition, the archway, the dome in front of the *mihrab,* and the adjacent *maqsura*, a private area set aside for the ruler, are ornamented with mosaics designed and executed by a Byzantine artisan. Small *tesserae* give the surfaces a shimmering aspect that adds to the complexity of this focal point. Overhead, arches are more ornate than in the remainder of the mosque. They are both scalloped and interlaced, with a filigree of delicate carvings. The upper piers have a stylized pilaster carved on the surface to break the form into smaller, more delicate elements. This is the only decorative device within the building that emphasizes the direction of Mecca, an indication of the importance of this place.

The scalloped dome in front of the *mihrab* is lavishly decorated with blue, green, and red mosaics on a gold background. The materials for the mosaics may have been gifts of the Byzantine emperor.

The Mezquita is an architectural homage to the Islamic influence upon Spanish culture that was curtailed—but never eliminated—after Catholic rulers took power in Córdoba in 1236. The building exists today because the Catholic population so admired it that they refused to demolish it, as had been proposed. In the sixteenth century, a cathedral was built within the mosque. The ribbed vaulting of the nave was inserted into the hypostyle hall, resting directly on existing keyhole arches. The small columns of this mainly late Gothic structure are an interesting counterpart to the delicate carvings of the *maqsura* and *mihrab*. This mixture of styles and functions produced a building that, in itself, shows the cross-pollination, clashes, and artistic exchanges between Catholic and Islamic Spain.

327

Inlays

Inlay is the art of carving a design into a substrate, usually stone or wood, and filling this area with a different material so that the surface is flush and a design is apparent. The term "damascening" is used when the inlay consists of metal inserted into metal, such as in the design of jewelry. The cloisonné technique is a method of introducing colorful elements into metalwork, using delicate wires soldered onto a metal substrate to create boundaries for enamel that is placed within these shapes.

Inlay has a long history. In the Middle East, the Canaanites in 1200 BCE and earlier used inlay techniques to decorate metal bowls and cedar furniture. Much later, the Greeks designed both furniture and tombs in this manner. This fact is mentioned in the *Odyssey*, in which Homer describes a wooden bed Odysseus made, inlaid with ivory, gold, and silver. In the Far East, artisans decorated bronzes with different inlaid metals, and in Korea, by 1150 CE, celadon pottery was created with inlay techniques that historians think may have been adapted from the earlier practice of bronze inlay.

While metal inlay was often gold or silver, a black alloy of silver, copper, and lead sulfides called *niello* was used by Roman and Byzantine artisans and possibly earlier. *Niello* was popular because of the color contrast it provided and its softness when heated. Later forms of this material, used by medieval and Renaissance artisans, were more difficult to use because the alloy was different, but even so, Russian, East Asian, and Islamic artisans continued this technique into the modern era.

Pietre dure (Italian for "hard stones") is an inlay technique, using rare and semiprecious stones, developed in Italy during the sixteenth century. In Florence, a workshop that created inlaid boxes, flasks, wall panels, and other objects was the center for this craft. Stones were selected for their rarity, color, and supposed curative properties.

Mughal Inlay

The Mughal Empire, established in the sixteenth century, brought *pietre dure* to South Asia, where it was called *parchin kari*. This intricate inlay has figurative designs, such as flowers, leaves, and geometric patterns. At the Taj Mahal in Agra, India, completed in 1653, the use of inlay begins at the entrance to the complex, where the sandstone gates are inlaid with colored marble, and continues in the main mausoleum, which is decorated with geometric floral and leaf patterns, and numerous poetic texts and passages taken from

Parchin kari work embellishes the exterior of the tomb of Itimad al-Dawlah, chief minister of the Mughal Emperor Jahangir, in Agra, India.

the Koran, all using the *parchin kari* technique. Also in Agra is another Mughal building featuring *parchin kari*, the tomb of Itimad al-Dawlah, built in 1628 by Queen Nur Jahan for her father. It is filled with intricate floral inlays of yellow porphyry, agate, jasper, and black marble. Other important Mughal structures using stone inlay include the seventeenth century tomb complexes of the Mughal Emperor Jahangir (at Shahdara, near Lahore, Pakistan), and the tomb of his father, Akbar the Great (near Agra).

Coptic Inlay

After the Muslim Arabs conquered Egypt in the seventh century CE, Coptic Egyptian architecture combined the imagery of Christian art with the geometric intricacy of Islamic-influenced ornament. This combination is prominently displayed on such objects as the inlay panels of the iconostasis—the Coptic church screen—which includes icons of saints, as well as ebony, ivory, and other highly valued semiprecious materials, which are arranged in geometric patterns.

Cosmati Work

Between about 1100 and 1300, an Italian inlay technique called Cosmati work, consisting of glass and marble *tesserae* (small tiles), was practiced, and used as inlay for church campaniles, furnishings, featured walls, and marble flooring. The people who carried on this craft came from one family, the Cosmati of Rome, and they practiced predominantly in and around the province of Rome, although some were invited to work in England. The intricate geometric patterns they used derived from earlier Greek and Roman tilework, and perhaps Islamic and Byzantine geometric ornament. The work consists of eye-catching, vividly colored regular tessellated patterns. Particularly notable is the nave floor of the Cathedral of San Cesareo in Terracina, near Rome, where small black, tan,

and white triangles and rectangles border boldly veined dark marble circles surrounded and bordered by white marble.

Parquet Inlay

Basketweave, herringbone, and other optically intriguing geometric patterns were common in both ancient Egyptian marquetry—inlaid wood, chiefly used in furniture—and the parquet flooring used much later in Baroque and Rococo architecture. This practice of parquet inlay was

Swirling bands of marble and glass characterize the Cosmati work on the floor of the high altar of Westminster Abbey, London. It dates from 1268.

revived in the seventeenth century in Dutch, German, and eventually English and French architecture, as well as in furniture design. All this was possible because of technical advances in the milling of wood, as well as the international trade in exotic hardwoods.

Inlay in Orvieto Cathedral

The medieval Italian architects Arnolfo di Cambio, Giovanni Ammanate, and Lorenzo Maitani were three of the important designers behind the great Gothic Cathedral of Orvieto, Italy, which was built from 1290 to 1500. The ornamentation owes a great debt to the geometric patterning of Islamic tile and inlay, particularly on the exterior. Inlay was used for interior decoration on the wood choir stalls designed in the fourteenth century by Sienese artisans, notably Pietro de Minella. A variety of woods, cut along the end grain into small geometric pieces, created patterns called *intarsia a toppo*. This was combined with images of religious figures, also inlaid in wood and rendered with a high degree of fine detail. Similarly, figures of saints were combined with geometric intarsia for the wooden lectern. This technique was also used in other medieval Italian churches, including the slightly later choir stalls in the Cappella dei Signori in Siena.

The choir stalls of Orvieto Cathedral, Italy, begun in about 1330, are inlaid with different types of wood to create a variety of patterns.

Taj Mahal
Agra, India

The Taj Mahal is a prime example of the integration of ornament and architecture. Located in Agra, in the Indian state of Uttar Pradesh, this Islamic building is one of the greatest works of architecture in the world. It was commissioned by the Mughal Emperor Shah Jahan (reigned 1628–1658) as a mausoleum for his wife, Mumtaz Mahal, who died in 1631 giving birth to his fourteenth child.

This completely symmetrical building sits prominently on a plinth measuring 1,110 sq ft (103 sq m). Beyond the plinth are four minarets placed symmetrically around the structure. The Taj Mahal is the centerpiece of a majestic complex that includes an entrance court, a gateway, a mosque, a guesthouse, and formal gardens with a reflecting pool.

The Illuminated Tomb

Construction work began the year after Mumtaz Mahal's death. Shah Jahan brought to Agra highly talented artisans and master builders from India and central and western Asia, including notable Persian and Turkish experts. Architects, draftsmen, masons, carpenters, calligraphers, inlayers, stucco plasterers, and builders specializing in dome construction techniques all made a contribution. A number of architects worked on the complex, including Ismail Khan, from Turkey, and Ustad Ahmad Lahori (Master Ahmad of Lahore). Construction lasted for 17 years, and required a labor force of about 20,000.

The setting, symmetry, and sparkling façades of the Taj Mahal make clear the building's importance. A rectangular reflecting pool leads the eye up to the pointed central arch set within a rectangular plane and from there to the central dome, which is capped with a delicate gilded bronze finial. Massive masonry walls are made to seem lightweight through the use of intricate stone inlay on the surfaces of almost white stone. Also contributing to an illusion of near weightlessness are the bright translucent marble, the delicate proportions and ornament, and the dramatic shadows formed by deep recesses in the façades. Because of the luminous exterior, Mughal writings referred to the Taj Mahal as the Rauza-i Munawara, the Illuminated Tomb.

Exquisite Ornament

From a distance, the Taj Mahal appears to be entirely white—it is clad in white marble from India's Makran region—but a closer look reveals colored stone inlay, which is used throughout the complex. Major elements are emphasized with floral and geometric patterns, as well as Koranic quotations, carved into the marble and filled with stone. This ornamental technique, called *parchin*

kari in South Asia and *pietre dure* in Europe, requires a sculptor to incise the shapes into the marble and then fill the form with precisely cut carved stone or other hard material. The infill used at the Taj Mahal consisted of mother of pearl, coral, and a variety of semiprecious and rare stones including agate, cornelian, bloodstone, turquoise, lapis lazuli, onyx, garnet, and jasper. Precious stones were also used, including sapphire, emerald, ruby, pearl, and topaz.

The building's ornamentation was carefully placed to emphasize particular forms. For example, a floral motif fills each spandrel panel above the pointed arches, creating a contrast between the white marble within the opening and the façade. The geometric floral motif banding the base of the main onion-shaped dome (*amrud*) calls attention to the slight bulging above. Surrounding the main dome, four kiosks (*chhatris*) capped with four miniature domes repeat the form, but without this emphasis of geometric banding. The smaller pavilions at the top of each minaret repeat the dome form yet again. Artisans also designed with marble alone. For example, each dome is topped with a carved marble lotus form, and the plinth that forms a base for the building is adorned with a blind marble arcade of arches, creating a play of light and shadow on the façades.

Inside the Taj Mahal, a central octagonal chamber is covered by a domed ceiling. This space houses a marble cenotaph for Mumtaz and one for her husband, Shah Jahan. These cenotaphs are purely ceremonial, as the deceased were

The perfect symmetry of the Taj Mahal is accentuated by the narrow pool that leads the eye toward the main dome. The four minarets are purely decorative, having no practical purpose.

buried in marble caskets in a crypt (*maqbarah*) below. The cenotaphs are surrounded by an octagonal screen wall (*jali*), which defines an inner space that feels even more significant because of the partition's intricate design. Piercings in the marble *jali* form complex filigree patterns that resemble metalwork, with lacy intertwining patterns. Mumtaz's cenotaph sits in the middle of this space on a marble floor patterned to receive the raised platform. Later, when Shah Jahan died, his cenotaph was added to the right of Mumtaz's. The white marble cenotaphs and caskets are decorated with calligraphy and highly stylized inlaid floral patterns in colorful rare and semiprecious stones. Flowering plant motifs were used in both the cenotaphs and the ornamentation of the building itself, notably as low-relief carved decorations on the building's exterior around the dado, or base, of the entrances.

Floral Motifs and Calligraphy

Geometric patterns adorn the complex's flooring, both exterior and interior. But most of the surface ornamentation is floral. This is fitting because floral embroidered cloth was a passion of Mumtaz. This type of cloth had become available during the seventeenth century when trade between Europe and India resulted in the production of Indian cloth made expressly for export. Textiles were embroidered with patterns combining Indian artistic traditions with flowers taken from European botanical albums. These motifs are similar to the floral designs used both in the Taj Mahal and in an earlier mausoleum Mumtaz had commissioned when her father died in 1641.

The abundance of floral design is contrasted by the black and white panels of calligraphy—passages are thematically related quotations from the Koran—that were also extensively used as a design motif. The chief calligrapher, an artisan from Shiraz (Iran), Amanat Khan Shirazi (also called Abd al-Haqq), wrote verses from the Koran (in Arabic) with ink on paper, and these full-size images were then transferred to the stone for incising by the stone carvers.

The elegant calligraphy and floral designs on the surfaces of the Taj Mahal unfold the building's spiritual essence, which a visitor first glimpses upon arrival when the pure symmetry and perfect geometry is reflected in the water and illuminated by the sky.

The main dome *(amrud)* of the Taj Mahal (left) was designed by Ismail Khan of Turkey. It is 65 ft (20 m) in diameter and 187 ft (57 m) high, and is topped by a finial of bronze (originally of gold).

At the center of the Taj Mahal is the cenotaph of Mumtaz Mahal (above), which is decorated with verses from the Koran (on the upper part) and floral designs (on the lower). Alongside her centotaph is that of her husband, Shah Jahan, placed here on his death in 1666.

Tiles

The expressive nature of tiles, with their variety of surfaces and coloration, has made them an invaluable tool for the ornamentation of buildings, from monumental works to regional vernacular architecture. In particular, the colors of tiles, their ability to reflect light, to be arranged into patterns, and to be painted and glazed, have provided artists with a uniquely flexible and expressive medium which also gives a durable surface.

A tile is a thin piece of hard material used for covering a surface. Many different materials are used for making tiles, and the tiles can be arranged with an almost limitless variety. Artisans have used regular and irregular pieces of tile as borders, friezes, murals, and ceiling and floor coverings, both inside and out, in free form as well as geometric patterns. As well as being purely decorative, wall and floor art in civic or religious buildings can serve to relate histories, legends, and concepts, and information about people and places.

Patterns and Types

Regular tesselated tiles are evenly spaced and can only be made from square, triangular, or hexagonal pieces. By combining all three shapes together in one design, several other patterns are possible. This technique is called Archimedean, or semiregular tiling. It was used in Islamic architecture, Italian medieval architecture, and other traditions, and is still found in contemporary work.

Encaustic tiles are unglazed tiles made from different colored clays, rather than glazes, to create patterns. They are formed by pressing clay into a carved mold to produce a depression for a later inlay of another clay or clays, which form a design

Elaborate, multicolored tilework covers the brick structure of the seventeenth-century Mosque of Sheikh Lotfollah, in Isfahan, Iran. The interior is similarly ornamented.

Tile Patterns and Types

Mosaic

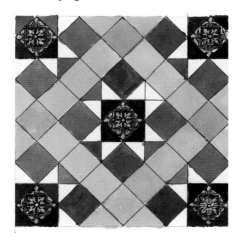

Tessellated tile

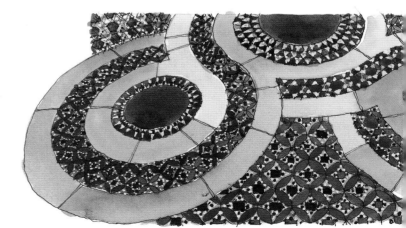

Opus Alexandrinum

Vividly colored tiles blanket the sinuous shapes and pinnacles of the gatehouses in the Parc Güell in Barcelona, Spain, designed by Antoni Gaudí. Originally intended as a privately owned garden city housing estate, the area was declared a public park in 1922.

century in Rome by the Cosmati family and became known as Cosmati work.

Mosaic *tesserae* were laid in various ways to achieve different effects. Geometrically regular tiles were laid in a grid pattern (known today as *opus regulatum*), and irregular tiles were laid in non-gridded or seemingly random fashion (today called *opus palladianum*). Sometimes, both techniques were mixed in one work, to create a textural contrast. Floor mosaics used trees, fruits, animals, and people in scenes bordered by a vocabulary of visually intriguing patterns that imitate braided ropes or appear to be interlocked scrolls. The Romans and Byzantines were masters of the mosaic.

Iranian Tilework

The ancient art of glazed tile manufacture seems to have been revived in Iran around the ninth century CE, and its products were detailed and exquisite. One fine example is the seventeenth-century Mosque of Sheikh Lotfollah in Isfahan, Iran, which is tiled both inside and out with interwoven floral patterns. Fields of differing color palettes and differing scales of floral patterns help define the architectural elements, including the arches below the dome. The dome's exterior is covered by tan enameled bricks with blue accents that unify the dome with the blue in the wall below. The interior dome surface is a brilliant mosaic in a golden color with buff-colored bricks creating a bold design infilled with a repeating floral mosaic. The tilework in Iran is a masterful blend of the floral and the geometric.

baked into the tile. Architectural uses of this technique can be found in buildings which date back to the thirteenth century. In the early nineteenth century, the invention of pressing machinery enabled manufacturers to produce such tiles again.

In Roman architecture, a technique called opus Alexandrinum was used, in which regular *tesserae* (small tiles) and pieces of marble, stone, and glass were arranged in patterns around discs of marble, which were often made by slicing up old columns. This was revived in the twelfth

Modern Interpretations

The Catalan architect Antoni Gaudí collaborated with the mosaicist Josep Maria Jujol to design the Parc Güell (Güell Park) on the slopes of the Montaña Pelada in Barcelona, Spain, constructed between 1900 and 1914. Gaudí and Jujol covered the sinuous organic shapes within the park using odd-shaped and broken pieces of mosaic tile *(trendacís)*. The shards are imbedded in grout to face curvilinear fountains, animals (including a playful dragon), and a terrace with a long, curving bench in the shape of a serpent. Beneath the terrace, a monochromatic tile surface of undulating white "clouds" creates the ceiling of a hypostyle hall which supports the terrace. The wavy roof forms of the buildings at the entrance to the park are also covered with the colorful, smooth shards.

The Brazilian architect Oscar Niemeyer designed the Church of São Francisco (St. Francis) in Pampulha, Belo Horizonte, Brazil, in 1943. The mosaic façade of the church, depicting scenes from the life of St. Francis, was designed by the Brazilian painter Cândido Portinari and is completely integrated into this work. The colors and surface treatment recall the strong tradition of *azulejos*—glazed ornamental tiles which were traditionally mostly blue and white, and were imported from Portugal during Brazil's colonial period to be used in the most important buildings, including churches. The *azulejo* tile-making technique had been brought to Portugal and Spain by the Moors.

The Mosaics of San Vitale

The Byzantines inherited a tradition of rich surface ornamentation from their Roman and Hellenistic predecessors and brought the art of the mosaic to its peak of perfection. The chancel of the Church of San Vitale in Ravenna, Italy, unquestionably a masterpiece of Byzantine architecture, is filled with a rich series of mosaics, all from around CE 540. These works are comprised of small, irregularly shaped *tesserae*, in vibrant colors, from many varieties of stone, glass, and glazed clays. The mosaics depict a mixture of religious and civic narratives, including images of Jesus Christ, angels, biblical events, and the Byzantine emperor and empress and other figures, including priests. Taken together, the church's mosaics have an extraordinary beauty and power.

In the mosaics of San Vitale, the Emperor Justinian is shown, flanked by priests and courtiers, carrying a bowl containing eucharistic bread.

333

Alhambra
Granada, Spain

The Alhambra, one of the few remaining well-preserved medieval palace complexes in Europe, is a remarkable embodiment of Moorish architecture and ornamentation. Built in the thirteenth and fourteenth centuries on the hill of Sabika, it overlooks Granada, which from 1300 was the last Moorish territory in Spain. The complex started out as a fortified citadel, initiated by the founder of the Nasrid Dynasty, Ibn al-Ahmar, who ruled Granada as Muhammad I. It evolved into a small city, with a palace sector for royalty in the northern part. This was the home of the Nasrids until 1492, when the Catholic Monarchs, Queen Isabella and King Ferdinand, defeated Abu 'abd Allah Muhammad XI, known as Boabdil, the last Moorish ruler of Granada.

The Alhambra includes towers, courtyards, and ceremonial spaces which are decorated with stone, stucco, tiles, and carvings. These decorative treatments contribute to the effect of demater-ialized walls and ceilings, hiding the structural aspects of vaults and domes. They also speak of the history and meaning of the buildings and the kingdom: one low-relief carving in Arabic states, "There is no conqueror but God," the motto of Muhammad I. While Córdoba's Mezquita (Great Mosque) is an early example of the Moorish style, both sturdy and bold, the Alhambra's interior spaces are characterized by the delicate filigree of ornamental details that cover surfaces with predominantly lacy forms, such as *muqarnas*—vaults ornamented to resemble honeycombs or stalactites—quotations from the Koran and poetry, and slender columns, pilasters, and inventive column capitals and impost blocks.

The Mexuar and Cuarto Dorado

The main Nasrid palace complex is known as the Casa Real Vieja (Old Royal Residence). The result of many building programs, it consists of courts, gardens, and halls for ceremonial purposes. Each room is filled with inventive and intricate ornamentation. Important rooms are adjacent to equally impressive courtyards which connect the many parts of the palace. Miradors (viewing porches) provide expansive views of the Alhambra gardens and of Granada beyond. Some of the most significant parts of the complex are described below.

A building called the Mexuar serves as the entrance to the Casa Real Vieja. It contains a long rectangular room entered from the south through a gate decorated with stucco. Inside the Mexuar, four short marble columns divide the front portion of the hall from a larger gallery

Decorating many of the Alhambra's walls are mosaics in complex vegetal or, as here, geometric patterns of great beauty. An inscription in one room likens the tiles on its walls and floors to brocade.

space and support impost blocks below a stucco-encrusted entablature with a gallery above. On the walls, tiles are arranged in diamond patterns on the lower wall and a carved frieze of text bands the wall above. "Everything you own comes from God," reads one inscription. The exact purpose of the Mexuar is not known, but the royal court may have been held here.

To the east of the Mexuar stands the Cuarto Dorado (Golden Court), known for its fine stuccowork and a corbeled frieze using a *muqarnas* form. Ornate stuccowork on the walls completely hides the structure behind. This ornamentation was clearly designed to make an impression, for the Cuarto Dorado was the royal entrance to the palace complex during the reign of Muhammad V in the second half of the fourteenth century.

The Courtyards

The Mexuar adjoins two courtyards, the Patio de los Arrayanes (Court of the Myrtles) and the Patio de los Leones (Court of the Lions). The Patio de los Arrayanes is distinctive for the long reflecting pool that runs along its axis. A portico with six slender columns frames the two short end walls, and above the north wall looms the Torre de Comares (Comares Tower). The water in the pool makes a contrast with the solidity of the walls, which are ornamented with ceramics, delicate and ornate wooden frames, and stucco decorated with geometric and vegetal patterns.

Water also plays an important role in the nearby Patio de los Leones. Four water channels terminate at the central fountain in the court,

At the Patio de los Arrayanes (Court of the Myrtles), surrounding buildings, including the delicate portico and the crenellated Torre de Comares (Comares Tower), are reflected in the narrow, myrtle-lined pool.

dividing the courtyard into four parts. This calming and cooling feature is augmented by the deep shadows created by an arcade framing the court on all four sides. On two ends, arcaded pavilions protrude into the space and provide a strong east–west axis, creating even deeper shade and blurring the division between interior and exterior. The courtyard was once planted with six orange trees, which were complemented by the vegetal designs throughout the complex.

Throughout the Alhambra, more than thirty inscriptions of poetry are carved in walls and on fountains. Poetry is prominently displayed in the Sala de los Reyes (Hall of the Kings), which is adjacent to the eastern end of the Patio de los Leones. There, the letters are interwoven with

vegetal forms, and surrounded by a combination of geometric and vegetal relief carving. Highly stylized calligraphy intertwines leaves and vines with phrases in Arabic written specifically for the Nasrid rulers.

The Sala de las Dos Hermanas (Hall of the Two Sisters) flanks the Patio de los Leones on the north, and the Sala de los Abencerrajes (Hall of the Abencerrajes) to the south. In both halls, the domes are completely covered with breathtaking white carved *muqarnas* vaults, which are delicately lit by small windows. In the Sala de las Dos Hermanas, the floor is paved with smooth marble, but the upper walls are of stucco, carved into shallow blind arches and intricate patterns of vegetal and geometric designs, as well as Arabic

The *muqarnas* vault of the Sala de las Dos Hermanas (Hall of the Two Sisters) is made up of numerous small stucco niches that create a dazzling honeycomb effect. Elsewhere in this hall, poetic inscriptions compare the room and its vault to the heavens.

poetry. Below are geometrically arranged tiles in dark colors offset with white and Arabic text.

The overall effect of such skillful combinations of intricate ornamentation—geometric, vegetal, and calligraphic—is to hide the structure of the Alhambra, whose surfaces seem to dissolve in a light diffused by texture, color and pattern. In this way, the rooms, passages, overlooks, courtyards, and porches retain a sense of mystery and wonder.

335

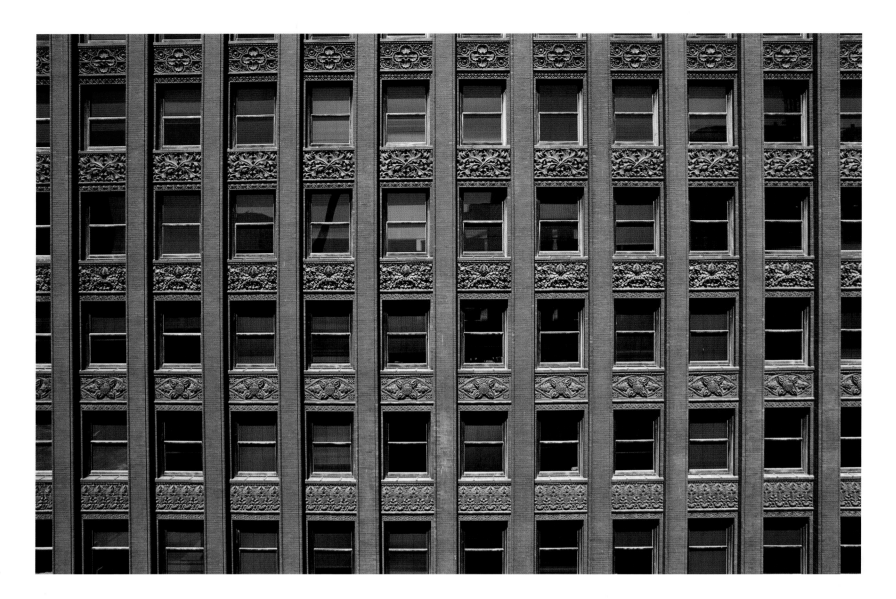

Pilasters

A pilaster is a slight protrusion from a wall, usually rectangular in section, and resembling a flattened column. While they may often be only decorative elements that give an opportunity to express dynamic form or a sense of order, pilasters also serve an important function, creating an architectural response to structural columns and piers.

Pilasters are often used as decorative covers for structural piers that are deeper than the walls they support. By contrast, the classical column is a fully cylindrical element, not attached to any wall. The half-column is defined as half round in section and engaged with a wall. Similarly, the three-quarter engaged column has a three-quarter-round section. Both engaged columns and pilasters can be structural, adding thickness to the wall section, but pilasters and engaged columns are often only ornamental.

Compositionally, pilasters can express the rhythm of the structural bays of a building and provide a sense of scale and harmony. In classical, neoclassical, and Greek revival buildings, pilasters have capitals, and can be fluted. In Baroque architecture, pilasters modulate walls and define bays and rhythms. For example, at the Residenz, a palace in Würzburg, Germany, the architect Balthasar Neumann used pilasters to create order and rhythm in the grand staircase hall, overlapping pilaster over pilaster for an extra sense of depth and modulation. Architects of the early skyscrapers, such as Dankmar Adler and Louis Sullivan, designed façades with multistoried pilasters to create a sense of order and emphasize height.

Roman Pilasters

A half-column's greater protrusion from the wall behind, and the greater shadow this produces, gives the impression that a half-column can carry more weight than the flatter pilaster. The Romans used this visual perception to great effect in their architecture. In multistoried buildings, Roman

Leon Battista Alberti adapted the classical orders using pilasters to create the elegant façade of the Palazzo Rucellai in Florence, Italy.

architects conveyed the idea that the building was more massive at the bottom and lighter in the upper stories through a progression of orders. This visual progression is clearly expressed in the Colosseum in Rome, where the substantial-looking Doric half-columns are attached to the huge piers on the lowest level, unifying their arcaded pier construction with the ancient Greek trabeated (post and beam) aesthetic the Romans respected. The more slender order of Ionic half-columns is on the second level, again attached to the structural piers, and the third level is decorated with even more delicate-looking Corinthian half-columns. On the fourth level is the lightest expression of all, the Corinthian pilaster, which carries through the theme of trabeated construction, but purely as decoration.

Renaissance Pilasters

Classical architectural vocabulary, and with it, the pilaster and the engaged half-column, was central to the design work of Renaissance architects. In about 1441, Filippo Brunelleschi created a new interior for the Medici family's San Lorenzo parish church in Florence. He articulated the Corinthian pilasters on the side aisle by using a gray stone, *pietra serena*, for the pilasters and other details, including the arcades, all set off against a wall of white stucco. The contrast unifies the pilasters, columns, cornices, and half-round arches that define the bays of the church.

As Renaissance architects experimented, they used the shallow pilaster as a way to make the façade of a building seem like a taut, almost weightless, screen. The Palazzo Rucellai, built in Florence by Leon Battista Alberti from 1455 to 1470, referred back to the Roman convention of a Doric order on the lowest level, Ionic on the second, and Corinthian on the third, but a taut, sleek façade was achieved through the expression of the orders entirely with pilasters, eliminating the more substantial-looking half-columns the Romans used. The pilaster on the façade continued to be used inventively by architects, in pairs, for example, and as colossal orders, spanning two or more stories. Giuliano da Sangallo's Basilica of Santa Maria delle Carceri in Prato, Italy, built in the late fifteenth century, uses both pairing and colossal orders to express the building's height and monumentality.

As a new generation of architects took pure Classicism and transformed it in Mannerist and then Baroque experimentation, the pilaster was key to the dynamic façades and interiors they created. Bernini's Sant'Andrea al Quirinale in Rome, completed in 1670, both inside and out uses pilasters with columns as a way to create a dynamic sculptural form. A human-scale entry porch supported by single-story columns is set before a main façade that is a full story higher, with a pediment supported by piers faced by two-story Corinthian pilasters. A second set of pilasters, which actually turn the corner of the façade, expresses the protrusion of the main pediment from the wall behind.

Santi Luca e Martina

The church of Santi Luca e Martina in Rome is an early Baroque design which already illustrates the emerging tendency toward plastic modeling. It is a two-story trabeated (post and beam) façade, incorporating both columns and pilasters, a combination which in itself creates a variety of depth and shadow. And contrary to the impression of a stable and rational structure, the whole surface seems to thrust and buckle as if the cylindrical shape is trying to burst out of the surrounding block. This arbitrary evocation of plastic forces completely overwhelms any reading of the conventional column and beam action which would normally be suggested by such a classical composition. The two horizontal entablatures seem less like beams than like belts trying to restrain the exploding façade. The pilasters, normally somewhat inert elements, are even more important than the columns, and give the projecting side elements the stability necessary to contain the bulging centre. The ornamental cartouche, which breaks through the segmental pediment on top, carries overtones of the earlier Mannerist style.

The church dedicated to Martina, a martyr under the Roman emperor Septimus Severus, was given to the members of St. Luke's Academy in 1588, and they added their patron saint to the dedication. It was remodeled by Pietro da Cortona between 1635 and 1650.

Statues

Whether carved from stone or wood, formed from terracotta, or cast in metal, statues may be purely decorative, or impart meaning and importance to architecture. Statuary has served this dual purpose in many cultures from ancient times until the present day. There are many ways statuary and architecture can be integrated, and a few of the possible strategies are discussed here.

Through the use of proportion, statues can help the viewer comprehend the scale of architectural elements, or conversely, fool the eye into misunderstanding scale and proportion. By relating a narrative, such as a biblical event, statues, particularly in groupings, can reinforce the purpose of a building. A single piece of colossal statuary can awe the observer or be a building's focus. Some statues are so large that they are themselves buildings, as is the Statue of Liberty in New York, designed by the sculptor Frédéric-Auguste Bartholdi and engineered by Gustave Eiffel. The statue's symbolism, including the broken chains at Liberty's feet to represent the end of bondage, sends a clear message.

Caryatids and other Statues in Ancient Greek Architecture

In ancient Greek architecture, statues of female figures called caryatids were sometimes used instead of Ionic columns. These were used at the sixth-century BCE Treasury of the Siphnians at Delphi, which also had a continuous frieze of relief sculpture across the entablature with statues of sphinxes and the winged victory goddess Nike posed on the roof. The sphinxes, caryatids, and the ever-watchful Nike served as symbolic guardians of the treasures kept within. This early Greek example of caryatids in architecture shows how the sculpture can be integrated into the structure and meaning of the building. Later Greek examples include the more famous porch of the Erechtheion, on the Acropolis of Athens, which is supported by six maidens.

The Statue of Liberty stands at the entrance to New York harbor, a symbol of political freedom. A gift to the American people from the people of France, it was inaugurated in October 1886.

A caryatid is a scuptural decoration with a structural function. Shown on the left are three of the six caryatids that support an entrance porch at the Erechtheion, on the Acropolis of Athens, Greece.

In both Indian Hindu temples and medieval European churches, statuary is a significant architectural element and a narrative device at the same time. Through size, placement, and iconographic conventions, groupings of statues come to be understood by the faithful.

Integrating Statues with Architecture

When statuary and architecture are envisioned together, they create a whole that is greater than the sum of their parts. Some statues exist purely for functional and decorative reasons. Gargoyles, for example, act as waterspouts while at the same time adding an ornamental flourish to building exteriors. Because of their practical and decorative dual function, gargoyles were used by many different cultures and periods, including ancient Greece, medieval Japan and Europe, and in the Gothic Revival architecture of the nineteenth century. Similar statues that do not have a waterspout function are called grotesques or chimeras. These types are among the many forms of delicate carving that are used to break down the mass of a building's façade, create interest, and call attention to particular details.

At the Gothic cathedral of Nôtre-Dame de Paris, gargoyles and chimeras abound, as do statues of saints and biblical figures, which, though decorative, have a mainly religious purpose: to remind the faithful of biblical events and direct their minds to religious matters. The three doorways of the main entrance (the westwerk) have statues depicting the life of the Virgin Mary, the Last Judgment, and the life of St. Anne. A number of statues at Nôtre-Dame were deliberately damaged because of the ways in which people

interpreted them. For example, the statues of biblical kings above the main entrance were thought to depict French kings, and were vandalized during the French Revolution.

In the Renaissance, architecture and statuary were sometimes conceived as a unified whole. Such was the case in the New Sacristy for the Medici tombs in San Lorenzo Church, Florence, Italy, designed by Michelangelo from 1520. He never completed the project, but the statues he and others carved were designed specifically for this space. The completed pieces, particularly the statues of Night and Day on the Tomb of Giuliano de' Medici, flow with the lines of the architecture. Although the design is unfinished,

Gargoyles such as these on Nôtre-Dame de Paris (above) are designed to take water from the roof and away from the building, but their grotesque design has given them a life of their own as pure decoration.

the possibilities of the unification of art and architecture are apparent here. Also during the Renaissance in Italy, large statues were placed on the tops of important buildings, including above the cornice of various palazzi, the pediments of Andrea Palladio's churches and villas, Jacopo Sansovino's Library of San Marco in Venice, and Michelangelo's buildings on the Piazza del Campidoglio in Rome.

Terracotta Warriors and Stone Buddhas

Between 221 and 205 BCE, more than 700,000 people were involved in the construction of the tomb of the First Emperor of the Qin Dynasty near present-day Xi'an in Shaanxi Province, China. Artisans created more than 8,000 life-size terracotta warriors, horses, and other figures, as well as models of palaces and towers, and tools and weapons, all buried in the emperor's chamber. This is not only one of the most extensive sculpture projects known, but also a representation of ultimate imperial power. The fully three-dimensional sculptures show a powerful sensitivity, with each warrior having unique qualities and looking almost like portraiture.

Another large-scale sculpture project took place in China between c. 460 and 490, when Buddhism from India took root. Stone carvings of Buddha and his disciples were commissioned by Wei Dynasty rulers for rock-cut temples and cells. Sandstone cliffs were carved into colossal figures over 42 ft (13 m) high, using a style that was clearly influenced by Indian Buddhist traditions.

Terracotta soldiers stand in ranks in the pit in which they were buried, at the tomb of the First Emperor. Each man originally held a long spear or halberd.

Painted Walls

Paint is any colored substance that is spread thinly over a surface for decoration or protection. The most ancient paintings that still survive were applied directly to stone surfaces protected from the weather and rendered in pure pigments. Later, paint was made from pigment suspended in a medium, such as water, egg, or oil, which made the pigment into a liquid or paste that was easier to apply.

From Tempera to Acrylics

Of the many types of paint, tempera, a mixture of pigment, water, and egg yolk, is one of the earliest known, used even by the Egyptians. Tempera became quite popular during medieval and Renaissance times, and was often applied to wooden panels that were stabilized with bracing and glue, and prepared with a gesso coating, a mixture of gypsum and glue. After painting, the panels were attached to a wall, as, for example, an altarpiece. The smooth, white surface of the panel was ideal for accepting paint, and, for different decorative effects, it could also be lightly incised with a stylus or have gold leaf applied.

In oil painting, pigments are mixed with oil, usually linseed, to form a paste. Oil paint originated in northern Europe in the fifteenth century, and spread to the rest of Europe by the sixteenth century. Like tempera, it was used on treated wood and gesso panels, but it has a number of advantages over the older medium. Oil stays moist longer than water-based paint, allowing the painter to mix colors easily, either on the painting itself or before the paint is applied. This allows for subtle transitions and variations in color and tone. The artist can also manipulate and change the work, and even scrape off the painted surface before it dries. And because the dried oil paint is flexible, it can be used on a variety of surfaces without cracking. Consequently, artists began to use oils on canvas and exploit its properties, applying the flexible medium thickly to add texture.

Like tempera, the modern medium of acrylic is a water-based paint. It is made from a suspension of pigments in a polymer emulsion, a type of plastic. It can be applied as thickly as oil paint or thinned to a watercolor consistency, which allows a painter to apply the colors in a number of ways, from traditional brushwork to airbrush.

Ancient Discoveries

Ancient wall paintings, one of the earliest forms of ornament that survive today, tell us much about the concerns of the people who created them. The very earliest paintings are made with pigments alone. In Australia, paintings of this type may be as much as 75,000 years old. In Arnhem Land, northern Australia, paintings from the oldest known style depict images of people and kangaroos. Later paintings are known

A white kangaroo, with its internal organs clearly shown, decorates a rock shelter in Arnhem Land, Australia. The tradition of Aboriginal rock art stretches back tens of thousands of years.

to express beliefs about the painters' relationship to the natural and supernatural worlds.

In the Spanish Pyrenees, archaeologists have found caves containing handprints and painted images of bison, boar, deer, and other animals from between 30,000 and 10,000 BCE. More than 300 wall paintings and engravings of animals—dating from as long ago as 30,000 BCE—including mammoths and hyenas, were discovered in Chauvet cave, France. The cave paintings of Lascaux, France, date from about 15,000 to 13,000 BCE, and depict horses, bulls, stags, and humans. These images were outlined first, and then colored with other pigments, in yellow, red, brown, and black, stored in tubes made from bone. More recent rock paintings from around 5000 BCE, found in Tassili, Algeria, show humans and domesticated cattle. We can only conjecture as to the significance of these works, but the large number of hunting scenes may mean that the paintings were associated with magical rites to ensure success during the hunt.

In Dura Europos, Syria, archaeologists found a synagogue, a Christian baptistery, and a house used for Christian worship, all of which date to about 240–245 CE. In the synagogue, wall paintings depict Old Testament scenes, and other panels were painted in a *trompe l'oeil* imitation of stone. Wall paintings in the baptistery were much

more modest, but later, as Christianity grew and churches were built, paintings and other art forms were used to depict saints and Bible stories, which ornamented churches to dramatic effect.

Indian Murals

Paintings with religious meanings can also be found inside the rock-cut Buddhist Chaitya halls of Ajanta, in Maharashtra, India. From around the first century BCE to about 500 CE, these caves were carved to create temples with the architectural features of freestanding buildings, such as rib vaulting and columns. Numerous colorful religious paintings, depicting acts of devotion, survive in four of the Chaityas. One painting, *Prince Distributing Alms*, shows a prince with his horses, assistants, and the poor, while another, *Worship of the Buddha*, uses shading to make the Buddha seem three-dimensional on the flat plane. The paintings were applied onto a white plaster finish, first drawn in brown outlines and modeled with black, brown, red, and cream paint, which was made with dry pigment mixed with a liquid binder, similar to tempera.

Painting in pre-Columbian America

The vast ceremonial complex of Teotihuacán, Mexico, dates from about 350 to 650 CE. High platforms, topped with temples, were once colorfully painted. The platform of Quetzalcóatl (a god in the form of a feathered serpent) is still covered with geometric carvings of the rain god Tlaloc, the storm god, and stylized serpent heads. Small shells and abstract geometric shapes are carved between these larger figures. Paint on these decorative elements would have emphasized the intricate designs. The whole city was decorated with hundreds of murals, particularly in its residential complexes, such as the so-called "Palace of the Jaguars." The paintings depicted architectural elements, rituals, human and animal figures, shells, leaves, abstract patterns, and Tlaloc.

The Maya, who lived in southern Mexico and neighboring parts of Central America, also produced wall paintings with strong colors and narrative content. The site of Bonampak, in Chiapas, Mexico, from the eighth century CE, has particularly vivid paintings of courtly life.

The paintings at Bonampak, Mexico, are some of the best preserved of the Mayan period. The artists used red, a mustard color, blue-green, and brown to show a wide variety of scenes of upper-class life, including battles, prisoners brought before the king, and, shown here, musicians performing in the presence of a lord.

The interior walls of the synagogue at Dura Europos, Syria (left), are covered in scenes from the Hebrew Bible. The paintings were completed in *c.* 245 CE, and the synagogue was buried about ten years later, when the city's Roman defenders used it in their preparations to repel attacking Persians.

Frescoes and Friezes

For thousands of years, frescoes and friezes have been employed by various cultures to embellish architecture. It is through such decorative elements that buildings speak to us about their purpose and place in the culture and the legends and beliefs of a people.

Frescoes

Tempera paint, made from pigment and egg yolk, can be applied directly to walls and ceilings coated with wet plaster, a technique called fresco. The wet plaster absorbs the paint, resulting in a long-lasting mural, integral to the wall surface. The word *fresco* is Italian for "fresh," and refers to the freshness of the surface, which must be painted over immediately, before it becomes too dry.

In classical Italian fresco painting, first a lime plaster undercoat called a scratch coat *(trullisatio)* is applied to the surface to be painted. Then, a brown coat *(arriccio)* of plaster covers the scratch coat. Finally, a sand coat *(arenato)* is applied and upon this, a final plaster topcoat *(intonaco)* is troweled on smoothly or brushed on in a more highly textured way to receive the final paint. It is on this wet, fresh plaster surface that the artist paints. For a large fresco, each day a new section of plaster must be freshly prepared for the artist. Each of these sections is called a *giornato*. The artist must work quickly to paint the *giornato*, because it takes only a few hours for the plaster to dry, and careful planning is required.

Frescoes are very durable. The graceful frescoes discovered in the ruins of the Minoan civilization in Crete date from about 1600 to 1400 BCE. The Minoans used *buon fresco*, a technique in which the plaster was painted with pigments mixed only with water. In the Roman towns of Pompeii and Herculaneum, frescoes of people and landscape adorned the interiors of many houses. They were rendered within a painted framework of architectural elements shown in perspective. Expensive materials such as marble were imitated in Roman frescoes—a cheaper way to include such decoration than using the real thing.

In medieval times, when few people were literate, one way for the Christian church to transmit its teachings was through ornament. Frescoes, along with statues, wall paintings, and stained-glass windows, became an important means of conveying Bible stories, the lives of the saints, and the consequences of sin. Romanesque church frescoes, such as those in the chapel of Castel Appiano, Italy, employed brilliant colors, and depicted saints and angels, rendered in a flat style. Nineteenth-century architects repeated the Romanesque fresco style in their buildings, along with the architectural style. One notable example in North America is Henry Hobson Richardson's Trinity Church in Boston, built in 1872, which is filled with John La Farge's murals.

One of the most extraordinary sets of frescoes in Europe is that of the Scrovegni Chapel in Padua, Italy, painted by Giotto, and completed in 1305. The cycle of paintings depicts the life of the Virgin Mary and her parents on two walls, with the Christian seven virtues and seven deadly sins illustrated below them. A two-panel scene of the Annunciation stands out from the other works because of the red background, a contrast to the blue used elsewhere. With their three-dimensional modeling and sense of movement and perspective, Giotto's frescoes set a precedent for Italian Renaissance fresco painting, practiced by numerous distinguished artists including Raphael, Correggio, and Michelangelo.

In the twentieth century, Mexican artists including Diego Rivera, Jose Orozco, and David Siqueiros revived the fresco in North America. The Detroit Museum of Art, Detroit, Michigan, commissioned Rivera in 1932 to cover an entire gallery with a fresco cycle called *Detroit Industry*, a commentary on capitalism.

Friezes

In classical architecture, the frieze is an architectural element positioned above the architrave and below the cornice. But more generally, the term frieze can be used to mean any horizontal architectural ornament of a building. Friezes have been employed as a narrative element in the architecture of many cultures. The Assyrian palace gates at Balawat, Iraq, which date from 883 to 859 BCE, were ornamented with a series of bronze frieze bands, which relate King Shalmaneser's discovery of the source of the Tigris River.

Classical Greek architects used different types of friezes to correspond with each order, Doric, Ionic, and Corinthian. The Doric frieze contained projecting blocks called triglyphs, which were positioned between relief sculptures in spaces called metopes. The sculptures functioned as a narrative element as well as an ornamental one, and the triglyphs are thought to be an

This restored fresco depicting dolphins and fish is from the Queen's megaron (apartments) in the Minoan Palace of Knossos, Crete.

The Pergamon Altar frieze, dating from 166-156 BCE, from Pergamon, Turkey (now in Berlin, Germany), depicts the struggle between the gods and the giants.

ornamental vestige of the ends of beams, once present in earlier wooden versions of the same building type. Ornament such as this—purely decorative versions of elements that were originally functional forms—is said to be mimetic. There are other such mimetic features present in Greek friezes. The early Ionic Greek buildings had a simple, unadorned frieze except for a trim of small decorative pieces called dentils, which were probably derived from a peg system that fastened elements of the roof structure together in earlier wood construction.

In later Ionic Greek architecture, for example, at the Treasury of the Siphnians at Delphi, of the sixth century BCE, continuous high-relief sculptural scenes covered the entire frieze. Later still, in Hellenistic and Roman times, builders adopted elements from classical Greek architecture, and Corinthian and Composite temple structures were also adorned with a continuous frieze of relief sculptures, providing a narrative relating to the building's dedication or function. An outstanding example is the altar frieze at Pergamon, Turkey, of the second century BCE.

Angkor Wat

A significant Hindu example of the use of friezes in architecture can be found at Angkor Wat, Cambodia, former capital of the Khmer Empire. This twelfth-century complex, made from soft gray sandstone, uses horizontal banding as a repeated theme. Bands consist of small repeated designs, as well as figures in sets of low- and high-relief sculptures. In this vast complex, armies, courtesans, dancers, and other figures are depicted in many friezes. In the Churning of the Sea of Milk Gallery, a bas-relief frieze 160-ft (49-m) long depicts a Hindu creation legend. In the frieze, gods, demons, the builder of the complex, and celestial dancers, work to create the essence of immortality.

Asuras (demons) pull on the tail of the serpent Vasuki to churn the cosmic sea, in a bas-relief in the Churning of the Sea of Milk Gallery at Angkor Wat in Cambodia.

Residenz
Würzburg, Germany

The former residence of the Würzburg prince-bishops is an outstanding example of Austrian/South German Baroque architecture and decoration. This palatial building gives us an understanding of the prodigious talent of European artists during the Baroque period, as well as the enormous wealth and power of the prince-bishops.

A bishopric was founded in the Würzburg region in 724. During medieval times, the city developed into a wealthy trade center, and a university was established in 1402. From the twelfth century, Würzburg was ruled by a prince-bishop. In 1720, Prince-Bishop Johann Philipp Franz von Schönborn commissioned the Residenz as a replacement for an earlier, more modest bishop's residence. The main architectural components were completed by 1744, when Friedrich Karl von Schönborn was prince-bishop. The many interior finishes, including frescoes and stuccowork, took until 1780 to complete.

Surrounding the palace are grand, formal French and naturalistic English gardens, which were planted within existing fortification walls. The palace itself is U-shaped, built around four main interior courts and a central entry court of honor. The symmetrical, cream-colored stone façade is in the French Baroque style; a dome with a slate roof rises in the center. The architect-engineer Balthasar Neumann was the principal designer, but many other prominent architects, including Johann Lucas von Hildebrandt and Maximilian von Welsch, contributed to the large complex. Although severely damaged in World War II, when most of the city was destroyed by Allied bombing, the Residenz has been skillfully restored, enabling us to appreciate this lavishly ornamented building once again.

The Frescoes of Tiepolo

Most notable among the elements that survived World War II are the court chapel, the Kaisersaal (Imperial Hall, a banqueting hall), the Weissesaal (White Hall), and the grand staircase, which contains one of the world's largest ceiling frescoes. It is painted on a vault that covers an area of about 60 x 100 ft (18 x 30 m), an enormous span that was made possible by the light and strong structure devised by Neumann.

The Venetian artist Giovanni Battista Tiepolo decorated the vault with a dynamic fresco of the four known continents (Europe, Asia, America, and Africa), which he represented by human figures, and with Apollo commanding his cloud-filled heavens in a chariot pulled across the sky by galloping horses. This colorful work is a dramatic contrast to the white staircase and white on white stucco walls that frame the painting. The blue sky of the fresco and the white staircase glow with light from the large windows, emphasizing the large volume. The walls were decorated with high-relief sculptures of cherubs and other figures, doorways, and blind window openings. Pilasters define a rhythm of bays on the upper landings, and the side walls are segmented by strings of small plaster roundels. Stucco was used not only here, in the staircase, but also applied as ornament throughout the Residenz, sometimes in white and sometimes in bright colors.

With more than 300 rooms, the Residenz bears witness to the wealth of its founders, the prince-bishops of Würzburg, whose palace it was. Napoleon called it "the nicest parsonage in Europe."

Neumann was careful to create a contrast between the staircase and the Kaisersaal, each extravagant in its own way. While the staircase stucco is a plain white, the stucco carvings in the Kaisersaal are brightly colored and gilded. Formal and highly ornamented, the Kaisersaal is oval in plan with optically dizzying patterned marble floors, a dome, veined marble pilasters, and white walls offsetting the tinted carving. Between the two spaces, the Weissesaal, dominated by white stuccowork, creates a moment of pause. In the Kaisersaal are three Tiepolo ceiling frescoes—*Apollo Leading Beatrice of Burgundy to the Genius of the German Nation*, *The Wedding of Frederick Barbarossa*, and *The Investiture of the Bishop Harold as Duke of Franconia*—all related to the political history of the prince-bishopric.

The artist was accompanied to Würzburg in 1750 by his two sons, who assisted their father with the frescoes. During his sojourn, Tiepolo painted not only these brilliant works at the Residenz, but in three years also painted two works for the court chapel, an altarpiece for an abbey, and a number of small commissions.

Leading off from the vestibule is the magnificent staircase, designed by Balthasar Neumann and decorated with frescoes by Tiepolo. The vault covers about 6,000 sq ft (540 sq m).

The centerpiece of the Residenz is the sumptuous Kaisersaal (Imperial Hall), where frescoes and stuccowork combine to dazzle the eye.

Stucco and other Decoration

The vast amount of stucco sculpture and ornamentation in the Residenz, ranging from classical pilasters to fanciful rocaille—stylized motifs in the form of scrolls or shells—required the use of many artisans and a master stucco artist, the Italian-Swiss sculptor Antonio Bossi. Bossi used bilateral symmetry and asymmetrical compositions, which included leaf, berry, flower petal, and cherub elements, in his designs. He worked closely with Tiepolo to create an almost seamless continuity between the frescoes and the surrounding stuccowork.

Patterned floors in the public areas of the palace help define the various rooms. Wood parquet is used in the antechambers on either side of the Kaisersaal, and in the string of rooms that follow beyond the antechambers. These rooms include the Grünlackiertes Zimmer (Green Lacquered Room), the Venezianisches Zimmer (Venetian Room), a mirror room, a gallery, and audience rooms. The most important spaces in the palace were designed to have special floor treatments.

The grandeur of the Kaisersaal, for example, is emphasized by its polished stone floor, with two colors defining a checkerboard background pattern for an array of arcs in a third, lighter color. This kind of refined geometric flooring contrasts with the simple and practical rough-cut stone floor of the entrance hall, which was made large enough for a carriage to enter.

The Hofkirche

In the southern wing of the Residenz is the Hofkirche (Court Chapel). It consists of three interlocking ovals, with sinuous balcony curves, supported by veined pink and gray, smooth marble columns with gilded Corinthian capitals. Several white Solomonic (twisted) columns, also with gilded Corinthian capitals, add another level of complexity to this highly ornamented space. Gilded stuccowork, paintings, and frescoes (by Johann Rudolf Byss) continue the decorative themes from the rest of the palace, but with an intensity that is designed to inspire awe and devotion in the worshiper.

Stucco decorations in the rocaille style by Antonio Bossi dominate the Weissesaal (White Hall). It was used as an antechamber to the Kaisersaal.

Stencils

Over the centuries, stenciling has been used in many cultures for decorating architectural surfaces, as well as objects and materials such as cloth, pottery, leather, and furnishings. Most stencils consist of designs cut into thin, water-resistant sheets of stiff paper, plastic, or metal. When placed over a surface, these allow ink, dye, or paint to be daubed, spread, or sprayed through the open areas of the pattern. Solid areas in the design block the ink or paint, allowing the background to show through. The same design can be used repeatedly, enabling the creation of borders, such as a frieze, or any other repeated pattern. Patterns with more than one color can be achieved by using one stencil for each color, with each stencil having registration marks, or a small point in the pattern, to ensure correct alignment between applications of color.

In a traditional paper stencil, the design itself is limited to areas that are connected to one another, because at least a thin strip of the stiff material (called a bridge) has to hold the solid areas together. This limitation can be a challenge for the designer. However, using a serigraph (screenprint or silkscreen) is a way to avoid this need for connections between the stencil pieces, because a fine cloth screen holds the design elements together. The modern serigraph is a very adaptable medium, and today designers use photography, digital technology, and plastics for new

effects. This variation on stenciling, in which a blocking material like a coating or film is adhered to silk or other finely woven cloth, works because the unblocked areas allow the ink to be squeezed through the cloth with a squeegee and the blocked areas are kept in place by the porous cloth. Probably originally developed in Japan, the serigraph is, to a large extent, an extension of a traditional Japanese string stenciling technique called *itoire-gata* in which fine threads create almost invisible connections between stripes, holding the "islands" of color blocking together.

History of Stenciling

It is likely that the very first stencils were tracings from the Paleolithic period, as found in paintings in several caves in what are now France and Spain. In Central Australia, hand and foot tracings of children and adults can be found in the Carnarvon Gorge, where there are thousands of such prints, including a tracing of a whole body. These early stencils are as much as 2,000 years old. Also found in Australian rock shelters are tracings of objects such as tools, including boomerangs and spears.

In China during the T'ang Dynasty (618–907 CE), sacred cave walls were decorated with stenciled images of the Buddha, a tradition that is still followed in Buddhist temples in parts of East Asia today. It was only during the twelfth

century, when paper from Asia was adopted in Europe, that stenciling became popular there.

In Japan and China, many different stenciling techniques were employed for applying delicate patterns to cloth, one being stenciling both sides of the cloth with a resist—a material that does not take up the dye—made from rice paste before dying the fabric. In Japan, during the sixteenth and seventeenth centuries, when these techniques were developed, the stencil design was cut with a sharp knife by skilled artisans who did not need so much as a preparatory sketch. The stencils themselves were made from paper, stiffened with persimmon juice for durability.

Along with woodblock printing, stenciling was key to the development of wallpaper patterns in the seventeenth century. In colonial America during the eighteenth century, stencils were used to decorate walls before wallpapers were readily available, and the technique was used for furniture decoration as well. The tradition continued well into the nineteenth century, and underwent a revival in the late twentieth century.

Louis Sullivan and Stenciling

Stenciling was made use of by a number of architects in Europe and the United States during the late nineteenth and early twentieth centuries. In the United States, the members of the Chicago School incorporated into their work ideas about

Stenciled designs in gold leaf on black lacquer (right) adorn the entrance to the Wat Xieng Thong Buddhist temple in Louangphrabang, Laos, which dates from the sixteenth century. The interior has similar work.

polychromy discussed in books and articles by the Chicago architect John Wellborn Root and the English art and architecture critic John Ruskin, as well as the color theory advanced by the French chemist M. E. Chevreul. Medieval veneers and mosaics also had an influence on these architects. It was through stenciling that these concepts were brought together, and expressed on the interiors of Louis Sullivan's buildings, and also in the works of Henry Hobson Richardson.

During the 1880s and 1890s, Sullivan and the designer Louis Millet experimented in marrying floral and interlocking patterns found in medieval art, with the use of innovative color theory. The Chicago Auditorium Building of 1889 and the Trading Room of the Chicago Stock Exchange Building of 1894 are prime examples of this treatment. The Auditorium Building represents a

breakthrough for Sullivan. In earlier projects, he had used monochrome stencil patterns on flat backgrounds, while here, he was bolder, using paired contrasting colors as well as tonal contrasts which added vibrancy. The geometric and foliated patterns follow the ribs of the ceiling, emphasizing the curved structure.

The Trading Room ceiling was covered with intricate stenciling consisting of many carefully registered colors following beams, trusses, and flat expanses, all stenciled with rusts, greens, yellows, oranges, and blues. The stenciled patterns overlay color upon color to create a rich glow with considerable depth, intended to bring nature inside the building. Sullivan used stenciling as part of his strategy to create a "color symphony," recalling the mottled background of greens and yellows encountered in the forest.

The lavish use of multicolored stencils to decorate interiors enjoyed a vogue during the Art Deco period of the mid-1920s to the late 1930s. The ceiling of the ballroom of Sheffield City Hall, England (below), has the original stencils from 1932.

Finishing Touches

Whether viewing a building from the outside or walking through its interior, the experience is dramatically impacted by the finishing touches. Materials, textures, connections, and details are used to define the scale, to give character, and ultimately to give life to otherwise uneventful spaces.

Floors

Everyone is familiar with floors as the horizontal planes that are traversed as one moves through a building's interior spaces. Much of the time, standing on the floor is one's only direct physical contact with a building. Like many architectural elements, floors vary greatly, depending on culture. As an example, traditional Japanese culture requires the removal of shoes upon entering a domestic dwelling.

Climate also plays a key role with regard to floors. In hot climates, cold, hard surfaces, such as tiles or stone, keep rooms cooler, as do raised floors with loosely fitted wood slats, which allow breezes to flow under the buildings and filter upward into the rooms. In cold climates, heated water is often circulated through tubes within the floor, resulting in warm floors that are pleasant to walk and sit on.

When discussing floors, there is often some confusion between the floor as a structural system and the floor as a decorative surface. These must relate to one another because the underlying structural system needs to support the visible material above. On occasion, a single material may serve both purposes, as seen with the earliest packed soil floors and in modern examples of concrete floors.

The great marble floors of St. Peter's Basilica in Rome employ a minimal palette of different colored stones. They are inlaid in strongly delineated patterns of massive scale, which ground the basilica's elaborate internal decorative scheme.

The practice of laying wooden floors as parquet dates from late seventeenth-century France. This floor is at Miramare Castle in Trieste, northern Italy, which was designed by Carl Junker, and built from 1856 to 1860 for Maximilian of Habsburg.

The Sound of a Floor

The sound of a floor has a definitive impact on how a user experiences an interior. Anyone who has had their footsteps echo throughout the space as they walk across the stone floors of a grand cathedral is familiar with this impact. In contrast, the hollow sound produced when walking across a poorly constructed floor reveals its inherent shoddiness.

One example of a building that utilized sound in a unique way is Nijo Castle in Kyoto, Japan. In the corridors of this royal residence, completed in 1603, a system of floorboards intentionally squeaks with every step; it has been nicknamed the "nightingale floor." Along with hidden alcoves for bodyguards, it was a precautionary measure to warn the shogun of an assassination attempt.

The sound of nightingales singing is produced by the nails or clamps rubbing against holes in the floorboards as a person walks above.

In the Farnsworth House, in Plano, Illinois, the floor is covered with a grid of pale travertine, laid in great rectangular slabs, over precast concrete. The same travertine is used for the entrance steps and the terrace. The house was designed by Mies van der Rohe and built between 1946 and 1951.

Structurally, floors are very important as they can brace a building laterally. Within the depth of the floor, space between structural members is often used for the building's systems, such as electricity and plumbing. Visually, the look of the floor has a great impact on how a space is perceived. Standard floor treatments are often used in unimportant rooms, whereas the more significant rooms and entranceways get more intricate and expensive treatments. Logistically, a floor's finished surface serves to make the floor useful within its given context. Industrial facilities will often utilize highly durable and cleanable surfaces, whereas carpets or rugs are used to add warmth and comfort to residential spaces.

Flooring Materials

There are many different types of decorative flooring materials. The differences between tile, wood, and carpet can make a dramatic difference to the feeling of a space. Additionally, within each material selection, the finish treatments can drastically alter the impression of the space.

Stone slabs, stone tiles, and stone mosaics have been employed throughout history for their beauty and durability. The inlaid marble floors at St. Peter's Basilica in Rome assure that the floors of this highly significant church are as impressive as its other architectural features. The inclusion of the engraver's name on each section and the subtle differences in engraving style add a personal touch to this vast basilica. Stone is also

the base material of terrazzo and concrete, but the poured application of floors made from these materials yields a very different aesthetic.

Floors of clay, ceramic, and even of glass tile remain popular for their beauty and durability. They are often used in water-prone areas such as kitchens and bathrooms.

Among the most popular of flooring materials, wood has been used for thousands of years, as much for its inherent beauty as its practicality. Because it is easier to work than stone, many common buildings were constructed of wood, and had wooden floors as well. The inlaid wood floors at the eighteenth-century Archbishop's Residenz in Wurzburg, Germany, and those at Miramare Castle in Trieste, Italy, are examples of the elegance of wooden flooring. Additionally, cork flooring, made from the bark of the cork oak, is known for its durability, soundproofing qualities, and its near impervious nature.

In many classical buildings, columns and blocks of marble were often sliced up and recycled as flooring, known as *opus Alexandrinum* (Alexandrian work). In the twelfth century, the Cosmati family of Rome specialised in a similar treatment in which discs sliced from old columns were surrounded by refined inlay patterns, often including gold and other mosaic tiles. This *opus Cosmati* was also used for tombs, altar rails, and other fittings across Europe.

The use of carpets originated in Asia and the Middle East. Carpets are generally loom-woven

and can include any variety of materials, the most common of which are textiles and grasses. Today, carpets are often permanently fixed to the floor below; they are considered "rugs" when they are smaller than a room and are laid atop another finished floor. Traditional Japanese interiors often consist of floors covered with woven grass rugs called tatami mats, and the room sizes are based on the proportions and dimensions of these standard-sized mats.

As science has progressed, new materials have become available, including resilient flooring that is available in sheet or tile format and seamless poured flooring. These products are generally known for their ease of cleaning and for their affordability, and are prevalent in institutional and industrial applications.

Specialty Floors

Today, there are numerous specialty floors that have been derived for highly specific purposes. In office buildings, raised flooring systems allow for maximum flexibility when the wiring for computers and other technology must frequently be moved and changed. Modern "sprung," or floating, floors allow dancers to minimize damage to their joints, and these same systems are being integrated into homes for older people and for play areas for children. Raised glass floors may be incorporated into archaeological areas, allowing visitors to see what lies below without causing damage to historic sites.

Paneling

Uses of Paneling

Throughout the centuries, paneling has been used to add warmth and a sense of character to spaces that are deserving of special treatment. In its current form, paneling has existed since the late medieval period.

Paneling is typically defined as the use of interlocking, rectangular planks of wood used to create a series of raised frame elements that hold inset panels to create a continuous surface. The vertical and horizontal framing elements, respectively called stiles and rails, are typically thicker than the panels that they surround. Although the panels can be made of a variety of materials, thin sheets of wood are the most common infill material. Flat panels and raised panels are the two basic panel types, but more decorative paneling will sometimes include an applied molding at the joints around the panel.

Paneling can be used to create interest in a variety of architectural applications, but in its surface form it is most often applied to ceilings and walls. It is used in freestanding elements, too: paneled doors are often found in residential design, and traditional cabinetwork frequently includes smaller paneled doors.

When applied to an entire wall, paneling can create a surface that has great visual impact. Historically, paneled walls would be highly detailed, but a powerful and simple example of modern paneling can be seen in Mies van der Rohe's Crown Hall building, located on the Illinois Institute of Technology campus in Chicago, Illinois, and built between 1950 and 1956. The interior of this open-plan building utilizes a centrally located wall covered with wood paneling, which divides the open space. Crown Hall is a very fine example of a modern paneling using simple, flat panels supported by a concealed structural system. The lack of traditional frames allows the grain of the wood to play a prominent role in the design.

When paneling is applied to the lower portion of the wall, typically below a chair, or dado, rail, it is referred to as a wainscot. Simpler versions of wainscoting utilize tongue-and-groove boards to create a wooden surface in place of the frame-and-panel system.

Within the traditional panel system, a variety of different materials has been used in the place

The Hall of Magdalen College, Oxford, England, was begun in 1474 and restored in 1902. It is notable for its linenfold paneling, in which the face of each wood panel resembles a sheet of linen hung with the folds vertical in a symmetrical pattern.

of wood panels to create unique designs. These include fabric panels, plasterwork, and painted frescoes. In addition, sometimes panels can be recessed to create niches for statuary or decorative items, thus blurring the boundaries between casework and paneling.

Designed by McKim, Mead & White, the Metcalfe House in Buffalo, New York, had a highly decorative inglenook that incorporated prominent oak paneling. The intimate areas adjoining the fireplace, inglenooks—which were popularized by their use in homes designed by Frank Lloyd Wright—create a place of gathering around the hearth. The scale of the paneling in the Metcalfe inglenook brought a human proportion to the space, which translated into a sense of comfort. The frame-and-panel system is used to cleverly juxtapose various types of inserts, such as traditional raised panels adjacent to niche panels in which objects of importance to the family are displayed. Wood screen panels allow glimpses of the stairwell, thus maintaining a connection to other parts of the home. Before the Metcalfe House was demolished, the inglenook and staircase were removed and re-installed in the American wing of the Metropolitan Museum of Art in New York.

Paneling Throughout History

Like many decorative features of contemporary architecture, the original use of paneling was highly utilitarian. Early paneling was developed as a means for making spaces seem comfortable and helping to insulate buildings. This extra layer of material added thickness to the walls, and was also helpful in obstructing drafts that would gust through the joints of stone walls. Another early use of paneling was to control the dampness that filtered up from the ground into buildings.

There had been versions of paneling used for centuries in different cultures and countries, but paneling as a defined system of stiles and rails is generally attributed to the English. Its decorative use can be seen in prominent buildings from the fourteenth century, but it was the early sixteenth century that saw the culmination of English paneling into a defining style of architecture.

The Salon de Diane (Salon of Diana) in the Palace of Versailles, France, has paneled doors and inlaid marble pilasters. The room was created for Louis XIV by the architect Louis Le Vau and the painter Charles Le Brun about 1671–1673.

The Lady Chapel, at the eastern end of Westminster Abbey in London, incorporates a prolific amount of interior paneling that creates a very elaborate and intense space. The paneling corresponds to the proportions found in the windows' tracery, resulting in a highly unified interior. The prominence of the orthogonal lines in both the tracery and paneling led to the late Gothic era of English design being identified as the Perpendicular Period. The chapel was commissioned by Henry VII and constructed between 1503 and 1519.

France is also well known for prominent paneling in its interior architecture. As they embraced decorative paneling, the French made modifications that conferred a distinct aesthetic, which became known as *boiserie*. The prominent feature of this seventeenth- and eighteenth-century paneling style is the elaborate decorative nature of the panels. Often they were intricately carved of wood, but the most fanciful rooms had paintings in place of wood panels. Early boiserie was left unpainted, thus expressing the character

of the wood, but later moldings were often painted or sometimes even gilded.

The Palace of Versailles, located just outside Paris, is a superb example of French paneling, which can be seen on both wall and ceiling surfaces. The gilded paneling is used to create continuity throughout the enormous palace, and a multitude of panel materials are effective in differentiating the spaces in which they are used. Fabric panels, for example, are employed to add elegant warmth to many bedchambers. Wood panels are carved into designs that complement the rooms in which they are installed. Most spectacularly, mirrored panels are incorporated into the 240-ft (72-m) long Galerie des Glaces (Hall of Mirrors).

In his house at 2 Willow Road, Hampstead, London, the modernist architect Ernö Goldfinger used simple wood panels to add warmth and beauty to a building structure with a concrete frame. The house was completed in 1939.

Château of Fontainebleau
Fontainebleau, France

Located 40 miles (65 km) south of Paris in the rural town of Fontainebleau, the Château of Fontainebleau is a gargantuan royal residence that housed French monarchs since the Middle Ages. In addition to its historic significance, it is an architectural marvel, and its interior is filled, seemingly to excess, with exquisite ornamentation. Every surface is alive with intricate three-dimensional detailing.

With the château's expansion in the early sixteenth century, the decision was made to develop the exterior in the French Gothic style. At the same time, the interior was evolving into France's first example of Renaissance architecture.

Fontainebleau's interior was an important move away from the medieval to the fashionable design developments taking place in Italy. After the successes of Fontainebleau, the path was paved for all of France to embrace these new design ideals. As the French continued to define

their interpretation of Renaissance thinking, a modified version of the movement began to spread throughout Europe.

The History of the Château

The Château of Fontainebleau is a somewhat bewildering assortment of ideas and architectural styles, because the complex was constructed and subsequently remodeled in several phases over nearly eight centuries.

François I, who reigned from 1515 to 1547, is credited with the prominent transformation of the château and, although the building has grown, many features from his plan still remain intact today. A medieval castle at Fontainebleau, set on a forested 42,000 acres (17,010 ha), had been used as a hunting lodge, and had fallen into disrepair. In 1530, François I decided that the castle should be renovated into a new royal residence, which would stand to symbolize the

modernization of the monarchy. Today, only a single tower remains from the medieval building.

Under the direction of Rosso Fiorentino, and later Francesco Primaticcio, a team of talented artisans with an affinity for the Mannerist style was assembled. With this team, which became known as the "first school of Fontainebleau," in charge of the interiors, the surfaces were painted in scenes that reflected their ideals. Dreamlike colors, exaggerated proportions, and surreal expressions, as well as with sexual undertones, dominate many of the highly allegorical scenes.

Subsequently, the château was remodeled by various monarchs. Henri IV greatly enlarged the Fontainebleau complex and embarked on a grand scheme for landscaping the gardens. Napoleon was the last ruler to have a significant impact and his rendition of the interior remains largely intact. The château is now listed as a UNESCO World Heritage Site.

The François I wing of the Château of Fontainebleau (left), designed by Gilles le Breton, was the first structure to be built around an old medieval castle. Begun in the early sixteenth century, the château was enlarged and remodeled over three centuries.

Significant Spaces

The wide variety of interior decoration employed throughout the Château of Fontainebleau ensures that visitors are awed and entertained at every moment of their journey through the hundreds of interlinked spaces. Many of the rooms have significant decorative and stylistic features, but expanding on notable rooms from different eras offers an understanding of the architectural progression of the château.

Known to be the first significant decorated gallery in France, the Galerie François I (Gallery of Francis I) is among the most important spaces created by Fiorentino's team. In addition to being a showpiece, the gallery was constructed to link two groups of buildings within the sprawling floor plan of the complex.

The gallery is filled with decorative surfaces and elements, but it is the upper walls with their playfully intertwined frescoes, paintings, and sculptural plasterwork that are the real highlights of the gallery. Sculpted plasterwork elements protrude spectacularly into the room, and they include highly animated cherubs, royal insignia, and elegant female forms, alongside 12 narrative frescoes. Austere walnut paneling on the lower portion of the walls provides a thoughtful balance to the abundant and colorful subject matter above. Likewise, the gallery's herringbone wood parquet floor and coffered ceiling are relatively simple and do not compete with the more ornate paneling and frescoes.

The sumptuous Salle de Bal (Ballroom; above) has recently been restored. Planned as an open-air loggia, glass windows were installed to protect it from harsh weather. The frescos by Francesco Primaticcio and his student Niccolo dell'Abate are full of movement, and the ceiling is richly decorated in silver and gold.

From the balcony of the La Chapelle de la Trinité (Trinity Chapel; below) can be seen the full splendor of the decoration, completed by a number of artists, notably Martin Fréminet, during Henri IV's reign.

Completed during Henri II's reign, the Salle de Bal (Ballroom) uses a wide array of materials which are offset against rich colors. The main body of the room has an elegant coffered walnut ceiling, complete with carving and gilding. The floor mimics the ceiling's octagonal and diamond design, but adds its own inlaid embellishments. The central space is lined with arched alcoves, each with a large window, offering more intimate spaces for socializing. The lower portions of the walls have elegant wood paneling that seamlessly integrates built-in wooden benches. Above them, the magnificent frescoes, mainly by Primaticcio, fill the space with life and color.

Constructed during many decades under the rule of multiple monarchs, the design of La Chapelle de la Trinité (Trinity Chapel) maintains a surprising amount of uniformity. Its stone altar commands attention when entering the chapel from the ground floor, but this splendid space is best viewed from the balcony, where the opulent ceiling and upper frescoes can be observed more closely. Although they were completed nearly a century after the "first school" painted frescoes at Fontainebleau, the art in the chapel stays true to the Mannerist style.

The room, originally known as the Galerie de Diane (Gallery of Diane), was converted by Napoleon into the palace library. Having been a gallery space, the library is a very linear room with a continuous barrel vault ceiling that runs the length of the space. Although it is still highly detailed, the library reflects a less flamboyant period, and the decoration is less sculpted than some other rooms of the palace. The long side walls host an alternating sequence of windows and tall book shelves, where the windows offer abundant light for reading.

The François I wing of the Château of Fontainebleau (left), designed by Gilles le Breton, was the first structure to be built around an old medieval castle. Begun in the early sixteenth century, the château was enlarged and remodeled over three centuries.

Significant Spaces

The wide variety of interior decoration employed throughout the Château of Fontainebleau ensures that visitors are awed and entertained at every moment of their journey through the hundreds of interlinked spaces. Many of the rooms have significant decorative and stylistic features, but expanding on notable rooms from different eras offers an understanding of the architectural progression of the château.

Known to be the first significant decorated gallery in France, the Galerie François I (Gallery of Francis I) is among the most important spaces created by Fiorentino's team. In addition to being a showpiece, the gallery was constructed to link two groups of buildings within the sprawling floor plan of the complex.

The gallery is filled with decorative surfaces and elements, but it is the upper walls with their playfully intertwined frescoes, paintings, and sculptural plasterwork that are the real highlights of the gallery. Sculpted plasterwork elements protrude spectacularly into the room, and they include highly animated cherubs, royal insignia, and elegant female forms, alongside 12 narrative frescoes. Austere walnut paneling on the lower portion of the walls provides a thoughtful balance to the abundant and colorful subject matter above. Likewise, the gallery's herringbone wood parquet floor and coffered ceiling are relatively simple and do not compete with the more ornate paneling and frescoes.

The sumptuous Salle de Bal (Ballroom; above) has recently been restored. Planned as an open-air loggia, glass windows were installed to protect it from harsh weather. The frescos by Francesco Primaticcio and his student Niccolo dell'Abate are full of movement, and the ceiling is richly decorated in silver and gold.

From the balcony of the La Chapelle de la Trinité (Trinity Chapel; below) can be seen the full splendor of the decoration, completed by a number of artists, notably Martin Fréminet, during Henri IV's reign.

Completed during Henri II's reign, the Salle de Bal (Ballroom) uses a wide array of materials which are offset against rich colors. The main body of the room has an elegant coffered walnut ceiling, complete with carving and gilding. The floor mimics the ceiling's octagonal and diamond design, but adds its own inlaid embellishments. The central space is lined with arched alcoves, each with a large window, offering more intimate spaces for socializing. The lower portions of the walls have elegant wood paneling that seamlessly integrates built-in wooden benches. Above them, the magnificent frescoes, mainly by Primaticcio, fill the space with life and color.

Constructed during many decades under the rule of multiple monarchs, the design of La Chapelle de la Trinité (Trinity Chapel) maintains a surprising amount of uniformity. Its stone altar commands attention when entering the chapel from the ground floor, but this splendid space is best viewed from the balcony, where the opulent ceiling and upper frescoes can be observed more closely. Although they were completed nearly a century after the "first school" painted frescoes at Fontainebleau, the art in the chapel stays true to the Mannerist style.

The room, originally known as the Galerie de Diane (Gallery of Diane), was converted by Napoleon into the palace library. Having been a gallery space, the library is a very linear room with a continuous barrel vault ceiling that runs the length of the space. Although it is still highly detailed, the library reflects a less flamboyant period, and the decoration is less sculpted than some other rooms of the palace. The long side walls host an alternating sequence of windows and tall book shelves, where the windows offer abundant light for reading.

Plaster

Plaster, the prevailing wall and ceiling finish for surfaces in buildings around the world, traditionally consists of mineral powder mixed with water. Though its composition varies slightly based on regional materials, plaster is so widely used because it is readily available, easily moldable, and fire resistant.

In addition to its standard use as a wall and ceiling finish, at different times in history more decorative uses of plaster have been in vogue. These more sculptural uses were often highly three-dimensional and eventually became to be considered works of fine art in their own right. An unusual use that has been made of plaster can be seen in theatrical and movie set design. Because it can be modified to resemble wood, stone, and numerous other materials, plaster is often used to create the fictitious spaces and elements that bring a cinema production to life.

A History of Plaster

The most primitive way plaster has been used involves earthen plasters, often pressed on the inner walls of rustic huts and cabins. Used to seal the walls against the outdoor elements, the plaster had the additional benefit of creating a reasonably smooth interior surface for decorating. Examples of plaster use can be seen throughout the ancient world. Intact relief paintings on plaster have been found in the corridors and chambers of Egypt's ancient pyramids. The works are well preserved, and testing has revealed that the composition of ancient plaster is chemically similar to the plaster used today.

In timber-framed buildings, the plaster was laid upon laths, which are small strips of timber nailed horizontally across the wall frame, with gaps in between. The rendering coat, (a lime or cement mortar), would push into the gaps and become firmly keyed onto the timber. The next or floating coat was of finer material such as lime and fine sand, and created the finished shape or surface plane. The final setting coat was a thin layer of lime or gypsum plaster which would be polished to a very smooth surface. In the late nineteenth century, expanded metal mesh was introduced as a substitute for timber lathing.

As more refined plaster mixtures came into existence and plasterwork developed as a craft, great artisans of the Renaissance period began to recognize its full potential as a material. The prominence of frescoes as a method of adding embellishment to interiors is the first example of this. Frescoes are created by first applying a thin layer of plaster to a surface. Wet pigment

In the anteroom at Syon House, in west London (above), completed in 1769, the English architect Robert Adam imitated Roman marble columns by using *scagliola*. This is an Italian technique in which coloring agents and other materials are added to plaster and the surface is polished.

At the Thermae Stabiane (Stabian Baths, above left) in Pompeii, Italy, the vividly colored stucco wall, and molded pilaster and frieze, are tantalizing evidence of interior decoration in the second century BCE.

is then added into the malleable plaster, which is manipulated to create an image. The plaster dries with the pigment actually imbedded in its surface, creating highly durable works of art.

The Sistine Chapel in the Vatican, Rome, home of the world's most famous fresco, registers as one of the most powerful spaces in the world. The chapel itself is quite small in scale, but two-thirds of each wall and the entirety of the ceiling are covered in frescoes. Dominating the ceiling is Michelangelo's series of nine paintings based on the Book of Genesis.

As ornamentation became increasingly more elaborate with the progression from Renaissance architecture to Baroque and Rococo, plasterwork broke new ground, and began to be viewed as a fine art. Early plasterwork had been considered sculptural when stenciled forms protruded just a fraction of an inch into the space. The next step was the introduction of decorative items such as plaster moldings, rosettes, frames, and pilasters that were used to adorn significant rooms.

As designers became increasingly bolder, their plasterwork became more three-dimensional, and eventually culminated in sculptures that appear to be minimally connected to the wall or ceiling surface. In place of the traditional flat application methods, the sculptural plaster techniques they employed utilized molds and jigs to create raised forms. After they had been fully cured, the forms could continue to be carved and sanded.

Types of Plaster

The earliest plasters were earthen mixtures that consisted of clay, sand, and a fibrous ingredient, such as straw, which helped to bind the mixture together. Over the centuries, more sophisticated mixtures were perfected, leading to more durable and attractive surfaces.

For many centuries, cement plaster, or stucco, has been used on exteriors. Originally consisting of lime, water, and a fine aggregate, such as sand, in today's mixtures the lime has been replaced with portland cement. Smooth surfaces or more textured effects can be achieved with cement

plaster. Venetian plaster, made of marble dust combined with sand and lime, is famous for its traditional color palette and hard, smooth finish.

Throughout history, gypsum plaster has been used to create attractive and durable walls in interiors. Gypsum is naturally fire-resistant, and it is combined with water and fine aggregate to create the plaster.

In the twentieth century, the construction standard shifted toward plaster board, usually referred to by the trade names "sheetrock" or "drywall", for interior walls and ceilings. Paper-covered sheets of pressed gypsum are screwed into the structure, then tape and plaster putty are applied to cover the seams. The traditional application of plaster is still used, however, on projects where its more hand-crafted appearance and additional strength are required.

Several decades after Robert Adam, the artist Antonio Canova decorated the ceiling of the Villa Rezzonico in Bassano del Grappa, near Venice, Italy, by sculpting the stark white plaster into highly decorative, three-dimensional Rococo patterns.

The Brilliant Influence of Luis Barragán

Twentieth-century Mexican architect Luis Barragán is recognized for his use of brilliantly colored plaster walls. Employing combinations of contrasting or toning colors to emphasize the vertical planes of his modernist structures, and often incorporating running and still water in internal and external spaces, Barragán completed relatively few buildings, but his mastery of space and light has influenced architects throughout the world. Much of his early work involved landscape design, and he embraced the local terrain and the traditional architectural patterns of Mexico to develop a distinctive, spare compositional style of pure planes using stucco, adobe, timber, and water, which, nevertheless, employed a modernist vocabulary. Barragán died in 1988.

In this contemporary garden in El Paso, Texas, the influence of Luis Barragán is evident in the brightly colored plaster walls and flat, vertical planes.

Cabinetwork

Unlike furniture, which is freestanding, cabinetwork is most often physically connected to a building, and therefore an integral part of the building's interior. The general purpose of cabinetwork is for storage or for the display of prominent objects.

Traditionally, cabinetwork was made of wood, and was a prominent component in a building's millwork. Defined as all the elements made of "finish-grade" wood and permanently affixed to the building, millwork commonly includes doors, mantels, interior trim, and stair components, as well as frames for doors, windows, and surface paneling—some of which are known for being intricately executed. Cabinetwork most often includes moving elements, such as drawers and doors, and is time-consuming to produce.

A History of Cabinetwork

The history of cabinetwork is intertwined with that of furniture, and the two remain closely related to this day. The main driving force behind the development of cabinetwork was military necessity. The earliest cabinets were simple wood boxes which were used for the transporting of military objects. Known as campaign chests, or war chests, these early cases had lids that allowed top access. Over time, it became apparent that side or front access was more convenient, and the basic form began to evolve. Eventually, the chests were placed on legs, and they began to resemble modern cabinetwork.

In the Western world, English cabinetmakers dominated the craft from its beginnings in the medieval period and throughout its early history. Because of their expense, cabinets were reserved for upper class and royal residences throughout much of this period. These cabinets were used to conceal valuables and important documents. They were also used as writing surfaces in an era when correspondence was an art as well as a social necessity. The sixteenth century saw a leap in the popularity of Dutch cabinetwork, with the English maintaining their strong influence.

Japan is renowned for its strong tradition of cabinetwork, which is called *tansu*. Very different stylistically from Western designs, these cabinets had an elegant simplicity that complemented their rectilinear form. Accents of hammered metal offered ornament and helped to strengthen the corners and edges.

Cabinetwork generally evolved along with the architectural styles of the day and is classified by period, according to its decoration. The Arts and Crafts Movement of the late nineteenth century celebrated the handmade crafts and allowed the artistry of the cabinetmaker to enjoy a surge in popularity. The movement was a reaction against the poor quality of the mass-produced furniture of the Industrial Revolution. The beauty and fine detailing of their Arts and Crafts cabinetwork encompassed staircases, architraves, and mantels, as well as furniture made for individual buildings.

In contemporary homes, cabinets are now mostly associated with kitchens and have a more functional, utilitarian aesthetic. In addition to

Tansu is the Japanese word for the wood cabinets that became widespread during the Edo period (1603–1868). In this house in Shinagawa, Tokyo (left), the tansu—both freestanding and built-in—display the characteristic fine joinery and ornate hardware and are both functional and works of art.

kitchen cabinetry, built-in shelving, wardrobes, and medicine cabinets are not uncommon in well-designed homes.

Components of Cabinetwork

With cabinetwork being made primarily of wood, there is a variety of joinery techniques that are used to ensure that every connection serves its purpose. Dovetail connections are often used at drawer corners to create a solid connection that effectively resists racking and pulling apart. Cabinet doors are traditionally made using the frame-and-panel construction system, with the frames often utilizing mortise-and-tenon or half-lap joints. Lesser quality contemporary cabinets often employ screws instead of the traditional wood-to-wood joinery.

Trees that are native to the region traditionally provided most of the material stock. Originally, solid slices of wood were used for cabinetwork, but plywood and veneers have become popular because they do not shrink and expand as solid wood does. In recent decades, metals, plastics, and synthetic materials have become popular alternatives to wood.

Typical cabinet hardware consists of hinges, as well as door and drawer pulls. These range from very simple to highly elaborate. Modern cabinets may have additional hardware, such as full extension drawer glides and self-closers.

The final step in the making of cabinetwork is its installation. Built-in cabinets are attached to the structure of the building to securely support their contents. This connection can occur at the wall, ceiling, or floor.

Uses of Cabinetwork

Cabinetwork is an integral part of many building types. In residential projects, cabinetwork is often utilized in kitchen, bath, closets, and other areas requiring storage. Houses of worship may display special items, such as relics, in cabinets. Custom-designed offices are also likely to use built-in cabinets. One building type whose primary use requires cabinetwork is the library. Historically, the perimeter of the room was surrounded with open shelves for books, and cabinets with glazed doors protected rare and special volumes.

In the Theological Library at the Strahov Monastery in Prague, Czech Republic, which was completed in 1679, the cabinetwork is a striking example of baroque extravagance. Thoughtfully integrated into the space, the tall stacks of shelves adorned with ornament are nestled into barrel vaults in some places, and elegantly wrap around columns in other locations. The bottom shelf is extended out to create a bench seat that runs the length of the library stacks.

An early twentieth-century example of library cabinetwork, at the Stockholm Public Library in Sweden, which was designed by Gunnar Asplund in the 1920s, utilizes a central cylinder of elegant bookshelves which hold the library's main book collection. The high, cylindrical volume of the reading room is clearly defined from the exterior of the library building, but once inside the geometry of the space becomes far more powerful as the visitor is completely engulfed by the finely finished, book-filled cabinetwork.

In many contemporary houses, the only cabinetwork is in the kitchen. Sleekly modern, long underbench cabinets in this Brazilian house (above) have been fashioned to provide a beautiful and utilitarian space.

The cabinetwork in the circular reading room of the Stockholm Public Library in Sweden (below) is an integral part of the space. The building, by Gunnar Asplund, references classic library architecture and its cabinetwork is influenced by Biedermeier furniture.

Architectural Metalwork

There are many different types of metal used in buildings. Further complicating matters, there is also a wide range of architectural applications in which the metals are incorporated. In modern construction, for instance, a single building might employ steel columns and beams, lead flashing, copper pipes, nickel-coated brass faucets, aluminum windows, and stainless steel handrails. Clearly, then, metalwork is prolifically integrated into both the exterior and interior of buildings in a variety of ways.

In modern architecture, the structural use of metal is generally separate from its ornamental use. However, the Library of Sainte Geneviève, in Paris, designed by Henri Labrouste and completed in 1850, offers a very striking example of these two uses being combined. This famous interior incorporates two rows of structural but delicately designed iron arches. This was criticised by the German architect Gottfried Semper. While he accepted the validity of decorative iron, he rejected its structural expression. He held that by its very nature the material called for thin forms, whereas architecture needed 'effects of mass.' Therefore iron could only be used in architecture as 'light accompaniment.'

A History of Metalwork

Being difficult to extract and manipulate, metal developed more slowly as a building material than its counterparts of wood and stone. But by the nineteenth century, science and industry had advanced to the point of making metalwork more feasible, and subsequently it became more economically viable as well.

Historically, metalwork used for architectural purposes contained a high percentage of iron and was generally painted to prevent rust. Painted iron offered a material that could be molded into ornate forms like plaster, but was durable enough to hold up outdoors. Cast iron was often used in railings and gates, and for decorative historic façades and exterior ornamentation.

By the late 1920s, stainless steel was sparkling from the decorative top of New York's Chrysler Building and the Empire State Building was sleekly ornamented with aluminum and nickel. The twentieth century also saw the introduction of metal panels to clad buildings, a practice taken to extremes by the architect Frank Gehry. In recent years, metal fins and perforated metal sheets have become popular exterior sun-shading details. In keeping with the Earth-friendly ideals

The beauty of cast iron owes much to the inherent tension between the hard, brittle material and the delicate, lace-like patterns into which it can be molded. The ironwork on these terrace houses in Sydney, Australia (right), is typical of ornamentation on nineteenth-century houses.

One of the most dazzling and extravagant uses of architectural ironwork is on the Chrysler Building in New York. An Art Deco masterpiece completed in 1930, its seven-tier spire is encased in stainless steel.

Hector Guimard's decorative entrances to the Paris Métro (below) are one of the best known examples of Art Nouveau metalwork. He developed several different entrance types—with balustrades, as here, and enclosed in fan-shaped pavilions.

that are prominent in contemporary architecture, these elements are cleverly located to prevent direct sunlight, and therefore heat, from entering a building in the summertime.

Decorative interior metalwork can be found in many residential and commercial buildings. Prominent historic uses of interior metalwork have included pressed metal ceilings, ornamental fireplace surrounds, and decorative radiator and grille covers. More modern examples may also include stainless steel railings, which sometimes incorporate metal cable systems, as well as metal doors, door jambs, and cabinets. More recently, stainless steel appliances and countertops have become extremely popular in residential kitchens.

Throughout history, door hardware, hinges, and decorative pulls have been predominantly made of metal due to its highly durable nature. This is an important role, as doorknobs can be likened to the "handshake" of a building.

The architects of the Art Deco Movement of the 1920s favored aluminum to create the sleek, rounded forms that were so prevalent in their interiors. The material embodied the ideal of the machine era that they were promoting.

War efforts have become highly dependent on metal for the fabrication of weapons and other equipment. During some wars, recycling efforts were implemented because of metal shortages, and these have sometimes resulted in the removal of architectural metalwork, with the inevitable consequence of altering the intended appearance and feeling of buildings.

Working with Metal

For many years, the two prominent types of metal found in architectural projects were cast iron and wrought iron. Cast iron elements are created by heating the metal to a liquid state and pouring it into molds. Wrought iron elements

are formed by heating the metal to a softened state, and then manipulating it with tools to get the desired shape. Today, the process is quite different. Large metal foundries produce sheets, bars, rods, and tubes of various types of metal. The appropriate components are then procured and manufactured to become readymade or custom architectural metalwork.

Designed by Carlo Scarpa, the Castelvecchio Museum, in Verona, Italy, is an excellent example of modern metalwork contributing successfully to the design of an interior. Built-in iron "stands" which showcase artifacts are used to create a well-ordered journey through this ancient castle. Although the metal elements all employ the same design language, no two pieces are the same. Some act as plinths, others as easels, and others as pedestals, and still others are attached to walls to create floating shelves. Metalwork, along with wood accents, also choreograph the visitor's path through the museum, with stairs and railings, and with metal grates that serve as doors. Scarpa has used the metalwork in a way that is at once unquestioningly functional as well as being highly ornamental.

The Experience Music Project building in Seattle, Washington, designed by Frank Gehry and constructed between 1999 and 2000, is a progressive example of how metalwork within an interior can create an extraordinary experience. Conceptually, the building was initially conceived as a smashed guitar from a Jimi Hendrix rock concert. Gehry's signature swooping metal forms twist their way from exterior to interior, where they act as space-defining elements. Many of these striking elements are painted, though one retains its natural metal color. With a mirror-polished finish, this unique element reflects its colorful neighbors. It also distorts and reflects the visitors below, creating exhilarating effects.

In his renovation at the Castelvecchio Museum in Verona, Italy, undertaken between 1956 and 1964, architect Carlo Scarpa has employed a variety of metal stands—from simple shelves to complex stages—to make an intriguing exhibition space.

Details

The theoretical approach, or the concept, of a building is expressed in many ways, such as how the building occupies its site, through the floor plan, and the sequence. In the cases where the physical construction of its details also reinforces this main idea, a building begins to achieve true success. This can be illustrated by studying the finishes of a building. As Mies van der Rohe is credited with saying, "God is in the details"—one of the most famous quotes in the architectural world.

Details are the elements that add character and make a building special. The connection between the fireplace and wall, the light cove that grazes a wall with light, the proportions of the entrance hall, and the aesthetic of the stair balustrades are common examples of details. Generally, details are used to identify significant areas that augment the experience of a space. Frank Lloyd Wright is known to have wanted to control every detail in his buildings, and often he would go even further and design the furniture as well. This ensured that every element in the building was working together to create an aesthetic consistent with his initial concept.

As architects moved away from their earlier role as master builders, a drawing type became necessary to convey how the architect meant for a project to be constructed. This led to the development of construction detail drawings, which show how the many varied pieces of a building come together. The details are typically drawn at a larger scale, sometimes even at full scale, in order for the builder to understand the difficult areas better.

Varying Types of Details

Details are used for different reasons in different buildings. Sometimes these details express the building's structure, at other times they relate directly to a use of the building, or they may be employed to create hierarchy within a space.

The carved cave temples at Ellora in India offer a superb example of detailing used to add hierarchy. In the fifth century CE, when monks began carving the earliest temples into the stone hillside, they added intricate carvings in certain areas while carving other surfaces into flat planes. The more intricate areas direct the visitors' gaze, thus creating a rich experiential quality.

The quintessential castle walls with tooth-like battlements at the top were not intended to be decorative, but were a defense mechanism. The taller section of the battlement walls protected the castle's archers, while the lower, open section offered a clear area from where they could take aim at their enemies.

The contemporary Japanese architect Tadao Ando is known for his elegant use of concrete. Formwork ties, which are necessary during the

Frank Lloyd Wright famously wanted to control every detail of his buildings—right down to the design of the furniture, and how it was arranged in a space. The linear style of his stained glass—as for the Robie House in Chicago—had much in common with that by Charles Rennie Mackintosh.

At the Teatro Armani in Milan, Italy, the architect Tadao Ando punctured massive concrete slabs with regularly spaced square holes, thereby creating a subtle, rich pattern and softening the severe modernity of an inherently utilitarian material.

pouring of concrete walls, are located to reveal elegant patterns once the formwork is removed. This leads to a thoughtful, sophisticated detail that offers insight into the process of constructing the building.

Details Throughout the Years

Historically, the details were most often applied or carved into surfaces toward the end of the construction process. These details generally relate to the architectural style of the day. In the past, when construction of a single edifice might take hundreds of years, the prevailing style had often advanced before a building was completed, and therefore it may have been designed as one style but finished as a mixture of styles. The two towers at the Cathedral of Chartres in France were built nearly four centuries apart, and have distinctly different detailing. The northern tower is more recent and uses additional ornament, a steeper spire, different arches, and is significantly taller than its southern counterpart.

In the historic building process, practicality required that the exterior shell of a structure be substantially completed before the interior work could begin, in order to protect the craftwork from the weather. For this reason, the detailing of interiors will often reflect a later style than that of the building's exterior.

After the lavish details of earlier architecture, the pendulum began to swing in the opposite direction with regard to ornament, and the early twentieth century witnessed the debate over the appropriateness of ornament in architecture. Later, the idea of expressing structural truth by exposing well-detailed structural elements was a drastic departure from previous thoughts. The culmination of this drive to simplify can be seen in minimalism, the sparse spaces of which reveal a deliberately limited use of details. Designers employed the purposeful application of materials, colors, and textures in place of ornament. Details do not compete for attention due to their limited use in such buildings.

The seeming simplification of design by the Modern Movement in fact led to details that were challenging to construct and required great skill and craftsmanship from the builder: for example, previous generations of architects had specified baseboards in order to conceal the awkward meeting of the wall and floor, but when the modernists deemed these too decorative, the edges of both the wall and the floor needed to be perfectly constructed.

The Thermal Baths at Vals

Peter Zumthor's thermal bath building in Vals, Switzerland, is a superb example of simple detailing that is used to create highly atmospheric spaces. The design contrasts cool, gray stone walls with the warmth of bronze railings, and light and water are employed to sculpt the spaces. The horizontal joints of the stonework mimic the horizontal lines of the water, and there is a subtle change in the texture of the stone at the waterline. Skylights inserted into narrow slots in the ceiling create a dramatic line of light that accentuates the fluidity of the water. Every detail of the building thus reinforces the importance of the bath on a variety of levels.

In the hands of Swiss architect Peter Zumthor, gray stone, bronze, light, and water combine to become something sensuous and mysterious.

Charles Rennie Mackintosh

The Glasgow School of Art in Scotland—a masterful essay in stone, metal, and glass—has a deliberately simple façade, relieved by the generous entrance bay, bold but uniform fenestration, and occasional Art Nouveau ornamentation.

Architect, furniture designer, and painter, Charles Rennie Mackintosh is recognized as Scotland's most influential designer. Born near Glasgow in 1868, he lived most of his years in Scotland, although later in life he spent some years in England and in southern France before his death in 1928.

Mackintosh studied at the Glasgow School of Art. Here he became part of a group of artists known as "The Four." The other members were Herbert MacNair, Frances Macdonald, and her sister Margaret Macdonald, who later became Mackintosh's wife. The group came to be a major influence on what became known as the Glasgow Style of architecture and design.

Initially, The Four created small-scale, easily transportable designs, such as furniture, posters, and other graphic-based pieces. Their work was exhibited in Glasgow, and then went on to be shown in London, Turin, and Vienna, where it influenced Viennese Art Nouveau as well as the Viennese Secessionists.

Design Principles

Combining his scholastic knowledge with his professional experience, it did not take long before Mackintosh began to develop his own confident, meaningful approach to design.

He strongly believed that the Gothic revival and Victorian styles that were popular at the time were inappropriate in the setting and climate of Scotland. Mackintosh respected the simplicity of Japanese design and the elegance of Art Nouveau, but was drawn to the local baronial style as a starting point. This was an important step toward his goal of achieving a distinct Scottish design language. Mackintosh felt that spaces should be designed based on their specific functions, and he is known for creating clear and elegant floor plans which provided effective lighting.

Although Scottish identity and functional spaces were signatures of Mackintosh's style, the single defining trait of his work is his meticulous attention to detail, which can be seen in all his design and architectural work.

Architectural Projects

Created for a design competition in 1901, the "House for an Art Lover" was based on the early theories of Mackintosh and Margaret Macdonald. The design was hailed for its inspiring originality, but was disqualified from the competition for not arriving by the deadline. More than 90 years later, the design was made a reality when the house was built in Glasgow's Bellahouston Park.

During his career Mackintosh designed several noteworthy buildings, but the new facility for his alma mater, the Glasgow School of Art, is his most significant and influential work. At the time of the project's design, he was working for the firm of Honeyman and Keppie, where he would later become a partner, and was entrusted with the project. Margaret Macdonald collaborated on the project's interior. From its design in 1896 to completion in 1909, the commission spanned several of the architect's prime years.

The Glasgow School of Art is a celebration of the styles Mackintosh passionately favored. The massive volume and austere stone walls are reminiscent of the Scottish baronial style, while the curving entry steps soften the façade and prepare the visitor for the other Art Nouveau detailing that will be encountered. The great windows are beautiful and utilitarian, and give the building a modern feel, which contrasts with the heavy but subtle stonework.

Located in Helensburgh, near Glasgow, the Hill House is the largest domestic building by Mackintosh. Completed in 1903, the exterior is in keeping with the palette and ideals of his earlier work. The interior offered the architect an unusual opportunity to design the fireplaces, the furniture, and even a fireplace tool set, which was crafted of pewter.

Among his most significant projects is the Willow Tea Rooms. It combines Mackintosh's architecture, interior design, and furniture design to create a cohesive environment. The owner of four different social tea rooms within Glasgow,

Mackintosh gave the library of the Glasgow School of Art an exposed, two-story skeleton of wood. The tall, linear space is unadorned with curves; instead, the architect concentrated such decorative details in the balustrades and the purpose-designed, wooden desks and chairs.

Kate Cranston became an important, long-term client for Mackintosh. He designed all four of the locations, but it was the Willow Tea Rooms where his ideals were comprehensively translated in the design of everything in the space, all the way down to the menus and wait staff uniforms.

The Willow Tea Rooms were situated in an existing four-story building, the façade of which was redesigned by Mackintosh. The interior of the tea rooms consisted of numerous spaces, each with their own thoughtful aesthetic. In the glamorous Room de Luxe, silver high-backed chairs and friezes of leaded mirror created the most prestigious room in the building. In sharp contrast to its elegance, the Gallery was designed as a masculine space where men could enjoy tea. A strong sense of verticality was still present, but a darker palette and distinct Asian influence gave the room a distinguished feel.

Furniture Design

Mackintosh well understood the importance of furniture in defining the atmosphere of a space, and he incorporated his own designs for furniture into his architectural commissions whenever possible. The furniture often becomes a defining feature in otherwise simple rooms.

His original high-backed chair—probably his most famous work—was designed for Cranston's Argyle Street Tea Rooms, and its tall vertical back would become a signature element in his future designs. The way he used straight lines and right angles juxtaposed with elegant Art Nouveau curved forms in the furniture created a pleasing balance that was echoed in the interior space.

In his residential commissions, Mackintosh often designed massive wooden beds, which were

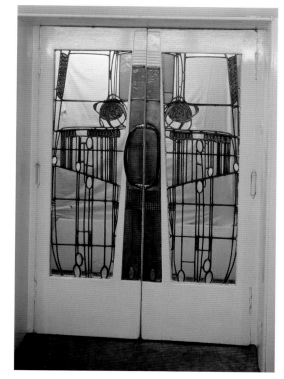

typically painted with light colors. Mackintosh's use of solid wood rather than paneling created a strong appearance and, used with prominent vertical headboards, gave the beds a considerable presence in the bedroom. The quintessential example of such a bed is found in the master bedroom at the Hill House.

Spanning the Arts and Crafts Movement, Art Nouveau, and early modernism, Charles Rennie Mackintosh's architecture, furniture, and interior designs have an important place in international design history, and ensure a lasting legacy for a talented architect and designer.

Incorporating furniture into the building—designing it within an architectural context—as Macintosh did at the Hill House, Helensburgh, in Glasgow (above), was a characteristic of the Arts and Crafts Movement, introduced by Philip Webb in the Red House that he designed for William Morris in 1859.

The stained glass doors of the Willow Tea Rooms in Glasgow (left), like every other detail of the interior decorative scheme, were designed by Mackintosh. This 1903 commission was the first time he had the opportunity to control all aspects of the design, including the external layout and the multilevel architectural spaces.

Reference

Chronology of Architecture

NEOLITHIC	6000–3000 BCE

ANCIENT NEAR EAST	
Sumerian	4500–2000 BCE
Babylonian	1900–500 BCE
Assyrian	1800–700 BCE
Hittite	1650–1200 BCE
Urartu	800–585 BCE
Achaemenid (Persian)	550–330 BCE

ANCIENT EGYPTIAN	
Archaic	3250–2700 BCE
Old Kingdom	2700–2200 BCE
Middle Kingdom	2200–1500 BCE
New Kingdom	1500–1000 BCE

INDIAN SUBCONTINENT	
Indus Valley	2500–1500 BCE
Hindu	1500 BCE–present
Buddhist	200 BCE–present
Jain	900 BCE–present
Mughal (Muslim)	1150 BCE–present

ANCIENT GREEK	
Minoan	2000–1450 BCE
Mycenaean	1600–1000 BCE
Archaic	1000–600 BCE
Classic	600–320 BCE
Hellenistic	320–30 BCE

CHINESE	
Shang dynasty	1600–1000 BCE
Zhou dynasty	1000–200 BCE
Han dynasty	200 BCE–CE 200
Tang dynasty	CE 600–1000
Song dynasty	CE 1000–1200
Ming dynasty	1370–1640
Qing dynasty	1640–1911
Modern	1911–present

PRE-COLUMBIAN (CENTRAL AND SOUTH AMERICA)	
Olmec	1500–800 BCE
Teotihuacán	300 BCE–CE 600
Maya	CE 200–900
Zapotec	CE 500–600
Toltec	CE 900–1100
Inca	1200–1533
Aztec	1300–1521

ROMAN	
Republican	500–30 BCE
Imperial	30 BCE–CE 300
Late antique/Early Christian	CE 300–500
Byzantine	CE 500–1500

JAPANESE	
Prehistoric	10,000–300 BCE
Ancient	300 BCE–CE 1200
Asuka and Nara	CE 550–790
Kamakura	CE 1185–1330
Muromachi	CE 1340–1580
Edo	1603–1867
Modern	1870–present

DARK AGES	
Ravennate	CE 400–790
Visigothic	CE 410–710
Merovingian	CE 486–771
Early Saxon	CE 600–800

ISLAMIC	
Umayyad Caliphate (Persia, Iraq, Egypt, Syria, Jordan, Palestine)	CE 630–700
Umayyad Caliphate (Spain)	CE 700–1000
Abbasid Caliphate (Persia, Iraq, Egypt, Syria, Jordan, Palestine)	CE 700–1000
Seljuk dynasty (Persia, Turkey, Iraq)	CE 400–700
Fatimid dynasty (Arabia, Egypt)	CE 400–600
Almoravid dynasty (Spain/Maghreb)	CE 1000–1200
Nasrid dynasty (Granada)	1200–1600
Safavid dynasty (Persia)	1430–1760
Mamluk Empire (Egypt, Arabia, Syria, Jordan, Palestine)	1250–1520
Ottoman Empire	1300–1920

EARLY MEDIEVAL	
Carolingian	CE 770–1000
Asturian	CE 800–900
Late Saxon	CE 800–1066

ROMANESQUE	CE 1000–1200

GOTHIC	
France	
Gothique à Lancettes	1130–1230
Rayonnant	1200–1280
Flamboyant	1280–1500
England	
Early English	1180–1275
Decorated	1275–1380
Perpendicular	1380–1520

RENAISSANCE	
Italian	1430–1530
European	1500–1700
Mannerism	1530–1600
Elizabethan (England)	1530–1600
Jacobean (England)	1600–1640

BAROQUE AND NEOCLASSICAL	
Baroque	1600–1725
Louis XIV (France)	1643–1715
Georgian (England)	1714–1800
Palladian Revival (England)	1715–1750
Rococo	1725–1775
Neoclassical and Style Gabriel (France)	1750–1800

ECLECTIC	
Empire style (France)	1800–1814
Regency (England)	1800–1840
Victorian (England)	1840–1900
Second Empire (France)	1850–1880
Art Nouveau/Jugendstil	1890–1910

TWENTIETH CENTURY	
Expressionism	1910–1925
Art Deco	1925–1939
Modernism	1910–1950
Bauhaus	1919–1933
International style	1925–1965
Brutalism	1950–1965
Postmodernism	1965–present

Please note that all these dates are approximate.

Glossary

abacus *See* DORIC.

abutment A mass of masonry that is designed to provide lateral support to a structure, and especially to contain the spread of an arched bridge or similar construction.

acropolis In the Greek world, a hill that is the focus of a town; commonly the original fortified settlement which later becomes the main location of religious and public buildings as the town expands below. Also used for the same feature in Hittite and other towns.

acroterion An ornament (such as a sphinx, chimera, PALMETTE, or ANTHEMION) above the roof line of a Greek temple, particularly at the corners and peak of the PEDIMENT; and by extension a piece of statuary in such a location, as in a Roman temple.

adobe The Spanish and Mexican term for an unbaked or sundried mud BRICK, used generally of such a brick when formed in a rectangular mold (unlike plano-convex and other early brick types). Other terms, such as *clay lump* or *batt*, are used in other cultures.

adytum The core sanctuary of a Greek temple, commonly a chamber or CELLA, but also an open courtyard such as the one for the oracle at the Temple of Apollo, Didyma, Turkey.

aedicule A frame such as a window surround, with a PEDIMENT carried on PILASTERS or COLONETTES, and giving the appearance of a small building.

Aeolic order A PRECLASSICAL order in which the CAPITAL consists of two spirals rising from a central point (as opposed to the two spirals joined laterally in the IONIC ORDER) found throughout the Near East, especially in Cyprus and Aeolis (in the west of modern Turkey), and corresponding to the ram's horn form in Anglo-Saxon architecture.

aggregate The solid materials, such as sand and gravel, which are bound by a cementitious substance to form CONCRETE.

aisle A passageway within a space, such as that running between seats or along the side of a church or auditorium.

ambulatory A walking space or aisle, particularly that following around the curve of a church APSE and passing behind the altar. Also the continuous passage around the central space in a DOUBLE-SHELLED plan.

amphitheater A circular or oval structure with ramped seats surrounding a central arena for performances, gladiatorial contests, or spectacles, and resembling two Roman theaters joined back-to-back, hence the name.

antae The wing walls projecting from the end of the CELLA or central chamber of a classical temple so as to create a porch, or a false porch, or OPISTHODOMOS, at the opposite end.

antefixae Palmettes or similar ornaments above the EAVE-line of a classical temple, generally corresponding to and masking the lines of imbrices (*see* IMBREX) or cover TILES.

anthemion A Greek ornamental device based upon the honeysuckle, with a flat base from which fronds radiate upward, each finishing in a spiral that turns in toward the central axis. It is commonly used in ANTEFIXAE and in continuous MOLDINGS of various sorts.

apse A semicircular or similar form projecting out of a building, typically at the eastern end of a church, or the end or side of a Roman secular BASILICA. In the eastern church it may contain the SYNTHRONON and CATHEDRA, the stepped bench for the clergy and throne of the bishop.

aqueduct A channel carrying water to a settlement with minimum practicable fall in level, by tunneling through mountains and bridging valleys; commonly used especially for the bridge portions of such a system, carried on one or more levels of masonry arcading.

arcade Strictly a row of ARCHES carried on COLUMNS or PIERS, but by extension an arcaded loggia, or more generally a row of shops opening off a loggia or covered passage.

arch A curved span across an opening—typically a semicircle, but also a lobe, a horseshoe, a point formed by two intersecting arcs, or other such form. It is an arch in a structural sense only if made up of radial BLOCKS or VOUSSOIRS, which are wholly or mainly subject to compression.

architrave The MOLDINGS surrounding a door or window opening on the vertical wall face.

archivolt The MOLDINGS concentrically following the curve of an ARCH, on the vertical face (as opposed to the INTRADOS).

arris The sharp edge formed by the intersection of two planes or surfaces, of which the groin is a special instance.

Art Deco A style characterized by brightly coloured geometric ornament, making use of ceramic finishes, GLASS, chrome, STAINLESS STEEL, and other new materials, and taking its name from the Exposition des Arts Décoratifs et Industriels Modernes, held in Paris in 1926.

Art Nouveau A style characterized by sinuous vegetable and geometric forms, especially in wrought IRON, and lurid or subfusc green and blue glazes, particularly characteristic of France and Belgium in about 1890 to 1910.

Arts and Crafts Movement A movement originating in Britain with the work of Morris, Webb, and others, in reaction to mass production and industrialization. It placed value on the skills and character of the craftsman-artist and on the integrity, color, and texture of natural materials.

ashlar Stonemasonry accurately dressed in rectangular BLOCKS with fine joints.

astylar Normally used of a FAÇADE, meaning without COLUMNS (rather than without style).

atlante (telamone) A giant male figure used to support a load in CLASSICAL, and later in MANNERIST, architecture. The notable classical example is the Temple of Olympeian Zeus, Agrigento, Sicily, Italy *c.* 480 BCE, which had such a figure set on the face of a wall between each pair of COLUMNS, helping to support the excessive span of the ENTABLATURE.

atrium A court within a building, particularly the partly unroofed axial courtyard of a Roman house, or a roofed well rising up through more than one level in a modern building.

bailey The outer wall or first line of defence of a castle or fortification, or the court enclosed by it; may be sacrificed under severe attack when the defenders retreat to a more defensible KEEP.

balloon frame A frame consisting of uniform-sized vertical STUDS rather than individual COLUMNS and framing members. These studs continue (or are spliced) through a two or more story wall height (perhaps the source of the term "balloon"). It was in established use by about 1850.

baluster, balustrade A *baluster* is a vertical piece, commonly turned in an ornamental profile, and a row of *balusters* supporting a handrail is known as a *balustrade*. The form was essentially invented during the Italian RENAISSANCE. By extension any perforated vertical panel with a handrail on top has become known as a balustrade.

banister A handrail or BALUSTRADE running with the slope of a staircase or RAMP.

baptistery A building, usually detached from a church, for the conduct of the Christian rite of baptism, especially one containing a full immersion font. They generally appeared from the fourth century CE and were commonly of compact square, octagonal, or circular forms.

Baroque A style in Europe in the seventeenth and eighteenth centuries, initiated by Italian architects such as Bernini and Borromini, characterised by flamboyance, virtuosic effects, theatricality, and illusionistic ceiling paintings.

barrel vault A ceiling in the form of a half cylinder (also *wagon vault*). *See* VAULT.

bas-relief A deep representational carving or an ornamental carving on a vertical surface (as distinct from low relief).

basilica A rectangular hall-like building, often with side AISLES defined by COLONNADES, used in Rome for law courts and other public purposes; also a private hall for performances or for cult worship. By extension a Christian building of long shedlike form, entered from the short end (initially the east, but later usually the west), with side aisles above which CLERESTORY lighting enters the NAVE, and with a timber roof structure. Today the term is often used to refer to a major church.

battlement An upward projection above the roof line behind which a defender could shelter while firing outward, commonly forming a rectangular series in a European castle. In Mesopotamia, Syria, and Crete, the form was commonly stepped; this form persists as an ornamental convention in the Roman Temple of Bel, Palmyra. The Islamic world tended to use the form known as a MERLON.

bay One of a series of more or less uniform structural or spatial divisions of a building.

bay window A window projecting from the exterior wall in a square, polygonal, or curved form and large enough for the interior space to be occupied.

bell tower A tower carrying a bell, principally in connection with a Christian church, but also for purposes such as fire alarm, marine warning, and public celebration. The Italian CAMPANILE is one of the earliest types.

belvedere A platform or pavilion for the enjoyment of a pleasing view, usually on a high point of ground or on the roof of a building.

bending stress The stress induced by placing a load on a beam or similar member, tending to cause it to bend downward and hence compressing the upper fibres and extending the lower ones—thus a combination of compression and tension stresses.

Bessemer converter A device that uses a blast of air to assist in burning out carbon and other elements from pig iron, purifying the IRON and rendering it suitable for STEEL manufacture.

bitumen A tarry hydrocarbon derived from petroleum naturally or by distillation, used in waterproofing mixtures, treated building papers, and dampproof course materials.

blind window An element in a wall giving the appearance of a window but without an opening or glazing, and serving only design purposes, especially to balance a real window.

block A building element of steeper or more cubic proportions than a brick, particularly a CONCRETE BLOCK.

boiserie Intricately carved wood paneling, the French equivalent of WAINSCOT, but often with raised MOLDINGS, gilding, and other elaborate decoration, used in the seventeenth and eighteenth centuries.

boss A knob, principally for ornament, either projecting from a plane surface such as a door, or covering the intersection of two or more RIBS in a GOTHIC VAULT.

breccia A rock consisting of stone fragments bound within a cementitious matrix. It was used for ornamental carvings, wall facings, and also used for COLUMNS in Minoan, Egyptian, and Roman architecture.

brick A rectangular clay element, either dried in the air (*see* ADOBE), or "burnt" or baked hard in a clamp or kiln. Traditionally, bricks of both types are either squarish flat plates; or of more blocklike proportions. The formation of a brick may be by hand using a rectangular mold; by extrusion, in which a strip of clay is squeezed out of a machine and sliced off (*see* EXTRUDE); or by mechanical pressing in a mold. The press can use a drier clay that distorts less, and can be burned sooner, and generally produces a brick of better quality. Burning takes place in a CLAMP OR KILN.

brick veneer The surfacing of a timber structure in a skin of BRICK. Although this occurs when an existing structure is refaced, the technique as a deliberate means of construction is relatively modern. By the early twentieth century it was popular in the United States.

broach *See* SPIRE.

bronze An alloy of copper and tin, hard enough to be used for tools before iron was available: hence the Bronze Age.

buttress A vertical or stepped strip running up the face of a wall to reinforce it at the point where it carries a vertical load or a lateral force, usually caused by an ARCH or arched roof structure on the opposite side.

buttress, flying A BUTTRESS in which the outward thrust is transferred through a raking and sometimes arched span of masonry to a lower wall structure or a detached pillar. The weight of the masonry, which may be augmented by a PINNACLE rising above the PILLAR, combines with the thrust to create a resultant force that descends at a steeper angle. This force can then be transmitted through the buttress structure to the ground.

Byzantine The style of art and architecture developed in the eastern empire ruled from Constantinople (formerly Byzantium, and today Istanbul, Turkey). The city was chosen as capital by Emperor Constantine and at first it was a Roman one. But over two centuries local forces gradually supervened. The Byzantine period is generally taken to begin with the accession of Justinian in CE 527. Churches tend to be centrally planned and domed, and equipped with the ICONOSTASIS (image screen) required by the eastern liturgy. They are rather dark, and their interior walls are given over to a skin of marble paneling and MOSAIC decoration. The mosaics are rich in gold, with figures tending to float; in very late Byzantine work, mosaics are often replaced by FRESCOES.

caisson A structure like an open box, to keep water or sediment from entering an area being excavated; the caisson may be incorporated into the building.

campanile The Italian form of bell tower, usually circular in early examples at Ravenna, but later generally square in plan.

cant A slope or angle, as in the canted courses used to form the arches of a pitched or NUBIAN VAULT.

cantilever An element projecting horizontally from a wall to carry a load.

capital An ornamental element that finishes the top of a COLUMN, and the form of which in CLASSICAL architecture principally defines the architectural ORDER, as in the DORIC, IONIC, and so on.

Carolingian Associated with the rule of Charlemagne (768–814), which attempted to revive the status and culture of Rome. There are architectural influences from San Vitale,

Ravenna, Italy, in the Palatine Chapel at Aachen, Germany; the PROPYLON gate of St. Peter's, Rome in gatehouse, Lorsch, Germany; the ring crypt of St. Peter's at Seligenstatt, Germany; VISIGOTHIC Spain at Germigny-des-Prés, France. Also includes novel elements of apparent barbarian origin, especially the composition of a building from simple geometric forms and the use of tall towers at Saint-Riquier Abbey, France.

caryatid A female figure used as a supporting element in place of a COLUMN, famously in the south porch of the Erechtheion, Athens, Greece.

casement window A window in which the SASH is hinged like a door, at the side, top, or bottom; often a symmetrical pair is used.

castellate To build or embellish in the manner of a castle, and in particular to provide with BATTLEMENTS.

catacomb An underground burial place used in Rome and elsewhere, from the second century CE onwards; often comprising a network of galleries with wall space for LOCULUS and arcosolium burials. They may also contain cult chapels and *cubiculi* (small rooms for family or group burials, and associated funeral feasts).

catenary The shape formed by a hanging chain, in which every element is in simple tension. In a true catenary, any applied load will be proportional to the length of the chain.

cathedra The throne of a bishop; in the eastern church typically at the back of the APSE and center of the SYNTHRONON.

cavity wall A wall consisting of two vertical leaves with a space between to provide thermal insulation and prevent the transfer of moisture from the exterior. In earlier BRICK (or hollow) walls, some of the bricks run horizontally across the space. In a true cavity wall, the leaves are structurally distinct but tied at intervals. As moisture can still pass across a common brick, special bricks were developed using dense clay with a glazed finish, and shaped in order to encourage water to drop into the cavity, or ramped up so as to bond into a higher course in the inner leaf. Metal ties were of four main types, and usually had a downward kink at the center to cause water to drop off.

cella The central chamber of a Greek temple, containing the cult image. It does not contain the altar, which is outside and normally detached from the temple building.

cement An adhesive or binding material such as a glue, but in building especially the materials used in MORTAR and CONCRETE, such as ROMAN CEMENT and PORTLAND CEMENT.

centering The timber framework required to support the underside of an ARCH, VAULT, or other superstructure during construction. It involves expensive carpentry using curved timbers, and is usually designed to be slid along (in the case of a BARREL VAULT), and/or to be used a number of times in the construction of a given building. It is sometimes recycled in subsequent projects.

chamfer A forty-five degree cut from what would otherwise be a right-angled ARRIS, as in the corner of a square timber PILLAR.

chamfer stop The place (usually near the top or the bottom) where a chamfered member returns to its rectangular form. The transition is usually made by a sloping triangular FILLET; more elaborate medieval scrolled forms are illustrated by the nineteenth-century architect and theorist Eugène Viollet-le-Duc as *congés*.

chevet In a church or cathedral, the (typically French) term for the east end in which the curve created by the APSE is elaborated with a semicircular AMBULATORY from which radiate projecting chapels.

choir The arm of a church to the liturgical east of the transept, occupied principally by the choir and clergy.

chord The upper or lower member of a TRUSS.

cladding The nonstructural surface material attached to the side of a building, generally some form of boarding or panel, and not used for a cement or other rendered surface.

clamp A pile of BRICKS arranged so as to burn without the permanent structure of a KILN. Coal dust or other fuel is commonly mixed into the clay itself, so that the brick literally burns rather than merely bakes. More fuel is laid between the lower layers of bricks, to spread the burning process. The outer faces of the pile are finished with waste or damaged bricks and sealed with mud or lime mortar. Fires are started at the side of the clamp to initiate the burning process, then the whole is sealed and left to burn for at least some days.

classical To do with antique Greece and Rome, as distinct from "classic," which generally means having a degree of perfection or enduring quality, but not specifically antique.

cleat A piece fastened to the side of a member, which in building is generally a continuous strip, and sometimes one of a pair between which an infill panel or planks may be secured.

clerestory A vertical surface created by a difference in roof levels, often pierced by window or other openings, such as those above the aisle roof of a church opening into the upper part of the nave. Also known as *clearstory*.

clinker *See* KILN, BRICK.

cob Mud used without formwork for building walls. It is often mixed with grass or straw, and sometimes small stones, and is placed in layers, each of which sets before the next is placed. Although the variation is enormous, according to the materials and the climate, a layer of 2 ft (60 cm) and a drying time of two weeks is fairly typical. Then the rough surface is pared off, and is almost invariably finished with a lime plaster. Where a similar soft mud mixture is used to infill a timber structure, rather than stand in its own right, it is called *pug*.

coffering Recessed square paneling, most particularly in a ceiling, as in the dome of the Pantheon, Rome.

colonette Small shaft or COLUMN, particularly one with a more ornamental than structural function, such as one set in the sides of a multiple-order GOTHIC doorway, or forming the side of an AEDICULE.

colonnade Uniform row of close-set COLUMNS, such as that surrounding a classical temple. A row of columns carrying ARCHES and set farther apart is an ARCADE.

column A vertical structural member designed to take compression, and of circular section, as distinct from a PIER or PILLAR.

Composite A classical ORDER introduced in Rome, in which the overall form of the CORINTHIAN capital is combined with the horizontal VOLUTES of the IONIC.

concrete An artificial stone created by binding AGGREGATE in LIME or CEMENT. It takes compression well, but not tension. It may be used as mass concrete (for example, in FOUNDATIONS); formed into BLOCKS; or reinforced. *Reinforced concrete* is an engineering material consisting of concrete containing STEEL or other reinforcement, so designed that the concrete is subject only to compression forces, whereas the reinforcement takes tension and shear forces, and sometimes a proportion of the compression as well. *Carbon concrete* is reinforced with fine carbon fibers, generally as grids, rather than with metal bars, each with clearly defined structural function.

concrete block CONCRETE cast into a block without reinforcement, for use as a masonry unit in construction. Solid concrete blocks were used in England in 1832, but were not a really practical form of construction until the hollow block was patented in 1887. This produced a unit more readily cured and lighter.

corbel To overlap one BLOCK past another, by means of which stone or other masonry can be made to span an opening or space. The blocks are subject to shear force and the technique is traditionally used in stone, but is occasionally done in BRICK or other materials.

corbel table A wall surface, the whole of which is CORBELED out beyond the lower one. An arcaded corbel table is one supported on a row of ARCHES, as is common in LOMBARDIC ARCHITECTURE, and was originally inspired by arcaded MACHICOLATION.

Corinthian order A CLASSICAL ORDER in which the CAPITAL is based on leaves of the acanthus plant. Early versions were used in small items such as lamps. The capital first appeared at an architectural scale to deal with specific compositional problems in the interior of the Temple of Apollo Epicurius at Bassai, Greece, in the late fifth century BCE. It continued to be used only in special interior situations until it appeared on a small scale externally in the choragic monument of Lysicrates, Athens, in 334 BCE, and then in the full-scale Temple of Zeus Olbius, Cilicia (Uzuncaburc, Turkey), in the 2nd century BCE. As used in Hellenistic work, the SHAFT and the ENTABLATURE are much the same as those of the IONIC, but in the Roman Corinthian it was often unfluted.

cornice The crowning horizontal element of the ENTABLATURE, or projection of the roof edge, often faced with a CYMA recta profile. Later used for the element at the top of an interior wall surface that makes the junction with the ceiling, commonly a cove with a series of parallel MOLDINGS above and below, but sometimes with dentils or other elaboration.

Cosmati work Medieval marble and MOSAIC decorative flooring and paneling work. Discs of marble or PORPHYRY, often made by sawing up antique columns, are surrounded by bands and spirals of marble and mosaic, set within an overall rectangular grid. The technique was revived in Rome around 1100 by craftsmen who included some members of the Cosmas family, from whom the collective name is derived. Their dominance in Rome ceased in the fourteenth century.

course A horizontal row of BRICKS or stones in a wall or a footing. *See* STRING COURSE.

crepidoma The base of a CLASSICAL temple, always consisting of three steps in a DORIC temple of the fifth century BCE, the top one being the STYLOBATE. Later, greater numbers of steps were common. In the Temple of Apollo, Didyma, the building is so large that a human cannot easily negotiate the crepidoma, and a smaller flight of steps is interpolated into the crepidoma on the entrance axis.

crossing The intersection of the NAVE and TRANSEPT in a church.

crow-stepped Stepping up on a slope, particularly in a crow-stepped GABLE, common around the Baltic and in Scotland; the gable steps up on either side with the projections higher than the sloping roof surface behind. Also known as *corbie-stepped*.

crypt A space below the floor of a church, usually to house relics or to accommodate sarcophagi or burials. An influential example was the *ring crypt* at St. Peter's Basilica, Rome, in the late sixth century CE. This consisted of a semicircular passage, which could be entered from the NAVE at either end, passing beneath the raised floor of the APSE. In the eighth century, it was imitated in churches in Rome and in CAROLINGIAN Germany. Very different was the *hall crypt*, which became popular in northern Italy and Germany as a burial place for notables. It was a rectangular space extending across the east end of a BASILICAN church, as at San Miniato, Florence, or across the whole TRANSEPT in such examples as St. Michael's, Hildesheim, Germany. It was usually roofed with groin VAULTING, carried on a square grid of columns. Crypts of more varied forms appear in France and elsewhere; a notable example is that of Saint-Denis, Paris, where members of the royal family were interred from MEROVINGIAN times (*c.* CE 500–750) onward.

cryptoporticus A vaulted underground passage, found in some Roman palaces and probably used for access by servants, but better known below public streets and fora, where it was used mainly for storage by traders operating above. A good example is that running along a street in Bosra, Syria, lit by small apertures raking up to the street gutter above. In the cryptoporticus surrounding three sides of a rectangle at Arles, France, each arm consisted of two BARREL-VAULTED corridors separated by segmental arcading on massive stone PIERS, and lit by means of windows in the vault, which slanted up to the open space of the enclosure above.

cubiculum A bedroom in ancient Rome and by extension a small squarish chamber for burials in a CATACOMB.

cupola A small dome.

curlicue An ornamental line curving capriciously, or in a tendrillike manner.

curtain wall A wall that hangs across the face of a building, as opposed to one that is loadbearing or that is created by infilling the panels of the structural frame. The term is used especially for a cladding of GLASS panes set within a metal framing system.

cut-and-cover method Construction of an underground tunnel by digging a trench and then roofing it, as opposed to tunneling.

cyma A MOLDING consisting of two contrary curves, like a shallow S. In the *cyma recta*, more usually used in CLASSICAL locations such as the CORNICE, the concave curve is the lower and the convex the upper; in the *cyma reversa* it is the opposite.

dado The lower level of a wall up to about chair-rail height, often distinguished by darker or more substantial decoration, a tradition originating in the Bronze Age when this level was often formed with ORTHOSTATS, while the walls above were of rubble or earth.

Dark Ages The period between the collapse of the western Roman empire and the emergence of the CAROLINGIANS, about the fourth to the early eighth centuries CE. This saw the cessation of large building projects, and the almost complete disappearance of the craft of stonemasonry. But it soon saw the emergence of new architectural traditions associated with the new nations, including LOMBARDIC, VISIGOTHIC, MEROVINGIAN and Saxon architecture. In the seventh and eighth centuries, the influence of Syrian refugees caused a revival of stonemasonry across Europe, generally associated with the use of the Syrian monolithic ARCH.

decking Strips (other than regular floorboards) laid to create a horizontal plane. Especially metal profiles with raised edges, used for flat or low-pitched roofing, and timber slats laid with spaces between for the floors of walkways, verandahs, or seating areas within gardens.

Deconstruction A term coined by the French philosopher Jacques Derrida in the 1960s, for the analysis of texts to expose meanings other than the purported ones. The process is necessarily subjective. In architecture, the term has been used to provide a rationale for inverting and subverting accepted conventions.

Decorated The second phase of English GOTHIC architecture, of the fourteenth century; more ornate than the EARLY ENGLISH. It is sometimes subdivided into *Geometric* and *Curvilinear* in reference to the change in the style of window TRACERY over this period.

dipteral Surrounded by two rows of COLUMNS, as in a larger CLASSICAL temple.

distyle Having two COLUMNS, for example between the ANTAE of the porch at the end of a small CLASSICAL temple.

dome A hemispherical, or occasionally semiovoid or other shaped ceiling or roof, usually in some form of masonry.

Doric order The earliest of the canonical CLASSICAL ORDERS, which emerged in Greece in the seventh century BCE. The CAPITAL consists of two elements: the *echinus*, which is circular with a gentle convex curve in profile, and the *abacus*, a flat square plate with vertical edges. Approximations to both can be found in earlier Minoan and Mycenaean architecture. The shaft is fluted, with 20 flutes, which are shallowly concave and meet at a sharp ARRIS. The profile of the shaft has the subtle curve called ENTASIS, and then flares out a little at the top, or TRACHELION, where it meets the abacus. The most striking aspect of the Greek Doric order is that the shaft runs straight to the floor or STYLOBATE without any form of base or MOLDING, or any closure of the fluting. The Romans added a base, and this was the form transmitted through the Italian Renaissance.

dormer window A vertical window projecting above a sloping roof surface, with a separate roof of its own.

dosseret block Essentially a variety of IMPOST BLOCK placed between the CAPITAL of the column and the SPRINGING of the arch above; however, the term is best confined to the type that is a flat plate with a classical profile, such as a CYMA recta. This type appears in some medieval buildings, such as Sant'Agata dei Goti, Rome, and in churches of the TUSCAN PROTO-RENAISSANCE, and was revived by Brunelleschi in the loggia of the Ospedale degli Innocenti, Florence.

double-hung window A window consisting of two SASHES, a lower one which can slide upward, and an upper (and outer) one which can slide downward. Normally each is counterbalanced with weights concealed in the boxing on either side, and connected to each sash by means of cords passing over pulleys at the top of the frame.

double shell A plan type used especially in centralized church plans, in which an inner space or NAVE, of circular, octagonal, or quatrefoil form, is separated by an ARCADE or COLONNADE from an AMBULATORY, the external wall of which is the same or a similar geometric shape. An early example of a circle within a circle is Santa Costanza, Rome.

dragon beam The word is a corruption of "diagonalis" or diagonal, but has been taken to derive from "dragging," in the sense of tying in a member that thrusts outward. It is a short horizontal beam, on the diagonal, into which the base of a HIP rafter is seated. It spans from the intersection of the wall plates at the corner of the building inward to an angle brace, which cuts across the corner. Its first known use is in Inigo Jones's Banqueting House in London, and may have come from an Italian source.

dressing The process of bringing rough stone to a smooth finished state.

drum In architecture, a cylinder upon which a DOME can be raised, the main purpose being to light the interior space by means of windows through the drum. This became the norm in BYZANTINE churches, but had the disadvantage of leaving the dome without lateral support, unless the drum was to be unduly thick or was to be reinforced with BUTTRESSES. In construction, a cylinder upon which a rope is wound for hoisting, in a winch or crane.

Early English The first phase of English GOTHIC architecture, essentially of the thirteenth century, characterized by narrow LANCET windows and simple external design. Also known as *Lancet*.

eave The overhanging edge of a roof.

echinus *See* DORIC.

embrasure An opening from which a defender may fire upon an attacker, being either the space between two BATTLEMENTS, or a wall opening with the sides splayed to allow the greatest range of firing angles from the interior and the least width for the entry of a projectile from outside.

encaustic tile A TILE, the body of which is pressed with a sunken design on the surface; the design is filled with clay of a contrasting colour. When baked, this creates a homogeneous tile with a pattern that will survive the wearing away of the surface. The technique was a medieval one revived in England in 1830 by Samuel Wright. Encaustic tiles were often used with others in TESSELLATED TILING.

engaged column A COLUMN which, rather than being freestanding, appears to be sunk to about half its depth into the surface of a wall.

entablature The part of a CLASSICAL building extending from the LINTEL to the top MOLDING of the CORNICE, usually above a COLONNADE.

entasis The subtle convex curvature in profile of a Greek DORIC column, and sometimes other types, which begins from a vertical line at the base and slants increasingly inward. It approximates to the arc of a very large circle, the center of which is on the same level as the column base. It can be seen as a bulge, maximizing somewhere between one-third to two-fifths of the column height, but the diameter at no point exceeds that of the base.

esonarthex *See* NARTHEX.

exedra A semicircular or rectangular space opening out of a larger chamber, commonly with seating; or a curved element opening out of the NAVE of a DOUBLE-SHELLED building, and reflected in the form of the AMBULATORY and in a corresponding exterior APSE.

Expressionism A movement in art and architecture that aims to achieve expressiveness by exaggeration and simplification.

exonarthex *See* NARTHEX.

expanded metal A sheet of metal punched with slots in a staggered pattern so that when pulled sideways the slots open out and the sheet becomes a diamond mesh. It was invented in the United States by J. F. Golding, who patented it in 1884 as a form of LATHING for PLASTER. By the 1890s, it was also being used to reinforce CONCRETE, less because of its suitability than because it was a way of avoiding patent restrictions governing other systems.

extrados The outer or upper face of an ARCH, as opposed to the INTRADOS.

extrude To squeeze out in a strip, like toothpaste. In making extruded BRICKS, a rectangular strip of clay is squeezed out through a die onto a conveyor belt. At intervals, a rack of wires is folded down to cut off a number of bricks. Using an appropriate die, it is also possible to extrude bricks of nonrectangular shapes, with striated faces, or with one or more voids through them. Extrusion is also used in the manufacture of other building materials, and is one of the ways of making lead pipes.

façade The main or public face of a building, or any face that is given a formal architectural treatment.

façadism The renovation of a building by rebuilding the interior so that essentially only the FAÇADE is authentic, a practice which is generally anathema to conservationists.

fachwerk *See* HALF TIMBER.

fanlight The glazed opening above a doorway, especially if it is semicircular or semielliptical with a radial pattern of glazing bars; a rectangular opening is a TRANSOM light.

fan vault A VAULT form used in English PERPENDICULAR GOTHIC in which the surface, instead of being made up of essentially cylindrical segments, as in earlier vaulting, consists of flaring cones rising from the COLUMN or point of support. A number of uniform RIBS radiate up from this point, and the distinction between transverse, diagonal and TIERCERON ribs necessarily disappears. There are also numerous ribs in the transverse direction and the vault surface itself can therefore be very thin, which makes it necessary to stabilize the lower part of the cone shape by filling it with ballast material.

fascia In CLASSICAL architecture, the flat face of the topmost MOLDING of the ENTABLATURE, or a flat face in the ARCHITRAVE of the entablature. By extension, it is a flat strip in the vertical plane covering the rafter ends at the edge of a roof.

fillet A flat band or ribbon; used in architecture of a flat strip separating two MOLDINGS, or running between the FLUTES of an IONIC or CORINTHIAN COLUMN.

finial An ornament on the end or peak of a roof, commonly in the form of a spike, a fleuron, a dragon, or a chimera.

First Romanesque *See* LOMBARDIC ARCHITECTURE.

Flamboyant The third main phase of the French GOTHIC style, current from the fourteenth to early sixteenth centuries, and named from its flamelike free-flowing window TRACERY.

flashing The covering of a junction in the building fabric to prevent the entry of water. For example, where a verandah roof joins the wall of a building, a strip of lead sheet may be built into the wall to cover the junction. Flashing is required in many other locations, including external door and window frames which project beyond the face of the wall, and where a parapet surrounds a flat roof.

flèche A slender SPIRE riding from a roof.

float glass A GLASS made by floating a ribbon of hot glass onto a liquid of greater density. The two surfaces are then fire polished to give undistorted vision and reflection.

flute A groove, usually a concave curve in section, in a location such as a COLUMN shaft, and used particularly where a number of such grooves are in parallel (known as *fluting*).

footing The lowest part of a building, resting on the FOUNDATION. A common type is *strip footing*, which runs continuously under the loadbearing walls, and may be of brick or stone, usually stepping out to a width much greater than the wall itself, or else of reinforced CONCRETE. A *pad footing*, placed under a column or point load, is usually square and steps out even further. The extent of the stepping out depends upon the bearing capacity of the soil; if the capacity is low, or the building is very heavy, it is more efficient to place the building on a *continuous slab*.

foundation The ground upon which a building stands. This is ideally solid rock, but usually a soil of sufficient bearing capacity can be found at some depth. Otherwise, where the soil is poor, it may be necessary to improve it by the addition of gravel or mass CONCRETE.

fresco A painting method used principally on walls, in which the colors are applied to fresh wet PLASTER so that they penetrate it and become integral to it when it sets.

frieze The central division of the classical ENTABLATURE; also a band of decoration at the top of an interior wall surface.

gable The vertical surface closing the end of a roof, and particularly the triangular end of a roof with two sloping faces. A gable roof is one that has two slopes and closes in this way, as opposed to a hipped roof (*see* HIP), which has four sloping faces and no vertical face. *See also* CROW-STEPPED.

gablet A small GABLE, especially a subsidiary gable within a complex roof shape, or one that is entirely ornamental.

gallery A covered walkway, particularly one partly open to one side, as in the upper part of a fortification, for the use of defending marksmen; an ARCADE around the top of a church APSE; or above the aisles on either side of a church NAVE (a tribune gallery).

gargoyle A spout to throw water from the roof away from the sides of a building. In CLASSICAL architecture, it is commonly a modeled terracotta or carved marble lion's face with a lead spout in its mouth. In GOTHIC architecture, it is a dragon, chimera, or other fanciful creature.

gesso Gypsum (PLASTER of Paris) or chalk, for use in painted or modeled decoration.

Gilardoni tile *See* MARSEILLES TILE.

girder A large loadbearing beam, including an open-web girder of iron or steel which is strictly a parallel-chorded TRUSS.

glass A translucent or transparent material usually made by fusing silica (quartz or sand) with an alkali. The earliest uses were for small vessels, irrelevant to architecture. The first use of small panes of glass for lighting building interiors cannot be established precisely, but they would have been formed by casting. The process of forming BLOWN GLASS may have been discovered by the Egyptians, but is more generally believed to have been invented at Sidon in the time of Alexander the Great. Its significant use dates from Roman times.

glass, blown GLASS formed from the "metal" (the term for molten glass) by blowing a bubble, which is then manipulated.

glass, blown cylinder (*commonly* sheet glass) GLASS blown to a bubble and then swung in a heated pit until it extends into a cylindrical shape. When the ends of the cylinder have been opened, and a cut run along the length, it is reheated and allowed to flatten into a rectangular sheet.

glass, crown Blown GLASS, in which the bubble is transferred to a punty (iron rod), and spun to create a flat disc, or *table*. The lump, or *bull's eye,* at the center severely limits the size of the pane that can be cut from the table.

glass, drawn cylinder GLASS produced by a mechanized process in which a cylinder is pulled up out of the molten "metal" to a height of 40 or 50 ft (12 or 15 m) at a controlled speed, to produce a long tube, which is then cut to the required sizes and flattened.

glass, plate Formed by pouring molten GLASS onto a flat table and spreading it mechanically, then grinding and polishing it. This process, invented in seventeenth-century France, produced much larger and finer sheets than the original system of casting flat pieces.

Gothic The medieval architectural style which first appeared in twelfth-century France, and spread to the rest of Europe, characterized by the pointed ARCH and the RIB VAULT, sometimes by the FLYING BUTTRESS, and usually by stained GLASS windows. In France there are three main phases: the "primaire" (GOTHIQUE À LANCETTES); and the "secondaire" (RAYONNANT) and "tertiaire" (FLAMBOYANT). In England, the equivalent phases are the EARLY ENGLISH, DECORATED and PERPENDICULAR.

Gothique à Lancettes The first phase of French GOTHIC architecture, of the twelfth century, using pointed ARCHES and geometric window TRACERY.

grillage A network of beams overlying each other at right angles, used below a building to spread the load on an unstable soil or to link the caps of PILES.

grisaille The painting of stained GLASS in a monochrome grey.

guttae Small conical projections under the TRIGLYPHS and mutules of the DORIC ENTABLATURE, possibly derived from TRENAILS in this position in an archetypal timber structure.

H-section A steel section with flanges wider than those of the commoner I-section.

half timber Frame and infill construction, used especially in medieval and later houses. The infill may consist of LEHMWICKEL, WATTLE AND DAUB, ADOBE, or baked brickwork; these panels are often plastered and whitewashed in contrast to a dark stained finish of the exposed timber frame.

haunch The lower side part of an ARCH or arched bridge.

Hellenistic The postCLASSICAL period of Greek and Greek-influenced architecture in Greece and the regions conquered by Alexander the Great, from Alexander's accession in 336 BCE until Roman rule, which came at various dates. Decoration was very rich and innovative, and the CORINTHIAN ORDER became popular. Temples reached sizes previously seen only in Asia Minor, and urban design became axial and monumental. Details were absorbed from conquered territories, such as Egypt and Syria, and such novel elements as broken and segmental PEDIMENTS were introduced.

hexastyle Having six COLUMNS, as in the end elevation of a CLASSICAL temple.

hip The angle where two roof slopes meet, usually at 45 degrees in plan; hence a hipped roof is one which slopes on four sides, as opposed to the two of a GABLE roof.

hydraulic In relation to LIME and CEMENT, having water-resistant properties. This means that it can be used for underwater works, or if used in an exposed position, such as in a STUCCOED wall surface, it will not be quickly washed way. A LIMESTONE with an appropriate proportion of clay, and burned to a higher temperature, will produce a hydraulic lime. Most cements are hydraulic.

hypostyle Filled with COLUMNS; used especially of the Egyptian hypostyle hall.

I-beam An iron or steel beam with a cross-section like the letter "I"; it has a much greater moment of inertia than the same amount of metal in a rectangular shape, and therefore resists bending much better.

iconostasis In the eastern or Orthodox church, a screen that separates the chancel from the NAVE, originally a lattice of COLUMNS, but by the fourteenth or fifteenth century a complete wall covered with icons of the Lord, the Virgin Mary and saints. Mass is conducted behind this screen.

imbrex (*pl.* imbrices) In a CLASSICAL tiled roof, the narrow tile that covers the joint between two TEGULAE.

impost block A BLOCK placed above the CAPITAL of a column and below the impost, or SPRINGING of an ARCH. Elements of three types are used in this position, and the terminology is confusing (*see* PULVINO and DOSSERET

BLOCK). "Impost block" represents a complete section of classical ENTABLATURE. According to implicit classical principles, an arch cannot be carried on a column, but can be placed above a beam or entablature. An impost block in the profile of an entablature permits the conceit that the arch is resting on a beam, and therefore is not in breach of the classical grammar. This device appears in medieval work at Hildesheim, Aachen, and elsewhere. It is used with full understanding by Brunelleschi, who uses the true impost block in his churches of San Lorenzo and Santo Spirito, Florence.

inlay Decorative material set into a base to produce a flush surface.

intercolumniation The clear distance between two COLUMNS.

inglenook A recessed BAY large enough to sit in, containing a fireplace. This allows the people in the nook to keep warm even if the fire is insufficient to heat the whole room.

insula Literally an island, but referring to a multistory residential block in ancient Rome or Ostia. The ground-floor street frontages were usually occupied by shops and businesses, the mezzanine level for storage or sleeping, and the upper floors for private apartments. There may be a LIGHT WELL at the center.

intarsia INLAID or MOSAIC woodwork.

intrados The inside or underneath face of an ARCH, as distinct from the EXTRADOS.

Ionic order The second of the canonical classical ORDERS, defined by a CAPITAL in which two downward SCROLLS are joined across the top (unlike those of the AEOLIC). The COLUMN shaft is FLUTED, with narrow FILLETS between the flutes, and has base MOLDINGS of either the Attic or the Asiatic type. Considerable variation is possible in the ENTABLATURE. The LINTEL, especially if it is large, may be stepped out slightly in three stages, each defined by a very fine astragal (or bead and reel) molding. There may or may not be a continuous sculpted FRIEZE above. The CORNICE is generally supported by a row of small blocks (*dentils*). The order presents a formal problem in that the spirals of the two scrolls are visible on the front face of the capital, but from the side only the edge of one scroll can be seen. Thus, a corner capital would face only one or other of the elevations, but not both. To deal with this, an odd capital was devised in which the scrolls appear on both faces at right angles, and on the corner are shortened and bent out together as a single projection at forty-five degrees. This clumsy device reduced the popularity of the Ionic and promoted the CORINTHIAN in Rome.

iron, cast Iron in its basic form, still containing carbon, which is formed by pouring into a mold. The result is a brittle material that is strong in compression but poor in tension and bending, and likely to fail under sudden changes of temperature (as when water is played upon it in fighting a fire).

iron, corrugated Sheet wrought iron, or later mild steel, rolled or pressed into an approximation of a sine curve in section. The idea of rolling or fluting sheet metal was not new, but Henry Robinson Palmer, engineer of the London Docks, experimented with its use for structural purposes in 1829. A thin sheet of flat iron can span only a very small distance, but its capacity is dramatically increased by corrugation. It is further increased if the corrugated sheet is curved or arched in the lengthwise direction, and this is what Robinson did in the BARREL-VAULTED iron roofs he built at the Docks. Because the sheets available were small, it was necessary to rivet them together in both the sideways and the lengthways directions; once done, this created a continuous roof surface so strong that it required only a wrought-iron tension rod across the base to make it self-sufficient.

iron, galvanized Galvanizing is coating iron with zinc, which has the property not merely of covering the surface but of reacting with corrosive elements before the iron does. The idea had existed since the eighteenth century, but the French chemist Stanislas Sorel brought it to a practical level, and in 1836 took out a French patent on the coating of iron with molten zinc, zinc paint, or zinc powder. Manufacture began in 1843.

iron, wrought Iron that has had most of the carbon and some other impurities removed, originally by burning them out in a small-scale "finery" (refinery); it may be done also by other means, including extensive rolling or working of the metal. Thus it is a commercially pure material, and its properties differ from those of CAST IRON. It can be hammered and worked into shape, and this working gives it a fibrous texture: it is more resilient than cast iron and can take tension, though it is not as strong as cast iron in compression. It is also more susceptible to rust.

jamb The vertical member at the side of a door or window opening.

jerkin-head roof A roof that ends in a GABLE surmounted by a small HIP, like an ordinary gable roof with the point sliced off on an angle.

jetty The projection of an upper floor beyond the lower one, common in medieval European architecture, causing buildings to overhang streets and footpaths.

joggle In a masonry ARCH, a deliberate step or irregularity in the joint between two VOUSSOIRS, so that one cannot slide past the other.

joist One of the smaller and uniformly sized beams carrying a floor or ceiling.

jubé *See* ROOD SCREEN.

keep A well-defended tower or stronghold within a larger fortification, to which the defenders can retreat if the outer walls are breached by an attacker. In Chinese architecture, known as a *donjon*.

keystone The topmost central VOUSSOIR of an ARCH, which is often made larger or more ornamental. Its structural function is the same as that of the other voussoirs but it is the last to be put in place and locks the arch.

kiln, brick A simple BRICK kiln is a walled but unroofed structure, the top of which is sealed on each occasion with loose bricks, clay, and similar; a cupola or circular kiln is fully domed over. As a kiln contains both the bricks and the fires in the one space, there is a risk of overburning bricks close to the flame *(clinkers)* and underburning those farther away *(called doughboys)*. A more uniform result is obtained from an *updraft kiln*, which has the fire below and the heat passing up through the bricks. Even better is a *downdraft kiln* in which the heat enters from the top, or is first directed to the top, and is sucked down through the bricks. A *continuous kiln*, the best known of which is the *Hoffman*, is generally circular or oval: the fire moves around the kiln so that at any one time bricks are being loaded at one point, and at others steamed, burned, cooled, and unloaded. In a *tunnel kiln*, the fire is in a fixed place and the bricks are passed slowly through on a railway.

lancet A narrow opening with a pointed head formed by two intersecting arcs of a circle, typical of early GOTHIC work. The word is also used to describe the style, characterized by these openings (often windows), which is more generally called EARLY ENGLISH.

lantern, roof A boxlike or GABLED structure on top of a roof, with side windows or openings to light or ventilate the space below.

lath A small strip of timber, especially one of those used as the base for PLASTERING. The laths are spaced apart, so the first coat of render or plaster squeezes through the gap and expands slightly so as to lock the material in place when it hardens.

lathing The layer of timber LATHS prepared to receive PLASTERING, or a metal mesh serving the same purpose, especially expanded metal.

lead light The term for stained GLASS or other glazing, consisting of small pieces set between *cames* (narrow lead strips).

lehmwickel A construction found in Germany, German-influenced areas, and northern France, consisting of timber stakes wound around with mud and straw to form a cylinder, a number of which are packed in parallel to fill a panel in a *fachwerk* or HALF-TIMBERED wall, or to span horizontally between ceiling joists. The technique is often mistaken for WATTLE AND DAUB.

lierne In English GOTHIC vaulting of the DECORATED period, a RIB other than a ridge rib which passes between two other ribs in the VAULT and does not terminate at the SPRINGING point: that is, it is not a TIERCERON or a transverse, wall, or diagonal rib.

light A window or glazing unit, especially as part of a larger grouping, as in a BAY WINDOW made up of two, three, or more lights, with areas of masonry or MULLIONS between them; or in a GOTHIC window in which the lights are separated by stone TRACERY (*see also* FANLIGHT). The word is not used of the panes within a SASH that are separated only by glazing bars, as in a typical Georgian or early Victorian window; nor of the separate quarries divided by lead cames in a leadlight window.

light well A well or unroofed space within a building, which provides a source of natural light to the adjacent rooms on each level.

lime A material used in MORTARS and primitive CONCRETE, the product of burning LIMESTONE or other materials consisting principally of calcium carbonate (such as marble, coral, or shells). When burned, the carbonate produces calcium oxide, or quicklime, plus carbon dioxide: $CaCO_3 = CaO + CO_2$. *Quicklime* is a corrosive and difficult substance, and is "slaked" by adding water to produce calcium hydroxide, a process generating considerable heat: $CaO + H_2O = Ca(OH)_2$. Calcium hydroxide, or *slaked lime*, is the material used for building purposes in mortar, STUCCO, and concrete. It reacts slowly with carbon dioxide in the air to turn into calcium carbonate: $Ca(OH)_2 + CO_2 = CaCO_3 + H_2O$. This reaction begins at the exposed surface, and has the advantage that if cracks develop in the structure, and new surfaces of lime are exposed, they begin setting.

limestone A rock consisting of calcium carbonate ($CaCO_3$), which is both used as a building stone in its own right, and burned to produce LIME. The stone tends to be soft when first cut, but to harden on exposure to the air—a useful property in early building, when quarrying tools were primitive.

linenfold paneling Timber paneling used in late medieval England in which each panel is carved in relief with the semblance of a linen cloth hanging in vertical symmetrical folds.

lintel The lower part of a classical ENTABLATURE, which is a beam spanning across the columns, and in modern usage the beam spanning the head of a door or window.

liturgical east Because Christian churches normally point to the east, it is convenient to refer always to the sanctuary as the east end. To avoid confusion, in those churches pointing in a different direction, the term is qualified, as the "liturgical east" end. The same is done, less commonly, of the liturgical south TRANSEPT, west entrance, and so on.

loculus A slot cut into the walls of a CATACOMB or other tomb chamber to take a body, either parallel with the wall face or at right angles.

loess Wind-deposited soil that may compact into something approaching a soft rock, particularly in Shaanxi province, China, where underground dwellings are excavated into it.

Lombardic architecture The architecture of northern Italy established under the Lombards, who arrived as invaders in CE 568. They had little architectural tradition of their own, but some structures of a CLASSICAL, BYZANTINE or VISIGOTHIC character were built in their territory. By 643 a guild of masons, the Comacini, had been established and their work was influenced by the style of Ravenna, which was embedded in the east side of their territory, and to use brick detailing such as PILASTER strips and CORBEL tables. By the late ninth century, they began using the same details in stone. The term "Lombardus" became synonymous with "stonemason" in much of Europe, and they were sought for projects at great distances. The style that spread across southern France and into Spanish Catalonia is sometimes called the PREMIER ART ROMAN or FIRST ROMANESQUE. Their influence is also seen to a lesser extent in the former Yugoslavia.

louvre Originally a sort of ventilating lantern-cum-chimney on the roof of a medieval building, but "louvre" came to mean the type of angled horizontal slat used in the sides of such a structure to allow the passage of air in and/or smoke out. It became a standard means of ventilating farm buildings, such as dairies and stables. It can be made to pivot on the horizontal axis, to adjust the amount of air or light admitted. It was also common in the Far East, especially in India as *jhilmils*. Means of linking the slats so they could be moved in unison by a single lever were improved from the early nineteenth century; later in the century American joinery companies specialized in very fine adjustable timber louvres set within frames that could themselves move in the manner of CASEMENT or DOUBLE-HUNG SASHES. GLASS louvres became common in the early twentieth century, especially for bathrooms.

lunette A crescent-shaped or semicircular panel or opening. In architecture, especially a window in the form of a semicircle with arc rising from a horizontal base.

machicolation A fortification device in which a defensive wall is crowned by a terrace or GALLERY that cantilevers out and is provided with openings through which missiles or boiling oil can be dropped on attackers.

Mannerism The artistic and architectural style that succeeded the High RENAISSANCE in Italy. It can be explained in two ways. The first is the usual cyclical reaction occurring when any style has reached perfection. The second is the circumstances in Rome that gave rise to a sense of unease and insecurity in the early sixteenth century: an outbreak of the plague in 1522; the artistically disastrous reign of Pope Adrian VI in 1522–1523; and, worst of all, the sack of Rome by Spanish troops in 1527. Mannerism tended to undermine CLASSICAL principles by distortion, exaggeration, and wit; its impact depended upon the viewer's understanding those principles.

mansard roof A roof with a steep lower face and shallower upper part, usually accommodating rooms within, and named from the architect François Mansart.

maqsura An enclosure used in an early mosque to protect the ruler from assassination, located near the MIHRAB. Also the screen enclosing the grave in an important mausoleum.

marquetry Wooden inlay work used in decorating furniture.

Marseilles tile A French roofing TILE in the general category of the *Gilardoni tile*, which was introduced in the 1840s by the Gilardoni brothers of Alsace, using newly available pressing machinery. Tiles are rectangular, with a central rib or diamond for strengthening, a beaded overlocking side joint for weatherproofing, and a bullnose toe overlapping an upward flange at the head of the next tile. Marseille (referred to in the anglicized form as "Marseilles") was a major port of export, and a number of local manufacturers adopted a standardized design which was exported to India, South America, Australasia, and elsewhere, and hence became very influential.

masonry Properly built stone, BRICK, or occasionally CONCRETE work, but usually meaning stone unless otherwise qualified.

mastaba An Egyptian tomb in which the body is below ground level, and above ground is a rectangular platform with its sides sloped or "battered" at seventy-five degrees. Larger examples might contain a mortuary chapel and other rooms within the platform.

megalith A large stone used as part of a building or monument.

megaron An early house and temple form in the Greek and Aegean world, consisting of a single chamber entered from one end through a porch formed by the extended side walls or ANTAE. The opposite end was sometimes curved, though usually square. The megaron evolved into the CLASSICAL temple form.

menhir In prehistoric times, a single large upright stone used as a monument alone, or in an arrangement with others.

merlon A BATTLEMENT, particularly one in the Muslim world, with the top curved to form a point, or bifurcated.

Merovingian The architecture of Frankish Gaul under the Merovingian dynasty (*c.* 500–750) founded by Clovis, characterized by a greater survival of Roman forms than in most cultures of the DARK AGES; the use of classicizing marble CAPITALS from Pyrenean quarries; and the use of the PORTICUS.

metope A squarish recessed panel between each pair of TRIGLYPHS in the DORIC ENTABLATURE, sometimes left open in early examples, but otherwise commonly with relief decoration.

mihrab A niche that is the focus of prayer in a mosque, placed to indicate the direction of Mecca.

millwork A term for timber MOLDINGS, and by extension other joinery products.

minaret The tower of a mosque from which the *muezzin* issues the call to prayer.

Minimalism The absence of ornament, unnecessary structure, or complex forms: a strand of MODERNISM.

miter A right-angled joint in which the two arms are cut to meet at forty-five degrees.

moat The deep surrounding ditch of a fortification, whether dry or filled with water.

Modern Movement (*also* Modernism) The early twentieth-century movement to reject historical precedent and design upon a simple, rational, and functional basis. It embraces such approaches as the rejection of ornament of Loos, the industrial logic of the Bauhaus

school, the abstract massing of Le Corbusier, and the clarity of Mies van der Rohe.

moldings Small sections of various cross-section, often combined in parallel to create a form, such as a skirting or CORNICE. They are usually uniform along their length as if extruded; but in CLASSICAL architecture, where they are carved, they may be modeled in three dimensions. In PLASTERING, they are usually "run" by the plasterer drawing along a wooden section of the appropriate shape. In joinery, they are formed by specially shaped molding planes. By the mid-nineteenth century they were more commonly produced in mills.

monitor, roof A projecting LANTERN or continued raised section above the ridge of a roof, for the purpose of lighting or ventilation.

monolithic arch A stone LINTEL over an opening, with the bottom cut out in the form of an ARCH; structurally, it is a beam that has been weakened.

mortar The adhesive material of a masonry wall, consisting usually of LIME or CEMENT with sand, but in more primitive construction of mud, with or without a proportion of lime.

mortise and tenon A T-shaped joint in which the cross arm has a slot *(mortise)* cut through it, and the piece at right angles has its end narrowed to a tongue *(tenon)* to fit in. Sometimes, to prevent it coming apart, the tongue is made so long as to pass right through the other member, and a peg or TRENAIL put through it so that it cannot be withdrawn.

mosaic Small squarish tiles of stone, GLASS, or glazed TERRACOTTA, often including some of gold, and used to create abstract patterns or figurative designs.

motte In early medieval fortification, an earthen mound carrying a fortification, often surrounded by a BAILEY or larger walled area at natural ground level: hence motte-and-bailey.

mud brick *See* ADOBE.

muqarnas A form of VAULTING made up of concave segments to create a honeycomb or stalactite effect; evolved from the SQUINCH.

mullion The vertical structural division between the LIGHTS of a window.

narthex A full-width transverse space at the west or entrance end of a church, acting as a vestibule. An *exonarthex* is a narthex more open to the exterior and often attached like a PORTICO. An *esonarthex* is one within the body of the building and more open to the interior, a continuation of the side aisles at right angles.

nave The long arm of a church occupied principally by the congregation, especially if vaulted and resembling an inverted ship; also a similar volume in a secular building. It is distinguished from the AISLES (which are usually at the sides, often under lower roofs, and used more as passages than seating areas).

Neoclassicism A term often misused to refer to any architecture of a CLASSICAL character, but correctly confined to a specific movement of the eighteenth century to reapproach the classical tradition in two ways (which were not mutually exclusive). The first, strongest in Britain, was to use classical precedents with greater precision, and drew upon the writings of Stuart, Revett, Adam, Wood, and Chandler. The second, developed in France, was to reduce architecture to what were seen as the abstract fundamentals of classical architecture. Laugier, in particular, postulated a primitive form of hut as the antecedent of the classical temple, and accepted as proper elements of architecture the columns, the beams, and the sloping members necessary to create a pitched roof. Although walls were not so fundamental, he permitted them as a concession to human weakness. But he opposed the elaboration of the BAROQUE, including unnecessary elements such as PEDESTALS beneath columns, and especially opposed any element motivated by caprice (effectively anything descended from the work of Borromini). No actual buildings measured up fully to these criteria, but by the end of the century they had inspired the megalomaniac projects of Boullée, which were enormous, abstract, and evoked specific meanings such as the sphere of the cosmos. These *sublime* or emotionally muscular projects are known as ROMANTIC CLASSICISM.

niello A material used to fill engraved designs in silver and other metals; made of sulfur with silver, lead, or copper.

Nubian vault A BARREL VAULT constructed of leaning ARCHES so as to avoid the need for complicated carpentry to support it during construction. Against a vertical wall at one end, the base of an arch is begun, but is immediately cut off by the vertical surface. Successive arches are begun, each leaning against the last and becoming a little more complete, until a complete leaning arch is built. Other arches follow successively. Because of the lean, and the effect of friction, it is not necessary to support them from below. Such vaults were used in ancient Egypt and Mesopotamia, and today are used throughout the Middle East in mud brick construction. Also known as a *pitched vault*.

obelisk A giant four-sided tapering stone used as a monument in ancient Egypt. Many were looted and reused in Europe.

octastyle Having eight COLUMNS, as in the end elevation of a CLASSICAL temple.

oculus A circular opening or eye, especially the unglazed circular opening in the dome of a Roman building such as the Pantheon; also a conventional window of circular form.

ogee A curve reversing on itself to make a shallow S-shape, used in the late GOTHIC, and especially in eighteenth century "Gothick" work. Also a MOLDING of this shape in section, resembling the classical CYMA, often used in guttering and sometimes abbreviated to "OG."

opisthodomos The false porch of a Greek temple, which presents the same appearance as the true porch at the opposite end, but gives no access to the interior.

order *1.* In CLASSICAL architecture, a canonical combination of elements defined, first, by the form of the CAPITAL and, second, by the form of the COLUMN shaft. Wheareas the DORIC order has a specific form of ENTABLATURE, in other orders it is more negotiable. The classical Greek orders are the DORIC, IONIC, and CORINTHIAN. An earlier form of capital in the eastern Mediterranean region is referred to as the AEOLIC ORDER, but has no (known) characteristic shaft or entablature. The Romans modified the Greek orders, generally by making them more elaborate, and introduced the Tuscan and COMPOSITE. *2.* In medieval architecture, an assemblage of two COLONNETTES carrying a round or pointed arch, in a doorway or other opening, the term being used in the sense of two, three, or more orders, referring to the existence of that number of concentric sets.

ordonnance The ordering or formal disposition of the parts, particularly in the composition of a building in elevation.

oriel window A curved or polygonal window BAY projecting from upper level of a building.

orthostat (*also* orthostate) A large squared stone, generally as distinguished within a construction of rubble or mud brick. In the Bronze Age, it was common to form the base of a wall with a single course of orthostats with less substantial construction above (*see* DADO).

oubliette A small secret dungeon, usually with no windows and entered from a trap door.

Palladian To do with the architecture of Andrea Palladio (1508–1580); used not so much of his own buildings as those of the Palladian Revival in early eighteenth-century Britain.

palmette An ornament with radiating fronds like a palm leaf, used especially in classical Greek architecture, rising from a flat base.

parquet, parquetry Flooring of blocks of contrasting woods set in a geometric pattern.

pedestal A square base upon which a COLUMN or statue is raised.

pediment The triangular form at the end of a CLASSICAL temple, reflecting the pitched roof, with the periphery formed of projecting MOLDINGS and the center a recessed triangular panel (TYMPANUM). Also the same form used elsewhere, as in an AEDICULE. The curved or segmental pediment seems to have appeared in Hellenistic Egypt and was widely used in Roman and later architecture. The "broken" pediment, and various other deliberately incomplete forms, sometimes with one set within another, were also Hellenistic, used in Rome, and revived especially in the BAROQUE.

pendentive The geometric device used to connect the circular base of a DOME to a square or octagonal substructure. The visible face is a spherical triangle: part of the surface of a sphere as cut by two vertical planes and the horizontal plane at SPRINGING level. Structurally it may be monolithic, made of radial VOUSSOIRS like a true dome, or CORBELED horizontally.

peripteral Of a CLASSICAL temple, surrounded by a COLONNADE on all four sides.

peristyle A surrounding COLONNADE, either around a solid structure such as a CLASSICAL temple, or around a courtyard.

Perpendicular The third phase of English GOTHIC architecture, from the late fourteenth to the early sixteenth centuries, stressing gridlike vertical and horizontal divisions in windows and paneling, within which ARCHES are flatter and made up from four rather than two arcs of a circle; also employing the FAN VAULT.

piazza An Italian town square. The term, used by Inigo Jones for his Covent Garden Piazza, London, came to be associated with the recessed loggia that surrounded this square. It was used for the recessed loggia at the base of some tenement blocks, and by 1699 for a complete arcaded undercroft proposed at the Capitol, Williamsburg, Virginia. The word was then used in the United States and India for a verandah, and in the United States especially for a part of a verandah that was wider than the rest or partially screened. By the late nineteenth century even an unroofed platform might be called a piazza.

Picturesque A concept developed out of the landscape design in eighteenth-century Britain. The term at first implied nothing more than "worthy to appear in a picture," but it came to include a desire for variety in color, texture, and outline, as well as associational values:

those that aroused the intellect or emotions by reference to classical gods, national heroes, family members, and so on. The desire for naturalism encouraged the introduction of asymmetry in landscape design, in reaction to the dominant axiality of the BAROQUE. This was demonstrated in the evolving landscape designs of Kent, Brown, and Repton. The concept of the "sublime" was codified by Burke. The Picturesque itself was not an architectural style, but the principle that underlay the "cottage ornée" of the early nineteenth century, the castellated work of Nash and other architects, and domestic styles such as the Italianate.

pier A vertical masonry support, usually rectangular in plan but occasionally a cylinder (like a fat COLUMN).

pietra dura Semiprecious stones used in the manner of MOSAIC.

pietra serena A grey-blue sandstone often used in Tuscany in combination with lighter grey surfaces, from Brunelleschi onward.

pilaster A flat-faced representation of a COLUMN, set against, and projecting from, a wall surface. If abstracted by omitting the CAPITAL and simplifying the shaft, it becomes the *pilaster strip* used in Ravennate and LOMBARDIC ARCHITECTURE.

pile Either a tall shaft carrying a structure high above ground or over water, or a member driven into the ground by hammering so as to carry a building on a poor foundation. By extension, *sheet piling* consists of steel sections interlocking along the edge, so that they can slide past each other while being driven into the ground, but when complete they create a continuous wall that prevents an excavation from collapsing inwards. The *screw pile* invented by Alexander Mitchell was a flattish Archimedean screw that could be twisted into a sandy foundation below water level to support structures such as openwork lighthouses.

pillar An upright member more substantial than a COLUMN, either for monumental purposes or to carry a heavy load; commonly rectangular as in a PIER.

pinnacle A pointed decorative element often terminating some part of a roof.

pintle A pin upon which a door can rotate; more primitive than a hinge. It is sometimes used also for a PIVOT, but strictly is an upright metal pin which is cantilevered from the door frame, so that a ring attached to the side of the door can drop over it, allowing the door to swing. It can often be seen in old barns or industrial door openings in old factories.

pisé de terre Earth rammed in place between panels of shuttering or formwork, as distinct from soft mud (COB) and mud brick or ADOBE. It should be a dry gravelly loam, not a clay (which shrinks and cracks when used monolithically). It has been used extensively in China, and in the Mediterranean world from Phoenician North Africa to Spain and France.

pitch Slope, as in a roof, or a pitched VAULT. 'Pitched roof' generally implies a roof of two symmetrical slopes, as opposed to a monopitch or skillion roof.

pitched vault *See* NUBIAN VAULT.

pivot The most primitive method of swinging a door, in which one of the STILES is continued above and below, and finished in points that move in sockets in the frame above and below.

plaster A surfacing material for walls and ceilings, generally made from gypsum, though the term is also applied to other materials used in the same way, as in "LIME plaster."

platband A flat rectangular MOLDING or FASCIA projecting shallowly from a surface.

plinth The base of a structure, usually with vertical faces and somewhat wider than what it supports. It may be the lowest element of a PEDESTAL, or a complete base to a building, projecting like a skirting.

podium A raised platform or dais, but also the platform-like base of a structure, which may be the same as a PLINTH.

porphyry A hard, red, igneous crystalline stone popular in Egyptian and Roman architecture.

portal A formal entrance area or PORTICO incorporating a doorway.

portcullis A wooden or iron grille carried on chains and designed to be dropped quickly to close a gate or door in a fortress.

portico The formal axial entrance area of a CLASSICAL temple or public building, with a roof carried on COLUMNS, or the equivalent in a medieval or other building.

porticus A small squarish chamber, usually one of two or more placed symmetrically in the plan of a Saxon, MEROVINGIAN or VISIGOTHIC church, and sometimes occupying the whole area where AISLES might otherwise be found.

portland cement An "artificial" CEMENT, in that the main ingredients (essentially LIMESTONE and clay) are obtained separately and mixed to the desired proportions, rather than found in some naturally occurring

mixture as with ROMAN CEMENT. Several British and French patents were obtained for controlled mixtures of lime and clay in the early nineteenth century. In 1810, E. J. Dobbs obtained a British patent for mixing chalk or limestone with clay, burning it, and grinding the CLINKER, which are the essentials of cement manufacture. In 1822 Joseph Aspdin patented a material he called "portland cement," because of its supposed resemblance to Portland stone. These cements are cosmetic materials rather than structural ones. Today, the clinker, which consists of calcium silicates, is ground and is the main constituent.

post and beam The fundamental structural form in which vertical posts or columns, subject to compression, carry a horizontal beam, subject to bending stresses. Also known as *trabeation*.

Postmodernism The movement that followed and rejected MODERNISM, but which is not defined by any single principle. It tends to be characterized by contrivance, arbitrariness, wit, and contextual references.

pozzolana A volcanic ash found in many parts of Italy, containing silica and alumina. It gave ROMAN CEMENT its distinctive quality. Other materials with the same effect, such as Dutch trass, are sometimes referred to as "pozzolans."

Premier Art Roman *See* LOMBARDIC ARCHITECTURE.

propylaeum A formal columnar roofed gateway structure, most famously the Propylaea giving access to the Acropolis of Athens, Greece.

propylon The Latin equivalent of the Greek PROPYLAEUM, but used more generally of a gateway with columns rather than a distinctive structural type, as in the propylon gate of the old Basilica of St. Peter, Rome.

pug *See* COB.

pulvino Literally a cushion: a type of IMPOST BLOCK placed between the CAPITAL of a column and the springing of an ARCH above. The term is best reserved for one that is literally cushion-shaped, as in San Vitale, Ravenna.

purlin One of the small beams supporting a roof surface and running transverse to the roof slope, typically resting on top of the RAFTERS or roof principals. In a larger and more complicated roof, a larger *underpurlin* may be required to support the rafters from below, again running transverse to the slope.

qanat A technique originating in ancient Persia used for drawing water from subterranean sources without pumping. It consists of a series of vertical shafts that are connected to a single horizontal shaft leading from a raised water source to an outlet at a lower elevation. Qanats are still used in the Middle East.

quadripartite vault In GOTHIC architecture, a VAULT in which four surfaces or "compartments" meet at a central point, divided by diagonals in plan (see SEXPARTITE VAULT).

quoin A corner BLOCK in walling, usually larger or more prominent, and more formally dressed, than adjoining masonry. Commonly the quoins are alternately large and small as they rise, so as to key into the body of the wall.

raft A continuous slab FOOTING extending beneath the whole plan area of a building, used in unstable soils where it is not cost-effective to provide separate strip and pad footings for each element of the load. Raft slabs are made especially in reinforced CONCRETE.

rafter A sloping member in a roof frame that defines the shape of the surface, and normally extends from RIDGE to EAVE. It may support small timbers (*battens*) running transversely, or a continuous layer of boarding (*sarking*), to which the roof surfacing material is fixed.

rail One or more horizontal pieces of wood that join with the vertical STILES and a central panel to form a door or window.

ramp An inclined plane, with each end at a different elevation to the other. Commonly used to provide access to buildings for individuals who have difficulty with stairs. The slope is often around 20:1 horizontal distance to vertical elevation.

Rayonnant The second main phase of French GOTHIC architecture, current in the twelfth century and characterized by circular windows with radiating TRACERY.

Renaissance The revival of CLASSICAL culture and humanist learning which began in Italy in the fourteenth and fifteenth centuries and spread across Europe. The term means "re-birth" and can be used in other contexts, but is generally varied, as in "renascence," or qualified, as in "CAROLINGIAN Renaissance," to avoid confusion. The main predecessors of the Italian Renaissance are as follows. The Sixtine Renaissance, during the papacy of Sixtus III (432–440), revived TRABEATION and CLASSICAL proportions at a time when Italy had been influenced by the ARCADING and steeper cross-sections of the East. The Carolingian Renaissance of about 800, initiated by Charlemagne, aimed to reinstate imperial Roman culture but included significant elements from BYZANTINE and other cultures. The TUSCAN PROTO-RENAISSANCE is the most significant. The Renaissance

proper in architecture begins in the early fifteenth century with the work of Brunelleschi in Florence, and Alberti in Florence and elsewhere. The *High Renaissance*, exemplified in the work of Bramante, is more centered in Rome. This gives way to MANNERISM, though PALLADIO pursues in his own way what are essentially Renaissance ideals.

represented structure The convention whereby the face of a building represents a structure that is not the real one. The classic example is the Colosseum, Rome, which is in fact an ARCHED and VAULTED structure, but has a complete system of COLUMNS and ENTABLATURES on its face with no structural function whatever. The resultant combination, an arch on PIERS behind a TRABEATED BAY, was a standard element in the RENAISSANCE work of Alberti and others. Another form is seen in the NAVE of many GOTHIC cathedrals: the forces in the vault are depicted as passing through its RIBS (which may or may not be true), and thence down the face of the wall to the floor by slender COLONETTES, which are far too thin to stand in their own right, much less to carry any load, but they complete an aesthetically satisfying fiction.

revetment Veneer or paneling, such as thin slabs of marble covering the face of a wall.

rib A molded length of material, usually stone, with an apparent structural function. Although not without precedents in Roman architecture, it is essentially an invention of the late ROMANESQUE, and was first applied to vaulted roofing to run along the lines where two surfaces meet, which would otherwise be ARRISES. It then became a major characteristic of the Gothic style: in the late Gothic it was often placed arbitrarily on the face of the VAULT, as in the TIERCERON and LIERNE, or might depart from the surface and cut across the void. Where the ribs seem to wander arbitrarily across the surface, as in some Czech examples, this is called a *free vault*. It is a vexed question whether the vault rib in its original form serves a structural purpose such as to carry load; a constructional one, such as to hold up sections of the vault until the last stone locks the completed vault; or an aesthetic one (the rib covers what would otherwise be an arris, which is difficult to form in a true line, and creates a satisfying represented structure).

ridge The top line of a roof structure, running in a horizontal, or near horizontal, direction. In a timber roof, a wooden member may be placed here. It has no structural function as the RAFTERS on either side bear against each other, but is convenient in the construction process.

riser The vertical elements in stairs, occasionally decorated with TILES or artistic reliefs.

rocaille Shell-like decoration, used especially in the ROCOCO style.

Rococo A period of art and architecture from eighteenth-century France with a characteristic playfulness. Features include elaborate ornamentation, light colors, usage of curves, and integration of sculpture, artworks, and furniture into the design of a room.

Roman cement This term is used in two senses. The CEMENT used by the Romans is a LIME that is improved by the addition of POZZOLANA (volcanic ash). But as commonly used, it refers to the discovery by Englishman James Parker of naturally occurring septaria nodules that burn to produce a cement, patented by him in 1796. The nodules were a natural combination of LIMESTONE and clay and the material is essentially like a HYDRAULIC lime but better.

Romanesque The medieval style that emerged in Europe in about CE 1000 and was superseded by the GOTHIC from the mid-twelfth century on, depending upon the location. To some extent, a revival of Roman architecture as it uses the semicircular ARCH and revives the use of BARREL and intersecting groin VAULTING. But it is diverse. The timber roof is prominent in Britain and Germany; Roman traditions are much stronger in Provence, France; external wall treatment differs between the Lombardic region in Italy and northern Europe; and in Burgundy, France, steep proportions and pointed arches seem to presage the GOTHIC.

Romantic Classicism *See* NEOCLASSICISM

rood screen An openwork screen dividing the chancel of a church from the NAVE and carrying a "rood" or cross, found in some English GOTHIC churches, and especially in the Gothic Revival work of A. W. N. Pugin. The *jubé* is the French equivalent.

rose window A large circular window with radiating TRACERY, used mainly in France. It should be distinguished from a *wheel window*, which is usually much smaller, has radiating elements resembling the spokes of a wheel, and is found in England and northern Italy.

rustication Stonework that is left with a rough finish, with protruding blocks, often with deep grooves between each block. The style became popular in the RENAISSANCE, particularly for the lower floors of a large building.

sash A movable frame containing GLASS in a CASEMENT, DOUBLE-HUNG, or other window.

sawtooth A roof profile in which vertical or near-vertical areas of glass alternate with sloping surfaces in a profile resembling that of a saw. The glass faces away from direct sun, so the light remains as uniform as possible throughout the day. The form was mainly promoted in the nineteenth century for single-story mills. The sawtooth profile was taken up for use in factories and industrial buildings.

scroll A spiral decoration. In architecture, it is used most prominently to effect the transition between the central panel of a RENAISSANCE or BAROQUE church FAÇADE and the lower sides.

sexpartite vault In GOTHIC architecture, a VAULT in which six surfaces *(compartments)* meet at a central point, divided by two diagonals and one transverse rib in plan. *See* QUADRIPARTITE VAULT.

shaft A slender column, as in GOTHIC architecture.

shear stress A stress, which causes elements to shear or slide past each other.

shingle A flat piece of timber used in roofing or wall surfacing, such as a TILE, but sometimes restricted to a sawn piece, as distinguished from a split piece *(shake)*.

sill Originally a horizontal beam or piece of timber, especially a *ground sill*, or horizontal piece of timber forming the base of a wall, particularly in box-frame construction. Now used for the near-horizontal surface at the base of a window, or sometimes a door, opening.

skyscraper An exceptionally tall building, defined subjectively, but especially one depending upon a passenger elevator to make it commercially viable.

spandrel A recessed or nonstructural infill panel, such as the rectangle above or below a window, or the area between an ARCH and its rectangular surround.

spire A steep pointed roof on a GOTHIC tower, best distinguished from a STEEPLE. It may be a steep square pyramid, but more commonly is octagonal in plan, and either has PINNACLES at the corners of the square base from which it rises, or triangular FILLETS or BROACHES sloping in from the corner.

spoils The reuse of materials in new buildings or monuments. It has been a common practice since antiquity. A good example of the use of spoils is the church of San Salvatore, Spoleto, Italy, believed to date from the fourth century CE onwards. Also known as *spolia*.

springing The point at the base of an ARCH where the curvature begins.

squinch A means of spanning the corner of a square space to create an octagon, especially to support a polygonal or circular shape such as a drum or a dome. The form is commonly arched but is distinct from the spherical triangle of the PENDENTIVE.

stainless steel A term embracing a range of alloys containing iron and 11 percent or more of chromium, and more especially austenitic stainless steel, which contains 18 percent of chromium and 8 percent of nickel, developed by Edward Maurer in 1909–12. *See* STEEL.

steddle A mushroom-shaped stone or timber shaft with an overlapping cap used in Europe to support granaries and other structures to prevent vermin from entering the building. Also known as *staddle* or *dottle*.

steel A pure form of iron containing no more than 0.25 percent carbon, and able to be worked well. Widely used from the 1870s.

steeple A tall tower, usually attached to a church, topped with a SPIRE, a feature of Christian architecture since early medieval times. Often steeples are used as bell towers.

stile The vertical framing member forming either side of a door (meaning the door itself, not the frame surrounding the opening).

stoa A Greek building featuring a covered walkway or PORTICO with a roof supported by COLONNADES. Typically, it was open along one side with a wall or rooms on the other, and was commonly used for markets and for other public gatherings.

string course A narrow continuous band of BRICKWORK that runs horizontally across the face of a building, often to highlight the junction between floors. A common feature of medieval architecture.

strut A short structural member, such as a metal rod or wooden beam, taking compressive loads.

stucco A CEMENT mixture made from LIME, sand, and water used for coating interior or exterior surfaces of buildings. It has also been used decoratively, particularly in BAROQUE, ROCOCO, and Islamic architecture.

stud A relatively slight, vertical timber member, originally used within panels of a timber-framed wall and serving to support external cladding, such as weatherboard, and/or an interior surface such as PLASTER. In some nineteenth-century construction, the main framing members were eliminated, leaving a wall framed entirely in studs, hence *stud frame*.

stump A round or square timber post, or a precast CONCRETE post, supporting a building, otherwise known as a BLOCK or PILE.

stylobate The topmost level or step of the CREPIDOMA that forms the foundation of many classical Greek buildings.

synthronon A stepped bench for the seating of the clergy, running around the inside of the APSE in an eastern church.

tegula (*pl.* tegulae) In a CLASSICAL tiled roof, the larger TILE laid to cover the roof surface, but requiring an IMBREX (a convex tile) to waterproof the joint.

telamone *See* ATLANTE

tempera A type of paint made by combining pigments, with egg yolk acting as the binder. It is one of the oldest forms of paint, dating back to ancient Egypt, made mainly obsolete by the invention of oil paints around the 1500s.

terracotta From the Italian, meaning "baked earth," it is a hard red-brown ceramic used for artistic purposes as well as building materials, such as BRICKS and roofing TILES.

tessellated tiling A tautologous term, as "tessellated" means composed of small TILES, but usually referring to the combination of tiles of square, triangular, or other shapes, and contrasting colors, laid to form geometric patterns. Often ENCAUSTIC TILES are included.

tessera (*pl.* tesserae) The individual elements in a MOSAIC, often GLASS or ceramic in the shape of a square or a cube.

tetrakionon A four-way monumental ARCH, especially one straddling the intersection of two streets in Roman North Africa or Syria.

tetrastyle Having four COLUMNS, as in the end elevation of a small CLASSICAL temple.

thatch A roof covering made from plant stalks, such as straw, reeds, or heather, built up into many layers. It has been used in cultures from the tropics through to Africa, Europe, and Asia.

tierceron In GOTHIC VAULTING, a RIB that ascends from the springing to the ridge (or a transverse ridge), but continues past it like a transverse or diagonal rib.

tie rods A cylindrical metal rod used to handle tensile loads, often used to support, brace, or reinforce structures such as roof beams.

tile A plate, usually of baked clay, for flooring, cladding, or roofing, including TESSELLATED and ENCAUSTIC TILES. A flat tile for roofing is a *crown tile* or *shingle tile*; other roofing tiles are shaped in cross-section to make them more weatherproof and reduce the necessary overlap. The *Flemish tile* is an asymmetrical "S" in cross-section. The *Cordoba or Spanish tile* is a semicylinder, or a slightly tapered shape, to be laid alternately face up and face down. The CLASSICAL tiles are the TEGULA and IMBREX. From the mid-nineteenth century on, the mechanical press allowed production of tiles of variable thicknesses and complicated forms, including overlocking edges, reducing the need for overlap: the MARSEILLES TILE is the most prominent example.

tongue and groove A type of joinery where two panels of wood can be made to fit flush by carving out a *groove* in one edge and a ridge *(tongue)* in the other. It is often used in wood flooring and WAINSCOTING.

trabeation *See* POST AND BEAM

tracery The stonework dividing up the LIGHTS of a medieval window, usually in *bars* of uniform thickness, although there also occurs *plate tracery*, which gives the appearance of having been cut from a flat plate of stone.

trachelion The top section of a DORIC column shaft where it reaches its narrowest diameter then flares out slightly to meet the CAPITAL.

transept The cross arm of a church at right angles to the NAVE, the origins of which are debatable. In the Dark Ages, some churches had a cruciform (cross-shaped) interior volume, but truly cruciform plans were rare before the ROMANESQUE period.

transom A horizontal bar that divides a window or separates a door from a window above it. It can also refer to the small window above the door, also called a FANLIGHT or *transom light*.

tread The horizontal elements in a set of stairs.

trenail A wooden nail.

triforium In the NAVE elevation of a church, the intermediate level between the ARCADE of the AISLE and the CLERESTORY windows above. It might be decorated with blind arcading or have open ARCHES into a GALLERY or passage. Its name does not derive from it being one of three levels, but from the fact that at Canterbury Cathedral it had three openings per bay, a common feature in other churches as well.

triglyph A BLOCK forming one of a series in a DORIC FRIEZE, thought to represent the beam ends in archetypal timber construction. The block has three vertical grooves in it and GUTTAE projecting below.

trilithon A structure consisting of two vertical posts supporting a single horizontal LINTEL, often made from stone. The most famous example is Stonehenge.

truss A support structure composed of multiple beams typically formed into triangles for strength. Commonly seen in bridges, or inside buildings as roof supports.

turnbuckle A device for adjusting the tension or length of TIE RODS or guy wires. It consists of a metal loop with two eyelets with opposite threading at the ends. The tension can be adjusted by rotating the loop.

turret A small tower projecting from the wall of a building, originally used in medieval times as a defensive structure but subsequently it became a decorative feature. The turret top can be open with crenellations or closed, often with a conical roof.

Tuscan Proto-Renaissance The school of ROMANESQUE architecture in and around Florence around 1050 to 1120 showing strong classicizing tendencies, relying much upon white and black marble REVETMENT, and exemplified by the BAPTISTERY of San Giovanni and the church of San Miniato, Florence, Italy. It made use of COSMATI WORK and was the source of much of the detailing later used by Brunelleschi.

tympanum The drumlike face recessed within a PEDIMENT, often carrying relief sculpture.

vault A solid masonry roof of a curved section. The semicylindrical BARREL VAULT is the simplest example. The *groin vault* is created by the intersection of two barrel vaults, creating an ARRIS or groin at forty-five degrees on plan. The DOME can be regarded as a form of vault, but is usually distinguished from it. The highest development is the RIBBED vaulting of the GOTHIC period. *See* NUBIAN VAULT.

vernacular A form of architecture utilizing local materials and knowledge, used mainly in the construction of dwellings and private buildings. Contrasted with buildings designed by professional architects.

vestibule A hall, lobby, or passage between the entrance and the interior of a building. It has been used since ancient Roman times and is a common feature of churches.

viaduct A bridge consisting of a series of short contiguous spans intended to carry road or rail traffic. Viaducts originated in Roman times.

Visigothic To do with the Visigoths, a tribe from near the Black Sea, which sacked Rome in CE 410, and moved on to settle permanently in western France and Spain, where they ruled until defeated by the Arabs in 710. The horseshoe ARCH and the lobed plan are characteristics of their architecture. Their banded arches may derive from BYZANTINE

sources; their use of the PORTICUS is shared with other cultures of the DARK AGES, and their later use of the monolithic arch can be attributed to the influence of Syrian refugees.

volute A spiral ornament as in the IONIC and AEOLIC CAPITALS.

voussoir A wedge-shaped BLOCK forming an ARCH.

wainscot Wooden wall paneling, especially as applying to the lower, or DADO, level of a wall, and commonly in oak.

Warren girder A form of TRUSS where all members are formed to make equilateral triangles with no vertical members. Named after inventor, British engineer James Warren.

wattle and daub A building material dating to prehistoric times, consisting of a lattice of interwoven wooden stakes, branches, or twigs *(wattles)*, and daubed in clay, mud, or dung.

westwerk A large entrance structure typically found on the western face of CAROLINGIAN or ROMANESQUE-style churches. It consists of two large towers or STEEPLES with multiple stories in between, a VESTIBULE leading to the NAVE, and a chapel above.

wind-catcher A ventilation device used in traditional Middle Eastern architecture intended to draw cool air up through a building.

ziggurat A stepped or terraced pyramid first built by the ancient Sumerians in the Mesopotamian valley. They contain no internal chambers but are believed to have been used as platforms for temples or shrines.

Z-purlin A pressed steel section with a vertical web, a top flange turning at right angles in one direction, and a bottom flange in the opposite direction. One of a number of forms (including the C-PURLIN) made from sheet steel of uniform thickness, and are lightweight, structurally efficient, and easy to manufacture.

Index

Plain numbers indicate references in the body text. Italicized numbers indicate references in image captions, while bold numbers indicate references in feature boxes.

Acknowledgments

The Publisher would like to thank Dannielle Doggett for editing the index, as well as Jo Collard, Scott Forbes, Janet Healey, Lynn Lewis, and Stephen Smedley for their help during the conceptualization process prior to production. Special thanks goes to Tim Dean for contributing text to the glossary.

Captions for preliminary pages and openers

Page 1: A plaster ceiling from the Casa Milà designed by Antoni Gaudi, and built in Barcelona, Spain, between 1900 and 1914

Pages 2–3: Clouds reflected in a highly polished geodesic dome

Pages 4–5: A view of the Gothic façade of Cologne Cathedral, Germany at night

Page 7: The Great Jaguar Temple in the Mayan city of Tikal, Guatemala, dating from the fourth century BCE

Page 10: Two electricians at work on the lights of the Eiffel Tower, during its construction in 1889

Pages 12–13: A view of the Great Pyramid at Giza in Egypt, built in the middle of the third millennium BCE

Pages 46–47: Two of the four pyramids in the courtyard of the Louvre Museum in Paris, designed by I.M. Pei, and completed in 1989

Pages 86–8: Building the Lexington Avenue line subway tunnels beneath the Harlem River, New York, in 1913

Pages 106–107: The façade of the Guggenheim Museum, Bilbao, Spain, designed by Frank Gehry in 1997

Pages 144–145: The decorated arched doorway and brass doors of the Dar el-Makhzen or Royal Palace in Fez, Morocco, dating from the seventeenth century

Pages 164–165: Some of the columns and the roof of the restored Temple of Kom Ombo, close to the Nile, in Egypt; it was begun in the reign of Ptolomes VI around 180 BCE

Pages 194–195: The dome of the Mosque of Sheikh Lotfollah built in 1615, on the eastern side of the Naghsh-e Jahan Square, in Isfahan, Iran

Pages 236–237: The tiled roofs of stone towers of the medieval town walls in Tallinn, Estoniaß

Pages 278–279: Spiral staircase in the Temple of the Winds, Mount Stewart, County Down, Ireland; designed by James 'Athenian' Stuart in the 1780s

Pages 298–299: Entrance hall of a contemporary hotel in Los Cabos, Mexico

Pages 320–321: A gargoyle on the roof of the Gothic cathedral of Nôtre-Dame de Paris

Pages 348–349: Fitted diamond-shaped doors on cupboards in the house of Japanese architect Kasai Kiyoshi

Pages 366–367: The arch which forms part of the façade of the Temple of Hadrian, in Ephesus, Turkey, built before 138 CE

Photographic Credits

t=top; b=bottom; l=left; r=right; c=centre

AA = Picture Desk, The Art Archive
AAAC = Ancient Art and Architecture Collection
AKG = akg-images
ARCAID = ARCAID
CB = Corbis
GI = Getty Images
IS = Istock
PL = photolibrary.com
WF = Werner Forman Archive

1 CB/ Ramon Manent, 2–3 GI/Michael Banks, 4–5 GI/Jorg Greuel, 7 AA/Gianni Dagli Orti, 8tl WF, 8tc GI/Bruno De Hogues, 8tr AA/Culver Pictures, 9tl GI/Panoramic Images, 9tc GI/Martin Child, 9tr GI/Adam Jones, 8bl AA/Gianni Dagli Orti, 8bc GI/Medioimages/Photodisc, 8br GI, 9bl GI/Shalom Ormsby, 9bc GI/Richard T. Nowitz, 9br CB/Michael Freeman, 10 GI/Fox Photos,12–13 WF, 14 AA/Gianni Dagli Orti, 15t Aga Khan Trust for Culture/Christopher Little, 15b PL, 16t PL, 16b AA/Gianni Dagli Orti, 17 AKG/ A.F.Kersting, 18l PL, 18r CB/Michael Freeman, 19 ARCAID/Chuck Choi, 19–20 ARCAID/ Gollings Photography, 20–21 CB/Jon Sparks, 21t GI/Nico Tondini, 21b CB/Chris Hellier,22b CB/ Kazuyoshi Nomachi, 22t CB/Peter M. Wilson, 23 AA/Alfredo Dagli Orti, 24t GI/De Agostini, 24b CB/Lindsay Hebberd, 25t CB/Louis laurent Grandadam, 25b PL, 26t AA/Gianni Dagli Orti, 26b AKG/Erich Lessing, 27 GI/Donald Nausbaum, 30–31 CB/AA, 30 AA/Museo Capitolino rome/Gianni Dagli Orti, 31 AKG/ Walter Limot, 32t AA/Duomo Florence/Alfredo Dagli Orti, 32b CB/Douglas Kirkland, 33t CB/ Sergio Pitamitz, 33b CB/Christophe Boisvieux, 34b CB/ARCAID Richard Bryant, 34t CB/JAI/ Michele Falzone, 35 CB/Giraud Philippe, 36t CB/ Patrick Ward, 36b PL, 37 PL, 38 CB/l. Clarke, 38–39 CB/George H. H. Huey, 39 AKG/Gerard Degeorge, 40 GI/John Elk III, 41b AKG/Orsi Battaglini, 41t AKG/Bildarchiv Monheim, 42t AKG/Herve Champollion, 42b CB/Atlantide Phototravel, 43t AKG/Bildarchiv Monheim, 43b PL, 44 CB/Thomas A. Heinz, 44–45 AA/Manuel Cohen, 45 CB/Bettmann, 46–47 GI/Bruno De Hogues, 48 AAAC/C.M.Dixon, 48–49 GI/Adam Jones, 49 CB/Gianni Dagli Orti, 50t CB/ Wolfgang Kaehler, 50b CB/Bob Krist, 51t CB/ Ashley Cooper, 51b CB/E.O. Hoppé, 52 GI/ Tomonari Tsuji, 53c AA/ Egyptian Museum Turin/ Gianni Dagli Orti, 53t CB/E.O. Hoppé, 54 CB/ Ric Ergenbright, 55tr CB/Kazuyoshi Nomachi, 55tl CB/Lowell Georgia, 56–57 CB/Peter Adams/ zefa, 57t CB/Yann Arthus-Bertrand, 57b CB/ Thelma Sanders; Eye Ubiquitous, 58 AA/Gianni Dagli Orti, 59t CB/Roger Wood, 59b CB/ Stephanie Colasanti, 61t GI/Richard Nowitz, 61b CB/Yann Arthus-Bertrand, 62–63 CB/Charles & Josette Lenars, 63t CB/Yann Arthus-Bertrand, 63b CB/The Art Archive, 64 CB/Werner Forman, 65l ARCAID/Lucinda Lambton,65r PL, 66–67 CB/ Robert Estall, 67t AA/Museo della Civilta Romana Rome/Gianni Dagli Orti, 67b GI/Hulton Archive,68t Library of Congress, 69r AA/ Culver Pictures, 69l GI/Andrew Wakeford, 70l CB/ Hoberman Collection, 71r GI/Time & Life Pictures, 71l CB/Hulton-Deutsch-Collection, 72t CB/Alan Schein Photography, 72b CB/ Bettmann,73t CB/Jose Fuste Raga,73b CB/Lake County Museum, 74 CB/David Lees, 74–75 ARCAID/Bill Tingey, 75b PL,76 CB/Adam Woolfitt/Robert Harding World Imagery, 77t Architectural Association School of Architecture Photo Library, 77b IS, 78t AKG, 78b FL/Karolina Krolikowska, 79 FL/David Harding, 80t GI/Jake Fitzjones, 80b Mary Evans, 80–81 PL, 82 CB/ Edifice, 83 CB/ARCAID/Nicholas Kane, 84t CB/ James L. Amos, 84b CB/Michael S. Yamashita, 85 IS/ Nikada, 106–107 GI/Panoramic Images, 108b CB/Paul Almasy, 108t CB/Bettmann, 109 GI/ Louie Psihoyos, 110 CB/Yann Arthus-Bertrand, 111l Picture Media/Reuters, 111r Mary Evans, 112b PL, 112t GI/Time & Life Pictures, 113 PL, 114l PL, 114r AA/ Neil Setchfield, 115 CB/ Michael Freeman, 116–117 CB/The Irish Image Collection, 116 PL, 117 CB/Vanni Archive, 118b CB/Adam Woolfitt, 118t PL, 119b GI/De Agostini, 119t PL, 120b CB/Craig Lovell, 120t CB/Dave G. Houser, 121b CB/Kevin Schafer, 121t WF, 122b AA/Gianni Dagli Orti, 122t AA/ Gianni Dagli Orti, 123 CB/Adam Woolfitt, 125b CB/Frans Lemmens/zefa, 125t CB/Blaine Harrington III, 126–127 CB/Roy Rainford/ Robert Harding World Imagery, 126b CB/Araldo de Luca, 127b CB/Construction Photography, 127t GI/Gary Ombler, 128 CB/ARCAID/Will Pryce/Thames & Hudson, 128–129 PL, 130b CB/Roger Wood, 130t GI/Reza Estakhrian, 131 CB/Christophe Boisvieux, 132b GI/Egyptian, 132t CB/Peter Johnson, 133 PL, 134 AKG/ British Library, 135 PL, 136b CB/Bettmann, 136t CB/Angelo Hornak, 137 PL, 138b GI/French School, 138t CB/Vanni Archive, 138–139 PL, 140b CB/Pitchal Frederic, 140t CB/Thomas A.

140b CB/Pitchal Frederic, 140t CB/Thomas A. Heinz, 141b PL, 141t CB/Edifice, 142–143 PL, 142t CB/Alfredo Aldai/epa, 143t PL, 143b PL, 86–87 AA/Culver Pictures, 88b AA/National Museum Damascus Syria/Gianni Dagli Orti, 88t WF, 89t AA/Neil Setchfield, 89b WF, 90 AA/Culver Pictures, 91t CB/zefa/José Fuste Raga, 91b CB/Angelo Hornak, 92 GI/Panoramic Images, 93t CB/Bruno Morandi/Robert Harding World Imagery, 93b CB/Julia Waterlow; Eye Ubiquitous, 94t Global Book Publishing, 94–95 CB/Fernando Alda, 95t CB/Angelo Hornak, 96bl AKG/Erich Lessing, 96br CB/Nicolas Sapieha, 97 CB/Massimo Listri, 98t AKG/Paul Almasy, 98bl AA/Eileen Tweedy, 98br GI, 99 CB/Klaus Hackenberg/zefa, 100t CB/Stefano Bianchetti, 100b CB/Construction Photography, 101tl CB/Ashley Cooper, 101tr GI/Robin MacDougall, 102t CB/Chris Hellier, 103t GI/Stephen Frink, 103b CB/Michael Busselle, 104b CB/Andrew Holbrooke, 104–105 GI/Insy Shah, 105b GI/Bruno Muff, 144–145 GI/Martin Child, 146 CB/The Irish Image Collection, 146–147 CB/Hubert Stadler, 147l Miles Lewis, 147r PL, 148b CB/Clay Perry, 148t PL, 149b PL, 149c AA/Eileen Tweedy, 150 CB/Michael S. Yamashita, 151 CB/Eye Ubiquitous/Paul Seheult, 152r AA/Mireille Vautier, 152l GI/De Agostini/Getty Images, 153l AKG/Erich Lessing, 153r ARCAID/Guy Montagu-Pollock, 154 PL, 155 AA/Gianni Dagli Orti, 156b AA/Gianni Dagli Orti, 156t AA/Gianni Dagli Orti, 157 AKG/Andrea Jemolo, 158 AKG/Herve Champollion, 159 AA/Gianni Dagli Orti, 160b AKG/Herve Champollion, 160t AKG/Herve Champollion, 161b PL, 161t PL, 162 CB/epa/Alfred, 163 GI/Bertrand Rieger, 164–165 GI/Adam Jones, 166 WF, 167b GI/Sylvain Grandadam, 167t GI/Ken Gillham, 168–169 AA/Gianni Dagli Orti, 169 AAAC/R Ashworth, 170–171 AA/Manuel Cohen, 171 CB/Jason Hawkes, 172l CB/Alinari Archives, 172r AA/Gianni Dagli Orti, 173b ARCAID/Paul M.r. Maeyaert, 173t AA/Gianni Dagli Orti, 174 ARCAID/Florian Monheim, 175b AAAC/G Tortoli, 175t AAAC/James Lynch, 176 AKG/François Guénet, 178 WF, 179 CB/Chris Hellier, 180 GI/Guy Vanderelst, 180–181 GI/Medioimages/Photodisc, 181 GI/Dorling Kindersley, 182 AA/Gianni Dagli Orti, 183b CB/Adam Woolfitt, 183t AA/Stephanie Colasanti, 184b AA/Manuel Cohen, 184t PL, 184–185 AA/Manuel Cohen, 186 AKG/Jean–louis Nou, 186t GI/Adam Crowley, 187 AA/Gianni Dagli Orti, 188–189 AAAC/J Ormerod, 188 AKG/Stefan Drechsel, 189b AKG/Nimatallah, 189t CB/Art on File, 190b japan-photo.de/Hartmut Pohling, 190t CB/Amet Jean Pierre, 191 ARCAID/Peter Aaron, 192 AAAC/James Lynch, 193 CB/ARCAID/John Gollings, 194–195 AA/Gianni Dagli Orti, 196t CB, 197 CB/Christophe Boisvieux, 198 PL, 199 CB/Tom Bean, 201 GI/John Heseltine, 202 GI/Firecrest Pictures, 203b GI/AFP, 203t CB/Bettmann, 204b CB/Charles & Josette Lenars, 204–205 CB/Thinkstock, 205b AA/Gianni Dagli Orti, 206 CB/Mimmo Jodice, 207 PL 208 Aga Khan Trust

for Culture, 209b Aga Khan Trust for Culture, 209c Aga Khan Trust for Culture, 209t Aga Khan Trust for Culture, 210b PL, 210–211 AA/Gianni Dagli Orti, 212l GI/Andrew Ward/Life File, 212–213 PL , 214 CB/Vanni Archive, 215 CB/Giraud Phillipe, 216 CB/Ruggero Vanni, 216–217 CB/Adam Woolfitt, 217b M.I.T/G.E. Kidder Smith, Courtesy of Kidder Smith Collection, Rotch Visual Collections, 218 PL, 219r CB/Paul Almasy, 219l PL, 220–221 CB/Bernard Annebicque, 221 GI/Renaud Visage, 222 CB/Christophe Boisvieux, 223l AA/Nicolas Sapieha, 223r GI/Travelpix Ltd, 224 AKG/Andrea Jemolo, 225t PL, 225b CB/Alinari Archives, 226–227 PL, 227t AA/Gianni Dagli Orti, 228 CB/Paul H. Kuiper, 229t CB/Adam Woolfitt, 229c PL, 230 GI/Hulton Archive, 231l CB/Robert Holmes, 231r CB/Ashley Cooper, 232 PL, 233 CB/James Leynse, 232–233 CB/Pawel Libera, 234 PL, 235c ARCAID/Richard Bryant, 235t PL, 236–237 GI/Medioimages/Photodisc, 238 CB/Roger Wood, 239b CB/Adam Woolfitt, 239t CB/JAI/Walter Bibikow, 240 CB/Jason Hawkes, 240–241 CB/Yann Arthus-Bertrand, 242–243 AKG/Hervé Champollion, 242 CB/Roger Wood, 243t CB/Roger Wood, 244 AA/National Archaeological Museum Athens/Gianni Dagli Orti, 245 AA/Gianni Dagli Orti, 246l AA/Chateau Lafitte France/Alfredo Dagli Orti, 246r CB/Skyscan, 247 CB/epa/Andy Rain, 248 CB/Sergio Pitamitz, 249b CB/Michael Freeman, 249t CB/Sandro Vannini, 250b PL, 250t AKG/John Hios, 251b AA/Manuel Cohen, 251t GI/Medford Taylor, 252 PL, 252–253 CB/Wolfgang Kaehler, 254 AKG/Rainer Hackenberg, 255b CB/Craig Lovell, 255c CB/Charles & Josette Lenars, 256 CB/Michel Gounot, 257 AA/Jarrold Publishing, 258 CB/David Clapp/ARCAID, 258–259 GI/Charlie Waite, 259 CB/Tom Grill, 260 PL, 261b CB/Marcus Vetter, 261t PL, 262 CB/Martin Jones, 262–263 PL, 263 CB/Wolfgang Kaehler, 264 PL, 264–265 PL, 265 CB/Craig Lovell, 266–267 Anthony Browell, 267b Glenn Murcutt, 267c Glenn Murcutt, 268 CB/Edifice, 268–269 PL, 269 CB/Morton Beebe, 270 PL, 271t PL, 271b CB/Angelo Hornak, 272 AA/Alfredo Dagli Orti, 273t AKG, 273b PL, 274 AA/Gianni Dagli Orti, 275 CB/Tom Grill, 276 WF, 276–277 CB/José Fuste Raga/zefa, 277 CB/JAI/Jane Sweeney, 278–279 GI, 280t PL, 280b ARCAID/Le Corbusier & Pierre Jeanneret/Richard Bryant, 281t GI/Arvind Garg, 281b CB/Angelo Hornak, 282 PL, 283t PL, 283b PL, 284t AA/Gianni Dagli Orti, 284b CB/Jon Hicks, 285t CB/Clay Perry, 285b AA/Nicolas Sapieha, 286–287 GI/Panoramic Images, 286t GI/Dave Bartruff, 287t CB/Atlantide Phototravel, 288t CB/Mimmo Jodice, 289t AKG/Erich Lessing, 289b GI/Panoramic Images, 290b CB/ARCAID/David Clapp, 290–291 CB/Sandro Vannini, 292t AKG/Andrea Jemolo, 293t CB/Atlantide Phototravel, 293b AA/Gianni Dagli Orti, 294b CB/Peter Aprahamian, 295t CB/Blaine Harrington III, 295b CB/Angelo Hornak, 296t GI/DEA/C. SAPPA, 297t CB/ARCAID/Nicholas Kane, 297b PL, 298–299 GI/Shalom

Ormsby, 300 AA/Neil Setchfield, 301b CB/Atlantide Phototravel, 301t WF, 302–303 GI/Panoramic Images, 303b CB/Angelo Hornak, 305t AAAC/R.R. Bell, 305b ARCAID/Florian Monheim/Bildarchiv-Monheim, 306l CB/Donald Nausbaum, 306–307 ARCAID/Mark Fiennes, 307t GI/Krzysztof Dydynski, 308t CB/Vanni Archive, 308b CB/G.E. Kidder Smith, 309t ARCAID/Pierre Chareau/Michael Halberstadt, 309b CB/Richard Schulman, 310b PL, 311b ARCAID/Greene and Greene/Mark Fiennes, 311t AA/Victoria and Albert Museum London/Sally Chappell, 312b AKG/Archives CDA/St–Genes, 312–313 PL, 313t GI/National Geographic, 314t CB/Nathalie Darbellay/Sygma, 315b ARCAID/Sir John Soane/Richard Bryant, 315t AA/Alfredo Dagli Orti, 316t GI/Frans Lemmens, 316b GI/Time & Life Pictures, 317tl GI/Hiroshi Watanabe, 317tr GI/Ryan McVay, 318b GI/Tim Graham, 319t WF, 319cr GI/Krzysztof Dydynski, 320–321 GI/Richard T. Nowitz, 322t AA/Gianni Dagli Orti, 322b AA/Gianni Dagli Orti, 323 CB/Antoine Gyori, 324t CB/Angelo Hornak, 324b AA/Archaeological Museum Istanbul/Gianni Dagli Orti, 325 PL, 326 CB/Vittoriano Rastelli, 327 CB/John and Lisa Merrill, 328 CB/Adam Woolfitt, 329t CB/Angelo Hornak, 329b PL, 330 GI/Glowimages, 331r GI/Win Initiative, 331l CB/Bob Krist, 332 CB/Arthur Thévenart, 333t GI/Marco Simoni, 333b PL, 334b CB/Bettmann, 334t CB/Adam Woolfitt, 335 CB/Paul Almasy, 336b AKG/Erich Lessing, 336t CB/Thomas A. Heinz, 337 PL, 338t AA/Neil Setchfield, 338b CB/Bob Krist, 339b GI/John Wang, 339t CB/Annebicque Bernard, 340 GI/Richard I'Anson, 341b CB/Charles & Josette Lenars, 341t AKG/Erich Lessing, 342–343 CB/Ruggero Vanni, 342 CB/Bettmann, 343 CB/Michael Freeman, 344b ARCAID/Florian Monheim/Bildarchiv-Monheim, 344t ARCAID / Florian Monheim/Bildarchiv-Monheim, 345b CB/Adam Woolfitt, 345t ARCAID/Florian Monheim/Bildarchiv–Monheim, 346 Global Book Publishing, 347b PL, 347t PL, 348–349 CB/Michael Freeman, 350t GI/David Tomlinson, 350b CB/Elio Ciol, 351tl CB/ARCAID/Alan Weintraub, 351tr Madeline Miraglia, 352 PL, 353t PL, 353b CB/ARCAID/Nicholas Kane, 354 CB/Paul Almasy, 355t CB/Robert Holmes, 355b CB/Ludovic Maisant, 356tl CB/Mimmo Jodice, 356tr CB/Adam Woolfitt, 357t GI/Roger Viollet, 357b PL, 358t CB/Michael Freeman, 359t CB/ARCAID/Alan Weintraub, 359b PL, 360b CB/Richard Hamilton Smith, 361tl Global Book Publishing, 361tr CB/Stefano Bianchetti, 361b CB/Massimo Listri, 362 CB/Farrell Grehan, 363–364 ARCAID/Tadao Ando Architect & Associates/Richard Bryant, 363b ARCAID/Peter Zumthor/Nicholas Kane, 364t GI/Chris Close, 364b CB/Barry Lewis, 365 CB/Thomas A. Heinz, 365c CB/Angelo Hornak, 366–367 GI/Glowimages, **Endpapers** IS/Constantinos Gerakis, **Cover (small)** PL, **Cover (large)** GI/Robert Adam, **Spine** IS/Lisa Marzano, **Back** AA/Manuel Cohen.

Architectura

ELEMENTS OF ARCHITECTURAL STYLE

Produced by Global Book Publishing
Level 8, 15 Orion Road
Lane Cove, NSW 2066, Australia
Ph: (612) 9425 5800
Fax: (612) 9425 5804
Email: rightsmanager@globalpub.com.au